Praise for *The Handbook of English for Specific Pur*

"*The Handbook of English for Specific Purposes* would make an excellent addition to school or university collections. It could also be an excellent textbook for a dedicated course on ESP in a teacher education program . . . The *Handbook* provides a broad overview of the field, with sections specifically oriented to teachers, administrators and/or teacher educators ('ESP and language skills', 'ESP and pedagogy'), as well as to researchers ('Areas of ESP research', 'Research perspectives and methodologies in ESP research')."

English Australia Journal, March 2013

"Until then, *The Handbook of English for Specific Purposes* fills the vacuum. More than a handbook, it is a companion to all researchers in ESP studies."

S. Isani / Asp, November 2013

"English for specific purposes has undergone a process of diversification in recent years. This volume provides a complete overview of today's ESP research, which makes it compulsory reading for any scholar in the field."

Inmaculada Fortanet Gómez, Universitat Jaume I

"This *Handbook* is an excellent state-of-the-art survey of research in the field of English for specific purposes. As it is both authoritative and user-friendly, it is a precious reference work for both scholars and students."

Maurizio Gotti, Università di Bergamo

"This excellent volume covers the latest scholarship, research methods, and teaching practices in various areas of ESP. The chapters provide in-depth and accessibly-written perspectives on how ESP intersects with genre analysis, discourse communities, corpus linguistics, multimodal texts, and critical pedagogy."

Sunny Hyon, California State University

Blackwell Handbooks in Linguistics

This outstanding multi-volume series covers all the major subdisciplines within linguistics today and, when complete, will offer a comprehensive survey of linguistics as a whole.

The Handbook of English for Specific Purposes

Edited by

Brian Paltridge and Sue Starfield

WILEY Blackwell

This paperback edition first published 2014
© 2013 John Wiley and Sons, Inc.

Edition history: John Wiley & Sons, Inc. (hardback, 2013)

Registered Office
John Wiley & Sons Ltd, The Atrium, Southern Gate, Chichester, West Sussex, PO19 8SQ, UK

Editorial Offices
350 Main Street, Malden, MA 02148-5020, USA
9600 Garsington Road, Oxford, OX4 2DQ, UK
The Atrium, Southern Gate, Chichester, West Sussex, PO19 8SQ, UK

For details of our global editorial offices, for customer services, and for information about how to apply for permission to reuse the copyright material in this book please see our website at www.wiley.com/wiley-blackwell.

The right of Brian Paltridge and Sue Starfieldto be identified as the authors of the editorial material in this work has been asserted in accordance with the UK Copyright, Designs and Patents Act 1988.

Library of Congress Cataloging-in-Publication Data

The handbook of English for specifi c purposes / edited by Brian Paltridge and Sue Starfi eld.
       p. cm.
    Includes index.
    ISBN 978-0-470-65532-0 (hardcover : alk. paper)
    ISBN 978-1-118-94155-3 (paperback : alk. paper)
    1. English language–Study and teaching.   I. Paltridge, Brian.   II. Starfi eld, Sue, 1952–
LB1576.H2334 2012
372.6–dc23

                                   2012015791

A catalogue record for this book is available from the British Library.

Cover image: *Einstein's Dream* diptych by Gerrit Greve © Gerrit Greve / Corbis.

Set in 10/12 pt Palatino by Toppan Best-set Premedia Limited
Printed and bound in Malaysia by Vivar Printing Sdn Bhd

2   2015

Contents

Notes on Contributors

Francesca Bargiela-Chiappini is Honorary Associate Professor in the Centre of Applied Linguistics, University of Warwick, UK. She has published widely on business discourse and intercultural business communication.

Diane Belcher is Professor of Applied Linguistics at Georgia State University, a former co-editor of the journal *English for Specific Purposes*, and current co-editor of *TESOL Quarterly*. She also co-edits a teacher reference series titled *Michigan Series on Teaching Multilingual Writers*. She has authored a number of articles on advanced academic literacy and is currently at work on her seventh edited volume, on critical and corpus-based approaches to intercultural rhetoric.

Joel Bloch teaches ESL composition at The Ohio State University, Columbus, Ohio. He is the author of the book *Technologies in the Second Language Composition Classroom* and has authored several papers on intercultural rhetoric, plagiarism, and technology. He is currently completing a book on plagiarism and intellectual property law and researching multimodal literacies in the academic writing classroom.

Susan Bosher is Professor and Director of ESL in the English Department, St. Catherine University, St. Paul, Minnesota. She has taught an English for Nursing course for pre-nursing immigrant and international students since 2000. In addition, she has authored an English for Nursing textbook and co-edited a collection of essays for nurse educators on creating a more culturally inclusive environment in nursing education. She has also conducted workshops for nursing faculty on numerous topics related to ESL students in nursing.

Maggie Charles is a Tutor at Oxford University Language Centre, in the UK, where she specializes in teaching academic writing to graduates. She has published work on the pedagogical applications of corpus linguistics, the study of stance/evaluation and discipline-specific discourse, and has recently co-edited a volume entitled *Academic Writing: At the Interface of Corpus and Discourse* (with Diane Pecorari and Susan Hunston). She is also a consultant on academic writing for the *Oxford Advanced Learner's Dictionary*.

Liz T. Chiang is a doctoral student in the Department of Language and Literacy Education in the Faculty of Education at the University of British Columbia, Canada. Her research interests include racial inequality, non-/native-speaker, and second language education.

Ulla Connor is the Barbara E. and Karl R. Zimmer Chair in Intercultural Communication at Indiana University in Indianapolis. Her research and teaching has been on multilingual writers. She is the author of numerous articles as well as the author of *Writing Across Languages* (1996) and *Intercultural Rhetoric in Second Language Writing* (2011). She is the founding organizer of the international conference Intercultural Rhetoric and Written Discourse.

Averil Coxhead is a Senior Lecturer in Applied Linguistics in the School of Linguistics and Applied Language Studies, Victoria University of Wellington, New Zealand. She is currently developing several vocabulary size tests, investigating approaches to teaching specialized vocabulary at secondary school level, and researching the phraseology of the Academic Word List.

Dan Douglas is an Emeritus Professor in the Applied Linguistics program at Iowa State University. He has published extensively on language assessment and language for specific purposes.

Dacia Dressen-Hammouda is currently an Associate Professor of English and Director of the Masters Program in Technical Documentation Design at Blaise Pascal University, Clermont-Ferrand, France. Her research interests include discoursal silence and writing expertise, L1/L2 writing pedagogy, genre analysis, ESP/EAP, intercultural technical communication and user studies.

Christine B. Feak is a Lecturer in English for Academic Purposes at the University of Michigan English Language Institute, Ann Arbor, Michigan, where she teaches both speaking and writing courses. In addition to co-authoring textbooks with John Swales on academic writing, she is co-author of *Academic Interactions: Communicating on Campus*, a corpus-informed academic speaking textbook.

Gibson Ferguson is a Senior Lecturer at the University of Sheffield, UK, and Director of the MA programme in Applied Linguistics. He researches in the areas of language policy, teacher education and ESP/EMP and has published in such journals as *English for Specific Purposes*, *International Journal of Applied Linguistics*, *International Journal of Bilingual Education and Bilingualism*, and *World Englishes*. He is also the author of *Language Planning and Education* (2006).

John Flowerdew is a Professor in the Department of English, City University of Hong Kong. His research interests include discourse analysis and English for specific purposes. Among other books, he has published *Academic Listening: Research Perspectives*; *Research Perspectives on English for Academic Purposes* (with Matthew Peacock); *Academic Discourse, Second Language Listening: Theory and Practice* (with Lindsay Miller); and *Lexical Cohesion and Corpus Linguistics* (with Michaela Mahlberg). His latest books are *Advances in Discourse Studies* (edited with Vijay Bhatia and Rodney Jones) and *Critical Discourse Analysis in Historiography*.

Lynne Flowerdew teaches and carries out research at the Hong Kong University of Science and Technology. Her research and teaching interests include corpus linguistics, genre analysis and EAP/ESP curriculum design and methodology. She has published widely in different areas of corpus linguistics in international journals and refereed edited collections. Her most recent books are *New Trends in Corpora and Language Learning*, co-edited with Ana Frankenberg-Garcia and Guy Aston, and an authored book *Corpora and Language Education*.

Christine C. M. Goh is Associate Professor of Applied Linguistics in the National Institute of Education, Singapore (Nanyang Technological University). Her interests include development and assessment of listening and speaking, and the role of metacognition in L2 learning. She has authored many international journal articles, books and book chapters on these topics.

Alan Hirvela is an Associate Professor at Ohio State University. He taught previously at the Chinese University of Hong Kong. In addition to his article and book publications, he is currently co-editor (with Diane Belcher) of *TESOL Quarterly*.

Ken Hyland is Professor of Applied Linguistics and Director of the Centre for Applied English Studies at the University of Hong Kong. He has published over 150 articles and 14 books on language education and academic writing. He was founding co-editor of the *Journal of English for Academic Purposes* and is now co-editor of *Applied Linguistics*.

Ann M. Johns, Professor Emerita of Linguistics and Writing Studies (San Diego State University), has devoted her academic career to ESP issues. Her research in the 1970s and 1980s was on English for Business and Economics (EBE); but she soon turned to, and has remained with, English for Academic Purposes (EAP), especially as it relates to novice students. Her five books and her more than sixty articles and book chapters focus principally upon genre pedagogies and student learning in secondary and post-secondary contexts both in the United States and abroad. She served as co-editor of *English for Specific Purposes Journal* (1985–93), and she continues to review manuscripts from five international journals.

Ryuko Kubota is Professor in the Department of Language and Literacy Education in the Faculty of Education at the University of British Columbia, Canada.

She has many publications in edited books and journals such as *English for Specific Purposes, Journal of Second Language Writing,* and *TESOL Quarterly.* Her research interests include critical applied linguistics and second language writing.

Meredith Marra is a member of the Wellington Language in the Workplace Project team and a Senior Lecturer at Victoria University of Wellington, New Zealand, where she teaches a range of courses in sociolinguistics and workplace discourse. Her primary research interest is the language of business meetings, and she has published in the areas of humor and gender in workplace interactions. Her latest research focuses on intercultural interaction involving skilled migrants in the New Zealand workplace.

Carol Lynn Moder is Professor of Linguistics and TESL at Oklahoma State University. From 2004–2006, she held contract grants with the International Training Division of the US Federal Aviation Administration to develop an Aviation English curriculum for International Air Traffic Controllers. She served as a consultant to ICAO in 2005, participating in the development of the CD of ICAO rating samples.

Hilary Nesi is a Professor in English language at Coventry University, UK. Her research interests include English for Academic Purposes, and the design and use of lexical reference tools. She was principal investigator for the project to create the *BASE* corpus of British Academic Spoken English, and for the *BAWE* corpus project "An Investigation of Genres of Assessed Writing in British Higher Education".

Catherine Nickerson is a Professor in the College of Business at Zayed University in the United Arab Emirates. She has held senior positions in India and in the Netherlands, and has also lived and worked in the United States and the United Kingdom. Her current research interests include the use of English as an international language in business contexts and the communication of corporate social responsibility.

Jill Northcott is a Lecturer and Head of English for Business and Law at the English Language Teaching Centre (formerly IALS), University of Edinburgh, UK.

Brian Paltridge is Professor of TESOL at the University of Sydney, Australia. He has published in the areas of English for specific purposes, genre analysis, academic writing, and discourse analysis. He is a former editor of the journal *English for Specific Purposes*.

Jean Parkinson is a Lecturer in Applied Linguistics in the School of Linguistics and Applied Language Studies, Victoria University of Wellington, New Zealand. She has published in the areas of language for science and technology and writing pedagogy. Her current interest is in the language used to discuss qualitative and quantitative research results.

Paul Prior is a Professor of English and the Center for Writing Studies at the University of Illinois at Urbana-Champaign. Extending earlier studies of genre, voicing, literate activity, chronotopic lamination, and disciplinarity, he is currently working on studies of semiotic remediation practices in academic and everyday settings.

William Rozycki is a Professor in the Center for Language Research, University of Aizu, and chair of the IEEE Professional Communication Society, Japan chapter. His research interest is the discourse of engineering, with a special focus on the oral presentation practices of non-native English-speaking engineers.

Sue Starfield is an Associate Professor in the School of Education and Director of the Learning Centre at the University of New South Wales, Australia. She is co-editor of the journal *English for Specific Purposes* and co-author of *Thesis and Dissertation Writing in a Second Language*. Her research interests include advanced academic writing and research genres and identity in academic writing.

Paul Thompson is a Senior Lecturer in Corpus Linguistics in the Department of English at the University of Birmingham, UK, and Director of the Centre for Corpus Research. He is currently developing large-scale multidisciplinary corpora of doctoral theses and of research articles, and is also involved in the development of corpus-informed language learning materials for second language learners.

Zuocheng Zhang is Lecturer in TESOL Education at the University of New England, Australia. His research interests focus on business discourse, English for specific purposes, multimodality, and discourse and identities and he has published extensively in these areas. He is currently collaborating on a research project on contemporary Chinese business discourse supported by the Program for Innovative Research Team and the "211 Program" at the University of International Business and Economics, Beijing, China.

Acknowledgments

We are especially grateful to all the authors whose chapters ensure the *Handbook of English for Specific Purposes* will make a substantial contribution to the field. We thank Danielle Descoteaux and Julia Kirk at Wiley-Blackwell for their support and encouragement in this venture, also to Louise Ennis for her very careful copy editing of the book. We are, as always, thankful to our families and life partners for their forbearance as we pursue our scholarly endeavors.

Every effort has been made to trace copyright holders and to obtain their permission for the use of copyright material in this book. We apologize for any errors or omissions in this and would be grateful if notified of any corrections that should be incorporated in future reprints or editions of this book.

Introduction

Overview of the Handbook

The *Handbook of English for Specific Purposes* is a state of the art survey of research in the field of English for specific purposes (ESP). Each chapter of the book presents a review of a particular topic in English for specific purposes research. The chapters have been specially written for the *Handbook* by authors who have a high level of expertise and are well regarded in the field of English for specific purposes research. Each chapter includes comprehensive reviews of research in the area being discussed, as well as indications for further research directions in relation to the particular topic.

The audience for the *Handbook* is students, teachers, and researchers with an interest in English for specific purposes research, as well as people working in the areas of language studies, language teaching, and applied linguistics more generally. The *Handbook* is aimed at upper level undergraduate students as well as graduate students undertaking masters and doctoral degrees in TESOL, English language teaching, and applied linguistics. The book is also a reference work for scholars with an interest in researching this particular area of language teaching and learning. The book does not assume a background in the area of English for specific purposes, but is, at the same time, sufficiently advanced to meet the needs of researchers in this area. The *Handbook* aims to be a user-friendly yet authoritative reference work for students and researchers in the area of English for specific purposes.

The Handbook of English for Specific Purposes, First Edition.
Edited by Brian Paltridge and Sue Starfield.
© 2013 John Wiley & Sons, Inc. Published 2013 by John Wiley & Sons, Inc.

What is English for Specific Purposes?

English for specific purposes (ESP) refers to the teaching and learning of English as a second or foreign language where the goal of the learners is to use English in a particular domain. The teaching of English for specific purposes, in its early days, was largely motivated by the need to communicate across languages in areas such as commerce and technology (see Benesch 2001, Johns, this volume, Starfield 2012 for reviews of these developments). This has now expanded to include other areas such as English for academic purposes (EAP), English for occupational purposes (EOP), English for vocational purposes (EVP), English for medical purposes (EMP), English for business purposes (EBP), English for legal purposes (ELP), and English for sociocultural purposes (ESCP) (Belcher 2009).

A key feature of an ESP course is that the content and aims of the course are oriented to the specific needs of the learners. ESP courses, then, focus on the language, skills, and genres appropriate to the specific activities the learners need to carry out in English. Typically (although not always) ESP students are adult learners. They are also often a homogeneous group in terms of learning goals, although not always in terms of language proficiency. Key issues in the teaching of English for specific purposes are how to identify learner needs, the nature of the genres that learners need to be able to produce as well as participate in, and how we can know that our learners have been able to do this successfully, and, if not, what we can do to help them to do this. These (and many other) issues are discussed in this *Handbook*.

Research Directions in English for Specific Purposes

In a chapter (Paltridge and Starfield 2011) we wrote for the *Handbook of Research in Second Language Teaching and Learning* we looked at current research trends in English for specific purposes as they appeared in the pages of the journal *English for Specific Purposes*. The main themes we identified were studies that took a genre perspective on ESP language use, corpus studies of specific purposes uses of English, studies which examined the use of English as a lingua franca in specific purpose settings, and research into advanced academic literacies. We also found that studies that looked at issues of identity in ESP teaching and learning and ethnographic approaches to examining ESP texts and contexts were increasing in their popularity.

Belcher et al.'s (2011) *New Directions in English for Specific Purposes Research* takes this discussion further by pointing to other issues that are attracting the interest of ESP researchers. One of these is the issue of disciplinary language and ESP teaching. Hyland (2002, 2004, 2011) in the area of EAP, for example, has shown how the use of language varies in terms of rhetorical patterns and linguistic features across disciplines, especially in their written genres, arguing that this needs to be accounted for in the teaching and researching of specific purpose genres. ESP studies have also considered contextual aspects of specific purpose genres, taking up Swales' (1993) argument for the need to go beyond structural and linguistic examinations of texts in order to better understand social and contextual features of genres (see Paltridge and Wang 2011; Swales and Rogers 1995 for further discussion of this). Research in ESP, then, has increasingly moved from linguistic descriptions, on their own, to studies which aim to understand why genres are shaped as they are, and how they achieve their particular goals.

Classroom-based research has also come to more prominence in ESP publications. A key researcher in this area is Cheng (2011) who discusses learner, teacher, and institutional factors that impact on ESP teaching and learning. He points to the need to better understand how learner needs and expectations are translated into learning objectives in ESP classes, as well as how ESP students interpret these objectives and use them to guide their own learning. Cheng also discusses the relationship between input materials and output activities and the criteria that ESP teachers use to judge whether their input materials are suitable for their students and the learning objectives of the course. He discusses the issue of appropriate methodologies in ESP classes as well as classroom-based assessment in ESP settings. Cheng's research helps us to understand some of these questions. There are still, however, many questions in this area that need future research.

Identity continues to be a research interest in the area of ESP as well as the use of English as a lingua franca in specific purpose settings. Genre studies continue to attract interest, although they are now becoming increasingly more complex and multi-method than they once were (see Flowerdew 2011, Tardy 2011 for further discussion of this). There is an ever-increasing use of ethnographic techniques in ESP research (see Dressen-Hammouda, this volume; Starfield 2011) and the issue of learner needs is becoming more complex and more focused, not just on what learners need to do, but also on who they want to become (Belcher and Lukkarila 2011). Corpus studies have continued to have an important place in ESP research and critical discourse analysis, as well as critical perspectives more generally, which have started to gain more prominence in ESP research (see e.g. Kandil and Belcher 2011; Starfield 2011, this volume). Research in ESP, then, while still specific, is also increasingly critical and ethnographic at the same time as it maintains its materials-driven, learner-centered and needs-responsive focus (Belcher 2009; Dudley-Evans and St. John 1998). As Johns in the first chapter of this volume points out, ESP research has come a long way since its early days in the 1960s. It has perhaps moved in ways that early teachers and researchers might not have expected, or anticipated. Some of these developments are reflected in the chapters of this *Handbook*.

There are most certainly, however, other developments that are yet to come, as very clearly articulated by Diane Belcher in the final chapter of the *Handbook*. In her chapter, Belcher points to the important role that ESP can play in increasing access and options for learners in their current and future worlds of work, study, and everyday life. In particular, she points to how research into specific purpose language use as well as ESP professional practice more generally, can help do this.

REFERENCES

Belcher, D. (2009) What ESP is and can be:
An introduction. In D. Belcher (ed.),
*English for Specific Purposes in Theory and
Practice*. 1–20. Ann Arbor, MI: University
of Michigan Press.

Belcher, D., Johns, A. M., and Paltridge, B.
(eds.) (2011) *New Directions in English for
Specific Purposes Research*. Ann Arbor, MI:
University of Michigan Press.

Belcher, D. and Lukkarila, L. (2011)
Identity in the ESP context: Putting the
learner front and center in needs
analysis. In D. Belcher, A. M. Johns, and
B. Paltridge (eds.), *New Directions in
English for Specific Purposes Research*.
73–93. Ann Arbor, MI: University of
Michigan Press.

Benesch, S. (2001) *Critical English for
Academic Purposes*. Mahwah, NJ:
Lawrence Erlbaum.

Cheng, A. (2011) ESP classroom-based
research: Basic considerations and future
research questions. In D. Belcher, A. M.
Johns, and B. Paltridge (eds.), *New
Directions in English for Specific Purposes
Research*. 44–72. Ann Arbor, MI:
University of Michigan Press.

Dudley-Evans, T. and St John, M. J.
(1998) *Developments in English for
Specific Purposes: A Multi-Disciplinary
Approach*. Cambridge: Cambridge
University Press.

Hyland, K. (2002) Specificity revisited:
How far should we go? *English for
Specific Purposes* 21: 385–95.

Hyland, K. (2004) *Genre and Second
Language Writing*. Ann Arbor, MI: The
University of Michigan Press.

Hyland, K. (2011) Disciplinary specificity:
Discourse, context and ESP. In D.
Belcher, A. M. Johns, and B. Paltridge

(eds.), *New Directions in English for
Specific Purposes Research*. 6–24. Ann
Arbor, MI: University of Michigan Press.

Kandil, M. and Belcher, D. (2011) ESP and
corpus-informed critical discourse
analysis: Understanding the power of
genres of power. In D. Belcher, A. M.
Johns, and B. Paltridge (eds.), *New
Directions in English for Specific Purposes
Research*. 252–70. Ann Arbor, MI:
University of Michigan Press.

Paltridge, B. and Starfield, S. (2011)
Research in English for specific
purposes. In E. Hinkel (ed.), *Handbook of
Research in Second Language Teaching and
Learning*, Volume 2. 106–21. London:
Routledge.

Paltridge, B. and Wang, W. (2011)
Contextualising ESP research: Media
discourses in China and Australia. In D.
Belcher, A. M. Johns, and B. Paltridge
(eds.), *New Directions in English for
Specific Purposes Research*. 25–43. Ann
Arbor, MI: University of Michigan Press.

Starfield, S. (2011) Doing critical
ethnographic research into academic
writing: The theory of the methodology.
In D. Belcher, A. M. Johns, and B.
Paltridge (eds.), *New Directions in English
for Specific Purposes Research*. 174–96. Ann
Arbor, MI: University of Michigan Press.

Starfield, S. (2012) The historical
development of languages for specific
purposes. In C. A. Chapelle (ed.), *The
Encyclopedia of Applied Linguistics*.
Oxford: Wiley-Blackwell.

Swales, J. M. and Rogers, P. (1995)
Discourse and the projection of
corporate culture: The mission
statement. *Discourse and Society* 6:
223–42.

1 The History of English for Specific Purposes Research

ANN M. JOHNS

Introduction

Reviewing the history of English for specific purposes (ESP) research presents at least three problems: the first is deciding when the review should begin, that is, at what point in ESP's long history. This problem was solved by taking the lead from John Swales (1988), whose movement history, *Episodes in ESP*, begins in the early 1960s. The second problem is more difficult: though much of the research cited in this review was written for international journals, there has always been considerable localized, on-site ESP/LSP research that is either unpublished, published in a language other than English, or in local journals. For example, there are, or have been, regional ESP journals in Brazil (*ESPecialist*) as well as conferences and research publications in other parts of Latin America (see Horsella and Llopis de Segura 2003), where the Latin American ESP community has been active for many years[1]. In Europe, *ASP: la revue du GERAS* (see e.g. Gledhill 2011) and *Ibérica*, the official journal of AELFE, the European Association of Languages for Specific Purposes, often publish relevant articles (see e.g. Bhatia 2002). The European Association for the Teaching of Academic Writing (EATAW) conferences include a variety of papers that could fall under the ESP rubric (see Futász and Timár 2006). IATEFL also has a special interest group in ESP http://espsig. iatefl.org/ which publishes research reports (http://espsig.iatefl.org/). At this writing, at least three other publications are also available: the *Asian ESP Journal* (http://www.asian-esp-journal.com/), *ESP World* (http://www.esp-world.info), and the international (currently print and online) journal, *English for Specific Purposes (ESPJ)*. Because of this wide variety of possibilities, it is sometimes difficult to make clear-cut decisions about trends in research or which articles to cite.

The Handbook of English for Specific Purposes, First Edition.
Edited by Brian Paltridge and Sue Starfield.
© 2013 John Wiley & Sons, Inc. Published 2013 by John Wiley & Sons, Inc.

A third problem confronts the reviewer, as well: making a clear distinction between research and practice. Unlike many other research areas in theoretical and applied linguistics, ESP has been, at its core, a practitioners' movement, devoted to establishing, through careful research, the needs and relevant discourse features for a targeted group of students (see e.g. Richterich and Chancerel 1977). As Belcher (2009a: 3) points out in her edited collection:

> ESP specialists accept the responsibility for finding out what their learners will likely need (and want) to be able to read, write, speak and comprehend as listeners to achieve their goals.

This conflation of research and pedagogical practice may explain why John Swales' ground-breaking *Episodes* (1988) history includes eleven pedagogical pieces and only three other entries that would be considered research by the current reviewers of *ESPJ* or why *Issues in ESP* (Waters 1982) includes five chapters on research-based pedagogies. This may be why Tom Huckin and Leslie Olsen, respected ESP researchers, wrote *Technical Writing and Professional Communication for Nonnative Speakers* (1991) for the classroom, or why Michael Long's (2005) research-based collection is devoted exclusively to needs assessment, fundamental to ESP curriculum design. No doubt this is why Ken Hyland, a prolific English for academic purposes (EAP) researcher, addresses teaching approaches in his volume titled, *Genre and Second Language Writing* (2004), why Helen Basturkmen (2006, 2010) combined research on learning and pedagogy in her ESP overview volumes, or why Swales and Feak (2000, 2004, 2009, 2011a, 2011b, Feak and Swales 2009, 2011) have produced pedagogical volumes that apply current ESP research to teaching. Undoubtedly, there are more published and unpublished examples of this research/teaching interaction in many parts of the world.

Given the frequent – and required – conflation of research and pedagogical practice in ESP, how can a history of *research*, in contrast to systematic preparation for teaching practices, be written? To identify some distinctions between the two, four sources have been consulted: Hatch and Farhady (1982), whose volume on applied linguistics research design remains one of the best, even today; Martin Hewings' "A History of ESP through *English for Specific Purposes (ESPJ)*" (2001); Peter Masters' "Research in ESP" (2005), and the international journal *English for Specific Purposes* (ESPJ), founded as *The ESP Journal* in 1981.

Hatch and Farhady defined research as "a systematic way for searching for answers to appropriate questions . . ." The researcher's task is viewed as "asking the appropriate questions, selecting the best and optimally the shortest ways to find answers, and interpreting the findings in a way which we can justify" (1982: 1). On the other hand, in his 2005 overview of ESP research, Peter Master, who served as *ESPJ* co-editor, includes a variety of pieces on course design which might not qualify under the Hatch and Farhady definition; thus his view of the nature of ESP research is considerably broader, influenced, no doubt, by his pedagogical practice. However, as Hewings points out, and which should be clear from the discussion that follows, since its inception, the premier international journal,

English for Specific Purposes (ESPJ), has become increasingly empirical, as exploratory and course design papers have become relatively rare. Not surprisingly, the number of *ESPJ* articles on program description has decreased significantly: from 36 in the first five volumes to 10 in volumes 16–20 (Hewings 2001: 1). One result of this move toward empiricism is that the journal has now been included in the prestigious Social Science Citation Index (SSCI) "which is widely used as an indicator of quality research publications in, for example, US tenure committees and the UK Research Assessment Exercise" (Hewings 2001: 1).

Using these sources and my own experiences as a previous *ESPJ* co-editor and researcher, I have divided the research history that follows into four sections: The Early Years (1962–1981), The Recent Past (1981–1990), The Modern Era (1990–2011), and The Future (2011 plus), principally citing the articles in *ESPJ* as evidence, but drawing from a number of other sources as well.

The Early Years 1962–1981 (From Text-based Counts to "Rhetorical Devices")

This review begins in the years following World War II, where Swales (1988) began in *Episodes in ESP.* At that time, the central focus of ESP research was English for science and technology (EST) in academic contexts, an interest that remains strong to this day. In the first years of this period, research tended to be descriptive, involving statistical grammar counts within written discourses. Swales' first example in *Episodes,* by Barber (1962), was devoted to counting grammatical features across genres (textbooks and journal articles), in an attempt to determine some general sentence-level characteristics of EST. However, as Swales noted, this type of work "had descriptive validity but little explanatory force" (1988: 59). So this approach was soon overridden, as influential EST researchers, John Lackstrom, Larry Selinker, and Louis P. Trimble (see e.g. Lackstrom et al. 1972), began to dominate the field. For these North American authors from what was called "the [University of] Washington School," the relationships between EST grammar or lexicon and the authors' rhetorical purposes in texts were central, a connection that continues to be the focus of much of the ESP discourse analysis. Their "Grammar and Technical English" (1972), republished and discussed in *Episodes* (1988: 58–68), had a major impact. Joined by Mary Todd Trimble, Louis Trimble, and Karl Drobnic (1978) they edited a collection that also focussed upon science and technology. Along with chapters on curriculum design, this publication included sections on contrastive discourse analyses for Spanish, Macedonian, and Japanese, investigating both lexical and grammatical EST features.

In addition to contrastive analysis studies, a forward-looking chapter in the Trimble, Trimble, and Drobnic volume called "Purpose, device, and level in rhetorical theory" was contributed by a Washington School colleague, Robert Bley-Vroman. There, the author laid out the goals of ESP rhetorical theory as "establish[ing] a correspondence of purpose with device," with "device" referring to "the linguistic means by which the author achieves his [sic] end" (1978: 280). In general, these scholars' research, though ground-breaking, did not involve efforts to interview students or disciplinary experts to verify their hypotheses gleaned from texts.

Nonetheless, Washington School work represented an important turning point for ESP, with rhetorical concerns, particularly as they were inferred from "devices" within the text, becoming a central research focus. Probably the most famous of the studies in this period is found in Tarone et al. (1981), which appeared in the first volume of what was then called *The ESP Journal*, established by Grace Burkhart at the American University in Washington, DC and was reprinted, with commentary, in *Episodes in ESP* (1988: 174–187). In contrast to some of their predecessors, Tarone and her colleagues were not attempting to generalize about features of scientific language across genres; instead, they focussed on one arguably central characteristic of scientific prose, syntactic *voice,* as it had been argued that about 25 percent of the verbs in research articles are in the passive (Swales 2011). Whereas Barber was concerned with counts of grammatical items across EST, Tarone and her colleagues were testing hypotheses about the functions of a specific grammatical feature as it influenced rhetorical decisions among a narrow range of research articles in astrophysics. Another relatively new characteristic of this 1981 study was the involvement of an expert as a "specialist informant" with whom Tarone and the other applied linguists tested their conclusions.

Through the Tarone et al. study and the Washington School work precedents were set that can be found in much of what has been published in succeeding years. Among other contributions, these researchers brought to the fore two influential approaches in ESP methodology identified by Selinker (1988) in his research overview: "consultations with subject-specialist informants," and "rhetorical/ grammatical analyses" of specific types of texts, generally in science and technology disciplines. In less internationally conspicuous, more localized work, content specialists were also beginning to be consulted. For example, in a Regional English Language Centre/Singpore University publication edited by Jack C. Richards (1976), there appeared a chapter titled "The language of science from the viewpoint of the writer of science" (Godman: 71–78).

The trend towards more narrowly defined ESP research topics and texts, found in Tarone et al., was influential then, and remains central (see Hyland 2011). Dudley-Evans (2001: 311), in his final comment as *ESPJ* editor, noted that these trends toward in-depth, empirical and focussed work have continued:

> . . . as ESP research becomes more sophisticated and the range of its activity much broader, it has inevitably developed a much more focussed approach that looks at more detailed questions.

Though this is a review of ESP *research,* it is important to note that ESP coursebooks, often supported by the British Council, as well as published and unpublished research were being distributed widely in the EFL world, particularly in the Middle East and Latin America. Among the most famous were the *Nucleus* series, edited by Martin Bates and Tony Dudley-Evans (1976–80), Ewer and Latorre's (1969) *A Course in Basic Scientific English,* and John Swales' *Writing Scientific English* (1971/6) (see also Ewer 1971).

The More Recent Past: 1981–1990 (Broadening the Scope/Introducing Central Concepts)

A second historical period in ESP is bounded by the work of John Swales, whose seminal "Aspects of Article Introductions," first appeared in the United Kingdom in 1981. The approach described there became widely recognized when it appeared in augmented form in *Genre Analysis* (1990), initiating a research boom that has yet to end.

ESP leaders were also making an effort to expand the movement's horizons. Near the close of this period, the editors of *ESPJ,* John Swales and Ann Johns (1987: 163), expressed their concerns that ESP continued to be limited and was therefore considered irrelevant by most of the TESOL community; however, they promised to broaden the journal's scope, saying in the editorial for Vol. 6 (3):

> . . . as (ESP) researchers and practitioners have produced more refined studies, they have limited the scope and interest in ESP, principally to English for Science and Technology in an academic context. As a result, many TESOL professionals, working in content-based instruction and vocational ESL, do not think of themselves as part of ESP.
>   . . . We are attempting, through this journal and elsewhere to break from ESP's self-imposed limit in order to return to Strevens' original broad definition of ESP (1977), which included English for academic purposes, English for occupational purposes (also called VESL). . . .

The attempt to widen ESP's scope by the *English for Specific Purposes Journal* was certainly made and, as a result, the 1981–1990 period may have been the most inclusive in terms of topics for published research and pedagogical practice. During this period, special issues of the journal were devoted to teacher training (Vol. 2(1), 1983, in honor of Jack Ewer); to Vocational ESP (Vol. 3(2), 1984, guest edited by JoAnn Crandall); to interlanguage (Vol. 6(2), 1987, guest edited by Larry Selinker), and to training of international teaching assistants (Vol. 8(2), 1989, guest edited by Richard Young). In addition, submitted articles to issues that were not "special" predicted much of what was to come. The most frequently appearing of these topics are discussed below.

Needs assessment

During these early years of *ESPJ* publication, there appeared a considerable number of articles on needs assessment, the core of ESP practitioner work; though as West (1984) showed in her discussion of vocational ESL (VESL), research into student needs had become increasingly empirical, triangulated, and complex over time. Jacobson (1986), also breaking new ground, concentrated upon the strategic, rather than grammatical or discourse competence needs of students in a physics lab. In an Italian setting (1988), Tarantino used a face-to-face questionnaire interview to measure the macro- and micro-level needs of 53 EST researchers and students.

Linguistic devices and their rhetorical purposes

The interest in linguistic "devices," particularly as they related to rhetorical purposes, remained popular throughout the 1980s. Adams-Smith (1984) explored the problems that L2 speakers may have with distinguishing between objective statements of fact and author-marked observations in written texts. Malcolm's (1987) functional account of tense usage in the *Journal of Pediatrics* and Hanania and Akhtar's (1985) study of the rhetorical functions of certain verb forms in biology, chemistry, and physics theses demonstrated the potential for this approach. Though much of the research that connected linguistic elements with their rhetorical functions was completed on written texts, Rounds (1987) took on spoken English in her study of the rhetorical realizations of personal pronouns in a university mathematics classroom.

Technology: Posters, telexes, slides, and computer-mediated instruction

Though computers were not widely employed between 1981 and 1990, various researchers studied the technologies available. Betty Lou DuBois (1980), whose interest was in the juxtaposition of the visual with the verbal, studied the use of slides in biomedical speeches and later (1985), the design and presentation of posters at biomedical meetings. Zak and Dudley-Evans (1986) examined two features of the telex: word omission and word abbreviation, suggesting how they might be taught in Business English. Research involving computers did appear in Murray's (1988) longitudinal study of this "new medium of communication" in a business environment. In her article, the author juxtaposed CmC (computer-mediated instruction) with more traditional forms of written communication. In other ESP research contexts, the computer was also gaining in importance. In August, 1988, for example, Eindhoven University of Technology, in the Netherlands, held a Languages for Specific Purposes (LSP) conference which combined papers on more traditional topics (e.g. word counts within disciplinary discourses) with forward-looking papers such as "Technical communication via computational abstracts" (Harvey and Horsella 1988).

Other, less common, topics in ESP research

In addition to the special issue on interlanguage, the *ESPJ* also touched on topics that were common in the more "general" ESL/EFL areas, such as error analysis. Doushaq (1986), for example, published a piece on stylistic errors made among

Arab students of English for academic purposes (EAP). Though error analysis was no longer a major ESP research topic, other subjects, which continue to be popular, began to appear in the literature, such as early research on learning strategies, an area that is increasingly important to research in the early twenty-first century (see Tardy 2006). Adamson (1990) employed a case study approach to 15 ESL students, investigating both the effective and ineffective strategies (e.g. note-taking and using dictionaries) that were applied to academic classrooms, concluding that English for academic purposes is best taught along with academic content. Tedick (1990) studied the impact of students' subjective knowledge on their writing performance. Nonetheless, as Johns (1988) and Tardy (2006) have indicated, much more still needs to be done to study strategies and to determine how EAP classroom skills can be transferred to content classes or assignments in post-secondary institutions.

Others examined academic writing assignments. Horowitz (1986) classified essay examination prompts in research that has had broad implications for future work. In like manner, Braine (1989) examined students' writing assignments in two undergraduate courses in science and technology.

Central ESP concepts: Genre and rhetorical moves

The term *genre,* which continues to be highly salient in ESP research, began to appear in the ESP literature, often as linguistic "devices" were contrasted among text types. Morrow (1989), for example, contrasted the use of conjuncts in two genres: business news stories and academic journal articles. First, like Barber (1962), he counted the number of conjuncts; but then he commented on communicative and pragmatic functions of these linguistic elements within the texts studied. Gunawardena (1989) compared the uses of the present perfect in the rhetorical divisions within biology and biochemistry research articles. Hopkins and Dudley-Evans (1988), drawing from Swales' 1981 "Aspects" article, conducted a genre-based investigation of discussion sections in published articles and student dissertations, contrasting the rhetorical components of each. Interestingly enough, the issue of genre "volatility," important to current research and theory, was raised by Tinberg (1988: 211), who found differences in rhetorical purposes between examples of two texts within the same genre, resulting from

> . . . competing constraints on the author to stay within the bounds of the general community's genre, while at the same time developing a strong and persuasive argument within the smaller community of his/her paradigm.

The other, related, key term which has become central to ESP research is *rhetorical moves,* discussed in Swales' "Aspects of Article Introductions" (1981). It gained particular popularity in Britain during this period (e.g. Hopkins and Dudley-Evans 1988) and in other parts of the world after the publication of *Genre Analysis* in 1990. Here's what John Swales (2004: 226), with his characteristic modesty, has to say about the significance of his work:

The Create-a-Research Space (CARS) model for RA (research article) introductions in *Genre Analysis* has apparently been quite successful, in both descriptive and pedagogical terms. There are presumably a number of reasons: It was relatively simple, functional, corpus-based, sui-generis for the part-genre for which it applies and, at least in its early days, perhaps offered a schema that had not been widely available. A further predisposing element for the largely positive response may have been its strong metaphorical coloring – that of ecological competition for research space in a tightly contested territory.

Thus, during this second historical period, from the initial publication of *English for Specific Purposes* and "Aspects of Article Introductions" in the early 1980s to the appearance of *Genre Analysis* (1990), the two major terms in the field, *genre* and *rhetorical moves*, were introduced and discussed; and many of the current topics and research approaches were already in place. What was missing, among other things, was the sophisticated use of the computer for gathering corpus data, topics relating to additional ESP areas, and, more triangulated, critical, and contextualized methodological approaches. It should be pointed out, however, that despite the varied topics mentioned in this section, much of ESP research continued to operate within a narrow topical range, as the principal interest of researchers often focussed on English for academic purposes, particularly science and technology (EST) at the post-secondary or graduate level. In addition, written discourse continued to be the preferred data for analysis, according to Hewings' (2001) study.

The Modern Age: 1990–2011 (New International Journals, Genre, and Corpus Studies Take Center Stage)

The introduction and importance of new international journals

The next period, 1990–2011, is identified here as the "Modern age in ESP." During this period, two new international journals appeared, both of which included research articles that might have been published in *ESPJ*. The *Journal of Second Language Writing (JSLW)* was founded in 1991 by Ilona Leki and Tony Silva; and though many of its early articles focussed on writing processes or student errors, topics that have not been central to ESP research, in the 2000s, articles about academic argumentation, text analysis, and other issues that overlap with ESP interests appeared with increasing frequency. In 2007, Ken Hyland published "Genre pedagogy: Language, literacy, and L2 writing instruction" in *JSLW*, after which a number of genre-based, ESP-like research articles appeared, eventually resulting in a special issue (20(1), 2011a), edited by Christine Tardy, on "The future of genre in second language writing: A North American perspective."

In 2001, responding to the overwhelming number of articles in *ESPJ* and else-where on academic texts, students, and contexts, Liz Hamp-Lyons and Ken Hyland established the *Journal of English for Academic Purposes (JEAP)*. Though there are many examples of *ESPJ*-like articles in this journal, two will be offered as evidence here. In 2004, Samraj examined the discourse features of graduate student research papers "in order to increase our understanding of this heterogeneous genre and the dimensions along which it can vary across sub-disciplines" (2004: 5). Halleck and Connor (2006), using the increasingly popular corpus methodologies, exam-ined the rhetorical moves in TESOL conference proposals. ESP-related articles also continued to appear in more inclusive applied linguistics journals (see e.g. Johns 1993 on argumentation in engineering). Like *ESPJ*, *JEAP* published special issues on topics and methodologies that often expanded the journal's scope and pre-dicted research topics or methodologies for the future. These included "Evaluation in academic discourse," "Contrastive rhetoric in EAP," "Academic English in secondary schools," and "Corpus-based EAP," all of which overlap with ESP interests.

What makes these new international journals and *ESPJ* central to an under-standing of ESP research in the twenty-first century is the fact that, in many parts of the world, academics are now required to publish in international journals (preferably those on the Social Science Citation Index) in order to be promoted in their home institutions. This move results, in many cases, from the efforts on the part of the administrators of individual institutions and national educational organizations to boost university rankings internationally. An article on the inter-national "rankings race" (Hazelkorn 2011: 2) included these comments:

> [To improve their university's positions in the rankings], institutions are restructur-ing to create larger, more research-intensive units, or altering the balance between teaching and research or between undergraduate and graduate activities. Resources are being redirected towards . . . faculty members who are more prolific, particularly on the international level, and thus likeliest to move the [international ranking] indi-cators upward.

Not surprisingly, *English for Specific Purposes*, as well as other international publications (especially those on the SSCI), have experienced a rapid increase in international submissions. During 2010, for example, the largest number of sub-missions to *ESPJ* were from Taiwan (23) and the second largest from China (21). Below this group were the United States (16), Iran (11), and Malaysia (10) (Pal-tridge, personal communication, March 9, 2011). It must be noted, however, that since the *ESPJ* acceptance rate is about 25 percent, a considerable number of the total number of submissions have not been published.

Intercultural rhetorics

The interest in contrastive discourse analysis, while evolving into "intercultural rhetorics" has always been woven into ESP research (see Connor 2002, 2004). An earlier collection on this topic was edited by Swales and Mustafa (1984) and included this representative chapter, "Textual approximation in the teaching of academic writing to Arab students: A contrastive approach," by Clive Holes. In 1990, Salager-Meyer's contrasts between metaphors in French and Spanish Medical English research articles appeared in *ESPJ*. Elsewhere, Vijay Bhatia has edited, with Christopher Candlin and others, two major intercultural books on legal discourse (2003, 2008). This interest in intercultural rhetorics continues to this day (Connor 2004), often in English as a foreign language contexts (e.g. Perales-Escudero and Swales 2011). A useful intercultural turn has been taken by Mauranen (2005, 2011) and her colleagues (e.g. Björkman 2009, Hülmbauer 2009) who have pursued the topic of English as a lingua franca through the extensive ELFA (English as a lingua franca in academic settings) Project.

Genre: The central concept

Another important characteristic of the 1990–2011 period is the dominance of *genre* in ESP research, since Swales' *Genre Analysis* (1990) initiated a remarkably productive topic for scholars. Studies of advanced academic genres continue to predominate, a concern for those who believe that the most intransigent academic issues can be found in novice undergraduate education (see Benesch 1996; Johns 1997). Bhatia's (1993, 2004, 2008) continuing work has demonstrated, however, that genre analysis can and should be completed on professional genres, as well. This interest in (expository) genres continues to enrich research both within the ESP community (e.g. Tardy 2009, 2011b) and among genre theorists and practitioners from other theoretical schools (see Bawarshi and Reiff 2010).

As Hyon pointed out (1996), there are three acknowledged theories and research paths in genre studies, representing different views and pedagogical goals, and there continue to be tensions among them (Johns 2011; Tardy 2011a). In an effort to resolve some of the theoretical and pedagogical differences, some experts have been working towards theory, research, and pedagogical convergences, moves that should be very productive for future ESP research (Artemeva et al. 2011; Bawarshi and Reiff 2010; Flowerdew 2011; Johns 2002; Johns et al. 2006; Swales 2009).

Before continuing, it is important to look more closely at what has resulted from the ground-breaking ESP work by John Swales. What types of genre research based upon the "rhetorical moves" discussed in *Genre Analysis* (1990) have taken place? A full response to this question would require a book; however, for the purposes of this review, a few of the many examples from *ESPJ* that build directly upon the 1990 volume will be noted here. In the special issue of the journal devoted to a Latin American ESP conference (1992), Salager-Meyer reported on "A text type and move analysis study of verb tense and modality distribution in Medical English abstracts." Also relevant are Kanoksilapathan's (2005) article on the rhetorical structures of biochemistry research articles; Lorés' (2004) study of research article abstracts, touching on both structure and theme; Holmes' (1997) investigation of discussion sections in three disciplines; Nwogu's (1997) article investigating the medical research paper, and Samraj and Monk's (2008) paper in which they examined statements of purpose in graduate student applications.

Although genre analysis that stems from Swales' 1990 "moves" work still appears to be productive, especially in intercultural rhetoric studies (e.g. Ono 2011; Ren and Yuying 2011), most genre research published in international journals now focusses on other issues (see Bhatia 2004 for an overview). One area of research related directly to pedagogy is the development of learner genre awareness. In her meta-analysis of research into first and second language genre learning, for example, Tardy (2006: 81) found that the vast majority of the studies took place in post-secondary academic contexts, 24 of which were in undergraduate classes, while 28 were in graduate school contexts. She found 12 learning/acquisition studies of professionals and interns, and only 8 among young learners and secondary students.

John Swales moved on many years ago from his 1990 classic approach in *Genre Analysis* to propose different ways for examining a genre and discussing its implications. A 2002 publication written with a graduate student, Stephanie Lindemann, employed a case study to focus on the importance of investigating how students "get from the macro- to the micro-level" in their writing processes, particularly as they attempt to produce a complex text, in this case, a literature review for a research paper. In this publication, the authors noted that very little had been done to examine the actual processes that students undertake when attempting difficult tasks, an area that continues to be productive. Swales has also introduced nomenclature that has become integral to ESP research and parlance. His *Other Floors, Other Voices* (1998) brought "textography" into the ESP lexicon, as he studied the interactions of texts and contexts in three distinct discourse communities, using written work, interviews, observations, and other data. A "textographies" approach has been extended by Paltridge, another productive ESP researcher and practitioner, in his more recent work (2008; Paltridge et al. 2011). In "Occluded genres in the academy: The case of the submission letter," Swales (1996) brought another term into the ESP vernacular while reporting his study of submission letters to *ESPJ*. This "occluded" concept (genres which are difficult to obtain examples of) has been extended by Hyon (2008) in her case study of university retention-promotion-tenure reports. These forays did not prevent Swales from returning to an earlier period of careful linguistic analysis as in his 1997 discussion of the "missing complement," a feature characteristic of the cuneiform EST tablet presented to him at an ESP Special Interest Section meeting at a TESOL Conference.

Corpus studies

The modern period also marks the dominant use of corpus research, particularly in analyses of written academic genres, though some important work has been completed on oral language, as well, as seen in the University of Michigan's corpus of spoken academic English, MICASE (see Simpson-Vlach and Leicher 2006). Ken Hyland's many publications focussing on the relationships between writers and readers of academic texts represent some of the most frequently cited among the ESP corpus studies. His work on metadiscourse, "those aspects of text which explicitly refer to the organization of the discourse or the writer's stance towards either its content or the reader" (Hyland 2005a: 109) and his "interpersonal model of metadiscourse," presented in an article co-written with Tse (Hyland and Tse 2004), have been influential. Hyland (2005b: 49) also focussed on "textual voice or community-recognized personality" as he spoke of writer stance; writer engagement then dealt with the ways in which writers relate to their readers. Complementing this text-based research with interviews with specialist informants, he explored differences between the "hard" disciplines, such as the sciences and the disciplines viewed as "soft," e.g. the social sciences and humanities.

These issues of interpersonality and interactivity in written discourse increased in importance during this period, so much so that one aspect, "evaluative language," became the focus of a special issue of *JEAP* (Vol. 2(4), 2003), edited by Marina Bondi and Anna Mauranen. Working from the Hunston and Thompson definition of evaluation, an "expression of the speaker or writer's attitude or stance towards, or viewpoint on, or feelings about the entities or propositions that he or she is talking about" (Hunston and Thompson 2000: 5), the contributors to this issue examined and critiqued evaluative language and its purposes within and among academic discourses.

Prominent researchers

In addition to John Swales, there are individuals who have made special contributions to ESP throughout its history, several of whom will be discussed here. Vijay Bhatia is probably the most prominent ESP research voice in areas outside of academia. His volume entitled *Analyzing Genre: Language Use in Professional Settings* (1993) began his long research and publication path related to professional writing, particularly in the law, as he wrote, edited or co-edited volumes on viewing the law with international perspectives (see e.g. Bhatia et al. 2008) and on diversity and tolerance in socio-legal contexts (Wagner and Bhatia 2009), while contributing to a growing understanding of ESP genre theory (Bhatia 2004, 2009). Using genre as a base, he has moved beyond the language and the law to study broader research interests such as discourse realizations (see e.g. his work on creativity and accessibility in written professional discourse, 2008, and research methodologies, 2002).

Charles Bazerman's historical studies (see especially, *Shaping Written Knowledge: The Genre and Activity of the Experimental Article*, 1988, http://www.education.ucsb.edu/bazerman/), as well as his work with colleagues on the act of writing (see Bazerman and Prior 2004), have been valuable to theorists, researchers, and practitioners. In recent years, he has edited a series called "Rhetoric, knowledge, and society," volumes reporting on influential studies in the field of writing, both academic (e.g. Prior 1998) and professional (e.g. Winsor 1996). Bazerman also creates alliances among genre theorists, as seen at the Writing Research Across Borders Conference that he convened in 2011 as well as among faculty across the disciplines (Bazerman and Paradis 1991; Bazerman and Prior 2005). One of his principal interests is building bridges among researchers from different parts of the world through both his international conferences and publications (e.g. Bazerman et al. 2009).

Diane Belcher has made major contributions to research internationally as co-editor of *English for Specific Purposes* (1998–2008) and, at this writing, of *TESOL Quarterly*. Her work in editing ESP volumes on research and practice (Belcher 2009a; Belcher, et al. 2011) and her ESP survey articles (e.g. 2006) have enabled students and professionals throughout the world to appreciate the contributions of modern ESP. In addition, her research on publication in a diverse world (e.g. 2007, 2009b) has explored the obstacles and triumphs of the international scholar.

Brian Paltridge, a former co-editor, with Sue Starfield, of *English for Specific Purposes Journal* and co-editor of the collection, *New Directions in English for Specific Purposes Research* (Belcher et al. 2011). Like Belcher, many of this ESP expert's major contributions are found in his publications that make difficult concepts and current research accessible to the student and practicing teacher. With Starfield, for example, he has produced *Thesis and Dissertation Writing in a Second Language* (Paltridge and Starfield 2007). In addition, his volumes on discourse analysis (e.g. Paltridge 2012) and *Genre and the Language Learning Classroom* (Paltridge 2001) and his state-of-the-art reviews (e.g. Paltridge 2004) are read widely. And like Belcher and many ESP researchers, he devotes most of his attention to graduate students and scholars, with particular focus on China (e.g. Paltridge 2007), where his university has established a joint masters program with Fudan University in Shanghai.

Though as of this writing, Anthony (Tony) Dudley-Evans and Maggie Jo St John are not publishing in ESP, it is important to note that their *Developments in English for Specific Purposes: A Multi-Disciplinary Approach* (1998), in its twelfth printing, continues to be a required teacher education coursebook in many parts of the world. Because of his earlier, research-driven pedagogical work, Tony is the only person who appears twice in *Episodes in ESP* (1988), once as co-author, with Martin Bates, of *Nucleus General Science* (1976) and once with Tim Johns, a remarkable scholar as well, with an article on team-teaching in the sciences (Johns and Dudley Evans 1980). Later, Tony became an expert in the discourse of economics, co-authoring a volume with Henderson on the subject (Dudley-Evans and Henderson 1990). Maggie Jo's interest is the English of Business; and in addition to co-editing a special issue on this topic in *ESPJ* (Vol. 15(1) 1996), she has written two books for EFL business students (1992 and 1994). At this writing, she is actively promoting, through Twitter and elsewhere, volunteer work and English language teaching in the mountains of northern Nicaragua through her direction of the NEST Trust (http://www.thenesttrust.org.uk).

In addition to discussing individual researchers/practitioners who have played central roles, it is important to note there are areas in the world experiencing a burst of energy among a group of researchers, sometimes addressing the same topics or methodologies in different ways. Earlier in this review, the significant number of submissions to *ESPJ* from China and Taiwan was mentioned; the *Asian*

ESP Journal (http://www.asian-esp-journal.com/) publishes articles from this region, as well, with authors discussing a variety of subjects often using current methodologies. Throughout Europe, researchers also remain active, particularly as they study the use of English among L2 speakers (e.g. Mauranen 2011). The Spanish and Portuguese-speaking world, particularly Latin America, continues to publish papers (see the *ESPecialist*) and hold research conferences (see Horsella and Llopis de Segura 2003). In addition, there have been a considerable number of research efforts in Spain. From the relatively new Universitat Jaume I (James I University), established in 1993 to pursue studies of technology, comes an article by Santiago Posteguillo (2002) demonstrating how online activity has blurred genres and changes our view of language, arguing that there should be online sub-areas for each ESP specialty (e.g. e-BE, for electronic Business English; e-ME for electronic Medical English), since in each specialty, there are specific digital applications. Other members of the Universitat Jaume I faculty, Inmaculada Fortanet-Gómez, Juan Carlos Palmer-Silvera, and Miguel Ruiz-Garrido, are involved in studies of intercultural rhetoric (2011). From Ana I. Moreno at the University of Léon comes an article that employed a common writing assignment, the cause/effect analytical essay, to demonstrate that researchers need to match their theoretical descriptions of particular discourse types to actual classroom instructions and texts (2003). The University of Zaragoza also has an active faculty (see e.g. Pérez-Llantada, 2009) where corpora play a significant role in the research process.

Mohamed Daoud, an ESP specialist who is active in promoting research-informed ESP teaching in North Africa (1996, 2000), has reported that he, his students, and his colleagues are very active, particularly in writing course-related and textbook projects, as well as theses and dissertations on needs analysis, skill and strategy development, and genre studies. However, as is the case in a number of regions in the world, there is much more happening in ESP than one would assume from examining international journals.

The Future

What will the future bring? It appears that English for specific purposes is moving in the following directions:

International authorship.   As it becomes more important for international scholars to publish in SSCI journals, an increasing number of quality submissions will be made from across the world, not only to *ESPJ* but to other international applied linguistics journals (e.g. *JEAP, JSLW, TESOL Quarterly*) that publish ESP-related work. Unfortunately, this may affect regional journals which often are more focussed on the local needs of ESP students, including pedagogical practices.

Researcher roles.   Because ESP has been, and continues to be, a practitioner move-ment – based upon the research necessary to meet the needs and analyze the discourses and contexts of target student populations, researchers will continue to view themselves as taking one or several professional roles. In their widely circulated overview of ESP theory, research, and teaching, Dudley-Evans and St John (1998: 13–17) listed five key roles of the ESP practitioner: teacher, course-designer and materials provider, collaborator (often with a subject or vocational specialist), researcher, and evaluator. Though the role of the researcher has been emphasized in this review, the collaborative role is one that is essential in a number of ESP contexts; and in these situations, research and teaching often interact. Here, for example, is a discussion of collaborative vocational ESL work taking place in the United States (Johns and Price, in press):

> With the collaboration of CTE instructors and employers, Price [an ESP Consultant] and her colleagues have [conducted needs assessments] and created curricula designed to help students to transfer their skills seamlessly into employment or their job training classes.

Varied methodologies and triangulation.   For those considering the central mandate of ESP, an appropriate and thorough needs analysis, it might be best to consult Michael Long's extensive introduction in his collection (2005), devoted exclusively to needs analysis. Among other chapters in the volume are found a variety of approaches, including case studies, task-based foci, and sociological perspectives as well as combinations of these. Other researchers, like Tardy (2011b), have argued for multi-methodological approaches to genre analysis in order to capture [genre's] "dynamic, situated, and intertextual nature." However, at the time of this writing (2011), it appears that corpus linguistics approaches to text continue to dominate submissions to *ESPJ* and the research scene. The editors of ESPJ note, for example, that there have been an increasing number of submissions that employ corpus approaches to the analysis of lexical bundles (Paltridge, personal communication, February 12, 2011).

There are also promising efforts to increasingly contextualize and critique ESP approaches. An examination of the 2011 volume, *New Directions in English for Specific Purposes Research*, makes this clear. In this volume, Paltridge and Wang (2011) discuss ways of contextualizing ESP research, analyzing media texts in China and Australia as an example of this. And though ESP tends to portray itself as "scientific" and "objective," there have always been those who challenge this view (e.g. Benesch 1996, 1999), referring to ESP as "assimilationist," for not enabling students to critique their study environments or texts. In *New Directions*, the term "*critical*" is used with both discourse analysis and ethnography. Kandil and Belcher (2011) report on a corpus-informed study, a critical discourse analysis of the genres of power. Combining a strong contextual approach (ethnography) with a critical focus, Starfield (2011) and Johns and Makalela (2011) discuss their studies, both of which took place in South Africa.

Multimodalities.   Gunther Kress (2010) and his colleagues have provided the applied linguistics leadership in approaching texts, and learning, as multimodal. In a 2003 presentation, he argued that there are linked shifts in representation and dissemination [of information]: that is, from the constellation of mode or writing and medium of the book/page to the constellation of mode of image and medium of screen . . . [This results in] shifts in authority, in changes in forms of reading, shifts in shapes of knowledge and in forms of human engagement with the local and natural world (2003: 3).

Traditionally, especially sciences and technology (EST) and vocational/technical English, coursebooks have identified visual information as central to students' learning (e.g. Kerridge 1988; Yates et al. 1988), and Johns (1998) has discussed interactions of the visual and the verbal in economics, so it is surprising that so little research has been completed either on the visual/verbal interaction in texts or on academic or nonacademic visual rhetoric.

In an excellent volume called *Critical Graphicacy: Understanding Visual Representation Practices in School Science,* Roth et al. (2005) speak of the ways in which visual displays can be employed, and by extension, should be a focus of ESP research. Visual images are used:

to present data, illustrate abstract concepts, organize complex sets of information, facilitate the integration of new knowledge with existing knowledge, enhance information retention, mediate thinking processes, and improve problem solving (Roth et al. 2005: 208–09).

Certainly there is much to study in this list, in addition to the uses of visual information for business and vocational ESP.

Varied locales.   It should be evident from this review that post-secondary academic *texts,* particularly those written by graduate students, have been the preferred sites for ESP research, perhaps because this has been the interest of some of the best-known ESP researchers (Swales, Hyland, Belcher, Paltridge). However, if ESP is to become a more universally-accepted movement, then, as Tardy (2006) points out, more researchers need to make classrooms the center of some of their work (see also Cheng 2011). Some of these classrooms should be in vocational or professional schools (see Johns and Price in press) or in secondary classrooms (see *JEAP* special issue: Academic English in Secondary Schools, 2006, Vol. 5(4)). Interestingly enough, ESP for business professionals has been the fastest-growing area in pedagogical practice (St John 1998). Though the language and discourses of the professions have always been an integral part of the North American genre school and technical writing programs, except for Bhatia and Bazerman's early work, the business, law and other professions have been underrepresented in ESP research. This, too, needs to change.

Locales can also be viewed as vantage points, that is, from the point of view of different stakeholders in an ESP enterprise. In *New Directions* (2011), Belcher and Lukkarila argue that learner identity, particularly the cultural identity of learners, needs to be given greater attention in a needs analysis. Though these authors acknowledge the extensive work in identity studies (e.g. Block 2007; Canagarajah

2004), there is little in *ESPJ* or other ESP publications that considers the intercultural identities of students.

The future of genre studies

It appears that genre as a research topic is nowhere near exhausted. Because it offers possibilities for increasingly complex discussions of text, context, writer, audience, language, and other issues, it may continue to intrigue researchers and ESP practitioners for many years to come. As mentioned earlier, an important recent development in genre studies is the attempt to examine theoretical views (Bawarshi and Reiff 2010) with dispassion and, particularly in the case of Charles Bazerman (WRAB II) and John Swales (2009), to find shared interests among the genre schools. What are these and what research questions might they engender? Here is a list of what most experts, whatever their theoretical views, may recognize as researchable, offered by Swales (2009: 148):

- That in studying genres and genre production, we need to recognize a balance between the constraints of current or previous contexts and expectations of a discourse community and writer/speaker choice.
- That context "colors the realization of genre exemplars,"
- That "genres and genre sets are always evolving in response to various exigencies" and finally
- That in terms of pedagogies and learning, and as a consequence of the other features of genres, "[we need] a more nuanced approach to genre-awareness and acquisition".

As a result of these efforts by the most creative and well-published authors in genre studies, ESP may, in fact, become much more specific and contextualized, and there will be more studies of whether various "nuanced" genre-awareness approaches in the classroom (see Johns 2009) are, in fact, effective, especially in L2 classrooms.

Conclusion

ESP has come a long way in terms of research practices since its inception in the 1960s, but genre, a topic initiated in 1981, remains with us. In addition, other topics and methodologies have opened the way for learner-centered approaches, advocated by Hutchinson and Waters (1987), and later, by Tardy (2006). There will probably be further interest in classroom-based research and in studies in less-popular academic locales, such as secondary and vocational schools or in regions where English is the lingua franca. Perhaps, unfortunately, for the needs of local students and international scholars, research may become more centralized in international journals, though online publications may mitigate some of these issues.

Four words may serve to summarize what the future may bring to ESP: *variety*, in topics, methodologies, rhetorics (e.g. the visual and multimodal), writer's stance, and more; *context*, as the locales for research become diversified, bring to the fore the specific contexts of classrooms, businesses, online media – and in learners' cognition – *complexity*, realized through methodological triangulation, and finally, *critique*, not only of the researcher's work and pedagogies but of the researcher him/herself, through self-reflection.

NOTE

1   See *English for Specific Purposes* 11(2), special issue on the 2nd Latin American ESP Conference, Santiago, Chile, November 1990.

REFERENCES

Adamson, H. D. (1990) ESL students' use of academic skills in content courses. *English for Specific Purposes* 9: 67–88.

Adams-Smith, D. (1984) Medical discourse: Aspects of authors' comment. *ESP Journal* 3: 25–36.

Artemeva, N., Bawarshi, A., Byrnes, H., Devitt, A., Fox, J., Giltrow, J., Pare, A., et al. (2011) Converging Streams? Rhetorical and textual approaches to genre research and pedagogy. Symposium, Writing Across Research Borders II. February 17–20. Washington DC: George Mason University.

Barber, C. L. (1962) Some measurable characteristics of modern scientific prose. *Contributions to English Syntax and Philology*, Gothenburg Studies in English, 14. Reprinted, with a commentary, in J. M. Swales (ed.) (1988) *Episodes in ESP: A Source and Reference Book on the Development of English for Science and Technology*. 1–15. New York: Prentice-Hall.

Basturkmen, H. (2006) *Ideas and Options for English for Specific Purposes*. Mahwah, NJ: Lawrence Erlbaum.

Basturkmen, H. (2010) *Developing Courses in English for Specific Purposes*. Basingstoke, UK: Palgrave/ Macmillan.

Bates, M. and Dudley-Evans, T. (Series eds.) (1976–80) *Nucleus: English for Science and Technology*. Harlow: Longman.

Bawarshi, A. and Reiff, M. -J. (2010) *Genre: An Introduction to History, Theory, Research and Pedagogy*. West Layfayette, IN: Parlor Press.

Bazerman, C. (1988) *Shaping Written Knowledge: The Genre and Activity of the Experimental Article*. Madison, WI: University of Wisconsin Press.

Bazerman, C. and Paradis, J. (eds.) (1991) *Textual Dynamics and the Professions*. Madison, WI: University of Wisconsin Press.

Bazerman, C. and Prior, P. (eds.) (2004) *What Writing Does and How it Does it*. Mahwah, NJ: Lawrence Erlbaum.

Bazerman, C. and Prior, P. (2005). Participating in emergent socio-literate worlds: Genre, disciplinarity, interdisciplinarity. In R. Beach, J. Green, and M. Kamil (eds.) *Multidisciplinary*

Perspectives on Literacy Research. 2nd ed. 133–78. Cresskill, NJ: Hampton Press.

Bazerman, C., Bonini, A., and Figueiredo, D. (eds.) (2009) *Genre in a Changing World*. West Lafayette, IN: Parlor Press.

Belcher, D. (2006) English for specific purposes: Teaching to the perceived needs and imagined futures in the world of work, study, and everyday life. *TESOL Quarterly* 40: 133–56.

Belcher, D. (2007) Seeking acceptance in an English-only research world. *Journal of Second Language Writing* 16: 1–22.

Belcher, D. (ed.) (2009a) *English for Specific Purposes in Theory and Practice*. Ann Arbor, MI: University of Michigan Press.

Belcher, D. (2009b) How research space is created in a diverse research world. *Journal of Second Language Writing* 18: 221–34.

Belcher, D., Johns, A. M., and Paltridge, B. (eds.) (2011) *New Directions in English for Specific Purposes Research*. Ann Arbor, MI: University of Michigan Press.

Belcher, D. and Lukkarila, L. (2011) Identity in the ESP context: Putting the learner front and center in needs analysis. In D. Belcher, A. M. Johns, and B. Paltridge (eds.) *New Directions in English for Specific Purposes Research*. 73–93. Ann Arbor, MI: University of Michigan Press.

Benesch, S. (1996) Needs analysis and curriculum in EAP: An example of a critical approach. *TESOL Quarterly* 30: 723–38.

Benesch, S. (1999) Rights analysis: Studying power relations in an academic setting. *English for Specific Purposes* 18: 313–27.

Bhatia, V. (1987) Textual mapping in British legislative writing. *World Englishes* 6: 1–10.

Bhatia, V. (1993). *Analyzing Genre: Language Use in Professional Settings*. London: Longman.

Bhatia, V. (2002) Applied genre analysis: A multi-perspective model. *Ibérica* 4: 3–19.

Bhatia, V. (2004) *Worlds of Written Discourse: A Genre-Based View*. London: Continuum.

Bhatia, V. (2008) Creativity and accessibility in written professional discourse. *World Englishes* 27: 319–26.

Bhatia, V. (2009) Intertextual patterns in English legal discourse. In D. Belcher (ed.), *English for Specific Purposes in Theory And Practice*. 186–204. Ann Arbor, MI: University of Michigan Press.

Bhatia, V., Candlin, C., Egnberg, J., and Trosborg, A. (eds.) (2003) *Multilingual and Multicultural Contexts: An International Perspective*. New York: Peter Lang.

Bhatia, V., Candlin, C., and Evangelisti Allori, P. (eds.) (2008) *Language, Culture and the Law: The Formulation of Legal Concepts Across Systems and Cultures*. New York: Peter Lang.

Bley-Vroman, R. (1978) Purpose, device, and level in rhetorical theory. In M. Trimble, L. Trimble, and K. Drobnic (eds.) *English for Specific Purposes: Science and Technology*. 278–88. Corvallis, OR: English Language Institute, Oregon State University.

Block, D. (2007) The rise of identity in SLA research, post Firth and Wagner (1997). *The Modern Language Journal* 91: 863–76.

Björkman, B. (2009) From code to discourse in spoken ELF. In A. Mauranen and E. Ranta (eds.), *English as a Lingua Franca: Studies and Findings*. 225–53. Newcastle, UK: Cambridge Scholars Publishing.

Bondi, M, and Mauranen, A. (eds.) (2003) Evaluation in academic discourse. Special issue of *Journal of English for Academic Purposes*, Vol. 2(4).

Braine, G. (1989) Writing in science and technology: An analysis of assignments from ten undergraduate courses. *English for Specific Purposes* 8: 3–16.

Canagarajah, S. (2004) Multilingual writers and the struggle for voice in academic discourse. In A. Pavlenko and A. Blackledge (eds.), *Negotiation of Identities in Multilingual Contexts*. 266–89. Clevedon, UK: Multilingual Matters.

Cheng, A. (2011) Language features as the pathways to genre: Students' attention to non-prototypical features and its implications. *Journal of Second Language Writing* 20: 69–82.

Connor, U. (2002) New directions in contrastive rhetoric. *TESOL Quarterly* 36: 493–510.

Connor, U. (2004) Intercultural rhetoric research: Beyond texts. *Journal of English for Academic Purposes* 3: 291–304.

Daoud, M. (1996) English language development in Tunisia. *TESOL Quarterly* 30: 598–605.

Daoud, M. (2000) LSP in North Africa: Status, problems, and challenges. *Annual Review of Applied Linguistics* 30: 77–06.

DuBois, B. L. (1980) The use of slides in biomedical speeches. *ESP Journal* 1: 45–50.

DuBois, B. L. (1985) Popularization at the highest level: Poster sessions at biomedical meetings. *International Journal of the Sociology of Language* 56: 67–84.

Dudley-Evans, T. (2001) Editorial. *English for Specific Purposes* 10: 311–12.

Dudley-Evans, T. and Henderson, W. (1990) *The Language of Economics: The Analysis of Economics Discourse*. London: Modern English Publications (in cooperation with the British Council).

Dudley-Evans, T. and St John, M. J. (1998) *Developments in English for Specific Purposes: A Multi-Disciplinary Approach*. Cambridge: Cambridge University Press.

Doushaq, H. (1986) An investigation into stylistic errors of Arab students learning English for Academic Purposes. *English for Specific Purposes* 5: 27–40.

ELFA Project (http://www.eng.helsinki.fi/elfa).

English for Specific purposes (1990) Special issue on Latin America 11(2).

ESP World (http://www.esp-world.info).

Ewer, J. R. (1971) Further notes on developing an English programme for students of science and technology, *English Language Teaching* 26, 1, and 3. Reprinted, with commentary, in J. M. Swales (ed.) (1988) *Episodes in ESP: A Source and Reference Book on the Development of English for Science and Technology*. 45–57. New York: Prentice-Hall.

Ewer, J. R. and G. Latorre (1969) *A Course in Basic Scientific English*. London: Longman.

Feak, C. B. and J. M. Swales (2009) *Telling a Research Story: Writing a Literature Review*. Ann Arbor, MI: University of Michigan Press.

Feak, C. B. and J. M. Swales (2011) *Creating Contexts: Writing Introductions Across Genres*. Ann Arbor, MI: University of Michigan Press.

Flowerdew, J. (2011). Reconciling contrasting approaches to genre analysis: The whole can equal more than the sum of the parts. In D. Belcher, A. M. Johns, and B. Paltridge (eds.), *New Directions in English for Specific Purposes Research*. 119–44. Ann Arbor, MI: University of Michigan Press.

Futász, R. and Timár, E. (2006) Academic writing: Teaching online and face to face. EATAW Conference 2005. *Journal of Second Language Writing* 15: 147–49.

Fortanet-Gómez, I., Palmer-Silveira, J. C., and Ruiz-Girrido, M. (2011) *Empirical Intercultural Students of Professional and Academic Discourses*. Presentations at the Writing Research Across Borders II Conference, February 17–20. Washington DC: George Mason University.

Gledhill, C. (2011) The "lexicogrammar" approach to analyzing phraseology and collocation in ESP texts. *ASP: La revue du GERAS* 59: 5–23.

Godman, A. (1976) The language of science from the viewpoint of the writer of science textbooks. In J. Richards (ed.), *Teaching English for Science and Technology* (Anthology Series 2). 71–9. Singapore: Regional English Language Centre/Singapore University Press.

Gunawardena, C. N. (1989) The present perfect in rhetorical divisions of biology and biochemistry journal articles. *English for Specific Purposes* 8: 265–74.

Halleck, G. and Connor, U. (2006) Rhetorical moves in TESOL conference proposals. *Journal of English for Academic Purposes* 5: 70–86.

Hanania, E. and Akhtar, K. (1985) Verb form and rhetorical function in science writing: A study of MS theses in biology, chemistry, and physics. *The ESP Journal* 4: 49–58.

Harvey, A. and Horsella, M. (1988, August 3–6). *Technical Communication via Computational Abstracts: Implications for ESP*. Paper presented at the Second International Eindhoven LSP Conference, Eindhoven, the Netherlands.

Hatch, E. and Farhady, H. (1982) *Research Design and Statistics for Applied Linguistics*. Rowley, MA: Newbury House.

Hazelkorn, E. (2011, March 13). Questions abound as the college-rankings race goes global. *The Chronicle of Higher Education*: 1–4.

Hewings, M. (2001) A history of ESP through *English for Specific Purposes*. Accessed March 2, 2011 from http://www.esp-world.info/Articles_3/Hewings_paper.htm.

Holes, C. (1984) Textual approximation in the teaching of academic writing to Arab students: A contrastive approach. In J. M. Swales and H. Mustafa (eds.), *English for Specific Purposes in the Arab World*. 228–42. Birmingham, UK: The Language Studies Unit, University of Aston.

Holmes, R. (1997) Genre analysis and the social sciences: An investigation of the structure of research article discussion sections in three disciplines. *English for Specific Purposes* 16: 321–38.

Hopkins, A. and Dudley-Evans, A. (1988) A genre-based investigation of the discussion sections in articles and dissertations. *English for Specific Purposes* 7: 113–21.

Horowitz, D. (1986) What professors actually require: Academic tasks for the ESL classroom. *TESOL Quarterly* 20: 445–62.

Horsella, M. and G. Llopis de Segura. (2003) Survey of Latin American English for Specific Purposes Colloquia. In G. Saravia et al. (eds.), *Advances in ESP Research in Latin America*. Proceedings of the VIII Latin American ESP Colloquium, Córdoba, Argentina: Comunicarte Education.

Huckin, T. N. and Olsen, L. A. (1991) *Technical Writing and Professional Communication for Nonnative Speakers of English.*, 2nd ed. New York: McGraw-Hill.

Hülmbauer, C. (2009) "We don't take the right way. We just take the way we think you will understand" – The shifting relationship between correctness and effectiveness in ELF. In A. Mauranen and E. Ranta (eds.), *English as a Lingua Franca: Studies and Findings*, 323–47. Newcastle, UK: Cambridge Scholars Publishing.

Hunston, S. and G. Thompson (2000) Evaluation: An introduction. In S. Hunston and G. Thompson (eds.), *Evaluation in Text: Authorial Stance and the Construction of Discourse*. 1–27. Oxford: Oxford University Press.

Hutchinson, T. and A. Waters (1987) *English for Specific Purposes: A Learning-Centred Approach*. Cambridge: Cambridge University Press.

Hyland, K. (2004) *Genre and Second Language Writing*. Ann Arbor, MI: University of Michigan Press.

Hyland, K. (2005a) *Metadiscourse*. London: Continuum.

Hyland, K. (2005b) Stance and engagement: A model of interaction in academic discourse. *Discourse Studies* 7: 173–92.

Hyland, K. (2007) Genre pedagogy: Language, literacy and L2 writing instruction. *Journal of Second Language Writing* 16: 148–64.

Hyland, K. (2011) Disciplinary specificity: Discourse, context, and ESP. In D. Belcher, A. M. Johns, and B. Paltridge (eds.), *New Directions in English for Specific Purposes Research*. 6–24. Ann Arbor, MI: University of Michigan Press.

Hyland, K. and Tse, P. (2004) Metadiscourse in academic writing: A reappraisal. *Applied Linguistics* 25: 156–77.

Hyon, S. (1996) Genres in three traditions: Implications for ESL. *TESOL Quarterly* 10: 693–722.

Hyon, S. (2008) Convention and inventiveness in an occluded academic genre: A case study of retention-promotion-tenure reports. *English for Specific Purposes* 27: 175–93.

Jacobson, W. H. (1986) An assessment of communication needs of non-native speakers of English in an undergraduate physics lab. *English for Specific Purposes* 5: 173–88.

Johns, A. M. (1988) The discourse communities dilemma: Identifying transferable skills for the academic milieu. *English for Specific Purposes* 7: 55–60.

Johns, A. M. (1993) Written argumentation for real audiences: Suggestions for teacher research and classroom practice. *TESOL Quarterly* 27: 75–90.

Johns, A. M. (1997) *Text, Role and Context: Developing Academic Literacies*. New York: Cambridge University Press

Johns, A. M. (1998) The visual and the verbal: A case study in macroeconomics. *English for Specific Purposes* 17: 183–98.

Johns, A. M. (ed.) (2002) *Genre in the Classroom: Multiple Perspectives*. Mahwah, NJ: Lawrence Erlbaum.

Johns, A. M. (2009) Genre awareness for the novice academic student: An on-going quest. *Language Teaching* 41: 237–52.

Johns, A. M. (2011) The future of genre in L2 writing: Fundamental, but contested,

instructional decisions. *Journal of Second Language Writing* 20: 56–68.

Johns, A. M., Bawarshi, A., Coe, R., Hyland, K., Paltridge, B., and Reiff, M. J. (2006) Crossing the boundaries of genre studies: Commentaries by experts. *Journal of Second Language Writing* 15: 234–49.

Johns, T. and Dudley-Evans, A. (1980) An experiment in team-teaching of overseas post-graduate students of transportation and plant biology. *Team Teaching in ESP*: 137–55. London: The British Council/ETIC. Reprinted, with a commentary, in J. M. Swales (ed.) (1988) *Episodes in ESP: A Source and Reference Book on the Development of English for Science and Technology*. New York: Prentice-Hall.

Johns, A. M. and Makalela, L. (2011) Needs analysis, critical ethnography, and context: Perspectives from the client and the consultant. In D. Belcher, A. M. Johns, and B. Paltridge (eds.), *New Directions in English for Specific Purposes Research*. 197–221. Ann Arbor, MI: University of Michigan Press.

Johns, A. M. and Price, D. (in press) English for specific purposes. In M. Celce-Murcia, D. M. Brinton, and M. A. Snow (eds.), *Teaching English as a Second or Foreign Language*. 4th ed. Boston: Heinle Cengage.

Journal of English for Academic Purposes (Special issues cited): Vol. 2(4) (2003) Evaluation in academic discourse (M. Bondi and A. Mauranen, guest eds.). Vol. 3(4) (2004) Contrastive rhetoric in EAP (U. Connor, guest ed.), Vol. 5(4) (2006) Academic English in secondary schools (A. M. Johns and M. A. Snow, guest eds.) Vol. 6(4) (2007) Corpus-based EAP pedagogy (P. Thompson, guest ed.)

Journal of Second Language Writing Tardy, C. (ed.) Vol 20(1) (2011). Special issue: The future of genre in second language writing: A North American perspective.

Kanoksilapatham, B. (2005) Rhetorical structure of biochemistry research articles. *English for Specific Purposes* 24: 269–82.

Kerridge, D. (1988) *Presenting Facts and Figures*. London: Longman.

Kress, G. (2010) *Multimodality: A Social Semiotic Approach to Contemporary Communication*. London: Routledge.

Lackstrom, J. E., Selinker, L., and Trimble, L. P. (1972) Grammar and technical English. *English Teaching Forum:* X(5). Reprinted, with a commentary, in J. M. Swales (ed.) (1988), *Episodes in ESP: A Source and Reference Book on the Development of English for Science and Technology*. 58–68. New York: Prentice-Hall.

Long, M. (2005) Methodological issues in learner needs analysis. In M. Long (ed.), *Second Language Needs Analysis*. 19–76. Cambridge: Cambridge University Press.

Mead, R. and Henderson, W. (1983) Conditional form and meaning in economics text. *ESP Journal* 2: 139–1.

Lorés, R. (2004) On RA abstracts: From rhetorical structure to thematic organization. *English for Specific Purposes* 23: 280–303.

Malcolm, L. (1987) What rules govern tense usage in scientific articles? *English for Specific Purposes* 6: 31–44.

Master, P. (2005) Research in English for specific purposes. In E. Hinkel (ed.), *Handbook of Research in Second Language Teaching and Learning*. 99–116. Mahwah, NJ: Lawrence Erlbaum.

Mauranen, A. (2005). English as a lingua franca – An unknown language? In G. Cortese and A. Duszak (eds.), *Identity, Community, Discourse: English in Intercultural Settings*. 269–93. Frankfurt: Peter Lang.

Mauranen, A. (2011) English as the lingua franca of the academic world. In D. Belcher, A. M. Johns, and B. Paltridge (eds.), *New Directions in English for Specific Purposes Research*. 94–117. Ann Arbor, MI: University of Michigan Press.

MICASE (Michigan Corpus of Academic Spoken English) (http://micase.elicorpora.info/).

Moreno, A. (2003) Matching theoretical descriptions of discourse and practical applications of teaching: The cause of causal metatext. *English for Specific Purposes* 22: 265–95.

Morrow, P. R. (1989) Conjunct use in business news stories and academic journal articles: A comparative study. *English for Specific Purposes* 8: 239–54.

Murray, D. E. (1988). Computer-mediated communication: Implications for ESP. *English for Specific Purposes* 7: 3–18.

Nwogu, K. N. (1997) The medical research paper: Structure and functions. *English for Specific Purposes* 16: 119–38.

Ono, M. (2011) A genre analysis of the overall organization and introductory chapters of Japanese and English literature PhD theses. Paper presented at Writing Research Across Borders II, 17–20 February. Washington DC: George Mason University.

Paltridge, B. (2001) *Genre and the Language Learning Classroom*. Ann Arbor, MI: University of Michigan Press.

Paltridge, B. (2004) State of the art review: Academic writing. *Language Teaching* 37: 87–105.

Paltridge, B. (2012) *Discourse Analysis*. 2nd ed. London: Continuum.

Paltridge, B. (2007) Beyond the text: An examination of Chinese college English writing. *University of Sydney Papers in TESOL* 2: 149–66.

Paltridge, B. (2008). Textographies and the research and teaching of writing. *Iberica: Journal of the European Association of Language for Specific Purposes* 15: 9–23.

Paltridge, B. and Starfield, S. (2007) *Thesis and Dissertation Writing in a Second Language*. London: Routledge.

Paltridge, B., Starfield, S., Ravelli, L., Nicholson, S., and Tuckwell, K. (2011) Doctoral writing in the visual and performing arts: Two ends of a continuum. *Studies in Higher Education.* DOI: 10.1080/03075079.2011.562285.

Paltridge, B. and Wang, W. (2011) Contextualizing ESP research: Media discourses in China and Australia. In D. Belcher, A. M. Johns, and B. Paltridge (eds.), *New Directions in English for Specific Purposes Research.* 25–43. Ann Arbor, MI: University of Michigan Press.

Peráles-Escudero, M. and Swales, J. M. (2011) Tracing convergence and divergence in pairs of Spanish and English research article abstracts. *Iberica*: 49–70.

Pérez-Llantada, C. (2009) Textual, genre and social features of spoken grammar: A corpus-based approach. *Language Learning and Technology* 13: 40–58.

Posteguillo, S. (2002) Netlinguistics and English for internet purposes. *Ibérica* 4: 21–38.

Prior, P. (1998). *Writing/Disciplinarity: A Sociolhistorical Account of Literate Activity in the Academy.* Mahwah, NJ: Lawrence Erlbaum.

Ren, H. and Yuying, L. (2011) A comparison study on the rhetorical moves of abstracts in published research articles and Master's foreign-language theses. *English Language Teaching* 4: 162–66.

Richards, J. C. (ed.) (1976) *Teaching English for Science and Technology (Selected papers from the RELC Seminar on the teaching and learning of English for scientific and technological purposes in Southeast Asia).* Singapore: SEAMEO Regional English Language Centre, Singapore University Press.

Richterich, R. and Chancerel, J. L. (1977) *Identifying the Needs of Adults Learning a Foreign Language.* Oxford: Pergamon Press.

Roth, W.-M., Pozzer-Ardenghi, L., and Young Han, J. (2005) *Critical Graphicacy: Understanding Visual Representation Practices in School Science.* New York: Springer.

Rounds, P. (1987) Multifunctional personal pronoun use in an educational setting. *English for Specific Purposes* 6: 13–30.

Salager-Meyer, F. (1990) Metaphors in medical English prose: A comparative study with French and Spanish. *English for Specific Purposes* 9: 145–59.

Salager-Meyer, F. (1992) A text-type and move analysis of verb tense and modality distribution in medical English abstracts. *English for Specific Purposes* 11: 93–115.

Samraj, B. (2004) Discourse features of the student-produced academic research paper: Variations across disciplinary courses. *Journal of English for Academic Purposes* 3: 5–22.

Samraj, B. and Monk, L. (2008) The statement of purpose in graduate program applications: Genre structure and disciplinary variation. *English for Specific Purposes* 27: 193–211.

Selinker, L. (1988) Using research methods in LSP: Two approaches to applied discourse analysis. In M. L. Tickoo (ed.), *ESP: State of the Art.* 33–52. Singapore: SEAMEO Regional Language Centre.

Selinker, L., Todd Trimble, M., and Trimble, L. (1976). Presuppositional rhetorical information in EST discourse. *TESOL Quarterly* 10: 281–90.

St John, M. J. (1998).Business is booming: Business English in the 90s. *English for Specific Purposes* 15: 3–18.

Simpson-Vlach, R. C. and Leicher, S. (2006) *The MICASE Handbook.* Ann Arbor, MI: University of Michigan Press.

Starfield, S. (2011) Doing critical ethnographic research into academic writing: The theory of the methodology. In D. Belcher, A. M. Johns, and B. Paltridge (eds.), *New Directions in English for Specific Purposes Research.* 174–96. Ann Arbor, MI: University of Michigan Press.

Swales, J. M. (1971/1976) *Writing Scientific English.* London: Thomas Nelson & New York: Cengage.

Swales, J. M. (1981) *Aspects of Article Introductions.* Birmingham, UK: Aston

University, The Language Studies Unit. Republished University of Michigan Press (2011).

Swales, J. M. (1988). *Episodes in ESP: A Source and Reference Book on the Development of English for Science and Technology.* 2nd impression. New York: Prentice-Hall.

Swales, J. M. (1990). *Genre Analysis: English in Academic and Research Settings.* Cambridge: Cambridge University Press.

Swales, J. M. (1996) Occluded genres in the academy: The case of the submission letter. In E. Ventola & A. Mauranen (eds.), *Academic Writing; Intercultural and Textual Issues.* 45–58. Amsterdam: John Benjamins.

Swales, J. M. (1997) The world's earlier-known technical texts: A brief note. *English for Specific Purposes* 16: 153–5.

Swales, J. M. (1998) *Other Floors, Other Voices: A Textography of a Small University Building.* Mahwah, NJ: Lawrence Erlbaum.

Swales, J. M. (2004) *Research Genres: Exploration and Applications.* New York: Cambridge University Press.

Swales, J. M. (2009) Worlds of genre. In C. Bazerman, A. Bonini, and D. Figueredo (eds.), *Genre in a Changing World.* 1–13. West Lafayette, IN: Parlor Press.

Swales, J. M. (2011) Coda: Reflections on the future of genre and L2 writing. *Journal of Second Language Writing* 20: 83–5.

Swales, J. M. and Feak, C. B. (2000) *English in Today's Research World: A Writing Guide.* Ann Arbor, MI: University of Michigan Press.

Swales, J. M. and Feak, C. B. (2004) *Academic Writing for Graduate Students: Essential Tasks and Skills.* 2nd ed. Ann Arbor, MI: University of Michigan Press.

Swales, J. M. and Feak, C. B. (2011a) *Navigating Academia: Writing Supporting Genres.* Ann Arbor, MI: University of Michigan Press.

Swales, J. M. and Feak, C. B. (2011b) *Creating Contexts: Writing Introductions Across Genres.* Ann Arbor, MI: University of Michigan Press.

Swales, J. M. and Johns, A. M. (1987) Editorial. *English for Specific Purposes* 6: 163.

Swales, J. M. and Lindemann, S. (2002) Teaching the literature review to international graduate students. In A. M. Johns (ed.), *Genre in the Classroom: Multiple Perspectives.* 105–20. Mahwah: NJ: Lawrence Erlbaum.

Swales, J. M. and Mustafa, H. (eds.) (1984) *English for Specific Purposes in the Arab World.* Birmingham, UK: The Language Studies Unit, University of Aston.

Tarantino, M. (1988) Italian in-field EST users self-assess their macro- and micro-level needs: A case study. *English for Specific Purposes* 7: 33–54.

Tardy, C. (2006) Researching first and second language genre learning: A comparative review and a look ahead. *Journal of Second Language Writing* 15: 79–101.

Tardy, C. (2009) *Building Genre Knowledge.* West Lafayette, IN: Parlor Press.

Tardy, C. (2011a) Editorial. *Journal of Second Language Writing* 20: 1–5.

Tardy, C. (2011b) ESP and multi-method approaches to genre analysis. In D. Belcher, A. M. Johns, and B. Paltridge (eds.), *New Directions in English for Specific Purposes Research.* 145–73. Ann Arbor, MI: University of Michigan Press.

Tarone, E., Dwyer, S., Gillette, S., and Icke, V. (1981) On the use of the passive in astrophysics journal papers. *ESP Journal* 1: 123–40. Reprinted, with a commentary, in J. M. Swales (ed.) (1988), *Episodes in ESP: A Source And Reference Book on The Development of English for Science and Technology.* 188–205. New York: Prentice-Hall.

Tedick, D. (1990) ESL writing assessment: Subject-matter knowledge and its impact on performance. *English for Specific Purposes* 9: 123–43.

Tinberg, R. J. (1988) The pH of a volatile genre. *English for Specific Purposes* 7: 205–12.

Trimble, M. T., Trimble, L., and Drobnic, K. (1978) *English for Specific Purposes: Science and Technology*. English Language Institute: Oregon State University.

Wagner, A. and Bhatia, V. (eds.) (2009) *Diversity and Tolerance in Socio-Legal Contexts: Explorations in the Semiotics of the Law*. Aldershot, UK and Burlington, VT: Ashgate Publishers.

Waters, A. (ed.) (1982) *Issues in ESP*. Lancaster, UK: Lancaster Practical papers in English Language Education, Vol. 5.

West, L. L. (1984) Needs assessment in occupation-specific VESL or how to decide what to teach. *The ESP Journal* 3: 143–52.

Winsor, D. A. (1996) *Writing Like an Engineer: A Rhetorical Education*. Mahwah, NJ: Lawrence Erlbaum.

Yates, C., St John, M. J., and Fitzpatrick, A. (1988) *Technical English for Industry*. London: Longman.

Zak, H. and Dudley-Evans, T. (1986). Features of word omission and abbreviation in telexes. *English for Specific Purposes* 5: 59–72.

Part I   ESP and Language Skills

This section of the *Handbook* provides a state of the art look at the relationship between ESP and the key areas of speaking, listening, reading, writing and vocabulary. While for the purposes of this volume it has been necessary to separate these into distinct chapters, it is important to acknowledge, as several of the authors in the section do, that in the classroom, they are of course, less easily separable. ESP pedagogies have tended to focus on identifying – often through needs analyses – sets of transferable generic language and literacy skills that are seen to be applicable in the majority of academic and workplace settings. More recent approaches such as the "academic literacies" approach (Lea and Street 1998) understand that "skills" are always located within specific contexts and communities and form part of sets of social practices – that is, distinct ways of thinking, feeling, believing, valuing, and acting – that also shape learner and teacher identities (Gee 1990; Prior, this volume).

Not only do the chapters in this section trace the history of developments in each of these areas, they also provide an extensive assessment of current approaches to both research and pedagogy as well as outlining avenues for future research. As more and more academic institutions in countries where English is not the native language offer "English medium instruction," there is renewed interest in teaching and researching these five language skills within new and diverse academic contexts. Not only learners but their teachers, too, become the object of study.

Chapters in this section, therefore, also explore the implications of English as a lingua franca (ELF) for both English for academic purposes (EAP) and English for occupational purposes (EOP), raising questions about the usefulness of distinctions between native and non-native speakers or even between English as a

The Handbook of English for Specific Purposes, First Edition.
Edited by Brian Paltridge and Sue Starfield.
© 2013 John Wiley & Sons, Inc. Published 2013 by John Wiley & Sons, Inc.

second language (ESL) and English for specific purposes (ESP) that have been dominant in ESP. These questions also remind us that learner identity is implicated in all skills development, that learners come to any learning context with a history, desires, needs and wants that will shape how they learn what is being taught (Kanno and Norton 2003).

As several of the authors of these important chapters tell us, developments in technology are impacting on research and pedagogy in exciting ways that are of relevance for both teachers and researchers. Corpus linguistics, for example, is central to studies of vocabulary and large corpora of academic lectures and other oral communications are now available for analysis and the development of authentic learning materials. As Christine Feak and Christine Goh point out, historically research into written genres has tended to take precedence over studies of oral communication in ESP, possibly because, as is the case with EAP, they have been seen as more critical to success. Until fairly recently, as Feak reminds us, there were also significant methodological barriers to collecting spoken data. It is now possible to collect and code large amounts of spoken data using relatively inexpensive yet powerful equipment. In all these skills areas learners are being expected to engage with texts that are increasingly multimodal, and frequently digital, increasing demands on both learners and teachers while suggesting interesting research possibilities.

In Christine Feak's chapter on speaking, she discusses the development of speaking corpora such as the Michigan Corpus of Academic Spoken English (MICASE), the British Academic Spoken English corpus (BASE), the English as a Lingua Franca in Academic Settings corpus (ELFA), and the Vienna Oxford International Corpus of English (VOICE) and the possibilities they afford for deepening our understanding of speaking across contexts and in lingua franca settings. The chapter reviews studies of speaking in academic settings, and in a number of workplace and professional settings, some of which are fairly well known and others of growing importance such as call centers and aviation (see Moder, this volume). Our attention is also drawn to emerging areas of research such as conference presentations and humor and we are asked to reflect on taken for granted assumptions about native and non-native speakers' speaking needs and the extent to which ELF speakers want to achieve native speaker-like competence.

Christine Goh's up to date review of research on ESP listening examines the construct of ESP listening and provides a detailed account of what is involved in the development of listening skills and the metacognitive processes needed for successful listening. She identifies a need for more research into listening in non-academic contexts as most of the studies she reviews have been in EAP settings. She clearly identifies areas for further research and provides recommendations for teaching.

Alan Hirvela's chapter provides a thorough review of ESP approaches to teaching reading from the early days of ESP to the present day. While earlier approaches may have focussed more on discrete reading skills, current approaches tend to adopt more situated and integrated approaches. Clearly as he points out, reading and writing have had a reciprocal relationship from the early work of John Swales (1981) on article introductions to more recent work on genre pedagogy as the analysis of specialized texts is seen as key to students' learning to ultimately reproduce these genres. Although the focus in this chapter is on reading in academic contexts, the theoretical and pedagogical concerns noted would be applicable to other contexts too.

Ken Hyland's chapter pursues the notion that writing, like the other skills discussed in this section, is not a generic transferable skill but is a literacy practice, highly dependent on the specific social contexts in which particular texts are produced and received. He identifies three approaches to ESP writing research: genre analysis, contextual studies which move beyond looking solely at rhetorical structure to more qualitative explorations of the environment in which texts are being produced via, for example, methods such as observation, surveys, diaries, interviews and focus group discussions, and critical studies which focus on "how social relations, identity, knowledge and power are constructed through written (and spoken) texts" and how ideologies work to ensure that some texts have greater social value than others.

In her chapter on vocabulary, Averil Coxhead, opens her discussion of this topic by posing the apparently straightforward question "What vocabulary do ESP learners need?" Beginning with an examination of definitions of specialized or technical vocabulary and of different approaches to conceptualizing vocabulary and ESP, she then moves beyond single words to lexical patterning in ESP, illustrating that, in fact, there are no simple answers to this question. She concludes by looking at some of the challenges for bringing ESP research on vocabulary into classrooms.

REFERENCES

Gee, J. P. (1990) *Social Linguistics and Literacies: Ideology in Discourses*. London: The Falmer Press.

Kanno, Y. and Norton, B. (2003) Imagined communities and educational possibilities: Introduction. *Journal of Language, Identity and Education* 2: 241–49.

Lea, M. and Street, B. (1998) Student writing in higher education: An academic literacies approach. *Studies in Higher Education* 23: 157–72.

Swales, J. M. (1981) Aspects of article Introductions. *Aston ESP Research Reports* 1. Birmingham, UK: Language Studies Unit, University of Aston at Birmingham. Republished University of Michigan Press (2011).

2 ESP and Speaking

CHRISTINE B. FEAK

Introduction

The research lens of English for specific purposes (ESP) would appear to be overall somewhat more focussed on writing than speaking. One factor contributing to this phenomenon is that in some ESP contexts, specifically English for academic purposes (EAP), written genres rather than oral genres have been considered as more central to professional success. Another, perhaps more important, factor may be the relative ease with which written data can be obtained and compiled into a usable form for analysis. Unlike the case of writing, significant methodological barriers to collecting speaking data along with subsequent transcribing have posed challenges to research. The ESP research landscape, however, is changing largely due to the ease with which speech corpora can now be created. While only a decade ago researchers were dependent on sometimes costly and time-consuming methods to collect speech samples, today technology has greatly simplified the process. Now, data can be collected in almost any speaking environment via a handheld audio/video recorder or even an off-the-shelf mobile phone (Hughes et al. 2010).

As corpora become more widely created and distributed, perspectives on learners, learner needs, and curriculum design are changing. Of significance here is the realization that most oral communication in English occurs among speakers who do not share a common first language. Indeed, as Seidlhofer (2001: 134) explains, English in these interactions is a lingua franca "far-removed from its native speakers' linguacultural norms and identities."

The widespread use of English as a lingua franca (ELF) has prompted a refocussing of some ESP speaking research toward the ELF perspective, which increasingly questions the need for English language learners to acquire native speaker-like

The Handbook of English for Specific Purposes, First Edition.
Edited by Brian Paltridge and Sue Starfield.
© 2013 John Wiley & Sons, Inc. Published 2013 by John Wiley & Sons, Inc.

target forms. This view is particularly prominent in studies of oral business communication (Charles 2007) and emerging in English for academic purposes (see Pilkinton-Pihko 2010). In this regard, Charles (2007: 263) reasonably questions why ELF speakers should, "shape their mutual communication around a fictitious native speaker (NS) (particularly in the absence of one)? Why could they not shape it around their own, shared, communicational needs?" Together with questions regarding native speaker speech norms, are growing uncertainties surrounding notions of "native speakerness" and of native speaker competence. While the issue of how native speakers can or should be defined is beyond the scope of this chapter, whether native speakers are necessarily competent in all speaking contexts or more competent than non-native speakers (NNS) is a matter of increasingly relevant debate, as will be discussed later.

Our work in ESP has been to assist learners in their efforts to acquire the language they need or perhaps desire to achieve academic, professional, or occupational goals. This remains fundamental to the field. What has been evolving in many cases, however, is the learners, the context of their language use, as well as teaching and assessment practices that best address these changes. As indicated, second language (L2) users of English today are more likely to engage in NNS–NNS encounters and therefore have a greater interest in becoming competent L2 speakers of English rather than achieving native speaker competency. In this context, native speakers, who constitute the minority, must now become sensitive to ELF and perhaps accommodate L2 speakers. If native speaker competence is not a primary goal, then current assessments of language proficiency based on NS criteria may no longer be appropriate. Here I explore these developments in ESP speaking research, beginning with a brief overview of some current directions in ESP speaking scholarship, followed by a more detailed discussion of areas where our thinking about speaker status should perhaps be broadened. The chapter concludes by exploring EAP research on conference presentations, which highlights the need to create ESP speaking curricula that consider sociopragmatic awareness in the learning of speech genres. This research also supports the argument made nearly two decades ago that the distinction between native and non-native speakers is neither constructive (Swales 1993) nor defensible.

Corpora: An Overview

As described elsewhere in this volume, both large and small corpora are foundational to ESP research. Principal among the larger ESP speaking corpora are those focussing on academic speech settings: the Michigan Corpus of Academic Spoken English (MICASE) (http://quod.lib.umich.edu/m/micase/), the British Academic Spoken English corpus (BASE) (http://www2.warwick.ac.uk/fac/soc/al/research/collect/base), and the English as a Lingua Franca in Academic Settings corpus (ELFA) (http://www.helsinki.fi/englanti/elfa/elfacorpus.html). Other speech corpora have a broader scope including the Corpus of Spoken, Professional American English (CSPA) (http://www.athel.com/cspa.html), which contains transcripts of White House press conferences and university faculty meetings; the Hong Kong Corpus of Spoken English (HKCSE) (http://rcpce.engl.polyu.edu.hk/HKCSE/), which is comprised of four sub-corpora (academic, business, conversation and public); and the Vienna Oxford International Corpus of English (VOICE) (http://www.univie.ac.at/voice/), which has captured speech events in professional, educational, and leisure settings. The ELFA and VOICE corpora are significant in that their emphases allow for comparisons of ELF and English in Anglophone environments. Indeed, studies comparing academic ELF and English in Anglophone academic settings (specifically based on MICASE) have revealed relevant differences in how speakers communicate in these contexts. In the case of ELF, speakers were shown to make considerable effort to prevent misunderstanding through the use of self-repairs and other means of clarifying (e.g. reformulation, repetition, and co-construction); in the native speaker context, self-repairs tended to not involve syntactic reformulations, but rather paraphrases of longer points that had been made (Mauranen 2006).

The availability of corpora such as MICASE on the internet has hastened the pace of research on English for academic purposes speaking. Although many hands may not exactly make light work, the research output of many scholars worldwide examining the same data has led to growth in our explorations and understanding of EAP speaking. (As an example, see the summary of MICASE research at http://micase.elicorpora.info/micase-publications-and-presentations).

Areas of Inquiry: An Overview

English for academic purposes speaking

Of the many areas of EAP speaking, some, such as university lectures (Crawford Camiciottoli 2005; Fortanet 2004; Mauranen 2009) have received greater research attention than others. However, a small, but growing literature is available on under-explored, occluded academic encounters such as office hours (Limberg 2007; Reinhardt 2010), classroom talk (Csomay 2006), project groups in US university settings (Axelson 2007) and small group discussion in post-graduate courses in the US (Kim 2006). Two studies of office hours are particularly relevant here, one by Limberg (2007) investigating the structure and another by Reinhardt (2010) examining differences between international graduate students who teach in US universities – International Teaching Assistants (ITAs) – and practicing academics. Research here has shown that office hours generally follow a five-phase structure, all of which are intended to accomplish a particular goal (Limberg 2007).

1. Prefacing Sequence: Summons – Answer (e.g. knocking at the door/entry);
2. Opening (identification/recognition/greeting);
3. Outlining academic business (motivation for visit);

4.   Negotiating academic business (discussion; co-constructing a solution);
5.   Closing (leave-taking; expression of gratitude; reference to future encounters; exit).

A central goal of an office hour visit is the negotiation of academic business, e.g. homework assistance. Successful negotiation requires the encounter to be supportive, inclusive, and centered on the learner (Limberg 2007; Rienhardt 2010). While some office hours are uncomplicated, others are more complex, calling for the instructor to probe to isolate the student's concern and provide a workable solution that may involve some negotiation with the student. Thus, the interactional demands of office hours can be quite complicated and challenging in terms of language skill and intercultural awareness – particularly for ITAs who may be struggling with their own teacher identity. Specifically, ITAs have been found to perceive themselves as inadequate when dealing with US students. While the causes of this perception are multifaceted, they may be partly attributable to influences from the ITAs' previous, non-Anglophone academic cultures (Reinhardt 2010) on their teaching and interactional styles, which may confound their ability to interact with US students. Some evidence for this is seen in the speech of those ITAs who use fewer inclusion and involvement statements with their students (e.g. the use of *we* to denote that the instructor and the student are working together on a problem or issue as in this MICASE citation, "okay so then when we do the plot of it we're gonna have five . . ." (Simpson et al. 2002). The lack of inclusion signals, then, gives rise to the perception of ITA detachment and unsupportive office hours.

The potential challenges and threats to identity experienced by non-native speakers of English when interacting with US students may also exist in US classrooms. Classrooms have been described as particularly stressful for graduate students from non-Anglophone countries who see themselves as less capable, but nonetheless eager to contribute to classroom and small-group discussions (Axelson and Bogart 2010; Kim 2006). Here, challenges can be attributed to the dominant class group, consisting of domestic students who set a "tone" for a classroom that can easily exclude international students. This can cause international students to be reluctant to participate, negatively affecting the learning environment. Equally unfortunate is that in such a classroom environment, domestic students seem "unlikely to learn" or benefit from (Axelson and Bogart 2010) the classroom diversity, which has great potential to be a source of new, rich multicultural perspectives. As a result, learning opportunities for all students may be lost. Although it is not clear whether similar issues exist in university classes where English is a lingua franca, one could envision other dominant groups potentially exerting a comparable influence, a possibility that is worthy of investigation.

Despite a possible uncertain cultural identity or feelings of marginalization, international students are still expected to demonstrate content and speaking genre expertise in classrooms, particularly for oral presentations. One unique pedagogical presentation genre is the design studio presentation typical of architecture programs. Studies have emphasized the rhetorical nature of these talks as well as the effectiveness of different speaker styles. Typical styles have been described as the rather unsuccessful "janitor's tour" common among novice presenters for whom the simple creation of a narrative is challenging; the more effective "emerging architect" who is becoming familiar with the conventions of the pedagogical genre; and the confident "playful near-expert" with genre awareness (Morton 2009: 221). These categorizations highlight the importance of a developmental trajectory in a student's socialization into the discipline and awareness of the relevant speech genres, which then enables students to engage in strategic decision-making while creating their presentations (Morton 2009).

Instrumental to successful design presentations is the speaker's ability to both explain the design and help listeners experience or "see" a structure as if it actually exists (Swales et al. 2001). This involves the use of a "narrative style, effective images, and dynamic grammar" (Morton 2009: 217) together with the ability to create multimodal demonstrations incorporating sound, music, and animation. By establishing a convincing narrative style a student supports the effort to draw the listener into his or her world, and helps establish rapport, the latter of which is also seen as highly relevant in other ESP speaking contexts, such as conferences, as will be discussed later.

The need to develop a convincing speaking style is also emerging in another unique context known as the Three Minute Thesis (3MT) competition. The high-pressure 3MT competition has its origins at the University of Queensland, Australia, but has now expanded to many universities in Australia and New Zealand. The goal of the competitions is twofold: to encourage PhD students to fine tune their oral presentation skills and to help them develop the ability to share their research with nonexpert listeners (Skrbis, McDonald, and Miscamble 2010). The three-minute time limit is also well-suited to help PhD students prepare for opportunities to spontaneously discuss their work with others outside the competition and the students' departments, such as at conferences (Skrbis et al. 2010). As the name indicates, students have three minutes to present their research topic and are allowed a single slide. Presentations are judged in terms of communication style, comprehension, and engagement; prizes are awarded. Many of the winning presentations are available on YouTube; the 2011 winner of the University of New South Wales competition, for instance, can be seen at http://www.youtube.com/watch?v=b-b4vcaytoa. Although as of this writing no published studies of these oral presentations are available, this is certainly an area worthy of research attention.

In looking at the 3MT, it would be interesting to know how these talks compare to the related writing, an issue that continues to be explored in other speaking contexts (Ädel 2010; Csomay 2006; Swales and Burke 2003). The query posed by (Swales 2001: 37) over a decade ago asking whether "academic speech is 'more like' casual conversation or more like academic writing," remains open to debate and can at best be answered as "it depends." Overall, the MICASE data points to an affinity toward conversation (Swales and Malczewsk 2001) and the same proclivity is found in classroom talk (Csomay 2006). If, however, we consider classroom lectures, evidence points to more similarities with writing (Thøgersen and

Airey 2011); moreover, in the context of oral presentations, evidence shows that some "talk" is first written to be spoken later, particularly among those less confident in their presentation ability (Webber 2005), and also contains aspects of written language.

Apart from office hours, surprisingly, widespread interest in ITA concerns seems to have somewhat waned despite some unresolved issues. As suggested above, how we can best support ITAs in office hour teaching is worthy of additional research. Another relevant issue is whether ITA training programs should be offered by the department in which the teaching will occur or be conducted by EAP specialists (Gorsuch 2006). This question underlies the broader debate of whether ITA training is a matter of language training or of enculturation into the teaching norms of a discipline, and parallels ongoing discussion in the larger EAP context regarding the potential advantages of discipline-specific courses in comparison to those with multidisciplinary representation. While not necessarily a matter of one perspective or the other, certainly the advantages of each must be weighed up in EAP course design.

Unlike interest in ITA issues, increasing attention is being given to academics teaching in English worldwide. Similar to the "facilitated diffusion" of English into global business endeavors, English has become a primary education lingua franca in non-Anglophone countries where content and language integrated learning (CLIL) is becoming well established (Räisänen and Fortanet-Gómez 2008). Reasons for interest in CLIL, the most common language of which is English, followed by German, include increasing mobility among student populations and university interest in enlarging the potential student pool (Björkman 2011; Coleman 2006; Crawford Camiciottoli 2005; Labi 2011). According to Coleman (2006), 30 percent of European universities offer at least one program taught in English; this figure rises to 100 percent in Finland and the Netherlands. A similar move toward English is evident in Turkey where all of the elite private universities have at least one English-medium program (Coleman 2006).

The emergence of English-medium CLIL is not uncontroversial given potential barriers this may create, particularly in disciplines where language is "central to debate [and] meaningful scholarly discourse can be a challenge" (Labi 2011: 24). Of some concern is the inadequate language skills of students and perhaps more so of faculty. Although ITAs must demonstrate English proficiency prior to teaching, universities where English is the lingua franca hesitate to assess the language ability of professors (Labi 2011), despite potential problems. For example, like the ITAs investigated in Reinhardt (2010), lecturers at a Swedish technical university where English is the lingua franca were found to employ fewer expected pragmatic strategies that would be typical of student–student small group interactions (Björkman 2011), suggesting a possible distancing effect. Similarly, changes in rhetorical style, as compared to a speaker's first language, have also been found to contribute to teaching that is slower, more monologic and less interactive (Thøgersen and Airey 2011). Further, a study by Pilkinton-Pihko (2010) revealed that lecturers themselves saw some deficiencies in how they used English in the classroom; nevertheless, as many ELF speakers, they did not assess their abilities against native speaker norms (Pilkinton-Pihko 2010). Even more significant than language competence, however, is the "perceived threat to cultural identity and the status of the native language as a language of science" (Coleman 2006: 6). Thus, academic ELF may be more a lingua non grata rather than lingua franca. Despite criticisms of the Englishization of higher education, Coleman (2006) suggests a possible inevitable move toward diglossia with one language being used for local communication and English for more utilitarian purposes.

ESP speaking beyond academia

While the growth in academic ELF parallels the global expansion of English, the move toward English for utilitarian purposes is neither a recent phenomenon, nor limited to academia. Beyond EAP, the tradition of ESP speaking research continues in professional settings, including the rather well-established fields of Business (Kankaaranta and Louhiala-Salminen 2010) and Medicine (Hoekje 2006; Pilotto, Duncan, and Anderson-Wurf 2007), discussed in detail in Nickerson (this volume). Some relatively new lines of inquiry have emerged such as business calls (Bowles 2006) and call centers (Forey and Lockwood 2007; Hood and Forey 2008) and the high stakes aviation context where clear communication is a precondition to safe navigation (Aiguo 2007; Sullivan and Girginer 2002; Tajima 2004; Moder this volume). The field is moving forward in other novel directions, as demonstrated by work in some heretofore unexplored environments such as those of French mountain guides (Wozniak 2010), land surveyors in Hong Kong (Cheng and Mok 2008), hospitality workers in Taiwan (Su 2009), construction industry engineers in Asia (Handford and Matous 2011), and driving school translators in Japan (Freiermuth 2007).

   While sometimes it seems that the availability of corpora, rather than learner need, drives some ESP speaking research, needs analysis aimed toward creating pedagogical materials has remained strong. For instance, materials for driving school translators in Japan emphasized precision in imperative constructions rather than longer, but more polite requests (*Turn right* vs. *Could you please turn right*) (Freiermuth 2007). In construction, the grammatical accuracy was found less important than the ability to understand nonverbal forms of communication. Interestingly, contractors working at construction sites, require an "ability to encode and understand the symbols which carry meaning (such as diagrams and photographs)" (Handford and Matous 2011: 97). Nonverbal communication skills, including gesturing, are instrumental for successful communication in construction environments with high noise levels and where speakers have a "high level of shared professional knowledge, and a relatively less confident grasp of the language (when compared to the speakers' L1s)" (Handford and Matous 2011: 97). This does not suggest that interpersonal aspects of communication are unimportant; on the contrary, as with business communication, clear messages and avoiding face-threatening acts are important. What is unique is the heavy reliance on visual communication. In the mountaineering context, however, guides are more concerned about being able to interact with their clients using ELF in a positive manner, particularly under less than ideal physical circumstances. Less than ideal circumstances may also affect communications in business call centers, which have increasingly been outsourced to countries such as India and the Philippines. Calls may involve a frustrated or angry caller and thus require great skill on the part of the agent. For instance, as Hood and Forey (2008) note, silence may be important in addressing fluctuating levels of emotion in problematic interactions. Also significant in these interactions is the agents' language, which can be characterized as "addressee-focussed, polite, and elaborated; primarily planned and procedural; and constantly managed and monitored" (Friginal 2008: 101). Finally, research has shown that it may be important in ESP speaking course design to consider that some speakers inevitably must straddle two ESP contexts – one academic and one professional, as in the case of some land surveyors (Cheng and Mok 2008) and civil engineers (Kaewpet 2009) who spend time in both university courses and work settings. Given these wide-ranging ESP speaking contexts, it appears that a progressively greater burden is being imposed on ESP instructors and course designers to meet the needs of their learners.

Changing perspectives within ESP speaking

The predominance of interactions between speakers of different L1s strongly suggests that the onus of successful spoken communication should be borne by all speakers, whether non-native or native speakers of English (Frank 2000). If we assume that absolute distinctions among speakers are perhaps unconstructive and that no group has the linguistic upper hand, native speakers (however this may be determined) may also need language training that heightens their awareness of and sensitivity to language differences (Kankaaranta and Louhiala-Salminen 2010; Yamazaki 2010) and offers strategies for effective communication. Reason to do so is explored more closely in the following discussion of Aviation English.

Challenges to native speaker privilege and competence are growing in aviation where the communication stakes are quite high and limited opportunities for multiple forms of repair are the norm (see Moder, this volume). Aviation English (or Airspeak) consists of the fixed forms of an international language established for communications between air traffic controllers (ATC) and pilots (Howard 2008). Aviation English (AE) has its own protocols, pronunciation, and "grammar." Much of the language is scripted (i.e. composed to be spoken); prescribed phrases are required along with a set order in which the discourse evolves. For instance, "Taxi into position and hold" has a specific meaning shared with no other sanctioned expression (Howard 2008: 373). Non-essential talk, which is common in other speaking interactions, is absent and the discourse is exclusively task-oriented. Provided the correct forms have been learned, the limited flexibility in the communication format is thought to facilitate information exchange (Howard 2008). Even so, reports of AE breakdowns leading to crashes are not infrequent (Tajima 2004). To lessen the possibility of disaster due to communication breakdowns the International United Nations Civil Aviation Organisation (ICAO), which codifies practices, standards and requirements for international air navigation, in 2004 mandated that pilots and ATCs demonstrate an acceptable ability to communicate in AE (Alderson 2009).

Although AE research and courses existed prior to the ICAO mandate, AE course development and valid assessments to measure proficiency have become important areas of ESP speaking inquiry. Further, calls have been made to create AE corpora (Alderson 2009), but significant challenges exist in doing so. One challenge involves gaining access to actual communications between ATC and pilots (Sullivan and Girginer 2002). For instance, in their study of AE at Ataturk International Airport in Istanbul, Turkey, Sullivan and Girginer required permission from no fewer than four administrative levels (the Turkish State Airport Administration, the Civil Defense Department, the airport police, and the deputy governor of the airport) before gaining clearance to enter the control tower to observe the communications between Turkish ATCs and pilots from various L1s.

The small number of corpus-based studies of AE offer some interesting findings and arguments. Significantly, regardless of the L1 of pilots and ATCs, deviations from prescribed scripts are not uncommon. In the Turkish data, for instance, numbers were inappropriately relayed; further deviations occurred in greetings, closings, the use of Turkish between L1 Turkish pilots and ATCs, and the use of colloquial expressions by L1 English speakers (e.g. *chop* vs. *turbulence*) (Sullivan and Girginer 2002). While the use of Turkish in Turkish airspace may seem appropriate or desirable, this can prevent non-Turkish speaking pilots on other aircraft from following the communications in an airspace, potentially compromising safety.

Deviations were also abundant in an AE corpus of communications at several Midwestern US airports. Significantly, 36 percent of the pilot-ATC turns failed to follow required scripts and instead involved colloquial expressions, e.g. *gotcha* vs. *affirmative*, which could lead to misunderstanding. Deviations have been attributed to inconsistencies in the meanings of terms common to both AE and general English. For example, in AE *hold* means *stop*, but colloquially can mean *continue* or *maintain* as in *hold your course* (Jones 2003).

Other AE studies have highlighted distractions due to multitasking that could lead to breakdowns in pilot-ATC communication (Howard 2008). Like speaking deviations, distractions are relevant regardless of the speakers' L1; however, this problem may be somewhat more pertinent for L2 speakers. Specifically, in a simulated ATC-pilot navigation task involving either a high or low level of distraction, L2 English speakers who were less proficient in English retained information less accurately than L1 English speakers. Moreover, the former produced more accented and less fluent speech in situations involving a significant distraction (Farris et al. 2008).

The effects of deviations and distractions on successful ATC-pilot communications have implications for the AE proficiency certification mandate. As Alderson (2009) notes, it may both be necessary to assess language use under stressful conditions and to require native speaker pilots and ATCs to undergo the same testing procedures as those whose L1 is not English. The need to require certification of all ATCS and pilots seems reasonable in view of studies demonstrating that native speakers of English may be less capable users of AE due to deficits in language awareness regarding their use of idioms and colloquial English (Alderson 2009). Thus, in Alderson's view, being a native speaker of English, however defined, is not necessarily indicative of competence.

AE research suggests that being a native speaker of English should not necessarily be equated with competence. In this respect, we are reminded from our own experience that often non-native speakers of a language may in fact be more proficient than native speakers. Apart from knowledge of grammar and vocabulary, one important factor contributing to this difference may be familiarity with a particular speech genre or communicative goals of a speech event. While a certain level of language proficiency is necessary, equally important is a speaker's experience. If we agree that this is the case, then why does it seem that so little ESP research is extended to support native speakers as well? To explore this further, the next section provides a discussion of ESP speaking in conference settings.

The conference forum

Conferences have been the focus of considerable research, much of which is summarized in *The Language of Conferencing* (Ventola, Shalom, and Thompson 2002). As is known, conferences are a forum for many speech events ranging from informal networking talk to the genre cluster of more formal presentations. Within this genre cluster posters have received renewed attention (MacIntosh-Murray 2007), while nascent research on argumentation strategies in conference discussion sessions has emerged (Vassileva 2009), along with analyses of presentations.

Conference presentations (CP) are undoubtedly essential for scholars to fully participate in the ongoing activity of their disciplines (Ventola et al. 2002). Conference papers and posters were the focus of early work in ESP speaking, most notably conducted by Dubois (1985, 1987) who was indeed ahead of her time in noting differences between spoken and written academic language (e.g. the use of approximations and what she described as the "strikingly casual" nature of numerical expressions in biology talks). While the published research article genre may be more highly valued than CPs for career advancement, CPs offer meaningful opportunities for presenters to gain insights into their work. Significantly, they are a means to disseminate new research, for which presenters receive immediate audience feedback that may contribute to diversifying or fine-tuning the work before publication – or even abandoning research if feedback is significantly negative. CPs may also help to prevent duplicative efforts early on or help to establish networks by enabling researchers to identify others engaged in similar projects (Grushcow 2004).

Common CPs include panel presentations (roundtables) offering multiple perspectives on a topic, posters, and papers, the latter two highlighting research of one individual or research group. To my knowledge, no published research has explored panel presentations and the complex interplay among speakers, suggesting a fruitful area for research. Thus, this section focusses on posters and paper presentations. Posters in many fields "suffer in esteem" (Dubois 1985: 81) and are viewed as "poor country cousins" (Swales and Feak 2000: 81) to paper presentations. Indeed, the poster as a genre "has been struggling to find a niche for itself as a viable alternative to the traditional conference presentation" (Swales 2004: 64).

Despite perceptions that a poster invitation signals lesser quality, other factors contribute to the diminished respect for posters, namely the timing and location of poster sessions (MacIntosh-Murray 2007). This is particularly relevant when we consider that sessions often occur in spaces too small to accommodate a large number of attendees; located in rooms that are difficult to find; and take place during conference schedule breaks, placing them in competition with more important "social genres" (Shalom 2002) such as networking with others. This potentially substandard environment, may cause speakers to forgo a conference to present a poster rather than a paper (MacIntosh-Murray 2007), which in turn may further diminish the perceived value of the genre.

Typical poster presentations require speakers to remain at their assigned location for a specified period of time, during which they have opportunities to interact with and obtain feedback from attendees. Unlike paper CP presenters, poster presenters engage in one-on-one interactions, the nature of which can be stressful and unpredictable because the audience has greater control over whether, with whom, for how long, and how to engage in conversation about the research (MacIntosh-Murray 2007). Lacking the control afforded by a CP paper, poster presenters must be adept at reading the audience on many levels including interest in the research and the amount and level of detail to provide (Dubois 1985). For this reason, many students, particularly inexperienced presenters, prefer typical timed oral presentations followed by a prescribed amount of time for audience interaction during the Q and A. Students also prefer paper CPs because of the communicative burden of the dual role of the poster as a display that should stand on its own and serve as a backdrop for audience interaction (MacIntosh-Murray 2007).

The perceived lower status of poster presentations has perhaps constrained the research interest in the genre compared to paper presentations. However, research is emerging to reflect ongoing efforts to elevate the genre at professional meetings, principally in biomedicine and the life sciences. Emergent forms of poster sessions involve a seated audience and session chair (MacIntosh-Murray 2007) and offer presenters time to discuss their posters projected as a slide. Presentation time is short (2–5 minutes) and audience commentary may be solicited. In another format, posters are presented in small groups, one member of which is a discussant who provides feedback. These new formats suggest that some posters are approximating traditional paper presentations, albeit in an extremely truncated form that may require a special set of speaking skills for presenters, much like those needed for success in the 3MT described earlier.

The movement toward novel forms of poster presentations gives rise to some important implications. For one, due to time constraints, new instantiations of the poster genre may leave little opportunity for the repair or recasting of ideas. For another, these new formats may disadvantage some less fluent or inexperienced presenters. Studies have shown, for example, a "slow-down" effect in English for L2 speakers (regardless of fluency), ranging from 25 percent to 45 percent slower than that of speakers whose L1 is English (Hincks 2010). This slow-down effect has also been found among university lecturers teaching in English rather than their native language and attributed to a lecturing style that more resembles written English and includes frequent repetitions (Thøgersen and Airey 2011).

Interestingly, while many academics consider an invitation to present a poster as a consolation prize (MacIntosh-Murray 2007), this genre appears to be valued as a final course project and a means to showcase and stimulate graduate student research. Indeed, a search for the term "poster session" on the websites of many major research institutions reveals how common they have become and how they are valued. At one university, for instance, posters are described as

> . . . a phenomenal way to get feedback on your dissertation from . . . scholars, whether your dissertation is just a seedling of an idea or almost complete. The poster session has a reputation of being an "accelerating incubator" – an experience that will move your ideas forward in a short amount of time (ICOS 2011).

Given this description one cannot help but wonder whether posters in a conference forum and posters in an educational setting are indeed the same genre. Although they may share structure, style, and content, significant differences in the audience, purpose, and the perceived value of the communicative event cannot be ignored.

Paper conference presentations (paper CPs) have been the focus of a small, but growing, number of studies (Rowley-Jolivet and Carter-Thomas 2005a, 2005b; Webber 2005) that have examined the genre in terms of move structure, conversational features, and the need to establish a personal connection with the audience. As with research article introductions, introductions to paper CPs have been suggested to follow a move structure (Rowley-Jolivet and Carter-Thomas 2005a). Table 2.1 outlines the three moves based on Rowley-Jolivet and Carter-Thomas (2005a).

As suggested by Table 2.1, achieving one's communicative purpose in a paper CP introduction requires the creation of a unique context shaped by the speaker's need to acknowledge and establish rapport with the audience.

A similar need to establish rapport was found by Wulff, Swales, and Keller (2009) in their study of the post-presentation discussion at a small, highly specialized conference in applied linguistics. Session chairs at this conference largely limited their role to that of announcing the start, near close, and close of the discussion, typically marking the discoursal shift from presentation to discussion by the transition *okay*, the use of inclusive *we*, and an indication of the time available for questions. For instance, "Okay, we have (about) # minutes for questions." Another feature of this conference was the frequency of humor and laughter. While humor has been extensively studied in other fields – see Attardo (2008) and Norrick (2010) for useful reviews – this topic is under-researched in the ESP speaking literature (Lee 2004). Humor at this conference, which was attended by many

Table 2.1   Move Model for paper CP introductions (based on Rowley-Jolivet and Carter-Thomas 2005a)

Move A. Setting up the framework
1.   Meeting interpersonal aims: Establishing rapport and projecting a persona
     Examples:
     • Greeting
     • Joking
     • Offering personal anecdotes
     • Making light-hearted remarks
     • Thanking the audience for being present at a less than ideal time or
       expressing thanks to collaborators or those providing financial support.
2.   Meeting discoursal aims: Preparing the audience
     Examples:
     • Presenting the topic in a light different from what was previously stated
       or written
     • Enhancing the contribution of the research by using evaluative language
       to indicate novelty (possibly absent from the title or abstract)
     • Indicating one's stance toward the topic (possibly absent from the title
       or abstract)
     • Outlining the talk.

Move B. Contextualizing the framework
Situating the talk within the larger conference experience or research area
     Examples:
     • Referring to other presentations/conference events or other acts of
       intertextuality
     • Alluding to previous work likely to be familiar to attendees (Literature
       reviews, typical of research article introductions, are absent due to time
       constraints and the cognitive burden this would place on the listeners.
       The talk is situated by assuming shared knowledge.)

Move C. Indicating the research rationale
1.   Stating motivation
     Examples:
     • Highlighting problems, gaps or counter-claims
     • Asserting relevance, centrality or need
     • Establishing the continuation of previous work.
2.   Responding to the motivators
     Examples:
     • Raising questions
     • Stating hypothesis
     • Previewing results or solutions
     • Outlining research goals.

individuals who knew each other to some extent, was frequent, on average one general laughter episode every 90 seconds. These results are consistent with those for dissertation defenses in which laughter was common among committee members who appeared to have amiable relationships (Swales 2004). While the broader implications of humor and laughter for conference presentations remain unclear, we can, nonetheless, conclude that at least for a small conference attended largely by a cohesive group, humor is initiated by both presenters and listeners and serves as an indicator of a positive shared experience. As such, further research on how an "atmosphere of cooperative interaction" (Webber 2005) is established is worthy of further research and pedagogical attention.

CP research also suggests that mode of expression is important for all ESP research. Specifically, in some ESP studies considerable effort has been made to compare speaking and writing differences and similarities so as to determine whether some ESP speech is more like writing or conversation, as mentioned previously. While the writing–speaking continuum is significant, it is equally relevant that the two skills be viewed as complementary in some speaking or perhaps all ESP genres. For instance, CPs are typically multimodal (Prior 2009; Tardy 2005; Ventola et al. 2002) and "multimedial," since preparing and conveying information may require writers and speakers to employ a range of semiotic media, including visual, written and spoken elements, as well as technology (e.g. computers and innovative interfaces that enable sophisticated information to be shared). Indeed, there is growing awareness that ESP speaking (and writing) is not only situated within a genre cluster or chain consisting of a blend of spoken and written genres and sub-genres as well as other texts (Räisänen 2002), but also emerges from processes involving listening and reading.

The CP findings are relevant for all presenters regardless of their L1. While proficiency in English may contribute to successful CP or other speaking events, experience in a particular environment and the relevant genres is also a necessary precondition for success. In the case of CPs, all junior academics, regardless of their L1, would benefit from knowledge of the genre structure and ways to achieve one's speaking aims. Thus, given the difficulties in establishing an unequivocal distinction between native and non-native speakers, ESP speaking scholarship should consider the potential needs of all who could benefit from explicit instruction and feedback. For instance, the outsourcing of calls in our global economy may indeed compel native English speaker callers to learn ways to accommodate agents from different cultural and linguistic backgrounds rather than expect agents to completely acquiesce to the cultural and linguistic norms of the callers.

Conclusions and Future Directions

Traditionally, the impetus for ESP research has been to address the unique needs of English language learners and users. As Belcher (2006) stresses, the boundaries among researchers, instructors, materials designers, and curriculum developers are often unclear. And indeed, much recent work in ESP speaking continues to be aimed at providing appropriate, tailor-made instruction. Research to date has revealed how disciplinary communities differ in target language uses and aims. While instruction has typically emphasized language accuracy relative to native speakers for effective communication, today appropriate instruction in many areas should be less so, emphasizing more the need to address the myriad of other considerations. For instance, in some ESP speaking contexts, besides language, matters of cross-cultural awareness may be essential in the curriculum, as suggested by the needs analysis of mountain guides (Wozniak 2010) and medical professionals (Hoekje 2006; Pilotto, Duncan, and Anderson-Wurf 2007). Other relevant considerations in curriculum design include how and when to best integrate pragmatics in a curriculum. We do not know, for instance, when to introduce strategies for humor and rapport building, which are important for certain business interactions (Kankaaranta and Louhiala-Salminen 2010) and various academic contexts such as dissertation defenses (Swales 2004) and professional conferences (Rowley-Jolivet and Carter-Thomas 2005a; Wulff, Swales, and Keller 2009).

The ESP speaking research has been varied and insightful, but it remains unclear how much of this work is being "repurposed" in the form of teaching materials. Central to ESP is the perspective that it is an approach to *teaching*. As such, it is surprising that in comparison to other approaches to English language teaching, relatively few pedagogical materials are readily available. While many studies indicate that research has been undertaken to inform teaching, the materials developed are largely occluded, shared to a much lesser extent than the actual research. Given the wealth of information on how English is used, efforts to develop and make available evidence-based instructional materials are needed, together with accounts of their evolution and research to evaluate effectiveness.

REFERENCES

Ädel, A. (2010) Just to give you kind of a map of where we are going: A taxonomy of metadiscourse in spoken and written academic English. *Nordic Journal of English Studies* 9: 69–97.

Aiguo, W. (2007) Teaching aviation English in the Chinese context: Developing ESP theory in a non-English speaking country. *English for Specific Purposes* 26: 121–28.

Alderson, C. (2009) Air safety, language assessment policy, and policy implementation. *Annual Review of Applied Linguistics* 29: 168–87.

Attardo, S. (2008) Semantics and pragmatics of humor. *Language and Linguistics Compass* 2: 1203–15.

Axelson, E. (2007) Vocatives: A double-edged strategy in intercultural discourse among graduate students. *Pragmatics* 17: 95–122.

Axelson, E. and Bogart, P. (2010) *Leveraging a global student body to maximize learning.* Provost's Seminar on Teaching, November 2010. Ann Arbor, MI, Michigan.

Belcher, D. (2006) English for specific purposes: Teaching to perceived needs and imagined futures in worlds of work, study, and everyday life. *TESOL Quarterly* 30: 133–56.

Björkman, B. (2011) Pragmatic strategies in English as a lingua franca: Ways of achieving communicative effectiveness. *Journal of Pragmatics* 43: 950–64.

Bowles, H. (2006) Bridging the gap between conversation analysis and ESP: An applied study of the opening sequences of NS and NNS service telephone calls. *English for Specific Purposes* 25: 332–57.

Charles, M. (2007) Language matters in global communication. *Journal of Business Communication* 44: 260–82.

Cheng, W. and Mok, E. (2008) Discourse processes and products: Land surveyors in Hong Kong. *English for Specific Purposes* 27: 57–73.

Coleman, J. A. (2006) English-medium teaching in European higher education. *Language Teaching* 39: 1–14.

Crawford Camiciottoli, B. (2005) Adjusting a business lecture for an international audience: A case study. *English for Specific Purpsoses* 24: 183–99.

Csomay, E. (2006) Academic talk in American university classrooms: Crossing the boundaries of oral-literate discourse. *English for Academic Purposes* 5: 117–35.

Dubois, B. L. (1985) Popularization at the highest level: Poster sessions at biomedical meetings. *International Journal of the Sociology of Language* 56: 67–84.

Dubois, B. L. (1987) Something on the order of around forty to forty-four: Imprecise numerical expressions in biomedical slide talks. *Language in Society* 16: 527–41.

Farris, C., Trofimovich, P., Segalowitz, N., and Gatbonton, E. (2008) Air traffic communication in a second language: Implications of cognitive factors for training and assessment. *TESOL Quarterly* 42: 397–410.

Forey, G. and Lockwood, J. (2007) "I'd love to put someone in jail for this": An initial investigation of English in the business processing outsourcing (bpo) industry *English for Specific Purposes* 26: 308–26.

Fortanet, I. (2004) The use of "we" in university lectures: Reference and function. *English for Specific Purposes* 15: 45–66.

Frank, R. (2000) Medical communication: Non-native English speaking patients and native English speaking professionals. *English for Specific Purposes* 19: 31–62.

Freiermuth, M. (2007). ESP needs washback and the fine tuning of driving instruction. *Simulation and Gaming* 38: 35–47.

Friginal, E. (2008) Linguistic variation in the discourse of outsourced call centers. *Discourse Studies* 10: 715–36.

Gorsuch, G. (2006) Discipline specific practica for international teaching assistants. *English for Specific Purposes* 25: 90–108.

Grushcow, J. (2004) Measuring secrecy: A cost of the patent system revealed. *Journal of Legal Studies* 33: 59–83.

Handford, M. and Matous, P. (2011) Lexicogrammar in the international construction industry: A corpus-based case study of Japanese-Hong Kong on-site interactions in English. *English for Specific Purposes* 30: 87–100.

Hincks, R. (2010) Speaking rate and information content in English lingua franca oral presentations. *English for Specific Purposes* 29: 4–18.

Hoekje, B. (2006) Medical discourse and ESP courses for international medical graduates (IMGs). *English for Specific Purposes* 26: 327–43.

Hood, S. and Forey, G. (2008) The interpersonal dynamics of call-centre interactions: Co-constructing the rise and fall of emotion. *Discourse & Communication* 2: 389–409.

Howard, J. W. III (2008) "Tower, am I cleared to land?": Problematic communication in aviation discourse. *Human Communication Research* 34: 370–91.

Hughes, T., Nakajima, K., Ha, L., Vasu, A., Moreno, P., and LeBeau, M. (2010, Sept.) *Building transcribed speech corpora quickly and cheaply for many languages.* Paper presented at the 11th Annual Conference of the International Speech Communication Association, 26–30 Sept., Makuhari, Chiba, Japan.

ICOS (2011) Interdisciplinary committee on organizational studies dissertation poster session. Retrieved February 1, 2011, from http://www.icos.umich.edu/content/icos-dissertation-poster-session.

Jones, R. K. (2003) Miscommunication between pilots and air traffic control. *Language Problems & Language Planning* 27: 233–48.

Kaewpet, C. (2009) Communication needs of Thai civil engineering students. *English for Specific Puposes*, 28: 266–78.

Kankaaranta, A. and Louhiala-Salminen, L. (2010) "English? – oh it's just work": A study of BELF user's perceptions. *English for Specific Purposes* 29: 204–09.

Kim, S. (2006) Academic oral communication needs of East Asian international graduate students in non-science and non-engineering fields. *English for Specific Purposes* 25: 479–89.

Labi, A. (2011, Feb. 18). Europe's push to teach in English creates barriers in the classroom. *The Chronicle of Higher Education* LVII: A23–A24.

Lee, D. (2004) *Humor in spoken academic discourse.* Paper presented at the 5th North American Symposium on Corpus Linguistics and Language Teaching, May 2004, Montclair State University, New Jersey, USA.

Limberg, H. (2007) Discourse structure of academic talk in university office hour interactions. *Discourse Studies* 9: 176–93.

MacIntosh-Murray, A. (2007) Poster presentations as a genre in knowledge communication: A case study of forms, norms, and values. *Science Communication* 28: 347–76.

Mauranen, A. (2006) Signaling and preventing misunderstanding in English as a lingua franca communication. *International Journal of the Sociology of Language* 177: 123–50.

Mauranen, A. (2009) Spoken rhetoric: How do natives and non-natives fare? In E. Suomela-Salmi and F. Dervin (eds.), *Cross-Linguistic and Cross-Cultural Perspectives on Academic Discourse.* 199–218. Amsterdam: John Benjamins.

Morton, J. (2009) Genre and disciplinary competence: A case study of contextualisation in an academic speech genre. *English for Specific Purposes* 28: 217–29.

Norrick, N. R. (2010) Humor in interaction. *Language and Linguistics Compass* 4: 232–44.

Pilkinton-Pihko, D. (2010) English as a lingua franca lecturers' self-perceptions of their language use. *Helsinki English Studies* 6: 58–74.

Pilotto, L., Duncan, G., and Anderson-Wurf, J. (2007) Issues for clinicians training international medical graduates: A systematic review. *Medical Journal of Australia* 87: 225–28.

Prior, P. (2009) From speech genres to mediated multimodal genre systems: Bakhtin, Voloshinov, and the question of writing. In C. Bazerman, A. Bonini, and D. Figueiredo (eds.), *Genre in a Changing World.* 17–34. West Lafayette, IN: Parlor Press.

Räisänen, C. (2002) The conference forum: A system of interrelated genres and discursive practices. In E. Ventola, C. Shalom, and S. Thompson (eds.), *The Language of Conferencing.* 69–93. New York: Peter Lang.

Räisänen, C. and Fortanet-Gómez, I. (2008) The state of ESP teaching and learning in Western European higher education after Bologna. In I. Fortanet-Gómez and C. Räisänen (eds.), *ESP in European*

Higher Education. 11–51. Amsterdam: John Benjamins.

Reinhardt, J. (2010) Directives in office hour consultations: A corpus-informed investigation of learner and expert usage. *English for Specific Purposes* 29: 94–107.

Rowley-Jolivet, E. and Carter-Thomas, S. (2005a) The rhetoric of conference presentation introductions: Context, argument and interaction. *International Journal of Applied Linguistics* 15: 45–69.

Rowley-Jolivet, E. and Carter-Thomas, S. (2005b) Scientific conference Englishes: Epistemic and language community variations. In G. Cortese and A. Duszak (eds.), *Identity, Community, Discourse.* 295–320. Bern: Peter Lang.

Seidlhofer, B. (2001) Closing a conceptual gap: The case for a description of English as a lingua franca. *International Journal of Applied Linguistics* 11: 133–58.

Shalom, C. (2002) The academic conference: A forum for enacting genre knowledge. In E. Ventola, C. Shalom, and S. Thompson (eds.), *The Language of Conferencing*: 51–68. New York: Peter Lang.

Simpson, R. C., Briggs, S. L., Ovens, J., and Swales, J. M. (2002) *The Michigan Corpus of Academic Spoken English.* Ann Arbor, MI. Accessed Feb. 2, 2012 at http://quod.lib.umich.edu/m/micase/.

Skrbis, Z., McDonald, D., and Miscamble, T. (2010, April) *The three minute thesis (3MT).* Paper presented at the Proceedings of the 2010 Quality in Postgraduate Research Conference, Adelaide, Australia.

Su, S. (2009) Designing and delivering an English for hospitality syllabus: A Taiwanese case study. *RELC Journal* 40: 280–313.

Sullivan, P. and Girginer, H. (2002) The use of discourse analysis to enhance ESP teacher knowledge: An example using aviation English. *English for Specific Purposes* 21: 397–404.

Swales, J. M. (1993) The English language and its teachers: Thoughts past, present, and future. *ELT Journal* 47: 283–91.

Swales, J. M. (2001) Metatalk in American academic talk: The cases of "point" and "thing". *Journal of English Linguistics* 29: 34–54.

Swales, J. M. (2004) *Research Genres.* Cambridge: Cambridge University Press.

Swales, J. M., Barks, D., Ostermann, A., and Simpson, R. (2001) Between critique and accomodation: Reflections on an EAP course for masters of architecture students. *English for Specific Purposes* 20: 439–58.

Swales, J. M. and Burke, A. (2003) "It's really fascinating work": Differences in evaluative adjectives across academic registers. *Corpus Analysis: Language Structure and Use* 1–18. Amsterdam: Rodopi.

Swales, J. M. and Feak, C. B. 2000. *English in Today's Research World.* Ann Arbor, MI: University of Michigan Press.

Swales, J. M. and Malczewski, B. (2001) Discourse management and new-episode flags in MICASE. In R. Simpson (ed.), *Corpus Linguistics in North America.* Ann Arbor, MI: University of Michigan Press.

Tajima, A. (2004) Fatal miscommunication: English in aviation safety. *World Englishes* 23: 451–70.

Tardy, C. (2005) Expressions of disciplinarity and individuality in a multimodal genre. *Computers and Composition* 22: 319–36.

Thøgersen, J. and Airey, J. (2011) Lecturing undergraduate science in Danish and in English: A comparison of speaking rate and rhetorical style. *English for Specific Purposes* 30: 209–21.

Vassileva, I. (2009) Argumentative strategies in conference discussion sections. In E. Suomela-Salmi and F. Dervin (eds.), *Cross-Linguistic and Cross-Cultural Perspectives on Academic Discourse.* 219–240. Amsterdam: John Benjamins.

Ventola, E., Shalom, C., and Thompson, S. (2002) *The Language of Conferencing*. Frankfurt, Germany: Peter Lang.

Webber, P. (2005) Interactive features in medical conference monologue. *English for Specific Purposes* 24: 157–81.

Wozniak, S. (2010) Language needs analysis from a perspective of international professional mobility: The case of French mountain guides. *English for Specific Purposes* 29: 243–52.

Wulff, S., Swales J. M., and Keller, K. (2009) "We have about seven minutes for questions": The discussion sessions from a specialized conference. *English for Specific Purposes* 28: 79–92.

Yamazaki, C. A. (2010) *The racial dimensions of language discrimination against international teaching assistants and a proposed program for reducing discrimination on campus*. Masters thesis. University of California, Davis, CA.

3 ESP and Listening

CHRISTINE C. M. GOH

Introduction

In a recent review of materials for English for specific purposes (ESP), McDonough (2010) identified over 20 professional areas in which English was needed for effective communication. These included aviation, commerce, customer care, engineering, finance, human resources, information technology, law, law enforcement, maritime communication, media, medicine, nursing, telecommunications, and tourism. Two points arising from McDonough's review are particularly relevant to the discussion of ESP and listening in this chapter. Firstly, for most if not all of the materials surveyed, the explicit emphasis was on learning specialized vocabulary. While grammar and language skills (speaking, listening, reading and writing) are also important in many of the materials she described, the emphasis given to each of these areas was uneven. Where oral communication skills are crucial to an area of work (for example, aviation and maritime communication) the focus tended to be on speaking and the correct pronunciation of technical words. On the whole, attention to listening in the materials McDonough surveyed took the form of tried-and-tested language teaching techniques (e.g. gap filling, sentence/ dialogue completion, picture questions and labeling diagrams) while, in other cases where speaking was emphasized, attention to listening was incidental. Secondly, there is a disjunction between ESP teaching and research. McDonough observed that many of the materials she reviewed did not seem to have been based on research. Although this observation was about ESP in general, it is especially true of listening in the area of English for occupational purposes, where so little research has been carried out. In academic listening, where more research has been conducted over the past few decades, we are beginning to see materials that pay

The Handbook of English for Specific Purposes, First Edition.
Edited by Brian Paltridge and Sue Starfield.
© 2013 John Wiley & Sons, Inc. Published 2013 by John Wiley & Sons, Inc.

greater attention to issues such as culture and discourse that are based on research. It is not difficult, then, to see the extreme imbalance in the discussion of listening in these two areas of ESP research. (see below)

A further point that merits consideration in our discussion of ESP listening is the limited interface between general ESL listening and listening for specific purposes. Although the labels they bear seem to imply differences between the two types of listening, in fact the two share many fundamental characteristics. Fulcher's (1999) discussion of content validity in English for academic purposes (EAP) tests offers insights that can help illuminate this. He argued that EAP testing within the broader framework of ESP had focussed too much on subject knowledge and this had detracted from the main purpose of drawing valid inferences about language knowledge, skills or abilities from test scores. This situation had arisen, Fulcher reasoned, as a result of the perceived need within EAP to be "authentic" by ensuring that relevant content from real life is included. Fulcher further highlighted research which showed that variance in EAP test scores had been mostly due to language proficiency, not subject knowledge. From Fulcher's discussion, we may draw the following implication for ESP listening: While specificity of subject/domain content for ESP listening is useful, it is the general ability to listen in the target language (ESL listening competence) that would have a greater impact on learners' overall ESP listening performance.

One reason for the perceived differences between ESP and ESL listening is the assumption that learners who require ESP training already possess some level of proficiency in the language that enables them to communicate in English. Learning materials for these learners therefore tend to focus on developing the specific vocabulary of the field of work or study, a conclusion that McDonough (2010) drew from her survey of current ESP materials. In the aviation industry, for example, pilots, air traffic controllers and ground crew are expected to use and recognize phrases specific to their area of work so that they can communicate effectively with speakers of English from different countries. Similarly, students enrolled in English-speaking universities are expected to have a level of mastery of English as indicated by scores on international standardized tests of English such as the Test of English as a Foreign Language (TOEFL), the IELTS (International English Language Testing Service) test, and the Michigan English Language Assessment Battery (MELAB). The purpose of academic listening instruction in tertiary institutions is typically to develop skills such as lecture comprehension that will help these students participate and succeed in academic or academic-related discourse.

Feak and Salehzadeh (2001), in discussing the challenges in developing a video listening placement assessment, noted that some academic listening programs also valued, amongst other things, students being active in the classroom beyond the act of note-taking. It is important therefore that EAP learners have strong listening comprehension skills not only for understanding lectures but also for interacting with others in face-to-face communication. Equal attention should therefore be given to helping learners improve their basic comprehension processes and to addressing comprehension problems they face as second language listeners. In some English for occupational purposes (EOP) contexts, the basic listening proficiency of learners may be even weaker than that of those studying in tertiary institutions. In other words, ESP listening teachers could do more by way of pedagogy to enhance comprehension processes that influence how learners make sense of what they hear in a language over which they have inadequate control. It would be beneficial to the field therefore if material writers and researchers were cognizant of the discussion and research in general second language (L2) listening, and their possible implications for ESP listening pedagogy. In what follows, I draw on theoretical insights about general ESL listening to explore the construct of listening for specific purposes and review research carried out into ESP listening, with reference mainly to EAP listening, where the main focus of the research has been. Subsequently, I suggest directions for future research and implications for materials and instruction.

Exploring the Construct of ESP Listening

The goal of second language listening instruction is to develop active listeners and this is also the goal of the more defined area of ESP listening. The term "active listener" refers to "someone who constructs reasonable interpretations on the basis of an underspecified input and recognizes when more specific information is required. The active listener asks for the needed information" (Brown 1990: 172). To listen actively, language learners need to:

- have an available source of relevant knowledge to support cognitive processing;
- use listening skills to facilitate comprehension and interaction;
- engage in metacognitive processes to enhance and regulate their own comprehension and listening development. (Goh 2005; Vandergrift and Goh 2012).

Active listening can occur in all types of listening contexts and is not restricted to situations where the individual is interacting with others. It is needed when one is talking to another person (interactive listening) or when listening to a talk or a lecture (one-way listening). In interactive listening, listeners engage their interlocutors in repeating and explaining messages to obtain greater clarity in their attempt to construct an understanding of the message (Dörnyei and Kormos 1998; Farrell and Mallard 2006; Vandergrift 1997, 2006). In one-way listening, where the context does not allow them to do this, active listeners will make use of appropriate strategies to cope with difficulties and facilitate their comprehension by making predictions or drawing inferences, as well as monitoring and evaluating their understanding (Goh 2002, Vandergrift 2003).

ESP listening as a construct has many similarities to ESL listening. It involves the same cognitive processes that draw from a number of similar knowledge sources to process spoken input, and requires the use of the same core (or "macro") skills that enable effective attention to information in accord with the purpose for listening. Where the two types of listening differ is in the additional skills and specific types of knowledge required for EAP and EOP purposes (see below).

ESP learning materials are typically developed for learners who have roughly an intermediate level of proficiency (McDonough 2010). One might also assume that such learners are able to understand spoken discourse on everyday topics and can participate in a selected range of spoken interactions by making appropriate responses. In reality, however, this may not always be the case, with some learners needing to work hard to build up their rather low level of listening ability while at the same time learning to develop new skills needed for their specific domains. This is where a learner's development of ESL listening and ESP listening competence overlap. It is useful, therefore, to conceptualize ESL and ESP listening development as being interrelated, instead of considering ESP listening development as an "add on" to a set of skills that learners already possess.

While undergoing training in ESP listening skills, a learner is likely to be concurrently developing his or her second language listening competence. Research suggests that the listening problems encountered by learners in both general English and ESP contexts are similar and are linked mainly to factors that influence fundamental cognitive processes, for example: accents (Goh 2000; Rogerson-Revell 2007), vocabulary (Dudley-Evans and Johns 1981; Kelly 1991; Littlemore 2001; Meccarty 2000; Olsen and Huckin 1990), and the demands of interactive listening that require quick and appropriate responses (Ferris and Tagg 1996a; Vandergrift 1997, 2006).

Cognitive processes and knowledge sources

To recognize the sounds they hear, and construct meaning from the spoken text, all second language listeners need three types of knowledge: knowledge about the language (phonology, syntax, and vocabulary), knowledge about language use (discourse and pragmatic), and knowledge about context, facts and experiences (prior or background knowledge, or "schema"). Successful listening comprehension is the result of the interplay of two types of processing that draw on these knowledge types: bottom-up (sounds- and text-driven) processing and top-down (schema-driven) processing (Brown 1990; Field 1998; Vandergrift and Goh 2012). Bottom-up processing involves the decoding of sounds, while top-down processing uses prior knowledge to help listeners draw constrained inferences. For optimal comprehension of input, both sets of processes interact in a harmonious manner to enable the listener to construct an understanding of the message. The accuracy of learners' interpretation, however, can just as easily be affected and constrained by either top-down processing or bottom-up processing (Davis and Johnsrude 2007; Field 2004; Tsui and Fullilove 1998). Knowledge about language and language use, which affects overall language proficiency plays an important role in second language listening comprehension. When learners can apply this knowledge quickly or in an automatized manner during listening, they will have more cognitive capacity for deep meaning construction to occur (Anderson 1995;

Field 2008; Rost 2002; Vandergrift and Goh) 2012). These two types of knowledge are elaborated on below.

Listening comprehension is built upon effective sound discrimination (Wolvin and Coakley 2000) which is dependent on listeners' knowledge of the English sound system and ability to convert those sounds to recognizable words or strings of words in a process called perception or perceptual processing (Anderson 1995). While this ability is largely automatized or "second nature" in first language listening, it requires a range of word recognition and segmenting skills in second language listening (Brown 1990; Field 2008). Less proficient listeners are generally slow at doing this and suffer interference in their echoic memory, a type of sensory memory that retains aural input long enough for processing (Greenberg and Roscoe 1988). Comprehension is affected when word recognition and segmentation skills are not adequately automatized (Segalowitz and Segalowitz 1993).

Syntactic knowledge, or knowing how information is structured grammatically in an utterance, is needed for parsing. This is a process by which an utterance is segmented according to meaning units based on the grammar of the language in order for the listener to create a composite mental representation of the combined meaning of the words (Anderson 1995). Listeners' syntactic knowledge is also helped by their knowledge about how tense and aspect are indicated in the English language. Research suggests that some second language listeners rely heavily on syntactic clues to process what they hear (Conrad 1985; Wolff 1987) and there are indications of a fairly strong correlation between grammar knowledge and listening comprehension (Meccarty 2000). Another source of knowledge for comprehension is vocabulary or lexical knowledge and it includes not only knowing the literal meaning of words but also other semantic references of the same words when they are used in variety of contexts. Vocabulary has been shown to be a key factor affecting the outcome of L2 comprehension even in advanced learners (Bonk 2000; Kelly 1991).

ESP listening is similarly dependent on knowledge about language forms and vocabulary that directly facilitates the perception and parsing of spoken input. Vocabulary remains a challenge for ESP listeners since each discipline has its body of technical and specialized terms that have to be additionally acquired. Furthermore, even after a learner has encountered these words and become familiar with their meanings, they may still have problems recognizing the words in a stream of speech. Another challenge related to vocabulary is ESP listeners' lack of familiarity with idiomatic and fixed expressions that may be used by their interlocutors or lecturers (for example, "off the beaten track/path"), or other expressions which may have specific sociocultural connotations (for example, "a sandwich short of a picnic"). International university students' comprehension of lectures has been shown to be affected by their inability to understand some of the expressions that their lecturers use (Dudley-Evans and Johns 1981; Huang and Finn 2009; Littlemore 2001).

In addition to drawing on their knowledge of language forms and vocabulary, second language listeners as a whole need to rely on knowledge of discourse. They need to understand how the speech that they are listening to can unfold in predictable ways according to what the speaking event might be. Second language learners use their knowledge of the structure of a genre to facilitate listening comprehension and recall (Wolff 1989) while those who are involved in two-way or interactional listening can also predict the development of a conversation if they have some prior knowledge of how the discourse in that context is typically structured (for example, service encounters, a joke or a retelling of an anecdote). Knowledge of discourse structures in ESP listening is related to current discussions of genres and ESP (see Paltridge, this volume) but, on the whole, apart from academic lectures, spoken genres have not been as well-described in ESP. The relevance of this knowledge is often found in discussions about EAP listening where it is argued that knowledge about the discourse structure of lectures can assist lecture comprehension (Tauroza and Allison 1994; Young 1994). It has also been argued that since the discourse structures of lectures across different disciplines may vary, it would be useful for EAP listeners to learn about these variations through instruction (Dudley-Evans 1994).

Discourse knowledge in lecture comprehension is also related to a learner's ability to recognize discourse signals. In first language lecture comprehension, it has been shown that the amount of lecture notes taken by students is positively related to the lecturer's use of discourse signals (Rickards et al. 1997). Second language students, however, have benefitted differently from discourse signaling (or "rhetorical cueing"), with some groups appearing not to have been helped by their lecturer's use of it (Dunkel and Davis 1994). Some studies, on the other hand, have indicated that discourse signaling improves EAP listeners' understanding and recall (Eslami and Eslami-Rasekh 2007; Jung 2003).

There are two possible reasons why the findings may, so far, have been inconclusive. Firstly, as noted by Chaudron and Richards (1986), and Flowerdew and Tauroza (1995), the specific impact of signaling from macro discourse markers and micro discourse markers is still unclear. Discourse markers are words and phrases that join ideas together, show attitude and organize an extended piece of spoken text. Macro or global markers (e.g. "Moving on now to," "It's important to notice that") signal a change in topic or a point of emphasis while micro or local markers (e.g. "Well," "So,") signal intentions and logical connections at the clausal level. Secondly, learners' ability to benefit from discourse signaling is closely affected by perceptual processing. In other words, discourse markers are only helpful if learners can recognize these words and phrases when processing the aural input.

Another type of knowledge about language that all second language listeners need is pragmatic knowledge. Rost (2002: 40) observed for L2 listening that from "a pragmatic perspective, listening is an intention to complete a communication process." Pragmatic knowledge is just as important for general listening as it is for listening for specific academic or occupational purposes. In many listening contexts of an interactive nature, listeners have to interpret what they hear and respond appropriately by first understanding the function of an utterance and its intended effect. Demonstrating pragmatic knowledge through behaviors such as asking for repetitions, rephrasing statements for clarification and backchanneling, are important for all second language learners (Brice and Montgomery 1996).

Receipt tokens that ("mmm," "yeah," "mm hm") provide speakers with crucial indicators of listeners' feedback are a sign of good listenership (McCarthy 2003) and also help second language speakers remain longer in an interaction (Gardner 1998).

Listening skills and metacognitive processes

Listening is carried out in different ways at different times because the reasons for listening change from one listening event or context to the next. Effective listeners will use a number of enabling skills in order to achieve their desired comprehension goal. Discussing ESP listening, Dudley-Evans and St John (1998: 95) proposed two macro-skills for EAP and EOP listening: "listening (to monologue)" and "listening and speaking," and each in turn consists of several micro-skills. I suggest that these macro-skills are in fact contexts in which listening takes place: one-way listening and interactive listening, as mentioned earlier in this chapter. For greater clarity on listening comprehension processes it is more helpful to consider the core comprehension skills that effective listeners use either singly or in combination in order to achieve their desired comprehension goals (Vandergrift and Goh 2012):

Listen for details	understand and identify specific information
Listen for main ideas	understand and summarize key points in a text
Listen for global understanding	understand the gist of the message
Listen and infer	fill in the gaps in one's understanding by using knowledge about the language forms and use, and relevant prior knowledge
Listen and predict	anticipate what one will hear
Listen selectively	pay attention to specific parts of the message by ignoring other parts.

Each of the above core skills can be further differentiated into sub-skills, for example, listeners can make inferences using a number of contextual and linguistic cues depending on the context for listening. Dudley-Evans and St John (1998) also highlighted several micro-skills for both one-way and interactional ESP listening contexts. If we consider the interactive or bidirectional nature of ESP listening in situations such as seminar discussions and professional conversations, it becomes clear that many of the skills that learners need when participating in a discussion are in fact similar to those needed for everyday conversations. These skills relate to turn-taking and include recognizing turn-giving cues, and gaining the floor, as well as using a variety of questions to check understanding, seek clarifications and probe for more information. Second language speakers in general need these skills as well as others (e.g. backchanneling, recognizing gestures and other nonverbal cues), in order to manage spoken interactions in interactive listening events. The overlaps between listening in ESP and non-ESP contexts can also be seen in some of the features of academic listening identified by Flowerdew

(1994), such as the ability to distinguish what is relevant from what is not, a sub-skill that Richards (1983) also highlighted. While Richards' (1983) early attempt at differentiating conversational listening from academic listening was useful, many of the skills that are needed in one type of listening are also important to the other even though the contexts for listening differ.

Nevertheless, depending on the demands on listening in learners' respective EAP or EOP contexts, new skills may need to be added to their existing reper-toires. In academic listening, particularly in lecture comprehension, learners will need to learn to recognize specific types of discourse cues in extended discourse, take notes and integrate incoming messages with information from other sources such as lecture notes and reference materials (Flowerdew 1994; Flowerdew and Miller 2005; Richards 1983). In other ESP domains, such as Business English, the type of listening skills needed may be affected, for example, by the size of a meeting, with many business people feeling more at ease and confident in small meetings compared with larger ones (Rogerson-Revell 2007). Given the nature of business discussions, which involve not only negotiations for meaning but also business outcomes, business people also need to be able to listen critically and respond quickly and accurately at such meetings. Not having enough time to think and respond is a complaint common of many business people who are non-English native speakers. Thus, while ESP listening shares many common features with ESL listening, it also has unique features as a result of specific requirements of communication contexts. ESP listening development may therefore require more high-level listening skills that are relevant to academic demands as well as workplace related competency.

In addition to knowledge and skills, L2 listeners also need to engage in meta-cognitive processes that include strategies for facilitating comprehension and coping with listening difficulties. Just as importantly, these processes will also allow listeners to monitor their own comprehension and overall listening develop-ment. Listening strategies are effortful and conscious behaviors, and they play important roles in facilitating listening comprehension and overall listening devel-opment (Chamot 1995). These are used for manipulating and transforming the spoken input, managing and regulating cognitive processes, managing emotions and exploiting resources to assist comprehension (Vandergrift and Goh 2012). To do this well, learners must develop a strong awareness of their mental processes and improve their capacity to manage these processes (Goh 2008). Proficient L2 listeners have been found to use not only more but also more effective and appro-priate strategies to enhance their comprehension (Macaro, Graham, and Vander-plank 2007) and heightened metacognitive awareness about listening has been found to be a characteristic that is common to proficient L2 listeners (Vandergrift et al. 2006). There is currently little information on how ESP listeners engage in metacognitive processes and how these processes in turn influence their listening comprehension. Nevertheless, given the fundamental importance of cognitive processing in listening, there are reasons to expect that metacognitive processes have the same impact on ESP listening comprehension. Research is needed to verify this claim.

Researching ESP Listening

Listening in EAP contexts has captured the attention of researchers and ELT experts over the last three decades, with much of the research focussing on lecture comprehension. However, the same amount of research interest in listening is not evident for (most) other EOP contexts. Of the, over twenty, professional areas that McDonough (2010) identified, ESP listening for nonacademic purposes has yet to attract research in any substantial way. There is therefore still a lack of empirical evidence that could inform listening materials and instruction for specific purposes in the workplace. Belcher (2006) has discussed this dearth of research in workplace listening competencies, observing that it is very much a reflection of the overall ESP reality.

Research and scholarly discussions in academic listening have provided the field of ESP with valuable information on listening processes, instructors and materials. Researchers have been particularly interested in the perceptions of students and lecturers, the challenges they have each faced and the strategies they have reported using. Students from a variety of discipline backgrounds have been consulted, including engineering, nursing, culinary arts, English, business, medical, arts and humanities and the sciences. Likewise, lecturer studies have been from diverse disciplines at undergraduate and graduate levels, and from varied language backgrounds, such as native English speakers and Chinese as first language (L1) speakers. Research into ESP listening has continued to adopt one of three research methodologies: psychometric studies, discourse analysis or ethnography (Flowerdew 1994).

A variety of data collection methods have become increasingly popular, such as surveys, interviews, observations, journals/dairies and case studies. Benson's (1989) case study provided valuable insights on how an individual student coped with the academic listening task, but few other studies have used this strategy of inquiry, with surveys appearing to be the favored data collection method. These methods are used in research into other areas of EOP listening while data triangulation has also been employed through the use of multiple data collection methods. For example, in studying hotel maids' language needs during spoken interactions, Jasso-Aguilar (1999) demonstrated the value of insiders' perspectives through a combination of participant observation, unstructured interviews and questionnaires.

On the other end of the spectrum of research methods is the use of corpora for identifying features of authentic academic spoken English discourse (see Nesi, this volume). The BASE (British Academic Spoken English) corpus, for example, consists of 160 lectures and 40 seminars recorded in a variety of departments in two British universities (see http://www2.warwick.ac.uk/fac/soc/al/research/collect/base/.) The BASE Plus corpus (at the same website as the BASE corpus) is a larger collection of spoken texts and offers researchers opportunities to examine spoken academic discourse and this has diverse implications for ESP listening research and material. The MICASE (Michigan Corpus of Academic

Spoken English) which offers similar opportunities is a collection of nearly 1.8 million words of transcribed speech from events such as lectures, classroom discussions, lab sections, seminars and advising sessions (see http://micase.elicorpora.info/).

The sections that follow will present a synthesis of some of the key findings on ESP listening research and discussions, drawing information from EAP research as well as (wherever possible) findings from studies of workplace listening.

Developing academic listening skills

Good listening comprehension has been shown to contribute significantly to academic performance (Jeon 2007). In a survey of tertiary-level students and their professors, Sawaki and Nissan (2009) identified 17 core activities in academic contexts where listening is essential, more than those identified in a study by Powers (1986) and in Jordan's (1997) recommended list. Besides the all important lecture, other activities included listening to instructors explaining course requirements, assignments and deadlines as well as listening to classmates' reports, questions and summaries.

In spite of its importance, listening continues to pose a challenge to many EAP learners. Areas of difficulties in lecture comprehension and interactive listening include:

- coping with inadequate general English language proficiency which causes difficulties in understanding and remembering information during lectures (Huang 2004, 2005; Huang and Finn 2009), participating in more interactive forms of oral interaction during lessons (Ferris and Tagg 1996a; Lucas and Murry 2002; Mason 1994) and responding to questions in class (Ferris 1998; Huang and Finn 2009);
- recognizing the functions of nonverbal cues (gestures and facial expressions) in authentic lectures (Huang and Finn 2009), which are lacking in written text or scripted lectures;
- recognizing syntactic, phonological or nonverbal clues that signal the end of turns (Dudley-Evans and St John 1998);
- being well prepared for different degrees and types of interaction expected according to different class sizes, disciplines and class types (e.g. graduate vs. undergraduate) (Ferris and Tagg 1996b);
- handling the considerable variety of lecturers' preferred lecturing styles: reading style, conversational style, rhetorical style and report-and-discuss style (Dudley-Evans 1994; Ferris and Tagg 1996b);
- responding to what is required during lectures and at the same time comprehending and extracting salient points from them (Ferris and Tagg 1996a);
- improving note-taking skills (Ferris 1998; Flowerdew 1994) – there are indications of a relationship between the amount of notes that students take and their test performance (Olmos and Lusung-Oyzon 2008) and academic learning (Chaudron, Loschky, and Cook 1994);

- integrating listening to the lecturer, taking notes and processing of visual information that accompany lectures (Gruba 2004);
- understanding the use of metaphorical language by lecturers (Dudley-Evans and Johns 1981; Littlemore 2001, Littlemnore et al. 2011) and;
- coping with anxiety when required to participate actively in class (Arnold 2000).

The above challenges are to some extent affected by general language proficiency level and listening ability. For example, the study by Dunkel and Davis (1994) showed there was a relationship between learners' proficiency and fluency and the quantity (measured by word count and idea units) and quality of students' lecture notes. A study by Olsen and Huckin (1990) revealed that students could be distinguished by the types of strategies they used for recognizing lecturer intent when taking notes. Information-driven strategies were employed by students who simply wanted to identify and learn facts while point-driven strategies were used by students who attempted to distinguish major points from supporting ideas. The strategies used by the second group suggests that the learners were able to go beyond listening for details to using more sophisticated skills such as drawing inferences and listening for main points and global understanding.

Tauroza and Allison (1994) proposed a constituent structure of lectures that comprised five "idea units": topic, introduction, problem, solution, and evaluation. To investigate whether students recognized these idea units, they investigated 50 students' recall of a lecture and found that a majority of the students managed to differentiate the topic from the introduction, as well as three key details of the solution but only a small percentage of them could accurately identify the other idea units. The higher-ability students were generally more successful at understanding the evaluation of the solution by the lecturer, suggesting that more complex listening skills were required for this part of the lecture. The researchers speculated that the students who misunderstood the evaluation section may have performed a "local interpretation," which according to Brown and Yule (1983) is the attempt to understand something based exclusively on the context that is unfolding. Proficient listeners, on the other hand, make use of a more global context so that they can arrive at a coherent interpretation that is consistent with textual evidence (Tauroza and Allison 1994). An overreliance on the local interpretation of a message can lead students to misunderstand a lecture. These listening problems have also been observed in research on general second language listening ability and strategy use.

Improving general listening proficiency is a challenge for many EAP learners. Despite gaining admittance into academic programs on account of their scores in standardized tests, many learners still have difficulties processing low-level information quickly to facilitate higher-level meaning construction. As cognitive processes during listening are recursive and reiterative (Anderson 1995), students who do not have adequate decoding or bottom-up skills will struggle to keep up with the transient input and this will affect deep processing that can lead to better recall (Goh 2000). Huang (2004) and Huang and Finn (2009) observed that tertiary-level

ESL students who demonstrated adequate language competence in proficiency tests such as the TOEFL still encountered difficulty with academic listening, an area that they also found more challenging than reading and speaking. A perception study of medical college students in Taiwan and their teachers showed that the students were keen to improve their listening skill, which they felt was the weakest of the four skills, and felt they still needed a general English course (Chia et al. 1999). Chinese EAP students studying in Singapore also considered listening to be their weakest skill, and some of them also felt they had little control over its development (Liu 2005).

ESP listeners can be supported through textbooks and classroom activities, but as Flowerdew and Miller (1997) noted, many of the EAP textbooks they examined did not address the need to develop learners' strategic competence. They identified several ways in which EAP students could be supported through more effective material preparation, instruction and lecture delivery:

- help learners attend to features of spoken language: micro-structuring; false starts, redundancies and repetitions; body language;
- integrate audio input with other media: use of visual aids; integration with pre- and post-reading and tutorial discussion.

In view of the challenges that second language learners face in academic settings, lecturers have been advised to:

- use interpersonal strategies to show empathy with students to make their lectures less threatening and create a more conducive learning environment (Flowerdew and Miller 1997);
- help students develop better discourse knowledge for lectures (Dudley-Evans 1994; Young 1994);
- structure the lecture by using a narrative thread to hold the lecture together, macro-markers and rhetorical questions (Crawford Camiciottoli 2004; Flowerdew and Miller 1997);
- give students more time to take notes by including more pauses and hesitations (Dunkel 1988);
- be cognizant of cultural diversity in classes and its implications for teaching (Leki 2001; Miller 2009), and;
- prepare learners with effective learning strategies and help them make preparations for subject-matter lectures (Ferris and Tagg 1996a).

Miller (2009) summarized a series of studies he conducted in Hong Kong with Flowerdew from 1992–2000 and identified four dimensions to lecturing in the students' second language which lecturers should take into account in order to support students in their learning and understanding:

Ethnic – the difficulties a lecturer from one ethnic background has when presenting lectures to students from a different cultural background;

Local – when aspects of the local setting assist students to comprehend the lecture
   content;

Academic – practices peculiar to educational institutions, e,g. teacher-centered
   instruction vs. student-centered learning;

Disciplinary – the realization that each discipline has specialized vocabulary and
   specific ways of presenting information.

He also identified language and pedagogical features in lectures which students found useful, including simplification, use of examples, lecture handouts
(and mapping of the lecture with a handout), use of visuals and staging of lectures.
Previously, Flowerdew and Miller (1996) had identified sociocultural features of
lectures delivered in students' second language, which could have an impact on
comprehension and learning:

Purpose of lectures – While both lecturers and students considered lectures to be
   important, lecturers saw lectures as a means for them to develop students'
   thinking skills and creativity whereas students saw them as mainly a means for
   them to receive information.

Roles of lecturers – Lecturers took on a variety of roles, e.g. "prioritizer of information," "mediator to the local situation," and language teacher.

Styles of lecturing – Lecturers often adopted a traditional monologic style of lecturing even though they would have liked to use a more participatory style. Students, however, were often unresponsive towards this more interactive style of
   learning.

Simplification – Lecturers took into consideration, though with limited success,
   students' linguistic problems. They tried to slow down their speech, avoided
   using complex or unusual words, and repeated themselves more. Students
   seemed to find repetition to be the most beneficial of these strategies for helping
   them to comprehend lectures more effectively.

Listener behavior – Lecturers expressed their difficulty in getting students' attention
   while students expressed that they were bored, unable to adapt to the lax classroom discipline, or had to use their mother tongue to help each other understand the lectures better.

Humor – Although injecting humor into a lecture was seen to be useful, foreign
   lecturers stated that their use of humor had been unsuccessful due to cultural
   or linguistic barriers between themselves and students.

Instructors and materials

The ESP instructor is often perceived to be 'a provider of materials – selecting
material that is available, adapting it as necessary and supplementing it' in order
to meet learners' needs (Dudley-Evans and St John 1998: 185). At the same time,
instructors need to be aware of changes in the lecturing and teaching style in
their universities. In the United States, for example, there is a move towards less
formal and more interactive styles in academic settings (Ferris and Tagg 1996b).

Furthermore, instructors need to understand differences between authentic lecture discourse and written text or scripted lectures in EAP classes when preparing students for lectures. Instructors should strive to provide or use authentic materials for authentic purposes: thus, learners should be exposed to lectures delivered at an authentic speed and given practice in engaging with other participants in real-time interaction (Dudley-Evans and St John 1998). For example, ESP learners preparing for the hospitality industry need to be well-versed in the "hospitality language" that corresponds to the different stages of the arrival-departure hospitality cycle (Blue and Harun 2003).

With regard to teaching lecture comprehension, Young (1994) offered a model of analysis of the discourse structure of academic lectures. Discourse structures are described in terms of metadiscourse phases (discourse structuring, conclusion, and evaluation) as well as the content phases (theory and examples). These descriptions, Young claimed, would be useful for the selection of appropriate instructional materials as well as provide teachers with the tools to raise learners' awareness of the structure of the generic type of academic lectures. While Young's proposed model provides a detailed linguistic description of different phases of a lecture, it would have to be simplified before EAP teachers are able to apply it to ESP listening instruction.

Recent ESP teaching materials that address a wide range of professional areas tend to assume that teachers have full access to various technologies and that students are able to acquire broader language skills outside class although this may not necessarily be true of all contexts (McDonough 2010). McDonough observed that information technology appears to play a vital role with the internet being central to student activities and teacher support. Chan (2009: 12), in her review of Business English materials, showed that the materials in general offer plenty of opportunities for practicing speaking and listening, although the approach is usually to "present information through written or spoken texts with concomitant emphasis on reading and listening." She also pointed out that the materials were not authentic, did not focus much on developing awareness about language and the learning process, and did not draw on empirical research, a point also noted by McDonough, for EOP materials in general.

Future directions for ESP listening research

The use of English in tertiary institutions is quite phenomenal as we see a rise in the number of universities in many traditionally non-English speaking countries offering courses taught in English (Coleman 2006; Wilkinson 2005). Although ESP is flourishing, courses and materials development are still not well supported by research (McDonough 2010; St John 1996) and this has "hindered ESP's professionalization as a self-standing discipline in universities, and as a discipline that complements skills courses in training for non-native speakers" (Dudley-Evans and St John 1998: 230). A constant diversifying in purposes for the use of English in specific fields and occupations has made a description and definition of ESP problematic (Belcher 2006; St John 1996). In addition, with the growing number of genres identified in ESP and the emphasis given to literacy development in EAP, researchers would also have to "find ways to facilitate practitioners' conceptualization and operationalization of a more broadly inclusive multiliteracies approach to fostering and assessing genre competence" (Belcher 2004: 177).

In discussions of academic and workplace literacies, the importance of listening and speaking, or oracy, is often overshadowed by reading and writing. Clearly greater emphasis needs to be given to researching oral skills, particularly listening. Given the diversity in socioeducational contexts in which ESP teaching is conducted, there is also a need for empirical research on different scales in the classroom or workplace that can contribute to a better understanding of the needs of different groups of language learners (see, e.g. hospitality studies by Jasso-Aguilar 1999; Su 2009). Ongoing efforts in the analysis of discourse and rhetoric will help us further understand the influence of cultures in both one-way and interactive listening processes. More attention should also be paid to varieties of English as an international language that "may help ESP rethink its conceptualization of *expertise*, or proficient specialist language use, long the target of ESP research efforts" (Belcher 2006: 150).

The paucity of published research and materials on listening, particularly in professional and vocational discourse settings needs to be addressed so that practitioners can have a clearer understanding of the nature of listening expertise or what it takes for someone to communicate competently in their area of work. This would help derive what Belcher (2004: 177) refers to as "research-based definitions of community-specific expertise" with respect to listening. This is particularly true of ESP listening in English for occupational purposes (EOP), which has not benefitted from insights derived from research. Academic listening, on the other hand, has had a relatively longer period of scholarly engagement. Further research is also needed to examine ways of exploiting technologies for improving ESP learners' listening skills; for example, using web-based instruction and cooperative learning to help learners improve communication skills (Wang 2009).

Thus, the challenge in ESP listening is not just about finding ways of feeding research findings into course development, it is also about driving more research into the diverse workplace contexts where listening plays a critical role. As research into academic listening continues to develop, it would be useful for researchers to find ways of strengthening the interface between general ESL/EFL listening and ESP listening. One possible area is in the study of ESP learners' metacognition in relation to listening (Goh 2008). Research into learners' metacognitive awareness and metacognitive instruction in ESL has shown its relevance and contribution to listening development (see e.g. Cross 2010; Graham and Macaro 2008; Mareschal 2007, Vandergrift and Tafaghodtari 2010). A similar focus in ESP listening would help to elucidate internal and external factors (other than perceived problems which have been widely studied to date) that influence successful listening performance for academic and occupational purposes. In this regard, the following could be considered:

- The ESP learner's listening self-concept could be explored for its effects on listening comprehension, anxiety, motivation, and learning to listen for specific purposes.
- The ESP learner's metacognitive knowledge as it relates to both academic-learning and workplace-specific listening situations and beyond could be examined for its role in comprehension.
- The effects of knowledge about language and language use on listening performance could be investigated in different types of ESP listening.
- The way effective ESP listeners combine skills and strategies in one-way and interactive listening events could be described as this can provide valuable insights for teaching.
- More in-depth case and ethnographic studies of individual learners in different learning and cultural contexts could be carried out to provide rich data on how individual learners develop their listening in and outside the classroom.
- Metacognitive instruction in listening for academic and professional/vocational purposes could be conducted and its effects on lecture comprehension and interactive listening examined.
- The relationship between general second language listening proficiency and ESP listening proficiency could be investigated to examine the interrelationships between the two types of listening.
- The relationship between listening performance in standardized language proficiency tests and listening achievement in ESP courses could help establish how well the former predicts the latter.
- ESP listeners' critical awareness of the way spoken language influences perceptions and understanding could be investigated to support a critical pedagogic approach to ESP listening.

Recommendations for Teaching

Needs assessment, content-based teaching methods, and content-area informed instructors are generally accepted as integral to specific-purpose teaching, though the definition of these concepts and how they are realized are still being debated (Belcher 2006). Many teachers would agree that a key purpose of their teaching would be to demystify the academic or institutional discourse that learners face (Dudley-Evans and St John 1998). The methodology of respective disciplines and professions should therefore be reflected in ESP teaching (Dudley-Evans and St John 1998). More specifically, ESP listening instructors and material developers could benefit from what various ESP researchers have highlighted in their discussions of ESP and listening, namely:

- Be aware that learners may have different perceptions of tasks and situations, objectives and needs (Jasso-Aguilar 1999). "EAP pragmatism" of teachers will ensure a "willingness to recognize and investigate the diverse goals, strategies, tactics and contexts that actual EAP experience subsumes" (Allison 1996: 98), thereby helping students to succeed in various settings.

- Do not assume that learners are necessarily motivated to learn because the curriculum is expected to meet their academic or occupational needs (Chia et al. 1999). Motivate students to learn (Chan 2009; Su 2009), even to the extent of going beyond the needs in the workplace (Jasso-Aguilar 1999; St John 1996).
- Recognize that many language learners are new to their field (McDonough 2010), have different aspiration and anxiety levels (Su 2009), and their listening proficiency may be influenced by a lack of "linguistic intelligence" (Mahdavy 2008) or general language proficiency.
- Make course evaluation in ESP courses an imperative so as to achieve a deeper understanding about how learning experiences and processes can affect ESP learners (Su 2009).
- Be aware of underlying differences in sociocultural discourse conventions or linguistic competence which could lead to problems in listening and affect other people's impression of ESP learners (Rogerson-Revell 2007; St John 1996).
- Use a variety of techniques to help ESP learners improve their listening in the classroom (Chia et al.1999).
- Facilitate cooperative learning by assigning each student a lecture buddy to help them in their listening comprehension (Mendelsohn 2002).
- Evaluate materials for their overall goals and to ensure that there is fitness for purpose based on the needs of learners in a specific area of studies or work (McDonough 2010).
- Harness the potential of technological innovations in ESP teaching (Belcher 2004; Dudley-Evans and St John 1998) for generating teaching materials relevant to actual occupational situations and maximizing the advantages of on-site teaching. Teachers would need to be able to incorporate them into their pedagogy and prepare their students to use them effectively. (Hyland and Hamp-Lyons 2002).
- Accept training and support if ESP teachers are not specialists in the particular field. For example, teachers may need training on how to pronounce domain-specific terminology (McDonough 2010; Su 2009) and learn how to create the kind of interaction that is expected between the students, who are professionals in their field, and the teacher who is not (McDonough 2010).

Concluding Remarks

Much has been achieved in the area of ESP listening by way of research into academic listening and the development of EAP materials. EOP listening, however, has not been able to benefit from similar kinds of research insights. Given the diversity in the range of EAP and workplace English learning needs, it has been suggested that the scope of ESP be redefined by excluding EAP (Harding 2007). If we were to adopt this stand and consider the coverage of ESP listening through a non-EAP professional and vocational lens, it would become immediately clear that this area of ESP listening research is in dire need of support from the field as a whole. The small but growing number of studies in listening for occupational purposes is an encouraging sign but more can be done within the ESP community to support it. Finally, given the difficulty in separating general listening abilities from ESP listening abilities, it would be useful to adopt an approach in the research and teaching of ESP listening that integrates the best of theory and practice in both learning contexts.

REFERENCES

Anderson, J. R. (1995) *Cognitive Psychology and its Implications*. 4th ed. New York: Freeman.

Allison, D. (1996) Pragmatist discourse and English for academic purposes. *English for Specific Purposes* 15: 85–103.

Arnold, J. (2000) Seeing through listening comprehension exam anxiety. *TESOL Quarterly* 34: 777–86.

Belcher, D. (2004) Trends in teaching English for specific purposes. *Annual Review of Applied Linguistics* 24: 165–86.

Belcher, D. (2006) English for specific purposes: Teaching to perceived needs and imagined futures in worlds of work, study, and everyday life. *TESOL Quarterly* 40: 133–56.

Benson, M. J. (1989) The academic listening task: A case study. *TESOL Quarterly* 23: 421–45.

Blue, G. M. and Harun, M. (2003) Hospitality language as a professional skill. *English for Specific Purposes* 22: 73–91.

Bonk, W. J. (2000) Second language lexical knowledge and listening comprehension. *International Journal of Listening* 14: 14–31.

Brice, A. and Montgomery, J. (1996) Adolescent pragmatic skills: A comparison of Latino students in English as a Second Language and speech and language programs. *Language, Speech, and Hearing Services in Schools* 27: 68–81.

Brown, G. (1990). *Listening to Spoken English*. London: Longman.

Brown, G. and Yule, G. (1983) *Teaching the Spoken Language: An Approach Based on the Analysis of Conversational English*. Cambridge: Cambridge University Press.

Chamot, A. U. (1995) Learning strategies and listening comprehension. In D. J. Mendelsohn and J. Rubin (eds.), *A Guide for the Teaching of Second Language Listening*. 13–130. San Diego, CA: Dominie Press.

Chan, C. S. C. (2009) Forging a link between research and pedagogy: A holistic framework for evaluating business English materials. *English for Specific Purposes* 28: 125–36.

Chaudron, C. and Richards, J. C. (1986) The effect of discourse markers on the comprehension of lectures. *Applied Linguistics* 7: 113–27.

Chaudron, C., Loschky, L., and Cook, J. (1994) Second language listening comprehension and lecture note-taking. In John Flowerdew (ed.), *Academic Listening: Research Perspectives*. 75–92. New York: Cambridge University Press.

Chia, H-U., Johnson, R., Chia, H-L., and Olive, F. (1999) English for college students in Taiwan: A study of perceptions of English needs in a medical context. *English for Specific Purposes* 18: 107–19.

Coleman, J. A. (2006) English-medium teaching in European higher education. *Language Teaching* 39: 1–14.

Conrad, L. (1985) Semantic versus syntactic cues in listening comprehension. *Studies in Second Language Acquisition* 7: 59–69.

Crawford Camiciottoli, B. C. (2004) Interactive discourse structuring in L2 guest lectures: Some insights from a comparative corpus-based study. *Journal of English for Academic Purposes* 3: 39–54.

Cross, J. (2010) Raising L2 listeners' metacognitive awareness: A sociocultural theory perspective. *Language Awareness* 19: 281–97.

Davis, M. H. and Johnsrude, I. S. (2007) Hearing speech sounds: Top-down influences on the interface between audition and speech perception. *Hearing Research* 229: 132–47.

Dörnyei, Z. and Kormos, J. (1998) Problem-solving mechanisms in L2 communication: A psycholinguistic perspective. *Studies in Second Language Acquisition* 20, 349–85.

Dudley-Evans, T., and Johns, T. F. (1981) A team-teaching approach to lecture comprehension for overseas students. In *The Teaching of Listening Comprehension*. 30–46. London: The British Council.

Dudley-Evans, T. (1994) Variations in the discourse patterns favoured by different disciplines and their pedagogical implications. In J. Flowerdew (ed.), *Academic Listening: Research Perspectives*. 146–165. New York: Cambridge University Press.

Dudley-Evans, T. and St John, M. J. (1998) *Developments in English for Specific Purposes: A Multi-Disciplinary Approach*. New York: Cambridge University Press.

Dunkel, P. (1988) Academic listening and note taking for L1/L2 students: The need to investigate the utility of the axioms of good note taking. *TESL Canada Journal* 6: 11–26.

Dunkel, P. and Davis, J. N. (1994) The effects of rhetorical signaling cues on the recall of English lecture information by speakers of English as a native and second language. In J. Flowerdew (ed.), *Academic Listening: Research Perspectives*. 55–74. New York: Cambridge University Press.

Eslami, Z. R. and Eslami-Rasekh, A. (2007) Discourse markers in academic lectures. *Asian EFL Journal* 9: 22–38.

Farrell, T. S. C. and Mallard, C. (2006) The use of reception strategies by learners of French as a Foreign Language. *The Modern Language Journal* 90: 338–52.

Feak, C. B. and Salehzadeh, E. (2001) Challenges and issues in developing an EAP video listening placement assessment: A view from one program. *English for Specific Purposes* 20: 477–93.

Ferris, D. (1998) Students' views of academic aural/oral skills: A comparative needs analysis. *TESOL Quarterly* 32: 289–318.

Ferris, D. and Tagg, T. (1996a) Academic listening/speaking tasks for ESL students: Problems, suggestions, and implications. *TESOL Quarterly* 30: 297–320.

Ferris, D. and Tagg, T. (1996b) Academic oral communication needs of EAP learners: What subject-matter instructors actually require. *TESOL Quarterly* 30: 31–58.

Field, J. (2004) An insight into listeners' problems: Too much bottom-up or too much top-down? *System* 32: 363–77.

Field, J. (2008) *Listening in the Langauge Classroom*. Cambridge: Cambridge University Press.

Flowerdew, J. (ed.) (1994) *Academic Listening: Research Perspectives*. New York: Cambridge University Press.

Flowerdew, J. and Miller, L. (1996) Lectures in a second language: Notes towards a cultural grammar. *English for Specific Purposes* 15: 121–40.

Flowerdew, J. and Miller, L. (1997) The teaching of academic listening comprehension and the question of

authenticity. *English for Specific Purposes*
16: 27–46.

Flowerdew, J. and Miller, L. (2005) *Second
Language Listening: Theory and Practice.*
New York: Cambridge University Press.

Flowerdew, J. and Tauroza, S. (1995) The
effect of discourse markers on second
language lecture comprehension. *Studies
in Second Language Acquisition* 17:
435–58.

Fulcher, G. (1999) Assessment in English
for academic purposes: Putting content
validity in its place. *Applied Linguistics*
20: 221–36.

Gardner, R. (1998) Between speaking and
listening: The vocalisation of
understandings. *Applied Linguistics* 19:
204–24.

Goh, C. C. M. (2000) A cognitive
perspective on language learners'
listening comprehension problems.
System 28: 55–75.

Goh, C. C. M. (2002) *Teaching Listening in
the Language Classroom.* Singapore:
SEAMEO Regional Language Centre.

Goh, C. C. M. (2005) Second language
listening expertise. In K. Johnson (ed.),
*Expertise in Second Language Learning and
Teaching.* 64–84. Basingstoke, UK:
Palgrave Macmillan.

Goh, C. C. M. (2008) Metacognitive
instruction for second language listening
development: Theory, practice and
research implications. *RELC Journal* 39:
188–213.

Graham, S. and Macaro, E. (2008) Strategy
instruction in listening for lower-
intermediate learners of French.
Language Learning 58: 747–83.

Greenberg, S. N. and Roscoe, S. (1988)
Echoic memory interference and
comprehension in a foreign language.
Language Learning 38: 209–19.

Gruba, P. (2004) Understanding digitized
second language videotext. *Computer
Assisted Language Learning* 17: 51–82.

Harding, K. (2007) *English for Specific
Purposes.* Oxford: Oxford University
Press.

Huang, J. (2004) Voices from Chinese
students: Professors' use of English
affects academic listening. *College
Student Journal* 38: 212–24.

Huang, J. (2005) Challenges of academic
listening in English: Reports by Chinese
students. *College Student Journal* 39:
553–70.

Huang, J. and Finn, A. (2009) Academic
listening tests for ESOL students:
Availability, concerns, and solutions.
*International Journal of Applied Educational
Studies* 6: 46–55.

Hyland, K. and Hamp-Lyons, L. (2002)
EAP: Issues and directions. *Journal of
English for Academic Purposes* 1: 1–12.

Jasso-Aguilar, R. (1999) Sources, methods
and triangulation in needs analysis: A
critical perspective in a case study of
Waikiki hotel maids. *English for Specific
Purposes* 18: 27–46.

Jeon, J. (2007) *A study of listening
comprehension of academic lectures within
the construction-integration model.*
Doctoral dissertation, Ohio State
University, IL.

Jordan, R. R. (1997) *English for Academic
Purposes: A Guide and Resource Book for
Teachers.* Cambridge: Cambridge
University Press.

Jung, E. H. S. (2003) The role of discourse
signaling cues in second language
listening comprehension. *The Modern
Language Journal* 87: 562–77.

Kelly, P. (1991) Lexical ignorance: The
main obstacle to listening
comprehension with advanced foreign
language learners. *International Review of
Applied Linguistics* 29: 135–49.

Leki, I. (2001) A narrow thinking system:
Nonnative-English-speaking students in
group projects across the curriculum.
TESOL Quarterly 35: 39–67.

Littlemore, J. (2001). The use of metaphor
in university lectures and the problems
that it causes for overseas students.
Teaching in Higher Education 6: 333–49.

Littlemore, J., Chen, P., Trautman K., and
Barnden, J. (2011) Difficulties in

metaphor comprehension faced by international students whose first language is not English. *Applied Linguistics*, DOI: 10.1093/applin/amr009.

Liu, X. (2005) Teaching academic listening. In K. P. Foong and M. Vallance (eds.), *Teaching English to Chinese ESL Students: Classroom Practices*. 30–47. Singapore: Pearson Longman.

Lucas, C. J. and Murry, J. W. (2002) *New Faculty: A Practical Guide for Academic Beginners*. New York: Palgrave Macmillan.

Macaro, E., Graham, S. and Vanderplank, R. (2007) A review of listening strategies: Focus on sources of knowledge and on success. In E. Macaro and A. Cohen (eds.), *Language Learner Strategies: 30 Years of Research and Practice*. 165–85. Oxford: Oxford University Press.

Mahdavy, B. (2008) The role of multiple intelligences (MI) in listening proficiency: A comparison of TOEFL and IELTS listening tests from an MI perspective. *Asian EFL Journal* 10: 109–26.

Mareschal, D. (2007) *Neuroconstructivism: How the Brain Constructs Cognition*. Oxford: Oxford University Press.

Mason, A. (1994) By dint of: Student and lecturer perceptions of lecture comprehension strategies in first-term graduate study. In J. Flowerdew (ed.), *Academic Listening: Research Perspectives*. 199–218. New York: Cambridge University Press.

McCarthy, M. (2003) Talking back: "Small" interactional response tokens in everyday conversation. *Research on Language and Social Interaction* 36: 22–63.

McDonough, J. (2010) English for specific purposes: A survey review of current materials. *ELT Journal* 64: 462–77.

Meccarty, F. H. (2000) Lexical and grammatical knowledge in reading and listening comprehension by foreign language learners of Spanish. *Applied Language Learning* 11: 323–48.

Mendelsohn, D. (2002) The lecture buddy project: An experiment in EAP listening comprehension. *TESL Canada Journal* 20: 64–73.

Miller, L. (2009) Engineering lectures in a second langauge: What factors facilitate students' listening comprehension? *Asian EFL Journal* 11: 8–30.

Olmos, O. L. and Lusung-Oyzon, M. V. P. (2008) Effects of prior knowledge and lesson outline on note taking and test scores. *Education Quarterly* 66: 71–86.

Olsen, L. A. and T. H. Huckin (1990) Point-driven understanding in engineering lecture comprehension. *English for Specific Purposes* 9: 33–47.

Powers, D. E. (1986) Academic demands related to listening skills. *Language Testing* 3: 1–38.

Richards, J. C. (1983) Listening comprehension: Approach, design, procedure. *TESOL Quarterly* 17: 219–40.

Rickards, J. P., Fajen, B. R., Sullivan, J. F., and Gillespie, G. (1997) Signaling, notetaking, and field independence-dependence in text comprehension and recall. *Journal of Educational Psychology* 89: 508–17.

Rogerson-Revell, P. (2007) Using English for international business: A European case study. *English for Specific Purposes* 26: 103–20.

Rost, M. (2002) *Teaching and Researching Listening*. London: Longman.

Sawaki, Y. and Nissan, S. (2009) *Criterion-related validity of the TOEFL® iBT listening section* (TOEFL iBT™ Report No. iBT-08). Princeton, NJ: ETS.

Segalowitz, N. S. and Segalowitz, S. J. (1993) Skilled performance practice and the differentiation of speed up automatization effects: Evidence from second language word recognition. *Applied Psycholinguistics* 14: 369–85.

St John, M. J. (1996) Business is booming: Business English in the 1990s. *English for Specific Purposes* 15: 3–18.

Su, S. W. (2009) Designing and delivering an English for hospitality syllabus: A

Taiwanese case study. *RELC Journal: A Journal of Language Teaching and Research* 40: 280–313.

Tauroza, S. and Allison, D. (1994) Expectation–driven understanding in information systems lecture comprehension. In J. Flowerdew (ed.), *Academic Listening: Research Perspectives*. 35–54. New York: Cambridge University Press.

Tsui, A. and Fullilove, J. (1998) Bottom-up or top-down processing as a discriminator of L2 listening performance. *Applied Linguistics* 19: 432–51.

Vandergrift, L. (1997) The comprehension strategies of second language (French) listeners: A descriptive study. *Foreign Language Annals* 30: 387–409.

Vandergrift, L. (2003) Orchestrating strategy use: Toward a model of the skilled second language listener. *Language Learning* 53: 463–96.

Vandergrift, L. (2006) Second language listening: Listening ability or language proficiency? *The Modern Language Journal* 90: 6–18.

Vandergrift, L. and Goh, C. C. M. (2012) *Teaching and Learning Second Language Listening: Metacognition in Action*. New York: Routledge.

Vandergrift, L., Goh, C. M. H., Mareschal, C. J., and Tafaghodtari, M. H. (2006) The Metacognitive Awareness Listening Questionnaire (MALQ): Development and validation. *Language Learning* 56: 431–62.

Vandergrift, L. and Tafaghodtari, M. H. (2010) Teaching L2 learners how to listen does make a difference: An empirical study. *Language Learning* 60: 470–97.

Wang, M. J. (2009) Web based projects enhancing English language and generic skills development for Asian hospitality industry students. *Australasian Journal of Educational Technology* 25: 611–26.

Wilkinson, B. (2005) Where is English taking universities? *Guardian Weekly*, Accessed March 18, 2011 at http://www.guardian.co.uk/education/2005/mar/18/tefl.

Wolff, D. (1987) Some assumptions about second language text comprehension. *Studies in Second Language Acquisition* 9: 307–26.

Wolff, D. (1989) Identification of text-type as a strategic device in L2 comprehension. In H. W. Dechert and M. Raupach (eds.), *Interlingual Processes*. 137–50. Tubingen, Germany: Gunter Nann.

Wolvin, A. D. and Coakely, C. G. (2000) Listening education in the 21st Century. *International Journal of Listening* 14: 143–52.

Young, L. (1994) University lectures macro-structures and micro-features. In J. Flowerdew (ed.), *Academic Listening: Research Perspectives*. 159–76. New York: Cambridge University Press.

4 ESP and Reading

ALAN HIRVELA

Introduction

Reading occupies what might be called a curious place in English for specific purposes (ESP). On the one hand, as Jordan (1997: 51) has observed, "In any self-assessment or questionnaire-based survey, students almost always cite reading as the skill causing them the least difficulty." Thus, there would not seem to be much reason to address it in ESP. On the other hand, reading is at the heart of much of what ESP students do, both in acquiring knowledge of target community discourse and in conjunction with the use of another skill, such as writing. Thus, says McDonough (1984: 70), "It will come as no surprise to most people to discover that, in ESP terms, by far the most significant skill is that of reading." Then, too, even if many students rank reading as the "least difficult" of the skills, "this does not mean that students have no problems at all with reading" (Jordan 1997: 51). There are, then, important reasons to focus on reading in ESP courses and conduct research in this area.

In this chapter I look at the place of reading in ESP, first by briefly exploring its historical roots in the field and then by discussing more recent pedagogical perspectives and research findings concerning its use.

Foundations of Reading in ESP

Foundational aspects

To gain a better understanding of current perspectives on and approaches to ESP and reading, it is helpful to see where reading has come from as related

The Handbook of English for Specific Purposes, First Edition.
Edited by Brian Paltridge and Sue Starfield.
© 2013 John Wiley & Sons, Inc. Published 2013 by John Wiley & Sons, Inc.

to ESP. Like ESP itself, interest in reading began to shift in the 1970s. As Peter Strevens (1977: 109) commented while noting a significant pedagogical change taking place at that time: "the pendulum may have swung too far in the direction of speech, and many teachers are now seeking to increase the effort applied to learning and teaching a command of the written language, and especially to the learning and teaching of reading." Reinforcing this different view of reading, McDonough (1984: 70) pointed out that "English is the language of textbooks and journals." In other words, for very many learners, English is a "library language," especially in English as a foreign language (EFL) contexts. Thus, there was a new climate in which to approach reading.

From register analysis to discourse analysis

Reading's ascendancy in ESP coincides with important shifts in ESP itself. Hutchinson and Waters (1987: 13), in a historical review of ESP's development, identify an initial stage in which, they say, "the analysis had been of the surface forms of the language" in the form of register analysis, that is, the study at the sentence level of the use of language in different communicative settings, such as the language used by nurses, airplane mechanics, and bank tellers. In this stage, the teaching of reading received minimal attention. It was, say Hutchinson and Waters (1987: 10), at the next stage of development that reading pedagogy in ESP took major steps forward: "Whereas in the first stage of its development, ESP had focused on language at the sentence level, the second phase of development shifted attention to the level above the sentence, as ESP became closely involved with the emerging field of discourse or rhetorical analysis." This change in emphasis created an opening for new approaches to reading.

The changing tides with respect to reading can be seen in its early phase in the United Kingdom via the landmark ESP textbook series developed by Allen and Widdowson (1974), *English in Focus*, in which they began to look at longer stretches of texts, not individual sentences or short passages, and the ways in which authors structured those texts so as to guide the ways in which readers would read them. As Widdowson (1979) explained, they were interested in how discoursal elements in the texts "primed" the reading and understanding of them. Equipping students to identify and make use of these priming devices became a central focus of ESP reading instruction, as reflected in the teaching approaches portrayed in the *English in Focus* series and in another groundbreaking text, *Episodes in ESP* (Swales 1985), where there was further explication of how to teach the analysis and use of target community discourse via discourse analysis, especially in the sciences.

English for science and technology (EST) was in fact a primary site for the creation of the foundations of ESP reading instruction and research that continue to exert a heavy influence today. In addition to the important EST work taking place in the United Kingdom, at the University of Washington in the United States a group led by Louis and Mary Todd Trimble as well as Larry Selinker was also developing a discourse analysis approach to reading. In his book *English for Science and Technology: A Discourse Approach*, Louis Trimble (1985: 14), drawing on the same ideas at the heart of discourse analysis, set forth the ideas and practices of what he and team members called a rhetorical approach:

> The rhetorical approach to teaching non-native speakers how to read (and secondarily how to write) scientific and technical English discourse is built around three main rhetorical concepts: (1) the nature of the EST paragraph; (2) the rhetorical techniques most commonly used in written EST discourse; and (3) the rhetorical functions most frequently found in written EST discourse.

The University of Washington group also built upon the important notion of the *transfer* of knowledge and skills from one skill to another. As Trimble (1985: 14) explained:

> Here, I only wish to point out that we have writing best approached as a transfer technique. That is, we have the students consciously practice the rhetorical concepts they have found in their reading by giving them writing exercises designed to make them choose rhetorical elements most appropriate for a given purpose and a given level of reader.

To enhance this transfer process, according to Trimble (1985: 160), "Visual-verbal relationships are a very useful tool to exploit when teaching reading or when transferring the teaching emphasis to writing." In this approach, students might bring to class authentic samples of figures portraying, say, the operation of a device and then analyze the descriptive paragraph(s) accompanying the figures. Later they can write their own descriptions that mimic the rhetorical features seen in the authentic samples.

With this emphasis on authentic texts drawn from various disciplinary or vocational communities and the analysis of their properties as forms of discourse, ESP was positioning reading, like writing, as a *situated* activity. While in ESP courses students might still be taught a generic set of core reading comprehension skills applicable to a broad range of reading situations (e.g. reading textbooks), there was an increasing emphasis on linking the learning (and teaching) of reading to specific rhetorical and communicative contexts, with the needs for reading varying across these contexts. Dudley-Evans and St John (1998), in *Developments in English for Specific Purposes,* capture this changing situation in their observation that reading was increasingly being taught from the perspective of texts as providing information rather than their purely linguistic properties. In the same vein, T. Johns and Davies (1983) used the acronyms TALO (text as linguistic object) and TAVI (text as a vehicle of information) to portray these two essential views of texts and to advocate for an emphasis on TAVI in ESP reading pedagogy. The ESP reader thus had to learn how to identify and extract relevant information from the text as a vehicle, especially because, as the emerging field of genre analysis was demonstrating, the placement and arrangement of such information differs from one discipline to another.

Genre analysis

Discussion of the role of genre in ESP must begin with the extremely influential work of John Swales, "the doyen of ESP genre studies" (Hyland 2004: 43). As Swales (1990: 58) explains in his seminal book, *Genre Analysis: English in Academic and Research Settings*:

> A genre comprises a class of communicative events, the members of which share some set of communicative purposes. These purposes are recognized by expert members of the parent discourse community, and thereby constitute the rationale for the genre. This rationale shapes the schematic structure of the discourse and influences and constrains choice of content and style.

With the use of genre analysis techniques, ESP students can be taught how to recognize (as readers) and mimic (as writers) the "schematic structure" of texts in their chosen discourse communities.

In the late 1970s and early 80s, Swales and other ESP specialists, operating mostly in the United Kingdom, began analyzing the properties of specific kinds of texts in various disciplines. In his teaching and research at the University of Aston in the early 1980s, for example, Swales focussed in particular on the introductory section of scholarly research articles. This is where he began creating his "moves analysis" framework (Swales 1981) that has since been a core feature of genre research and pedagogy in ESP, including reading pedagogy. From a teaching perspective, he developed at Aston a two-pronged approach: "The class-work can be divided into two kinds: study of Article Introductions and writing tasks" (Swales 1983: 197). The "study," or initial portion, of this approach was in fact the reading dimension, in which students were asked to analyze article introductions from academic journals in their chosen discourse community, followed by their own attempts to write such introductions. This shift from analysis in reading to use of information gained through analysis in writing became a core pedagogical instrument in the approaches to ESP that developed later and constitute the core activities in the field today.

Emerging Perspectives and Research on Reading

In this section of the chapter I will review how ESP specialists have treated reading since the foundations discussed in the first section of the chapter were established. Thus, the discussion will review work published over the past 25 years approximately. Due to space limitations, the discussion cannot be exhaustive. Instead, I focus on the most representative work that has appeared. For the most part the discussion is organized around categories related to the treatment of reading in order to provide an orderly look at the various directions in which reading has been dealt with. Much of the work discussed will have its roots in pedagogy, in keeping with Belcher's (2004: 166) identification of ESP's "pragmatism – its eagerness to be responsive to learners' target language academic and occupational needs" as a central driving force in the field. As such, the literature on reading tends to focus on how it should be taught. In that regard, Bruce (2011: 140) captures the current situation in the following terms:

> Reading is sometimes taught on its own as a separate skill, sometimes in conjunction with writing, and sometimes as a component of a study skills programme. Whether a single skill or an integrated approach is taken, the main focus of reading instruction often tends to be the development of sub-skills related to extracting different types of information from texts, such as skimming for gist and scanning for specific details.

At the same time, says Jordan (1997: 143), it must be remembered that "When students read, it is for a *purpose*." This, he says, is the "starting point" for reading-related instruction.

Another perspective guiding the discussion in this section comes from Johns, Paltridge, and Belcher (2011: 3), who note that "the research into language and discourses/genres is the most evolved and sophisticated in ESP." Genre-related work is especially dominant, whether in the form of Swalesian "moves analyses" of texts in different disciplinary communities or the use of genre as a teaching tool in the ESP classroom. With respect to reading research and pedagogy, genre plays a very strong role and will be seen, directly or indirectly, in much of what follows.

In this section I will look at reading within two primary frameworks suggested earlier by Bruce (2011): (1) as a stand-alone skill, as in the case of courses dedicated to teaching students how to read, and (2) in an integrated skills framework.

Reading as a Stand-Alone Skill

Given its importance in ESP as established in the first section of this chapter, reading is often taught as a skill in its own right. Within this context, there are several areas of coverage. These are discussed in the remainder of this section.

Teaching reading skills

Reading teachers naturally want to know what to teach students in ESP reading courses, with improving reading comprehension a driving goal. This has led to interest in building students' knowledge of valuable reading strategies and a related focus on the rhetorical features of target community texts. As an initial way of activating this process, Huang, Cheng, and Chern (2006) have explored the use of carefully selected pre-reading materials (taken from longer discipline-specific texts students will read later) to prime students' reading skills in a reading course, including general purposes reading skills that have already been built. In fact, says Moore (1983: 120), in ESP, "the student rarely comes "blind" to the business of reading." In the case of technically oriented areas like EST, says Moore

(1983: 120), "the most necessary skill is that of locating the relevant or desired information" in the text, and so pedagogy is oriented toward a "location" mode.

However, much of the work related to comprehension building revolves around instantiating core reading skills and discourse analytic skills. In this regard, Crawford Camiciottoli (2003: 37) looked at the explicit teaching of metadiscourse features to undergraduates at an Italian university via the use of those features in economics textbooks. She explored the effects of this instruction on their reading comprehension and concluded that "metadiscourse can have a positive influence on comprehension" and so should play a greater role in ESP courses. Li and Munby (1996: 210), via a qualitative study of the metacognitive reading strategy use of two Chinese graduate students at a university in Australia, concluded that some of the comprehension strategies taught in general purpose English courses may not be useful in specialized English reading and that students need to be taught "to vary their strategies as the reading requires". Thus, students need to be taught flexible use of reading strategies and to be equipped with a wide array of metacognitive strategies, including those applicable to specific types of discourse in different disciplines. In another study focussing on metacognition, Dhieb-Henia (2003) looked at the effects of metacognitive strategy training among university students in Tunisia studying biology and concluded that such strategy training enhanced their comprehension of research articles in that discipline.

With respect to an explicit focus on rhetorical features of texts, Martinez (2002) describes a study focussing on exposing undergraduate EST students at a university in Spain to five versions of an authentic scientific text. While the content of the text remained the same, variations of rhetorical features were used to organize the content in different ways. Students' written recall of the information in each version of the text was compared, as was their identification of the rhetorical pattern of organization used in each passage, and the impact of each approach to organization on reading comprehension was analyzed. She found that the more the students recognized and understood the rhetorical features guiding organization of the text, the more effectively they read, thus reinforcing the explicit teaching of rhetorical features in ESP courses where reading is taught.

As for other reading strategy-related approaches, in a study of undergraduate engineering students in Egypt, Pritchard and Nasr (2004) identified positive values accruing from training students in using textual and contextual clues and exposing them to authentic texts in their discipline. Also worth noting is work by Hall et al. (1986: 152), who were interested in the problems encountered by EST students at a university in Thailand and created a course approach based on careful "information structuring" of the ways in which ideas were organized, with a particular emphasis on what they called "macro-cohesion" (links between content ranging across the texts and outside the texts) and "micro-cohesion," that is, "discourse connections between sentences." In their view, an appropriately coordinated arrangement of these levels of information-structuring in a reading course helps prepare students for the reading of their discipline specific texts. This approach built on one described earlier by Blanton (1984: 44) in one of the first reading-related articles to appear in the journal *English for Specific Purposes*. She proposed a "hierarchical model" of reading instruction in which students in a reading course work through a carefully sequenced set of reading tasks that help them understand what she calls "the hierarchical nature of academic discourse" (as opposed to a linear model).

Looking more broadly at the development of reading skills and improved comprehension, Spector-Cohen, Kirschner, and Wexler (2001) advocate an approach which includes four parts: a focus on linguistic forms, the teaching of reading strategies, introduction to typical academic genre/rhetorical forms, and what they refer to as "criterion tasks," that is, a set of tasks associated with performance at each stage of their reading syllabus.

Textbooks

In addition to how students should read, what they have to read and comprehend is also a key issue for ESP reading specialists. In this regard, textbooks have long been a topic of interest, particularly since this is the genre most commonly faced by students (Myers 1992). They are also likely to be students' first exposure to writing in their target discourse community. Here, Swales (1995: 3) observes, "Studies of textbook discourse have so far been largely restricted to introductory textbooks in standard undergraduate fields," and so it is these textbooks that are most likely to be used in ESP reading courses.

Especially noteworthy in this regard are two studies by Love (1991, 1993) of textbooks in the field of geology. Asserting that ESP students may be stymied by discipline-specific texts because their already existing schema for reading are not appropriate for comprehending specialized texts, Love (1991: 91) believes that "This seems likely to be a particular problem for students encountering their first textbook in a new subject, since they may have little background knowledge to draw on." In her rhetorical and grammatical analysis of introductory geology textbooks, she found that they strive to create "a cognitive model for the discipline" (1991: 89). That is, they "establish the discourse of the discipline, and thus 'acculturate' the beginning student into the new field" (1993: 197). This is because "the introductory textbooks within a particular academic discipline will exhibit both a schematic structure and a set of lexico-grammatical patterns which reflect and, to a certain extent, construct the epistemology of the discipline" (1993: 216–217). In this way they help students establish and instantiate the schema they need in order to go on to more sophisticated reading in that discipline. The job of ESP teachers, she says, is to help students "explore these characteristics of the texts" (1993: 217).

While Love focusses on the benefits of introductory textbooks, others have noted their limitations. Myers (1992: 13), for example, published an influential comparative analysis of the features of textbooks and journal articles. In drawing attention to the limitations of textbooks, he explained that "To mention some practical issues, textbooks will not show students how pronouns or hedges might be used in their writing, because textbooks do not represent the sort of interaction in which these modifications are necessary, and textbooks will not show how references or illustrations are used rhetorically, because textbooks use them peda-gogically." Hyland (1994, 1999), too, has discussed the limitations of textbooks compared to articles, especially in the context of the use of hedges (1994) and the use of metadiscourse (1999). In his 1999 paper, where he reported on a study of 21 introductory textbooks in 3 disciplines and a similar corpus of research based articles, Hyland found that "the ways textbook authors represent themselves, organize their arguments, and signal their attitudes to both their statements and their readers differ markedly" and that "these differences mean that textbooks provide limited rhetorical guidance to students seeking information from research sources or learning appropriate forms of written argument" (1999: 3). With respect to reading, he concluded that "Problems of reading relate to the fact that learning a discipline through the linguistic forms of textbooks does not introduce students to the full range of conventions within which the socio-cultural system of the discipline is encoded" (1999: 22), thus restricting the value of textbooks in ESP reading courses.

Swales (1995: 4), commenting on the limitations of textbooks, made the impor-tant point that "standard introductory textbooks are rarely little more than con-servative encapsulations of prevailing paradigms." Pedagogically speaking, said Myers (1992: 9), the solution is this: "If we, as teachers, keep several genres in mind, instead of focussing on textbooks as the genre that students first encounter, we may be able to help students respond more easily, and more critically, to the texts they encounter later in their careers."

Vocabulary

Vocabulary occupies an important place in both native language and second/ foreign language reading scholarship, since the words on the page are the starting point for reading. Thus, it is not surprising to see some emphasis on vocabulary in the ESP reading literature. However, given the nature of reading specialized texts, especially their vocabulary, the treatment of vocabulary in ESP courses may in some ways be more challenging than in general purpose English courses. Wil-liams (1985: 121) noted, for example, that "a typical two-or three-hour a week ESP course would not have the time or space necessary to teach all of the specialized vocabulary students would need to learn" and that "teaching of a pre-determined word-stock is unnatural." To account for this situation, he discussed five vocabu-lary learning strategies suitable for ESP: "(1) inferring from context, (2) identifying lexical familiarization, (3) unchaining nominal compounds, (4) synonym search and (5) word analysis" (1985: 122).

The article by Williams represents a more traditional approach to literature on reading, especially in the context of vocabulary, that is, a pre-corpus approach. The much more common focus that has emerged since the early 1980s, at least with respect to vocabulary, has been resources and insights gleaned from the field of corpus linguistics, usually in combination with genre analysis, that is, studying language as used within specific genres located inside particular disciplinary domains. (See Coxhead, this volume, for a detailed discussion of corpus-based research on vocabulary). For instance, Salager (1983), in one of the early corpus-based ESP studies, constructed a corpus of vocabulary used in Medical English texts. Her purposes were to investigate the application of corpus research techniques in the ESP context and to look into ways in which the results of the construction of a corpus could be used for ESP teaching purposes. Narrowing the focus of a corpus-based approach, Moss (1992) studied the importance of cognate recognition among Spanish students enrolled in university level ESP courses. Moss created a corpus of cognates found in a set of texts commonly read by these students in order to test students' ability to recognize them. In this way she could identify those aspects of cognate recognition that caused the most difficulty. Based on her findings, she recommended, as a pedagogical approach in ESP courses, "a strategy of structured and graded practice in cognate recognition" (1992: 141).

Ward (1999, 2001, 2009), combining an interest in textbooks and vocabulary, has studied the experiences of undergraduate engineering students in Thailand in reading English language textbooks in their chosen disciplines. In his 1999 study, he used a corpus-based approach to address the question: how large a vocabulary do EAP engineering students need? Noting that a common assumption in the literature is that, for general purposes reading, a vocabulary of at least 3,000 target language "word families" is necessary to read efficiently, he asked if the study of a specialized engineering corpus would achieve the same effects for students of engineering. (As explained in Ward, 1999: 310, "word families" represent all of the word forms – inflected forms and specified derivative forms – related to a headword. He gives the example of the headword use and such related words as used/uses/using/usable/usefulness/useless/users/user.) He constructed such a corpus from engineering textbooks used at his university and, after analyzing the predictive power of that corpus against more commonly known general word list corpora, concluded that engineering students would benefit more from early exposure to an engineering English corpus and, in combination with that corpus, would need a general vocabulary of only 2,000 word families. His 2001 study addressed vocabulary from a different direction by looking at how engineering students "get around the problem of textbook reading" due to their vocabulary problems (2001: 141). Based on responses to a questionnaire he administered, he found that the students avoided the vocabulary by "concentrating their attention on the applications, and especially the examples, given in those textbooks" (2001: 151). In his 2009 study he explored the issue of a growing reliance on engineering textbooks being written in or translated into the Thai language, thus limiting students' exposure to engineering vocabulary in English, despite the fact that they would need that vocabulary for graduate level study of engineering. He found significant vocabulary-related problems among the undergraduate engineering students that made reading of textbooks written in English difficult at best and recommended closer cooperation between engineering and English language teaching faculty such that students would receive more exposure to specialized English vocabulary.

Another area of vocabulary coverage concerns "subtechnical vocabulary" that is, not the specialized or technical terminology of a discipline, but rather "items which are neither highly technical and specific to a certain field of knowledge nor obviously general in the sense of being everyday words which are not used in a distinctive way in specialized texts" (Baker 1988: 91). Examples cited by Baker include such expressions as "others have said," "one explanation is," and "it has been pointed out by." Baker explored this topic in the area of Medical English by constructing a corpus drawn from Medical English journals. Words were categorized into what she called "three bands: General Lexis, Specialised Lexis, and Sub-technical/Rhetorical items" (1988: 91). Her interest was in words and phrases used for rhetorical/organizational purposes. Based on her analysis of patterns found in her corpus, she concluded that "the genre of medical journal articles is highly conventionalized and restricted in its patterning" (1988: 103) and that, in terms of ESP course pedagogy, once the most common rhetorical items have been identified, "learners should be given a great deal of exposure to these items in order to appreciate how to make use of the information in the text" (1988: 103). That is, for more effective specialized reading, they need to know more than the primary terminology of the discipline; just as important for reading comprehension is knowing the collocations that perform the rhetorical or organizing functions that link parts of sentences and thus provide deeper understanding of texts.

Marshall and Gilmour (1993: 69) have also studied subtechnical vocabulary, which they define as "the words which express the relations which exist between the key scientific concepts." They describe a study of the reading ability of over 2,000 English for science and technology (EST) students (grade 7 to university level) in Papua New Guinea that identified problems they had in processing subtechnical vocabulary. They tested students' knowledge of 45 subtechnical terms from an already existing corpus. As a remedy for this problem with subtechnical vocabulary, they encourage a pedagogy that emphasizes pre-reading exercises and extensive reading aimed at sensitizing students to the use of such vocabulary. They also assert that ESP teachers should not simply teach "lists of scientific and technical words" but instead should also "teach the contexts and structural relations within which the words have meaning" (1993: 75).

Reading in Integrated Skills Contexts

While there has been important work in the context of reading as a stand-alone skill, of considerable interest among many ESP specialists has been an integrated skills approach, with reading seen as a stepping stone to other skills or as complementing them. In the latter category, there has been some interest in connections between speaking and reading (e.g. Kelly and Khrishnan 1995; Murphy 1996). For the most part, though, the emphasis has been on the linking of reading and writing, building on the earlier work, cited previously, concerning EST.

As Jordan (1997: 143) explains:

> Reading, as a skill, is normally linked with writing. This is a fundamental characteristic of the target academic situation in which students are typically reading books

and journals, noting, summarizing, paraphrasing, and then writing essays, etc. In practice material for reading, the link with writing is normally included. Although the focus may be on various reading strategies and comprehension practice, the resultant exercises usually involve writing (apart from some multiple-choice questions and yes/no, true/false formats).

As Hirvela (2004) has noted, reading serves writing, with input gained through reading playing an important role in what students write and how they write. This is where genre analysis, especially, has been influential in the domain of reading and ESP. What students learn about genres, especially as they conduct their own genre analyses, as readers/writers, lays a foundation for how they then reproduce those genres themselves. In this section, then, I look at reading as it has been related to writing.

Genre-based approaches

Hyland (2004: 5) has observed that "Today, genre is one of the most important and influential concepts in language education." In much genre-based work in ESP, students, as readers, are repeatedly exposed to texts exemplifying the genres they must learn to understand and reproduce as they seek to gain membership in their chosen disciplinary communities. This process starts with the reading and analysis of these genres and culminates in students writing those same genres, such as literature reviews. Through this genre-based combination of reading and writing, they seek to develop what Johns (1997) refers to as socioliterate competence, that is, an understanding of the socially constructed nature of genres as well the components of literacy necessary for their creation. Within this framework, she says, "students are constantly involved in research into texts, roles, and contexts and into the strategies they employ in completing literacy tasks within specific situations" 1997: 15), a scenario "in which literacy classes become laboratories for the study of texts, roles, and contexts" (1997: 19).

Of particular importance is that, through the exposure and analysis experienced through genre-based reading, students acquire knowledge of what Paltridge (1997) calls "frames," that is, an awareness of certain core genre features which allows them to put texts they encounter into the appropriate frames and then process and understand them based on the textual properties of those frames. In this way genre-based reading instruction provides a kind of scaffolding or schema building that improves genre-based reading and is eventually transferred to writing.

In a comprehensive review of genre-based studies across many contexts and including both native language and second language students, Tardy (2006: 90–91) concluded with respect to the effects of genre-based instruction that

At a range of educational levels, at least some learners appear to be motivated by genre-based instruction and can develop a metalanguage for talking about texts through such instruction. Similarly, the rhetorical consciousness-raising of genre-based reading instruction may increase students' ability to locate information in texts and develop a better understanding of texts' rhetorical elements.

One way in which combined reading-writing genre-based teaching encouraging this "rhetorical consciousness-raising" takes place is in pedagogical settings where an EAP/ESP course is linked to a "content" course within students' target disciplinary community, and where the ESP teacher works in tandem with the content course teacher, who possesses expertise in that particular domain. Underlying this approach is what Johns (1988), among others, has called the "discourse communities dilemma" (or debate). That is, on the one hand, students need exposure to and must acquire command of target community discourse; on the other hand, ESP teachers cannot hope or expect to be equipped with sufficient knowledge of the various disciplines students seek to join. This is where the joint cooperation of the ESP teacher and the disciplinary expert addresses such a dilemma. Johns (1995, 1997), Kasper (1995), and Mustafa (1995) have provided detailed descriptions of how this kind of arrangement can equip ESP teachers to design appropriate courses in which students experience meaningful reading and analysis of relevant genres and begin learning how to write them. This can involve using the content course materials and assignments in the EAP/ESP course or having students themselves locate and work with relevant materials (such as in a portfolio approach to be discussed shortly). In these course combination scenarios, reading is the starting point for students' understanding of genres and serves as the foundation from which they draw the linguistic and rhetorical information they need to then produce genres as they transfer that information from reading to writing.

The more traditional approach in which ESP courses themselves are the site of genre-based reading and writing remains a strong one, as described in detail in book-length explorations of genre-based instruction (e.g. Hyland 2004; Johns 2002; Paltridge 2001). Hyland (2007) also shows how EAP/ESP teachers can learn, through teacher education courses, ways in which to create these important genre-based reading-writing connections that facilitate transfer of genre knowledge from reading to writing.

A number of studies have investigated the effects of such genre-based instruction. For example, Henry and Roseberry (1998) compared two groups of undergraduate students at a university in Negara Brunei Darussalam: one received genre-based instruction and the other did not. On the whole, the group which engaged in genre-based reading and writing outperformed the nongenre group, suggesting positive effects for genre-based instruction. Hyon (2001, 2002) looked at the long-term effects of a genre-based course, with a particular focus on reading but also the impact of this genre-based reading on writing. One year after completing a genre-based reading course, eight students (five graduate students, two undergraduates, and one university employee) were interviewed to see how the genre-based reading instruction had affected their subsequent reading and writing. On the whole, Hyon found modest long-term effects for the course, with some students retaining and using more of the genre-based reading input than others.

Swales and Lindemann (2002) investigated the effects of a graduate level EAP course on the literature review writing of graduate students. Noting that "several stages of reading as well as writing are involved in the process of composing a literature review" and that "transforming those separate readings into a succinct and coherent account of a disciplinary or interdisciplinary line of research demands a particular kind of reading-writing connection" (2002: 117), they developed a genre-based pedagogy which facilitated that kind of connection, using the metaphor of "architectures" to capture the various structures and properties that students need to acquire relative to literature review writing in their disciplinary community. They reported overall positive effects of the approach.

Another look at this kind of approach is described by Parkinson et al. (2007), who developed and taught a genre-based reading-writing course for science students at a university in South Africa. Their approach emphasized a carefully scaffolded series of reading tasks, including pre-reading activities, discussion, and vocabulary and comprehension exercises. The students read excerpts from science textbooks as well as popular and research-based science journal articles. They found that both reading comprehension and written expression "improved significantly" as a result of their scaffolded approach (2007: 459).

Hirvela (2001) explored a different approach to linking reading, writing, and genre in a study of students' reading of and writing about a wide-ranging set of genres via a combination of literary and nonliterary texts in an EAP writing course at an American university. He looked at students' responses to the different text types and how they used the texts in their writing and found positive results concerning both the literary and nonliterary texts. Based on these findings, he argued for a combination of literary and specialist texts in ESP and EAP courses within an integrated reading-writing pedagogy. This study expanded on his earlier work (Hirvela 1993), in which he focussed on the use of literary texts (science fiction short stories) with undergraduate EST students in Hong Kong and reported positive transfer from their specialized literary reading to their science-based writing, leading him to propose a Literature for specific purposes framework for ESP.

A different, and somewhat mixed, view of genre-based reading-writing instruction emerges in a recent article by Dovey (2010). She explores two instructional contexts in which a genre-based approach was used with post-graduate students studying information technology at a university in Australia. The emphasis in the course was on the development of source-based writing skills. Of particular interest in this study was the "generic ladder" scaffolding approach mentioned earlier in Swales and Lindemann (2002) and also discussed in a previously cited work by Hyland (2007). In the first iteration of the course, the students were taken through a carefully sequenced set of genre-based tasks, some involving reading and others writing, intended to culminate in the writing of a literature review. The students did not progress as expected, both from task to task and overall, and so the course was redesigned. The reading activities remained essentially the same, while more scaffolding was added to the writing-related activities. In general, in the revised course they sought to create more integration of reading-writing tasks and a move from "an orientation around genre toward an orientation around processes" (2007: 54). That is, there was less exposure to authentic genre samples as they moved toward an increased focus on the processes involved in successfully performing the assigned tasks. The writing of a literature review remained the culminating course task. The course revision resulted, overall, in improved student performance as well as more positive student evaluations of the course, leading the author to conclude that "With the emerging hegemony of genre-based approaches in EAP, the assumption that exposure to expert product is sufficient could result in a failure to address the full range of students' needs" (2007: 59). That is, transfer of knowledge gained through reading "expert products" is limited unless there is an effective combination of process-oriented tasks that provide appropriately deep levels of scaffolding.

Portfolios

While normally associated with writing, portfolios have also been presented as useful in the development of ESP reading ability, especially in conjunction with writing. Drawing on the core notions of genre analysis and what Frodesen (1995: 344) describes as an approach to instruction in which students become "ethnographers of their disciplines," ESP students are asked to discuss in their portfolios what they have learned in their reading of different genres of texts in their chosen disciplinary community. Johns (1995, 1997) has been an especially strong proponent of this approach to EAP and ESP instruction, first by asking students to compile what she calls a "reading portfolio" that provides the results of their disciplinary reading (i.e. what they have learned about genres in their discipline) before moving on to a "writing portfolio" in which they provide samples of their own disciplinary writing, drawing in part on the input and insights reported in their reading portfolios. Hirvela (1997) has discussed a similar approach using what he calls a "disciplinary portfolio" pedagogy. Here, too, in concert with Frodesen's notion of students as ethnographers, students provide a detailed analysis of what they have learned through their disciplinary reading, what he calls "sensitizing them to the demands and tendencies" of the genres of their chosen disciplinary community (1997: 83). In his portfolio pedagogy, the students complete several reading-related tasks, such as a detailed genre analysis of five published articles appearing in journals within their target disciplinary community and a collection and analysis of the manuscript submission guidelines for several academic journals in their field. As with the work of Johns, Hirvela also asks the students to relate the findings from their ESP-based reading to their writing, thus reinforcing the common pattern of linking reading with another skill.

Conclusion

This chapter has shown that, in terms of both teaching and research, a wide range of approaches to the treatment of reading in ESP-related contexts has emerged over the past three decades, especially under the influence of the groundbreaking work discussed earlier on discourse and genre analysis. The chapter has also demonstrated that reading is a vibrant area of ESP that continues to attract attention in the realms of pedagogy and research, despite perceptions that it is not as challenging to acquire or use as other skills.

As discussed briefly earlier, a key notion of reading that has evolved in ESP is its *situated* nature in specialized discourse contexts. While there are certain reading strategies that can be taught as stand-alone components of a reading course (e.g. skimming and scanning), in helping students navigate the complex textual worlds of specific disciplines, reading's situatedness also requires an accounting of both the overt and the less obvious (but just as important) features and subtleties of disciplinary discourse. This is where they need to develop the socioliterate competence Johns (1997), cited earlier, aims at creating in the classroom; this is how they gain deeper and more meaningful engagement with target community texts. Discourse and genre analysis continue to play major roles in this endeavor.

However, not all discourse or genre practices are transparent and amenable to easy identification through discourse and genre analysis. Hirvela (1997), citing Brandt (1990) and White (1983), has written of the "invisible discourse" of disciplinary communities, that is, the unwritten or vaguely articulated characteristics and properties of such communities, where to some extent students have to "read between the lines" in order to make effective use of their reading. Basturkmen (2006: 137) frames this in the context of helping students acquire what she calls "underlying knowledge" as well as more direct knowledge of genres and genre practices. Thus, as we move forward in ESP reading research and pedagogy, it is important to supplement long-existing discourse and genre-based practices with new approaches aimed at helping ESP readers negotiate the complicated nuances of this "invisible discourse" they must gain command of, in addition to the more visible discourse they encounter as readers so as to further develop the very important "underlying knowledge" of which Basturkmen (2006) speaks. Helping readers meaningfully engage what is invisible or semi-visible in addition to what is visible, particularly in the new world of digital literacy, is perhaps the next challenge for ESP reading specialists. Conducting this work is likely to involve a combination of both the existing tools provided by discourse and genre analysis and perhaps new tools tailored more specifically to the analysis of texts in the digital world.

REFERENCES

Allen, J. P. B. and Widdowson, H. G. (eds.) (1974) 1974 and later years. *English in Focus series*. Oxford: Oxford University Press.

Baker, M. (1988) Sub-technical vocabulary and the ESP teacher: An analysis of some rhetorical items in medical journal articles. *Reading in a Foreign Language* 4: 91–105.

Basturkmen, H. (2006) *Ideas and Options in English for Specific Purposes*. Mahwah, NJ: Lawrence Erlbaum.

Belcher, D. (2004) Trends in teaching English for specific purposes. *International Review of Applied Linguistics (IRAL)* 24: 165–86.

Belcher, D., Johns, A. M., and Paltridge, B. (eds.) (2011) *New Directions in English for Specific Purposes Research.* Ann Arbor, MI: University of Michigan Press.

Blanton, L. (1984) Using a hierarchical model to teach academic reading to advanced ESL students: How to make a long story short. *English for Specific Purposes* 3: 37–46.

Brandt, D. (1990) *Literacy as Involvement: The Acts of Writers.* Carbonsdale and Evansville, IN: The Southern Illinois University Press.

Bruce, I. (2011) *Theory and Concepts of English for Academic Purposes.* Basingstoke, UK: Palgrave Macmillan.

Crawford Camiciottoli, B. (2003) Metadiscourse and ESP reading comprehension: An exploratory study. *Reading in a Foreign Language* 15: 28–44.

Dhieb-Henia, N. (2003) Evaluating the effectiveness of metacognitive strategy training for reading research articles in an ESP context. *English for Specific Purposes* 22: 387–417.

Dovey, T. (2010) Facilitating writing from sources: A focus on both process and product. *Journal of English for Academic Purposes* 9: 45–60.

Dudley-Evans, T. and St John, M. J. (1998) *Developments in English for Specific Purposes: A Multi-Disciplinary Approach.* Cambridge: Cambridge University Press.

Frodesen, J. (1995) Negotiating the syllabus: A learning-centered, interactive approach to ESL graduate student writing course design. In D. Belcher and G. Braine (eds.), *Academic Writing in a Second Language: Essays on Research and Pedagogy.* 331–50. Norwood, NJ: Ablex.

Hall, D., Hawkey, R., Kenny, B., and Storer, G. (1986) Patterns of thought in scientific writing: A course in information structuring for engineering students. *English for Specific Purposes* 5: 147–60.

Henry, A. and Roseberry, R. L. (1998) An evaluation of a genre-based approach to the teaching of EAP/ESP writing. *TESOL Quarterly* 32: 147–56.

Hirvela, A. (1990) ESP and literature: A reassessment. *English for Specific Purposes* 9: 237–52.

Hirvela, A. (1993) A study of the integration of literature and communicative language teaching. Unpublished doctoral thesis. Stirling UK: University of Stirling.

Hirvela, A. (1997) "Disciplinary portfolios" and EAP writing instruction. *English for Specific Purposes* 16: 83–100.

Hirvela, A. (2001) Incorporating reading into EAP writing courses. In J. Flowerdew and M. Peacock (eds.), *Research Perspectives on English for Academic Purposes.* 330–46. Cambridge: Cambridge University Press.

Hirvela, A. (2004) *Connecting Reading and Writing in Second Language Writing Instruction.* Ann Arbor, MI: University of Michigan Press.

Huang, S. C., Cheng, Y. S., and Chern, C. L. (2006) Pre-reading materials from subject matter texts – Learner choices and the underlying learner characteristics. *Journal of English for Academic Purposes* 5: 193–206.

Hutchinson, T. and Waters, A. (1987) *English for Specific Purposes: A Learning-Centered Approach.* Cambridge: Cambridge University Press.

Hyland, K. (1994) Hedging in academic writing and EAP textbooks. *English for Specific Purposes* 13: 239–56.

Hyland, K. (1999) Talking to students: Metadiscourse in introductory coursebooks. *English for Specific Purposes* 18: 3–26.

Hyland, K. (2004) *Genre and Second Language Writing.* Ann Arbor, MI: University of Michigan Press.

Hyland, K. (2007) Genre pedagogy: Language, literacy and L2 writing instruction. *Journal of Second Language Writing* 16: 148–64.

Hyon, S. (2001) Long-term effects of genre-based instruction: A follow-up study of an EAP reading course. *English for Specific Purposes* 20: 417–38.

Hyon, S. (2002) Genre and ESL reading: A classroom study. In A. M. Johns (ed.), *Genre in the Classroom: Multiple Perspectives*. 121–41. Mahwah, NJ: Lawrence Erlbaum.

Johns, A. M. (1988) The discourse community dilemma: Identifying transferable skills for the academic milieu. *English for Specific Purposes* 7: 55–60.

Johns, A. M. (1995) Teaching classroom and authentic genres: Initiating students into academic cultures and discourses. In D. Belcher and G. Braine (eds.), *Academic Writing in a Second Language: Essays on Research and Pedagogy*. 277–92. Norwood, NJ: Ablex.

Johns, A. M. (1997) *Text, Role, and Context: Developing Academic Literacies*. Cambridge: Cambridge University Press.

Johns, A. M. (ed.) (2002) *Genre in the Classroom: Multiple Perspectives*. Mahwah, NJ: Lawrence Erlbaum.

Johns, A. M., Paltridge, B., and Belcher, D. (2011) Introduction: New directions for ESP research. In D. Belcher, A. M. Johns, and B. Paltridge (eds.), *New Directions in English for Specific Purposes Research*. 1–4. Ann Arbor, MI: University of Michigan Press.

Johns, T. and Davies, F. (1983) Text as a vehicle for information: The classroom use of written texts in teaching reading in a foreign language. *Reading in a Foreign Language* 1: 1–19.

Jordan, R. R. (1997) *English for Academic Purposes: A Guide and Resource Book for Teachers*. Cambridge: Cambridge University Press.

Kasper, L. F. (1995) Theory and practice in content-based ESL reading instruction. *English for Specific Purposes* 14: 223–30.

Kelly, R. K., and Krishnan, L. A. (1995) "Fiction talk" in the ESP classroom. *English for Specific Purposes* 14: 77–6.

Li, S. and Munby, H. (1996) Metacognitive strategies in second language academic reading: A qualitative investigation. *English for Specific Purposes* 15: 199–216.

Love, A. M. (1991) Process and product in Geology: An investigation of some discourse features of two introductory textbooks. *English for Specific Purposes* 10: 89–109.

Love, A. M. (1993) Lexico-grammatical features of Geology textbooks: Process and product revisited. *English for Specific Purposes* 12: 197–218.

Marshall, S. and Gilmour, M. (1993) Lexical knowledge and reading comprehension in Papua New Guinea. *English for Specific Purposes* 12: 69–81.

Martinez, A. C. L. (2002) Empirical examination of EFL readers' use of rhetorical information. *English for Specific Purposes* 21: 81–98.

McDonough, J. (1984) *ESP in Perspective: A Practical Guide*. London: Collins ELT.

Moore, C. J. (1983) EST readers: Some principles for their design and use. *Reading in a Foreign Language* 1: 119–30.

Moss, G. (1992) Cognate recognition: Its importance in the teaching of ESP reading courses to Spanish speakers. *English for Specific Purposes* 11: 141–58.

Murphy, J. M. (1996) Integrating listening and reading in EAP programs. *English for Specific Purposes* 15: 105–20.

Mustafa, Z. (1995) The effect of genre awareness on linguistic transfer. *English for Specific Purposes* 14: 247–56.

Myers, G. A. (1992) Textbooks and the sociology of scientific knowledge. *English for Specific Purposes* 11: 3–17.

Paltridge, B. (1997) *Genre, Frames and Writing in Research Settings*. Amsterdam: John Benjamins.

Paltridge, B. (2001) *Genre and the Language Learning Classroom*. Ann Arbor, MI: University of Michigan Press.

Parkinson, J., Jackson, L., Kirkwood, T., and Padayachee, V. (2007) A scaffolded reading and writing course for foundation level science students. *English for Specific Purposes* 26: 443–61.

Pritchard, R. M. O. and Nasr, A. (2004) Improving reading performance among Egyptian engineering students: Principles and practices. *English for Specific Purposes* 23: 425–45.

Salager, F. (1983) The lexis of fundamental medical English: Classifactory framework and rhetorical function (a statistical approach). *Reading in a Foreign Language* 1: 54–64.

Spector-Cohen, E., Kirschner, M., and Wexler, C. (2001) Designing EAP reading courses at the university level. *English for Specific Purposes* 20: 367–86.

Strevens, P. (1977) *New Orientations in the Teaching of English.* Oxford: Oxford University Press.

Swales, J. M. (1981) Aspects of article Introductions. *Aston ESP Research Reports* 1. Birmingham, UK: Language Studies Unit, The University of Aston at Birmingham. Republished University of Michigan Press 2011.

Swales, J. M. (1983) Developing materials for writing scholarly introductions. In R. R. Jordan (ed.), *Case Studies in ELT.* 188–200. London: Collins ELT.

Swales, J. M. (ed.) (1985) *Episodes in ESP: A Source and Reference Book on the Development of English for Science and Technology.* Oxford: Pergamon.

Swales, J. M. (1990) *Genre Analysis: English in Academic and Research Settings.* Cambridge: Cambridge University Press.

Swales, J. M. (1995) The role of the textbook in EAP writing research. *English for Specific Purposes* 14: 3–18.

Swales, J. M. and Lindemann, S. (2002) Teaching the literature review to international graduate students. In A. M. Johns (ed.), *Genre in the Classroom: Multiple Perspectives.* 105–20. Mahwah, NJ: Lawrence Erlbaum.

Tardy, C. M. (2006) Researching first and second language learning: A comparative review and a look ahead. *Journal of Second Language Writing* 15: 79–101.

Trimble, L. (1985) *English for Science and Technology: A Discourse Approach.* Cambridge: Cambridge University Press.

Ward, J. (1999) How large a vocabulary do EAP engineering students need? *Reading in a Foreign Language* 12: 309–23.

Ward, J. (2001) EST: Evading scientific text. *English for Specific Purposes* 20: 141–52.

Ward, J. (2009) EAP reading and lexis for Thai engineering undergraduates. *Journal of English for Academic Purposes* 8: 294–301.

Widdowson, H. G. (1979) *Explorations in Applied Linguistics.* Oxford: Oxford University Press.

White, J. B. (1983) The invisible discourse of the law: Reflections on legal literacy and general education. In R. W. Bailey and R. M. Fosheim (eds.), *Literacy for Life: The Demand for Reading and Writing.* 137–50. New York: Modern Language Association.

Williams, R. (1985) Teaching vocabulary recognition strategies in ESP reading. *English for Specific Purposes* 4: 121–31.

5 ESP and Writing

KEN HYLAND

Introduction

The challenge of ESP writing

Writing is perhaps *the* central activity of institutions. Complex social activities like educating students, keeping records, engaging with customers, selling products, demonstrating learning and disseminating ideas largely depend on it. Not only is it hard to imagine modern academic and corporate life without essays, commercial letters, emails, medical reports and minutes of meetings, but writing is also a key feature of every student's experience. While multimedia and electronic technologies are beginning to influence learning and how we assess it, in many domains conventional writing remains the way in which students both consolidate their learning and demonstrate their understanding of their subjects. With the continuing dominance of English as the global language of business and scholarship, writing in *English* assumes an enormous importance for students in higher education and on professional training courses. Countless individuals around the world must now gain fluency in the conventions of writing in English to understand their disciplines, to establish their careers or to successfully navigate their learning.

Written texts, in fact, dominate the lives of all students, even those in emergent, practice-based courses not previously thought of as involving heavy literacy demands, as Baynham (2000: 17) illustrates when he asks us to think of:

> The harassed first-year nursing student, hurrying from lecture to tutorial, backpack full of photocopied journal articles, notes, and guidelines for an essay on the sociology of nursing, a clinical report, a case study, a reflective journal.

The Handbook of English for Specific Purposes, First Edition.
Edited by Brian Paltridge and Sue Starfield.
© 2013 John Wiley & Sons, Inc. Published 2013 by John Wiley & Sons, Inc.

These kinds of experiences are extremely challenging to students and can be especially daunting to those who are writing in a second language. This is not only because different languages seem to have different ways of organizing ideas and structuring arguments but because students' prior writing experiences in the home, school or elsewhere do not prepare them for the literacy expectations of their university or professional workplace. Their trusted ways of writing are no longer valued as legitimate for making meaning in these new institutional contexts and they find the greater formality, impersonality, nominalization, and incongruence of these discourses mysterious and alien (see e.g. Lillis 2001).

Moreover, their experience in their new context underlines for students that writing (and reading) are not just key elements of learning and professional practice, but that it cannot be regarded as an homogeneous and transferable skill which they can take with them as they move across different courses and assignments. In this chapter I map something of the territory of ESP writing, sketching how we study it, what we know about it, and illustrating how this impacts on the practice of teaching and research.

ESP Conceptions of Writing

Unlike older "process" traditions which saw writing as a kind of generic skill which could be taught by modeling expert practices, ESP conceptions of writing focus on assisting students towards competence in particular target genres. Teachers do not simply "teach writing" but teach particular kinds of writing which are valued and expected in some academic or professional contexts. The literacy demands of the modern world, therefore, challenge ESP teachers to recognize that their task involves far more than simply controlling linguistic error or polishing style. Instead it encourages them to respond to a complex diversity of genres, contexts and practices.

In recent years the field of ESP has become increasingly sensitive to the ways in which texts are written and responded to by individuals acting as members of social groups. Ideas such as *communicative competence* in applied linguistics (Canale and Swain 1980), *situated learning* in education (Lave and Wenger 1991), and *social constructionism* in the social sciences (Berger and Luckmann 1966) have contributed to a view that places community at the heart of writing and speech. Basically, it encourages us to see that not all writing is the same and that that we use language to accomplish particular purposes and engage with others as members of social groups. For these reasons, the concept of *needs* (see L. Flowerdew, this volume) retains its position as a key feature of ESP practice while ESP itself steadfastly concerns itself with communication, rather than isolated bits of language, and with the processes by which texts are created and used as much as with texts themselves.

Of relevance here is the notion of "academic literacies," which rejects:

> the ways language is treated as though it were a thing, distanced from both teacher and learner and imposing on them external rules and requirements as though they were but passive recipients (Street 1995: 114).

Instead, literacy is something we do. Street characterizes literacy as a verb, an activity "located in the interactions between people" (Barton and Hamilton 1998: 3). From a student's point of view, a dominant feature of academic literacy is the requirement to switch practices between one setting and another, to control a range of genres appropriate to each setting, and to handle the meanings and identities that each evokes. One problem for students, however, is that while achievement is assessed by various institutionalized forms of writing, what it means to write in this way is rarely made explicit to students. A failure to recognize that conventions of writing are embedded in the epistemological and social practices of communities means that writing is a black box to students, particularly as subject lecturers themselves have difficulty in explaining what they mean (Ivanič 1998). The academic literacies position (Lea and Street 1999) therefore encourages us to see that writing must be understood as the crucial process by which students make sense not only of the subject knowledge they encounter through their studies, but also how they can make it mean something for themselves.

The ESP literature is coming to understand this and to recognize that the difficulties students experience with writing are often not due to technical aspects of grammar and organization, but the ways that different strands of their learning interact with each other and with their previous experiences. Entering the academy means making a "cultural shift" in order to take on identities as members of those communities. Gee (1996: 155) stresses the importance of this shift:

> [S]omeone cannot engage in a discourse in a less than fluent manner. You are either in it or you're not. Discourses are connected with displays of identity – failing to display an identity fully is tantamount to announcing you do not have that identity – at best you are a pretender or a beginner.

In other words, we cannot view writing as simply the medium through which students present what they have learned without consideration of its deeper cultural and epistemological underpinnings.

An important implication of these observations has been a commitment to contextual relevance in ESP. By finding ways of helping students to gain control over the texts they are asked to write ESP seeks to involve them in their studies and encourage them to take active responsibility for their learning. At the same time, an exploration of their target genres helps learners to see the assumptions and values, which are implicit in those genres and to understand something of the relationships and interests in that context. In other words, seeing "needs," contexts, and genres together locates writing in a wider frame while providing a basis for both developing the skills students' need to participate in new communities and their abilities to critically understand those communities. So while ESP continues to be heavily involved in syllabus design, needs analysis and materials development, it has also moved to become a more theoretically grounded and research informed enterprise.

ESP Approaches to Writing Research

Textual studies

While there are a number of ways of studying texts, genre analysis has become established as the most widely used and productive methodology in ESP writing research (Hyland 2004a; Johns 2002). A genre approach to writing looks beyond the struggles of individual writers to make meanings and delves beneath the surface structures of texts as products to understand how writing actually works as communication. This is an approach which assumes that texts are always a response to a particular communicative setting and which attempts to reveal the purposes and functions which linguistic forms serve in texts. The writer is seen as having certain goals and intentions, certain relationships to his or her readers, and certain information to convey, and the forms a text takes are resources used to accomplish these. Writing is therefore seen as mediated by the institutions and cultures in which it occurs, so that every text carries the purposes of the writer and expectations about how information should be structured and writer-reader relationships conveyed (Hyland 2009).

Genres in ESP are usually regarded as staged, structured events, designed to perform various communicative purposes by specific discourse communities (Swales 2004). The term reminds us that when we write we follow conventions for organising messages because we want our readers to recognize our purposes and we all have a repertoire of linguistic responses to call on to communicate in familiar situations. Writers therefore anticipate what readers expect from a text and how they are likely to respond to it: they use the rhetorical conventions, interpersonal tone, grammatical features, argument structure, and so on that readers are most likely to recognize and expect. ESP research into texts thus seeks to show how language forms work as resources for accomplishing goals by describing the stages which help writers to set out their thoughts in ways readers can easily follow, and identifying salient features of texts which allow them to engage effectively with their readers.

Genre approaches in ESP therefore attempt to explicate the lexico-grammatical and discursive patterns of particular genres to identify their recognisable structural identity. This work follows the move analysis work pioneered by Swales' (1990) which seeks to identify the recognisable stages of particular institutional genres and the constraints on regular move sequences. *Moves* are the typical rhetorical steps that writers or speakers use to develop their social purposes and

Table 5.1   The move structure of auditors' reports (Flowerdew and Wan 2010)

Move	*Frequency*
Summary of credible actions taken – tells readers that statements were audited according to recognized standards	25
Address responsibilities – details responsibilities of main players to show the auditors acted independently	25
Opinion – positive judgment of accounts	20
or	
Emphasis of matters – draws attention to some issue in the financial statements	5
or	
Basis for qualified opinion + qualified opinion – states exceptions, as when something is misreported or when auditor was unable to corroborate something	4
or	
Basis for disclaimer + disclaimer of opinion – auditor is unable to complete the audit and is not willing to give an opinion	1

analysts often make several passes through the texts in a corpus to identify what each move is doing, its boundaries, its typical realisations, and how it contributes to the text as a whole. A recent example of this kind of analysis is that by Flowerdew and Wan (2010) of the company audit report. The auditors' report is a text of about two pages produced for public and private company annual reports and intended to inform and assure readers of the accuracy of the financial statements prepared by the company. Their study of 25 such reports found that this is a highly formulaic text, which, like many genres in the corporate world, is based on existing templates which the auditors follow. Table 5.1, shows the structure, functions and frequency of each move in their corpus.

The frequencies shown in Table 5.1 indicate that the genre has two obligatory moves (or more accurately, two strongly prototypical moves) and that there are options for the third move depending upon whether the auditors are happy with the audit. Where the evaluation is positive, then there is a simple "opinion move" which expresses the positive evaluation of the auditors and that the opinion conforms with international standards. Where auditors want to draw attention to some issues, they opt instead for an "emphasis of matters." Where the audit does not give the company the all-clear then this is signaled in a separate qualified opinion, disclaimer of opinion or adverse opinion. Before each of these moves there is an explanatory move labeled basis for qualified/disclaimer of/adverse opinion which provides a warrant for the opinion that has been chosen. This explanatory move is less formulaic than the others in the audit report and can vary in content from report to report, but generally it is heavily hedged to avoid threatening the face of the company.

While analyzing moves (or *schematic structures*) has proved an invaluable way of looking at texts, analysts are increasingly aware of the dangers of oversimplifying by assuming blocks of texts to be mono-functional and ignoring writers' complex purposes and "private intentions" (Bhatia 1999). There is also the problem of validating analyses to ensure they are not simply products of the analyst's intuitions (Crookes 1986). Transitions from one move to another in a text are always motivated outside the text as writers respond to their social context, but analysts have not always been able to identify the ways these shifts are explicitly signaled by lexico-grammatical patterning.

Contextual studies

ESP research has not been entirely focussed on the printed page, however. Treating texts as purely textual artifacts can mean that while students are often able to handle the forms of professional genres when they go out to work, they are often unprepared "for the discursive realities of the professional world" (Bhatia 2008: 161), a consequence which is particularly problematic in legal contexts, for instance. Text analyses, then, are frequently accompanied in ESP research by more qualitative investigations to fill out the context in which the particular genre is created and used, using observation, surveys, diaries, interviews and focus group discussions (Hyland 2011). Thus research has explored ethnographic case studies (Prior 1998), reader responses (Locker 1999) and interviews with insider informants (Hyland 2004a). In the study reported above on audit reports, for example, the researchers observed the auditing process in situ and conducted in-depth interviews with four auditors and a technical manager. Such approaches infuse text analyses with greater validity and offer richer understandings about the production and use of genres in different contexts.

More fully explicit ethnographic studies have also been used to explore writing contexts and to take professional practices more seriously. Prior's (1998) study of the contexts and processes of graduate student writing at a US university is a classic example of this kind of research. Drawing on transcripts of seminar discussions, student texts, observations of institutional contexts, tutor feedback and interviews with students and tutors, Prior provides an in-depth account of the ways students in four fields negotiated their writing tasks and so became socialized into their disciplinary communities. Swales' (1998) "textography" of his building at the University of Michigan, is also a milestone of research in this regard. By combining discourse analyses with extensive observations and interviews, Swales traces the workings of individuals and of systems of texts to provide a richly detailed picture of the professional lives, commitments and projects of individuals in three diverse academic cultures working on different floors of a university building: the computer centre, the Herbarium and the English Language Institute.

Ethnographic research has also been conducted into professional workplaces, although these mainly focus on talk, and particularly on the talk that occurs in meetings (see Holmes 2011 for a recent overview). Studies into written professional discourse are relatively rare, although there are a number of studies which focus on the collaboration that goes on around the creation of corporate documents such as environmental reports (Gollin 1999), committee papers (Baxter, Boswood, and Pierson-Smith 2002), and legal documents (Gunnarsson 2009) or how computer-mediated technologies facilitate collaboration in writing projects (Hewett and Robidoux 2010). One study worth mentioning here is that conducted by Smart (2008) who, as an employee of the Bank of Canada, collected data over 23 years into the practices of the Bank's economists. Drawing on interviews, observations and documents, he depicts the culture of a professional community and discovers how the economists orchestrated the Bank's external communications with the media, the government, financial markets, trades unions and academia. In all these studies, research reveals how workplace writing is not an isolated act of creation but part of a socially organized and structured set of activities influenced by power, dominance, friendship, and group feeling (Gunnarsson 2009).

While criticized by researchers from more positivist traditions for a perceived lack of rigor, imprecision and subjectivity, ethnography claims to offer a richer, first-hand interpretation based on interaction with a local context. For analysts of academic and professional writing it suggests methods for studying texts in ways that are "situated," offering an alternative perspective to an exclusive focus on texts. Through a variety of qualitative methods we get a sense of the individual voices and the kinds of insights which only close observation and detailed analysis can reveal.

Critical studies

Although they take a number of different forms drawing on diverse theoretical concepts and methods, it is conventional to lump these together under the heading of critical discourse analysis (CDA). This views language as a form of social practice and attempts "to unpack the ideological underpinnings of discourse that have become so naturalized over time that we begin to treat them as common, acceptable and natural features of discourse" (Teo 2000: 1). CDA therefore links language to the activities that surround it, focussing on how social relations, identity, knowledge and power are constructed through written (and spoken) texts. This overtly political agenda distinguishes CDA from other kinds of discourse analysis and widens the lens of specific purposes teaching to take the sociopolitical context of teaching and learning into account. It attempts to show that the discourses of the academy and the workplace are not transparent or impartial means for getting things done or describing the world, but work to construct, regulate and control knowledge, social relations and institutions. This means that some kinds of writing, or what are called "literacy practices," possess authority because they represent the currently dominant ideological ways of depicting relationships and realities and these exercise control of language users.

The complexity and prestige of certain professional and academic literacies work to exclude many individuals, preventing their access to academic success or membership of professional communities. For those entering university it forces them to make a "cultural shift" in order to take on alien identities as members of those communities (e.g. Ivanič 1998). Successful writing therefore means representing yourself in a way valued by your discipline or profession, adopting the values, beliefs, and identities which such discourses embody. As a result, students often feel uncomfortable with the "me" they portray in their academic writing, finding a conflict between the identities required to write successfully and those they bring with them (e.g. Phan 2009)

While CDA does not subscribe to any single method, Fairclough (2003) draws on Systemic Functional Linguistics (SFL) (Halliday 1994) to analyze concrete instances of discourse. In this model, language is seen as systems of linguistic features offering choices to users, but these choices are circumscribed in situations of unequal power. SFL offers CDA a sophisticated way of analyzing the relations between language and social contexts, making it possible to ground concerns of power and ideology in the details of discourse. To examine actual instances of texts, CDA typically looks at features such as:

- Vocabulary – particularly how metaphor encodes ideologies;
- Transitivity – which can show, for instance, who is presented as having agency and who is acted upon;
- Nominalization and passivization – how processes and actors can be obscured;
- Mood and modality – which help reveal interpersonal relationships;
- Theme – how the first element of a clause can be used to foreground information or presuppose reader beliefs;
- Text structure – how text episodes are marked in texts;
- Intertextuality and interdiscursivity – the effects of other texts and styles on texts, such as where commercial discourses colonize those in other spheres.

It has to be admitted that research conducted from a critical perspective is fairly scarce in the professional writing literature. There are, however, several studies that show how language is used to influence readers or achieve control in written professional writing in different contexts. Harrison and Young's (2004) analysis of the phrasal construction of a memo from a senior manager, for example, shows how he uses bureaucratic language to distance himself from unpopular decisions. Lassen (2004), for instance, reveals how implicit meanings are conveyed in an environmental press release, while Hyland (2004b) discusses how a writer uses modality, formality and thematic choices to disguise a reprimand as an information text.

In academic contexts, research has explored the ways that the conventions of disciplinary writing can create tensions for students. The fact that specific forms and wordings are marked as more or less appropriate or more or less prescribed, can often create conflicts with the experiences students bring from their home community and the habits of meaning they have learnt there. The discourses and practices of their disciplines support identities very different from those they bring with them so that authoring becomes a complex negotiation of one's sense of self and the institutional regulation of meaning-making. The studies by Ivanič (1998) and Lillis (2001) into the experiences of "non-traditional" students in British higher education show how such regulation can be seen as confining and perhaps even threatening. This feeling of opposition between the new identity they are being asked to assume and those they are already comfortable with can provoke resistance. Both Lin (2000), in the case of Hong Kong students, and Canagarajah (1999) in the case of Sri Lankan Tamils, show how students passively resist the assumptions and values, which they are assumed to share by using the language.

This critically-oriented research thus re-establishes the intrinsic relationship between knowledge, writing and identity and raises issues of relevance and legitimacy in relation to writing practices.

Research in ESP Writing

It is perhaps unsurprising given ESP's explicitly pedagogical orientation, that most research has followed a genre perspective as this most easily provides teachers with descriptions of texts that can be translated into syllabuses and materials (e.g Hyland 2004b, Johns 2002, Swales and Feak 2004). Table 5.2 shows some of the written academic and professional genres that have been studied in ESP

Table 5.2   Some written genres studied in ESP research

Academic Written Genres

Research articles	Book reviews
Conference abstracts	Textbooks
PhD dissertations	Grant proposals
Submission letters	Peer review reports
Undergraduate essays	article bios
Teacher feedback	acknowledgments
Editors' letters	lab reports

Professional Written Genres

Business letters	arbitration judgments
Environmental reports	mission statements
Business emails	committee papers
Direct mail sales letters	legal contracts
Company annual reports	legal cases
Medical case notes	Engineering reports

research. The great majority of this research, however, has focussed on academic genres with much less attention being paid to professional or workplace genres.

As can be seen from Table 5.2, a range of written academic genres have been studied in recent years. These include undergraduate essays (Bruce 2010; Hyland 2009), student dissertations and theses (Hyland 2004c; Petrić 2007), research articles (Basturkmen 2009), scientific letters (Hyland 2004a), and book reviews (Hyland and Diani 2009), as well as various "occluded," or hidden, genres such as the MBA "thought essay" (Loudermilk 2007) and peer review reports on journal submissions (Fortanet 2008). Research is also beginning to appear on the role of multimedia and electronic communication in academic writing. This focusses mainly on Computer Mediated Communication in distance learning (e.g. Coffin and Hewings 2005), but also includes research on the use of wikis (Myers 2010) and hypertext environments (Bloch 2008).

Together this research demonstrates the distinctive differences in the genres of the academy where particular purposes and audiences lead writers to employ very different rhetorical choices.

Research on professional written genres has tended to focus mainly on the business letter (Van Nus 1999), and more recently, on how this is recycled as part of other genres such as emails and annual reports (Gotti and Gillaerts 2005). Emails themselves have also figured in genre analyses of business texts (e.g. Jensen 2009), as have the various parts of company annual reports (Hyland 1998). Outside of business contexts, considerable research is beginning to emerge on legal and medical genres such as invitations for bids (Belotti 2006), legal judgements (Mazzi 2006) and medical research reports (Williams 1996). Unlike much of the academic writing research, however, a great deal of professional writing research has been motivated less by pedagogical concerns that by the desire to gain an understanding of how people communicate effectively and strategically in organisations.

Research has also pointed to cultural specificity in rhetorical preferences (e.g. Connor 2002). Although *culture* remains a controversial term, one influential version of culture regards it as a historically transmitted and systematic network of meanings which allow us to understand, develop and communicate our knowledge and beliefs about the world. Culture is seen as inextricably bound up with language (Kramsch 1993), so that cultural factors have the potential to influence perception, language, learning, and communication. Although it is far from conclusive, in fact, results are hotly contested (e.g. Atkinson 2004), discourse analytic research suggests that the schemata of second language (L2) and first language (L1) writers differ in their preferred ways of organising ideas which can influence academic writing (e.g. Hinkel 2002). These conclusions have been supported by a range of studies over the past decade comparing the features of research articles in various countries (e.g. Molino 2010), student essays (Kubota 1998), and conference abstracts (Yakhontova 2002). In business contexts too, issues of culture have been explored, particularly in the use of English as a business lingua franca (BELF) in multinational companies (Nickerson 2005). While we cannot simply predict the ways people are likely to write on the basis of assumed cultural traits, discourse studies have shown that students' first language and prior learning come to influence ways of organising ideas and structuring arguments when writing in English at university.

It is difficult to summarize such a massive body of research into academic and professional genres, but it is possible to identify five broad findings:

1. That texts are systematically structured to secure readers' agreement or understanding;
2. That these community-specific ways of producing agreement represent rhetorical preferences that are specific to particular contexts;
3. That language groups have different ways of expressing ideas and negotiating writer-reader relationships and that these represent serious challenges to students understanding of themselves and their fields;
4. That professional writing is distinguished by its expert character, its specialized goal orientation, and its conventionalized form;
5. That there is frequently a disconnect between authentic written language and that in textbooks.

Together these studies help capture something of the ways language is used in the academy and workplace, producing a rich vein of findings which continues to inform both teaching and our understanding of the practices of professional and academic communities.

Specific Purposes Writing Instruction

ESP practitioners have made considerable use of these findings to determine what is to be learned and to organize instruction around the genres that learners need and the social contexts in which they will operate. Texts and tasks are therefore selected according to learners' needs and genres are modeled explicitly to provide learners with something to aim for: an understanding of what readers are likely to expect.

The demands of the modern workplace and university therefore mean that ESP recognizes the specificity of writing done in different domains and in the instruction that leads to competence in such domains (Belcher 2009; Hyland 2002). Successful writing does not occur in a vacuum but depends on an understanding of a professional context (Hyland and Bondi 2006), so that texts produced in legal, medical, technical, and business fields differ enormously from each other and often from one site to another. In fact, even students in fairly cognate fields such as nursing and midwifery, for example, are given very different writing assignments (Gimenez 2009). Students in practice-based or interdisciplinary degrees in particular may find that they face literacy demands which span several fields, so that business students, for example, may be expected to confront texts from accountancy, economics, financial management, corporate organisation, marketing, statistics, and so on.

There is, then, a marked diversity of task and texts in different fields and a considerable body of research testifies to the fact that the writing tasks students have to do at university are specific to discipline (e.g. Hyland 2002; Prior 1998). In the humanities and social sciences, for example, analyzing and synthesising multiple sources is important, while in science and technology, activity-based skills such as describing procedures, defining objects, and planning solutions are required (Hyland 2009). Genre and lexis also vary considerably so that the structure of common formats such as the experimental lab report can differ completely across different technical and engineering disciplines (Braine 1995) and even the lexis students are expected to use in particular fields varies enormously (Hyland and Tse 2007).

An important consequence of this is that ESP continues to base instruction on a study of the texts students will need in their target contexts rather than our impressions of writing. While all teaching starts with where the students are and takes their backgrounds, language proficiencies, teaching and learning preferences into account, ESP focusses on the world outside the writing classroom by going beyond grammar and vocabulary to prepare students for their future experiences using the most detailed needs analysis that time allows. This seeks to ensure that learning to write is related to the genres that students will confront and the contexts in which they will confront them: it is the means of establishing the *how* and *what* of a course. An analysis of students' writing needs not only helps to determine the genres and content of a course, but also its objectives, materials, and tasks of a course (Dudley-Evans and St John 1998). Decisions about what to teach and how to teach it, however, are not neutral professional questions but are likely to reflect the ideologies of the most powerful parties in any context, notably the teacher, the employer or the funding body, with important consequences for learners (Benesch 2001).

Many of these considerations are implemented in specific purposes programs by focussing on both the purposes for which people are learning a language and the kinds of language performance that are necessary to meet those purposes. Generally this has meant employing either *text-based, content-based,* or *consciousness-raising approaches.*

Text-based syllabuses (Feez 1998) organize instruction around the genres that learners need and the social contexts in which they will operate (Hyland 2004b). This involves adopting a scaffolded pedagogy to guide learners towards control of key genres based on whole texts selected in relation to learner needs (e.g. Johns 2002). In ESP classrooms it often involves active and sustained support by a teacher who models appropriate strategies for meeting particular purposes, guides students in their use of the strategies, and provides a meaningful and relevant context for using the strategies. A *content-based syllabus* (Mohan 1986), on the other hand, focusses on subject content as a carrier of language rather than a focus on language itself. For some practitioners, this simply means adopting any relevant themes from the students' field as a way of providing sheltered assistance towards their transition into a new community. For others it means taking a more immersion-like approach with close cooperation with the specialist subject teacher and varying degrees of subject-language integration (Dudley-Evans and St John 1998).

Finally, *a consciousness-raising approach* (Swales 1990) is an explicit attempt to avoid simplistic and formulaic approaches to writing specialist texts and the prescriptive teaching of target genres. In particular, it seeks to harness students' understandings of their fields by placing greater emphasis on exploratory, context-sensitive and research-informed understandings, which promote both learner awareness and learner autonomy. Essentially, *rhetorical consciousness-raising* is a "top down" approach to understanding language that encourages learners to analyze, compare and manipulate representative samples of a target discourse. Focussing on language is not therefore an end in itself but a means of teaching learners to use language effectively by encouraging them to experience for themselves the effect that grammatical choices have on creating meanings. Swales and Feak's (2004) textbook *Academic Writing for Graduate Students*, for instance, draws on an EAP research tradition to both develop in novice research writers a sensitivity to the language used in different academic genres and insights into the conventions and expectations of their target communities. This is principally accomplished by encouraging students to analyze text extracts, often through comparison with other genres.

Looking to the Future

Predictions are never easy, but one certainty is that ESP's concern with mapping the discourses and communicative challenges of the modern workplace and classroom will continue. This distinctive approach to language teaching, based on identification of the specific language features, discourse practices and communicative skills of target groups, and committed to developing teaching practices that recognize the particular subject-matter needs and expertise of learners, remain its core strength. ESP is, in essence, research-based language education and the applied nature of the field has been its strength, tempering a possible overindulgence in theory with a practical utility. It is possible, however, to anticipate some potential developments in the coming years.

First, it is likely that the expansion of studies into new specialist professional fields and written genres will continue. There are numerous genres that we know little about and others that are emergent and described only superficially. Many student genres, such as counselling case notes, reflexive journals and clinical reports, remain to be described while analyses of more occluded research genres (Swales 1996), such as referees reports and responses to editors' decisions, would greatly assist novice writers in the publication process. We also know little about the ways that genres form "constellations" with neighbouring genres nor about the "genre sets" that a particular individual or group engages in, or how spoken and written texts cluster together in a given social activity (Swales 2004). In addition, and as I have mentioned earlier, the mix of academic subjects now offered to students impact on the genres they have to participate in, compounding the challenges of writing in the disciplines with novel literacy practices that have barely been described. Moreover, literacy demands are made ever more complex by the increase in the use of electronic written texts, the growth of workplace *generification* (Swales 2004), and the proliferation of written genres into ever more areas of our professional lives. Control of these genres can pose considerable communicative challenges to all professionals, but for ESP teachers they demand a pedagogical response as well.

Second, it is also clear that much remains to be learnt and considerable research undertaken before we are able to identify more precisely the notion of "community" and how it relates to the professions and the discoursal conventions that they routinely employ in written texts. Nor is it yet understood how our memberships of different groups influence our participation in workplace discourses. For now, the term *profession* might be seen as a shorthand form for the various identities, roles, positions, relationships, reputations, reward systems, and other dimensions of social practices constructed and expressed through language use. Community, profession, and discipline, together with the practices that define expertise in them, are concepts which need to be further refined through the analyses of texts and contexts.

Third, ESP conceptions of literacy and writing instruction need to come to terms with the challenges posed by critical perspectives of literacy and teaching. Long-standing debates in the field have failed to resolve the issue of pragmatism versus criticality. This cuts to the heart of the *ethics* of ESP and the charge that in helping learners to develop their professional communicative competence, teachers reinforce conformity to an unexamined institutional and social order. The question, essentially, is whether ESP is a pragmatic exercise, working to help students to fit unquestioningly into subordinate roles in their professions, disciplines and courses, or whether it has a responsibility to help students understand the power relations of those contexts (e.g. Allison 1996; Pennycook 1997). This question is of central relevance to ESP writing teachers and it is becoming increasingly clear that the reciprocal relationship between theory and practice is a central concern for students, instructors, and the institutional contexts in which they meet (see Benesch 2009).

A fourth broad area is that of understanding the increasing role of multimodal and electronic texts in professional contexts. Scientific and technical texts have always been multimodal, but reports, brochures, publicity materials and research papers are now far more heavily influenced by graphic design than ever before and the growing challenge to the page by the screen as the dominant medium of communication means that images are ever more important in meaning-making. Analytical tools developed by Kress and Van Leeuwen (2006) and others provide a starting point for researchers and teachers to explain how visuals have been organized for maximum effect, while considerably more work needs to be done to understand the role of multimedia and hypertext in corporate and academic communication and the genres that students will need to control as part of their repertoire of writing skills.

Fifth, ESP writing instruction needs to pay greater attention to the contexts of professional writing and the ways in which writers collaborate to produce corporate documents of various kinds. While academic assignments are generally written individually, the university is a temporary and idiosyncratic environment which does not reflect the realities of corporate and scientific text construction. In those contexts, activities are less focussed on the individual than on the transactions and collaborations of working in teams and groups, and for second language speakers, often with less engagement with native English speaker interlocutors and texts. One major difference between instruction for academic and workplace contexts is that there is less consensus on the skills, language and communicative behaviors required in academic environments (St John 1996). It is also possible that text expectations may not only be linked to the values and conventions of particular discourse communities but to either national or corporate contexts, so that communication strategies, status relationships and cultural differences are likely to impact far more on successful interaction.

These are among the key issues that are emerging as important challenges which ESP writing teachers and researchers will need to confront.

Conclusions

ESP writing instruction is essentially a practically oriented activity committed to demystifying prestigious forms of discourse, unlocking students' creative and expressive abilities, and facilitating their access to greater life chances. The fact that it is grounded in the descriptions of texts and practices, however, means that it also seeks to provide teachers and students with a way of understanding how writing is shaped by individuals making language choices in social contexts, and so contributes to both theory and practice. In particular, it shows how ESP has nothing to do with topping up generic writing skills that learners have failed to master at school, but involves developing new kinds of literacy: equipping learners with the communicative skills to participate in particular academic and professional cultures. While these ideas have been around for some time, ESP takes them seriously and seeks to operationalize them in instruction by encouraging a view of writing as both understanding particular communicative genres and a reflective practice which relates texts to the cognitive, social and linguistic demands of specific professions and disciplines.

REFERENCES

Allison, D. (1996) Pragmatist discourse and English for Academic Purposes. *English for Specific Purposes* 15: 85–103.

Atkinson, D. (2004) Contrasting rhetorics/ contrasting cultures: Why contrastive rhetoric needs a better conceptualization of culture. *Journal of English for Academic Purposes* 3: 277–89.

Barton, D. and Hamilton, M. (1998) *Local Literacies*. London: Routledge.

Basturkmen, H. (2009) Commenting on results in published research articles and masters dissertations in language teaching. *Journal of English for Academic Purposes* 8: 241–51.

Baxter, R., Boswood, T., and Pierson-Smith, A. (2002) An ESP programme for management in the horse-racing business. In T. Orr (ed.), *English for Specific Purposes*. 117–46. Alexandra, VA: TESOL.

Baynham, M. (2000) Academic writing in new and emergent discipline areas. In M. Lea and B. Stierer (eds.), *Student Writing in Higher Education: New Contexts*. 17–31. Buckingham, UK: SRHE and Open University Press.

Belcher, D. (2009) What ESP is and can be: An introduction. In D. Belcher (ed.), *English for Specific Purposes in Theory and Practice*. 1–20. Ann Arbor MI: University of Michigan Press.

Belotti, U. (2006) Genre characteristics of invitations for bids. In V. Bhatia and M. Gotti (eds.), *Explorations in Specialized Genres*. 210–46. Bern: Peter Lang.

Benesch, S. (2001) *Critical English for Academic Purposes*. Mahwah, NJ: Lawrence Erlbaum.

Benesch, S. (2009) Theorizing and practicing critical English for academic purposes. *Journal of English for Academic Purposes* 8: 81–5.

Berger, P. and Luckmann, T. (1966) *The Social Construction of Reality*. London: Penguin.

Bhatia, V. K. (1999) Integrating products, processes, and participants in professional writing. In C. N. Candlin and K. Hyland (eds.), *Writing: Texts, Processes and Practices*. 21–39. Harlow, UK: Longman.

Bhatia, V. K. (2008) Towards a critical genre analysis. In V. Bhatia, J. Flowerdew, and R. Jones (eds.), *Advances in Discourse Studies*. 166–77. London: Routledge.

Bloch, J. (2008) *Technologies in the Second Language Classroom*. Ann Arbor MI: University of Michigan Press.

Braine, G. (1995) Writing in the natural sciences and engineering. In D. Belcher and G. Braine (eds.), *Academic Writing in a Second Language: Essays on Research and Pedagogy*. 113–34. Norwood, NJ: Ablex.

Bruce, I. (2010) Textual and discoursal resources used in the essay genre in sociology and English. *Journal of English for Academic Purposes* 9: 153–66.

Canagarajah, S. (1999) *Resisting Linguistic Imperialism in English Teaching*. Oxford: Oxford University Press.

Canale, M. and Swain, M. (1980). Theoretical bases of communicative approaches to second language teaching and testing. *Applied Linguistics* 1: 1–47.

Coffin, C. and Hewings, A. (2005) Engaging electronically: Using CMC to develop students' argumentation skills in higher education. *Language and Education* 19: 32–49.

Connor, U. (2002) New directions in contrastive rhetoric. *TESOL Quarterly* 36: 493–510.

Crookes, G. (1986) Towards a validated analysis of scientific text structure. *Applied Linguistics* 7: 57–70.

Dudley-Evans, T. and St John, M. J. (1998). *Developments in English for Specific Purposes*. Cambridge: Cambridge University Press.

Fairclough, N. (2003) *Analyzing Discourse*. London: Routledge.

Feez, S. (1998) *Text-Based Syllabus Design*. Sydney: National Centre for English Language Teaching and Research, Macquarie University.

Flowerdew, J. and Wan, A. (2010) The linguistic and the contextual in applied genre analysis: The case of the company audit report. *English for Specific Purposes* 29: 78–93.

Fortanet, I. (2008) Evaluative language in peer review referee reports. *Journal of English for Academic Purposes* 7: 27–37.

Gee, J. (1996) *Social Linguistics and Literacies: Ideology in Discourses*. London: Taylor and Francis.

Gimenez, J. (2009) Beyond the academic essay: Discipline-specific writing in nursing and midwifery. *Journal of English for Academic Purposes* 7: 151–64.

Gollin, S. (1999) "Why? I thought we'd talked about it before": Collaborative writing in a professional workplace setting. In C. N. Candlin and K. Hyland (eds.), *Writing: Texts, processes and practices*. 267–90. London: Longman.

Gotti, M. and Gillaerts, P. (2005) *Genre Variation in Business Letters*. Bern: Peter Lang.

Gunnarsson, B. L. (2009) *Professional Discourse*. London: Continuum.

Halliday, M. A. K. (1994) *An Introduction to Functional Grammar*. 2nd ed. London: Edward Arnold.

Harrison, C. and Young, L. (2004) Bureaucratic discourse: Writing in the "comfort zone". In L. Young and C. Harrison (eds.), *Systemic Functional Linguistics and Critical Discourse Analysis*. 231–46. London: Continuum.

Hewett, B. and Robidoux, C. (eds.) (2010) *Virtual Collaborative Writing in rhe Workplace: Computer-Mediated Communication Technologies and Processes*. Hershey, PA: IGI Global.

Hinkel, E. (2002) *Second Language Writers' Text*. Mahwah, NJ: Lawrence Erlbaum.

Holmes, J. (2011) Workplace discourse. In K. Hyland and B. Paltridge (eds.), *Continuum Companion to Discourse Analysis*. 185–98. London: Continuum.

Hyland, K. (1998) Exploring corporate rhetoric: Metadiscourse in the CEO's letter. *Journal of Business Communication* 35: 224–45.

Hyland, K. (2002) Specificity revisited: How far should we go now? *English for Specific Purposes* 21: 385–95.

Hyland, K. (2004a) *Disciplinary Discourses*. Ann Arbor MI: University of Michigan Press.

Hyland, K. (2004b) *Genre and Second Language Writing*. Ann Arbor: University of Michigan Press.

Hyland, K. (2004c.) Disciplinary interactions: Metadiscourse in L2 postgraduate writing. *Journal of Second Language Writing* 13: 133–51.

Hyland, K. (2009) *Academic Discourse*. London: Continuum.

Hyland, K. (2011) Academic discourse. In K. Hyland and B. Paltridge (eds.), *Continuum Companion to Discourse Analysis*. 171–84. London: Continuum.

Hyland, K. and Bondi, M. (eds.) (2006) *Academic Discourse Across Disciplines*. Frankfurt: Peter Lang.

Hyland, K. and Diani, G. (eds.) (2009) *Academic Evaluation: Review Genres in University Settings*. London: Palgrave Macmillan.

Hyland, K. and Tse, P. (2007) Is there an "academic vocabulary"? *TESOL Quarterly* 41: 235–54.

Ivanič, R. (1998) *Writing and Identity: The Discoursal Construction of Identity in Academic Writing*. Amsterdam: Benjamins.

Jensen, A. (2009) Discourse strategies in professional e-mail negotiation: A case study. *English for Specific Purposes* 28(1): 4–18.

Johns, A. M. (ed.) (2002) *Genre in the Classroom: Multiple Perspectives*. Mahwah, NJ: Lawrence Erlbaum.

Kramsch, C. (1993) *Context and Culture in Language Teaching*. Oxford: Oxford University Press.

Kress, G. and Van Leeuwen, T. (2006) *Reading Images: The Grammar of Visual Design*. 2nd ed. London: Routledge.

Kubota, R. (1998) Ideologies of English in Japan. *World Englishes* 17: 295–306.

Lassen, I. (2004) Resources in biotechnology press releases: Patterns of theme/rheme and given/new. In L.

Young and C. Harrison (eds.), *Systemic Functional Linguistics and Critical Discourse Analysis*. 264–79. London: Continuum.

Lave, J. and Wenger, E. (1991) *Situated Learning: Legitimate Peripheral Participation* Cambridge: Cambridge University Press.

Lea, M. and Street, B. (1999) Writing as academic literacies: Understanding textual practices in higher education. In C. N. Candlin and K. Hyland (eds.), *Writing: Texts, Processes and Practice*. 62–81. London: Longman.

Lillis, T. (2001) *Student Writing: Access, Regulation, Desire*. London: Routledge.

Lin, A. M. Y. (2000) Resistance and creativity in English reading lessons in Hong Kong. *Language, Culture and Curriculum* 12: 285–96.

Locker, K. (1999) Factors in reader response to negative letters: Experimental evidence for changing what we teach. *Journal of Business and Technical Communication* 13: 5–48.

Loudermilk, B. (2007) Occluded academic genres: An analysis of the MBA thought essay. *Journal of English for Academic Purposes* 6: 190–205.

Mazzi, D. (2006) "This is an attractive argument, but . . ." Argumentative conflicts as an interpretive key to the discourse of judges. In V. Bhatia and M. Gotti (eds.), *Explorations in Specialized Genres*. 271–90. Bern, Peter Lang.

Mohan, B. (1986) *Language and Content*. Reading, MA: Addison Wesley.

Molino, A. (2010) Personal and impersonal authorial references: A contrastive study of English and Italian Linguistics research articles. *Journal of English for Academic Purposes*: 86–101.

Myers, G. (2010) *The Discourse of Blogs and Wikis*. London: Continuum.

Nickerson, C. (2005) English as a *lingua franca* in international business contexts. *English for Specific Purposes* 24: 367–80.

Paltridge, B. (2002) Thesis and dissertation writing: an examination of published advice and actual practice. *English for Specific Purposes* 21: 125–43.

Pennycook, A. (1997) Vulgar pragmatism, critical pragmatism, and EAP. *English for Specific Purposes* 16: 253–69.

Petrić, B. (2007) Rhetorical functions of citations in high- and low-rated master's theses. *Journal of English for Academic Purposes* 6: 238–53.

Phan, L. H. (2009) Strategic, passionate, but academic: "Am I allowed in my writing?" *Journal of English for Academic Purposes* 8: 134–46.

Prior, P. (1998) *Writing/Disciplinarity: A Sociohistoric Account of Literate Activity in the Academy*. Hillsdale, NJ: Lawrence Erlbaum.

Smart, G. (2008) Ethnographic-based discourse analysis: Uses, issues and prospects. In V. Bhatia, J. Flowerdew, and R. Jones (eds.), *Advances in Discourse Studies* 56–66. London and New York: Routledge.

St John, M. J. (1996) Business is booming: Business English in the 1990s. *English for Specific Purposes* 15: 13–18.

Street, B. V. (1995) *Social literacies: Critical approaches to literacy in development, ethnography and education*. New York: Longman.

Swales, J. M. (1990) *Genre Analysis: English in Academic and Research Settings*. Cambridge: Cambridge University Press.

Swales, J. M. (1996) Occluded genres in the academy: The case of the submission letter. In E. Ventola and A. Mauranen (eds.), *Academic Writing: Intercultural and Textual Issues*. 45–58. Amsterdam: John Benjamins.

Swales, J. M. (1998) *Other floors, Other Voices: A Textography of a Small University Building*. Mahwah, NJ: Lawrence Erlbaum.

Swales, J. M. (2004) *Research Genres*. New York: Cambridge University Press.

Swales, J. M. and Feak, C. B. (2004) *Academic Writing for Graduate Students: Essential Tasks and Skills*. 2nd ed. Ann Arbor, MI: University of Michigan Press.

Teo, P. (2000) Racism in the news: A critical discourse analysis of news reporting in two Australian newspapers. *Discourse and Society* 11: 7–49.

Van Nus, M. (1999) Can we count on your bookings of potatoes to Madeira? Corporate context and discourse practices in direct sales letters. In F. Bargiela-Chiappini and C. Nickerson (eds.), *Writing Business: Genres, Media and Discourses*. 181–206. London: Longman.

Williams, I. (1996) A contextual study of lexical verbs in two types of medical research report: Clinical and experimental. *English for Specific Purposes* 15: 175–97.

Yakhontova, T. (2002) "Selling" or "telling"? The issue of cultural variation in research genres. In J. Flowerdew (ed.), *Academic Discourse*. 216–32. London: Longman.

6 Vocabulary and ESP

AVERIL COXHEAD

Introduction

Research into vocabulary and English for specific purposes (ESP) is driven primarily by the question, "What vocabulary do ESP learners need?" The problem is that this seemingly simple question does not have a particularly straightforward answer. It is more than likely that the question would be met with more questions about the kind of ESP the learners are focussed on, whether they all have the same goals, their level of proficiency, the context, and the amount of time available for learning. This reasonably complex area of research spans a wide range of teaching and research endeavors, from English for academic purposes (EAP) through to English for very particular purposes such as engineering and medicine. It covers everyday words that take on specialized meanings in particular contexts (think of *monitor* in computer science and *weight* in physics) and words that occur in a very narrow range of usage (such as *photosynthesis*). The chapter begins with an examination of definitions of specialized or technical vocabulary and moves on to different approaches to conceptualizing vocabulary and ESP. The focus then moves beyond single words to lexical patterning in ESP. The chapter ends with some challenges for bringing ESP research on vocabulary into classrooms.

What is Vocabulary for English for Specific Purposes and Why is it Important?

ESP vocabulary can be referred to in the literature by very different names from one study to another. These terms include special purpose, specialized, technical,

The Handbook of English for Specific Purposes, First Edition.
Edited by Brian Paltridge and Sue Starfield.
© 2013 John Wiley & Sons, Inc. Published 2013 by John Wiley & Sons, Inc.

sub-technical, and semi-technical vocabulary. In essence, such terms usually refer to the vocabulary of a particular area of study or professional use. The range of a word is important in ESP. That is, a specialized word would have a narrow range of use within a particular subject area. This means that specialized words are expected to belong to a particular subject area at university or to a professional discipline. People outside that academic or professional sphere might have some knowledge of this vocabulary but the people inside these areas of language use would be expected to be able to understand and use this language fluently. It is worthwhile keeping in mind, however, that specialized vocabulary does not always mean long Graeco-Latin words or highly technical words that are not used in everyday language. Some perfectly ordinary everyday words can carry very specific meanings in particular contexts. Nation (2008) points out that *by-pass* and *neck* are high frequency words in medicine but they also occur outside that specialized context. Crawford Camiciottoli (2007) lists *market* and *price* as words that can be found in everyday language but are also used in business studies. This problem is discussed later in the chapter when challenges in vocabulary and ESP are considered.

Vocabulary in ESP is important for several reasons. First of all, teachers and learners need to know that precious classroom time is directly related to their language needs. They should be reading material that contains key ideas and the language of their field and writing using those ideas and language. Woodward-Kron (2008: 246) carried out a longitudinal study of undergraduate students' academic writing in education and found that students' knowledge of a discipline is closely tied to the specialized language of that discipline. Secondly, understanding and using this special purposes vocabulary shows that these learners belong to a particular group. Learners need that language to show understanding, "make meaning and engage with disciplinary knowledge" (Woodward-Kron 2008: 246). This point is particularly important if learners are to become fully-fledged members of a particular community.

Another important point to make is that the size of this specialized vocabulary is not fully established. As Nation (2008:10) states, "we do not know a lot about technical vocabularies but they probably range in size from around 1,000 words to 5,000 words depending on the subject area." This means that ESP learners may face an extremely large learning task to fully develop their understanding and use of specialized vocabulary in their subject area at university or in a professional context.

Conceptualizing Vocabulary and ESP

Basturkmen (2006) outlines two fundamental perspectives on language for specific purposes. One approach posits that English has a common core of words all learners should know. In this view, specialization begins once learners establish that common core. The other approach conceptualizes all language as being for specific purposes (Basturkmen 2006) which means specialization should begin early. The key point here is where specialization should begin for language learners. Early specialization is easier to conceptualize and operationalize in learning contexts where all students are moving through the same educational system at the same age with a shared first language and language goals. Teachers whose students have a mix of academic purposes face a different task to teachers of classes with a single academic purpose. Compare, for example, a group of undergraduate engineering students in Venezuela and a group of pre-university students in an English for academic purposes program in New Zealand. The Venezuelan group will have a single subject area to focus on, whereas the New Zealand group may be planning to study very different academic subject areas, including business, economics, geology, design, music, and biology. Later in this chapter, various studies into vocabulary in ESP that look at specialization for language learners will be explored.

Identifying Vocabulary for ESP

According to Read (2007), methods for identifying vocabulary for specific purposes have varied greatly and have lacked systematicity. Nation (2008) points out that very few statistical studies have been carried out in technical vocabulary. This section looks at several ways to identify vocabulary for ESP, including consultation with experts in a particular field, working with specialized dictionaries, developing rating scales, and using techniques from corpus linguistics.

Consulting experts and technical dictionaries to identify specialized vocabulary

One approach to identifying specialized vocabulary is to consult experts in a particular field to help identify technical vocabulary (Schmitt 2010). Schmitt lists various difficulties with this method, including the fact that it is likely several experts on the same topic might well produce quite different lists, depending on variables such as their level of knowledge of the subject, the systematicity of their approach to developing the list, and how difficult it is to identify the technical words. Schmitt suggests that technical dictionaries may well have been developed using this method.

Technical dictionaries have been employed to help identify specialized vocabulary. Chung and Nation (2004: 254–55) outlined their experiences of using technical dictionaries to help decide whether a word is technical in nature. The authors note that while this technique may seem relatively straightforward, it demands a great deal of decision-making. These decisions include the size of the dictionary, whether just the single form of a word is to be taken into consideration or word family members, and the position of the word in main or sub-entries in the dictionary. The researchers report that this technique was around 80 percent accurate in identifying technical vocabulary.

Using a scale to identify specialized vocabulary

Categorization of words has also been done using a scale. Chung and Nation (2003) devized a four-step scale to categorise technical vocabulary in an applied linguistics textbook and an anatomy textbook. Step 1 on the scale represents words with meanings that have no specific connection to a subject area, for example *between*, *amounts*, and *early*. Step 2 contains words which are minimally related to the subject area, for example *supports*, *part*, and *protects* in anatomy. Step 3 is for words that are more closely related to the subject area, such as *neck*, *heart*, and *breathing* in anatomy. Step 4 is for words that relate closely to the technical subject area. These words would not be known generally, for example *fascia* and *pedicle* (2003: 105).

Using this scale, Chung and Nation (2003) found that one in every three words in the anatomy text was technical, compared to one word in five in the applied linguistics text. Why is this finding of one word in three being technical in an anatomy text important? Firstly, this new definition of technical vocabulary is vastly different from earlier estimates. Previously, estimates believed this figure to be close to 5 percent (Coxhead 1998; Nation 2001) which is much lower than the 33 percent finding in Chung and Nation (2003). Also, the variation in technical vocabulary between the two subject areas suggests that professionals in anatomy face a higher vocabulary learning challenge than those in applied linguistics. It could be the case that the applied linguistics text was more accessible for its readership than the anatomy text. Developing new scales means new ways of classifying technical words, so different results from different studies have to be accompanied by a clear understanding of how principles of selection and classification have taken place, just as Chung and Nation (2003) do in their study.

Corpus-based studies to identify specialized vocabulary

A corpus is a body of texts of written or spoken language. Corpus studies have contributed a great deal to our quest to identify and understand more about specialized vocabulary. They have been particularly useful for developing word lists for use in language classrooms and for independent study. Corpus-based studies allow for larger-scale investigations of words in context. They should be relatively easy to replicate. An example of a corpus-linguistic approach as a way to classify specialized vocabulary comes from Crawford Camiciottoli (2007). She divided the words in her Business Studies Lecture Corpus (BSLC) into five main semantic categories. These categories are in Table 6.1. Crawford Camiciottoli (2007) uses several corpora to compare her findings, including a more widely based corpus of different academic disciplines.

This corpus-based approach yields a very different view of specialized vocabulary than the Chung and Nation (2003) scale. Whereas Crawford Camiciottoli focusses on the relationship between the function of the lexical items in her corpus to business studies, Chung and Nation (2003) focus on the closeness of the relationship between the words and the subject area. That is, Chung and Nation's

Table 6.1 Semantic divisions in a Business Studies Lecture Corpus (BSLC), adapted from Crawford Camiciottoli (2007: 128)

Semantic category	Examples
related to business	turnover, inflation, supply
related to business entities and actors	firms, clusters, investors
related to business activities	production, input/output
related to business activities and economic trends	failing, deal, international, dynamic
related to increasing business performance	price, cost, percentage

(2003) scale indicates the likelihood of finding the words in other subject areas whereas the Crawford Camiciottoli (2007) categorization is concerned with the meaning relationships of the words being used in a specialized area. Categorization is important in corpus-based studies because while the computer takes a very short time to sort through a corpus, it takes many hours for humans to work through the output of the computer (Byrd and Coxhead 2010). Overlaps between categories or fuzziness between borders of a scale can be problematic.

Crawford Camiciottoli (2007) demonstrates how corpus-based research can provide a different approach to identifying vocabulary for ESP. Mike Nelson (nd) has also examined the vocabulary of Business English using a corpus linguistics approach but his study uses both spoken and written data. Nelson created two corpora for his study. The first contains Business English books (approximately 600,000 words) the second is the Business English Corpus (BEC) (approximately 1 million words). This corpus was made up of written and spoken texts. Nelson collected and categorized the written and spoken texts in his corpus into four main areas. These areas are writing about business (business books, journals, and articles), writing to do business (annual reports, faxes, letters, etc.), talking about business (interviews and radio and TV business reports) and speaking to do business (for example, meetings, speeches, and presentations). Nelson used a smaller version of the British National Corpus (BNC) to compare Business English to general English (go to http://users.utu.fi/micnel/business_english_lexis_site.htm). Table 6.2 shows the top ten lemmas from the Nelson (nd) and Crawford Camiciottoli (2007) corpus-based studies of Business English. A lemma is usually made up of a headword and its inflected forms (Nation 2001: 7). An example of a lemma in Crawford Camiciottoli (2007: 125) is *argue*, with its inflected forms (*argue*, *argues*, *argued*, *argument*, and *arguments*).

Nelson's top ten are "key words." That is, these words appear significantly more frequently in Business English than they do in general English. Crawford Camiciottoli's top ten key words (2007) are frequency-based. That is, *firm* was the

Table 6.2   Comparison of top ten words in business studies in Nelson (nd) and Crawford Camiciottoli (2007: 129)

Frequency order	Nelson's (nd) "most key words"	Crawford Camiciottoli (2007)
1	business	firm
2	company	company
3	market	produce
4	customer	economy
5	OK	price
6	product	percent
7	sale	work
8	fax	market
9	management	retire
10	price	invest

most frequent specialized word (occurring 423 times in the corpus), *company* was the next most frequent at 378, and so on.

Table 6.2 demonstrates how results from seemingly similar studies can be quite different. The Crawford Camiciottoli study identifies 174 technical words and uses lemmas as the base unit of counting.

A common core approach: The academic word list (AWL)

A well-known example of a corpus linguistics common core approach (see Basturkmen 2006 above) is the Academic Word List (Coxhead 2000). This list was designed as a potential tool for teachers and learners to help bridge more general everyday language that they might have encountered and used in high schools and language schools and the more specialized and Graeco-Latin language of written academic English. Coxhead used the first two thousand word families of West's (1953) *A General Service List of English Words* (GSL) to represent common core vocabulary in the development of the AWL using a written academic corpus. The first principle for selecting word families for the AWL was that the GSL words should not be included in the AWL. The GSL was used because it is a well-principled list. However, drawbacks with using the list (noted at the time and subsequently) are that the list is now very old (see Coxhead 2000; Nation and Webb 2010; Schmitt 2010) and does not contain more up-to-date but everyday words such as *computer* and *television*. Despite these problems, the West list is still reliable in its coverage figures over different corpora and has yet to be replaced.

Other principles for selecting word families for the AWL were the frequency of the words, their range across 28 academic subject areas, and the uniformity of their occurrence in the four academic disciplines of the corpus. The AWL contains 570 word families (an example of a word family is *environment, environmental, environmentalist, environmentalists, environmentally,* and *environments*). The word families were built up to level six of affixation according to Bauer and Nation (1993) (for more on the AWL see Coxhead 2000, 2006, 2011, and nd). The list covers 10 percent of the academic corpus it was based on. In subsequent studies over a variety of corpora, the list covers between 9 percent and 11 percent of academic texts, as can be seen in Table 6.3. In this table, the AWL coverage is ranked from the highest over a small corpus of academic texts (Cobb and Horst 2004) through

Table 6.3 Coverage of the AWL over various corpora (adapted from Coxhead 2011: 356)

Study	Corpus	Number of running words	Percentage of AWL coverage
Cobb and Horst (2004)	*Learned* section of the Brown corpus (Francis and Kucera 1979)	14,283 words	11.60
Konstantakis (2007)	Business	1 million words	11.51
Ward (2009)	Engineering	271,000 words	11.3
Vongpumivitch, Huang, and Chang (2009)	Applied linguistics research papers	1.5 million words	11.17
Hyland and Tse (2007)	Sciences, engineering, and social sciences, written by professional and student writers	3,292,600 words	10.6
Li and Qian (2010)	Finance	6.3 million words	10.46
Chen and Ge (2007)	Medical research articles	190,425 words	10.073
Martínez, Beck, and Panza (2009)	Agricultural sciences research articles	826,416-words	9.06
Coxhead and Hirsh (2007)	University level science texts	1.5 million words	8.96
Coxhead, Stevens, and Tinkle (in press)	Pathway series of secondary science textbooks	279,733 words	7.05
Coxhead (unreported)	Newspapers	1 million words	4.5
Coxhead (2000)	Fiction	3,500,000 words	1.4

to the lowest in fiction (Coxhead 2000). In a study of a series of secondary school science textbooks, Coxhead, Stevens, and Tinkle (2010) find that the AWL has coverage of 7.05 percent (see Table 6.3). Compare this figure to the other studies of university level texts where the coverage, on average, is 10 percent. This lower coverage figure indicates that while words in the AWL do occur in these secondary school texts, they are not as frequent as in university level texts.

Subsequent studies building on the methodology of the AWL include a pilot science-specific word list (Coxhead and Hirsh 2007), and a medical academic word list (Wang, Liang, and Ge 2008).

Coxhead and Hirsh (2007) used the GSL and the AWL as a core vocabulary in their study of specialized vocabulary in a corpus of 1.7 million words of first-year university science texts. The fourteen subject areas in the study included: agricultural sciences, biology, chemistry, computer science, ecology, engineering and technology, geography, geology, horticulture, mathematics, nursing and midwifery, physics, sport and health science, and veterinary and animal science. The coverage of the 318 word families in the science list over the corpus was 3.79 percent. A word family is based on a headword and both inflected and derived forms up to level six of the Bauer and Nation (1993) scale of affixes. Figure 6.1 below contains two examples of word families from Coxhead and Hirsh (2007: 12). Word families contain more members, usually, than a lemma.

Specialized medical vocabulary

Wang et al.'s (2008) medical word list was compiled using the GSL as a common core, but not the AWL. A consequence of this approach is overlap between the AWL and the medical word list. Six of the ten most frequent words in the Wang et al. list also occur in the AWL, for example, *data, significant, analyze, respond, factor,* and *method*. The other four in the medical word list top ten are *cell, muscular,*

diagnose	molecule
diagnosable	molecular
diagnosed	molecules
diagnosing	biomolecular
diagnoses	biomolecule
diagnosis	biomolecules
diagnostic	intermolecular
diagnostically	intramolecular
diagnostician	macromolecule
diagnosticians	macromolecules
diagnostics	
undiagnosed	

Figure 6.1   Examples of word families from Coxhead and Hirsh (2007: 12).

protein, and *clinic*. This medical word list is an example of early specialization, which means that learners with particular academic subjects in mind can focus early on the specialized vocabulary of their subject area rather than working on more general academic vocabulary. Hyland and Tse (2007) argue that learners need to develop a more disciplinary-based vocabulary because words behave in different ways depending on the context in which they occur. Their corpus-based study involved an examination of the distribution of some AWL words in three academic disciplines: sciences, engineering, and social sciences. The corpus contained texts written by professional and student writers. Hyland and Tse (2007) found examples of the same words behaving differently in subject areas, such as *process* occurring more often as a noun than as a verb in science and engineering than in social sciences. Such work expands our understanding of how words behave in different contexts. It also supports teachers and learners in their decisions on which words to focus on for specific purposes and why.

Early specialization: Ward's English list of basic engineering words

An example of early specialization for vocabulary learning is Ward's (2009) development of an English word list of basic engineering to support lower proficiency undergraduates. This study followed on from Ward (1999), where he examined engineering texts to determine the number of words students would need to know and found that 2000 word families covered up to 95 percent of a foundation-level engineering text from his textbook corpus. In the 2009 study, Ward was concerned that the list could be used by learners with little knowledge of vocabulary and grammar in English, would be useful for low-level language learners, and cover all different disciplines of engineering. Ward's final list contains 299 word types and covers 16.4 percent of a corpus of engineering textbooks. The top ten words from Ward's list are *system, shown, equation, example, value, design, used, section, flow,* and *given*. Of these 299 word types, 188 are also in the GSL 1000 list, 28 are in the GSL 2000, and 78 are in the AWL.

This section has looked across a range of studies into specialized vocabulary using different approaches. It has demonstrated the decisions and considerations of researchers when conducting their research. It has also shown that corpus-based studies in particular areas have made a major contribution to our understanding of specialized vocabulary.

Metaphor as an Example of Specialized Vocabulary

In a study of four university lectures from a spoken academic corpus, Littlemore et al. (2010) found that the average metaphoric density was 4.1 percent. Out of 132 (on average) items that second language participants found problematic in a lecture, 50 (38 percent) were used metaphorically. Of those problematic ones, the students were not able to explain the meaning of almost 50 percent of the metaphors that were used. The most important point here is that key or difficult concepts in a lecture might well be expressed through metaphor. Students who are not able to follow the metaphors are likely to misunderstand the lecture or not understand the key points at all.

Business studies in ESP have been the subject of several investigations into metaphor. One example is Charteris-Black and Musolff (2003), who compare the use of metaphors for euro trading in two corpora of financial reporting, one British and the other German. In the English data, three main clusters of metaphorical meaning were found. These three clusters, in order of frequency are:

> The value of the euro is an entity that *moves up and down*. The second cluster concern states of *health or strength* and can be summarized as the state of the euro is a state of health/strength. The third is related to notions of *combat* and physical struggle and can be summarized as euro trading is physical combat. There are two main sub-types of combat: boxing and general war metaphors (2003: 159, italics added).

Examples of these three clusters include *low/lower, fall/fell, downside* for movement; *support, weak,* and *ailing* for health/strength; and *batter, hit,* and *impact* for physical combat. According to the authors, both corpora reflect the movement and health or strength, but the German data showed more concern with stability than combat. It is interesting to note that health metaphors are used more often in winter than in summer (Boers 1997).

Boers (1997) finds that exposure to health, fitness, and fighting metaphors affects the language used by one hundred business and economics university students in a problem-solving activity, and to some extent, the decisions they make in response to a socioeconomic issue. Skorczynska Sznajder (2010) examines the use of war, health, and sports metaphors in a Business English textbook corpus and a business journal article/business periodical corpus and also finds implications for how learners respond to metaphor in language and in thought. She writes:

> Approaches to specialist vocabulary instruction through conceptual metaphors are necessary to enhance students' understanding of a discipline, especially if the learners are to be aware of possible social effects derived from conceptualizing a particular discipline through ideologically-motivated metaphors, as in the case of war metaphors in business and economic discourse (Skorczynska Sznajder 2010: 40).

Littlemore et al. (2010: 202) suggest that teaching second language speakers to recognize and understand metaphor in academic lectures "is no luxury" in English for academic purposes classes. Cultural differences can affect metaphor use. An EAP student of mine from Sri Lanka made a joke about being "opening bat" in a series of seminars in our class. He meant that he was the first speaker. As the only other person in the room who knew anything about the game of cricket, I was the only person who understood his joke.

Metaphors can consist of one or more words in a string and so they bridge the earlier part of this chapter looking at identifying single words with the next section on investigating longer strings of words as vocabulary in ESP.

Looking Beyond the Single Word at Lexical Patterning in ESP

Recently, more and more research is being carried out into multiword units in English for specific purposes. For example, Pinna's study of dentistry (2007) examines words on their own as well as clusters of two and three words together. Pinna finds key relationships between words such as "bone" to other words such as "graft" and "cortical." Crawford Camiciottoli (2007) finds some interesting examples of word compounds in her 109,449 word corpus of twelve business lectures. The most frequent were *bottom-up*, *cost-cutting*, and *cure-all*. Crawford Camiciottoli cautions that the speaking style of one lecturer can have a major impact on the frequency of the use of compounds. Larger-scale corpora with multiple speakers can go some way towards mitigating this particular problem. A quick search through the 152 transcripts or 1,848,364 words using the freely available and well-designed Michigan Corpus of Academic Spoken English (MICASE) (University of Michigan English Language Institute, nd, http://quod.lib.umich.edu/m/micase/) uncovers one example each of *cure-all/cure all* and *bottom-up/bottom up*. In the 3,500,000 word written academic corpus Coxhead (2000) developed for the AWL, *cost-cutting* occurs twice, and *bottom-up/bottom up* three times each. It could be that more recent corpora would deliver more occurrences of these words as these words and others that are coined gain use and spread widely.

The first two columns in Table 6.4 show Nelson's (nd) list of two and three-word phrases in his business studies corpora. The two-word phrases are much more closely aligned with the central notions of business than the far more general three-word phrases in this table.

Table 6.4 Most frequent two and three-word phrases in Nelson (nd) and Crawford Camiciottoli (2007)

Two-word phrases Nelson (nd)	Three-word phrases Nelson (nd)	Three-word lexical bundles Crawford Camiciottoli (2007: 131)
interest rates	a lot of	local productive systems
cash flow	one of the	option value model
market share	the end of	factors of production
stock market	in order to	the GDP deflator
Wall Street	we need to	high-tech companies

Table 6.4 also includes data on lexical bundles in the Crawford Camiciottoli study (see the final column). Byrd and Coxhead (2010: 32) define lexical bundles as a combination of "three or more words that are repeated without change for a set number of times in a particular corpus." Crawford Camiciottoli (2007) comments that there were few three-word bundles specific to business studies in her corpus. The most frequent was *local productive systems* which occurred 63 times. The frequency dropped quickly down to the fifth bundle, *high-tech companies* with 12 occurrences. This point is interesting because Biber, Conrad, and Cortes (2004) found lexical bundles occurred more often in classroom discourse than in written academic texts (for another comparison of lexical bundles in speaking and writing in academic contexts, see Pickering and Byrd 2008).

Lexical bundle research is part of a wider research endeavor that looks into the nature of formulaic sequences or phrases. Biber and his colleagues in Arizona have carried out well-principled, large-scale studies into lexical bundles in a variety of university texts and disciplines (see, for example, Biber 2006; Biber and Barbieri 2007; Biber, Conrad, and Cortes 2004). One of the key contributions of these studies is to demonstrate how lexical bundles can differ in areas such as newspaper prose, academic writing, conversational English, and fiction. Cortes (2004) found that history and biology students did not use lexical bundles often in their writing. Instead, they tended to use a small number of bundles in their writing but not in the same way as professional writers in the field. Biber, Conrad, and Cortes (2004) developed a taxonomy of bundles including discourse organizers, such as *on the other hand*, and stance expressions, such as *well I don't know* (see Byrd and Coxhead 2010 and Pickering and Byrd 2008 for more on classifying bundles using this taxonomy). Hyland (2008) also examined student and published writing in his corpus of electrical engineering, biology, business studies, and applied linguistics texts. In this study, Hyland (2008) shows how useful it can be to develop analytical systems that are closely adapted to the nature of the discourse from which the bundles are taken.

Byrd and Coxhead (2010) identified 73 lexical bundles that occurred at least 20 times per million words (that is, 9,904 occurrences in total) across 3.5 million words of arts, commerce, law, and science in Coxhead's written academic corpus from the AWL study. Law contained the largest percentage of lexical bundles at 5.44 percent, followed by Commerce at 2.65 percent of the total words in four-word set phrases. Seventy-three of the bundles are shared across all four disciplines (each bundle occurring at least 20 times per million words). After applying a uniformity principle, this list was pared down to 35 bundles. When this smaller list of bundles is compared to other lists developed by Biber, Conrad, and Cortes (2004) in university teaching and textbooks, and Hyland (2008), 21 bundles occurred in all three lists.

A recent study into the phraseology of academic texts comes from Simpson-Vlach and Ellis (2010) and their Academic Formulas List (AFL). This list was developed through an analysis of a corpus of academic speech, a corpus of academic writing and two matching non-academic corpora for comparison purposes. The researchers present three sub-lists. The first is the "core" AFL list of written and spoken formulas, and the others are the first 200 formulas of the spoken and written formulas from the different academic corpora. The authors categorize items from the three lists into various functions, for example, formulas of contrast and comparison such as *and the same* and *as opposed to* from the core AFL; *(nothing) to do* and *the same thing* which is primarily from spoken data; and *be related to the* and *is more likely* which is primarily from the written data. Readers might be interested to note that *blah, blah, blah* is a vagueness marker that is in the primarily spoken sub-list of the AFL (Simpson-Vlach and Ellis 2010).

With more and more such carefully designed and ground-breaking studies, a great deal more can be discovered about the kinds of multiword units needed by EAP and ESP students.

What are Some Challenges for Vocabulary in ESP?

One difficulty with identifying vocabulary for ESP is what to do with everyday words that take on a particular meaning in a specialized context, as mentioned early on in this chapter. Sutarsyah, Nation, and Kennedy's (1994) study found 34 words (such as *cost*, *supply*, and *average*) that were clearly connected to economics. These words appeared once out of every ten words on average. Furthermore, around twenty of these words are also in the first 1,000 words of the GSL (West 1953). The researchers compared the frequency of these words in the economics text and in a general academic corpus and found the words occurred more frequently in the specialized text.

These everyday words with specialized meanings could present some difficulties for teachers as learners struggle to learn new meanings and concepts for words that are already established in their lexicon in a particular way. In an interview as part of a study of specialized vocabulary in secondary school teaching in New Zealand, a secondary school science teacher explained that:

> Teaching biology is like teaching a language subject. For every known word students are familiar with, there is a biology word. For example, *dissolve* is not scientific English. It refers to solubility and insolubility. It relates to solute and solvent. Students have to be able to explain this meaning in a scientific context. If they use a scientific word in general terms, it will not be used in the correct way in normal language.

The point to make here is that the knowledge of the everyday meaning of the word is well established for this teacher's students. They know that sugar, for example, dissolves in water. But in their secondary school studies, these everyday words also have a specialized meaning, which makes words become technical. This new technical meaning requires her learners to build their knowledge of both the concept of a word and its meaning. The teacher uses a variety of techniques to teach these new meanings in the scientific context. She might deliberately not talk about a word like *respiration* using its everyday meaning in class. Instead, the teacher might just talk about *respiration* in chemical processes. In contrast, she might explore misconceptions about words with her students through asking their opinion of the meaning of a word, highlighting any misconception that arises, and giving the scientific point of view. Another approach is to break down words such as *photosynthesis* to show their constituent word parts.

Another reason why vocabulary in ESP can be challenging, according to Crawford Camiciottoli (2007: 138) is that specialized vocabulary "evolves and renews itself according to changing interests within communities of practice." In the case of Business English, as Crawford Camiciottoli notes, it is important to consider how professional texts in business and academic texts (including lectures as academic input) might use specialized vocabulary. That is, do university level texts contain the same vocabulary as professional texts in the same subject area?

Bringing Special Vocabulary into the Classroom

The purpose and methods of any corpus study need to be clear to teachers before they bring research findings into the classroom (Harding 2007). Byrd and Coxhead (2010: 51) list some questions teachers and learners might use to find out more about a list of specialized words including:

> Was the list derived from written and spoken corpora? What kinds of texts were included in the corpus? Are they representative of the reading of undergraduate or postgraduate learners? What principles of selection were used? How has the list been evaluated?

Nation (2001) outlines the kinds of knowledge learners need for understanding and using words. This kind of knowledge is important for everyday language and specialized words. Table 6.5 outlines the kind of knowledge learners need to produce a word in writing, including aspects of form, meaning, and use. A challenge for teachers and learners is ensuring that these kinds of learning are given attention as well as time and opportunity to develop.

One way to approach this teaching and learning problem is to apply Nation's four strands (2007) to create a balanced vocabulary program. Nation's four strands are meaning-focussed input (learning through reading and listening), meaning-focussed output (where learning is through writing and speaking), language-focussed learning (comprised of deliberate study of aspects of words such as how they are pronounced and spelled for example), and fluency development. Nation recommends that teachers consider the strands when designing vocabulary activities for the classroom. Hirsh and Coxhead (2009: 8) provide examples of activities that integrate Nation's four strands and a science-specific word list including, for example, using split information tasks with reading texts which fit into two of Nation's strands; meaning-focussed input and meaning-focussed output.

Table 6.5   Knowledge required for production of a word in writing (adapted from Nation 2001: 27)

Form		How is the word written and spelled?
Meaning	Form and meaning	What word form can be used to express this meaning?
	Concepts and referents	What items can this concept refer to?
	Associations	What other words can we use instead of this one?
Use	Grammatical function	In what patterns must we use this word?
	Collocations	What words or types of words must we use with this one?
	Constraints of use (register, frequency . . .)	Where, when, and how often can we use this word?

Another difficulty is that teachers tend to lack information on the use of target words and bundles (Byrd and Coxhead 2010). A good example of the kind of detail teachers need comes from Simpson-Vlach and Ellis (2010), who provide a rich description of the pragmatic functions they ascribe to various academic formulas. Figure 6.2 contains another example where Byrd and Coxhead (2010: 53) outline three main patterns for *on the basis of* from a written academic corpus. Figure 6.2 shows these three patterns and examples adapted from Byrd and Coxhead (2010: 53).

Note that the bundles in Figure 6.2 are surrounded by relatively dense academic prose. For some students, the bundle itself might not be as much of a challenge as the language that flanks it.

Currently, teachers and learners do not have many options in accessing corpora freely. One way to get such data is to use Tom Cobb's excellent website, the Compeat Lexical Tutor http://www.lextutor.ca/) (see Coxhead and Byrd (2007) for more on multiword units and how Cobb's website can be used to prepare writing teachers to teach academic grammar and vocabulary). Corpora such as MICASE lead the way in allowing teachers and learners to search online for examples of key words, lexical bundles, and formulas in use. (For more on various corpora that are available, see Schmitt 2010).

Conclusion

This chapter has looked at vocabulary in ESP from several perspectives. A great deal of research effort has gone into considering the nature of specialized vocabulary. This effort, however, does not equate in any way to the efforts that teachers

a. **Used at the beginning of a sentence:** In this use, *on the basis of* functions both to provide a transition and to specify methods or data used to carry out a process. This use needs an extended context to show how the phrase transitions and justifies as shown in this example from the AWL corpus:

... Clyne's research provides valuable information on the distribution of a large number of these languages in Australia (Clyne 1985, 1991; Clyne and Kipp1996). **On the basis of** *his analyses, Clyne also identifies a number of "unequivocally important" factors as relevant in accounting for different rates of language shift in different communities....*

b. **Used as an adverbial of reason in a passive sentence or clause to explain the way that a decision was made or data handled:**

Meanwhile, unskilled and unassisted migrants, most notably from Southern Europe, were accepted **on the basis of** *nomination by relatives in Australia....*

c. **Meaning strengthened or diminished with an adverbial:** *apparently, largely, normally, only, partly, primarily, purely, simply,* and *solely.*
Only for L. notosaurus was the decision on its specific distinction made **solely on the basis of** *allopatric data.*

Figure 6.2   Three main patterns for *on the basis of* (adapted from Byrd and Coxhead 2010: 53).

and learners make when teaching and learning vocabulary for ESP. Future research might focus on the nature of multiword units in different subjects and contexts in ESP, more research into vocabulary in ESP in languages other than English, and the development and use of multimodal corpora in this fast-moving field.

REFERENCES

Basturkmen, H. (2006) *Ideas and Options in English for Specific Purposes*. Mahwah, NJ: Lawrence Erlbaum.

Bauer, L. and Nation, P. (1993) Word families. *International Journal of Lexicography* 6: 253–79.

Biber, D. (2006) *University Language*. Amsterdam: John Benjamins.

Biber, D., Conrad, S., and Cortes, V. (2004) *If you look at . . .* : Lexical bundles in university teaching and textbooks. *Applied Linguistics* 25(3): 371–405.

Biber, D. and Barbieri, F. (2007) Lexical bundles in university spoken and written registers. *English for Specific Purposes* 26: 263–86.

Boers, F. (1997) "No pain, no gain" in a free market rhetoric: A test for cognitive semantics? *Metaphor and Symbol* 12: 231–41.

Byrd, P. and Coxhead, A. (2010) On the other hand: Lexical bundles in academic writing and in the teaching of EAP. *University of Sydney Papers in TESOL* 5:

31–64. Accessed February 2, 2012 at http://www-faculty.edfac.usyd.edu.au/projects/usp_in_tesol/volume05.htm.

Charteris-Black, J., and Musolff, A. A-. (2003) "Battered hero" or "innocent victim"? A comparative study of metaphors for euro trading in British and German financial reporting, *English for Specific Purposes* 22: 153–76.

Chen, Q. and Ge, G. (2007) A corpus-based lexical study on frequency and distribution of Coxhead's AWL word families in medical research articles. *English for Specific Purposes* 26: 502–14.

Chung, T. and Nation, P. (2003) Technical vocabulary in specialised texts. *Reading in a Foreign Language* 15: 103–16.

Chung, T. and Nation, P. (2004) Identifying technical vocabulary. *System* 32: 251–63.

Cobb, T. (nd) The Compleat Lexical Tutor. Accessed February 7, 2011 at http://www.lextutor.ca/ accessed.

Cobb, T. and Horst, M. (2004) Is there room for an AWL in French? In P. Bogaards and B. Laufer. (eds.), *Vocabulary in a Second Language: Selection, Acquisition, and Testing*. 15–38. Amsterdam: John Benjamins.

Cortes, V. (2004) Lexical bundles in published and student disciplinary writing: Examples from history and biology. *English for Specific Purposes* 23: 397–423.

Coxhead, A. (nd) The Academic Word List. Accessed January 14, 2011 at http://www.victoria.ac.nz/lals/staff/averil-coxhead.

Coxhead, A. (1998) The development and evaluation of a new academic word list. Unpublished MA thesis, Victoria University of Wellington, New Zealand.

Coxhead, A. (2000) A new academic word list. *TESOL Quarterly* 34(2): 213–38.

Coxhead, A. (2006). *Essentials of Teaching Academic Vocabulary*. Boston: Houghton Mifflin.

Coxhead, A. (2011) The academic word list 10 years On: Research and teaching implications. *TESOL Quarterly* 45: 355–62.

Coxhead, A. and Byrd, P. (2007) Preparing writing teachers to teach the vocabulary and grammar of academic prose. *Journal of Second Language Writing* 16: 129–47.

Coxhead, A. and Hirsh, D. (2007) A pilot science word list for EAP. *Revue Française de Linguistique Appliquée* XII: 65–78.

Coxhead, A., Stevens, L., and Tinkle. J. (2010) Why might secondary science textbooks be difficult to read? *New Zealand Studies in AppliedLlinguistics* 16(2): 35–52.

Crawford Camiciottoli, B. (2007) *The Language of Business Studies Lectures*. Amsterdam: John Benjamins.

Harding, K. (2007) *English for Specific Purposes*. Oxford: Oxford University Press.

Hirsh, D. and Coxhead, A. (2009) Ten ways of focussing on science-specific vocabulary in EAP. *EA Journal* 25: 5–16.

Hyland, K. (2008) *As can be seen*: Lexical bundles and disciplinary variation. *English for Specific Purposes* 27: 4–21.

Hyland, K and Tse, P. (2007) Is there an "academic vocabulary"? *TESOL Quarterly* 41: 235–53.

Konstantakis, N. (2007). Creating a Business Word List for teaching Business English. *Elia*, 7:, 79–102.

Li, Y. and Qian, D. (2010) Profiling the Academic Word List (AWL) in a financial corpus. *System* 38: 402–11.

Littlemore, J., Chen, P., Tang, P. L., Koester, A., and Barnden, J. (2010). The use of metaphor and metonomy in academic and professional discourse and their challenges for learners and teachers of English. In S. De Knop, F. Boers, and A. De Rycker (Eds.), *Fostering language teaching efficiency through cognitive linguistics*. 189–211. Berlin: Mouton de Gruyter.

Martínez, I. A., Beck, S. C., and Panza, C. B. (2009). Academic vocabulary in agriculture research articles. *English for Specific Purposes*, 28:, 183–198.

Nation, P. (2001) *Learning Vocabulary in Another Language*. Cambridge: Cambridge University Press.

Nation, P. (2007) The four strands. *Innovation in Language Learning and Teaching* 1: 2–13.

Nation, P. (2008) *Teaching Vocabulary: Strategies and Techniques*. Boston: Heinle Cengage.

Nation, P. and Webb, S. (2010) *Researching and Analyzing Vocabulary*. Boston: Heinle Cengage.

Nelson, M. (nd) Mike Nelson's Business English Lexis Site. Accessed at February 3, 2011 http://users.utu.fi/micnel/business_english_lexis_site.htm.

Pickering, L. and Byrd, P. (2008) In D. Belcher and A. Hirvela (eds.), *The Oral-Literate Connection: Perspectives on L2 Speaking, Writing, and Other Media Interactions*. 110–32. Ann Arbor, MI: University of Michigan Press.

Pinna, A. (2007) Exploiting LSP corpora in the study of foreign languages. In D. Gálová (ed.), *Languages for Specific Purposes: Searching for Common Solutions*. 146–62. Newcastle, UK: Cambridge Scholars Publishing.

Read, J. (2007) Second language vocabulary assessment. *International Journal of English Studies* 7: 105–25.

Schmitt, N. (2010) *Researching Vocabulary*. Basingstoke, UK: Palgrave Macmillan.

Simpson-Vlach, R. and Ellis, N. (2010) An academic formulas list: New methods in phraseology research. *Applied Linguistics* 31(4): 487–512.

Skorczynska Sznajder, H. (2010) A corpus-based evaluation of metaphors in a

Business English textbook. *English for Specific Purposes* 29: 30–42.

Sutarsyah, C., Nation, P., and Kennedy, G. (1994) How useful is EAP vocabulary for ESP? A corpus based case study. *RELC Journal* 25(2): 34–50.

University of Michigan English Language Institute (nd) The Michigan Corpus of Academic Spoken English (MICASE). Ann Arbor, MI: University of Michigan English Language Institute. Accessed at February 12, 2012. http://quod.lib.umich.edu/m/micase/.

Viphavee V., Ju-yu Huang, J., Yu-Chia Chang, Y. C. (2009). Frequency analysis of the words in the Academic Word List (AWL) and non-AWL content words in applied linguistics research papers. *English for Specific Purposes*, 28: 33–41.

Wang J., Liang, S. I., and Ge, G. (2008) Establishment of a medical academic word list. *English for Specific Purposes* 27: 442–58.

Ward, J. (1999) How large a vocabulary do EAP engineering students need? *Reading in a Foreign Language* 12(2): 309–24.

Ward, J. (2009) A basic engineering English word list for less proficient foundation engineering undergraduates. *English for Specific Purposes* 28(3): 170–82.

West, M. (1953) *A General Service List of English Words*. London: Longman, Green and Co.

Woodward-Kron, R. (2008) More than just jargon – the nature and roles of specialist knowledge in learning disciplinary knowledge. *Journal of English for Academic Purposes* 7: 234–49.

Part II Areas of ESP Research

Belcher's (2009) volume *English for Specific Purposes in Theory and Practice* provides examples of the many areas in which English for specific purposes (ESP) teachers are now working and which are also increasingly the focus of research. This includes well-established fields such as English for academic purposes through to newer areas such as the use of English in call-center communications (Lockwood et al. 2009). Other areas, such as Business English are reconsidered from the points of view of intercultural communication (Planken and Nickerson 2009) and the increasing use of multimodality in written communications (Nickerson and Planken 2009). English for academic purposes (EAP) is extended into more specialized areas such as graduate writing (Feak 2009), writing for publication (Hyland 2009) and English for academic purposes in the context of secondary school education (Cruickshank 2009). Each of these chapters point to the many new directions in which ESP teaching and research is heading. Equally, an increasing number of authors of ESP research are no longer from what Kachru (2011) describes as the "Inner Circle" of countries that use English. ESP research is clearly not the property of the English-speaking world, nor is it taking place in solely English-speaking countries, a point made by Belcher in the closing chapter of this volume.

ESP research, then, has come a long way, there are many new locations in which it is taking place, and there are new and exciting directions in which it is heading. This section of the *Handbook* reviews key areas of ESP research, both in terms of where they have come from, as well as where they are going.

In the opening chapter of this section Maggie Charles reviews research in the area of English for academic purposes. In particular, she discusses corpus-based EAP research, genre-based EAP research, and research that examines EAP as a set

The Handbook of English for Specific Purposes, First Edition.
Edited by Brian Paltridge and Sue Starfield.
© 2013 John Wiley & Sons, Inc. Published 2013 by John Wiley & Sons, Inc.

of social practices within institutional and global contexts. In the chapter on English for science and technology (EST) Jean Parkinson reviews work on the rhetorical structures of EST genres, the language and vocabulary of EST texts, as well as visual elements and multimodal aspects of EST genres. The chapter by Meredith Marra, which follows, outlines research into English in the workplace, much of it based on a sociolinguistics framework. She discusses, in particular, research into the use of English in corporate and professional environments. To illustrate the points she is making she describes a workplace communication project for skilled migrants that she is currently involved in at her university. Francesca Bargiela-Chiappini and Zuocheng Zhang in their chapter on Business English, after an overview of developments in Business English research, focus on a rather different context, the use of English for business purposes in Asia, in particular Japan and China. Much of the work they describe, importantly, has been carried out by non-native speaker researchers who bring very interesting insiders' perspectives to their research.

Jill Northcott's chapter on Legal English reviews research developments in the areas of forensic linguistics, language and the law, and translation studies. She then discusses the impact of the common law origins of Legal English before describing specific developments in research into Legal English. In her chapter on Aviation English, Carol Lynn Moder expands on a topic that first came up in Christine Feak's chapter on ESP and speaking. As Feak points out in her chapter, communication in aviation settings is extremely high-stakes and is, as she says, a precondition to safe aircraft navigation. In the chapter on English for medical purposes (EMP) Gibson Ferguson provides an overview of health communication research, before turning to the rise of English as an international language of medical research. He then discusses language-related research in English for medical purposes, including genre studies and research into grammatical and vocabulary features of Medical English. He concludes his chapter with a discussion of types of EMP courses and teaching materials. The chapter by Susan Bosher which follows describes English for nursing research and, in particular, academic strategies and skills, discipline-specific skills, and cultural skills and content in English for nursing courses. Language tasks and skills required of nurses in clinical settings are also discussed as are specific language and communication needs of students in this area.

The final chapters in this section represent developments in ESP research that have only relatively recently gained prominence in the area. The chapter on thesis and dissertation writing by Paul Thompson describes a further area that is gaining increased attention in ESP research. Theses and dissertations, as Thompson points out, differ from other advanced academic genres such as research articles in their purposes, scale, audience, and the requirements they need to meet. They have not, however, been as extensively researched as research articles, partly due to the size of theses and dissertations as texts for analysis (Swales 1990; Thompson 1999) as well as the difficulty, on occasion, of gaining sets of sample texts. Thompson reviews the research that has been carried out in this area as well as pointing to areas of further research needed on this topic.

The chapter by John Flowerdew reviews research in an equally new area, the use of English for research publication purposes. As he points out, the amount of research publication in English across the world is huge and there is an ever-increasing number of authors who are writing for publication in their second language. There are, however, many inequalities in this publishing and the dominance of English is a significant contributor to this. Flowerdew describes theory and methods that have been employed in research in this area as a way of trying to understand the challenges these writers face as well as finding ways in which they can be supported in this process.

REFERENCES

Belcher, D. (2009) (ed.) *English for Specific Purposes in Theory And Practice*. Ann Arbor. MI: University of Michigan Press.

Cruickshank, K. (2009) EAP in secondary schools. In D. Belcher (ed.), *English For Specific Purposes in Theory and Practice*. 22–40. Ann Arbor, MI: University of Michigan Press.

Feak, C. B. (2009) Setting the stage for scholarly evaluation: Research commentaries in the EAP graduate writing curriculum. In D. Belcher (ed.), *English for Specific Purposes in Theory and Practice*. 60–82. Ann Arbor, MI: University of Michigan Press.

Kachru, Y. (2011) World Englishes: Contexts and relevance for language education. In E. Hinkel (ed.), *Handbook of Research in Second Language Teaching and Learning*. 2nd ed. 155–73. Mahwah, NJ: Lawrence Erlbaum.

Hyland, K. (2009) English for professional academic purposes: Writing for scholarly publication. In D. Belcher (ed.), *English for Specific Purposes in Theory and Practice*. 83–105. Ann Arbor, MI: University of Michigan Press.

Lockwood, J., Forey, G., and Elias, N. (2009) Call center communication: Measurement processes in non-English speaking contexts. In D. Belcher (ed.), *English for Specific Purposes in Theory and Practice*. 165–85. Ann Arbor, MI: University of Michigan Press.

Nickerson, C. and Planken, B. (2009) English for specific business purposes: Written business English and the increasing influence of multimodality. In D. Belcher (ed.), *English for Specific Purposes in Theory and Practice*. 127–42. Ann Arbor, MI: University of Michigan Press.

Planken, B. and Nickerson, C. (2009) English for specific business purposes: Intercultural issues and the use of business English. In D. Belcher (ed.), *English for Specific Purposes in Theory and Practice*. 107–26. Ann Arbor, MI: University of Michigan Press.

Swales, J. M. (1990) *Genre Analysis. English in Academic and Research Settings*. Cambridge: Cambridge University Press.

Thompson, P. (1999) Exploring the contexts of writing: Interviews with PhD supervisors. In P. Thompson (ed.), *Issues in EAP Writing Research and Instruction*. 37–54. Reading, UK: Centre for Applied Language Studies, University of Reading.

7 English for Academic Purposes

MAGGIE CHARLES

Introduction

English for academic purposes (EAP) is concerned with researching and teaching the English needed by those who use the language to perform academic tasks. The field originally arose out of the wider area of English for specific purposes (ESP) and over the last two decades has increased enormously in importance, driven by the global growth in the use of English for employment, as well as academic research. Although most often applied to university level contexts and non-native speakers of English (NNSE), the term is very broad, covering, for example, both the requirements of native-speaker (NSE) secondary school students who have to read textbooks and write essays, as well as those of academics who need to give conference presentations and write research articles (RA). EAP has thus become a major research field in its own right, responding to the demands of a widening circle of users by providing increasingly sophisticated accounts of academic discourse and translating these insights into pedagogically valid methods and materials.

I will address this extensive topic by viewing EAP from three angles, each based on a different approach: corpus-based work, genre analysis, and investigation of the social context. The chapter therefore moves from a narrow-angle to a wide-angle view of EAP. It starts by surveying the contribution of corpora to the detailed description of academic discourse and its pedagogy; in the next section, attention shifts to whole texts and groups of texts examined through the use of genre analysis; finally, the view widens to consider EAP as constituting a set of social practices within institutional and global contexts. Each section highlights some of the issues that currently concern members of the field, points out areas

The Handbook of English for Specific Purposes, First Edition.
Edited by Brian Paltridge and Sue Starfield.
© 2013 John Wiley & Sons, Inc. Published 2013 by John Wiley & Sons, Inc.

that are currently under-represented in the literature and offers some suggestions for future research. The chapter shows how, although the priorities of these three approaches diverge, researchers are increasingly combining and integrating all three to achieve multifaceted and "thicker" accounts of EAP.

EAP and Corpora

A corpus can be defined as a collection of texts compiled according to set criteria and in EAP, as in many other areas of language study, their use has had an enormous impact. In particular, descriptions of academic discourse derived from large corpora have been used in the production of reference materials (e.g. Biber et al. 1999). Several large EAP corpora have also recently become available to researchers and teachers, including the British Academic Written Corpus (BAWE) (http://wwwm.coventry.ac.uk/researchnet/BAWE) and the Michigan Corpus of Upper-level Student Papers (MICUSP) (http://micusp.elicorpora.info/), both of which contain high-grade texts written by undergraduate and graduate students. The equivalent corpora for spoken discourse are the Michigan Corpus of Academic speech (MICASE) (http://quod.lib.umich.edu/m/micase/), which contains material from several different types of speech events and the British Academic Spoken English Corpus (BASE) (http://wwwm.coventry.ac.uk/researchnet/base), which consists of lectures and seminars. Small specialist corpora also have an important role to play in researching and teaching EAP (Tribble 2002) and many studies are based on corpora that are specialized by discipline and/or genre.

Corpora are often considered to have two major roles in language learning, both of which are relevant to their role in EAP: *direct* and *indirect* (Leech 1997). Their *direct* role is as a pedagogic tool; they are used with or by students for language learning purposes in the classroom. Their *indirect* use is to provide the data and research knowledge upon which pedagogical materials are based. I will deal first with some of the indirect uses.

Corpus investigation allows the observation of repeated patterns in large quantities of data and thus enables evidence-based descriptions of academic registers to be provided. In particular, the technique of multidimensional analysis, pioneered by Biber and co-workers, has described the distinguishing features of spoken and written university discourse (Biber 2006). This work shows, for example, that spoken registers (e.g. class teaching, service encounters) are characterized by features typical of interpersonal involvement and spontaneous production, while written registers (e.g. administrative information, textbooks) exhibit features associated with prepared production and high informational content. Biber and Gray (2010) go further to argue that traditional descriptions of academic writing as elaborate and explicit are misguided. They find that academic writing is typically characterized by modification within the noun phrase and is thus compressed rather than elaborate. They make the point that this condensed style is less explicit and therefore more difficult for novices to handle. Register description using multidimensional analysis has also been carried out on written learner discourse. Research on the BAWE corpus shows that at each academic level from first year undergraduate to Masters there is a gradual increase in informational features and a concomitant decrease in narrative features of the texts (Nesi and Gardner 2011). Thus students gradually adjust their production so that their writing comes to reflect the typical features of expert academic registers.

The compilation of large-scale learner corpora such as the International Corpus of Learner English (http://www.uclouvain.be/en-cecl-icle.html) has facilitated comparisons between first language (L1) and second language (L2) production. Set up by Granger and co-workers (Granger et al. 2009), this corpus consists of essays written in English by students from many different L1 backgrounds and investigations of this data have shown systematic variation in L2 production according to students' L1 (Gilquin, Granger, and Paquot 2007). Learner corpora have also been valuable in pinpointing several areas of particular difficulty for L2 learners, including for example, collocation (Nesselhauf 2003) and metadiscourse (Hyland 2005; Luzón Marco 2010). In a recent critical review of the field, Granger (2009) argues that the rigorous analysis of learner corpora has an important role to play in the design of appropriate corpus-informed pedagogical materials for EAP.

Another focus of corpus studies has been on describing the specific features of academic discourse and its phraseology and one of its achievements has been to reveal the characteristics of different disciplines and genres (e.g. Hyland 2000). Recent examples include Camiciottoli's (2007) analysis of the language of business studies lectures, work on the expression of stance (Fløttum, Dahl, and Kinn 2006; Tognini-Bonelli and Del Lungo Camiciotti 2005) and on individual lexico-grammatical features such as introductory *it* patterns (Groom 2005) and conditionals (Carter-Thomas and Rowley-Jolivet 2008). A particularly active strand of this research examines recurrent word sequences, known also as "lexical bundles," "formulaic sequences," multi-word units," and "n-grams." Biber, Conrad, and Cortes (2004) stress their importance and identify their three major functions: constructing stance, organizing discourse, and making reference. Lexical bundles have been found to vary in structure and function according to spoken and written registers (Biber et al. 2004) as well as discipline and genre (Hyland 2008). Given that they characterize the expert discourse of specific academic communities, it is especially important for novice members to master their use (Hyland and Tse 2007). However, differences have been reported between L1 and L2 production: L1 experts use the widest range of bundles and L2 students use certain expressions which are not employed by professionals (Chen and Baker 2010; Römer 2009).

Specialist lexis is another important aspect of research in EAP and corpora have been used in the compilation of academic wordlists, one of the most recent and widely used being the Academic Word List (AWL) (Coxhead 2000). This aims to distinguish the most frequent items of general academic vocabulary, presenting them in 570 word families. However, the utility of general academic wordlists has been questioned by Hyland and Tse (2007), who argue that words are used in different ways in different disciplines and that only discipline-specific lists can be valid and pedagogically useful. In support of this view, Chen and Ge (2007) find that the AWL does not adequately account for the academic words in medical RAs. Paquot (2010) attempts to resolve the issue by distinguishing the core vocabulary of academic activities and proposes an Academic Keywords List. Recently, attention has been drawn to the importance of extending wordlists to incorporate frequent collocations (Coxhead 2008; Durrant 2009). To this end, Simpson-Vlach and Ellis (2010) present a list of 3–5 word formulaic expressions derived from spoken and written corpus data and selected according to a new empirically based measure called "formula teaching worth." Their lists distinguish formulas that are frequent in each register and items are grouped according to functional categories, making them particularly well suited to pedagogic use.

So far, then, we have reviewed some of the indirect applications of corpus work and highlighted their important contribution to the field of EAP. Next we turn attention to the direct use of corpus data with students. As early as 1991, Johns advocated "data-driven learning" (DDL), arguing that presenting language data directly to students fostered an inductive approach and led to greater learner autonomy. Johns' work was concerned with teaching academic writing to tertiary-level students and to date, most courses reported in the literature still have this aim. Kaltenböck and Mehlmauer-Larcher (2005) provide a useful list of linguistic features particularly suitable for corpus work, including, for example, lexis, semantic prosody, and grammaticality. Among recent studies with a lexico-grammatical focus are Cresswell's (2007) work on teaching connectors and two reports on the use of corpora to teach university-level grammar courses (Estling, Vannestål, and Lindquist 2007; Granath 2009). Mudraya (2006) integrates the lexical approach with DDL in a course for engineering students, while Hafner and Candlin (2007) introduce corpus use to improve students' legal writing assignments. A novel approach is taken by Lee and Swales (2006), whose doctoral students compile and consult personalized corpora in their own fields. In addition to reports on classroom applications, there have been recent studies describing online materials dealing with, for example, connectors (Tseng and Liou 2006) and academic lexis (Horst, Cobb, and Nicolae. 2005). Oksefjell Ebeling's (2009) course comprises a range of exercises on written discourse, while the MICASE website provides a wealth of material to practice spoken language.

However, criticisms that corpus approaches can appear "fragmented" have been voiced by among others Swales (2002) and L. Flowerdew (2002), who argues that corpus work in EAP has over-emphasized local lexico-grammatical concerns. She advocates a redressing of the balance in favor of more extended discourse patterns and there is some evidence that this is increasingly happening. Lynne Flowerdew (2008) herself presents a study on teaching the problem–solution pattern in student report writing; Charles (2007, 2011) uses corpora of theses to teach rhetorical functions; Bianchi and Pazzaglia (2007) describe materials on teaching the research article, and Gavioli (2005) on the abstract.

Research has recently also begun to focus on evaluating the effectiveness of direct corpus approaches and their acceptability to students. Frankenberg-Garcia (2005) gives an insight into how students of translation make use of corpora and describes some of the pitfalls they encounter, while Breyer (2009) stresses the value of concordance work in stimulating reflection on a teacher-training course. Detailed assessment has been carried out both through self-reporting by students (Charles 2011; Granath 2009; Yoon 2008; Yoon and Hirvela 2004) and by empirical means (Boulton 2010; Cobb 1997; Cresswell 2007). Significant improvements in learners' English have been shown for vocabulary and grammar/usage, but the evidence is not always clear-cut (Boulton 2009; Cresswell 2007) and attitudes, although often favorable, can also vary.

As this section has shown, corpora have contributed much to EAP, particularly in terms of indirect uses, which provide corpus data on written discourse. However, given the very wide range of disciplines and genres to be described, there are still many areas that are under-researched. The development of new, more specialized corpora, including learner corpora, would contribute much to this effort. As far as spoken academic discourse is concerned, there is even more to be done. In particular, the development of video corpora (Fortanet-Gómez and Querol-Julián 2010) and multimodal concordancers (Ackerley and Cocchetta 2007) offer exciting new possibilities. With regard to direct uses of corpora, as Römer (2010) points out, there is a general need to create more DDL and corpus-informed materials which take into account the views and needs of both teachers and learners. It is also vital to popularize corpus approaches through providing training and creating corpus tools that are user-friendly (L. Flowerdew 2009). Finally, if corpus approaches are really to take off, teachers must be convinced of their benefits, which entails further research to test their effectiveness.

EAP and Genre

The notion of genre has proved extremely valuable and productive in the analysis and pedagogy of EAP and has been associated with three different approaches deriving from different traditions (Hyon 1996). Seeing genre as "social action" (Miller 1984), the Rhetorical Genre Studies (RGS) approach emphasizes the dynamic nature of genres and focuses particularly upon the contextual circumstances of their production. A somewhat different emphasis is reflected in the definition of genre as a "staged, goal-oriented social process" (Martin and Rose 2003: 7), which is put forward by researchers who base their work on systemic functional linguistics (SFL) (Halliday 1994). Arising out of the need for explicit teaching of socially valued genres in schools, this work lays more stress on the linguistic and discoursal features that characterize specific genres. A similar text-based approach is shared by the ESP tradition of move analysis, which is particularly associated with the work of Swales (1990, 2004) and Bhatia (1993, 2004). In his seminal book *Genre Analysis*, Swales draws attention to the important role of the discourse community by defining a genre as "a class of communicative events, the members of which share some set of communicative purposes" (1990: 58).

Common to the three approaches, however, is a conception of genres as situated social practices and thus they all share a concern with both the social contexts as well as the linguistic features of genres. Indeed, Tardy (2011) argues that earlier tensions between the three traditions have now become productive, with researchers employing multiple approaches, while Swales (2011: 3) goes further to suggest that, as far as pedagogical applications are concerned, they have "largely coalesced." Certainly, recent research on genre has been widened and deepened not only by developing earlier lines of enquiry, but by combining approaches and by applying new tools and techniques.

Writing from an RGS perspective, Coe underlines the importance of the relationship between a genre and the situation that evokes it. He defines genre as a "culturally typical structure that embodies a socially-appropriate strategy for responding to varied situations" (Johns et al. 2006: 245). Thus the specific form that a genre takes is a realization of the strategy that has developed in response to a recurring situation. This emphasis on strategy leads to a concomitant stress on the features of the genre-evoking situation and RGS approaches often make use of ethnographic data in their analysis of social context, as illustrated by Reiff's student materials on analysing genres (Johns et al. 2006). Molle and Prior's (2008) study also employs ethnographic methods, which lead them to highlight three important dimensions of genres: their membership of sets and systems, their multimodality, and their hybridity. They suggest that investigation of these dimensions can serve as the basis for EAP courses that seek to develop an awareness of "multimodal genre systems."

The multimodal nature of genres is also highlighted by Martin and Rose (2008). They provide an updated account of the theory which underlies the SFL approach, defining genre as "a configuration of meanings, realized through language and attendant modalities of communication" (2008: 20). To illustrate the importance of multimodality, they extend the study of science genres to take account of the complex interplay between text and visuals. Martin and Rose also focus on the hybridity and blending of genres, exemplified in their analysis of the way in which the genres of report and argument have been fused to create a new school genre in ecology. Another recent SFL genre analysis is Coffin's (2006) book length study of historical discourse, which traces the increasing complexity of the genres encountered by pupils as they move through their secondary school years. In a further extension of the SFL approach, Nesi and Gardner (2011) employ multidimensional analysis as well as ethnographic methods. Both textual and ethnographic data are used to identify the genres of student writing and group them into 13 families, while multidimensional analysis highlights the differences between the genre families. Nesi and Gardner's work provides the first extensive description of the genres of assessed student writing and opens the possibility for further fine-grained analyses.

Swales, too, has expanded his earlier account, suggesting that genres can be understood in terms of six metaphors: as *frames for social action, language standards, biological species, families and prototypes, institutions,* and *speech acts* (Swales 2004: 68). These metaphors indicate some of the aspects of genre which can be highlighted in research. Certain of them, such as genre as *language standard* have been foregrounded in the literature, as exemplified by the work of Hyland on disciplinary differences between genres (2005, 2008). Others, however, such as genre as *biological species* have received less attention.

Move analysis has also been extended by the use of an ethnographic approach (Bhatia 2004) and by the incorporation of a cognitive dimension (Bruce 2008). It has been applied to a wider range of genres, focussing recently not only on expert RAs (Lim 2010), but also on student productions, especially theses (Bunton 2005; Kwan 2006; Samraj 2008) and on the comparison of expert and novice writing (Basturkmen 2009). Less studied and occluded genres have been investigated such as the course syllabus (Afros and Schryer 2009) and the funding proposal (Koutsantoni 2009). Spoken genres have also attracted some attention, with Aguilar's (2004) investigation of peer seminars and Lee's (2008) comparison of introductions to lectures in large and small classes. Another fertile area of application for move analysis lies in cross-linguistic contrastive studies; recently, for example, introductions in English have been compared with their counterparts in Chinese (Loi 2010) and Brazilian Portuguese (Hirano 2009).

Much of the early work on text-based approaches to genre used the tools of discourse analysis to identify generic elements by hand in relatively small numbers of texts. More recently, however, corpora have been used as the source of data, and the application of corpus-based approaches has become the norm. Indeed researchers are increasingly using corpus tools such as annotation and keyword identification to identify signals of moves and move boundaries. Lynne Flowerdew (1998) was one of the first to suggest the application of corpus techniques to the investigation of generic elements. Her (2008) work on student and professional reports shows how specific keywords are typically used to realize problem and solution moves in this genre, while in a similar vein, John Flowerdew and Forest (2009) examine the role of the keyword *research* in indicating a gap in the PhD literature review.

An important step towards fully automating the identification of generic structure has been taken by Biber and co-workers (Biber et al. 2007). In this work, the unit of analysis is the "vocabulary-based discourse unit" (VBDU), which is identified by automatically segmenting the text according to linguistic rather than functional criteria. VBDUs are analyzed and grouped using multidimensional and cluster analysis and then generic structure is distinguished by reference to sequences of preferred VBDU types. In an interesting comparison of approaches, Biber et al. present two contrasting analyses of biochemistry and biology research articles, one using the traditional method of coding generic elements manually according to their function and the other employing VBDU analysis. The two approaches show considerable, though not complete, agreement on generic structure and, as Biber et al. point out, VBDU analysis has the advantage that it can be implemented with large corpora, thus providing a sound quantitative basis for genre identification and description.

Presentations and descriptions related to the teaching of genres are less frequent in the literature (Johns 2011). However, pedagogical concerns are specifically addressed by Cargill and O'Connor (2006), who use expert collaborators in a workshop approach, while Cheng (2011) takes a rather different line, arguing that students can perceive the contextual dimensions of a genre from its textual features. In a wide-ranging discussion of genre-based writing instruction, Johns (2011) suggests that a suitable approach for novice EAP writers would be one that starts with attention to the text and progresses first to a consideration of context and finally to carrying out a critique. This development would allow for an integration of textual and contextual approaches to genre analysis and should thus enable students to gain better understanding and increased proficiency in their target genres.

As Tardy (2006) notes, genres are highly complex and the gradual combining and blending of approaches that has taken place reflects that complexity and has led to fuller accounts of genres. However, while much work has been done on the major disciplines and the most highly valued genres, there are still many that remain unexamined, with spoken genres, in particular, still under-researched. Another area which deserves further attention is that of genre networks (Swales 2004), establishing the intertextual links between genres and the recontextualizations necessitated by a move from one genre to another. There is also scope for more research on the application of corpus methods, particularly on developing corpus-assisted move analysis, with the eventual goal of automatic identification of generic structure. Finally, as noted above, there is a scarcity of work on the pedagogical applications of genre analysis, and more studies that present and evaluate genre-based instruction would be very valuable.

EAP and Social Context

We now turn attention to research that investigates EAP in its wider social context, including its position as a set of social practices both within institutions and globally. Early work of this type focussed on academic discourse as a socially constructed phenomenon and on the student's socialization into the disciplinary community (Bazerman 1988; Berkenkotter and Huckin 1995). More recent studies have employed a variety of approaches, often combining methods to shed light on the social dimensions of EAP practices. Thus Hyland (2009) uses corpus investigation together with interview data to examine engagement, as does Pecorari (2008), who investigates source use and plagiarism. Discourse-based interviews are also employed by Harwood (2009) to look at citation and by Kwan (2009) to elucidate the reading practices of doctoral students.

One of the approaches which seeks to foreground the social dimension of EAP is termed "academic literacies" (Lea and Street 2006). Employing a critical ethnographic perspective, researchers seek to move away from what they see as a bias towards the text and to examine EAP as embedded in its specific sociocultural context. This approach highlights the complex and contested nature of academic practices and the lack of equality in the power relations that underlie them. Thus Hasrati and Street (2009) examine student and supervisor interview data and take into consideration disciplinary differences in the funding environment in their account of the process of PhD topic choice, while Lillis (2001) examines the social practices affecting the writing of students entering higher education from backgrounds that are not traditionally academic. Academic literacies researchers take a stance that is essentially "transformative" (Lillis and Scott 2007), in that they acknowledge the legitimacy of the resources that students bring to the academy and seek to develop alternative practices that would validate them (Lea and Street 2006).

This transformative approach is often contrasted with the normative tendency of much EAP research, which identifies academic practices in order to induct students into them, accommodating rather than problematizing the status quo. The question of whether to adopt an accommodationist or critical stance originates in work on critical EAP (CEAP) by Pennycook (1997) and Benesch (2001), who argue that viewing EAP in pragmatic terms neglects the social and political context in which teaching takes place. Accordingly, CEAP stresses the importance of "reflexivity and interrogation" in "situated praxis" (Benesch 2009); it often draws on topics arising from the daily lives of students, encouraging them to reflect on and question the issue raised, a procedure which opens up the possibility of challenge or change. Thus Starfield and Ravelli (2006) argue for expanding the options available to students writing doctoral dissertations, while Casanave's (2010) study describes an instance of how such a modification of academic conventions may occur. A review of CEAP work is provided by Morgan and Ramanathan (2005) and further theoretical and pedagogical accounts can be found in the special issue of *Journal of English for Academic Purposes* (2009) and the volume edited by Norton and Toohey (2004).

Within the wider context of the global position of EAP, an area of increasing importance has arisen from the widespread adoption of English as the language of research publication and the position of NNSE scholars in relation to this globalized research world. English has been characterized not only as a lingua franca which facilitates the efficient dissemination of knowledge, but also as a *Tyrannosaurus Rex* which establishes a linguistic hegemony, thereby disadvantaging NNSE scholars and marginalizing their contribution to research (Swales 1997; Tardy 2004). Work in this area also takes into account the perspectives of scholars at the periphery, who operate outside the major centers of research production (Canagarajah 1996). It has led to the development of a new sub-field, English for research publication purposes (ERPP), with a special issue of *Journal of English for Academic Purposes* (2008) devoted to this topic.

Researchers in ERPP focus not just on linguistic issues, but more generally on the social and political circumstances which influence the participation of NNSE and/or "peripheral" scholars in the international research community. It has been pointed out by many that such scholars experience increasing pressure to publish in English (e.g. Belcher 2007; J. Flowerdew 2001; J. Flowerdew and Li 2009; Lillis and Curry 2010). This may be due to a number of factors, including institutional policies of recruitment and promotion, as well as the desire to contribute to the knowledge base and achieve international visibility. Despite this trend, as Flowerdew and Li (2009) note for the Chinese context, research in certain areas, for example, humanities and social sciences, may continue to flourish in more than one language and in some cases, the predominance of English may be resisted (Li 2007; Li and J. Flowerdew 2009).

There are several aspects of the globalization of the research world that may adversely affect NNSE scholars' ability to get published. The quality of the language is a key concern for J. Flowerdew (2008), who argues that "poor language" is an important factor in the rejection of manuscripts and that it exerts a disproportionately negative effect upon NNSE scholars. Salager-Meyer (2008) concurs, while Lillis and Curry (2010) note that the time cost involved in writing in an L2 may lead to a reduced research output. A further issue of concern is that cultural differences may affect the rhetorical structure of the text and that mismatches with reader expectations may be seen by reviewers and editors as evidence of incompetence. The extent to which diversity from rhetorical norms may be acceptable is queried by Ha (2009). However Belcher (2009) finds evidence to suggest a decrease in diversity, at least with regard to RA introductions.

Other issues that may affect publication success are a lack of resources and contact with leading research communities, which may make it difficult for peripheral scholars to keep up with current developments and to situate their work appropriately. This can make research from the periphery seem dated or too local to be of interest to an international audience and may lead to rejection by reviewers and editors. It has been argued that similar weaknesses may be characteristic of all novice writers (Casanave 2008; Swales 2004). Belcher (2007), for example, investigates the publication process by examining NNSE and NSE submissions from both central and peripheral research contexts and notes that reviewers mention many similar reasons for rejection, including lack of knowledge about relevant topics, the literature and the expectations of the journal. Nonetheless, while all novice scholars are likely to experience some of the same problems in getting their work published, there is a wealth of evidence which suggests that being an NNSE places extra burdens on the prospective research writer. These are well summarized by Uzuner (2008) in her review of work that investigates NNSE scholars' participation in global research.

Several studies have made suggestions for improving this situation. On an individual level, Belcher (2007) advises would-be contributors to journals to exercise patience and persistence, a view echoed by Salager-Meyer (2008), while reviewers and editors are recommended to be clear and constructive in their comments. Lillis and Curry's (2010) approach of compiling and analyzing text histories enables them to distinguish the crucial role of what they call "literacy brokers," that is mediators who are involved in shaping the text as it passes through various stages on the way to publication. Both Salager-Meyer (2008) and Li and J. Flowerdew (2009) address the wider sociopolitical context by calling for the establishment of regional centers, whose task would be to promote the visibility and strengthen the international importance of non-center research. A different approach is taken by, among others, Mauranen, Hynninen, and Ranta (2010), who regard English as a lingua franca (ELF) as a distinct variety of English. They argue that, as most users of EAP are not NSEs, it is important to question the traditional adherence to the NSE standard. Instead, they advocate researching the practices of effective users and have compiled the ELFA corpus of spoken academic ELF to facilitate further investigation.

From this brief review of approaches which take into account the social context of EAP, it is clear that there are several areas of research that are currently under development and are likely to grow in significance in the future. Work on ERPP is of major importance and it would be useful if the concept of "publication" were expanded to include spoken communication. Further research is needed, for example, on the stages involved in the delivery of a conference presentation, a seminar or a lecture and on the roles and practices of those involved. Studies which focus more widely on all the EAP needs of junior faculty members and which examine how these could be addressed would also be of great value. Another area where more work is still needed concerns novice EAP students. Here, longitudinal studies of students' development taking into account course demands and tutors' attitudes could help determine effective practices. In both these areas, the use of corpus techniques would have much to contribute. Finally, as in each of the two previous sections, more research that discusses and disseminates examples of pedagogical materials would be particularly welcome.

Conclusion

This chapter has attempted to cover a wide range of aspects of EAP, but it has necessarily reflected my own knowledge and interests as well as the key trends in the field. Thus much of the research reported here deals with written discourse, in large part because written production is still the main means of assessment in the academy and there has been a major research and pedagogical effort directed towards high-stakes written genres. Similarly, the chapter has tended to focus on tertiary level contexts, reflecting the fact that much of the impetus for EAP research has emanated from university settings, in which practitioners are better resourced to carry out this work. Such biases are to a certain extent inherent in the field. However, within the scope of a relatively short chapter, it has also not proved possible to deal in detail with many topics that deserve attention, in particular those concerned with the implementation of EAP programs such as needs analysis, course syllabi and teaching materials.

The threefold approach taken here has highlighted in turn the differing contributions made to the field by adopting a corpus, genre, or social context perspective. This approach has enabled connections to be drawn between the three perspectives, showing that each can enrich the others and bringing into focus the growing tendency for them to be meshed in practice. Thus we have seen that corpus techniques have begun to be applied to genre analysis and are often combined with ethnographic methods, while genre analyses increasingly draw on corpus data alongside information on social practices. The social context approaches reviewed here have been perhaps slower to incorporate corpus methods, but there are signs that their potential is beginning to be recognized (e.g. Starfield 2004). This merging and blending of approaches is a positive development that may be expected to continue in future, leading to a gradual widening and deepening of our knowledge and understanding of EAP.

REFERENCES

Ackerley, K. and Coccetta, F. (2007) Enriching language learning through a multimedia corpus. *ReCALL* 19: 351–70.

Afros, E. and Schryer, C. (2009) The genre of syllabus in higher education. *Journal of English for Academic Purposes* 8: 224–33.

Aguilar, M. (2004) The peer seminar, a spoken research process. *Journal of English for Academic Purposes* 3: 55–72.

Basturkmen, H. (2009) Commenting on results in published research articles and masters dissertations in language teaching. *Journal of English for Academic Purposes* 8: 241–51.

Bazerman, C. (1988) *Shaping Written Knowledge*. Madison, WI: University of Wisconsin Press.

Belcher, D. (2007) Seeking acceptance in an English-only research world. *Journal of Second Language Writing* 16: 1–22.

Belcher, D. (2009) How research space is created in a diverse research world. *Journal of Second Language Writing* 18: 221–34.

Benesch, S. (2001) *Critical English for Academic Purposes*. Mahwah, NJ: Lawrence Erlbaum.

Benesch, S. (2009) Theorizing and practising critical English for academic purposes. *Journal of English for Academic Purposes* 8: 81–5.

Berkenkotter, C. and Huckin, T. (1995) *Genre Knowledge in Disciplinary Communication: Cognition/Culture/Power*. Hillsdale, NJ: Lawrence Erlbaum.

Bhatia, V. (1993) *Analysing Genre: Language Use in Professional Settings*. London: Longman.

Bhatia, V. (2004) *Worlds of Written Discourse*. London: Continuum.

Bianchi, F. and Pazzaglia, R. (2007) Student writing of research articles in a foreign language: Metacognition and corpora. In R. Facchinetti (ed.), *Corpus Linguistics 25 Years On*. 261–87. Amsterdam: Rodopi.

Biber, D. (2006) *University Language*. Amsterdam: John Benjamins.

Biber, D., Connor, U., and Upton, T. (2007) *Discourse on the Move*. Amsterdam: John Benjamins.

Biber, D., Conrad, S., and Cortes, V. (2004) *If you look at . . .*: Lexical bundles in university teaching and textbooks. *Applied Linguistics* 25: 371–405.

Biber, D. and Gray, B. (2010) Challenging stereotypes about academic writing: Complexity, elaboration, explicitness. *Journal of English for Academic Purposes* 9: 2–20.

Biber, D., Johansson, S., Leech, G., Conrad, S., and Finegan, E. (1999) *Longman Grammar of Spoken and Written English*. Harlow, UK: Pearson Education.

Boulton, A. (2009) Testing the limits of data-driven learning: Language proficiency and training. *ReCALL* 21: 37–54.

Boulton, A. (2010) Data-driven learning: Taking the computer out of the equation. *Language Learning* 60: 534–72.

Breyer, Y. (2009) Learning and teaching with corpora: Reflections by student teachers. *Computer Assisted Language Learning* 22: 153–72.

Bruce, I. (2008) *Academic Writing and Genre*. London: Continuum.

Bunton, D. (2005) The structure of PhD conclusion chapters. *Journal of English for Academic Purposes* 4: 207–24.

Camiciottoli, B. C.- (2007) *The Language of Business Studies Lectures*. Amsterdam: John Benjamins.

Canagarajah, S. (1996) "Nondiscursive" requirements in academic publishing, the material resources of periphery scholars, and the politics of knowledge production. *Written Communication* 13: 435–72.

Cargill, M. and O'Connor, P. (2006) Developing Chinese scientists' skills for publishing in English: Evaluating collaborating-colleague workshops based on genre analysis. *Journal of English for Academic Purposes* 5: 207–21.

Carter-Thomas, S. and Rowley-Jolivet, E. (2008) *If*-conditionals in medical discourse: From theory to disciplinary practice. *Journal of English for Academic Purposes* 7: 191–205.

Casanave, C. P. (2008) The stigmatizing effect of Goffman's stigma label: A response to John Flowerdew. *Journal of English for Academic Purposes* 7: 264–67.

Casanave, C. P. (2010) Taking risks? A case study of three doctoral students writing qualitative dissertations at an American university in Japan. *Journal of Second Language Writing* 19: 1–16.

Charles, M. (2007) Reconciling top-down and bottom-up approaches to graduate writing: Using a corpus to teach rhetorical functions. *Journal of English for Academic Purposes* 6: 289–302.

Charles, M. (2011) Using hands-on concordancing to teach rhetorical functions: Evaluation and implications for EAP writing classes. In A. Frankenberg-Garcia, L. Flowerdew and G. Aston (eds.), *New Trends in Corpora and Language Learning*: 26–43. London: Continuum.

Chen, Q. and Ge, G. (2007) A corpus-based lexical study on frequency and distribution of Coxhead's AWL word families in medical research articles (RAs). *English for Specific Purposes* 26: 502–14.

Chen, Y. H. and Baker, P. (2010) Lexical bundles in L1 and L2 academic writing. *Language Learning and Technology* 14: 30–49.

Cheng, A. (2011) Language features as the pathways to genre: Students' attention to non-prototypical features and its implications. *Journal of Second Language Writing* 20: 69–82.

Cobb, T. (1997) Is there any measurable learning from hands-on concordancing? *System* 25: 301–15.

Coffin, C. (2006) *Historical Discourse: The Language of Time, Cause and Evaluation*. London: Continuum.

Coxhead, A. (2000) A new academic word list. *TESOL Quarterly* 34: 213–38.

Coxhead, A. (2008) Phraseology and English for academic purposes. In F. Meunier and S. Granger (eds.), *Phraseology in Foreign Language Learning and Teaching*. 149–61. Amsterdam: John Benjamins.

Cresswell, A. (2007) Getting to "know" connectors? Evaluating data-driven learning in a writing skills course. In E. Hidalgo, L. Quereda ,and J. Santana (eds.), *Corpora in the Foreign Language Classroom*. 267–87. Amsterdam: Rodopi.

Durrant, P. (2009) Investigating the viability of a collocation list for students of English for academic purposes. *English for Specific Purposes* 28: 157–69.

Ebeling, S. O. (2009) Oslo interactive English: Corpus-driven exercises on the web. In K. Aijmer (ed.), *Corpora and Language Teaching*. 67–82. Amsterdam: John Benjamins.

Estling V., Lindquist M., and Lindquist, H. (2007) Learning English grammar with a corpus: Experimenting with concordancing in a university grammar course. *ReCALL* 19: 329–50.

Fløttum, K., Dahl, T., and Kinn, T. (2006) *Academic Voices: Across Languages and Disciplines*. Amsterdam: John Benjamins.

Flowerdew, J. (2001) Attitudes of journal editors to nonnative speaker contributions. *TESOL Quarterly* 35: 121–50.

Flowerdew, J. (2008) Scholarly writers who use English as an additional language: What can Goffman's *"Stigma"* tell us? *Journal of English for Academic Purposes* 7: 77–86.

Flowerdew, J. and Forest, R. (2009) Schematic structure and lexico-grammatical realization in corpus-based genre analysis: The case of research in the PhD literature review. In M. Charles, D. Pecorari and S. Hunston (eds.), *Academic Writing: At the Interface of Corpus and Discourse*. 15–36. London: Continuum.

Flowerdew, J. and Li, Y. (2009) English or Chinese? The trade-off between local and international publication among Chinese academics in the humanities and social sciences. *Journal of Second Language Writing* 18: 1–16.

Flowerdew, L. (1998) Corpus linguistic techniques applied to textlinguistics. *System* 26: 541–52.

Flowerdew, L. (2002) Corpus-based analyses in EAP. In J. Flowerdew (ed.), *Academic Discourse*. 95–114. London: Longman.

Flowerdew, L. (2008) *Corpus-Based Analyses of the Problem-Solution Pattern*. Amsterdam: John Benjamins.

Flowerdew, L. (2009) Applying corpus linguistics to pedagogy. *International Journal of Corpus Linguistics* 14: 393–417.

Fortanet-Gómez, I. and Querol-Julián, M. (2010) The videocorpus as a multimodal tool for teaching. In M. C. Campoy-Cubillo, Bellés-Fortuno, B., and Gea-Valor, M. L. (eds.), *Corpus-Based Approaches to English Language Teaching*. 261–70. London: Continuum.

Frankenberg-Garcia, A. (2005) A peek into what today's language learners as researchers actually do. *International Journal of Lexicography* 18: 335–55.

Gavioli, L. (2005) *Exploring Corpora for ESP Learning*. Amsterdam: John Benjamins.

Gilquin, G., Granger, S., and Paquot, M. (2007) Learner corpora: The missing link in EAP pedagogy. *Journal of English for Academic Purposes* 6: 319–35.

Granath, S. (2009) Who benefits from learning how to use corpora? In K. Aijmer (ed.), *Corpora and Language Teaching*. 47–65. Amsterdam: John Benjamins.

Granger, S. (2009) The contribution of learner corpora to second language acquisition and foreign language teaching. In K. Aijmer (ed.), *Corpora and Language Teaching*. 13–32. Amsterdam: John Benjamins.

Granger, S., Dagneaux, E., Meunier, F., and Pacquot, M. (eds.) (2009) *International Corpus of Learner English*. Louvain-la-Neuve: Presses Universitaires de Louvain.

Groom, N. (2005) Pattern and meaning across genres and disciplines: An exploratory study. *Journal of English for Academic Purposes* 4: 257–77.

Ha, P. L. (2009) Strategic, passionate, but academic: Am I allowed in my writing? *Journal of English for Academic Purposes* 8: 134–46.

Hafner, C. and Candlin, C. (2007) Corpus tools as an affordance to learning in professional legal education. *Journal of English for Academic Purposes* 6: 303–18.

Halliday, M. A. K. (1994) *An Introduction to Functional Grammar*. 2nd ed. London: Edward Arnold.

Harwood, N. (2009) An interview-based study of the functions of citations in academic writing across two disciplines. *Journal of Pragmatics* 41: 497–518.

Hasrati, M. and Street, B. (2009) PhD topic arrangement in "D"iscourse communities of engineers and social sciences/humanities. *Journal of English for Academic Purposes* 9: 14–25.

Hirano, E. (2009) Research article introductions in English for specific purposes: A comparison between Brazilian Portuguese and English. *English for Specific Purposes* 28: 240–50.

Horst, M., Cobb, T., and Nicolae, I. (2005) Expanding academic vocabulary with an interactive on-line database. *Language Learning and Technology* 9: 90–110.

Hyland, K. (2000) *Disciplinary Discourses: Social Interactions in Academic Writing.* Harlow, UK: Longman.

Hyland, K. (2005) *Metadiscourse.* London: Continuum.

Hyland, K. (2008) *As can be seen*: Lexical bundles and disciplinary variation. *English for Specific Purposes* 27: 4–21.

Hyland, K. (2009) Corpus informed discourse analysis: the case of academic engagement. In M. Charles, D. Pecorari, and S. Hunston (eds.), *Academic Writing: At the Interface of Corpus and Discourse.* 110–128. London: Continuum.

Hyland, K. and Tse, P. (2007) Is there an "Academic Vocabulary"? *TESOL Quarterly*, 41: 235–53.

Hyon, S. (1996) Genre in three traditions: Implications for ESL. *TESOL Quarterly* 30: 693–722.

Johns, A. M. (2011) The future of genre in L2 writing: Fundamental, but contested, instructional decisions. *Journal of Second Language Writing* 20: 56–68.

Johns, A. M., Bawarshi, A., Coe, R., Hyland, K., Paltridge, B., Reiff, M. J., and Tardy, C. (2006). Crossing the boundaries of genre studies: Commentaries by experts. *Journal of Second Language Writing* 15: 234–49.

Johns, T. (1991) Should you be persuaded: Two samples of data-driven learning materials. In T. Johns and P. King (eds.), *Classroom Concordancing.* 1–16. Birmingham: ELR University of Birmingham.

Kaltenböck, G. and Mehlmauer-Larcher, B. (2005) Computer corpora and the language classroom: On the potential and limitations of computer corpora in language teaching. *ReCALL* 17: 65–84.

Koutsantoni, D. (2009). Persuading sponsors and securing funding: Rhetorical patterns in grant proposals. In M. Charles, D. Pecorari, and S. Hunston (eds.), *Academic Writing: At the Interface of Corpus and Discourse.* 37–57. London: Continuum.

Kwan, B. (2006) The schematic structure of literature reviews in doctoral theses of applied linguistics. *English for Specific Purposes* 25: 30–55.

Kwan, B. (2009) Reading in preparation for writing a PhD thesis: Case studies of experiences. *Journal of English for Academic Purposes* 8: 180–191.

Lea, M. and Street, B. (2006) The "academic literacies" model: Theory and application. *Theory into Practice* 45: 368–77.

Lee, D. and Swales, J. M. (2006) A corpus-based EAP course for NNS doctoral students: Moving from available specialized corpora to self-compiled corpora. *English for Specific Purposes* 25: 56–75.

Lee, J. (2008) Size matters: An exploratory comparison of small- and large-class university lecture introductions. *English for Specific Purposes* 28: 42–57.

Leech, G. (1997) Teaching and language corpora: A convergence. In A. Wichman, S. Fligelstone, T. McEnery and G. Knowles (eds.), *Teaching and Language Corpora.* 1–23. London: Longman.

Li, Y. (2007) Apprentice scholarly writing in a community of practice: An intraview of an NNES graduate student writing a research article. *TESOL Quarterly* 41: 55–79.

Li, Y. and Flowerdew, J. (2009) International engagement versus local commitment: Hong Kong academics in the humanities and social sciences writing for publication. *Journal of English for Academic Purposes* 8: 279–93.

Lillis, T. (2001) *Student Writing: Access, Regulation, Desire.* London: Routledge.

Lillis, T. and Curry, M. J. (2010) *Academic Writing in a Global Context.* London: Routledge.

Lillis, T. and Scott, M. (2007) Defining academic literacies research: Issues of epistemology, ideology and strategy. *Journal of Applied Linguistics* 4: 5–32.

Lim, J. (2010) Commenting on research results in applied linguistics and education: A comparative genre-based investigation. *Journal of English for Academic Purposes* 9: 280–94.

Loi, C. K. (2010) Research article introductions in Chinese and English: A comparative genre-based study. *Journal of English for Academic Purposes* 9: 267–79.

Luzón Marco, J. (2010) Analysis of organizing and rhetorical items in a learner corpus of technical writing. In M. C. Campoy-Cubillo, B. Bellés-Fortuno and M. L. Gea-Valor (eds.), *Corpus-Based Approaches to English Language Teaching.* 79–94. London: Continuum.

Martin, J. R. and Rose, D. (2003) *Working with Discourse: Meaning Beyond the Clause.* London: Continuum.

Martin, J. R. and Rose, D. (2008) *Genre Relations: Mapping Culture.* London: Equinox.

Mauranen, A., Hynninen, N. and Ranta, E. (2010) English as an academic lingua franca: The ELFA project. *English for Specific Purposes* 29: 183–90.

Miller, C. R. (1984) Genre as social action. *Quarterly Journal of Speech* 70: 151–67.

Molle, D. and Prior, P. (2008) Multimodal genre systems in EAP writing pedagogy: Reflecting on a needs analysis. *TESOL Quarterly* 42: 541–66.

Morgan, B. and Ramanathan, V. (2005) Critical literacies and language education: Global and local perspectives. *Annual Review of Applied Linguistics* 25: 151–69.

Mudraya, O. (2006) Engineering English: A lexical frequency instructional model. *English for Specific Purposes* 25: 235–56.

Nesi, H. and Gardner, S. (2011) *Genres Across the Disciplines: Student Writing in Higher Education.* Cambridge: Cambridge University Press.

Nesselhauf, N. (2003) The use of collocations by advanced learners of English and some implications for teaching. *Applied Linguistics* 24: 223–42.

Norton, B. and Toohey, K. (eds.) (2004) *Critical Pedagogies and Language Learning.* Cambridge: Cambridge University Press.

Paquot, M. (2010) *Academic Vocabulary in Learner Writing.* London: Continuum.

Pecorari, D. (2008) *Academic Writing and Plagiarism.* London: Continuum.

Pennycook, A. (1997) Vulgar pragmatism, critical pragmatism, and EAP. *English for Specific Purposes* 16: 253–69.

Römer, U. (2009) English in academia: Does nativeness matter? *Anglistik* 20: 89–100.

Römer, U. (2010) Using general and specialized corpora in English language teaching: Past, present and future. In M. C. Campoy-Cubillo, B. Bellés-Fortuno, and M. L. Gea-Valor (eds.), *Corpus-Based Approaches to English Language Teaching.* 18–35. London: Continuum.

Salager-Meyer, F. (2008) Scientific publishing in developing countries: Challenges for the future. *Journal of English for Academic Purposes* 7: 121–32.

Samraj, B. (2008) A discourse analysis of master's theses across disciplines with a focus on introductions. *Journal of English for Academic Purposes* 7: 55–67.

Simpson-Vlach, R. and Ellis, N. (2010) An academic formulas list: New methods in phraseology research. *Applied Linguistics* 31: 487–512.

Starfield, S. (2004) "Why does this feel empowering?" Thesis writing, concordancing and the corporatizing university. In B. Norton and K. Toohey (eds.), *Critical Pedagogies and Language Learning.* 138–57. Cambridge: Cambridge University Press.

Starfield, S. and Ravelli, L. (2006) "The writing of this thesis was a process that I could not explore with the positivistic detachment of the classical sociologist": Self and structure in new humanities research theses. *Journal of English for Academic Purposes* 5: 222–43.

Swales, J. M. (1990) *Genre Analysis.* Cambridge: Cambridge University Press.

Swales, J. M. (1997) English as *Tyrannosaurus Rex. World Englishes* 16: 373–82.

Swales, J. M. (2002) Integrated and fragmented worlds: EAP materials and corpus linguistics. In J. Flowerdew (ed.), *Academic Discourse.* 150–64. London: Longman.

Swales, J. M. (2004) *Research Genres.* Cambridge: Cambridge University Press.

Swales, J. M. (2011) Coda: Reflections on the future of genre and L2 writing. *Journal of Second Language Writing* 20: 83–5.

Tardy, C. (2004) The role of English in scientific communication: *Lingua franca* or *Tyrannosaurus Rex? Journal of English for Academic Purposes* 3: 247–69.

Tardy, C. (2006) Researching first and second language genre learning: A comparative review and a look ahead. *Journal of Second Language Writing* 15: 79–101.

Tardy, C. (2011) The history and future of genre in second language writing.

Journal of Second Language Writing 20: 1–5.

Tognini Bonelli, E. and G. Del Lungo Camiciotti, G. (eds.) (2005) *Strategies in Academic Discourse.* Amsterdam: John Benjamins.

Tribble, C. (2002) Corpora and corpus analysis: New windows on academic writing. In J. Flowerdew (ed.), *Academic Discourse.* 131–49. London: Longman.

Tseng, Y. C. and Liou, H. C. (2006) The effects of online conjunction materials on college EFL students' writing. *System* 34: 270–83.

Uzuner, S. (2008) Multilingual scholars' participation in core/global academic communities: A literature review. *Journal of English for Academic Purposes* 7: 250–63.

Yoon, H. (2008) More than a linguistic reference: The influence of corpus technology on L2 academic writing. *Language Learning and Technology* 12: 31–48.

Yoon, H. and Hirvela, A. (2004) ESL student attitudes towards corpus use in L2 writing. *Journal of Second Language Writing* 13: 257–83.

8 English for Science and Technology

JEAN PARKINSON

Introduction

The wide range of purposes and contexts in which English is used has made English for specific purposes (ESP) an eclectic discipline. Typically trained as writing or language teachers, ESP teachers work outside of their own disciplines, and must become ethnographers, exploring unfamiliar language varieties, disciplinary cultures and modes, and drawing on scholarship from a wide range of fields to do so. These include sociocultural studies, literacy studies, second language (L2) writing studies, rhetoric, and systemic functional linguistics.

Perhaps because of the rapid expansion of English for science and technology (EST) in the last 50 years, science and technology were an early focus for ESP researchers (e.g. Barber 1988; Bazerman 1984, 1988; Braine 1989; Halliday 1993a; Herbert 1965; Swales 1971, 1988). The initial interest of EST teachers and researchers was on linguistic forms (see Johns, this volume), with later emphasis on skills, a more recent focus has been on disciplinary socialization, and most recently a critical perspective, which considers how literacy practices express societal or disciplinary power differences. In tracing this expansion, Hyland (2006) notes that each expanded focus comprehends rather than replaces prior ones. I represent this expanding focus in Figure 8.1 and use it to organize this chapter, starting with the widest focus, disciplinary culture, and values.

The expanding focus of ESP

What does English for science and technology encompass? Halliday (1993a) comments that a text is recognized as scientific English because of the combined effect of clusters of features and, importantly, the relations of these features throughout

The Handbook of English for Specific Purposes, First Edition.
Edited by Brian Paltridge and Sue Starfield.
© 2013 John Wiley & Sons, Inc. Published 2013 by John Wiley & Sons, Inc.

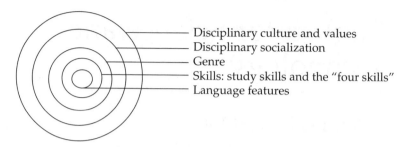

Disciplinary culture and values
Disciplinary socialization
Genre
Skills: study skills and the "four skills"
Language features

Figure 8.1   The expanding focus of ESP.

a text. Yet characteristic forms and vocabulary of science or technology should not be considered as separate from the genres in which they occur, because linguistic differences are part of what constitutes genre. Similarly the genres of science and technology partially constitute the various disciplines, and cannot be separated from them. Being a member of a discourse community involves using its characteristic language and genres, and also sharing its values (which are reflected in its language and genres), and taking on a role recognized by other members of the discourse community (Paltridge 2012).

This expanded perspective of ESP has replaced a notion of skills transferable between disciplines with the conception of specific literacies acquired in the context of the discipline. This creates a difficulty for EST teachers, who must provide access for their students into a discourse community of which they are usually not members. Spack (1988) noted this difficulty early on, suggesting that disciplinary discourse is too diverse and complex for ESP teachers to provide this access. Indeed, Mackiewicz (2004) outlines how humanities-trained writing tutors may give inappropriate advice to engineering students, for example. I outline below how EST practitioners have variously used employers, disciplinary teachers or students as resources to provide this insight.

To mitigate the status of EST teacher as disciplinary outsider, Smith Taylor (2007) suggests training discipline insiders in writing instruction to circumvent EST teachers' lack of insider knowledge. Stoller et al. (2005) stress the importance not only of working with discipline specialists in designing EST interventions, but of working towards a shared understanding with discipline specialists of what is valuable to them in writing, (e.g. content accuracy).

Swales and Lindeman (2002), teaching the literature review to graduate students, suggest that ESP instructors facilitate students' own investigation of disciplinary discourse. Pritchard and Nasr (2004), considering the teaching of reading to engineering students with greater disciplinary knowledge than their ESP reading teachers, suggest that students become informants to the teacher and classmates.

Collaboration with disciplinary experts is highly recommended if EST teachers are not knowledgeable about students' disciplines (Horn, Stoller, and Robinson

2008). Discipline and EST teachers can work together to identify the key features of genres. However, although collaborative approaches have been a key element in ESP methodology (Hyland 2007), collaboration is not always straightforward. Braine (2001) found reluctance among science and engineering professors, themselves L2 English speakers, to show him writing assignments they set for students. He speculated that they were ashamed of possible grammatical errors, and could see no value in a process approach to writing, having been educated through the grammar-translation method.

In addition to relying on employers, disciplinary teachers or students to ameliorate their outsider status, EST teachers also have available studies of the discourse features of science and technology texts, as well as studies of disciplinary cultures. I begin by reviewing studies of disciplinary cultures.

Culture and Values

To become a member of a science discourse community, a student needs to participate in and come to regard as natural, research science values: that science is quantitative, repeatable, and ideally free from bias. Engineering values by contrast are concerned with the design process and problem-solving within set specifications; associated discourse includes argument that links scientific phenomena to specific contexts (Archer 2008).

However, from a critical discourse perspective, disciplinary discourse is not equally accessible to everyone and the task of ESP teachers includes assisting students in unpacking their disciplines' ideological assumptions, rather than merely accepting and coming to share these. A critical perspective recognizes that science and technology are not context-free (Johnston, Lee, and McGregor 1996; Pennycook, 1997). Archer (2008), working in post-apartheid South Africa with students from underdeveloped rural communities, found a discontinuity between student expressions of suffering in rural communities, and the impersonal professional engineers' writing. Her work indicates the need to make professional conventions available to students, while ensuring that these are continuous with, not in opposition to, students' own values. Archer notes the value to developing countries of engineers who are knowledgeable about rural underdevelopment. To facilitate access to disciplinary discourse, EST teachers need awareness of such societal inequalities.

A discipline's culture may vary too between countries. Artemeva (1998) found that the different values in a North American and a Russian engineering company resulted in different views of rhetorical purpose, audience, organization, all expressed at the levels of sentence and paragraph organization, thematic structure and even content of periodic progress reports. The North American engineers saw an engineer's role as finding concrete solutions to technical problems, while the Russian engineers saw themselves as scientists. They were thus unwilling to frame this genre in ways expected by the report's North American audience.

Social constructionist studies of the talk, writing, and actions of scientists in research laboratories have been an important information source about disciplinary values. Latour and Woolgar (1979) studied how research findings become facts: generally we view facts as pre-existing, awaiting scientists' discovery. They suggest instead that facts are socially constructed (through intuition, data interpretation, collegial discussion, publication, etc.). They note that a statement gains factual status when recognized as true beyond a particular place and time, or its producers; it becomes part of the body of knowledge drawn upon by the community (Latour and Woolgar 1979).

Insight into discourse communities' values has come too from examination of the research article (RA), including Bazerman's (1988) study of its historical development. Discourse communities are driven by this published outcome of research, because publication represents community acceptance of research claims (Myers 1989). Linguistic and rhetorical features of RAs reflect this purpose. For example, the impersonal language of science RAs is a convention for expressing objectivity and the need to represent findings as separated from time and person. It reflects the desire to broaden applicability of a finding (not tied to the individual researcher) and also to make it appear that nature speaks for itself. Rhetorically, too, the RA presents the research process as more deliberate than it is. Researchers appear to follow a carefully planned path, rather than trying a number of possibilities; false starts and mistakes are not represented in the RA and opportunistic findings are represented rhetorically as part of a coherent research plan (see Flowerdew, this volume; Knorr-Cettina 1981).

Insight into the values of science and technology discourse communities is valuable to EST teachers from another perspective too, in that it helps them to assist students to access these communities. In the next section, I review an important trend in ESP, the focus on learners' socialization into a discourse for the purposes of becoming members of a target discourse community.

Integration into the EST Discourse Community

A disciplinary socialization perspective views students as not merely learning the registers and genres important in their disciplines, but as being enculturated into those disciplines by learning disciplinary values and behavior. This perspective draws on sociocultural theory, viewing discourse practices as learnt through interaction with those who have already mastered them (Duff 2010; Lemke 1990). A language socialization perspective may, however, represent the process of acquiring new literacy practices too simply. Lea and Street (1998) argue that acquiring disciplinary literacy requires a student to take on a new disciplinary identity, one with which they may not be comfortable, and which they may therefore resist.

These perspectives have led EST practitioners/researchers to use ethnographic methods in investigating the target discourse community. Vickers (2007: 624), for example, conceptualized a US computer engineering department as a "speech community containing communicative norms;" she viewed individuals as being competent members of this discourse community when they had an understanding of the range of activities that members participate in. Focussing on a single speech event, the team meeting, she describes the socialization of a NNS student into the discourse of a student design team. She traces how participation by the student, initially a peripheral member of the group, was scaffolded by core members who provided opportunities for design experiences. The student gained the confidence to suggest design solutions, initiate topics in discussions, and provide explanations. Considering engineering student writing from a similar perspective, Nelson (2000) aimed to socialize students into professional engineering culture by building peer review into engineering writing instruction.

Attention has been paid too to professional engineers' team meetings. Angouri (2010) compares recordings of engineers' meetings with their representation in ESP textbooks. Her findings include different turn-taking mechanisms, much overlapping talk, back-channelling, interactants extending or completing each others' utterances, and a lower degree of explicitness in the real data. By contrast, in the textbooks, speakers have non-overlapping turns in which speakers nominate the next speaker rather than speakers judging the appropriate place to take a turn. Angouri (2010) suggests how EST teachers can supplement textbook materials with real data to teach meeting interaction.

Also working in a language socialization paradigm, Chinn and Hilgers (2000) studied instructors in undergraduate science and engineering content courses. They characterized them as variously playing the role of corrector (where the goal was content mastery), journal editor (students peer-reviewed each other's work) and collaborator (collaborative assignments involved research and had multiple readers). Students of the editor- and collaborator-instructors learnt about genre in addition to content, while the collaborator-assignments gave students a sense of working within science or engineering, where collaboration and repeated review of writing are the norm.

Artemeva, Logie, and St Martin (1999), to assist students' integration into the engineering discourse community, based communication assignments on each student's chosen engineering area. This made the context seem more genuine for students, improving perceptions that the course served their needs. Their course, which included several engineering genres, focussed on audience and purpose, encouraging a sense of dialogue with instructor and peers. Similarly, Parkinson (2000) aimed to assist socialization into a discourse community by situating EST coursework in the content of undergraduate science students' subject areas. Students collected experimental data and wrote lab reports on this data, thus simulating students' disciplinary discursive contexts.

Research into EST Genres

To mitigate teachers' outsider status and gain insight into the genres and culture of these communities, researchers have worked on identifying key EST genres. Swales (2004) has noted that genres in any discipline or discourse community come in related sets, such as the RA and the lab report, the feasibility study and progress report, and the engineering presentation and design report. Much progress has been made also in analyzing the rhetorical and linguistic features of genres and identifying how they reflect the values and culture of the discourse community. The task is complicated by the fact that the key genres of these discourse communities are not identical with the genres demanded of students. Having identified work-related genres and/or pedagogical student genres, the EST teacher must consider how best to teach them in order to provide access to the discourse community. In the next section I review work on a range of science and engineering genres, starting with the RA.

Rhetorical features of the research article

Investigation of high stakes genres such as the RA have been valuable to EST teachers of graduate or professionals, who must read or write RAs. This investigation has also been valuable in revealing register features, and providing insight into the value system of particular science and technology disciplines and their discourse communities

In his study of the development of the RA, Bazerman (1988) indicates how the genre developed to convince readers who had not observed experiments. Newton, for example, represented himself in his writing as an ideal experimental scientist who isolates phenomena in a planned and orderly way. Newton's persuasive use of language has been influential, and Halliday (1993c) explores its continuing grammatical influence. Bazerman (1988) notes that literature survey length and number of references to the literature depends on how focussed the discipline is and the degree of consensus within it. As a discipline develops it becomes increasingly embedded in theory and knowledge rather than methods or instruments.

As a discipline, ESP regards students as benefitting from explicit instruction in genre structure. Much ESP work on RA structure has followed Swales' well-known CARS (create a research space) model (1981, 1984, 1990) on the moves in RA introductions. Considerable attention has been paid to the different sections, including Abstracts (Samraj 2005), Introductions (Swales 1981, 2004), Methods (Lim 2006; Wood 1982), Results (Brett 1994) and Discussions (Dudley-Evans 1994; Holmes 1997; Kanoksilapatham 2005; Parkinson 2011; Peacock 2002; Swales 1990).

Anthony (1999) studied software Engineering RA introductions, and found deviations from Swales' CARS model. Anthony suggests that research is needed in a wide range of fields so that these disciplinary variations can be available for ESP teachers unfamiliar with a particular discipline.

In reading pedagogy too, focus on genre has been of value. Stoller (2010) suggests ways for EST teachers to guide reading of chemistry texts, including consideration of purpose, audience, language, organization, and content. Students are sensitized by first considering linguistic and nonlinguistic features of nondisciplinary genres, then considering texts in the field written for an expert and non-expert audience, and finally focussing on the target genre.

Theses and dissertation

Theses and dissertations represent a genre similar in form to the RA. Paltridge (2002) found a number of alternative macro-structures and that advice in published handbooks did not match practice, indicating the value of specific instruction for graduate students. Koutsantoni (2006) compared rhetorical strategies used by engineering RA and thesis writers. She suggests the tendency of the student writers to hedge more, avoid personal attribution, distance themselves from their claims, and acknowledge limitations reflects different reader-writer power relationships in the two genres. She suggests a need for prospective engineers to be sensitized to expected community rhetorical strategies.

Studies of science textbooks

Science textbooks have been the subject of some study (Myers 1992, Schleppegrell 2004, Unsworth 1997, Young and Nguyen 2002). Textbooks are the main reading of science (Jackson, Meyer, and Parkinson 2006; Myers 1992) and engineering undergraduates (Parodi 2009), although Leventhal and Mynatt (1987) found that senior software engineering students read RAs. Swales (1995) notes that textbooks employ little hedging or human agency, and use abstract nominalizations as subjects of processes. In comparison with RA knowledge, textbook knowledge is not provisional (and thus has few citations), having been accepted by the science research community (Myers 1989). These differences mean that textbooks cannot easily be used as models for graduate students, who need to write RAs, or for undergraduate students, who need to write laboratory reports, a genre similar to RAs (Hyland 1998b).

Myers' (1992) comparison of these two genres found a number of register differences. Personal subjects such as *We* in RAs refer to researchers; in textbooks they refer to reader and writer. RAs are written in past tense for methods and in the present for well-accepted facts in the discipline. Textbooks are written largely in the present tense because textbooks limit information to published research that is already accepted by the research community, and are thus presented as all fact (Myers 1992). In RAs, almost all claims are hedged, while in textbooks there are few hedges (Hyland 2004; Parkinson and Adendorff 2005). RAs achieve cohesion through noun phrase repetition, while textbooks do so using logical connectors and a range of metadiscoursal markers (Hyland 2004). The main types of images associated with RAs are graphs and equations while textbooks use photographs and naturalistic drawings and diagrams (Pozzer-Ardenghiam and Roth 2010).

Pedagogical genres

A controversial issue in writing pedagogy has been whether genre should be explicitly taught. In the area of rhetorical genre studies some writing specialists (e.g. Freedman 1993), have avoided explicit instruction, because of the dynamic nature of genres and incidental student learning of genre features through immersion in the disciplinary culture, while others have focussed explicit teaching on context and situation rather than form (Giltrow and Stein 2009). ESP writing instruction has however favored explicit instruction on form, viewing it as of particular value to non-native speakers, who may find access to disciplinary cultures less easy than do native speakers.

Samraj (2004) notes that identically labeled texts may have distinct differences. EST teachers can therefore not rely on their own understanding of a genre, which may not coincide with that of the students' discipline. My own experience indicates that, compared with humanities essays, biology and geology essays are descriptive and do not expect writers to take a stance on an issue. Samraj (2004) examined the features of graduate research reports in two environmental science fields: conservation biology and wildlife behavior. She found that the first usually had a problem-solution structure and focussed on the environmental phenomenon, not the research. By contrast, wildlife behavior focussed on the research and tried to identify a gap in the field.

Artemeva and Fox (2010) used genre-competence assessment to see how well students identify and characterize rhetorical and textual features. They found that this ability is necessary but not sufficient for developing competence in writing engineering genres. Flowerdew (2000, 2003, 2008) considered good "apprentice" models, using high-performing student writing as models to teach the genre from the perspective of Hoey's (1983) situation-problem-response-evaluation pattern.

Laboratory reports

Braine's (1989) study of writing assignments in science and engineering courses found that most assignments were either lab or design reports (other writing included summary/reactions, case studies and library research papers). The lab report socializes students into core disciplinary values in experimental science including conventions for expressing objectivity, a value for quantitative methods, the need to show continuity of one's own findings with the literature, and a preference for mathematical models.

The lab report "encodes a scientific way of knowing in its structure" as Carter, Ferzli, and Wiebe (2007: 295) point out; the biology students in their study reported that the lab report encouraged them to act as scientists trying to solve a problem and it enabled them to view themselves as connected to the science community. Interestingly, they viewed their lab reports as more authoritative than textbooks and lecture notes, because they had used the register and ways of knowing of science.

The Introduction-Method-Results-Discussion organization of lab reports is similar to the experimental RA. The two genres also have similarities in purpose in that they report experimental results, although the RA must report new findings, while the lab report displays laboratory skills and understanding of accepted knowledge (Parkinson 2011). The lab report writer writes for a person grading the report, while the RA writer addresses peers.

Schleppegrell (2002) compared the lab reports of ESL Chemical Engineering writers to a well-written first language (L1) student's lab report. She found that the ESL students' difficulties were not merely ESL errors. Even if all errors were corrected, their lab reports would have a more restricted lexico-grammatical range than the L1 students'. For example to express assumptions, L1 writers used a range of grammar including *assume* as a verb, (passive, active, finite, and nonfinite), as an adjective, and as a noun as well as synonyms of *assume*. L2 writers by contrast depended on the imperative, or merely listed assumptions, because they lacked resources for expressing assumptions.

Smith Taylor (2007) notes that for many engineering students their main writing instruction is the grading of their reports by teaching assistants (TAs). For this reason she suggests training TAs in report grading, a further example of the collaborative approach taken by ESP. Interestingly, TAs focussed on content rather than surface form-related issues; they requested specificity, and probed validity. Use of a rubric led to about twice the proportion of coaching comments rather than authoritative comments.

Design reports

The design report is identified by Marshall (1991) as one of three important written engineering genres. (The other two he identified as important are the work experience report and the instruction manual). Design, usually taught through problem-based learning (PBL), is a key outcome for engineering education. PBL enculturates students into the activities of engineering by using group work, as practicing engineers do, to solve design problems. Students make and test the products of their designs. They report on this process in the design report as well as interim progress reports. Unlike a lab report, design reports consider the feasibility and cost of designs as well as match to specifications, not merely scientific/ technical elements.

Part of the same genre set as the design report is the design presentation. The work of Dannels (2003, 2009) illustrates how ESP teachers have investigated disciplinary communities' values and activities. In teaching the design presentation, Dannels (2003) found that although this genre was designed to simulate a workplace environment, professors had academic expectations. Students responded to these contradictory demands by addressing an academic rather than an industry audience and enacting an academic identity, but structured their presentations to show the influence of both academic and industry contexts. Dannels (2009) found that highly graded presentations were more likely to provide justifications for assumptions, evaluate their solutions and provide a personalized motivation. Lower-graded presentations used detached language and an impersonalized motivation. Dannels concludes that the higher-graded presenters were more skilled at negotiating a relationship with both the imagined professional audience and the real academic audience.

Olsen and Huckin (1990) studied another oral genre, the academic lecture in engineering. They found that students ignored the rhetorical problem-solution structure of the lecture. They understood the details, but ignored the main points and how they fitted together. They explain this failure as stemming from reliance on board notes, a focus on absorbing facts, and ignoring introductory remarks, prosodic markers, and rhetorical cues emphasizing main points. They suggest that the problem-solution-based nature of science and engineering is not stressed enough, either within the disciplines or within EST.

A Malaysian survey of professional engineers (Kassim and Ali 2010) suggested that ESP stress other oral genres including teleconferencing, and networking for contacts and advice. They suggest ESP courses for engineers should take into account workplace scenarios.

Language Features of EST

The grammatical and lexical features of language we use for specific purposes are by definition specialized and not a routine part of a native speaker's repertoire (Tudor 1997). Indeed corpus studies have shown how specialized the lexico-grammar and discourse strategies of disciplinary genres are (Paltridge 2009). Thus, ESP has tended to emphasize communication in the specialized target context rather than language teaching (Hyland 2007). Attention to language has been embedded in the teaching of key genres and language varieties learners will need to use in their disciplines.

Halliday's (1993b) influential analysis of the distinctive organization of written scientific text has shown how meaning in science tends to be expressed nominally rather than clausally, with meaning "buried" within the clause rather than explicitly signaled between clauses by use of conjunctions:

Clausal packaging of meaning:

Ozone	is destroyed	because	chlorine	reacts	with ozone
noun	verb	conj	noun	verb	prepositional group

Nominal packaging of meaning:

Reaction with chlorine	causes	ozone destruction
nominal group	verb	nominal group

Between these two examples, the actions *react* and *destroy* (most naturally or "congruently" expressed as verbs) become nominalized into the nouns *reaction* and *destruction*, a less expected, "less spoken" way of expressing this meaning. Similarly, the conjunction *because*, which signals the causal relation between two clauses is re-expressed as a verb, *causes*, and buried in a single clause, a less expected, "more written" way of expressing this meaning. Halliday (1993b) has labeled these more written uses of language "grammatical metaphor," because these meanings are metaphorical with respect to the grammar used to express them.

As Unsworth (1997) notes, the less congruent expression of written science makes this meaning less accessible. Mohan and Beckett (2003) studied the scaffolding of the acquisition of this nominalized writing in teacher talk. They found that the teachers of undergraduate science students recast student talk in more "literate," more nominalized and abstract ways. An example from their study is the following teacher recast:

S: To stop the brain's aging, *we can use our bodies and heads.*
T: So we can prevent our brain from getting weak *by being mentally and physically active*?

The student expresses meaning congruently, using a verb to talk about an action (use), and nouns (bodies, heads) to talk about objects. In the teacher's recast, the objects are construed as adverbs (mentally, physically) and the action as an adjective (active).

Packaging of meaning into nominalizations functions in science and engineering discourse to allow complex information to be compressed into a word, and it also allows a high level of abstraction e.g. *curvature of material surfaces* (Pueyo and Val 1996). Another important function of nominalization is allowing a process/action expressed in one clause to become, in the next clause, the theme about which a point can be made; this allows progress of the argument. An example from Halliday (1993b: 81) is:

Theme	Rheme
The atomic nucleus	*absorbs* energy in discrete units
Each *absorption*	absorbs energy in discrete units

Comparing the thematic structure of biology RA Method and Discussion sections, Martinez (2003) found that Method sections had simple literal experiential themes, referring to entities in the world; Discussions had more abstract and more multiple themes (i.e. a textual theme, linking the clause to other parts of the message, or an interpersonal theme, signaling writer attitude, in addition to an experiential element). An example of a multiple theme from her data is:

Therefore	it is possible that	classical MAP kinase isoforms	play a role in . . .
Textual theme	interpersonal theme	experiential theme	

She notes these sections' differing rhetorical goals: Method sections aim to describe methods in chronological order, while Discussions use abstract argument to convince readers. Martinez suggests raising awareness of this amongst L2 writers of RAs.

Vocabulary

Vocabulary as well as grammar differs from discipline to discipline. Ward (2009) estimated that his Thai engineering students knew only half of the 2000 most frequent English words as described in the General Service List (West 1953) and only 30 percent of academic words, yet had to read their textbooks in English. He identified 299 word types giving good coverage across five engineering subjects. These words are all from the General Service List plus the Academic Word List (Coxhead 2000) but are all distinctly engineering words (e.g. *system, equation, flow*). Mudraya (2006) distinguishes such sub-technical words, which have both an engineering and non-engineering meaning, from technical words, which have no exact synonym, resist semantic change, and have a narrow range of use, (e.g. *urethane*). She uses collocations to assist students to acquire both meanings. Ward (2007) used concordancing to study divergence in meaning in common sub-technical engineering words. His pedagogical suggestions include raising awareness of collocations, and teaching students to read collocates as chunks, not as single words.

Cortes (2004) and Hyland (2008) found lexical bundles (e.g. this result suggests) to be discipline-specific. Cortes (2004) found that RA writers use far more of these fixed expressions than do inexperienced writers (e.g. students at all levels, both native and non-native speakers). When students did use them, their use was not typical of use in the research articles, being more restricted and more repetitive in the bundles used. Cortes (2004) suggests that students might avoid the lexical bundles for fear of using them wrongly. A pedagogical implication of research in this area is to assist students in "noticing" the frequent use of the expressions.

Engagement, personal language, and citation practices

Language in science and technology is generally viewed as very impersonal. Students are encouraged by discipline specialists and ESP textbooks and teachers to avoid personal language in order to appear objective. Corpus studies have, however, shown that RAs do use personal pronouns, and that writers express stance and engagement in a number of ways.

Hyland (2001) studied personal pronouns in published RAs. On average in physics, biology, and electrical and mechanical engineering, there were 17.6 self mentions per RA including 11.9 personal pronouns. He notes that use of personal pronouns is a way of projecting a scholarly identity. It is important for students to be sensitized to their own disciplinary norms as norms vary between disciplines as Hyland found: for example on average there were 38.1 self mentions per RA in the humanities and social sciences. Kuo's (1999) study of engineering and applied physics journals suggests that personal pronouns show how writers view their own role in the research and their relationship with readers: *we* can refer to the writers themselves or to writer and readers or to the discipline as a whole.

What does this mean for personal language in undergraduate writing for EST students? Like all writers, students need to be sensitive to their audience, their professors, who expect a high level of impersonality. Luzon (2009) found different uses of *we* in undergraduate student engineering reports compared to the use of *we* in RAs. While noting the different purposes and audiences of these two genres, Luzon suggests students should analyze professional engineering reports for patterning of the pronoun. Harwood (2005), however, found the greater use of *I* in method sections of Computer Science MA projects than in RAs to be justified by the different audience and purpose of the student writers. He found that the student writing used *I* to highlight resourcefulness, justify procedures, and construct themselves as tenacious. He suggests corpus methods to draw students' attention to how the various requirements of different genres.

Hyland (1999) found that science RAs use fewer citations than humanities RAs, are less likely to quote their sources' names, or use them as an integral part of the sentence, employ fewer reporting verbs and do not represent their sources as taking a stance. He explains this in terms of the norms and culture of each discipline.

Koutsantoni (2004) considered how writers express attitude and evaluation in engineering RAs, looking specifically at attitude markers (e.g. *significantly*), certainty markers (e.g. *clearly*) and common knowledge markers (e.g. *it is widely accepted*). She suggests ESP materials should familiarize students with the preferred ways of limiting claims and of predisposing readers towards particular interpretations. Hyland (1998a) found fewer interpersonal markers in the science disciplines he studied than in the other disciplines. Hyland and Tse (2005) studied evaluative that-clauses (*We believe that . . .*) in RAs in a range of disciplines including biology, computer science, and electronic engineering. To evaluate their own findings, authors use this construction to mark the main argument, summarize purpose and express stance on the reliability of findings. Hyland and Tse suggest use of concordancing for exploration of these functions.

Modals and other hedges in academic writing function to soften what writers say and may even deliberately introduce an element of vagueness. They function variously to provide an accurate account of results (*approximately, about*), to signal the provisional nature of findings until accepted by the research community (*may be interpreted as*), protect the writer from claims of exaggeration and avoid offending other researchers (*we believe this is . . ..*) (Hyland 1996; Myers 1989).

Visual Elements and Multimodal Interpretation

Graphs and diagrams are an important part of science and technology discourse. Myers (2003) notes that diagrams are not an easily accessible language, but rather conventional depictions, which require disciplinary knowledge to understand; thus science and engineering students must learn to "read" images of molecules, flowcharts, graphs, micrographs, and so on. The social practices of engineering and science disciplines depend heavily on these visual forms, particularly graphs. Good control of a genre involves an understanding of how different modes – visual, written and oral – interact. Different modes offer different constraints and possibilities for making meaning. Archer (2006) used the poster as a tool to form links between the visual and the written, and between engineering culture new to her rural students and the culture students bring with them to university.

Mathematical discourse is a particular example of multimodal language. O'Halloran (2000) calls mathematics discourse multisemiotic in that it relies on language, maths symbolism, and visual elements. She shows that to participate in maths discourse requires shifting between these codes. Mathematical symbolism allows a precise, economical, complete statement of a particular relationship, which cannot be achieved in language alone. Molle and Prior (2008) found that writing in technology and mathematics-based sciences is likely to contain linguistically notated graphics and mathematical notation both on graphs and in the text. This makes collaboration with disciplinary specialists even more important for EST teachers, as understanding of equations, text, and visual elements and the meaning they make together is necessary for full understanding of texts in these disciplines.

Indications for Further Research Directions

Although much is known about the RA, much work on this genre is still necessary, particularly on sections other than the Introduction. Another area where research is needed is of variation between RAs in different disciplines. Corpus studies have emphasized the RA, comparing discourse in different disciplinary areas, and making comparisons with textbooks or dissertations and writing of graduate students, but seldom considering the writing of undergraduate students such as lab reports and design reports. Corpus studies of the language of professional design reports would also be valuable in guiding teachers of engineering writing. Another under-researched genre is the conference poster, an important genre for science and engineering graduate students. Some attention has been paid to oral science and engineering genres, but more work is needed. This includes meetings, formal presentations, conference presentations and everyday interaction in the laboratory or workplace. Mathematics discourse has also received little attention. More work is needed on how language, graphical interpretation, and mathematical expressions work together to make meaning. Finally, possibly because of its focus on classroom teaching, emphasis has been on practice; more attention could be paid to the construction of a theoretical framework for why we should teach in certain ways and how students acquire genre and register features.

Conclusion

This chapter has indicated the need for EST teachers to take account not only of lexis, grammar, and genres of science and engineering, but also to consider the disciplinary contexts into which students are being socialized, including the culture and values of these disciplines. The chapter has discussed how the typical position of EST teachers as disciplinary outsiders has led to the need to investigate these disciplines, their values, their genres, and the discourse features of their genres. Such investigations have used a number of approaches, most notably ethnographic studies of specific contexts, and discourse analysis of the genres and register features of these target disciplines. Written genres, especially the research article, have been the major focus of research to date. Further investigation of other written genres and of oral genres of science and technology, as well as further work on mathematical discourse would be of value to EST.

REFERENCES

Angouri, J. (2010) Using textbook and real-life data to teach turn-taking in business meetings. In N. Harwood (ed.), *English Language Teaching Materials: Theory and Practice*. 373–94. Cambridge: Cambridge University Press.

Anthony, L. (1999) Writing RA introductions in software engineering: How accurate is a standard model? *IEEE Transactions on Professional Communication* 42: 38–46.

Archer, A. (2006) A multimodal approach to academic "literacies": Problematising the visual/verbal divide. *Language and Education* 20: 449–62.

Archer, A. (2008) "The place is suffering": Enabling dialogue between students' discourses and academic literacy conventions in engineering. *English for Specific Purposes* 27: 255–66.

Artemeva, N. (1998) The writing consultant as cultural interpreter: Bridging cultural perspectives on the genre of the periodic engineering report. *Technical Communication Quarterly* 3: 285–99.

Artemeva, N. and Fox, J. (2010) Awareness versus production: Probing students' antecedent genre knowledge. *Journal of Business and Technical Communication* 24: 476–515.

Artemeva, N., Logie, S., and St Martin, J. (1999) From page to stage: How theories of genre and situated learning help introduce engineering students to discipline-specific communication. *Technical Communication Quarterly* 8: 301–16.

Barber, C. L. (1988) Some measurable characteristics of modern scientific prose. In J. M. Swales (ed.), *Episodes in ESP: A Source and Reference Book for the Development of English for Science And Technology*. 3–16. New York: Prentice Hall.

Bazerman, C. (1984) Modern evolution of the experimental report in physics: Spectroscopic articles in *Physical Review, 1893–1980. Social Studies in Science* 14: 163–196.

Bazerman, C. (1988) *Shaping Written Knowledge*. Madison, WI: University of Wisconsin Press.

Braine, G. (1989) Writing in science and technology: An analysis of assignments from ten undergraduate courses. *English for Specific Purposes* 8: 3–15.

Braine, G. (2001) When professors don't cooperate: A critical perspective on EAP research. *English for Specific Purposes* 20: 293–303.

Brett, P. (1994) A genre analysis of the results section of sociology articles. *English for Specific Purposes* 13: 47–59.

Carter, M., Ferzli, M., and Wiebe, E. N. (2007) Writing to learn by learning to write in the disciplines. *Journal of Business and Technical Communication* 21: 278–302.

Chinn, P. and Hilgers, T. (2000) From corrector to collaborator: The range of instructor roles in writing-based natural and applied science classes. *Journal of Research in Science Teaching* 37: 3–25.

Cortes, V. (2004) Lexical bundles in published and student disciplinary writing: Examples from history and biology. *English for Specific Purposes* 23: 397–423.

Coxhead, A. (2000) A new academic word list. *TESOL Quarterly* 34: 213–38.

Dannels, D. P. (2003) Teaching and learning design presentations in engineering: Contradictions between academic and workplace activity systems. *Journal of Business and Technical Communication* 17: 139–69.

Dannels, D. P. (2009) Features of success in engineering design presentations: A call for relational genre knowledge. *Journal of Business and Technical Communication* 23: 399–427.

Dudley-Evans, T. (1994) Genre analysis: An approach to text analysis for ESP. In M. Coulthard (ed.), *Advances in Written Text Analysis*. 219–28. London: Routledge.

Duff, P. A. (2010). Language socialization into academic discourse communities. *Annual Review of Applied Linguistics* 30: 169–92.

Flowerdew, L. (2000) Using a genre-based framework to teach organisational structure in academic writing. *ELT Journal* 54: 369–78.

Flowerdew, L. (2003) A combined corpus and systemic-functional analysis of the problem-solution pattern in a student and professional corpus of technical writing. *TESOL Quarterly* 37: 489–511.

Flowerdew, L. (2008) *Corpus-Based Analyses of the Problem-Solution Pattern: A Phraseological Approach*. Amsterdam: John Benjamins.

Freedman, A. (1993) Show and tell? The role of explicit teaching in the learning of new genres. *Research in the Teaching of English* 27: 222–51.

Giltrow, J. and Stein, D. (2009) Introduction. In J. Giltrow and D. Stein, (eds.), *Genres in the Internet: Issues in the Theory of Genre*. 1–26. Amsterdam: John Benjamins.

Halliday, M. A. K. (1993a) On the language of physical science. In M. A. K. Halliday and J. R. Martin (eds.), *Writing Science*. 54–68. London: The Falmer Press.

Halliday, M. A. K. (1993b) Some grammatical problems in scientific English. In M. A. K. Halliday and J. R. Martin (eds.), *Writing Science*. 69–85. London: The Falmer Press.

Halliday, M. A. K. (1993c) The construction of knowledge and value in the grammar of scientific discourse: Charles Darwin's *The Origin of the Species*. In M. A. K. Halliday and J. R. Martin (eds.), *Writing Science*. 86–105. London: The Falmer Press.

Harwood, N. (2005) "I hoped to counteract the memory problem, but I made no impact whatsoever": Discussing methods in computing science using I. *English for Specific Purposes* 24: 243–67.

Herbert, A. J. (1965) *The Structure of Technical English*. London: Longman.

Hoey, M. (1983) *On the Surface of Discourse*. London: George, Allen and Unwin.

Holmes, R. (1997) Genre analysis and the social sciences: An investigation of the structure of research article discussion sections in three disciplines. *English for Specific Purposes* 16: 321–37.

Horn, B, Stoller, F. L., and Robinson, M. S. (2008) Interdisciplinary collaboration: Two heads are better than one. *English Teaching Forum* 46: 2–13.

Hyland, K. (1996) Writing without Conviction? Hedging in science research articles. *Applied Linguistics* 17: 433–54.

Hyland, K. (1998a) Persuasion and context: the pragmatics of academic metadiscourse. *Journal of Pragmatics* 30: 437–55.

Hyland, K. (1998b) Talking to students: Metadiscourse in introductory coursebooks. *English for Specific Purposes* 18: 3–26.

Hyland, K. (1999) Academic attribution: Citation and the construction of disciplinary knowledge. *Applied Linguistics* 20: 341–67.

Hyland, K. (2001) Humble servants of the discipline? Self-mention in research articles. *English for Specific Purposes* 20: 207–26.

Hyland, K. (2004) *Disciplinary Discourses: Social Interactions in Academic Writing.* Ann Arbor MI: Michigan University Press.

Hyland, K. (2006) Study skills or academic literacy? In K. Hyland, *English for Academic Purposes: An Advanced Resource Book.* 16–23. New York: Routledge.

Hyland, K. (2007) English for specific purposes: Some influences and impacts. In J. Cummins and C. Davison (eds.), *International Handbook of English Language Teaching.* 391–402. New York: Springer.

Hyland, K. (2008) As can be seen: Lexical bundles and disciplinary variation. *English for Specific Purposes* 27: 4–21.

Hyland, K. and Tse, P. (2005) Hooking the reader: A corpus study of evaluative *that* in abstracts. *English for Specific Purposes* 24: 123–39.

Jackson, L., Meyer, W., and Parkinson, J. (2006) The writing tasks and reading assigned to undergraduate science students. *English for Specific Purposes* 25: 260–81.

Johnston, S, Lee, A., and McGregor, H. (1996) Engineering as captive discourse. *Phil and Tech* 1: 3-4.

Kanoksilapatham, B. (2005) Rhetorical structure of biochemistry RAs. *English for Specific Purposes* 24: 269–92.

Kassim, H. and Ali, F. (2010) English communicative events and skills needed at the workplace: Feedback from the industry. *English for Specific Purposes* 29: 168–82.

Knorr-Cetina, K. (1981) *The Manufacture of Knowledge: An Essay on the Constructivist*

Nature of Science. Oxford: Pergamon Press.

Koutsantoni, D. (2004) Attitude, certainty and allusions to common knowledge in scientific RAs. *Journal of English for Academic Purposes* 3: 163–82.

Koutsantoni, D. (2006) Rhetorical strategies in engineering RAs and research theses: Advanced academic literacy and relations of power. *Journal of English for Academic Purposes* 5: 19–36.

Kuo, C. H. (1999) The use of personal pronouns: Role relationships in scientific journal articles. *English for Specific Purposes* 18: 121–38.

Latour, B. and Woolgar, S. (1979) *Laboratory Life: The Construction of Scientific Facts.* New Jersey: Princeton University Press.

Lemke, J. L. (1990) *Talking Science: Language, Learning and Values.* Norwood, NJ: Ablex.

Leventhal, L. and Mynatt, B. (1987) Components of typical undergraduate software engineering courses: Results from a survey. *IEEE Transactions on Software Engineering* SE-13(11): 1193–99.

Lim, J. M. H. (2006) Method sections of management RAs: A pedagogically motivated qualitative study. *English for Specific Purposes* 25: 282–309.

Luzon, M. J. 2009. The use of *we* in a learner corpus of reports written by EFL Engineering students. *Journal of English for Academic Purposes* 8: 192–206.

Mackiewicz, J. (2004) The effects of tutor expertise in engineering writing: A linguisitic analysis of writing tutors' comments. *IEEE Transactions on Professional Communication* 47: 316–29.

Marshall, S. (1991) A genre-based approach to teaching report-writing. *English for Specific Purposes* 10: 3–13.

Martinez, I. (2003) Aspects of theme in the method and discussion sections of biology journal articles in English. *Journal of English for Academic Purposes* 2: 103–23.

Mohan, B. and Beckett, G. H. (2003) A functional approach to research on content-based language learning: Recasts in causal explanations. *The Modern Language Journal* 87: 421–32.

Molle, D. and Prior, P. (2008) Multimodal genre systems in EAP writing pedagogy: Reflecting on a needs analysis. *TESOL Quarterly* 42: 541–66.

Mudraya, O. (2006) Engineering English: A lexical frequency instructional model. *English for Specific Purposee* 25: 235–56.

Myers, G. (1989) The pragmatics of politeness in scientific articles. *Applied Linguistics* 10: 1–35.

Myers, G. (1992) Textbooks and the sociology of scientific knowledge. *English for Specific Purposes* 11: 3–17.

Myers, G. (2003) Words, pictures, and facts in academic discourse. *Iberica* 6: 3–13.

Nelson, S. (2000) Teaching collaborative writing and peer review techniques to engineering and technology undergraduates. 30th Annual Frontiers in Education Conference. Kansas City. Accessed February 2, 2012 at http://ieeexplore.ieee.org/stamp/stamp.jsp?arnumber=00896536.

O'Halloran, K. (2000) Classroom discourse in mathematics: A multisemiotic analysis. *Linguistics and Education* 10: 359–88.

Olsen, L. and Huckin, T. (1990) Point driven understanding in engineering lecture comprehension. *English for Specific Purposes* 9: 33-47.

Paltridge, B. (2002) Thesis and dissertation writing: An examination of published advice and actual practice. *English for Specific Purposes* 21: 125–43.

Paltridge, B. (2012) *Discourse Analysis.* 2nd ed. London: Continuum.

Paltridge, B. (2009) Afterword: Where have we come from and where are we now? In D. Belcher (ed), *English for Specific Purposes in Theory and Practice.* 289–96. Ann Arbor, MI: University of Michigan Press.

Parkinson, J. (2000) Acquiring scientific literacy through content and genre. *English for Specific Purposes* 19: 369–87.

Parkinson, J. (2011) The Discussion section as argument: The language used to prove knowledge claims. *English for Specific Purposes* 30: 164–75.

Parkinson, J. and Adendorff, R. (2005) Variable discursive constructions of three genres of science. *The Southern African Journal for Linguistics and Applied Language Studies* 23: 281–303.

Parodi, G. (2009) University genres in disciplinary domains. *Documentação de Estudos em Lingüística Teórica e Aplicada* 25: 401–26.

Peacock, M. (2002) Communicative moves in the discussion section of RAs. *System,* 30: 479–97.

Pennycook, A. (1997) Vulgar pragmatism, critical pragmatism and EAP. *English for Specific Purposes* 16: 253–69.

Pozzer-Ardenghiam, L. and Roth, W. -M. (2010) Toward a social practice perspective on the work of reading inscriptions in science texts. *Reading Psychology* 31: 228–53.

Pritchard, R. M. O. and Nasr, A. (2004) Improving reading performance among Egyptian engineering students: principles and practice. *English for Specific Purposes* 23: 425–45.

Pueyo, I. G. and Val, S. (1996) The construction of technicality in the field of plastics: A functional approach towards teaching technical terminology. *English for Specific Purposes* 15: 251–78.

Samraj, B. (2004) Discourse features of the student-produced academic research paper: Variations across disciplinary courses. *Journal of English for Academic Purposes* 3: 5–22.

Samraj, B. (2005) An exploration of a genre set: RA abstracts and introductions in two disciplines. *English for Specific Purposes* 24: 141–56.

Schleppegrell, M. J. (2002) Challenges of the science register for ESL students: Errors and meaning-making. In M. J. Schleppegrell and M. C. Colombi (eds.), *Developing Advanced Literacy in the First and Second Languages*. 119–42. Mahwah, NJ: Lawrence Erlbaum.

Schleppegrell, M. J. (2004) Functional grammar in school subjects. In M. J. Schleppegrell, *The Language of Schooling*. 113–45. Mahwah, NJ: Lawrence Erlbaum.

Smith Taylor, S. (2007) Comments on lab reports by mechanical engineering teaching assistants. *Journal of Business and Technical Communication* 21: 402–24.

Spack, R. (1988) Initiating ESL students into the academic discourse community: How far should we go? *TESOL Quarterly* 22: 29–52.

Stoller, F. (2010) Meet your ESP students' needs with a read-analyze-write approach. *Nineteenth International Symposium on English Teaching*. November 12–14, 2010. Taiwan.

Stoller, F. B., Horn, B., Grabe, W., and Robinson, M. (2005) Creating and validating assessment instruments for a discipline-specific writing course: An interdisciplinary approach. *Journal of Applied Linguistics* 2: 75–104.

Swales, J. M. (1971) *Writing Scientific English*. London: Nelson.

Swales, J. M. (1981) *Aspects of Article Introductions*. Birmingham, UK: The University of Aston, Language Studies Unit. Republished University of Michigan Press 2011.

Swales, J. M. (1984) Research into the structure of introductions to journal articles and its application to the teaching of academic writing. In R. Williams and J. Swales (eds.), *Common Ground: Shared Interests in ESP and Communication Studies* (ELT Documents No. 117). 77–86. Oxford: Pergamon Press.

Swales, J. M. (1988) *Episodes in ESP: A Source and Reference Book for the Development of English for Science and Technology*. New York: Prentice Hall.

Swales, J. M. (1990) *Genre Analysis: English in Academic and Research Settings*. Cambridge: Cambridge University Press.

Swales, J. M. (1995) The role of the textbook in EAP writing research. *English for Specific Purposes* 14: 3–18.

Swales, J. M. (2004) *Research Genres: Explorations and Applications*. Cambridge: Cambridge University Press.

Swales, J. M. and Lindemann, S. (2002) Teaching the literature review to international graduate students. In A. M Johns (ed.), *Genre in the Classroom*. 105–20. Mahwah, NJ: Lawrence Erlbaum.

Tudor, I. (1997) LSP or language education? In R. Howard and G. Brown (eds.), *Teacher Education for LSP*. 90–102. Clevedon, UK: Multilingual Matters.

Unsworth, L. (1997) Scaffolding reading of science explanations: Accessing the grammatical and visual forms of specialized knowledge. *Reading* 31: 30–42.

Vickers, C. (2007) Second language socialization through team interaction among electrical and computer engineering students. *The Modern Language Journal* 91: 621–40.

Ward, J. (2007) Collocation and technicality in EAP engineering. *Journal of English for Academic Purposes* 6: 18–35.

Ward, J. (2009) A basic engineering English word list for less proficient foundation engineering undergraduates. *English for Specific Purposes* 28: 170–82.

West, M. (1953) *A General Service List of English Words*. London: Longman.

Wood, A. (1982) An examination of the rhetorical structures of authentic chemistry texts. *Applied Linguistics* 3: 121–43.

Young, R. F. and Nguyen, H. T. (2002) Modes of meaning in high school science. *Applied Linguistics* 23: 348–72.

9 English in the Workplace

MEREDITH MARRA

Introduction

Teaching and researching English at work

Understanding the role and practice of English in the workplace is a key concern in English for special purposes (ESP). An increasingly globalized workforce and the overwhelming use of English as a de facto working language have created significant demand for workplace-specific courses. In parallel with this demand is the development of a field of (applied) sociolinguistic research which explores how people use language to negotiate their working lives. This chapter outlines the research that has been conducted in this area over the past two decades, identifying issues which can inform the teaching and learning of workplace English. If we consider ESP to be the conduit between academic research and practical applications (Basturkman 2006; Dudley-Evans and St John 1998), then this growing body of sociolinguistic work offers an exciting and productive pool of source material. As an illustration of the enormous potential for cross-fertilization, the chapter includes a description of a course which uses teaching materials developed from a corpus of naturally occurring workplace talk. The success of the interdisciplinary project which guides the course demonstrates that while the interaction of those working in ESP and those investigating workplace discourse has been limited to date, there is considerable scope for exploiting the synergies offered by the fields.

Before describing the research on English in the workplace, I start with two disclaimers. First, I acknowledge the reasonably narrow ESP focus covered in this chapter. While ESP for the workplace typically incorporates a wide range of contexts (including specific occupations such as healthcare, IT, factory workers, etc.,

The Handbook of English for Specific Purposes, First Edition.
Edited by Brian Paltridge and Sue Starfield.
© 2013 John Wiley & Sons, Inc. Published 2013 by John Wiley & Sons, Inc.

see Bosher, this volume; Ferguson, this volume; Northcott, this volume), the primary focus in this discussion is corporate and professional environments. The decision to concentrate on this area reflects the intersection of the interests of ESP specialists and the dominant environment in which sociolinguistic researchers have explored English in the workplace. Secondly, "discourse" features prominently throughout the chapter. By discourse I refer to interaction (spoken or written) produced in negotiation with others in a particular context (see also below). The importance of a situated approach to language use is increasingly recognized in the teaching of English, and is foundational for those who research English in the workplace from a discourse analytic perspective, like the authors described below.

Workplace Discourse Research

While ESP typically focusses on skills development and language learning, workplace discourse research is interested in identifying how language is used to achieve both task and people-oriented goals. This is clearly of relevance to those working in ESP; understanding more about how people communicate effectively in the workplace (as demonstrated by the analyses) has the potential to facilitate thorough needs analysis in similar workplace contexts. The discourse-based research which sits under the workplace banner has grown exponentially in the past twenty years, contributing to and benefitting from the wider "turn to discourse" in the social sciences. The range of qualitative analytic frameworks used for the empirical examination of language in use falls under the umbrella term "discourse analysis". There are many different schools and traditions following a range of theoretical assumptions and analytic tools. As such, discourse analysis acknowledges that there are multiple readings of any text, a strength, which emphasizes the complexity of talk. The overall goal of discourse analysts is to provide an understanding of social reality as it is produced by interactants, with each different approach offering a particular lens through which the analyst interprets the text.

Suspicious of the self-reported information provided by surveys and interviews, and in a move away from quantitative approaches, workplace discourse researchers typically collect and analyze naturally occurring talk to gain a greater understanding of the ways in which language in used on an everyday basis in the workplace context (e.g. Clyne 1994; Holmes and Stubbe 2003a; Koester 2006). This way of analyzing talk is also a reaction to the artificiality of experimental design, such as contrived groups and researcher-elicited language. These types of data often downplay the contextualized nature of workplace talk, where hierarchical differences, personal and long-term working relationships, and work histories (amongst other considerations) play an overt role in the way in which we design our talk. Instead, a discourse analytic approach relies on data which captures people talking at work, data which requires the cooperation of workplace participants and their colleagues.

A significant step in the establishment of the field of workplace discourse was the development of a methodology which created opportunities for precious access to "real" workplace talk. This permitted the analysis of authentic interaction rather than a reliance on intuitions and assumptions about communicative behavior, information which is notoriously unreliable (Angouri 2010; Kasper 1997). A particularly influential step toward this methodology was offered by Michael Clyne and his colleagues in their research on multicultural factories in Australia (see Clyne 1994). In their study, these researchers aimed to provide data on workplace communication in English between immigrants to Australia from different non-English speaking language and cultural backgrounds. The analysis drew on 182 hours of recordings involving 39 key informants derived from 8 workplaces, including factories, a catering section, offices, and meetings of a parents' group at a multicultural high school. In collecting this data, the team had preliminary meetings with management, unions and workers, followed by fieldworker visits where communication patterns were observed and then later recorded. Within this dataset were examples of a number of different communicative acts, such as receiving and making requests, instructions and complaints, and giving advice. A principal focus in the analysis was intercultural communication breakdown, and the researchers used triangulation in the form of participant interviews to support their understandings.

This Australian project was highly influential in establishing the feasibility of collecting authentic recordings as a source of information about workplace talk. The principles of data collection were taken up by the longstanding Language in the Workplace project (http://www.victoria.ac.nz/lals/lwp/) in New Zealand in 1996. Building on the research design, the research team (directed by Janet Holmes) developed a flexible methodology for working in white collar workplaces, this time involving New Zealand English speakers. The goal was a database of high quality, naturalistic interactional data recorded in everyday workplace contexts obtained using unobtrusive data collection processes. The data collection procedures needed to be achievable within a limited time frame and supported with sufficient demographic and contextual information to inform the analysis of the data. In achieving this goal, the team followed a philosophy which promoted ongoing, mutually-beneficial relationships, with workplace participants as co-researchers who were responsible for recording their own interactions based on negotiated research goals (see Holmes and Stubbe 2003a; Marra 2008 for descriptions; see also Roberts 2003 on "applied linguistics applied," a category for describing this kind of philosophy). The result was a participatory approach, which reduced the researchers' involvement in the physical collection of data to the absolute minimum to avoid distorting the naturalness of the interactions. In practice, volunteers recorded a range of everyday interactions at work over a period of two to three weeks, including social talk, telephone calls as well as "work-oriented" talk. For larger meetings, the team added video recording to aid speaker identification and provide access to relevant nonverbal contextual information. In establishing this design, a necessary and fruitful contribution has been the flexible and adaptable nature of the approach which has allowed the team to develop procedures for recording in factories, IT organizations, hospital wards, small regional workplaces, and more recently workplaces which operate following specific cultural norms based on a shared ethnicity other than the majority group (as reported in Holmes, Marra and Vine, 2011).

The success of this design for collecting good quality, everyday talk has meant that many other researchers have developed and adapted the application of the philosophy in workplaces around the world, including Angouri (2007) in multinational organizations in Europe, Schnurr and Chan (2011) in companies in Hong Kong, Ladegaard (2011) in global business corporations, as well as several researchers working in the United Kingdom (e.g. Koester 2010; Mullany 2007; Richards 2006). Consequently, there are many growing corpora of authentic workplace talk and analysis of these interactions provides useful information about how people talk in workplaces on an everyday basis.

A particularly important part of this philosophy is the role of the participants in the research. The ethics of recording in the workplace have always been a key consideration within the field, recognizing that the workplace is a high stakes environment with tangible consequences for the participants. Ethics committees at universities go to great lengths to ensure that any likely participant has fully understood how the data they contribute will be used and who will have access to it (i.e. genuine informed consent). Data is typically reported using pseudonyms and with any identifying information removed or replaced to protect the participants from potential risks, both seen and unforeseen. In practice this still relies on a certain level of mutual trust between the participants and researchers. As argued by Cameron (1985: 2), it is important to "break down the division between the researcher and the community," to avoid "researching on," and instead to "research with" the participants. The deliberate change from the term "subjects" in favor of the inclusive "participants" began to address the power imbalance of the research context; the process of researching with co-participants takes the ethical concern considerably further. As a number of researchers have noted, research is a form of social relationship, and one which is ongoing (Cameron et al. 1992; Garner, Raschka, and Sercombe 2006; Sarangi 2005). As workplace discourse researchers, our responsibility is to those we are working with, and mutually negotiated goals and benefits have been central to agreed practice. In terms of the data collected following these principles, it seems that the quality and scope reflects the positive relationships built between co-researchers (Holmes and Stubbe 2003a).

A group led by Sarangi and Candlin have developed the principle of the participants' cooperation and involvement even further, conducting research where professional participants become core members of the research team in order to understand the intricacies of professional practice alongside the analysis of the discourse. In the process they have established interdisciplinary research teams which draw on the in-group expertise of professional communities such as those working in law, healthcare, and management, engaging in analysis in collaboration with the skills and experience offered by applied linguists. The result is truly rich data and illuminating interpretations, built on extensive cooperation and long-term relationships (see Candlin 2006; Sarangi 2005,2007, and papers in Candlin and Sarangi 2011). The results have the potential to demonstrate the differences in the language used by various professional groups, with obvious application for those from non-English backgrounds working in these professions.

The language used by specific professional groups is one of a number of interests within the field. The terms professional, institutional, business and workplace discourse are all used by researchers, with various understandings of the boundaries between each. It seems that the overall goal, the disciplinary background and the particular theoretical stance each contribute to the distinctions made by researchers (see Bargiela-Chiappini and Zhang, this volume, for example). Others choose not to categorize their work, and instead adopt a more eclectic approach to their research. Because the field is still, for the most part, in its infancy (beyond the tradition of studying institutional talk within Conversation Analysis, e.g. Drew and Heritage 1992), individuals and research groups have often taken a wide-ranging focus, letting the data they have collected and their co-participants drive their research interests. This close engagement with co-participants has the advantage of resulting in good quality data which facilitates rigorous and systematic analysis. It has also meant that there is research in a number of areas, including analysis which explores both transactional (e.g.Gunnarsson 2009; Schnurr 2009; Vine 2004) and relational functions of workplace talk (Daly et al. 2004; Holmes and Marra 2004; Spencer-Oatey 2008). Despite this rather haphazard development, the resulting range of published research has much to offer those interested in accessing authentic language use at work, providing examples and analysis which can support both curriculum design and teaching materials.

The Importance of *Talk* at Work

"Talk," whether spoken or written, is central to this research (and naturally to ESP). Sarangi and Roberts argue that "workplaces are held together by communicative practices" (1999: 1); talk is how we "do" our work. An obvious focus for analysts is the tasks we achieve through language. Transactional/task-oriented interaction refers to the core, on-topic talk we expect in the workplace. Researchers have considered the way directives are enacted and interpreted (e.g. Vine 2009), the way meetings are run (e.g. Bilbow 1998; Rogerson-Revell 2008, Svennevig 2008) and the performance of leadership (e.g. Mullany 2010; Schnurr 2009). Others have focussed on problematic discourse and the negotiation of consensus (e.g. Firth 1995; Huisman 2001; Stubbe 2010), as well as the construction of various social identities in workplace talk, including gender (Baxter 2010; Holmes 2006; McCrae 2009; Mullany 2007) and ethnicity (Holmes, Marra and Vine, 2011). The researchers typically highlight the significance of context and group norms, establishing workplace interaction as a negotiation between colleagues.

Equally represented in the field is analysis of people-oriented, relational talk at work. The prevalence of small talk and humor in English-speaking workplaces (as evidenced by the empirical research) suggests that the misguided perception that relational talk is "dispensable" must be challenged (see argument in Fletcher

1999).The functions of humor at work have been investigated in detail, from goals of solidarity which emphasize shared group membership (Plester and Sayers 2007; Schnurr 2008) to those which enact power moves (Holmes and Marra 2002; Mullany 2004). A team that engages in practical jokes might use this behavior to cement inclusion and to encourage a productive working relationship. For example, Marra and Holmes (2007) describes an example of such a workplace: on April Fools' Day, new staff members were instructed to return a call to a "Mr Lion;" unbeknownst to them, the number they were given was for the local zoo. This served as an "initiation rite" which built solidarity in the team (and caused great amusement). Similarly small talk can function to "sugar the pill" in a particularly problematic request, or mitigate the effect of a criticism. Ignoring the relational aspects of workplace talk in favor of the transactional can mean describing only half the picture.

The relevance of people-oriented talk has proven particularly salient for those from non-English backgrounds. Clyne (1994) notes an interesting reaction to talk outside the socially sanctioned, task-focussed interaction we typically associate with work. He describes puzzlement from non-native speakers when native speakers engaged them in what they perceived as irrelevant, off-topic small talk. Having the skills to recognize and interpret such features in context (even if they do not initially extend to being able to produce these strategies) is something which can be immensely beneficial to those entering workplaces as non-native English speakers.

The overall trend which emerges is to emphasize the importance of both transactional and relational talk. Alongside business-oriented talk, an effective workplace participant must also understand "local ways of being sociable and local norms for managing small talk, humor and friendly chat" (Holmes 2005: 345). It is also clear that the same utterance can perform both functions simultaneously. Like all interaction, workplace talk is multifunctional and the relationship between form and function is complex.

Teaching Discourse Analysis: The Importance of Context

Embracing this perspective, there are increasing calls to encourage learners to develop analytic skills rather than teaching particular formulae or strategies. This also addresses various practical concerns, for example, how to meet the needs of learners from assorted backgrounds, on diverse career trajectories, and with different workplace goals. A focus on discourse analytic rather than English language skills encourages a move away from the decontextualized nature of some ESP materials and toward a focus which allows learners to assess and evaluate the English they meet in their own workplace interactions.

A useful model for such an approach is provided by Liddicoat et al. (2003). The exploratory process outlined in their model aims at facilitating the development of intercultural competence (Byram 1997). Learners are exposed to authentic interaction and encouraged to notice language use which is marked or distinctive (based on their experience and/or mother tongue norms). This is followed by reflection on the possible reasons for the particular language use, and their own response to the interaction. The next step is for the learners to use the language feature (*output*) and to experiment with new forms and strategies. In line with the cyclical nature of the model, learners are then encouraged to consider the interpersonal outcomes of using the new forms. This in turn leads to more reflection and experimentation, once again engaging with the reflexive nature of such an approach.

An added benefit of this approach is its potential as a method of empowering rather than simply shaping learners to fit or replicate majority group patterns (Eades 2004, Pennycook 2001). Byram (1997) notes that interactions involving learners will not be the same as native speaker interactions, and we must therefore be cautious of aiming for an unrealistic goal. A reflexive framework that draws on discourse analytic techniques facilitates opportunities for learners to "reflect on their own language experiences and practices and on the language practices of others in the institutions of which they are a part and in the wider society in which they live" (Clark and Ivanič 1997: 217; see also Pennycook 2001).

This style of learning, and specifically the emphasis on noticing, speaks to current debates on the importance of (socio) pragmatic instruction within English teaching for the workplace context. It has been argued, for example, that what are perceived to be English proficiency issues, can often be attributed to lack of understanding of culturally different communicative styles (Kasper 2006, Roberts 2005). The nuanced nature of meaning creation relies heavily on the "here and now," and this situated view of interaction encourages emphasis on local norms and understandings. Addressing this in language instruction involves moving beyond static forms and strategies which, while appealing from a learning and teaching perspective, are often inadequate for the contexts in which learners find themselves.

Researchers have produced persuasive arguments for emphasis to be placed on practical aspects of English in the form of sociopragmatic competence rather than grammatical accuracy (e.g. Lambert 2010; Forey and Lockwood 2007). However, developing pragmatic skills in another language has also been identified as extremely demanding (Clyne 2004; Myles 2005), and the viability of learning as a result of explicit instruction about pragmatic features (rather than simply exposure to these features) has been questioned. Nevertheless, authors such as Kasper and Rose (2002: 256) note that "without exception learners receiving instruction in pragmatics outperformed those who did not."

But how can we know which skills and features are most applicable for learners? The principles of researching with workplace co-participants, as described above (albeit in terms of data collection), provide one possibility. In an ideal world, teachers and learners would collaborate with those who are in the workplace contexts in which learners want or need to operate. However, this is often a practical impossibility. An obvious solution is greater interaction between workplace discourse researchers and ESP practitioners.

An Interdisciplinary Project: Workplace Communication for Skilled Migrants

By way of a study to illustrate a combined ESP – workplace discourse approach, I briefly describe an interdisciplinary project currently underway at Victoria University of Wellington in New Zealand. With the goal of facilitating the development of sociopragmatic competence, researchers from the Language in the Workplace project (described above) have joined with colleagues specializing in English language teaching to devise a course aimed at empowering skilled migrants who wish to enter New Zealand workplaces. The course consists of practical experience in workplaces, complemented by structured reflection in the classroom.

A concern for both the wider society and the New Zealand government is the struggle that professional migrants from non-English speaking backgrounds face in finding employment which recognizes their considerable expertise and experience. Stories of lawyers and doctors driving taxis and stacking supermarket shelves resonate across many countries. These migrants are frequently overlooked by prospective employers who continue to cite inadequate communication skills as a major obstacle (Henderson 2007; Podsialowski 2006; Spoonley and Davidson 2004), consistently underestimating the English language proficiency that migrants have reached.

Employment issues for migrants constitute an important topic for ESP and workplace researchers alike. As noted by Campbell and Roberts (2007) in their investigations of migrants engaging in job interviews in the United Kingdom, a particular issue is the importance of attending to both task and relational functions, and the challenge of marrying personal and professional discourse in culturally appropriate ways in job interviews. The ongoing work of Celia Roberts and colleagues (Campbell and Roberts 2007; Roberts, Davies, and Jupp 1992) has opened pathways for research in and outside the United Kingdom, especially research which pays attention to the gatekeeping role of the job interview (e.g. Kerekes 2005; Reissner-Roubicek 2010). The project at Victoria University of Wellington expands the focus to the practice of workplace talk (see also Marra, Holmes and Riddiford 2011 for a fuller description).

A lack of workplace communication training was identified as a concern in New Zealand and the university was contracted to provide an English language program which drew on the findings of the Language in the Workplace project and was suitable for skilled migrants who reached the benchmark of IELTS 6.0, and who had been unemployed or underemployed for at least two years. The selling point for the funders was the corpus of naturally occurring talk and the numerous analyses of effective communication between native speakers conducted over the previous decade. This data provided materials for teaching and facilitated relevant needs analysis for the skilled migrants who would participate in the course (see Newton and Riddiford 2010 for exemplification). Applied linguists at the university designed a curriculum which included both classroom instruction and supported workplace internships, with emphasis placed on the development of sociopragmatic skills to address social meaning in interaction. Built into the course were various tools to establish the progress of the students, including multiple data points such as discourse completion tasks (Blum-Kulka 1982), role plays and reflective interviews.

An important component in the ongoing development of the course was a parallel research project. Master has argued that ESP needs to "heed the repeated calls to establish its empirical validity" (2005: 111); that is, it needs to take it claims for validity beyond anecdotal success stories. The sociolinguists in the interdisciplinary team undertook research which aimed to evaluate the success of the program. A lack of appropriate assessment of class materials has been noted by Rose (2005) who argued that such evaluation rarely uses learners' day-to-day, face-to-face interactions as a measure of the success of teaching. It seemed natural for the Language in the Workplace team to apply their research procedures here, and migrants on the course have been tracked into their workplace contexts, recording samples of their workplace talk at the beginning and end of their internships. This research thus extends the use of authentic talk to incorporate assessment of the development of sociopragmatic skills (and in turn for developing future teaching practice).

To demonstrate the analytic perspective, I include two brief extracts which indicate the potential for insights offered by the approach. In example 1, Andrei, a workplace intern from Russia, is talking about his past work history with New Zealand colleague, Camille. Establishing his credentials as an experienced and competent professional seems like an obvious and acceptable topic of conversation. As the extract indicates, however, the method that Andrei uses does not have the consequences he necessarily expects.

Example 1

```
 1.  Andrei:   yes I er [clears throat] I was involved
                 in the same
 2.             similar to the similar work back in Europe
 3.  Camille:  oh right
 4.  Andrei:   er but for international er financial er
                 institutions like
 5.             international monetary fund //and the
                 world\
 6.  Camille:  /oh↑wow\\
 7.  Andrei:   bank and the European bank for
                 construction and development
 8.  Camille:  oh↓
 9.  Andrei:   and for our (    ) of ch- chairman and
                 deputy chairman
10.  Camille:  oh wow[1]
```

At a linguistic level, the problematic nature of this extract is not necessarily obvious. Despite some minor non-native features in his talk (e.g. *I was involved . . . to the similar work*) Andrei has no difficulty making himself understood. His experience is unquestionably impressive; he talks of working for the International Monetary Fund (lines 4–5) and with high ranking officials (line 9). There are, however, subtle hints from Camille that this interaction is not necessarily achieving a positive outcome for Andrei, and in particular that Andrei is not being self-deprecating enough for the particular community of practice in which he is operating. The indications of this, however, rely on nuanced readings of various features. One such indicator is the repetition of *oh (wow)* (lines 3, 6, 8, 10). The repetition of this form, and the corresponding intonation, makes it clear that Andrei has gone too far and his claims seem to be interpreted as boasting; this short utterance carries considerable pragmatic meaning. A micro-analytic focus also recognizes that the intonation is highly relevant. While the first occurrence sounds genuine, the others are progressively restrained: there is falling intonation in the second occurrence (as indicated in the transcript) and relatively flat intonation in the third. Systematic analysis of other interactions in this workplace makes it clear that it is important to behave in a way which does not seem boastful, in line with the widely recognized "tall poppy syndrome" prevalent in New Zealand society (i.e. a low tolerance of explicit demonstrations of power and status).

In a second example, Henry, a Chinese workplace intern, receives directions from his New Zealand colleague, Simon. Simon, Henry's workplace mentor, is describing the process for setting up new files in the company computer system.

Example 2

```
 1.  Simon:     set up a new folder and go add new folder
 2.  Henry:     mm
 3.  Simon:     because that automatically defaults to
                   what
 4.             the parent the parent folder
 5.             under here is the network folder ...
 6.  Justine:   mm
 7.  Simon:     so if I went
 8.             and go you know file new folder
 9.  Henry:     folder
10.  Simon:     and I've got to you know [types] put it
                   in ...
11.  Justine:   that's right yeah
12.  Henry:     mm mm mm
```

There is very little content in Henry's contributions which largely comprise of listenership devices in the form of minimal feedback (i.e. *mm*). However, Henry clearly understands what is going on, and is learning from his mentor's instructions. He uses appropriate signals to indicate that he is following, and that Simon should continue his explanation. In this interaction there is clear evidence of the success that some of the students achieve in developing their sociopragmatic competence within the workplace environment. Henry's minimal feedback in lines 2 and 12 matches the behavior of his New Zealand colleague, Justine (line 6). He also uses an appropriate echo of the information outlined by Simon in the form of *folder* (line 9). His workmates made specific reference to this communicative behavior, noting how well Henry integrated into their workplace from the outset. They provided positive evaluations of his proficiency in their evaluations, with his sociopragmatic and analytic skills arguably contributing to their assessments.

In each case the interns did not have significant issues with their English language ability, despite the ongoing concerns publically expressed by potential employers of skilled migrants. Instead of focussing on linguistic proficiency, the course encouraged them to develop discourse analytic skills to observe the behavior of those around them. Reactions (both positive and negative) alongside negotiation with interlocutors provide important information for learners as they navigate group norms and appropriate ways of behaving. By understanding group norms, the migrants have the opportunity to comply or flout community norms to achieve their desired goal, whether that is to be complicit in or to resist dominant patterns (see Holmes et al. 2011).

A rewarding number of the class members are now in jobs which more closely reflect their previous experience and expertise. The success of this program relies on the collaboration between researchers and ESP practitioners who work together to develop materials that reflect authentic workplace talk, and which address the needs of learners. This approach also encompasses the importance of context and the situated nature of language use at work.

A Need for Dialogue

Belcher (2004) argued that the perceived shortcomings of ESP were the focus on a narrow range of contexts and/or tasks in isolation from real life contexts. This speaks to the very heart of what workplace discourse research can offer. Sadly, a productive dialogue between practitioners and researchers is uncommon. Just as researchers work in negotiation with workplaces, it seems that there is an important need for researchers and practitioners to collaborate in ways which facilitate the development of appropriate, relevant teaching materials and approaches which help prepare learners for the realities of English at work (see also Dressen-Hammouda, this volume).

The disparate worlds of workplace researcher and those teaching English for the workplace are particularly apparent in the evaluation of teaching materials, an important part of the research agenda in ESP. More than twenty years ago Marion Williams (1988) questioned the relevance of textbook materials for teaching meeting talk, finding a considerable discrepancy between actual language use and the language prescribed (see also Angouri 2010; Chan 2009). Since then research has demonstrated a consistent mismatch between naturally occurring language use and the representations found in the textbooks (Barbieri and Eckhardt 2007; Wong 2002). Textbooks and textbook users have changed considerably, however (Edwards 2000, Harwood 2010). Those charged with the task of teaching English for the workplace are faced with complex challenges and pressures to meet the dynamic language and communication needs of students, as well as those of employers (Louhiala-Salminen 1996). The appeal of textbooks, as argued by Harwood (2005), lies in the fact that they allow teachers to use existing materials, rather than creating their own. He argues that good teachers use the materials selectively, not relying on, but referring to, the textbook. To enact this practice successfully, however, still involves an assumption that practitioners have an understanding of what authentic workplace talk looks like, and it remains common to focus on the need for, and more recently the relevance of, "authenticity" (e.g. Coupland 2007; Mishan 2005; Newton 2007). Once again we reach an issue of common interest, and one where greater interaction between the two worlds could provide fruitful discussions.

Since the early 1990s, researchers have investigated the myriad ways language is used in the workplace context including the role of discourse in the negotiation of power and politeness as well as the enactment of transactional and relational talk. There is continued recognition of the importance of English in the workplace, from Hong Kong (Evans 2010; So-mui and Mead 2000) to Finland (Louhiala-Salminen 1996) to Japan (Lambert 2010) and the Philippines (Forey and Lockwood 2007). This provides ongoing impetus for deeper understandings of how people use English in the workplace, including the ability of this research to support methods for preparing learners for the workplace environment.

By its very nature, ESP is at one level context-focussed; its goal is to investigate issues that relate specifically to what is required for the particular purpose, taking into account the needs of the learners (Basturkmen 2010). The disjoint between practitioners and researchers explored here seems to lie in the way in which this "context" is interpreted. The discourse analytic perspectives described above call for a view of context which is local and situated, well beyond the notion of simply a "corporate" or "business" environment in favor of an investigation which takes into consideration the micro-level detail of group norms and perspectives for understanding language in action, continually emphasizing the importance of contextual sensitivity. To address this in a way which meets the needs of a range of learners, the focus on teaching discourse analytic skills and encouraging a focus on sociopragmatic competence provides one possible option for ESP practitioners, an option which incorporates findings from research which investigates authentic workplace talk.

Conclusions and Future Directions

In this chapter, I have provided an overview of the findings and methodological approaches of discourse analysts who research English in the workplace. Throughout the discussion I have called for greater dialogue between these researchers and ESP practitioners who typically (and somewhat unhelpfully) engage in parallel academic worlds. As an illustration of the benefits of collaborative work, I have described a successful project which has been undertaken between Victoria University of Wellington's Language in the Workplace team and the teachers and students of a course which aims to facilitate the acquisition of workplace communication skills. Our research indicates the effectiveness of explicit classroom instruction alongside practical workplace experience for increasing learners' awareness of the sociopragmatic aspects of talk at work, and provides convincing evidence of participants' increased use of contextually appropriate talk.

This kind of interdisciplinary work will continue to be an integral feature of the field in the future; it brings together diverse viewpoints and theoretical perspectives that have the potential to deepen our understanding of language use in workplace settings. There are obvious benefits to be found by drawing on the skills of individuals from different disciplines, whether sociolinguists and applied linguists as described here, language specialists and academics from strategic management (e.g. Jackson et al. 2006), or collaborations between researchers and workplace professionals (as endorsed in the work of Sarangi 2005, 2007; and Candlin 2006). In each case, our knowledge is advanced by new perspectives and innovative approaches.

A second area in which we are likely to see new developments is the growing attention given to multimodal features of workplace interaction. Just as our focus has shifted from grammatical to sociopragmatic competence, researchers are increasingly interested in features of workplace talk beyond speech or writing (e.g. Filliettaz 2004). Advancements in technology have allowed us to capture gesture, body movement, and gaze in interaction. Their impact on interaction is widely recognized by analysts (e.g. Glenn and LeBaron 2011), and there have been recent campaigns for their inclusion in teaching programs, specifically in the area of pragmatic instruction (see Louw, Derwing, and Abbott 2010). This focus presents new challenges and exciting opportunities for workplace discourse researchers.

The dynamic lifecycle of research means that in addressing research questions we discover as many additional questions as we do answers. The body of research which specifically considers English in the workplace is continually growing, and greater engagement between practitioners and researchers will lead to productive and ongoing working relationships, with new and evolving research agendas tailored specifically to those issues most pressing for ESP.

Acknowledgment

In writing this chapter I have drawn on my ongoing research with the Language in the Workplace project in the School of Linguistics and Applied Language Studies at Victoria University; I acknowledge my long-standing collaborators in that work (especially Janet Holmes, Bernadette Vine, and Nicky Riddiford), as well as the numerous workplace co-participants who have allowed us to record their everyday talk. This chapter also draws on comparative research conducted with Jo Angouri at the University of the West of England, Bristol, to whom I express my thanks. I am also indebted to research assistant Doug Midgley for his help with this chapter.

NOTE

1   Transcription conventions: [ ] editorial and other information in square brackets; (oh) transcriber's best guess at an unclear utterance; //here\ overlapping talk; /here\\ – cut off talk; . . . section of transcript missing; ↑↓rising/falling intonation. All names are pseudonyms, and any identifying material has been removed.

REFERENCES

Angouri, J. (2007) Language in the workplace. A multimethod study of communicative activity in seven multinational companies situated in Europe. Unpublished PhD thesis, University of Essex, Colchester.

Angouri, J. (2010) Using textbooks and real life data to teach turn taking for business meetings. In N. Harwood (ed.), *English Language Teaching Materials: Theory and Practice*. 373–95. Cambridge: Cambridge University Press.

Barbieri, F. and Eckhardt, S. E. B. (2007) Applying corpus-based findings to form-focused instruction: The case of reported speech. *Language Teaching Research* 11: 319–46.

Basturkmen, H. (2006) *Ideas and Options in English for Specific Purposes*. Mahwah, NJ: Lawrence Erlbaum.

Basturkmen, H. (2010) *Developing Courses in English for Specific Purposes*. Basingstoke, UK: Palgrave Macmillan.

Baxter, J. (2010) *The Language of Female Leadership*. Basingstoke, UK: Palgrave Macmillan.

Belcher, D. (2004) Trends in teaching English for Specific Purposes. *Annual Review of Applied Linguistics* 24: 165–86.

Bilbow, G. T. (1998) Look who's talking: An analysis of "chair-talk" in business meetings. *Journal of Business and Technical Communication* 12: 157–97.

Blum-Kulka, S. (1982) Learning how to say what you mean in a second language: A study of speech act performance of learners of Hebrew as a second language. *Applied Linguistics* 3: 29–59.

Byram, M. (1997) *Teaching and Assessing Intercultural Communicative Competence*. Clevedon, UK: Multilingual Matters.

Campbell, S. and Roberts, C. (2007) Migration, ethnicity and competing discourses in the job interview: Synthesizing the institutional and personal. *Discourse and Society* 18: 243–71.

Cameron, D. (1985) "Respect, please!" – Subjects and objects in sociolinguistics. Unpublished manuscript.

Cameron, D., Frazer, E. Harvey, P. Rampton, B., and Richardson, K. (1992) *Researching Language: Issues of Power and Method*. London: Routledge.

Candlin, C. N. (2006) Accounting for interdiscursivity: Challenges to professional expertise. In M. Gotti and D. S. Giannone (eds.), *New Trends in*

Specialized Discourse Analysis. 21–45. Bern: Peter Lang Verlag.

Candlin, C. N. and Sarangi, S. (eds.) (2011) *Communication in Professions and Organisations* (Handbook of Applied Linguistics 3). Berlin: Mouton de Gruyter.

Chan, C. S. C. (2009) Forging a link between research and pedagogy: A holistic framework for evaluating business English materials. *English for Specific Purposes* 28: 125–36.

Clark, R. and Ivanič, R. (1997) *The Politics of Writing*. London: Routledge.

Clyne, M. (1994) *Inter-Cultural Communication at Work*. Cambridge: Cambridge University Press.

Coupland, N. (2007) *Style: Language Variation and Identity*. Cambridge: Cambridge University Press.

Daly, N., Holmes, J., Newton, J., and Stubbe, M. (2004) Expletives as solidarity signals in FTAs on the factory floor. *Journal of Pragmatics* 36: 945–64.

Drew, P. and Heritage, J. (eds.) (1992) *Talk at Work: Interaction in Institutional Settings*. Cambridge: Cambridge University Press.

Dudley-Evans, T. and St John, M. J. (1998) *Developments in English for Specific Purposes: A Multi-Disciplinary Approach*. Cambridge: Cambridge Universtiy Press.

Eades, D. (2004) Understanding Aboriginal English in the legal system: A critical sociolinguistics approach. *Applied Linguistics* 25: 491–512.

Edwards, N. (2000) Language for business: Effective needs assessment, syllabus design and materials preparation in a practical ESP case study. *English for Specific Purposes* 19: 291–96.

Evans, S. (2010) Business as usual: The use of English in the professional world in Hong Kong. *English for Specific Purposes* 29: 153–67.

Filliettaz, L. (2004) The multimodal negotiation of service encounters. In P. LeVine and R. Scollon (eds.), *Discourse and Technology: Multimodal Discourse*

Analysis. 88–100. Washington, DC: Georgetown University Press.

Firth, A. (1995) *The Discourse of Negotiation: Studies of Language in the Workplace*. Oxford: Pergamon Press.

Fletcher, J. K. (1999) *Disappearing Acts. Gender, Power, and Relational Practice at Work*. Cambridge, MA: MIT Press.

Forey, G. and Lockwood, J. (2007) "I'd love to put someone in jail for this": An initial investigation of English in the business processing outsourcing (BPO) industry. *English for Specific Purposes* 26: 308–26.

Garner, M., Raschka, C., and Sercombe, P. (2006) Sociolinguistic minorities, research and social relationships. *Journal of Multilingual and Multicultural Development* 27: 61–78.

Glenn, P. and LeBaron, C. (2011) Epistemic authority in employment interviews: Glancing, pointing, touching. *Discourse and Communication* 5: 3–22.

Gunnarsson, B. L. (2009) *Professional Discourse*. London: Continuum.

Harwood, N. (2005) What do we want EAP teaching materials for? *Journal of English for Academic Purposes* 4: 149–61.

Harwood, N. (ed.) (2010) *English Language Teaching Materials: Theory and Practice*. Cambridge: Cambridge University Press.

Henderson, A. (2007) English language proficiency and the employment of professional immigrants in New Zealand: How much is enough? *CACR Newsletter*, April 2, 2007.

Holmes, J. (2005) When small talk is a big deal: Sociolinguistic challenges in the workplace. In M. Long (ed.), *Second Language Needs Analysis*. 344–71. Cambridge: Cambridge University Press.

Holmes, J. (2006) *Gendered Talk at Work*. London: Blackwell.

Holmes, J., Joe, A., Marra, M., Newton, J., Riddiford, N., and Vine, B. (2011) Applying linguistic research to real world problems: The case of the Wellington Language in the Workplace Project. *Communication in Professions and*

Organisations (Handbook of Applied Linguistics 3). 533–49. Berlin: Mouton de Gruyter.

Holmes, J. and Marra, M. (2002) Over the edge? Subversive humour between colleagues and friends. *Humor* 15: 65–87.

Holmes, J. and Marra, M. (2004) Relational practice in the workplace: Women's talk or gendered discourse? *Language in Society* 33: 377–98.

Holmes, J., Marra, M., and Vine, B. (2011) *Leadership, Discourse and Ethnicity.* Oxford: Oxford University Press.

Holmes, J. and Stubbe, M. (2003a) *Power and Politeness in the Workplace.* London: Pearson Education.

Holmes, J. and Stubbe, M. (2003b) "Feminine" workplaces: Stereotype and reality. In J. Holmes and M. Meyerhoff (eds.), *Handbook of Language and Gender.* 573–99. Oxford: Blackwell.

Huisman, M. (2001) Decision-making in meetings as talk-in-interaction. *International Studies of Management and Organization* 31: 69–90.

Jackson, B., Pfeifer, D., and Vine. B. (2006) The co-leadership of transformational leadership: A discourse analysis. In J. Kennedy and L. Di Milia (eds.), *Proceedings of the 20th ANZAM Conference [electronic resource]: Management: Pragmatism, Philosophy, Priorities.* Rockhampton, Queensland: Faculty of Business and Informatics, Central Queensland University. Accessed February 2, 2011 at http://hdl.cqu.edu.au/10018/35954.

Kasper, G. (1997) *Can pragmatic competence be taught?* (NFLRC NetWork 6) Accessed May 31 2011 at http://nflrc.hawaii.edu/NetWorks/NW06.

Kasper, G. (2006) Speech acts in interaction: Towards discursive pragmatics. In K. Bardovi-Harlig, C. Félix-Brasdefer and A. Omar (eds.), *Pragmatics and Language Learning* vol. 1.1. 281–314. Honolulu: National Foreign Language Resource Center.

Kerekes, J. A. (2005) Before, during, and after the event: Getting the job (or not) in an employment interview. In K. Bardovi-Harlig and B. Hartford (eds.), *Interlanguage Pragmatics: Exploring Institutional Talk.* 99–131. Mahwah, NJ: Lawrence Erlbaum.

Koester, A. (2006) *Investigating Workplace Discourse.* London: Routledge.

Koester, A. (2010) *Workplace Discourse.* London: Continuum.

Ladegaard, H. J. (2011) "Doing power" at work: Responding to male and female management styles in a global business corporation. *Journal of Pragmatics* 43: 4–19.

Lambert, C. (2010) A task-based needs analysis: Putting principles into practice. *Language Teaching Research* 14: 99–112.

Liddicoat, A. J., Papademetre, L., Scarino, A., and Kohler, M. (2003) *Report on Intercultural Language Learning.* Canberra: Department of Education, Science and Training. Accessed May 31, 2011 at http://www1.curriculum.edu.au/nalsas/pdf/intercultural.pdf.

Louhiala-Salminen, L. (1996) The business communication classroom vs. reality: What should we teach today? *English for Specific Purposes* 15: 37–51.

Louw, K. J., Derwing, T. M., and Abbott, M. L. (2010) Teaching pragmatics to L2 learners for the workplace: The job interview. *The Canadian Modern Language Review [La Revue Canadienne des Langues Vivantes]* 66: 739–58.

McRae, S. (2009) It's a blokes thing: Gender, occupational roles and talk in the workplace. In P. Pichler and E. M. Eppler (eds.), *Gender and Spoken Interaction.* 163–185. London: Palgrave Macmillan.

Marra, M. (2008) Recording and analyzing talk across cultures. In H. Spencer-Oatey (ed.), *Culturally Speaking: Managing Rapport through Talk Across Cultures.* 2nd ed. 304–21. London: Continuum.

Marra, M. and Holmes, J. (2007) Humour across cultures: Joking in the multicultural workplace. In H. Kotthoff and H. Spencer-Oatey (eds.), *Intercultural Communication* (Handbook of Applied Linguistics 7). 153–72. Berlin and New York: Mouton de Gruyter.

Marra, M., Holmes, J., and Riddiford, N. (2011) New Zealand's Language in the Workplace project: Workplace communication for skilled migrants. In M. Krzanowski (ed.), *English for Work and the Workplace: Approaches, Curricula and Materials*. 93–106. Reading, UK: Garnet Education.

Master, P. (2005) Research in English for specific purposes. In E. Hinkel (ed.), *Handbook of Research in Second Language Teaching and Learning*. 99–115. Mahwah, NJ: Lawrence Erlbaum.

Mishan, F. (2005) *Designing Authenticity into Language Learning Materials*. Bristol, UK: Intellect.

Mullany, L. (2004) Gender, politeness and institutional power roles: Humour as a tactic to gain compliance in workplace business meetings. *Multilingua* 23: 13–37.

Mullany, L. (2007) *Gendered Discourse in Professional Communication*. Basingstoke, UK: Palgrave Macmillan.

Mullany, L. (2010) Gendered identities in the professional workplace. Negotiating the glass ceiling. In C. Llamas and D. Watts (eds.), *Language and Identity*. 179–91. Edinburgh: Edinburgh University Press.

Myles J. M. (2005) Communicative competence in the workplace: A look at the experiences of English second language engineering students during their professional internships. Unpublished PhD thesis: Queen's University, Kingston, Ontario.

Newton, J. (2007) Adapting authentic workplace talk for workplace communication training. In H. Kotthoff and H. Spencer-Oatey (eds.), *Intercultural Communication* (Handbook of Applied Linguistics 7). 519–37. Berlin: Mouton de Gruyter.

Newton, J. and Riddiford, N. (2010) *Workplace Talk in Action: An ESOL Resource*. Wellington, New Zealand: Victoria University of Wellington.

Pennycook, A. (2001) *Critical Applied Linguistics: A Critical Introduction*. Mahwah, NJ: Lawrence Erlbaum.

Plester, B. and Sayers , J. (2007) "Taking the piss": Functions of banter in the IT industry. *Humor* 20: 157–87.

Podsiadlowski, A. (2006) Faciliating migrants' entry and integration into the New Zealand workplace. Summaries of completed research. Accessed April 15, 2007 at http://www.victoria.ac.nz/cacr/research/migrantentry-com.aspx.

Reissner-Roubicek, S. (2010) Communication strategies in behavioural job interviews: The influence of discourse norms on graduate recruitment. Unpublished PhD thesis, University of Auckland, New Zealand.

Richards, K. (2006) *Language and Professional Identity: Aspects of Collaborative Interaction*. Basingstoke, UK: Palgrave Macmillan.

Roberts, C. (2003) Applied linguistics applied. In S. Sarangi and T. Van Leeuwen (eds.), *Applied Linguistics and Communities of Practice*. 132–49. London: Continuum.

Roberts, C. (2005) English in the workplace. In E. Hinkel (ed.), *Handbook of Research in Second Language Teaching and Learning*. 117–135. Mahwah, NJ: Lawrence Erlbaum.

Roberts, C., Davies, E., and Jupp, T. (1992) *Language and Discrimination: A Study of Communication in Multi-Ethnic Workplaces*. London: Longman.

Rogerson-Revell, P. (2008) Participation and performance in international business meetings. *English for Specific Purposes* 27: 338–60.

Rose, K. R. (2005) On the effects of instruction in second language pragmatics. *System* 33: 385–99.

Sarangi, S. (2005) The conditions and consequences of professional discourse studies. *Journal of Applied Linguistics* 2: 371–94.

Sarangi, S. (2007) Other-orientation in patient-centred healthcare communication: Unveiled ideology or discoursal ecology? In G. Garzone and S. Sarangi (eds.), *Discourse, Ideology and Ethics in Specialised Communication*. 39–71. Bern: Peter Lang.

Schnurr, S. (2008) Surviving in a man's world with a sense of humour: An analysis of women leaders' use of humour at work. *Leadership* 4: 299–319.

Schnurr, S. (2009) *Leadership Discourse at Work: Interactions of Humour, Gender and Workplace Culture*. Basingstoke, UK: Palgrave Macmillan.

Schnurr, S. and Chan, A. (2011) Exploring another side of co-leadership. Negotiating professional identities through face-work in disagreements. *Language in Society* 40: 187–209.

So-mui, F. L. and Mead, K. (2000) An analysis of English in the workplace: The communication needs of textile and clothing merchandisers. *English for Specific Purposes* 19: 351–68.

Spencer-Oatey, H. (2008) Face, (im)politeness and rapport. In H. Spencer-Oatey (ed.), *Culturally Speaking: Managing Rapport through Talk Across Cultures*. 2nd ed. 11–47. London: Continuum.

Spoonley, P. and Davidson, C. (2004) The changing world of work. In P. Spoonley, A. Dupuis and A. de Bruin (eds.), *Work and Working in Twenty-First Century New Zealand*. 17–40. Palmerston North, New Zealand: Dunmore Press.

Stubbe, M. (2010) "Was that my misunderstanding?": Managing miscommunication and problematic talk at work. Unpublished PhD thesis, Victoria University of Wellington, New Zealand.

Svennevig, J. (2008) Exploring leadership conversations. *Management Communication Quarterly* 21: 529–36.

Vine, B. (2004) *Getting Things Done at Work: The Discourse of Power in Workplace Interaction*. Amsterdam: John Benjamins.

Vine, B. (2009) Directives at work: Exploring the contextual complexity of workplace directives. *Journal of Pragmatics* 41: 1395–405.

Williams, M. (1988) Language taught for meetings and language used in meetings: Is there anything in common? *Applied Linguistics* 9: 45–58.

Wong, J. (2002) Applying conversation analysis in applied linguistics: Evaluating dialogue in English as a second language textbooks. *International Review of Applied Linguistics* 40: 37–60.

10 Business English

FRANCESCA BARGIELA-CHIAPPINI
AND ZUOCHENG ZHANG

Introduction: Where We Are Now

> Without research Business English foreign and second language learners will be hampered. With the growth of conferences and the increasing numbers of students studying Business English within MA courses, there will undoubtedly be much more research carried out and published (St John 1996: 15).

In the same year that Maggie Jo St John published the article from which this opening quotation is taken, Dudley-Evans and St John (1996) also compiled a report on Business English (BE) which again noted the limited research on the subject and the fact that such research had tended to concentrate on written communication while teaching focussed mostly on the spoken language. Moreover, they also identified two components of Business English, which they labeled "English for general business purposes" and "English for specific business purposes," respectively, the contents of which depend on the linguistic competence of the learners and their business experience. They also noted how the "underlying business culture is that of Western Europe and the United States of America" (Dudley-Evans and St John 1998: v) which they considered inappropriate. This is arguably one of the consequences of the international acceptance of "management," an ideology that took shape in the United States and the United Kingdom, and which is effectively propagated through the capillary network of management schools, and training managerial elites worldwide according to standardized MBA programs (Mintzberg 2004).

In this chapter, we hope to show how the notion of "Business English" has been adopted in local contexts to reflect often very different local circumstances, and we will take the cases of Japan and China to illustrate this point. Yet, while

The Handbook of English for Specific Purposes, First Edition.
Edited by Brian Paltridge and Sue Starfield.
© 2013 John Wiley & Sons, Inc. Published 2013 by John Wiley & Sons, Inc.

distinctive, these local histories also show how the Business English "brand" continues to be strongly influenced by Western preferences, especially in terms of which (native) English is deemed to be acceptable, and what theories and methods of international business and crosscultural management are taught alongside or as components of business communication programs.

Eleven years after St John's article, and from a very different context of practice, Zhang Zuocheng (Zhang 2005, 2007) proposed a discourse approach to Business English, which locates the practice and the teaching of the language within the discursivity of the business activities and contexts that generate them. Consequently, a pedagogic approach to Business English involves "the teaching of the system of strategic communication in international business in which participants adopt or adapt business conventions and procedures and make selective use of lexico-grammatical resources of English as well as visual and audio semiotic resources to achieve their communicative goals" (Zhang 2012).

This chapter offers an overview of Business English as seen from the perspective of business discourse, itself a composite of traditions and approaches (Bargiela-Chiappini 2009). It is hoped that this vantage point will provide complementary insights on Business English to those of other related chapters in this *Handbook*.

Following the historical note in the section below, which reveals the crucial role played by Western scholarship in the development of the field, the following section focusses on two distinct and significant local histories of Business English from outside the Western tradition, namely China and Japan. Lessons to be learned from these two contexts of practice will be discussed. In response to the call for a more research-based pedagogy of Business English (St John 1996; Dudley-Evans and St John 1998), the final section of this chapter sketches a possible new map for the field, which highlights its natural home within the social sciences and the advantages of new or renewed connections with a range of sympathetic disciplines and methodological approaches.

A Historical Overview: How We Got There

Business English is a recognized area of English for Specific Purposes (ESP) (Dudley-Evans and St John 1998; Hutchinson and Waters 1987; St John 1996). A number of Business English education programs are offered in quite different linguistic and social milieus across the world, notably the international Business English undergraduate program at Anglia Ruskin University in the United Kingdom, the Master's program of international business communication at Aalto University in Finland, and the Brazilian national ESP project (Celani 2008).

The position of this chapter within the handbook means that Business English looks up, figuratively-speaking, to English in the workplace (Marra, this volume), as well as down, to intercultural rhetoric (Connor and Rozycki, this volume) and English as a lingua franca (ELF) (Nickerson, this volume). Almost inevitably the trajectories of these chapters will cross at some point, perhaps more often than the individual authors had intended or planned. It seems to us that this is a sign of both a widening of horizons within each specific outlook as well as an increasing convergence towards research-based pedagogies. These developments have extended the purchase of "Business English" (BE) as a field of inquiry beyond the original focus on the needs of an idealized "Western" classroom setting, even though the "white Anglophone" teacher is still the preferred and, sometimes, only choice in certain parts of the world (we are grateful to Catherine Nickerson for this insight).

In this section, we will sketch a profile of the recent history of Business English since the 1990s and briefly recall salient developments as represented in relevant Anglophone literatures (for a historical perspective on ESP since the 1960s, the reader is referred to Dudley-Evans and St John 1998: Chapter 2).

In their 1998 landmark work *Developments in English for Specific Purposes: A Multi-Disciplinary Approach*, Dudley-Evans and St John (1998: 19) note that "ESP is an essentially materials-driven and teaching-led movement." The literature on business communication considerably enlarged the original, narrow view of Business English as the teaching of the language for vocational purposes through linking linguistic performance with actual business activities. The work of Catherine Nickerson (this volume) and Leena Louhiala-Salminen in Finland exemplifies the professional trajectory of many applied linguists who started as Business English teachers, migrated into being business communication teachers and are now teaching business discourse, especially to more senior students. It was when linguists and communication scholars began to look at what was happening in the field that finally a window was opened into a less neatly classifiable and ordered set of practices and ways of doing work. Suddenly, the gap between the English taught in the classroom and the English used in the workplace became apparent (de Beaugrande 2000; Louhiala-Salminen 1996; Nelson 2000, 2006).

Early linguistic analyses of business negotiations (Lampi 1986) and business meetings (Williams 1988) remained relatively isolated examples of empirical research in the use of English in business. It was not until the 1990s that discourse analysis, contrastive pragmatics, conversation analysis, occasionally combined with insights from ethnography, laid the foundations of a multimethod approach to "business discourse." In Europe, it was a group of Scandinavian scholars who established themselves as proponents of a discourse-based approach to business practices, especially intercultural negotiations: Mirija-Lisa Charles, Karl Ehlich, Ingrid Neumann, Anna Trosborg, Jan Ulijn, Johannes Wagner, and British-born Alan Firth, then working from Denmark. In the United States, the work of Laura Miller on Japan-US workplace interactions complemented Yamada Haru's work on Japanese-American meetings. In Australia, Michael Clyne, Helen Marriott, and Joan Mulholland were involved in the analysis of intercultural interaction in the workplace and business negotiations while in New Zealand, Janet Holmes and her collaborators set up a large collection of recordings from institutional and organizational settings (see Bargiela-Chiappini, Nickerson, and Planken 2007 for a fuller discussion; also Marra, this volume).

In the United Kingdom, Deidre Boden (1994) first documented the possibility of a multidisciplinary approach to the study of business meetings as organizational phenomena. Management and organization studies also influenced our own work (Bargiela-Chiappini and Harris 1997), even though the primary focus remained the pragmalinguistic analysis of meeting discourse. While a very fruitful decade for business discourse, the 1990s will probably be remembered for the fact that the vast majority of empirical research on situated language focussed on English as a lingua franca (see Nickerson, this volume) and, to a lesser extent, on "native" varieties of English (British, American, and Australian). Apart from scholars like Yamada Haru working on Japanese business discourse and Vijay Bhatia, who from Hong Kong became internationally-known for his work on the genres of institutional discourse, in the 1990s Asian scholarship was noticeable for its absence. Shanta Nair-Venuopal's (2000) analysis of the use of English alongside other languages in the Malaysian workplace inaugurated a decade when an increasing number of Asian authors first joined the growing movement of Western researchers taking a close interest in work practices and increasingly becoming more successful at obtaining access to corporate environments.

Perhaps unsurprisingly, English is the language that links most of the research conducted under the convenience label of "Asian business discourse(s)" (Bargiela-Chiappini and Gotti 2005; *Journal of Asian Pacific Communication* 15(2) 2005 and 16(1) 2006). This observation would seem to reflect the continuing dominance of English as *the* language of business worldwide. Yet, one of the most respected voices speaking on English matters, David Graddol (2006), warns that Mandarin and Spanish are slowly eroding the once unassailable supremacy of English. The Chinese government is promoting Mandarin as a second language through a widespread network of Confucius Institutes: the parallel will not be missed with another, equally powerful network, that of the British Council offices and their capillary action in promoting "the business of English." In 2005, Spanish became an alternative to English in Brazil's secondary schools, a move that is assisting the consolidation of Brazil as one of the largest and fastest growing economies outside India and China. Graddol predicted that the decline of the "old paradigm" – English as a foreign language – would endure for some time yet and that one of the signs of the "new paradigm" taking hold would be "the declining reverence of 'native speakers' as the gold standard of English" (2006: 66). The latter phenomenon is still far from noticeable at the time of writing (Nickerson personal communication) and will remain an academic projection while the "standard English" ideology continues to inspire EFL teachers (Wolff 2010).

Business English in Practice: Focus on Asia

In business discourse research at least, and especially, though not exclusively, in the "West," in the last two decades we have moved a long way from idealistic notions of English and language needs in business settings that were currency until the 1980s. In the same period, the growth of English "as an Asian language"

has consolidated into a phenomenon with potentially vast and long-term repercussions on the socioeconomic life of hundreds of millions of people, especially
in East Asia. In his commentary on the spread and use of English in Asia, Tom
McArthur (2003: 2) wrote:

> English is the lingua franca that Asians now share with one another and the rest of
> the world. One should also add however that it is now manifestly an Asian language
> in its own right. It has been thoroughly indigenized.

Perhaps it is appropriate in a section devoted to Business English in Asia, first
to attempt a definition of "Asia" for the purposes of our discussion. As McArthur
notes, for some "Asia" refers to East Asia but of course Asia begins in the West,
in the region that Europe refers to as the Near East and Middle East. This ethnocentric understanding of "Asia" has also been interrogated in relation to the rather
amorphous, yet politically laden, label of "Asian business discourse" (Bargiela-
Chiappini 2011). We agree with McArthur that we should avoid lumping together
the various "regions" that compose "Asia" when studying the spread and use of
English. Business English, in particular, has a very different history in, for example,
the Indian sub-continent and in East Asia. In this section, we will be looking at
two "case-studies," namely Japan and China, as illustrative of two different histories of Business English within East Asia, one closely related to the development
of American business communication (Japan) and the other to a more recent
attempt to define a localized field of pedagogy that has grown in response to the
huge demand for Business English by the fastest growing economy in the world
(China).

In her review of Business English research across the three circles of world
English (Kachru 1986), Catherine Nickerson notes how the study of American English lags behind that of other inner circle Englishes, with the exception of
course of contrastive studies, some of which were mentioned in the previous
section. The fact that, unlike their US business communication colleagues, European researchers in Business English would often be trained as applied linguists
and/or ESP teachers has arguably played a major role in the expansion of Business
English research outside the inner circle (Nickerson 2010). It is worth noting that
the English taught in Europe largely follows the UK model.

At the same time, inner circle Englishes have traditionally exported textbooks
on business communication to outer circle, and increasingly, to expanding circle
learners eager to share in the benefits of International Business English (IBE).
However, a survey of Business English textbooks from the United Kingdom and
the United States (Nelson 2000, 2006; cited in Nickerson 2010) found that their
contents bore little relevance to authentic workplace written and spoken English.
The discrepancy between teaching resources and actual work practices is nothing
new in inner circle contexts (see e.g. Williams 1988) but it is quite disconcerting
that shortcomings pointed out in the literature as early as the 1980s should continue to be propagated by influential publications exported all over the world. A
visit to the website of Pearson, one of the top education publishers in the United

States, is indeed instructive with respect to the type of textbooks, many running into several editions, sold under business communication and managerial communication (see http://www.pearsonhighered.com/educator/course/Business-Communication/91064983.page). If the contents of individual titles are anything to go by, one can only be dismayed at the lack of awareness of empirical research in workplace language, organizational discourse and business discourse of the last three decades in these publications.

A systematic critique of Business English textbooks on the market is beyond the scope of this chapter (but see the three-level coursebook *Business Advantage*, richly informed by empirical research in authentic workplace communication (Handford et al. 2011). Instead, we propose that we look at how Business English has developed in East Asia, in particular in two communities of users who have come to define two distinct understandings and trajectories of development of Business English practice and research. The choice of China and Japan was partly suggested by their contrasting traditions in Business English but also as examples of how different sociohistorical and economic developments have influenced the evolution of an academic field. In both countries, the origins of Business English can be traced to the teaching of English for business correspondence, mainly EFL for written communication, with a focus on lexicon and grammar. While Japan slowly moved away from the original narrow scope of Business English and eventually stopped using the label altogether in response to the changing economic policies of the country (Norisada 2003), China "stretched" the same label and expanded its scope to include complementary business and social scientific subjects (see Business English – China below). In this respect, China has probably followed a unique path in East Asia, culminating in the establishment of Bachelor of Arts degree programs in Business English at a number of the country's top universities. Whilst Japan has, over the last 70 years, developed its own brand of "business communication" in close collaboration with the United States, and has left to ESP the exclusive concerns for teaching materials design and testing, in China, Business English has become an umbrella concept that incorporates a range of subjects deemed to be necessary for the development of well-rounded specialists trained to satisfy the needs of the fastest growing economic power in the world.

The next two sections illustrate some of the work carried out in Japan and China under the banners of "business communication" and "business discourse" (Japan) and Business English (China). The first section, Business English-Japan, is based on an interview with Kameda Naoki by the first author on September 1, 2010. Before taking up his current professorial post, Kameda Naoki (Doshisha University, Kyoto) was owner and CEO of a manufacturing company and in this role he visited nearly 40 countries and did business with individuals from over 60 countries, mostly, though not exclusively, in English.

Business English-Japan

Attempts at tracing a chronology of Business English in Japan always seem to lead to "business communication," as if the two terms were considered synonymous.

According to Kameda (personal communication 2010), the term "business communication" was first used in Japan in the early part of the 1970s. The 1974 issue of the *Journal of Business English* (formerly *The Japan Business English Association Annual Studies*) carried papers by the pioneers of Japanese BE, namely Haneda Saburo, Ozaki Shigeru, and Nakamura Mikito. Not only did these individuals serve as executive directors of the Japan Business English Association but, through their work, they left an indelible mark on the field. Ozaki also published a monthly magazine with the telling title of *Business English* to which Kameda himself contributed as a young scholar. It was Ozaki who, in the early days of the field, first proposed a "human-oriented" perspective for the study of Business English that moved beyond linguistic analysis. He argued that:

> Business English is a tool with which [man] communicates with others, and it is always a human being that makes use of it. It follows, therefore, that the whole question of how best or most effectively [he] can communicate [his] ideas to others in Business English must be considered with [man], *i.e.* the one who uses Business English, at its center. The work that has hitherto been done in this area has tended to concentrate upon its linguistic aspects in total disregard of the existence of [men] (Ozaki 1975: 27).

In practical terms, Ozaki (1975: 30) suggested that individuals should adopt a "you-consideration" in their business interactions with a view to bridging the gap that separated them from their counterparts from other countries. His was an approach that acknowledged nearly four decades ago that mastering the linguistic subtleties of "Business English" was insufficient. Kameda followed in Ozaki's footsteps when he suggested, perhaps counter-intuitively for many, that *empathy* is "the secret to successful international business" (Kameda 1977; Kameda 2005: xiii). Empathic identification with business partners consists of suspending criticism, subjective judgement and unhelpful inferences. It is a mental attitude that is expressed in a "you-consideration" approach to intercultural communication, not to be confused with a "you-attitude," which Kameda dismisses as concerning "styles of expression . . . a technique for manipulating people with carefully chosen words and expressions" (Kameda 2005: 107).

The development of a humanistic perspective of business communication, which as far as we know is peculiar to the early Japanese tradition of Business English research, was embodied in business practice by Kameda himself as a CEO in his own company. In his interview, he took time to elaborate on how empathy and a "you-consideration" were his constant guiding principles in over two decades during which he accrued a portfolio of 1500 business negotiations, a large proportion of which he held in English with international business partners and clients.

Kameda's sensitivity to language use and his discussion of linguistic issues in the context of what he calls "international business," conveniently brought together and revisited in a monograph (Kameda 2005), exemplify the business communication approach to Business English that he shares with predecessors (e.g. Ozaki) and contemporaries (e.g. Norisada 2007, 2008), but also with the more recent and new discursive approach to business interaction adopted by scholars such as Tanaka (2006 2008, 2009, 2011), Fujio (2004) and Sunaoshi (2005). It is worth noting that through Ozaki's mentorship, Kameda was exposed to the work of other "fathers of the International Business Communication Association – Japan" (Kameda 2005: vi), namely Nakamura Mikito and Haneda Saburo who published in the 1970s and 1980s (Haneda 1976, 1986, 1989; Haneda and Shima 1982) and who influenced Kameda's own work. Of these authors, we have listed only the publications in English but there are many others in Japanese; some are cited in Kameda (2005).

Since its inception in the 1930s, the Japanese school of business communication, represented by the Japan Business Communication Association (JBCA) (formerly the Japan Business English Association), of which Business English is a substantive concern, has developed and maintained close ties with the American Association for Business Communication (ABC). This is reflected in a shared focus on application, be it to teaching or training. However, this has not hampered the development of an approach to communication in business that appears to be distinctive of Japanese scholarship. Kameda's work published in English, which we have been able to access more fully than the work of his contemporaries, describes the approach thus: "business is essentially about communication, and communication is essentially the formation of a relationship" (Kameda 2005: 1). This focus on the relationality of communication echoes Ozaki's concern for the human-centerdness of Business English research (Ozaki 1983: 53, cited in Kameda 2005: 18).

The values underlying this understanding of communication are subsumed under the "3Hs": "humanity: warm consideration for others; harmony: efforts not to hurt the feelings of others; and humility, or modesty" (Kameda 2005: 46). Space constraints do not allow us to examine the possible culture-specific roots of this value system; what is notable, however, is that the "other-consideration" driving this understanding of communication also includes the imperative of *self-understanding*. It is incumbent on international business negotiators to be fully aware of their own value system, ways of thinking and behavioral patterns. This includes an appreciation of discursive and pragmatic strategies that may be the cause of misunderstanding. For example, Japanese parsimonious, and at times elusive, use of verbal communication, the significance of silent communication, the preference for non-argumentativeness, all of which are "transferred" into ELF settings, may be easily misread in intercultural encounters (Kameda 2005). The possibility, indeed, the necessity, of empathetic communication is predicated on the premise that "no human beings are completely foreign to each other" (Kameda 2005: 109). A lesson from Japanese business communication is that Business English brings disparate individuals and groups to cooperate within a shared pragmalinguistic space in which the rules of engagement demand heightened self- and other-knowledge and a deep appreciation of the interplay between native linguistic and value systems and the "alien" cultural heritage of Business English which owes greatly to the United Kingdom and the United States.

There is also a new and growing interest in Japanese business discourse, more recent than the business communication tradition discussed thus far, but complementary to it, which finds its origins in the comparative analyses of US and Japanese negotiators conducted by Yamada Haru (1992) and Laura Miller (1994). Based on discourse analytic and pragmatic approaches to real-life business interactions conducted in English, this work lay the foundations of research-based business communication, both intra and intercultural, which focusses on interactional detail and seeks to interpret discursive strategies in the light of cultural, organizational and managerial ideologies. In the work of Tanaka Hiromasa and Fujio Misa (Fujio and Tanaka 2011), ELF interactions are scrutinized, as well as Japanese intracultural meetings and negotiations. The insights gained from such a two-pronged approach are beginning to build a fine-grained picture of Japanese business discourse in English and in Japanese that fills some of the gaps already highlighted by Japanese business communication scholars. For example, the sensitive issue of the role of English as a corporate language, endured rather than embraced in foreign companies based in Japan (Tanaka 2006) and the cultural assumptions revealed by ELF usage in Japanese-French negotiations (Tanaka 2008) cannot be appreciated without an understanding of Japanese interactional preferences in business settings, often expressed as concerns with "face" and "polite behavior" (Tanaka 2009; Tanaka 2011; Tanaka and Sugiyama 2010). In a similar vein, Fujio Misa (2004) points to the interactional significance of silence in meetings and the consequences of different interpretations of nonverbalization by Japanese and US participants. Finally, Sunaoshi (2005) in her study of Japanese-American factory workers adds further insights to the business discourse perspective, with potentially far-reaching consequence also for Business English pedagogy: the importance of the historical contexts that the interactants bring to the intercultural encounter and the concept of *understanding* as a process rather than a discrete experience, and one that must be shared between native and non-native speakers.

Business English-China

The launch of the *Asian ESP Journal* (http://asian-esp-journal.com/index.php) in 2003, a free access periodical that responds to the needs of teachers and trainers in Asia, reflects a dominant interest in pedagogic issues and applications, especially, although not exclusively, in East Asian countries. China is exemplary in this respect. The first activities foreshadowing the development of the field of Business English in China can be traced back to the early 1950s when language skills courses became available under the general banner of "translation" and prepared students to deal with business correspondence. Elements of business knowledge were included in such courses even though they were not identifiable as specific disciplines such as management or international law. With the opening of China to the outside world in the 1980s, more undergraduate courses began to offer business subjects such as management, economics, and international business law in association with language skills aimed to develop both written and spoken competences. Around the same period, university programs also first listed language for specific purposes as a specialist subject, which, in the Chinese education system, belonged to the arts, alongside foreign language and comparative literary studies.

Following a national change of emphasis of undergraduate programs towards broad-based education, at the end of the 1990s language for specific purposes (LSP) was dropped from university curricula. In the early 2000s, English language teachers in China were instrumental in bringing Business English back into the higher education curriculum after winning the argument at the national level on the social contribution of Business English to China, especially in response to the economy's pressing need for highly skilled graduates with combined language and business skills. The outcome of the policy change was the Ministry of Education's approval of the first Business English undergraduate courses. A significant aspect of this development was that top universities applied for and obtained ministerial approval to run such BA programs (Zhu, Wu, and Guo 2009). At the time of writing, thirty-two institutions nationwide have been granted approval, among them Guangdong University of Foreign Studies, Heilongjiang University, Shanghai University of Finance and Economics, Shanghai Institute of Foreign Trade, Shanghai International Studies University, the University of International Business and Economics, Xi'an International Studies University, and Yangzhou University.. The demand for places is huge and competition is steep.

Taking as an illustration the University of International Business and Economics (UIBE) in Beijing, one of the first three universities to run a BA in Business English, the first cohort of their four-year Business English undergraduate program graduated in 2011. Their Business English multidisciplinary curriculum is a composite of subjects organized in three core components of equal status: knowledge of business disciplines, business discourse, and professional practices where business discourse acts as a bridge between the other two components. While elements of "business knowledge" have been present since its inception in Business English teaching in China, the integrated curriculum of the current Business English program gives ample room to subjects such as economics, management, international business law, international trade, and so on, and relies on highly qualified academics in the individual disciplines to deliver courses of comparable level to those found in business degrees normally available in business schools. For a detailed discussion of the curriculum, refer to Zhang and Wang (2011)

The success of BA and MA degree programs in Business English now poses the issue of further development at the doctoral level, especially for students who are keen to specialize in the subject. Legitimization is a serious obstacle as Business English is not recognized as an academic discipline, not least because Chinese scholars have been arguing for some time that Business English lacks a dedicated theoretical and methodological apparatus. At the International Conference on Business English Studies held at Guangdong University of Foreign Studies in 2008 this concern was voiced by both senior academics representing institutions offering Business English programs and by Business English teachers. The current curricula are by definition multidisciplinary with subjects from the humanities and the social sciences; there is a case for going back to the foundational disciplines to look for a theoretical tradition that can form the backbone for possible future developments at the doctoral level. Meantime, Business English graduates continue to fill well-paid jobs in the private sector.

Given the emphasis placed on shaping the pedagogic resources required of Business English to meet the demands of a fast changing business and professional world, research has lagged behind. There is no shortage in China of linguists who are involved in the analysis of written and spoken business texts but what they lack is access to contexts of practice where it is possible to capture language in use through ethnographic methods. Decontextualized analysis is of limited use but access to the field is often dependent on personal contacts. The MA programs in Business English have proved very useful in bypassing access issues; their part-time students often work in business and government and therefore can gain privileged access to situated language use and can collect data for their dissertations. This in turn means that their supervisors, too, benefit from access to real-life Business English "data." A similar pattern of collaboration has been in place for some time at the Helsinki School of Economics (HSE), which offers MA programs in, among others, international business communication.

When teaching and research can build on collaboration between academics and practitioners and professionals, as it is the case at the Research Centre for Professional Communication in English (RCPCE) of the Polytechnic University of Hong Kong, the outcomes are distinctive and perhaps still quite unique in East Asia. The RCPCE's project portfolio is varied and underpinned by a combined linguistics and discursive approach to communicative professional practices. Examples of ongoing interdisciplinary RCPCE research includes both genre-specific projects such as "The discourse representations of financial analyst reports, . . . Discourse analysis and contrastive studies of court judgments . . . Surveying and construction engineering English" and region-wide investigations such as "A taxonomy of professional communicative competencies derived from the four key industries in Hong Kong" and "Learning and use of English for professional purposes in Hong Kong" (personal communication Winnie Cheng). While Hong Kong in general, and the RCPCE in particular, remains a beacon of professional English research, the first two ESP Asia conferences held in Chongqing in 2009 and in Ningbo in 2010 (under the auspices of the *Asian ESP Journal*) and the third one held in Xi'an in 2011 have attracted many scholars from mainland China who can now benefit from a dedicated forum to showcase their work and discuss their interests and concerns. The range of topics and approaches illustrated by the 2010 conference program (http://www.nottingham.edu.cn/conference/esp/Call%20 for%20papers.htm) is testimony to the growing number of Chinese ESP and Business English voices joining the international arena.

The two cases described above illustrate two very different patterns of evolution of Business English as a field of research and teaching: in Japan the establishment of the "Japanese English Teachers" Society in 1934 gathered English-language instructors based in universities, colleges and commercial high schools. In 1950, the Association changed its name to the "Japan Business English Association" and the focus of its members' teaching continued to be on written English competencies. It was not until 2002 that the new identity, Japan's Business Communication

Association, was finally approved by the general meeting, a long-coming recognition of the progressive change of emphasis in many of the members' interests and teaching profiles. Business English then morphed into business communication in Japan and is often associated with the work of a handful of influential scholars who strategically published in English and therefore made their work available beyond Japan. The same pattern, of a few individuals influencing profound developments in the field, is now repeating with the Japanese discourse analysts who, whilst still thin on the ground, are publishing in both Japanese and English, and are having their work noticed at international conferences. In contrast, China exemplifies an institutionalized development of Business English, with the creation of new and very competitive degree programs tailored to the needs of business. Research is still limited and often inspired by pedagogic issues (see however the special issue of the *Asian ESP Journal* on Chinese Business English, 2011).

Re-contextualizing Business English as a Research-Led Field of Practice

The orientation expressed in the call for papers of the 2nd ESP Asia conference seems to capture the thrust of future ESP research in Asia and beyond:

> As ESP grows in Asia, it needs to evolve practices that engage the ecologies in which it operates. Such ecologies include, on the one hand, sociolinguistic realities such as multilingualism and variation in global English(es), and, on the other hand, variable professional and academic cultures and practices in Asia (http://www.nottingham.edu.cn/conference/esp/call%20for%20papers.htm).

The enduring gap between research and practice in Business English prompted Catherine Nickerson (2005) to observe that textbooks of Business English continue to ignore research pointing to the need to integrate traditional teaching materials with findings from business practice. Her three-pronged approach to research and practice in English as a lingua franca and in English for special business purposes (ESBP) is motivated by "the pressing need to refer to the findings of research in the development of teaching materials" (Nickerson 2005: 376).

Reflecting on the many roles associated with ESP practitioners (Dudley-Evans and St John 1998), Laurence Anthony (2008) questions whether the desirable multi-role profile of the Business English professional could work in practice. Who has the time to be a Business English teacher, collaborator, researcher, course designer, materials provider and evaluator, asks Anthony, and where is the support for this multi-skilled professional? In her review article, Maggie Jo St John (1996: 8) singled out linguistic and nonlinguistic features of Business English that could drive a research-led pedagogy and concluded that "we must develop Business English research through an interdisciplinary approach that draws on techniques from fields such as applied linguistics, corpus linguistics and the social sciences."

Since then, pragmatics, sociolinguistics, conversation analysis and ethnomethod-ology, intercultural communication, Business English as a lingua franca (BELF) (see Nickerson, this volume), and intercultural rhetoric (see Connor and Rozycki, this volume), to name but a few, have populated the list of disciplines and approaches that have looked at intracultural and intercultural professional and business interaction. In this respect, we are now in a much better position than we were only fifteen years ago, with a consolidating body of empirical research in a number of languages, looking at both mediated and face-to-face communication, where English remains by far the most frequently analyzed language.

Alternative thinking in sociology suggests that a cosmopolitan outlook on international relations may be more fruitful than the current heavily partisan discourses of globalization and internationalism (Starke-Meyerring 2005). Cosmo-politanism's agenda includes concerns for justice and equality, as well as the economic and security concerns typical of international relations studies. In an attempt to open up the intellectual horizons of the field of Business English as an academic enterprise with tangible effects on the lives of hundreds of thousands of people, be they students, teachers, trainers, researchers, practitioners, and con-sumers, we could perhaps try to locate Business English research and practice within wider social, policy, and political debates. Business English is more than teaching or learning a skill, however specialized and marketable it may be, espe-cially in certain areas of the globe. It is opening up to a complex world of ideology and praxis with roots in systems of thought and values that are generally taken for granted by native speakers and often ignored by non-native learners and teachers, who may buy unquestioningly into the "Business English offer" as a package. Adaptation of ideas and models usually comes after adoption and following the realization that formulas and models emerging from a different world-view do not reflect local needs and are insensitive to local practices.

The cultural spread of Business English has generated renewed interest in updating pedagogy in line with business practices. "Business English-China," as it is known among Chinese authors, is a good example of such development, driven by the rising internal demand for graduates with specialist skills, and seeking to combine sensitivity to contextual peculiarities with lessons from extant international scholarship. As relevant literatures show, linguistics-applied has been at the forefront of innovative research in Business English that concen-trates on aspects of real life business, professional, and organizational interaction, both within and across "cultural" contexts. In his introduction to the 2002 edition of the *Oxford Handbook of Applied Linguistics*, Robert Kaplan (2002: ix) concludes, "the applied linguist has to have a broad exposure to all the social sciences." Echoing Kaplan, William Grabe defines applied linguistics as "a practice-driven discipline that addresses language-based problems in real-world contexts" (2002: 10) and calls on it to become a "mediating discipline" (2002: 9) across research and practice and also across a whole raft of disciplines such as psychology, education, anthropology, political science, sociology measurement, computer programming, literature, and/or economics. A discursive approach to researching and teaching

Business English would provide the mediating space in which the relevant social sciences could meet and engage in the formulation of a new agenda based on shared insights that would also be the first step towards possibly proposing Business English as a distinctive multidisciplinary field.

In the 2000s, discursive studies of English as a language of work in multinational companies (e.g. Nickerson 2000; Poncini 2004) have benefitted from an understanding of discourse as "contextual and intertextual, self-reflexive and self-critical, [. . . and] founded on the twofold notion of discourse as *situated action* and of *language at work*" (Bargiela-Chiappini and Nickerson 2002: 277, original emphasis). Building on the concern for research relevance expressed by applied linguistics and the wealth of insight from sociolinguistics, a (business) discourse approach to Business English can bridge the divisive gap between theory and practice that affects applied linguistics and which manifests itself in, among other -*isms*, the micro–macro dualism. Linguistics and pragmatics will continue to function as crucial disciplines in Business English research. However, as a forum for dialogue between the social sciences (Bargiela-Chiappini 2009), business discourse is inevitably multidisciplinary; in this respect, it is well positioned to act as host to Business English and encourage more discourse-based studies.

Looking over to the broad field of "the language of the workplace" (Marra, this volume), it is clear that interpretative research is already well-established and often challenges pedagogic and training prescriptions; it also welcomes dialogue with management and organization studies as well as anthropology, philosophy, ethics, social theory, semiotics, and perhaps a few others. Writing on workplace discourse from the perspective of applied linguistics, McGroarty (2002: 273) offers a characterization of what could be the potential scope of Business English:

> [l]anguage used in the workplace is never only about work; it expresses and shapes the social realities experienced by workers and spills over into the understandings of work, life, and people that carry over into other realms of individual and social experience. Hence, ongoing research on language uses in the professional and occupational activities belongs in the mainstream of contemporary applied linguistics. Without it, theorists, researchers and policymakers are likely to oversimplify the complexities and contradictions that connect the study of language and society.

Conclusion: Where We May Be Going

In the 1990s, Maggie Jo St John's review of ESP clearly identified its greatest strength in the range of effective textbooks, the product of a strong pedagogic tradition which also informed the professionalism of the teachers. Within this "materials-led movement" (St John 1996: 15), the role of the intuition of the materials writer is paramount; this, St John admits, was a cause of concern. In research-led Business English, findings from direct observation and analysis of (business) practices and languages are made available to the textbook author. Thus, for example, discourse-analytic research using ethnographic tools could shed light on the "generic features of different events such as meetings, [. . . .]

common features of effective communications, [. . .] the role of cultural influences and the way in which language and business strategies interact" (St John 1996: 15).

It is worth remembering that Business English began as a materials-led movement rather than a research-led movement that produced a number of successful textbooks and teaching resources inspired by writer's intuition about, or "informed understanding" of, business communication (St John 1996: 15). While adequate in the early days, this approach has serious limitations: discursive and ethnographic studies of business interactions conducted in the 1990s have demonstrated the complexity of the verbal strategies and contextual influences at play in real-life dyadic and multiparty talk. Perhaps paradoxically, the gap between pedagogy and praxis seems to have widened, especially in the field of intercultural business communication where English is very often deployed as a lingua franca: a cursory examination of some of the multi-edition US textbooks raises serious concerns about stereotypical and ethnocentric contents and an ignorance of the findings of a well-established tradition of empirical research in Europe, Australia, and New Zealand (but also see the work of Laura Miller 1994 on Japanese-American communication). Clearly, Business English needs to open up to the challenges raised by empirical research conducted within the discourse tradition, intercultural pragmatics, intercultural rhetoric (Connor and Rozycki, this volume), and intercultural communication, to name but a few of the relevant fields. There have already been some efforts in this direction. For example, Clarice Chan (2009) draws on empirical research in business meetings to develop a checklist which she uses in materials evaluation. Helen Spencer-Oatey and Peter Franklin (2009) exemplify the process of theory and practice informing and enriching each other in intercultural communication.

The deliberate focus on Asia of this chapter intends to offer a platform for the debates surrounding "English as an Asian Language;" these are not exclusive to the context of world Englishes scholarship but also animate a small but growing body of research focussed on English as a language of Asian business. This latest development is best appreciated in the development of Asian business discourse(s) (Bargiela-Chiappini 2011; Tanaka and Bargiela-Chiappini 2011), which is an attempt to widen the original Western scope of business discourse research to include alternative, indigenous perspectives and concerns. Attention to local practices means that findings from language needs analysis (e.g. Kawaguchi, Otha, and Ito 2009) that are useful to Business English need to be supplemented by qualitative research that taps into employees' understanding of what communication in the workplace is about. Unexpected findings include the realization that "lack of knowledge about one's language and lack of judgment as to its proper use causes miscommunication too" (Yamauchi and Orr 2008: 2) and the belief among some respondents that this is the most difficult component of communication. Emic interpretation emerging from, for example, interviews with employees, observation of their work practices and analysis of interactional data is invaluable to "correct" self-perceptions of communicative values and practices which are often spread by popular textbooks (Yamauchi and Orr 2008).

The dialogue between business discourse research, with its emphasis on the analysis of all aspects of communication in organizational settings, and Business English pedagogy, concerned with ensuring that students and trainees can operate effectively in the workplace, starts from the premise that English is no longer studied as a "foreign language" but rather as an international language; and as "an indispensable language for international communication in Asia" (Honna and Takeshita 2005: 379). The appropriation of (Business) English as one of the Asian languages (Honna 2003) is a first step towards the demythologization of its foreignness; it is also an invitation to move beyond prescriptive models in Business English teaching to adopt instead findings from descriptive and interpretative research that have been available for some time. Dialogue between disciplines for a fusion agenda for Business English teaching and research depends on sustained effort to bring together teachers and researchers, applied linguists and (organizational) discourse analysts and linguistic anthropologists. The current climate is favorable to multidisciplinary research, at least in the Anglophone countries, and is a fertile ground for such dialogue to take place with the blessings of academic institutions and funding bodies. Let us make the most of it while it lasts and work together towards the recognition of Business English as a mature, research-led scholarly enterprise as well as a practically useful academic subject and degree program.

Acknowledgments

Several colleagues have commented on this chapter, especially Catherine Nickerson, Tanaka Hiromasa, Kameda Naoki, and Meredith Marra. We thank them for their insightful and constructive feedback.

REFERENCES

Anthony, L. (2008) General purpose ESP program design. Plenary Speech given at the *Osaka University ESP Symposium*. Nov. 22, Osaka, Japan: Osaka University.

Bargiela-Chiappini, F. (2009) Introduction: Business discourse. In F. Bargiela-Chiappini (ed.), *The Handbook of Business Discourse*. 1–17. Edinburgh: Edinburgh University Press.

Bargiela-Chiappini, F. (2011) Asian business discourse(s). In J. Aritz and R. C. Walker (eds.), *Discourse Perspectives on Organizational Communication*. 59–79.

Madison, NJ: Fairleigh Dickinson University Press.

Bargiela-Chiappini, F. and Gotti, M. (eds.) (2005) *Asian Business Discourse(s)*. Bern: Peter Lang.

Bargiela-Chiappini, F. and Harris, S. (1997) *Managing Language: The Discourse of Corporate Meetings*. Amsterdam: John Benjamins.

Bargiela-Chiappini, F. and Nickerson, C. (2002) Business discourse: Old debates, new horizons. *International Review of Applied Linguistics in Language Teaching* 40: 273–86.

Bargiela-Chiappini, F., Nickerson, C. and Planken, B. (2007) *Business Discourse.* Basingstoke, UK: Palgrave Macmillan.

Boden, D. (1994) *The Business of Talk: Organizations in Action.* Cambridge: Polity Press.

Celani, M. A. A. (2008) When myth and reality meet: Reflections on ESP in Brazil. *English for Specific Purposes* 27: 412–23.

Chan, C. S. C. (2009) Forging a link between research and pedagogy: A holistic framework for evaluating Business English materials. *English for Specific Purposes* 28: 125–36.

de Beaugrande, R. (2000) User-friendly communication skills in the teaching and learning of Business English. *English for Specific Purposes* 19: 331–49.

Dudley-Evans, T. and St John, M. J. (1996) Report on Business English: A review of research and published teaching materials. Princeton, NJ: Educational Testing Service. Accessed May 5, 2011, http://www.ets.org/Media/research/pdf/toeic-rr-02.pdf.

Dudley-Evans, T. and St John, M. J. (1998) *Developments in English for Specific Purposes: A Multi-Disciplinary Approach.* Cambridge: Cambridge University Press.

Fujio, M. (2004) Silence during intercultural communication: A case study. *Corporate Communications* 9: 331–39.

Fujio, M. and Tanaka, H. (2011) "Harmonious disagreement" in Japanese business discourse. In J. Aritz and R. C. Walker (eds.), *Discourse Perspectives on Organizational Communication.* 81–98. Madison, NJ: Fairleigh Dickinson University Press.

Grabe, W. (2002) Applied linguistics: An emerging discipline for the twenty first century. In R. Kaplan (ed.), *The Oxford Handbook of Applied Linguistics:* 3–12. Oxford: Oxford University Press.

Graddol, D. (2006) *English Next.* Accessed October 3, 2010, http://www.britishcouncil.org/learning-research-englishnext.htm.

Handford, M., Lisboa, M., Koester, A., and Pitt, A. (2011). *Business Advantage (Upper Intermediate Level).* Cambridge: Cambridge University Press.

Haneda, S. (1976) On international cooperation for business communication studies. *The Journal of Business Communication* 13: 25–31.

Haneda, S. (1986) Japanese businessmen and English: Clumsy communicators' efforts to communicate. *Aoyama Business Review* 12: 1–25.

Haneda, S. (1989) *Business English for Telexing and Drafting.* Tokyo: Yuhikaku Ltd.

Haneda, S. and Shima, H. (1982) Japanese communication behavior as reflected in letter writing. *The Journal of Business Communication* 19: 19–32.

Honna, N. (2003) English is an Asian language: Some thoughts for action proposals. Fourteenth National Conference of the Japanese Association for Asian Englishes. Dec. 6. Nagoya, Japan: Chukyo University.

Honna, N. and Takeshita, Y. (2005) English language teaching in Japan: Policy plans and their implementation. *RELC Journal* 36: 363–83.

Hutchinson, T. and Waters, A. (1987) *English for Specific Purposes.* Cambridge: Cambridge University Press.

Journal of Asian Pacific Communication (2005) 15(2): 207–322; 2006 16(1): 1–158. Double Special Issue on Asian Business Discourse(s).

Kachru, B. (1986) *The Alchemy of English: The Spread, Functions and Models of Non-Native Englishes.* Oxford: Pergamon.

Kameda, N. (1977) Empathy in international business communication. *The ABC Bulletin, The American Business Communication Association* 40: 25–7.

Kameda, N. (2005) *Managing Global Business Communication.* Tokyo: Maruzen Co. Ltd.

Kaplan, R. (2002) Preface. In R. Kaplan (ed.), *The Oxford Handbook of Applied Linguistics.* v–x. Oxford: Oxford University Press.

Kawaguchi, K, Otha, R., and Ito, T. (2009) English language competencies needed by Japanese in manufacturing industry. 2009 IEEE International Professional Communication Conference, IPCC, 1–10.

Lampi, M. L. (1986) Linguistic components of strategy in business negotiations. Helsinki School of Economics Studies B-85. Helsinki: Helsinki School of Economics.

Louhiala-Salminen, L. (1996) The business communication classroom vs. reality: What should we teach today? *English for Specific Purposes* 15: 37–51.

McArthur, T. (2003) English as an Asian language. *English Today* 74(19): 19–22.

McGroarty, M. (2002) Language uses in professional contexts. In R. Kaplan (ed.), *The Oxford Handbook of Applied Linguistics.* 262–76. Oxford: Oxford University Press.

Miller, L. (1994) Japanese and American indirectness. *Pragmatics* 4: 221–38.

Mintzberg, H. (2004) *Managers, not MBAs: A Hard Look at the Soft Practice of Managing and Management Development.* San Francisco, CA: Berrett-Koehler Publishers.

Nair-Venuopal, S. (2000) *Language Choice and Communication in Malaysian Business.* Bangi: Penertbit UKM (Universiti Kengbansaan Malaysia Press).

Nelson, M. (2000) A corpus-based study of Business English and Business English teaching materials. Unpublished PhD thesis. Manchester, UK: University of Manchester.

Nelson, M. (2006) Semantic associations in Business English: A corpus-based analysis. *English for Specific Purposes* 25: 217–34.

Nickerson, C. (2000) *Playing the Corporate Language Game: An Investigation of the Genres and Discourse Strategies in English Used by Dutch Writers Working in Multinational Corporations.* Amsterdam, the Netherlands, and Atlanta, GA: Rodopi.

Nickerson, C. (2005) English as a lingua franca in international business contexts. (Editorial) *English for Specific Purposes* 24: 367–80.

Nickerson, C. (2010) The Englishes of business. In A. Kirkpatrick (ed.), *The Routledge Handbook of World Englishes.* 506–19. London: Routledge.

Norisada, T. (2003) Why we changed our name. *The Journal of Japan Business Communication Association* 62: 9–10.

Norisada, T. (2007) Relation-oriented communication in negotiation. *Kwansei Gakuin University Social Sciences Review* 11: 121–32.

Norisada, T. (2008) Language's influence on thoughts and action in business. *The Journal of International Business Communication* 67: 35–44.

Poncini, G. (2004) *Discursive Strategies in Multicultural Business Meetings.* Bern: Peter Lang.

Ozaki, S. (1975) Business English from a human point of view. *The Journal of Business Communication* 12: 27–31.

Ozaki, S. (1983) Nihonshiki Shogyou Eigo ni tsuite [On Japanese Style Business English], *Nihon Shogyou Eigo Gakkai Kenkyu Nenpo [The Japan Business English Association Annual Studies]* 43: 49–57.

Spencer-Oatey, H. and Franklin, P. (2009) *Intercultural Interaction: A Multidisciplinary Approach to Intercultural Communication.* Basingstoke, UK: Palgrave Macmillan.

St John, M. J. (1996) Business is booming: Business English in the 1990s. *English for Specific Purposes* 15: 3–18.

Starke-Meyerring, D. (2005) Meeting the challenges of globalization: A framework for global literacies in professional communication programs. *Journal of Business and Technical Communication* 19: 468–99.

Sunaoshi, Y. (2005) Historical context and intercultural communication: Interactions between Japanese and American factory workers in the American South. *Language in Society* 34: 185–217.

Tanaka, H. (2006) Emerging English-speaking business discourses in Japan. *Journal of Asian Pacific Communication* 16: 25–50.

Tanaka, H. (2008) Communications strategies and cultural assumptions: An analysis of French-Japanese business meetings. In S. Tietze (ed.), *International Management and Language*. 154–70. London: Routledge.

Tanaka, H. (2009) Japan. In F. Bargiela-Chiappini (ed.), *The Handbook of Business Discourse*. 332–44. Edinburgh: Edinburgh University Press.

Tanaka, H. (2011) Politeness in a Japanese intra-organizational meeting: Honorifics and socio-dialectal code switching. *Journal of Asian Pacific Communication* 21: 60–76.

Tanaka, H. and Bargiela-Chiappini, F. (2011) Asian business discourse(s). In J. P. Gee and M. Handford (eds.), The *Routledge Handbook of Discourse Analysis*. 455–69. New York: Routledge.

Tanaka, H. and Sugiyama, A. (2010) Language, power and politeness in business meetings in Japan. In P. Heinrich and C. Galan (eds.), *Language Life in Japan: Transformations and Prospects*. 170–85. New York: Routledge.

Williams, M. (1988) Language taught for meetings and language used in meetings: Is there anything in common? *Applied Linguistics* 9: 45–58.

Wolff, M. (2010) China's English mystery – The views of a China "foreign expert". *English Today* 26: 53–6.

Yamada, H. (1992) *American and Japanese Business Discourse*. Norwood, NJ: Ablex.

Yamauchi, K. and Orr, T. (2008) Communication problems in the modern Japanese workplace: An exploratory investigation of employee opinions. *Proceedings of the IEEE International Professional Communication Conference* (IPCC 2008, July 13–16). Montreal, Canada: IPCC.

Zhang, Z. (2005) *Business English: A Discourse Approach*. Beijing: University of International Business and Economics Press.

Zhang, Z. (2007) Towards an integrated approach to teaching Business English: A Chinese experience. *English for Specific Purposes* 26: 399–410.

Zhang, Z. (2012) Teaching Business English. In C. A. Chapelle (ed.), *The Encyclopedia of Applied Linguistics*. Boston, MA: Wiley-Blackwell.

Zhang, Z., and Wang, L. (2011) Curriculum development for Business English students in China: The case of UIBE. *The Asian ESP Journal* 7: 10–27.

Zhu, W., Wu, S., and Guo, T. (2009) Reflection into China's Business English teaching practices based on GDUFS graduates' employment status. *International Education Studies* 2(3): 30–3.

11 Legal English

JILL NORTHCOTT

Introduction

The growth in English for specific purposes (ESP) practice and research has waxed and waned with the growth and decline of global industries and their related professions. Legal English is no exception. Because English is currently acknowledged to be the lingua franca of international commercial and legal transactions, globalization has ensured an ongoing interest in this area of ESP practice. As ESP practitioners "a commitment to revealing the workings of other communicative worlds to our students by grounding pedagogical decisions in our understanding of target texts and practices" (Hyland 2002: 393) requires us to undertake and reflect upon relevant research. This focus underpins the following examination of Legal English research.

As ever, terminology can cause problems. The term Legal English (LE) has a variable meaning, understood by some to refer to legalese and by others as a shortcut for Anglo-American law, hence ESP practitioners have often eschewed the term in favor of English for legal purposes (ELP). Other acronyms have been developed to account for different subsets and so we have EALP (English for academic legal purposes), EOLP (English for occupational legal purposes) and EGLP (English for general legal purposes). In related fields other definitions prevail. However, in the discussion that follows, my understanding and use of the term Legal English equates with "English language education to enable L2 law professionals to operate in academic and professional contexts requiring the use of English" (Northcott 2009: 166). It follows from this that Legal English research is research undertaken primarily to promote this aim and thus support pedagogy. This, whilst concurring with the most applied of definitions of applied

The Handbook of English for Specific Purposes, First Edition.
Edited by Brian Paltridge and Sue Starfield.
© 2013 John Wiley & Sons, Inc. Published 2013 by John Wiley & Sons, Inc.

linguistics, encompasses a wider body of research than might at first be apparent. ESP is an essentially eclectic discipline and remains open to insights from many different fields.

My aim in this chapter, at least in part, concurs with the obligation, incumbent on all ESP teachers, "to engage in a degree of reflection that attempts to sort out the extent to which learners' purposes are actually served when the language practices of any target discourse community are actually taught" (Belcher 2009: 2). After an overview of research developments in the areas of forensic linguistics, language and the law, and translation studies, I consider the impact of the common law origins of Legal English before describing some specific Legal English research developments of particular interest to the ESP discourse community.

Language and the Law

The nature and properties of legal language provide material for a substantial part of the Legal English research agenda because a large part of ESP has focussed and continues to focus on the description and analysis of the target language and language practices of the particular discourse community to which the learners belong or aspire to belong. Research in this area can be found in a number of related applied linguistic sub-disciplines in addition to ESP. These are referred to variously as legal linguistics, language and the law, and forensic linguistics. Understandably, in what is essentially a multidisciplinary area, there is no common agreement on the demarcation points. It is in effect a contested area. Definitions would appear to depend on the definer's affiliation and academic background. For example, forensic linguistics is viewed, broadly, as a branch of applied linguistics including the study of the written language of the law and spoken legal discourse, with their related social justice issues, legal translation and interpreting as well as Legal English teaching and learning (Gibbons and Turell 2008). The narrower definition (Grant nd) characterizes it as "taking linguistic knowledge, methods and insight and applying these to the forensic context of law, investigation, trial, punishment and rehabilitation." Tiersma (2008b: 11) speaks of the "relatively fractured" language and law field and the lack of a common forum for all interested parties. He laments the fact that language and the law appears to be "an unappreciated discipline" (2008b: 9) with the emphasis on language, in US law schools, at least, typically limited to legal writing courses.

That lawyers view language as a tool not an object of study has not traditionally been seen as such a problem, however, for the ESP practitioner. ESP is, to quote Harding (2007: 6), "the language for getting things done." In other words, it begins from "a functional account of learner needs" rather than a structural approach to language. (Richards and Rodgers 2001: 21).

> In ESP the practical application and use of language overrides other aspects of language learning. The vocation can be anything from A to Z, from architects to zoologists, by way of bricklayers, lawyers and tour guides (Harding 2007: 6).

A common theme in the language and law literature is the lack of transparency and obscurity found in legal discourse, with its frequent use of formal words, deliberate use of expressions with flexible meanings, attempts at extreme precision, and complex syntactic constructions (e.g. Danet 1980; Maley 1987; Melinkoff 1963). This is attributed to both the historical development of the language and the desire for power. Mattila (2006: 10) takes the view that "the legal language, especially legal terminology, sometimes is almost a language museum. This is clearly demonstrated by Legal English." Developments in the history of the English language account in part for this. Anglo-Saxon, French, and Latin have all left their marks on the language of the law in English. Medieval French influence has left us with long, complicated sentences; Anglo-Saxon has given us alliterative phrases, the product of an oral tradition. Some of these have persisted (cf *to have and to hold* in the marriage service). Legal pairs (e.g. *null and void; peace and quiet; breaking and entering; cease and desist*) are the fossilized result of the legal language changing from French to English in the late medieval period. The question as to why these anachronisms have persisted in the legal language can be answered partly by the lawyer's need for certainty and precision. Moreover, using a language not well-known to the general populace, with obscurities and ambiguities combined with excessive use of ritualistic language, maintains the image of the law as something inaccessible, mysterious and frightening, enabling the state to maintain its authority and lawyers to hold on to power. Mattila shows how the development of the common law (the system in the United Kingdom, the United States and former colonial countries) further contributed to the process. A system originally developed to ensure a common system of justice throughout the country became increasingly conceptually complex. Subtle distinctions between cases required a complex terminology as each term needed to be interpreted, narrowly resulting in verbose statutes and contracts in contrast to civilian law (the system in continental Europe and its former colonies). Williams (2005) gives a detailed account of verbal constructions in legislative text, giving careful consideration to Plain Language (the movement to encourage simplification of legal and other public discourse) suggestions for change. He concludes that there are good reasons for keeping many of the constructions that at first sight appear archaic and obtuse.

The legal language dilemma is compounded by the system-bound nature of legal language. Brand (2009: 22) states the problem lucidly:

> The anatomist will have few difficulties in finding a term for 'spinal column' in a foreign language that precisely describes the body part [s]he means. The jurist is in a less comfortable position. Each national legal system uses terminology that does not necessarily correspond with the legal languages of other countries . . . concepts vary to such an extent in different legal systems that a literal translation is misleading at best.

There are those who maintain that the problems may have been overstated. Tiersma (2008a) gives his own account of the historical development of English legal language. Whilst conceding that claims of archaism, redundancy, and attention to precision, leading to difficulties for comprehension, are true, he also claims that the differences between legal language, both spoken and written, and ordinary language, are not so great. In fact, legal language can also be "innovative, casual and purposely vague" (2008a: 24). As evidence for the innovative nature of legal language, he cites the growth of different names for contracts resulting from the growth of internet sales. New legal terms have been coined, for example, for the different licenses that can be created online. "Shrinkwrap," "clickwrap," and "browsewrap" are terms used to show how a purchaser can agree to the terms of a license by, respectively, opening the box containing software, clicking on an icon on a website to show agreement with the terms and clicking on a notice taking the purchaser to a separate web page containing the full text of the license agreement. Moreover, Kryk-Kastovsky (2006: 13) defends the hypothesis that "the language of the law shares most of the pragmatic properties of colloquial language." She frames her analysis around selected pragmatic concepts, adpated primarily from a Gricean perspective as interpreted by Levinson (e.g. Levinson 1983), within the language of law. These concepts are presupposition, deixis, implicature, speech acts and power versus solidarity.

Spoken legal genres have received less attention than the more easily accessed written genres. Apart from courtroom discourse, which has been extensively analyzed and reported in the forensic linguistics literature (see Gibbons 1999), work has been done on the lawyer-client interview. This research is, however, confined to first language speakers of English interacting in common law jurisdictions. Maley et al. (1995) draw on audio-taped interviews in the Australian context to analyze the ways in which "clients and lawyers co-construct through their discourse, or discourses, the definition, exploration and sometimes the resolution, of the matter before them" (p.43).

Recent forensic linguistics research claims go beyond the fact that the difficulties in understanding the language of the law are one factor causing misunderstandings to show how the very nature of legal language can lead to social disadvantage for vulnerable groups. Eades (2008), for example, examines the central role of language in the failure of the law in cases involving children, intellectually disabled people, deaf people, dialect speakers and other minority group members. Mertz (2007) demonstrates how law students are trained to "think like a lawyer" through socialization into various specific language abilities, providing further empirical evidence for the inseparability of law and language and contributing to a firmer research base from which to understand the effects this has on society.

Translation Studies

Within translation studies there is an ongoing debate about the nature of legal translation. Some (e.g. Harvey 2002) claim that legal language is just one instance of specialized language and can threfore be approached in the same way. Others (e.g. Joseph 2007; Sãrcević 1997, 2001) claim that legal translation creates such unique problems that only legally qualified translators are fully competent in this area. This debate, which can become highly polarized in academic circles, has resulted in a tendency towards some mutually exclusive research by lawyers and linguists. There is, however, some interesting work in both legal translation and lexicography which is very valuable for the Legal English practitioner. Poon (2010) gives an account of the issues for consideration in developing a bilingual English-Chinese legal dictionary for use in Hong Kong. A bilingual legal system was implemented in Hong Kong post-1997 with the need to translate common law concepts into Chinese. In translating the ordinances (statutes), existing legal terms borrowed from China or Taiwan were found to be inappropriate because the legal systems are civilian not common law-based. For reasons already explored in this chapter, concepts and phrases are easier to interpret with reference to common law cases. Understanding is not enhanced by literal translations of legal terms. Although specialized dictionaries are generally intended for specialist communication, the purpose of the new dictionary was to enable the Chinese-speaking public to understand the law, motivated by the desire to ensure that Hong Kong's freedom and autonomy were not being undermined by Beijing. For a term or concept to be understood it is necessary to have:

1. definitions of a legal term;
2. a context showing how a legal term is interpreted;
3. sources of the relevant ordinances (statutes) and cases.

Poon maintains that the best way of understanding the meaning is to quote cases heard in courts because court interpretations form an integral part of the meaning of a legal term. What is needed is a translation of the brief facts of the cases and the *ratio decidendi* (the principles or reasoning for the decisions). There are clear implications for the teaching of legal vocabulary because a full understanding of common law terms requires an exploration of all of the steps outlined above.

Ng (2009: 372) provides us with an exciting ethnographic study of English and Cantonese use in the courts in Hong Kong in which he "urges scholars to acknowledge the constitutive role of language in the day-to-day operation of a common law system." Hong Kong is unique in that it is the only common law jurisdiction where "Chinese is used to articulate common law concepts such as *mens rea* and *actus reus*, equity and equitable interest, recklessness and negligence, among others."

Common Law as a Source of Difficulty

That English is the language of the common law has often been perceived as the root of many of the law-specific difficulties for Legal English learners (see Northcott 2006). These learners include both students preparing for post-graduate law study and practicing lawyers from continental Europe and other countries whose legal systems are based on civilian law. Legal language is system-bound which means that many legal terms denoting concepts derive their meanings from a particular legal system and can only be understood by reference to the specific legal system. Examples from English law include *equity* and *trust*. All legal systems contain terms with no comparable counterparts in another legal system but the problem is particularly acute when it involves a common law country. Language is seen to play a pivotal role in the common law because of the doctrine of *stare decisis* (Latin for 'to stand by that which is decided') whereby principles of law laid down in the decisions of the higher courts bind the lower courts.

> If the court in a previous decision determined that a certain word or form of words has a particular meaning, then it is necessary to use this word or form of words if you want to achieve that particular meaning (Beveridge 2000: 3).

In addition, the study of law itself varies between civil and common law jurisdictions. Civilian law is based on written statutes, which are general legal principles compiled into codes. Law students study these codes. English law, on the other hand, has not been completely codified. As well as long complex Acts of Parliament (fundamentally different from civilian statutes) students are required to read and understand sometimes long and complicated legal cases. The reasoning behind the decisions reached in the higher courts is also a source of binding law. Studying the common law can make heavy demands on students studying in a second language, because of both the difficulties involved in comprehending legal texts and different assumptions about how to interpret and apply the law. However, Engberg (2010) presents empirical evidence to show that interpretation problems stemming from judge-made law are not confined to the common law systems. Using the example of the development of the concept of *Mord* in German (the most serious kind of unlawful killing), he demonstrates that the interpretation of the relevant article in Swiss criminal law "depends on the background assumptions of the judge or legal expert" (2010: 59) and concludes that "it is difficult to assume that the statutory text should have a stable and objective meaning independent of who is reading it" (2010: 60). Goddard (2010: 48) posits the idea of a "comfort zone" for Legal English use, giving the example of the Slovak lawyer dealing with a contract written in English but governed by Slovak law as an illustration of Legal English outside the comfort zone of English used in common law contexts. This is a useful conceptualization for both teachers of Legal English, providing a standpoint from which to adopt appropriate pedagogical solutions.

Common Law Contracts

In addition to the difficulties inherent in working with cases, contracts are clearly a potential source of difficulty for the Legal English learner. Because of the importance assigned to the meaning of words and expressions by judges, in order to understand common law contracts it is necessary to know what the terms mean to a common law lawyer. In the increasingly globalized world of commercial contracts this can be a major barrier. As we have seen, there are differences between all legal systems. The problem is compounded in the case of international commercial contracts because of the use of English, the language of the common law, as the international language. There have been attempts to overcome this problem. The International Institute for the Unification of Private Law (UNIDROIT) tried to avoid the use of terminology peculiar to any given legal system by creating, where necessary, entirely new concepts with new terminology. However, even such attempts at legal harmonization as the UNCITRAL (the United Nations Commission on International Trade Law) model for international commercial arbitration law have not proved unproblematic (Gotti 2009). As the rules have been translated from English and integrated into the laws of different countries differences in practice have reemerged.

Triebel (2009) considers the practical language difficulties faced by German-speaking lawyers working with contracts in three specific situations: English contracts governed by common law; English contracts being interpreted by civil law courts; and contracts written in English but governed by the law of a civil law jurisdiction. Whilst it is important for common law lawyers to understand civil law drafting practices and vice versa, it is important to understand the fundamental difficulties in providing civil law equivalents for common law terms. In addition to some of the issues already considered in this paper, Triebel draws attention to the procedural origin of many common law terms. In other words, they were developed by the courts. In civil law these terms may be a matter of substantive law. This is not simply a translation problem as it also results in dilemmas of interpretation for the civil law courts. Orts Llopis (2007: 18) examines the difficulties involved in translating American contract law concepts into Spanish and reaches similar conclusions.

> . . . once terms like 'specific performance' or 'breach of contract' are incorporated into the everyday usage of international contracts, insurance policies, and other relevant documents, the Anglo-American perceptions and legal concepts attached to them can creep surreptitiously into the substantive law of the country of reception and may have deep consequences for the way commercial transactions are conducted.

Beveridge (2000) posits possible solutions for these difficulties, concluding that teaching Legal English to those involved in the legal process provides the best way of beginning to tackle the problems.

Legal English Research

The next section focusses on research areas central to ESP including research with broader application than just the legal field. Research in ESP generally has contributed substantially to the development of both the understanding and practice of Legal English.

Early (pre-1990s) Legal English teaching strained even the most resourceful of ESP practitioners. One solution to the dilemma was to draw on the resources of legal specialists. ESP practitioners without legal training themselves have been wary of trespassing on territory long considered to be sacrosanct to legal specialists who often consider themselves to be experts on both law and language. Early ESP literature (Swales 1982; White 1981) gives accounts of ESP teachers who learnt from experience that analyzing and understanding legal texts required a different approach from that adopted with other types of ESP. The usual strategies employed assumed that ESP texts were primarily informational. Legal texts, on the other hand, are frequently performative with intended legal effects. As White discovered, lawyers read legal cases in order to understand the reasoning of judges when reaching decisions that will become binding in future cases coming before the courts whereas the language teacher's comprehension questions were focussed on understanding the narrative of the case. The teacher's lack of understanding of the specialist subject may lead to confusion on the part of the student. Consequently, the team teaching experiments begun by Tony Dudley-Evans in the 1970s (Johns and Dudley-Evans 1978) seemed to point to the best way forward for English for legal purposes (ELP). Blue (1993) endorsed very close cooperation with subject specialists when teaching English for academic legal purposes (EALP). There are many accounts of English language program development for undergraduate law students operating with different levels of cooperation with legal specialists (Bruce 2002; Candlin, Bhatia, and Jensen 2002; Howe 1993; Morrison and Tshuma 1993; Smyth 1997). Northcott and Brown (2006) document a partnership between ESP teachers and legal specialists in the provision of short training courses for legislative translators. Using short extracts taken from a video corpus of legal seminars, parallels are drawn with the cooperation between lawyers and linguists in the translation teams and LE teachers working with legal specialists and the potentially "conflicting linguistic and legal agendas of the different discourse communities . . . and the perceived power imbalance between the two" (2006: 366).

The other options open to the non-legally trained English teacher were to conduct extensive needs analysis or/and engage in discourse analysis. In the former case, the conclusions drawn might then lead to courses to develop communication skills. Abo Mosallem (1984) gives an account of one such needs analysis for Egyptian police officers resulting in a course to develop basic communicative ability. Tadros (1989) provides us with an interesting example of the second. Her research impetus is from pedagogic need – a colleague needs help with a text which is too difficult for his first-year students at the University of Khartoum. However the resulting analysis, based on categorizing the text according to certain predictive categories, whilst of theoretical interest, comes no nearer to solving the problem. Needs analyses of specific situations requiring Legal English have become better suited for purpose. Deutch (2003) gives an account of a needs analysis of Israeli law students, recognizing the need for priority setting given the constraints imposed by non-legally qualified Legal English teachers. She acknowledges the positive role to be played by "any kind of cooperation" (2003:141) with legal specialists in minimizing the extents of these constraints.

Bhatia's early work on text easification (1979) both paved the way for more sophisticated genre frameworks for different types of legal text and held out the promise of a solution other than drawing on the expertise of the legal specialist in the classroom setting. Indeed the genre-analytical approach developed by Bhatia and subsequently taken up by other Legal English teachers in Hong Kong and other common law EALP contexts appears to have met with some success. Key genres identified and analyzed are case reports and statutes. Materials are then developed to aid both student comprehension of these genres and productive use to complete academic law assignments (Bhatia 1993, 2009). Further work on the analysis of specific legal writing genres such as the problem-question essay (Bhatia 1989; Bruce 2002; Harris 1997) has also contributed to this teaching methodology. In problem-question essays students apply existing case law to the solution of a different legal problem to demonstrate their legal reasoning skills and knowledge of the law.

Genre analysis has proved a useful tool. Bhatia's (1997) framework for understanding the language of the law, distinguishing genres as pedagogic, professional or academic, has been very influential in Legal English teaching. The methods advocated have been taken up and adapted for different teaching situations. Badger (2003) and Bowles (1995), for example, both write about the use of genre-based materials based on newspaper law reports. Reinhart (2007) has produced genre-based materials for US LLM (Master of Laws) students incorporating an analysis of the structure of legal holdings. The syntactic features of legislative text are described in Bhatia (1993). These include sentence length, nominalization, complex prepositional phrases, binomial and multinomial expressions, initial case descriptions, qualifications in legislative provisions and syntactic discontinuities. Other researchers (see Stewart Smith 1999 cited in De Klerk 2003: 92; Stubbs 1996) have identified similar features in legal text but without clearly distinguishing between different genres and communicative purposes the work is of limited relevance to ESP practitioners. The increasing sophistication of this type of analysis has developed alongside the availability of concordancing software and subsequent developments in corpus linguistics. These studies are pedagogically significant because in order to develop both receptive and productive skills students need familiarity with the generic structures of legal texts. Feak, Reinhart, and Sinsheimer (2000) attempt a genre analysis of law review notes. I have drawn on this analysis in order to develop my own writing materials for a pre-sessional course (Northcott 2006). Pedagogical applications for specialist corpora are continuing to receive the attention of researchers. Weber (2001) describes a task-based course incorporating the use of concordances for legal essay writing. Fan and Xu (2002) report on an online bilingual corpus in English and Chinese to facilitate the self-study of Legal English. Hafner and Candlin (2007) evaluate student use of a simple online concordancing tool in completing legal writing tasks such as drafting legal opinions of court pleadings. They find that students tend to use these tools as a quick-fix solution, using them to locate model texts, for example, rather than to identify lexical patterns and develop their writing skills. Paradoxically, the corpus (consisting of legal cases) was considered to be too specialized to be of much help for self-study.

Bruce (2002) describes a course for first-year law students at Hong Kong University integrating language and content. The article is of particular interest for its consideration of the narrow tightrope sometimes walked by ESP practitioners between teaching law and language. Lawyers and law students see the process of identifying legal reasoning and rhetorical moves and arbitrating on substantive points of law as inextricable. Substituting a disciplinary framework from linguistics for one from law can be counterproductive. Without close cooperation with legal specialists the case for teachers with a background in both teaching law and language is a compelling one.

There is evidence of increasing convergence between methods used for teaching both first language (L1) and second language (L2) law students. Various models (genre frameworks) have been developed to improve the ability of law students to write problem question essays. These essays, used extensively in undergraduate law programs in common law countries, require the law student to consider a set of facts and identify the legal issues raised, applying the law to the facts (see Tessuto 2011 for a comparison of the problem question essay with its Italian civil law counterpart). Strong (2003), writing primarily for English students, bases legal writing materials on CLEO (claim law evaluation outcome) as a useful framework. There is a need for more research to link the advice given in the books on legal method and guides to the law produced by legal academics and professionals (e.g. Bradney et al. 2000; Hanson 1999; Kenny 1994) with sound linguistic evidence. Northcott (2009) provides more detail on methods and materials for teaching academic Legal English to law students in both the common law context described and in civil law contexts.

Early claims for the uniqueness of law as a discipline have also come under scrutiny. From a social constructionist perspective, Berkenkotter and Huckin (1985) and Bizzell (1992) give credence to the view that because all disciplines and professions are created by the communicative practices of their members for particular audiences, teaching skills, and language cannot be divorced from content. The difference in the case of law may simply be one of accessibility (Bhatia 2009) because of the widely recognized and researched complexity of legal discourse (Goodrich 1987; Mattila 2006; Melinkoff 1963). Bhatia (2009: 187) also makes the point that "in almost all professional contexts discourses are becoming increasingly interdisciplinary, complex and dynamic."

Implications for Legal English Research and Practice

From the perspective of the ESP teacher, the difficulties in understanding legal language present challenges. Some practitioners have taken the view that obtaining a legal qualification is the best solution. Others take the view that this is a retrograde step, obscuring the language issues. Certainly, Legal English teaching experience that attempts to involve legal specialists is enlightening in this regard. No lawyer will give an answer to a question outside her often very narrow area of specialization, although ESP teachers often feel that they must be able to answer every question a learner asks. Neither professional legal qualifications, nor the more recent language and law qualifications, available in departments of forensic linguistics in Finland and the United Kingdom, suffice. ESP methods involving a learner-centered approach, which uses the knowledge of the learners and works in partnership with them to develop their competence in using the language of the law in the target contexts of use can provide a better solution. However, the need for authenticity and face validity, particularly in relation to the production of Legal English materials, requires some understanding of the law. With the best of pedagogic intentions, approaching text comprehension, for example, by adopting a purely discourse analytical approach can result in the production of materials which are linguist-friendly but over complex and demotivating for many learners. As with other branches of ESP, misrepresentations of subject content result in language teaching material being viewed with suspicion and can lead to loss of learner confidence. The dilemma is particularly acute for Legal English practitioners faced with the dual responsibility of making a difficult area more accessible whilst adhering to sound pedagogical principles as much of the research demonstrates.

There is a need for more research at the civil law–common law interface. If, as Beveridge (2000) believes, Legal English teaching is the main solution for those confronted with the difficulties involved in using English as a legal lingua franca, then more research into the interface is essential. In particular, there is a pressing need for more meaningful connections between the legal and linguistic discourse communities. These may become more of a possibility as the restrictive practices associated with the practice of law begin to crumble, and lawyers and linguists are recognized as equal players in the co-construction of legal discourses.

REFERENCES

Abo Mosallem, E. (1984) English for police officers in Egypt. *English for Specific Purposes* 3: 171–81.

Badger, R. (2003) Legal and general. Towards a genre analysis of newspaper law reports. *English for Specific Purposes* 22: 249–63.

Berkenkotter, C. and Huckin, T. (1995) *Genre Knowledge in Disciplinary Communication: Cognition,* *Culture, Power*. Mahwah, NJ: Lawrence Erlbaum.

Beveridge, B. J. (2000) Legal English – How it developed and why it is not appropriate for international commercial contracts. In E. Heikki and S. Mattila (eds.), *The Development of Legal Language. Papers from a Symposium on Legal Linguistics*. Finland: Kauppsakaari. Accessed Sept. 15, 2011, http://

www.tradulex.org/Hieronymus/ Beveridge.pdf.

Bizzell, P. (1992) *Academic Discourse and Critical Consciousness*. Pittsburgh: University of Pittsburgh Press.

Bowles, H. (1995) Why are newspaper law reports so hard to understand? *English for Specific Purposes* 14: 201–22.

Belcher, D. (2009) What ESP is and can be: An introduction. In D. Belcher (ed.), *English for Specific Purposes in Theory and Practice*, 1–20. Ann Arbor, MI: University of Michigan Press.

Bhatia, V. (1979) Simplification vs. easification: The case of cases. MA Thesis. University of Lancaster, UK.

Bhatia, V. (1993) *Analysing Genre: Language Use in Professional Settings*. London: Longman.

Bhatia, V. (1997) Language of the law. *Language Teaching* 20: 227–34.

Bhatia, V. (2009) Intertextual patterns in English legal discourse. In D. Belcher (ed.), *English for Specific Purposes in Theory and Practice*. 186–204. Ann Arbor, MI: University of Michigan Press.

Bradney, A., Cownie, F., Masson, J., Neal, A., and Newell, D. (2000) *How To Study Law*. 4th ed. London: Sweet and Maxwell.

Brand, O. (2009) Language as a barrier to comparative law. In F. Olsen, A. Lotz, and D. Stein (eds.), *Translation Issues in Language and Law*. 18–34. Basingstoke, UK: Palgrave Macmillan.

Bruce, N. (2002) Dovetailing language and content: Teaching balanced argument in legal probalem answer writing. *Journal of English for Specific Purposes* 21: 321–45.

Candlin, C., Bhatia, V., and Jensen, C. (2002) Developing legal writing materials for English second language learners: problems and perspectives. *English for Specific Purposes* 21: 299–320.

Deutch, Y. (2003) Needs analysis for academic Legal English courses in Israel: A model of setting prioities. *English for Academic Purposes* 3: 123–46.

Danet, B. (1980) Language in the legal process. *Law and Society Review* 14: 445–564.

de Klerk, V. (2003) Language and the law: Who has the upper hand? *AILA Review* 16: 89–103.

Eades, D. (2008) Language and disadvantage before the law. In J. Gibbons and M. T. Turell (eds.), *Dimensions of Forensic Linguistics*. 179–95. Amsterdam/Philadelphia: John Benjamins.

Engberg, J. (2010) Knowledge construction and legal discourse: The interdependence of perspective and visibility of characteristics. *Journal of Pragmatics* 42: 46–63.

Feak, C., Reinhart, S., and Sinsheimer, A. (2000) A preliminary analysis of law review notes. *English for Specific Purposes* 19: 197–220.

Frade, C. (2007) Power dynamics and Legal English. *World Englishes* 26: 48–61.

Gibbons, J. (1999) Language and the law. *Annual Review of Applied Linguistics* 19: 156–73.

Gibbons, J. and Turell, M. T. (eds.) (2008). *Dimensions of Forensic Linguistics*. Amsterdam: John Benjamins.

Goddard, C. (2010) Didactic aspects of Legal English. Dynamics of course preparation. In M. Gotti and C. Williams (eds.), *Legal English Across Cultures*. Special issue. *ESP Across Cultures* 7. Accessed Feb. 2, 2012, http://www.edipuglia.it/ESP/.

Goodrich, P. (1987) *Legal Discourse*. London: Macmillan

Gotti, M. (2009) Globalizing trends in legal discourse. In F. Olsen, A. Lotz, and D. Stein (eds.), *Translation Issues in Language and Law*: 55–75. Basingstoke, UK: Palgrave Macmillan.

Grant, T. (nd) What is forensic linguistics? Birmingham, UK: Aston University Centre for Forensic Linguistics. Accessed May 17, 2012 at http://www.forensiclinguistics.net/cfl_fl.html

Hafner, C. and Candlin, C. (2007) Corpus tools as an affordance to learning in professional legal education. *Journal of English for Academic Purposes* 6: 303–18.

Hanson, S. (1999) *Legal Method*. London: Cavendish

Harding, K. (2007) *English for Specific Purposes*. Oxford: Oxford University Press.

Harris, S. (1997) Procedural vocabulary in law case reports. *English for Specific Purposes* 16: 289–308.

Harvey, M. (2002) What's so special about legal translation? *Meta* 47: 177–85.

Howe, P. (1993) Planning a pre-sessional course in English for academic legal purposes. In G. Blue (ed.), *Language Learning and Success: Studying Through English*. 148–57. London: Macmillan.

Hyland, K. (2002) Specificity revisited: How far should we go now? *English for Specific Purposes* 21: 385–95.

Johns, T. and Dudley-Evans, T. (1978) Team-teaching of subject-specific English to overseas postgraduate students. *Birmingham University Teaching News* 5.

Joseph, J. (2007) Why legal translation is special: Genre, terminology and interpretative norms. In T. Lynch and J. Northcott (eds.), *Symposia for Language Teacher Educators: Educating Legal English Specialists and Teacher Education in Teaching English for Academic Purposes* (2006). CD-ROM. Edinburgh: IALS, University of Edinburgh.

Kenny, P. (1994) *Studying Law*. 3rd edn. London: Butterworths.

Kryk-Kastovsky, K. (2006) Legal pragmatics. In K. Brown (ed.), *Encyclopedia of Language and Linguistics*. 13–20. Oxford: Elsevier.

Langton, N. (2002) Hedging argument in legal writing. *Perspectives* 14: 16–52.

Levinson, S. (1983) *Pragmatics*. Cambridge: Cambridge University Press.

Maley, Y. (1987) The language of legislation. *Language and Society* 16: 25–48.

Maley, Y., Candlin, C., Crichton, J., and Koster, P. (1995) Orientations in lawyer-client interviews. *Forensic Linguistics* 2: 42–55.

Mattila, H. (2006) Legal language: History. In K. Brown (ed.), *Encyclopedia of Language and Linguistics*. 8–1. Oxford: Elsevier.

Melinkoff, D. (1963) *The Language of the Law*. Boston, MA: Little Brown.

Mertz, E. (2007) *The Language of Law School: Learning to "Think Like a Lawyer."* New York: Oxford University Press.

Morrison, A. and Tshuma, L. (1993) Consensus ad idem: English for Academic Legal Purposes at the University of Zimbabwe. In C. Rubagumya (ed.), *Teaching and Researching Language in African Classrooms*. 50–62. Clevedon, UK: Multilingual Matters.

Ng, K. H. (2009) "If I lie, I tell you, may heaven and earth destroy me." Language and legal consciousness in Hong Kong bilingual common law. *Law and Society Review* 43: 369–403.

Northcott, J. (2006) Law and language or language and law? The design and implementation of an English for the LL.M course. In D. Bartol, A. Duszak, H. Izdebski, and J. M. Pierrel (eds.), *Langue, Droit, Société*. Cahiers de DNPS. 435–45. Nancy: Université de Nancy.

Northcott, J. (2009) Teaching Legal English: Contexts and cases. In D. Belcher (ed.), *English for Specific Purposes in Theory and Practice*. 165–85. Ann Arbor, MI: University of Michigan Press.

Northcott, J. and Brown, G. D. (2006) Legal translator training: Partnership between teachers of English for legal purposes and legal specialists. *English for Specific Purposes* 25: 358–75.

Orts Llopis, M. A. (2007) The untranslatability of law? Lexical differences in Spanish and American contract law. *European Journal of English Studies* 11: 17–28.

Poon, W. Y. E. (2010) Strategies for creating a bilingual legal dictionary. *International Journal of Lexicography* 23: 83–107

Reinhart, S. (2007) *Strategies for Legal Case Reading and Vocabulary Development.* Ann Arbor, MI: University of Michigan Press.

Richards, J. and Rodgers, T. (2001) *Approaches and Methods in Language Teaching.* 2nd ed. Cambridge: Cambridge University Press.

Sãrcĕvić, S. (1997) *New Approach to Legal Translation.* The Hague: Kluwer Law International.

Sãrcĕvić, S. (2001) *Legal Translation: Preparation for Accession to the European Union.* CD-rom. Croatia: University of Rijeka Faculty of Law.

Smyth, S. (1997) Sentence first verdict later: Courting the law on a university in-sessional English language course. *ESP SIG Newsletter* 10: 15–20.

Strong, S. (2003) *How to Write Law Essays and Exams.* London: LexisNexis.

Swales, J. (1982) The case of cases in English for academic legal purposes. *International Review of Applied Linguistics* 20: 139–48.

Tadros, A. (1989) Predictive categories in university textbooks. *English for Specific Purposes* 8: 17–31.

Tessuto, G. (2011) Legal problem question answer genre across jurisdictions and cultures. *English for Specific Purposes* 30: 298–309.

Tiersma , P. (2008a) The nature of legal language. In J. Gibbons and M. T. Turell (eds.), *Dimensions of Forensic Linguistics.* 7–26. Amsterdam/Philadelphia, PA: John Benjamins.

Tiersma, P. (2008b) What is language and law? And does anyone care? In F. Olsen, A. Lorz, and D. Stein (eds.), *Law and Language: Theory and Society.* Düsseldorf: Düsseldorf University Press Available at SSRN http://papers.ssrn.com/sol3/papers.cfm?abstract_id=1352075.

Triebel, V. (2009) Pitfalls of English as a contract language. In F. Olsen, A. Lotz, and D. Stein (eds.), *Translation Issues in Language and Law.* 147–81. Basingstoke, UK: Palgrave Macmillan.

Weber, J. J. (2001) A concordance-and genre-informed approach to ESP essay writing. *ELT Journal* 55: 14–20.

White, G. (1981) The subject specialist and the ESP teacher. *Lexden Papers* 2: 9–14. Oxford: Lexden Centre.

Williams, C. (2005) *Tradition and Change in Legal English: Verbal Constructions in Prescriptive Texts.* Bern: Peter Lang.

12 Aviation English

CAROL LYNN MODER

Introduction

Aviation English describes the language used by pilots, air traffic controllers, and other personnel associated with the aviation industry. Although the term may encompass a wide variety of language use situations, including the language of airline mechanics, flight attendants, or ground service personnel, most research and teaching focus on the more specialized communication between pilots and air traffic controllers, often called radiotelephony.

The language used by flight attendants and other general aviation personnel, like many forms of English for specific purposes, uses conventional English pronunciation, structure, vocabulary, and interactional patterns, but adapts them to the purposes of the particular domain and context (Cutting 2011). The language of air traffic control is a more specialized and restricted variety, for which the language patterns are tightly regulated by professional and international standards. The language used among pilots and flight engineers in the cockpit is often a hybrid of specialized technical language and everyday language and may use varying amounts of English or other languages (Linde 1988; Nevile 2004; Wyss-Bühlmann 2005). Whereas the demands for the use of English by other aviation personnel vary widely by country and context, the use of English as the international language of air traffic control is officially mandated by the International Civil Aviation Organization (ICAO).

The ICAO is a specialized agency of the United Nations, whose role is to set standards for aviation safety and security and to promote cooperation in civil aviation among its 191 member states (ICAO nd Strategic Objectives). According to ICAO policy, pilots on international flights and air traffic controllers in airspaces

The Handbook of English for Specific Purposes, First Edition.
Edited by Brian Paltridge and Sue Starfield.
© 2013 John Wiley & Sons, Inc. Published 2013 by John Wiley & Sons, Inc.

that receive international flights must demonstrate the ability to communicate effectively in English, in addition to the language used by the station on the ground (ICAO 2004).

Because of a recent ICAO policy change regarding English language proficiency, Aviation English teaching and testing for pilots and air traffic controllers has become a major focus worldwide. In 1998, after a number of aviation accidents in which language was determined to be a contributing factor (see Cushing 1994 for some examples), ICAO commissioned a review of English proficiency requirements, focussing on the radio communication between pilots and air traffic controllers (Mathews 2004). In 2003, ICAO imposed new standards for Aviation English, which required pilots and air traffic controllers worldwide to reach by March 2008 uniform minimum English proficiency levels defined as Operational Level 4 by a prescribed rating scale. Meeting this deadline required member nations to put in place extensive training and testing procedures, which for many proved impossible within the time allotted between the adoption of the policy and the implementation date. ICAO has permitted various interim measures for nations that are making progress on compliance (Alderson 2009; ICAO nd Flight Safety Information Exchange).

The ICAO minimum acceptable proficiency level, Operational Level 4, requires pilots and air traffic controllers to demonstrate comprehensible pronunciation, intelligible fluency and delivery, and a vocabulary range sufficient to communicate on "common, concrete, and work-related topics" with the ability to paraphrase in unexpected circumstances. Very importantly, minimum acceptable comprehension and interaction skills are also specified. Comprehension must be "mostly accurate on common, concrete, and work-related topics" but "with a linguistic or situational complication or an unexpected turn of events, comprehension may be slower or require clarification strategies." Interaction must include responses that are "usually immediate, appropriate and informative" and personnel must initiate and maintain exchanges even in "an unexpected turn of events" and must deal with "apparent misunderstandings by checking, confirming, or clarifying" (ICAO 2004). These descriptors would be familiar to many ESP professionals. However, it is critical for ESP professionals working in Aviation English to understand the highly specialized context to which they apply.

Aviation English Discourse

Air traffic communication occurs entirely over radio frequencies and includes no face-to-face communication. The linguistic exchanges occur within a sociotechnical system supported by material anchors (Hutchins 1995, 1996, 2005). Controllers and pilots share information from charts, navigational aids, and flight plans. Most significant for the controller are radar displays, and most significant for the flight crew is the cockpit instrumentation. All communication within the cockpit and from the cockpit to the controller relies on speaker and hearer interpretations of these material symbols. Because most flights occur in highly regulated airspaces, most of the communication between pilots and controllers involves routine exchanges of predictable, shared information concerning the aircraft in the area, the parameters of the airport or airspace, and the expected actions at particular points in the flight. The specific language and exchange sequences required for routine pilot–controller communications is specified in professional training documents, most particularly in ICAO Document 4444 Air Traffic Management (ICAO 2001). The prescribed vocabulary and syntax are referred to as phraseology. Non-prescribed uses of more common English vocabulary and syntax are called "plain English" by aviation professionals.

Example 1 provides a sample of the prescribed phraseology of this highly specialized variety. All examples come from the radiotelephony portion of the Oklahoma State University Corpus of Aviation English (Moder and Halleck 2009, 2012). The call signs and reporting points have been modified to preserve anonymity.

Example 1

    PN395:   Center Control, Papa November tree-niner-fife at tree-tree-zero.
    CC: Papa November tree-niner-fife, Center Control, roger, maintain
              flight level tree-tree-zero, report at Dukka.
    PN395:   Report at Dukka, Papa November tree-niner-fife.

Example 1 is a routine communication between an en route controller, Center Control (CC), and the pilot of an aircraft with the call sign PN395 (Papa November tree-niner-fife). En-route air traffic controllers, or area controllers, typically monitor thousands of square miles of airspace and may also provide services for smaller airports in their area. For an aircraft that is already airborne, the en route controller monitors the direction, speed, and altitude (flight level) at which the aircraft flies and ensures that each aircraft is separated by an appropriate distance from other aircraft in the immediate area. Flight paths are typically well-established with well-mapped position points and typical flight levels and directions. The pilot and controller both have access to the intended flight plan and established flight paths and, in most cases, the controller also has radar information on the location of the aircraft.

Several distinctive aspects of the language of radiotelephony are illustrated in Example 1. The exchanges are brief, and the grammatical forms employed are limited. Most verbs occur in the imperative form and function words are limited to a small number of prepositions. The vocabulary is specialized and the use of numbers and letters is very prominent. Furthermore, the pronunciation of the letters and numbers follows the prescribed ICAO alphabet, which is also common to maritime and military contexts. Thus, "P" is read "Papa," and "N" as "November." All numbers are pronounced as single digits: the number "9" is pronounced "niner," the number "5" is pronounced "fife" and the number "3" is pronounced "tree." This last set of pronunciation features, though prescribed by the ICAO standard, is often not adopted by native speakers of English, who typically pronounce "3" and "5" in the usual plain English way. Also noteworthy is the use of identifiers (Center Control, Papa November tree-niner-fife) by each of the speakers in the exchange.

Research into the discourse of radiotelephony has helped to further specify the restricted grammatical features of the domain. Mell (2004, ICAO 2004) describes basic functions that are required in aviation work contexts. He describes content domains and functions and the grammatical forms used to express them, including imperatives and bare participles without auxiliaries (*leaving, cleared*). Citing results from the OSU aviation corpus, Moder and Halleck (2012) describe the most frequent verb forms as including those typically associated with various stages of a flight: *hold, turn, maintain, contact, land, cleared*, and *going*, as well as verbs of possession *have, get*, and *got*, and the perception verb *see*. As in Mell's study, these corpus results indicate that in radiotelephony, verbs most frequently occur in bare imperatives, with some verbs commonly occurring as bare *-ed* or *-ing* participles. The most common prepositions in the corpus were *to, of, at*, and *on*, prepositions typically associated with establishing locations, directions, or goals.

The context of the radiotelephony discourse situation also engenders specific interactional rules for exchanges. In Example 1 the pilot of PN395 is following his established flight plan and has just passed into the airspace overseen by Center Control. The purpose of his communication is to establish contact with the new controller. The pilot first identifies his addressee, Center Control, and then identifies himself, PN395 at the beginning of the communication. This identification at the initiation of an exchange, first of the intended addressee and then of the speaker, is a critical part of the discourse interaction in this context since all aircraft in the area tune to the same frequency. The use of a common language and frequency is critical for safety, since it ensures that all aircraft and control personnel have "situational awareness" of the aircraft in the area and their positions. When an exchange is initiated it is essential that the speaker and the addressee be clearly identified.

After this identification, the pilot states his flight level, 330, or 33,000 feet. At the beginning of his turn-at-talk, the controller identifies the aircraft and then identifies himself; he acknowledges his receipt of the information with the standard term "roger," then gives the pilot instructions to continue at the established flight level ("maintain flight level 330") and instructs him to report again when he reaches the reporting point on his flight plan called Dukka. The pilot acknowledges the new information in the controller's communication by repeating it ("Report at Dukka"). This repetition is called a readback and is an essential part of ensuring the information is correctly received. The pilot then concludes this first exchange by giving his call sign.

The next exchange follows the prescribed interactional pattern, but illustrates the non-prescribed addition of plain English expressions. In this exchange, the aircraft PN395 reaches the reporting point, Dukka, which is the boundary of Center Control's area. The pilot must terminate contact with Center Control and get the information necessary to contact the next control center at Melada. The exchange is provided in Example 2.

Example 2

> PN395: Center Control, Papa November tree-niner-fife is over Dukka
>
> CC: Papa November tree-niner-fife, Center Control, roger, radar service terminated, maintain three-three-zero, contact Melada one-two-fife decimal fife. **So long**.
>
> PN395: one-two-five-decimal five. **So long, sir**.

Most of the exchange in Example 2 follows the language and interactional patterns discussed above. Noteworthy in this example are the uses of the signoff phrase "So long" and the honorific "sir." Such signoff phrases and politeness markers are not part of prescribed phraseology, but are extremely common in radiotelephony discourse. In a study of fifteen hours of pilot–controller communication at a US airport, Howard (2008) found that signoffs occurred in seven percent of the exchanges, greetings in two percent, honorifics in two percent, and "please" and "thank you" in four percent. Researchers studying European and Australian contexts find similar uses (Nevile 2004; Sänne 1999; Wyss-Bühlmann 2005).

Other common uses of plain language in the radiotelephony context may be more problematic, especially when native speakers of English interact with non-native speakers. Example 3 presents a native English speaking pilot contacting a Spanish-speaking controller to request a deviation from the planned flight path because of weather. Although there is prescribed ICAO phraseology for this (Request weather deviation), the pilot uses plain English in his request ("we're deviating just a little bit left of course for weather").

Example 3

> A492: Center Control, Airline four-nine-two, **we're deviating just a little bit left of course for weather.**
>
> CC: Airline four-niner-two, Center Control, left deviation approved, after deviation fly direct to Omano.
>
> A492: Roger, after deviation, direct Omano, Airline four-nine-two.

Studies of transcripts of unexpected contexts indicate that pilots are more likely to use plain language to supplement phraseology in problematic or emergency situations (Linde 1988; Wyss-Bühlmann 2005). Example 4 illustrates one such use of plain English in an emergency communication. Here the pilot of A915 is alerting the controllers to a very serious situation. The emergency alert "mayday, mayday, mayday" is reserved for grave danger that requires immediate assistance. Following this prescribed alert, the pilot reports the plane has collided with birds after takeoff, an occurrence typically called "bird strike," resulting in damage to both engines. Note that the pilot uses plain English ("hit birds") and then uses full English syntax, including pronouns and auxiliaries, in the subsequent report. The controller's response also uses plain English ("okay" followed by a plain English question with rising intonation).

Example 4

> A 915:   Mayday mayday mayday, uh this is uh Airline nine-one-five, hit
>   birds, we've lost thrust both engines, we're turning back towards
>   airport.
> C: okay uh, you need to return to airport? turn left heading of uh
>   two-two-zero.

Many aviation professionals find such uses of non-prescribed syntax to be a potential cause of miscommunication, especially in unexpected contexts in international airspaces. Kim and Elder (2009) asked Korean pilots and controllers to listen to a recording of a communication in which an American pilot contacted a controller in Korean airspace because he was low on fuel and asked to be diverted to a nearby airport. There was some communication difficulty in the exchange, which the Korean aviation professionals attributed to the pilot's wordy use of plain English instead of more concise phraseology.

Comprehension and Negotiation of Meaning

The difficulty of comprehension in the radio channel makes the negotiation of meaning a critical skill in Aviation English. Comprehension is especially difficult in portions of the flight that involve the exchange of a great deal of rapidly presented information essential to flight safety, such as takeoff and landing. During these segments of the flight, aircraft are monitored by approach, or terminal, controllers. Approach controllers must ensure that departing aircraft are guided from the runway up into controlled airspace and approaching aircraft are guided down to the runway safely. At busy airports, approach controllers communicate concurrently with multiple aircraft at differing stages of flight. The flow of information is primarily from the controller to the pilot. Because of the typically heavy workload, controllers provide multiple pieces of information in a single turn in order to balance accuracy and efficiency. The pilot must attend to all of the information given and provide a readback to ensure comprehension accuracy. Example 5 presents an exchange between an approach controller and an aircraft approaching for landing.

Example 5

> AC: Airline four-zero-five, turn right heading zero-five-zero to intercept
>   the localizer, cleared for the ILS approach, reduce speed one-eight-
>   zero knots.
> A405:   Airline four-zero-five, right heading zero-five-zero to intercept the
>   localizer, **say again speed required please**.
> AC: Airline four-zero-five, one-eight-zero knots.
> A405:   one-eight-zero knots, Airline four-zero-five, **thank you.**

The controller identifies the aircraft addressed (Airline 405) and directs the pilot to turn the aircraft to the right until it reaches the heading of 050 degrees. The aircraft is flying an instrument landing system (ILS) approach with the help of signals from the antenna array near the end of the runway (the localizer). The controller also directs the aircraft to slow down to a speed of 180 knots. The pilot is given several pieces of key information in this one turn – the direction of the turn, the heading, and the speed. He reads back the first two pieces of information correctly but fails to recall the speed. He uses prescribed phraseology ("say again required speed") to request a repetition. He adds the politeness marker "please," possibly acknowledging that his request has made the exchange less efficient. After the controller repeats the speed, the pilot reads it back correctly and ends by thanking the controller for the repetition. Sänne (1999) identifies such uses of politeness markers as serving the relational function of orienting to the needs of others. He suggests these markers typically occur when the communication does not go according to expectations.

In spite of the amount of technical information conveyed in single turns, pilot–controller communication is surprisingly efficient, even in these critical segments of flight. In an examination of twelve hours of communication from departure and control sectors in the United States, Morrow, Rodvold, and Lee (1994: 246) found that only 12 percent or fewer of the transactions in each sample included understanding or information problems. However, even though problematic transactions occur with relatively low frequency, it is essential to aviation safety that the problems be detected and rectified immediately. Morrow, Rodvold, and Lee found that in problematic communications, pilots used phraseology ("Say again") in 25 percent of the transactions, plain English questions ("What was the heading?") in 35 percent, and repetitions with question intonation ("That was heading 180?") in 23 percent (1994: 247).

Example 6 illustrates the use of phraseology and intonation questions for the purposes of clarifying and repairing information in a complex communicative situation.

Example 6

A 364: Eastern Control, Airline tree-six-four, now reaching flight level two-five-zero, **request further low**.

EC: Airline three-six-four stand by . . .

EC: **Airline two-niner-six, confirm, requesting lower altitude?**
A 296: Airline two-nine-six, negative.

EC: Airline two-niner-six, roger.

EC: Airline tree-six-four, **confirm, requesting lower altitude?**
A 364: Airline tree-six-four, **roger, request two-one-zero**

EC: Airline tree-six-four, descend and maintain flight level **two-three-zero, correction two-one-zero**.

A 364: Airline tree-six-four, leaving two-five-zero for two-one-zero, **thank you**.

In Example 6, the approach controller (Eastern Control) is coordinating multiple aircraft during a heavy traffic period at an international airport. The pilot of one of the aircraft, A364, requests a change in altitude using unclear language ("request further low"). As is typical for such requests, the controller delays responding ("standby"), in order to check the other traffic in the area to determine the feasibility of the request. When the controller returns to the request, he is not certain which aircraft requested the change. He asks another pilot (A296) whether he requested the change ("confirm, requesting lower altitude?"). This query uses a combination of standard phraseology and rising question intonation to indicate uncertainty. The pilot of A296 indicates that he did not request the change ("negative"). The controller acknowledges this information ("roger") and then contacts A364 with the same query. The pilot of A364 responds positively, using the phrase "roger." According to standard phraseology, the positive response to a query would more appropriately be "affirm;" "roger" typically acknowledges that information has been received and understood, as in the preceding use by the controller. The pilot goes on to re-state the request, this time specifying the flight level requested ("request two-one-zero"). The controller approves this request, giving the pilot instructions to descend to the requested level and stay there. However, he misspeaks, giving the new flight level as 230, but he immediately self-repairs ("correction two-one-zero"). The pilot confirms his understanding that the controller has granted the requested flight level change ("leaving two-five-zero for two-one-zero"), and he thanks the controller. Here again, the expression of gratitude appears to acknowledge the additional workload created by the request.

The use of questions is one aspect of plain language that aviation professionals often assert does not have a role in radiotelephony. However, in a study of exchanges from Toronto Pearson Airport and Dublin Airport, Hinrich (2008) found that questions occurred frequently in pilot–controller communications. In twenty-four and a half hours of interactions, she found a total of 677 questions or 38.3 questions per hour (2008: 190). Questions were used roughly twice as frequently by the controllers (458 questions) as by the pilots (219 questions). On average, there were about 28 turns incorporating questions in every hour of recorded communication. The pilots used questions about 9 times per hour, and the controllers used 18 questions per hour (2008: 191). Approximately two thirds of the questions were syntactic interrogatives: "How long will you be on the ground?" "What was the distance again?" "May we maintain that speed?" "Is that okay?" One third were intonation questions: "We'd like to get just a little lower?" "Say again?" "Just reconfirm that was one-six-thousand?". The questions were used to seek information, but also to clarify, check, or repair information. Hinrich speculates that full WH-questions (such as Who, What, Where, Why questions), which are not approved phraseology, often occur when there are unanticipated changes to speakers' routine expectations. In these cases, the speakers use a full, direct question to verify or elaborate the unexpected information. The findings of the study suggest that the use of questions may signal a turn as negotiating meaning or managing the relational aspects of radiotelephony exchanges.

The preceding discussion has highlighted some of the major features of aviation discourse, including its specialized vocabulary, restricted syntax and interactional characteristics. The discussion has also provided details on commonly occurring plain language features, including greetings, signoffs, politeness markers, and questions. With this background established, we turn to a discussion of research that addresses key issues related to aviation language and considerations of safety and workplace efficiency.

Cognitive Load and Comprehension

As we have illustrated above, comprehension of complex information is central to safe and effective communication in the aviation domain. In most exchanges, information flows from the controller to the pilot, making the comprehension skills of the pilot critical. However, radio communication is only one small part of the work of flight crews in this sociotechnical system. The ability of flight crews to understand and manage radio communication is directly related to the cognitive load imposed on them by other tasks.

Farris et al. (2008) describe the multiple concurrent tasks pilots perform that require memory and processing demands in terms of cognitive workload. They suggest that high cognitive workload may interact with language proficiency to affect the ability of flight crews to adequately interact in radio communication with controllers. The cognitive load of communication becomes higher for the flight crew in critical stages of flight because of the need to coordinate flight procedures and information among the crew members in the cockpit in preparation for landing (see Goodwin (1996), Linde (1988), and Nevile (2004) for a detailed discussion of the cognitive and linguistic demands of the cockpit environment).

An additional factor that contributes to cognitive workload is the length of the controller messages. We saw an illustration of a pilot's failure to recall an extended message in Example 5 above. In a study of 268 turns-at-talk from approach control at Portland Airport, Barshi (1997) found that the message length varied from 2 to 6 pieces of information per controller turn. Most controller instructions contained 2 or 3 pieces of information, but about a fourth contained between 4 and 6. As the message length increased, the number of full and correct pilot readbacks decreased (1997: 25).

To compensate for the cognitive workload, Estival and Molesworth (2009) suggest that comprehension may be aided by greater emphasis on the prosodic features of message delivery – intonation, pauses, and stress. They suggest that the neutral prosodic contours and rapid delivery typically used by controllers may contribute to comprehension problems in radio communication for both native and non-native English speaking pilots.

A linguistic feature often related to cognitive workload is code-switching. Under normal flight conditions, code-switching may be an intentional interactional strategy. Wyss-Bühlmann (2005) found that communication in and around

Zurich airport reflected numerous instances of relationally motivated code-switching. Greetings, signoffs and expressions of gratitude were often given in the presumed language of the interlocutor ("gruezi," "schöne Abig," "adieu," "Danke schön"), establishing a friendly conversational tone (2005: 140–43).

In emergency contexts, code-switching appears to be a less intentional result of cognitive workload. Cookson (2009) discusses how code-switching may have contributed to the well-known collision of two aircraft in Zagreb airspace in 1976. The controller had been covering the heavily traveled Zagreb sector alone and was working under time pressure to resolve an imminent collision. Until the critical occurrence, the Yugoslavian flight crew had communicated with the controller entirely in English. The controller switched to his native language, which was also that of the flight crew, to give the crucial instructions to the aircraft. The pilot responded in that language as well. Unfortunately, the pilot of the other aircraft could not understand these instructions and was therefore unaware that the other plane had been mistakenly directed into its flight path. In this instance, language was a contributing factor, but the excessive workload placed on the controller was a major precondition for the accident.

Politeness and Mitigation

As we have seen, the role of politeness markers in Aviation English is contested. Such plain English phrases are proscribed in official training as impeding the efficiency of the information exchange, and they are discouraged by aviation-based researchers (Howard 2008; Morrow, Rodvold, and Lee 1994). However, researchers who take a discourse-based approach have suggested that the effectiveness of aviation communication should not be considered narrowly in terms of informational exchange alone, but more broadly in terms of the social aspects of the exchange (Hinrich 2008; Linde 1988; Sänne 2004; Wyss-Bühlmann 2005). These researchers suggest that because plain English acknowledges the interactional roles and goals of the participants, it can improve, rather than impede, the effectiveness of an exchange.

In a study of communication in the cockpit, Linde (1988) found that hierarchical relationships among members of the flight crew had a complex impact on their interactions. In reviewing transcripts of cockpit recorder data from eight aviation accidents, she found that requests made by more junior co-pilots to the captain were more likely to be mitigated or indirect. For example, she cites a case of an aircraft that overran the runway because of excessive speed. While the aircraft was approaching the runway too quickly, the co-pilot mentioned a tailwind and the possible slowness of the flaps, which reduce the speed. After the accident, he indicated that he had been trying to suggest to the captain that the plane was going too fast, but he had not explicitly and directly stated his observation. The captain did not interpret these indirect statements as warnings. Linde found that such mitigation was always present to some extent, but she also found that in emergencies the amount of mitigation decreased significantly. Linde's study has been cited by some researchers as ratifying the need to eliminate mitigation and politeness markers from aviation communication. However, it is important to highlight that Linde also found that the crews with the best safety records had higher rates of mitigation than crews with poor records. She posits that the relational information encoded by mitigation markers is key to maintaining the necessary hierarchical relations among flight crew members. She suggests that rather than training crew members to eliminate such language, they should be trained in effective ways to respectfully challenge a superior's assessment of a situation.

Politeness markers and mitigated requests are even more contested features in the context of pilot–controller communication. Example 7 illustrates the use of some contested features that mark politeness and mitigation.

Example 7 Airline two-nine-six, negative.

A2130:   Center Control Airline two-one-three-zero, request.
CC: Airline two-one-three-zero, Center Control, go ahead.
A2130:   **yes sir, like to uh get uh flight level three-nine-zero if we could, uh we were filed for that.**
CC: Airline two-one-three-zero, Center Control, standby **please**.
CC: Airline two-one-three-zero, climb and maintain flight level three-nine-zero.
A2130:   **okay** we're leaving three-five-zero for three-nine-zero, Airline two-one-three-zero, **thank you sir.**
CC: **You're welcome sir**.

Here the pilot, a native speaker of English, requests a change to a higher flight level, but instead of using established phraseology, he begins with an honorific ("sir") and issues a mitigated request using plain English ("like to get . . . if we could"). He continues by justifying the request ("we were filed for that"). The non-native speaking controller grants his request using standard phraseology. The pilot again uses plain English in his readback ("okay we're . . . ") and thanks the controller. The controller acknowledges the thanks with a plain English response.

In discussing similar polite, mitigated exchanges in Swedish airspace, Sänne (1999) reports that controllers have positive attitudes toward such friendly, personal contact with flight crews. He goes on to argue that the value of these expressions may be critical to making work-related interactions effective. Example 7 above can be considered as an illustration of this view. At the beginning of the exchange in the example, Airline 2130 is traveling at a lower than expected flight level. Because the lower flight level may increase fuel consumption, it is in the airline's best interest for the aircraft to move to a higher flight level. The pilot requests the change in very mitigated form ("like to get . . . if we could"). The mitigation seeks the controller's cooperation with the request while acknowledging that the controller may have a reason for asking the aircraft to continue to fly at a lower level. The pilot supports his request with a justification ("we

were cleared for that"). When the request is granted the pilot shows his acknowl-
edgement and appreciation of the cooperation ("thank you, sir"), to which the
controller responds with the polite response ("You're welcome").

Hinrich (2008) found that the modal "could" occurred frequently in requests
like these. Sänne (1999) argues that the use of these types of mitigation forms
by pilots and controllers is a strategy to accomplish cooperative actions effectively.
Pilots use them when their requests increase the controller's workload, and controllers use them when they are aware that the requests they are making are
unexpected or undesirable. The politeness and mitigation markers display that
control and authority are negotiated in this context, not determined absolutely by
position. The controller is responsible for giving directives in order to keep aircraft
safely separated, but the pilot is ultimately responsible for flying the aircraft safely.
Any controller or pilot request may be rejected on the grounds of safety, but otherwise pilots and controllers must try to work cooperatively to maintain efficiency.
One of Sänne's interviewees explains that in heavy traffic situations it is essential
that controllers maintain control through talk. To accomplish this, the controller
must lead the radio contact, anticipate the flight crews' actions, display authority,
and create social bonds by attending to flight crews' interests (1999: 220). Sänne
suggests that politeness markers, mitigated requests, and justifications help to
accomplish these social actions. Similarly, Wyss-Bühlmann (2005) in a study of
air traffic communication at Zurich airport has found that non-prescribed plain
language use – especially greetings, signoffs, "please" and "thank you," and mitigated questions – are used strategically to clarify meanings, solve problems of
understanding, and contribute to cooperative exchanges.

We see from the above discussion that there is a continuing tension between
the language recommended by policy and professional standards and the language actually used in authentic workplace communication. Although ICAO
standards require that routine communication be conducted entirely in prescribed
phraseology, actual language use evinces the same kind of variation found in
everyday language. The extent to which safety may be aided or impeded by features coding relational aspects of language, in particular markers of politeness and
cooperation, remains an open question.

Aviation English Curriculum Development
and Testing

In English for specific purposes teaching and testing, the task of the curriculum
or test designer is to mirror as accurately as possible the language, tasks, and
contexts of the target language situation. The discourse-based studies we have
discussed above provide background on authentic aviation discourse that would
be of value for those wishing to create authentic materials. In particular, Sänne
(1999), Nevile (2004), and Wyss-Bühlmann (2005), provide detailed descriptions
of the work-related contexts of pilots and controllers. Smith (2004) provides a
highly accessible overview of selected aviation topics designed for a general
audience.

A small number of studies have reported on the design of Aviation English teaching materials. Sullivan and Girginier (2002) discuss the use of discourse analysis to design materials for an ESP program in a Civil Aviation School in Turkey. They conducted an analysis of nine hours of recordings from the control center at Ataturk International Airport, supplemented by workplace observations and interviews and questionnaires distributed to Turkish controllers and pilots. Based on this material, they designed activities focussing on the pronunciation of numbers, the practice of readbacks, the repair of miscommunication, and the improvement of comprehension.

Wang (2007) describes the development of an Aviation English curriculum in China. The researcher briefly outlines the use of an approach highlighting phonetic and semantic contrasts in order to teach students key aspects of Aviation English pronunciation and vocabulary.

Focussing on the English required for ground staff at European airports, Cutting (2011) discusses the use of field observations to build dialogues that served to guide the development of classroom materials. The field notes were collated, and then experienced aviation teachers used them to write dialogues, which were next distributed to aviation professionals and trainers to determine their representativeness. The dialogues were grouped into sets of scenarios for security guards, ground handlers, catering staff, and bus drivers. Each set of scenarios was further analyzed to identify frequent forms and functions. The goal was to develop materials that would focus on the basic language features needed for learners with limited grammatical proficiency.

The testing of Aviation English has been the subject of numerous studies, particularly in response to the new ICAO proficiency requirements. Even before the new ICAO policy was established, testing of non-native speaking aviation professionals incorporated the distinctive interactional language features of radiotelephony in their design. One of the first studies of test design in this domain was by Teasdale (1996). He conducted a detailed discourse-based needs analysis, which included the transcription and analysis of twelve hours of authentic air traffic communication, supplemented with a questionnaire on language use. Based on the needs analysis, Teasdale outlined important recurring air traffic functions, such as understanding pilot readbacks and checking, confirming, or clarifying information when necessary.

Recent testing studies have focussed on the new ICAO proficiency guidelines. Clear overviews of the ICAO testing parameters and efforts by various countries to meet them are provided by Read and Knoch (2009) and Alderson (2009). Huhta (2009) describes the design of an aviation test in Finland, highlighting the conflicts that can arise between aviation experts and language specialists. Van Moere et al. (2009) describe the design and validation of a computer administered and scored test of Aviation English.

The question of how to define the domain of Aviation English for testing purposes is taken up in detail in Moder and Halleck (2009). The study investigates how and to what extent phraseology and plain English should be evaluated in Aviation English tests. Based on the performance of controllers on a variety of language test tasks, Moder and Halleck argue that it is essential to include both routine and unexpected radiotelephony tasks in Aviation English tests, making use of representative authentic combinations of phraseology and plain language.

Conclusions

Aviation English is an ESP domain in which common language features and professionally regulated standards interact to define a restricted variety designated for use in routine contexts, with a slightly more elaborated plain English variety needed for use in unusual or unexpected circumstances. Because ICAO governs Aviation English proficiency standards, ESP professionals should be cognizant of the ways in which the sociopolitical context affects language policy and use (see Moder and Halleck 2012 for a fuller discussion). Since public safety is at stake in the determination of the minimum proficiency level and its component features, it is imperative that proficiency standards be adequately validated through research. We have focussed on two key areas of interest in this regard. The question of cognitive workload and its impact on communication has been a continuing focus in aviation studies. Studies have just begun to tease out the positive and negative effects of the use of politeness markers and request mitigation features on the effectiveness of pilot–pilot and pilot–controller communication. More work needs to be done to elaborate the linguistic strategies that pilots and controllers can use to maintain communication under stress. In particular, there is a strong need to consider the extent to which the informational focus of radiotelephony training should be expanded to encompass relational features. The value of such relational features should be considered in terms of their possible contribution to more cooperative, efficient communication, but also in terms of their possible effect on communication involving aviation professionals who have attained only the minimum required proficiency level. A further issue is the need for native speakers of English to develop more effective paraphrasing strategies that rely on basic phraseology in order to accommodate the abilities of aviation professionals with widely varying English proficiency levels. ESP researchers, teachers, and test designers have much to contribute to the ongoing efforts to ensure that the English language proficiency levels of aviation professionals enable the greatest possible safety in international air travel.

REFERENCES

Alderson, C. (2009) Air safety, language assessment policy, and policy implementation: The case of Aviation English. *Annual Review of Applied Linguistics* 29: 168–87.

Barshi, I. (1997) *Effects of Linguistic Properties and Message Length on Misunderstandings in Aviation Communication.* PhD dissertation. Boulder, CO: University of Colorado.

Cookson, S. (2009) Zagreb and Tenerife: Airline accidents involving linguistic factors. *Australian Review of Applied Linguistics* 32(3): 22.1–22.14. Available at http://www.nla.gov.au/openpublish/index.php/aral/article/view/2029.

Cushing, S. (1994) *Fatal Words*. Chicago, IL: University of Chicago Press.

Cutting, J. (2011) English for airport ground staff. *English for Specific Purposes* 31: 3–13.

Estival, D. and Molesworth, B. (2009) A study of EL2 pilots' radio communication in the general aviation environment. *Australian Review of Applied Linguistics* 32(3): 24.1–24.16. available at http://www.nla.gov.au/openpublish/index.php/aral/article/view/2031/2414.

Farris, C., Trofimovich, P., Segalowitz, N., and Gatbonton, E. (2008) Air traffic communication in a second language: Implications of cognitive factors for training and assessment. *TESOL Quarterly* 42: 397–410.

Goodwin, M. (1996) Informings and announcements in their environment: Prosody within a multi-activity work setting. In E. Cooper-Kuhlen, M. Selting, and P. Drew (eds.), *Prosody in Conversation: Interactional Studies*. 436–61. Cambridge University Press, Cambridge.

Hinrich, S. -W. (2008) *The Use of Questions in International Pilot and Air Traffic Controller Communication*. PhD dissertation. Stillwater, OK: Oklahoma State University.

Howard, J. W. (2008) "Tower, am I cleared to land?": Problematic communication in aviation discourse. *Human Communication Research* 34: 370–91.

Huhta, A. (2009) An analysis of the quality of English testing for aviation purposes in Finland. *Australian Review of Applied Linguistics* 32(3): 26.1–26.14. Available at http://www.nla.gov.au/openpublish/index.php/aral/article/view/2033/2416

Hutchins, E. (1995) How a cockpit remembers its speeds. *Cognitive Science* 19: 265–88.

Hutchins, E. (1996) Distributed cognition in an airline cockpit. In Y. Engeström and D. Middleton (eds.), *Cognition and Communication at Work*. 15–34. Cambridge: Cambridge University Press.

Hutchins, E. (2005) Material anchors for cognitive blends. *Journal of Pragmatics* 37: 1555–77.

International Civil Aviation Organization (ICAO) (2001) Document 444: Air Traffic Management. Montreal: ICAO

International Civil Aviation Organization (ICAO) (2004) Manual on the implementation of ICAO Language Proficiency Requirements. Montreal: International Civil Aviation Organization.

International Civil Aviation Organization (ICAO) (nd) Flight Safety Information Exchange. *Language Proficiency Requirements*. Accessed Feb. 20, 2012 at http://legacy.icao.int/fsix/lp.cfm (20 February, 2012.)

International Civil Aviation Organization (ICAO) (nd) *Strategic Objectives of ICAO*. Accessed June 9, 2009 at http://www.icao.int/icao/en/strategic_objectives.htm.

Kim, H. and Elder, C. (2009) Understanding Aviation English as a lingua franca. *Australian Review of Applied Linguistics* 32(3): 23.1–23.17. Available at http://www.nla.gov.au/openpublish/index.php/aral/article/view/2030/2413.

Linde, C. (1988) The quantitative study of communicative success: Politeness and accidents in aviation discourse. *Language in Society* 17: 375–99.

Mathews, E. (2004) New provisions for English language proficiency are expected to improve aviation safety. *ICAO Journal* 59(1): 4–6.

Mell, J. (2004) Language training and testing in aviation need to focus on job-specific competencies. *ICAO Journal* 59(1): 12–14, 27.

Moder, C. L. and Halleck, G. B. (2009) Planes, politics and oral proficiency: Testing international air traffic controllers. *Australian Review of Applied Linguistics* 32(3): 25.1–25.16. Available at http://www.nla.gov.au/openpublish/index.php/aral/article/view/2032.

Moder, C. L. and Halleck, G. B. (2012) Designing language tests for specific social uses. In G. Fulcher and F. Davidson (eds.), *Routledge Handbook of Language Testing*. Abingdon, UK: Routledge.

Morrow, D., Rodvold, M., and Lee, A. (1994) Nonroutine transactions in controller-pilot communication. *Discourse Processes* 17: 235–58.

Nevile, M. (2004) *Beyond the Black Box: Talk in Interaction in the Airline Cockpit*. Aldershot, UK: Ashgate.

Read, J. and Knoch, U. (2009) Clearing the air: Applied linguistic perspectives on aviation communication. *Australian Review of Applied Linguistics* 32(3): 21.1–21.11. Available at http://www.nla.gov.au/openpublish/index.php/aral/article/view/2028.

Sänne, J. M. (1999) *Creating Safety in Air Traffic Control*. Lund: Arkiv Förlag

Smith, P. (2004) *Ask the Pilot: Everything You Need to Know About Air Travel*. New York: Riverhead Books.

Sullivan, P. and Girginer, H. (2002) The use of discourse analysis to enhance ESP teacher knowledge: An example of Aviation English. *English for Specific Purposes* 21: 397–404.

Teasdale, A. (1996) Content validity in tests for well-defined LSP domains: An approach to defining what is to be tested. In M. Milanovic and N. Saville (eds.), *Performance Testing, Cognition and Assessment: Selected Papers from the 15th Language Testing Research Colloquium*. Cambridge: Cambridge University Press.

Van Moere, A., Suzuki, M., Downey, R., and Cheng, J. (2009) Implementing ICAO language proficiency requirements in the Versant Aviation English Test. *Australian Review of Applied Linguistics* 32(3): 27.1–27.17. Available at http://www.nla.gov.au/openpublish/index.php/aral/article/view/2034/2417.

Wang, A. (2006) Teaching Aviation English in the Chinese context: Developing ESP theory in a non-English speaking country. *English for Specific Purposes* 26: 121–28.

Wyss-Bühlmann, E. (2005) *Variation and Co-Operative Communication Strategies in Air Traffic Control English*. Bern: Peter Lang.

13 English for Medical Purposes

GIBSON FERGUSON

Introduction

Language plays a significant role in most professions but perhaps nowhere more so than in medicine, where effective communication is widely recognized as important to clinical outcomes. Unsurprisingly, then, there is a large body of literature on communication in medical settings within which we can – for the purposes of this chapter – distinguish two partially overlapping categories. The first is literature of particular relevance to English for medical purposes (EMP), a pedagogic and research enterprise focusing on improving the English language skills of non-Anglophone health professionals. The second wider category, some of which is also relevant to EMP, is literature on health care communication, and especially doctor–patient communication (see e.g. Ainsworth-Vaughn 1998; Hunter 1991; Mishler 1984). Drawing on a variety of methodologies – from medical sociology as well from linguistics (e.g. conversation analysis, microethnography, interactional sociolinguistics) – this work aims to advance our understanding of communication in health settings and thus contribute to improvements in clinical practice. Outputs are published in medical journals (e.g. the *British Medical Journal*), in dedicated specialized journals (e.g. *Communication and Medicine*) as well as in the linguistic literature (see e.g. Sarangi and Roberts 1999), and are so extensive that a full review lies beyond the scope of this chapter. Nevertheless, because health communication research is adjacent to, and has been influential in EMP, a brief outline of key features of research may be useful, summaries of which are in Ainsworth-Vaughn 2001; Fleischman 2001; and Hydén and Mishler 1999.

The Handbook of English for Specific Purposes, First Edition.
Edited by Brian Paltridge and Sue Starfield.

Health Communication Research: An Overview

As mentioned, this literature gives particular prominence to doctor–patient encounters, which, since the 1980s, have been studied applying a variety of discourse analytic approaches to recordings and transcripts. The research highlights the ritualistic aspects of consultations as well as the power asymmetry between doctor and patient as discursively signaled, for example, by control of questioning and topic development. Some accounts point to the inherently conflictual nature of such encounters: patients try to give expression to their subjective experiences of their illness and how it impacts on their daily lives; doctors strive to direct the course of the interview so as to accomplish their clinical tasks as economically as possible, and in so doing may ignore, interrupt or suppress patients' accounts. Mishler (1984) characterizes this, famously, as a struggle between "the voice of the lifeworld" and "the voice of medicine." In other analyses, however, patients are seen as more compliant: offered the opportunity to comment or question, they decline, implicitly submitting to the doctor's expert authority (ten Have 1989).

One of the more frequently studied linguistic features of such interactions, as one might expect, is the role, form, and frequency of questions. Findings, at least as regards frequency, tend to confirm the asymmetrical power-relations of medical consultations. West (1984) found that only 9 percent of questions were asked by patients though Ainsworth-Vaughn (2001) reports a higher percentage of around 38 percent, with frequency subject to the influences of diagnosis, gender, and initial versus repeat visit.

Beyond this feature, there has also been considerable interest in the areas of the delivery of diagnoses (see e.g. Maynard 1992), patient, and doctor narratives, and, more recently, oral examinations for medical institutions. Narratives, to select but one of these, are widely recognized to be an important constitutive element of medical discourse. Patients' stories are clearly one source of information for clinical problem solving but from the patient's perspective they also serve other functions. They are, for example, a means of making sense of their experience of illness, of exploring their sense of self and how it undergoes change in the course of an illness (Fleischman 2001). Referring to the structure of illness narratives, Hawkins (1990) goes so far as to suggest a similarity with three-part conversion stories: there is the time before the illness, the crisis of disease onset (conversion), and the resolution (life after conversion). Doctors' stories meanwhile, as analyzed by Hunter (1991), are substantially medical retellings or reinterpretations of patients' stories by doctors for other doctors. These may take the form of case reports, case conference presentations, or medical chart entries but in all cases, patient narratives of illness tend to be recast, using the language of medicine, into cases of disease; that is, patients become objectified cases with their subjective experiences stripped away, this producing what Hunter (1991) refers to as the "incommensurability" of doctor and patient narratives.

Amongst other more specialized, but hardly esoteric, topics of interest in the medical and linguistics literature are the uses of euphemism and metaphor. The former is widely used by both doctors and patients to evade direct reference to distressing, embarrassing, or taboo subjects – death and dying, taboo body parts, bodily emissions, for example. Death, for instance, is a difficult subject to broach in medical interviews across many cultures (see e.g. Tsai 2010), and consequently is a topic that has spawned a variety of euphemisms in many different languages. Allan and Burridge (1991) offer an extended discussion of euphemism and its motivations in medicine and other fields.

Metaphors, meanwhile, are a pervasive feature of medical discourse, as they are in other fields. Particularly common is the "medicine is war" metaphor, in which disease features as the enemy, doctors as fighters, and technologies as weapons, and "the body is a machine" metaphor, where body parts have mechanical functions and counterparts (e.g. heart – pump; brain – computer; digestive organs – plumbing system) (see Fleischman 2001; Mintz 1992; van Rijn-van Tongeren 1997). Van Tongeren (1997) views metaphors in medicine as having three main functions: a catachretic function (to fill vocabulary gaps), a didactic function (to explain the novel or unfamiliar by reference to the familiar), and a theory-constitutive function (to explore novel, little understood phenomena for which there are no well-established terms). Didactic metaphors are, of course, particularly common in doctor–patient encounters when doctors seek to explain pathologies and treatments to patients. If these are useful functions, metaphors also have their drawbacks (Hodgkin 1985): "the medicine is war" metaphor, for instance, tends to assign patients a largely passive role and can precipitate feelings of personal failure in those who do not overcome their illness; the "body is a machine" metaphor, meanwhile, has dehumanizing potential.

This last point links to a pervasive, and not infrequently criticized, feature of contemporary biomedical discourse, which is that it tends to employ an abstract, "distancing" language (see e.g. Mintz 1992) in which the disease entity is fore-grounded, and patients appear only as cases subsumed into abstracted statistical aggregates. A particularly incisive, and critical, account of this tendency toward abstraction can be found in Anspach's (1988) analysis of the language of case presentations. This draws attention to the following linguistic features that are claimed to index tacit values and epistemological assumptions:

- Depersonalization, which is more than just the use of impersonal vocabulary but includes what Anspach (1988: 363) refers to as "the separation of biological processes from the individual" as exemplified below:

  The patient is a 21 year old Gravida III . . . black female 32 week gestation, by her dates. She states that. . . .

- Omission of the agent through the use of agentless passives or existential "there" constructions, which can take on particular significance if the procedure turns out to be problematic or controversial.
- The use of technology as agent (e.g. *"Follow–up CT scan showed . . ."*). By deleting mention of the agent and the interpretative process these usages, in Ansbach's (1988) opinion, take objectification to a further level.

- The use of reporting verbs. Patients are typically assigned non-factive predicators (e.g. *state, claim, report, deny, etc.*) and doctors factive ones (e.g. *note, observe, record, find, etc.*). The effect is to highlight the subjectivity of patients' accounts, which stands in contrast to the apparent objectivity of those of doctors.

This overview of aspects of health communication research is, of course, necessarily limited and partial. Our main focus has to be on research more directly related to EMP and its ultimately pedagogical goals, but as we turn to this it is as well to keep in mind the vast hinterland of communication research directed primarily at improving medical practice.

The Rise of English as an International Language of Medical Research

The existence of EMP owes much, of course, to the late twentieth-century emergence of English as the foremost international language of science and medicine. Prior to this, in the middle ages, Latin had been the lingua franca of Western medicine, with medical learning sustained by the Latin translation of Greek and Arabic texts (Taavitsainen 2006), and even today traces of Latin's former preeminence persist in medical abbreviations and anatomical terminology, to give but two examples. From the seventeenth century onward one sees an increased use of national languages (German, English, French) in medical texts, and by the early twentieth century English had emerged as one of several international languages of medical science, the others being German and French. These, however, have since lost status relative to English, whose dominance in medical research is documented in a number of publications. Maher (1986), for example, shows how the proportion of journal articles in English indexed in the comprehensive Index Medicus database rose from 53.3 percent in 1966 to 72.2 percent in 1980, and how international conferences are dominated by the language. Giannoni (2008), meanwhile, reports that more than 99 percent of Italian-authored biomedical research publications are now in English, with the national language reserved for less research-intensive local publications. A similar situation obtains in Scandinavia, where PhD students and medical researchers almost overwhelmingly elect to publish their theses and research papers in English (Gunnarsson 2009). A Swedish language medical journal – *Läkartigningen* – remains but only provides an outlet for non-research-intensive work.

This dominance may be convenient for transnational medical communication but also has drawbacks. One, felt particularly keenly in Scandinavia, is that the inroads made by English in medicine, and science more generally, may precipitate a gradual loss of specialized registers and lexis from national languages (see e.g. Berg, Hult, and King 2001; Gunnarsson 2000). Another concern is that the dominance of English may disadvantage non-Anglophone researchers relative to native speakers in their quest for international publication, producing a situation of linguistic inequality (see e.g. Carli and Ammon 2007). In the medical field Benfield and Howard (2000), for example, worry that critical comments on writing/language quality may be substantially more frequent for non-Anglophone researchers than their Anglophone counterparts, while Benfield and Feak (2006) ask the relatively privileged latter group to take more responsibility for assisting their non-Anglophone peers – possibly through co-publication.

The situation outlined above might lead one to believe that research writing and reading would feature prominently among the needs of EMP students internationally, and while this does appear to be the case, the picture – as revealed in EMP textbooks and materials – is somewhat more complicated, since these often retain a significant focus on spoken interaction in medical settings, as we shall see later. A variety of factors can be invoked here. One is that medical professionals seeking to migrate to, or practice in, Anglophone countries (e.g. Austaliasia, United Kingdom, United States) continue to constitute a significant constituency of EMP learners. Another is that the internationalization of higher education has stimulated an increased use of English as a medium of medical education in such places as China (see *chinaenglish.com*) and Russia, augmenting its traditional role in medical education in many postcolonial countries. Finally, there is also the widespread perception learners have that skills in spoken interaction are an essential component of foreign language proficiency.

However, if research writing and reading are not quite so prominent in teaching materials as one might predict from the global sociolinguistics of English, they certainly have an important place in language-related EMP research, to which we now turn.

Language–Related Research in EMP

There is a considerable body of language-related EMP research, more so in fact than on materials, methodology, or course design. Much of this focuses on intra-professional communication, and especially on written genres, though there is also work on such spoken genres as conference presentations and case conferences. For convenience we divide this review of research into three categories – genre studies, studies of specific grammatical features, and vocabulary studies – though there are obvious links between these levels.

Genre studies

Written medical genres include research articles, abstracts, case reports, review articles, peer reviews, letters to the editor, book reviews, and letters of referral. Pride of place among these, however, must go to two key genres – the research article (RA) and the case report, even though the latter is now considerably diminished in importance. For both we have good diachronic as well synchronic analyses.

The case report, to take this first, is essentially a narrative of a single case, recording the course of a patient's disease from diagnosis through treatment to outcome usually accompanied by some professional commentary. Drawing on a corpus of case reports from the *British Medical Journal* (BMJ) and *The Lancet* covering the period 1850–1995, Taavitsaianen and Pahta (2000) highlight substantial changes in the genre between the nineteenth and twentieth centuries, and argue that these reflect both epistemological developments and changes in the medical discourse community. Reports from the nineteenth century, for instance, exhibit a high degree of authorial involvement, retain some features of an oral mode of expression, and have abundant expressions of stance and effect, as in the following example:

> I will now mention a case in which jaundice prevailed to a greater or lesser degree for eighteen months, with ultimate cure . . . He had some head–affection and was accordingly very strictly dieted: and to this restricted diet I impute his attack. . . . (Taavitsainen and Pahta 2000: 64)

By the twentieth century, however, the doctor's role is largely suppressed and the discourse is characterized by greater impersonality as reflected in the increased use of passives and inanimate subjects, more frequent complex noun phrases, and greater use of third person narrative. The structure of case reports also becomes more uniform and conventionalized, and there are fewer of them such that they now almost exclusively report highly unusual diseases or unusual manifestations of more common illnesses. Tavitsainen and Pahta (2000) attribute these changes to the vastly increased size of the medical discourse community, to a reorientation of the doctor–patient relationship, and to an epistemological shift to more probabilistic forms of medical research based on large volumes of clinical data.

Interestingly, this evolutionary path is not dissimilar to that followed by the medical journal article, as comprehensively documented in Atkinson's (1992) diachronic study of rhetorical and linguistic changes in the *Edinburgh Medical Journal* between 1735 and 1985. At the rhetorical level the main changes observed by Atkinson (1992) can be summarized as showing:

- a shift from reports based on a small number of medical events to abstractions deriving from a large volume of cases;
- a gradual move to a non-author centered discourse style;
- a gradual shift from a narrative mode to a more abstract discussion of disease and treatment, and, from 1945, a move toward a highly conventionalized and now familiar IMRD structure for research articles (Introduction, Methods, Results, Discussion);
- a move toward a laboratory science model of medicine.

For studying the linguistic features of the register, Atkinson (1992) utilizes Biber's (1988) multidimensional approach, according to which co-occurrences of features, rather than single features, are mapped on to underlying dimensions, or scales, of variation (e.g. the informational vs. involved dimensions of textual production). His analysis reveals a gradual shift from involved to informational production, from narrative to non-narrative concerns, toward explicit reference and away from overt expression of persuasion. Below is a brief 1985 example illustrating an informational rather than involved text; that is, one characterized by dense noun phrases, a high type–token ratio, many attributive adjectives, and conversely few personal pronouns or "private" verbs (e.g. think, feel):

> In a patient with proven chronic duodenal ulceration the development of a metabolic alkalosis due to recurrent vomiting of undigested food suggests a diagnosis of pyloric stenosis or gastric outlet obstruction at the level of the pylorus . . . (Atkinson 1992: 356).

Moving to the present, Nwogu (1997) – drawing inspiration from Swales's seminal work on genre – models the internal schematic structure of the contemporary medical research article (RA) as in Table 13.1.

As is evident, the analysis shown in Table 13.1 utilizes the familiar Swalesian notion of moves, or text segments, each of which has a specific information function and a characteristic lexico-grammatical realization. For example, move 4 (describing data collection procedures) is, according to Nwogu (1997), characterized by explicit lexemes (e.g. *"The study population includes . . ."*), the use of the passive to indicate source of data, and the use of present/past tense to indicate sample size. These moves, their constituent elements, and the linguistic realizations together provide a schematic map of the RA, one intended to assist the novice RA author. But genres, of course, are not static constructs, and it is, therefore, no surprise to find that Nwogu's model has since been updated by Li and Ge (2009), who argue that moves 1 and 6 above are now obligatory and not

Table 13.1   The structure of the medical research article (RA) after Nwogu (1997: 135)

Major IMRD Sections	Moves	Content of Moves
Introduction	Move 1	Presenting background information
	Move 2	Reviewing related research (including limitations of)
	Move 3	Presenting new research
Methods	Move 4	Describing data collection procedure
	Move 5	Describing experimental procedures
	Move 6	Describing data analysis procedures
Results	Move 7	Indicating consistent observation
	Move 8	Indicating non-consistent observation
Discussion	Move 9	Highlighting overall research outcome
	Move 10	Explaining specific research outcomes
	Move 11	Stating research conclusions

optional as before, while move 9 has become an optional instead of obligatory move. They also note an increased use of first person plural pronouns reflecting a trend towards multiple authorship.

Closely related to the RA is the abstract genre, whose importance has risen with the growth in the medical literature and emergence of online databases, many of which provide free access to abstracts but not to the articles themselves. In such circumstances efficient information retrieval is clearly a priority, and for this reason medical journals increasingly require structured abstracts with explicit headings for RAs, the reporting of clinical trials and informative reviews (see e.g. Lock 1988). *The Lancet*, for example, requires the following explicit headings within the abstract: background, methods, results, clinical implications.

Reflecting their academic importance, there is a considerable body of ESP/EAP research on abstracts but few of these publications have a specific focus on medicine. Exceptions, now of considerable vintage, include a paper by Salager-Meyer (1990), which concludes that only 52 percent of her sampled abstracts from three genres (RAs, case reports, review articles) conform to journals' structural guidelines for abstracts. A subsequent paper (Salager-Meyer 1992) investigates the distribution of verb tenses and modal verbs across the major constituent moves of the abstract.

Next in importance to RAs and case reports is the medical review article, a synoptic genre which synthesizes findings from a diversity of studies to present a comprehensive, state-of-the art picture of a particular disease or treatment. Usually composed by an authoritative figure, the value of reviews is widely acknowledged: busy clinicians with no time to peruse unmanageable quantities of research increasingly resort to reviews as a convenient information resource, one that can also prevent researchers from meandering down already well-explored paths (Mulrow 1994). Somewhat surprisingly, however, there appears to be comparatively little published EMP research on this genre. This contrasts with the medical literature, where the quality of reviews has been widely discussed. Mulrow (1987), for example, was one of the first authors to draw attention to the poor scientific quality of non-systematic, narrative reviews, which have now been largely superseded by what are known as systematic reviews (Mulrow 1994) or meta-analyses. Even so, measuring their sample of 158 review articles against 10 established quality criteria, McAlister et al. (1999) report that comparatively few meet the highest methodological standards.

There are also studies of less prominent medical genres, which we can mention, if not comment on. These would include letters to the editor (Magnet and Carnet 2006), consensus statements (Mungra 2007), peer reviews (Mungra and Webber 2010), journal editorials (Giannoni 2008) and book reviews (Salager–Meyer, Ariza, and Berbesi 2007).

Moving on to spoken communication, conference presentations are one of the most important intra-professional genres, and one where non-Anglophones are often less at ease than in written communication. Research here is less abundant than for written genres but not negligible. Dubois (1985, 1987), for example, is the author of some early publications: the 1985 paper offers advice on the design and presentation of conference posters while the 1987 paper investigates imprecise numerical expressions in biomedical slide talks. (e.g. "almost 50 percent in heart rate"). These, Dubois concludes, function to ease the audience's aural processing load or to foreground more precise numerical measurements, but they may also reflect the preliminary nature of the findings reported.

More recent work on medical conferences can be found in Webber (2002, 2005) and Rowley-Jolivet (2002). Webber (2002) examines the question-answer phase at the end of the presentation, a phase reputed to present special difficulties for non-Anglophone speakers, and distinguishes five types of question, one of which, amounting to no less than thirty percent of her sample, conveys implicit or explicit criticisms of the presentation. For example:

Q: Are we sure that these substances work in the way we think they do. What do we know about mechanisms of x in lowering cholesterol levels? (Webber 2002: 235).

Reactions to questions, Webber finds, may take various forms: evasion, convergence, confrontation even.

Rowley-Jolivet (2002) views conference presentations as an intermediate stage in the construction of fully-fledged scientific claims, occupying a place between the initial laboratory work with all its contextual imperfections and the highly conventionalized rhetoric of the final refereed RA. And because they often report novel or preliminary work at an early stage in the claim-making process, they exhibit quite different characteristics from RAs. For example, unlike RAs, conference presentations refer to the vicissitudes of data-gathering, sometimes almost in confessional mode. For example:

There's been no specific protocol. It's just been by gosh and by golly a little bit (Rowley-Jolivet 2002: 109).

They also allow explicit criticism of other researchers, and they give greater prominence to the researcher and their decision-making processes. For example:

We thought we were being very smart in doing this. However, we ruined our study in a sense because we have what we call crossover (Rowley-Jolivet 2002: 116).

In somewhat similar vein, Webber (2005) draws attention to interactive features in medical conference monologues, ones that clearly distinguish this genre from the RA. These include: (a) frequent use of second person "you" and first person "I," signaling a higher degree of speaker involvement and conscious effort to engage the audience; (b) the use of specific discourse markers: e.g. "now" to indicate a new discourse unit; "so" to signal a discourse transition–point, and (c) the use of imprecise quantifiers (e.g. "about").

Collectively these various findings contribute to greater understanding of the conference presentation genre, its role in the elaboration of scientific claims, and its marked difference from written genres such as the RA. But, as Webber remarks, there is scope for further research – for example into differences between "native" and "non-native" conference presentations.

Studies of grammatical features

Many EMP genre studies combine investigation of rhetorical structure with study of the genre's lexico-grammatical features but every now and then papers appear that focus exclusively on a specific grammatical feature. Examples here would include hedges (Salager-Meyer 1994) and if-conditionals (Carter-Thomas and Rowley-Jolivet 2008; Ferguson 2001). The former of these is so widely discussed in the literature on scientific discourse that in the interests of brevity we pass immediately to if-conditionals.

The two papers above that focus on this construction differ slightly in the genres sampled: both cover RAs and journal editorials, but whereas Ferguson examines if-conditionals in doctor–patient consultations, the Carter-Thomas paper analyses conference presentations. That apart, the underlying motivations of both are broadly similar: to expose limitations in conventional pedagogical descriptions of if-conditionals and to show how genre-sensitive the forms and functions of this structure can be. Also comparable are many of the findings. Both papers show, for example, that the traditional type 1, 2, and 3 conditionals account for only a small proportion of instances across all medical genres, and that a wide variety of mixed verb forms are employed across the subordinate if-clause (the protasis) and the main clause (the apodosis). Both also demonstrate that course-of-event, or "factual" conditionals – to use the Carter-Thomas terminology – taking a past + past or present + present form, are common in the RA genre, particularly in the Methods section where they function to provide operational definitions or state eligibility criteria. For example:

> Patients entered the study if they satisfied the WHO criteria.

In the Discussion section, on the other hand, there is, as one might expect, a somewhat greater number of hypothetical (or "refocusing") conditionals as the writing here becomes more argumentative and speculative.

Journal editorials seek to present information and recommendations in an authoritative, assured tone. Thus, course of event conditionals do occur – mainly to express generalizations – but at a lower frequency than in the RA. More frequent, by contrast are hypothetical (or "refocusing") conditionals in argumentative or speculative contexts. A further distinctive feature of journal editorials, noted in both papers, is the frequency of if–conditionals incorporating modal verbs, which function to qualify the scope of recommendations, to modulate predictions, and to hedge generalizations.

Turning to the spoken genres, Carter-Thomas and Rowley-Jolivet (2008) draw attention to a frequent and distinctive use of what they call "discourse management" conditionals that speakers deploy to guide the audience through the conference presentation. For example:

> If you take a look at the median palliative index . . . (Carter-Thomas and Rowley–Jolivet 2008: 199).

Such polite directives, often without an apodosis, are also a notable feature of the more interactive doctor–patient consultation, where one also finds conditionals in interrogative contexts and jointly performed constructions. For example:

> Doctor: And if it was to happen now . . .
> Patient: I'd sort of have to look up, like that.

While there are differences between these two papers, there is agreement on a pedagogical issue of wider import, which is that EMP learners, hoping to use conditionals as a multifunctional resource, need to have their attention drawn to how the forms and functions of if-conditionals co-vary with differences in genre. The same is true, one suspects, of other constructions yet to be fully investigated.

Vocabulary studies

Even by the standards of other disciplines, medicine is well known for its large corpus of technical or specialized terms, mostly borrowed from Greek and Latin – sometimes with little morphological adaptation (e.g. *diabetes, embolus*). Chung and Nation (2003) estimated, for example, that technical words, defined as ones with a narrow range of occurrence and largely unknown in general use, accounted for as much as 37.6 percent of all word types in an anatomy text as against 16.3 percent of types in an applied linguistics text.

Given such proportions, and the salience of technical words in medical texts, it is hardly surprising that the pedagogical treatment of this category of vocabulary is widely debated in EMP circles, a common view being that this vocabulary is better learnt, and more commonly learnt, in the course of studying medicine, and that in any case semi–technical and lower frequency general vocabulary tend to be more problematic areas for the intermediate-level EMP student. This is a view with some validity but it also tends to oversimplify matters, for one can imagine a number of contexts in which sustained attention to items of technical vocabulary could become necessary. Much depends, for instance, on the first language (L1) background of the EMP student, their level of medical knowledge, the particular pedagogic activity in which the word occurs, the degree to which the word is important in the ongoing pedagogical activity, the availability of Medical English dictionaries, and which aspect of word knowledge is at stake. EMP students do not uncommonly have a sound knowledge of the meaning of a technical term yet struggle over its pronunciation, which the teacher may well be able to assist with. And even if the EMP teacher does not engage with teaching technical words directly, they can, in Chung and Nation's (2003) view, equip students with strategies for learning such vocabulary: for example, through fostering students' skills in recognizing technical words, interpreting definitions, and relating word senses to core meanings.

Meanwhile, beyond strictly technical terms, there is a category of semi-technical and academic medical vocabulary that has received research attention recently, the goal being to inform vocabulary teaching and learning priorities. Chen and Ge (2007), for example, investigate the degree to which Coxhead's (2000) Academic Word List (AWL) provides coverage of medical RAs. They find that it accounts for around 10 percent of running words, a not unreasonable proportion, but that only 51.2 percent of AWL words occur with any frequency in medical RAs, while, conversely, low-frequency words in these RAs have high frequency in the AWL. A case is thus made for an independent academic medical word list, which is exactly what Wang, Liang, and Ge (2008) provide. Using very similar word selection criteria as Coxhead – range, frequency, specialized occurrence – they compile a Medical Academic Word List (MAWL) comprizing 623 word families that account for 12.24 percent of tokens in the RAs sampled from a range of medical specialities. Only 54.9 percent of these 623 word families are also in the AWL, indicating a significant difference between the specific lexical repertoire of academic medicine and that of Coxhead's more general academic corpus. Useful though the MAWL is, it is not without limitations: it only samples medical RAs, for example, and thus there is scope for further research on the use and distribution of medical vocabulary in other genres as well as on vocabulary learning and teaching.

Courses, Activities and Materials in EMP

Types of EMP courses

There are a great variety of EMP courses around the world though we have few detailed accounts of these, at least in the international literature. It is clear, however, that such courses can, and do, vary along multiple dimensions as follows:

- in duration (i.e. short intensive vs. longer courses),
- in target audience (e.g. clinicians vs. medical researchers vs. pre-medical students vs. medical students in the clinical phase of their training),
- in medical speciality (e.g. cardiologists, oncologists, urologists, etc.),
- in skills, genres, and medical situations (e.g. English for doctor–patient consultations , English for medical congresses, English for report/journal article writing, etc.).

With respect to the latter category, one of the more useful needs analysis checklists remains that of Allwright and Allwright (1977: 58), a version of which is in Table 13.2.

Table 13.2   English contact situations of potential difficulty for non-Anglophone doctors (after Allwright and Allwright 1977: 58)

1	Rapid reading of textbooks/professional journals/papers for information
2	Detailed study of textbooks/journals/papers, etc.
3	Writing papers/reports/articles in English for publication/symposia/ conferences
4	Corresponding with English-speaking colleagues on professional matters
5	Understanding lectures/papers in English delivered orally at conferences, medical meetings, symposia, etc.
6	Giving papers/lectures in English at conferences, medical meetings, symposia, etc.
7	Participating in (i.e. understanding and contributing to) formal discussion at conferences, etc.
8	Participating in (i.e. understanding and contributing to) informal discussion at conferences, etc.
9	Participating in post-graduate courses in English-speaking medical institutions
10	Entertaining/being entertained
11	Doing clinical work with English-speaking patients
12	Doing clinical work with English-speaking colleagues

In some cases needs may be restricted to one or two of the above categories, generating a course of highly specific scope (e.g. English for medical congresses for Dutch cardiologists). In the majority of instances, however, needs will be more diffuse, and in this situation logistics and economics may dictate a more broadly–based course (e.g. English for doctors).

Sociolinguistic evidence suggests that the major need worldwide is in the area of English for medical research (e.g. reading and writing journal articles; speaking at medical conferences), but, as noted previously, a considerable number of EMP courses also encompass doctor–patient communication skills. An example would be the course described by Basturkmen (2010), which caters to overseas-trained doctors seeking to pass registration examinations and work in New Zealand. This focuses almost exclusively on doctor–patient communication. Materials, based on prior observation of medical consultations, were specially written for the target group and take participants through the typical sequence, and associated language, of doctor–patient consultations.

Another example of an EMP course with a significant focus on spoken communication is that described by Shi et al. (2001) from the very different context of Hong Kong, where English still plays a considerable role in medical education. This course was designed to serve the needs of medical students entering the clinical phase of their training and encountering the specific challenge of negotiating ward teaching sessions in which they were expected, having elicited case histories from patients in Cantonese, to report the case details to their tutor in technical Medical English. Course content was based on an analysis of video recordings of ward teaching sessions, and, like the New Zealand course above, made use of role-play/simulation exercises to rehearse language and skills useful in the clinical context.

Among other useful accounts of EMP courses are Maclean (1997), who describes an experiential EMP teacher education course in which the trainer worked along-side trainees in delivering an English for medical congresses course to Cuban doctors, and Wood and Head (2004), who describe the use of problem-based learning tasks in a course for pre-medical students in Brunei.

Course content and activities

It is possible, indeed common, to build an EMP course around a sequence of relevant language items (e.g. medical terminology). Preferable, however, and more communicative, might be a course consisting of what Allwright and Allwright (1977: 59) refer to as "a planned sequence of pedagogically useful activities," with prominence given to authentic texts and tasks. These activities might include some, or all, of the following:

- *Simulated case conferences*: A course participant presents a case to the class of doctors (or alternatively the class may read the case report or listen to a recording and take notes). Groups or pairs then make differential diagnoses and suggest investigations/treatment. During the discussion the teacher takes notes on language difficulties for subsequent feedback and at the end presents the clinical solution from the source material (see Allwright and Allwright 1977).
- *Listen and report:* Paired or individual participants listen to a talk on a medical topic, take notes and report back to another pair who have heard a different talk.
- *Read and report:* Individual participants, or pairs, read a medical journal article, take notes and summarize what they have read for another pair with a different article.
- *Listening to a talk from a guest speaker doctor.*
- *Preparing and presenting short talks:* These may be based on a case, or on a medical topic the participant has previously researched. The teacher may record such talks for feedback purposes.
- *Doctor–patient role-plays.*
- *Medical English pronunciation practice in the language laboratory.*

An example of a course incorporating these activities (and others) is the three-week intensive "English for Medicine" course run at the University of Edinburgh. This caters mainly to European doctors and students wishing to develop their proficiency in using English in a range of professional contexts, and is based on the following key design principles: (a) a variety of activity mode and type across the day and the week; (b) the use of authentic texts and tasks wherever possible; (c) prioritization of listening and speaking; and (d) plentiful communicative practice – students interact and communicate; teachers function more as planners, orchestrators and monitors of student activity than as language instructors.

For a further example – this time of a more specific course and its constituent activities – we can refer to an intensive, one-week "English for Medical Congresses" course devized by Joan Maclean, former Head of the Medical English unit at the University of Edinburgh, and aimed at preparing non-Anglophone doctors for speaking at international congresses. The key organizing principle of the course is rehearsal: replicating as closely as possible the target activities of congresses – e.g. listening to speakers, presenting short papers, talking to posters, fielding questions, writing abstracts, etc. Course content is a series of activities arranged in a sequence of input, practice and feedback loops. Input consists of analysis of video-recorded conference presentations with elicitation of features of good and bad presentations, remedial pronunciation work, information on discourse signalling expressions, help with writing abstracts for the end of course mini-conference, and some work on grammar and vocabulary (e.g. for talking to graphs and tables). Practice activities include listening in pairs to a recorded medical talk and giving a summary report to another pair, practice in describing/interpreting graphs/tables and in using discourse markers, practice in transposing data into visual form and indicating the main points, writing abstracts, giving informal mini-talks, rehearsal of mini-conference talks, and presentations at the mini-conference. Feedback is regarded as a crucially important component of the course and for this reason many practice sessions are video or audio recorded for subsequent group or individual feedback, focusing on language, pronunciation, and delivery style. Grading and sequencing is achieved in two main ways: through a gradual move from short, informal talks to small groups to longer, more formal presentations to larger audiences, and through a steady increase in the intensity of feedback. This culminates in the video-recording of mini-conference presentations and the delivery of individualized writing feedback. Throughout the week the teacher's primary roles are as activator of resources, animator of activities, and provider of feedback (see Maclean 1997).

EMP materials

Teaching materials for EMP are based either on locally produced exploitations of authentic medical texts or on commercially published textbooks, or some combination of both. The first option is often preferable in that it enables the teacher to tailor the course contents more precisely to the specific needs and profile of the target group. But there are obvious drawbacks and pitfalls: writing materials for a specific group is time-consuming and may be uneconomic unless materials can be banked for later re-use; it also requires skill, creativity, and, almost invariably, consultation with a medically-trained informant.

Useful sources of material that can be turned to classroom exploitation include texts for educating medical students or for keeping clinicians up to date. For example, the textbook *100 Cases in Clinical Medicine* (Pattinson et al. 2007) provides a ready source of case material for simulated case conference discussion, and besides this there is an abundance of medical journal articles, medical journalism, recorded talks and podcasts designed for a professional audience, and online videos (e.g. see http://www.bmj.com/site/video/), which are all exploitable in EMP classrooms.

Meanwhile, among better-known contemporary EMP textbooks one would include *English in Medicine* (Glendinning and Holmström 2005), *Professional English in Use: Medicine* (Glendinning and Howard 2007), and *Good Practice* (McCullagh and Wright 2008). Interestingly, all these place strong emphasis on doctor–patient interaction, with some books following the sequence of the medical consultation from presenting complaint through examination and diagnosis to treatment. *English in Medicine* gives priority to listening and speaking and exploits such authentic medical texts as prescribing information leaflets, case notes, clinical biochemistry results, prescriptions, discharge summaries for a range of listening, reading, discussion, and pair-speaking activities. *Professional English in Use*, by contrast, is designed principally for self-study and, accordingly, listening gives way to a greater emphasis on medical vocabulary. The third book, *Good Practice* again focuses heavily on doctor–patient interaction but can be considered innovative in that it goes beyond the language necessary for consultations to encompass such additional areas as cultural awareness, non-verbal communication, empathetic listening, and intonation that all contribute to effective patient-centered consultations. To this end considerable use is made of DVD recordings of consultations, which provide a solid basis for student analysis and discussion.

Conclusion and Future Directions

It has not been possible in a chapter of this size to cover all aspects of EMP research and practice, taking in, for example, such areas as EMP testing, teacher education and corpora. Nevertheless, the chapter has illustrated the vibrancy of EMP, a field that over the last 15 years or so has accumulated a significant body of language–related research. Even so, there is considerable scope for future research as there remain genres (e.g. the review article), grammatical features (e.g. concessive clauses), and aspects of medical vocabulary (e.g. the vocabulary of textbooks) that have yet to be fully explored. Spoken genres – doctor–patient consultations, case conferences, and medical congress presentations – are also a fertile area for further research, particularly if it explores differences (and similarities) between the language used by Anglophone professionals and their non-Anglophone international counterparts.

Much less abundant in the literature, meanwhile, are accounts, analyses, or evaluations of EMP practice, which it is hoped will appear to complement descriptive research on medical discourse. Of particular interest, because of their scarcity, would be academic studies of the use, impact, and effectiveness of technological innovations (e.g. online interactive materials, discussion boards, podcasts, weblogs, etc.), which are increasingly common features of EMP pedagogy as in other branches of ESP.

REFERENCES

Ainsworth-Vaughn, N. (1998) *Claiming Power in Doctor–Patient talk*. Oxford: Oxford University Press.

Ainsworth-Vaughn, N. (2001) The discourse of medical encounters. In D. Schiffrin, D. Tannen, and H. Hamilton (eds.), *The Handbook of Discourse Analysis*. 453–69. Oxford: Blackwell.

Allan, K. and Burridge, K. (1991) *Euphemism and Dysphemism: Language Used as a Shield and Weapon*. Oxford: Oxford University Press.

Allwright, J. and Allwright, R. (1977) An approach to the teaching of medical English. In S. Holden (ed.), *English for Specific Purposes*. 58–62. London: Modern English Publications.

Anspach, R. (1988) Notes on the sociology of medical discourse: The language of case presentation. *Journal of Health and Social Behaviour* 29: 357–75.

Atkinson, D. (1992) The evolution of medical research writing from 1735 to 1985: The case of the *Edinburgh Medical Journal*. *Applied Linguistics* 13: 337–4.

Basturkmen, H. (2010) *Developing Courses in English for Specific Purposes*. Basingstoke, UK: Palgrave Macmillan.

Benfield, J. and Feak, C. (2006) How authors can cope with the burden of English as an international language. *Chest* 129: 1728–30.

Benfield, J. and Howard, K. (2000) The language of science. *European Journal of Cardio-Thoracic Surgery* 18: 642–8.

Berg, C., Hult, F. and King, K. (2001) Shaping the climate for language shift? English in Sweden's elite domains. *World Englishes* 20: 305–19.

Biber, D. (1988) *Variation Across Speech and Writing*. Cambridge: Cambridge University Press.

Carli, A. and Ammon, U. (eds.) (2007) *Linguistic Inequality in Scientific Communication Today. AILA Review 20*. Amsterdam: John Benjamins.

Carter-Thomas, S. and Rowley-Jolivet, E. (2008) If-conditionals in medical discourse: From theory to disciplinary practice. *Journal of English for Academic Purposes* 7: 191–205.

Chen, Q. and Ge, G. C. (2007) A corpus-based lexical study on frequency and distribution of Coxhead's AWL word families in medical research articles (RAs). *English for Specific Purposes* 26: 502–14.

Chung, T. and Nation, P. (2003) Technical vocabulary in specialised texts. *Reading in a Foreign Language* 15: 103–16.

Coxhead, A. (2000) A new academic word list. TESOL *Quarterly* 34: 213–38.

Dubois, B. (1985) Poster sessions at biomedical meetings: Design and presentation. *The ESP Journal* 4: 37–48.

Dubois, B. (1987) Something on the order of around forty to forty-four: Imprecise numerical expressions in biomedical slide talks. *Language and Society* 16: 527–41.

Ferguson, G. (2001) If you pop over there. A corpus-based study of conditionals in medical discourse. *English for Specific Purposes* 20: 61–82.

Fleischman, S. (2001) Language and medicine. In D. Schiffrin, D. Tannen and H. Hamilton (eds.), *The Handbook of Discourse Analysis*. 470–502. Oxford: Blackwell.

Giannoni, D. (2008) Medical writing at the periphery: The case of Italian journal editorials. *Journal of English for Academic Purposes* 7: 97–107.

Glendinning, E. and Holmström, B. (2005) *English in Medicine*. 3rd ed. Cambridge: Cambridge University Press.

Glendinning, E. and Howard, R. (2007) *Professional English in Use: Medicine*. Cambridge: Cambridge University Press.

Gunnarsson, B. L. (2000) Swedish tomorrow – A product of the linguistic dominance of English? *Current Issues in Language and Society* 7: 51–69.

Gunnarsson, B. L. (2009) *Professional Discourse*. London: Continuum.

ten Have, P. (1989) The consultation as genre. In B. Torode (ed.), *Text and Talk*. 115–35. Dordrecht, Netherlands: Foris.

Hawkins, A. (1990) A change of heart: The paradigm of regeneration in medical and religious narrative. *Perspectives in Biology and Medicine* 33: 547–59.

Hodgkin, P. (1985) Medicine is war. *British Medical Journal* 291: 1820–1.

Hunter, K. (1991) *Doctor's Stories: The Narrative Structure of Medical Knowledge*. Princeton, NJ: Princeton University Press.

Hydén, L. C. and Mishler, E. (1999) Language and Medicine. *Annual Review of Applied Linguistics* 19: 174–92.

Li, L. J. and Ge, G. C. (2009) Genre analysis: Structural and linguistic evolution of the English–medium medical research article (1985–2004). *English for Specific Purposes* 28: 93–104.

Lock, S. (1988) Structured abstract: Now required for all papers reporting clinical trials. *British Medical Journal* 297: 156.

Maclean, J. (1997) Professional preparation: A technique for LSP teacher education. In R. Howard and G. Brown. (eds.), *Teacher Education for LSP*. 158–75. Clevedon, UK: Multilingual Matters.

Magnet, A. and Carnet, D. (2006. Letters to the editor: Still vigorous after all these years? *English for Specific Purposes* 25: 173–99.

Maher, J. (1986) The development of English as an international language of medicine. *Applied Linguistics* 7: 206–18.

Maynard, D. (1992) On clinicians co-implicating recipients' perspectives in the delivery of diagnostic news. In P. Drew and J. Heritage (eds.), *Talk at Work: Interaction in Institutional Setting*. 331–58. Cambridge: Cambridge University Press.

McAlister, F., Clark, H., Walraven, C., Straus, S., Lawson, F., Moher, D., and Mulrow, C. (1999) The medical review article revisited: has the science improved? *Annals of Internal Medicine* 131: 947–51.

McCullagh, M. and Wright, R. (2008) *Good Practice*. Cambridge: Cambridge University Press.

Mintz, D. (1992) What's in a word: The distancing function of language in medicine. *The Journal of Medical Humanities* 13: 223–33.

Mishler, E. (1984) *The Discourse of Medicine: Dialectics of Medical Interviews*. Norwood, NJ: Ablex.

Mulrow, C. (1987) The medical review article: State of the science. *Annals of Internal Medicine* 106: 485–88.

Mulrow, C. (1994) Systematic reviews: Rationale for systematic reviews. *British Medical Journal* 309: 597. Accessed May 21, 2 at http://www.bmj.com/content/309/6954/597.full.

Mungra, P. (2007) A research and discussion note: The macrostructure of consensus statements. *English for Specific Purposes* 26: 79–89.

Mungra, P. and Webber, P. (2010) Peer review process in medical research publications: Language and content comments. *English for Specific Purposes* 29: 43–53.

Nwogu, K. (1997) The medical research paper: Structure and functions. *English for Specific Purposes* 16: 119–38.

Rowley-Jolivet, E. (2002) Science in the making: Scientific conference presentations and the construction of facts. In E. Ventola, C. Shalom, and S.

Thompson (eds.), *The Language of Conferencing*. 95–125. Frankfurt: Peter Lang.

Salager-Meyer, F. (1990) Discoursal flaws in medical English abstracts: An analysis per research and text type. *Text* 10: 365–84.

Salager-Meyer, F. (1992) A text-type and move analysis study of verb tense and modality distribution in medical English abstracts. *English for Specific Purposes* 11: 93–113.

Salager-Meyer, F. (1994) Hedges and textual communicative function in medical English written discourse. *English for Specific Purposes* 13: 149–70.

Salager-Meyer, F., Ariza, M. A., and Berbesi, M. (2007). Collegiality, critique and the construction of scientific argumentation in medical book reviews: A diachronic approach. *Journal of Pragmatics* 39: 1758–74.

Sarangi, S. and Roberts, C (eds.) (1999) *Talk, Work and Institutional Order: Discourse in Medical, Mediation and Management Settings*. Berlin: Mouton de Gruyter.

Shi, L., Corcos, R., and Storey, A. (2001) Using student performance data to develop an English course for clinical training. *English for Specific Purposes* 20: 267–91.

Taavitsainen, I. (2006) Medical communication: Lingua francas. In K.

Brown (ed.), *Encyclopedia of Language and Linguistics*. 643–44. 2nd ed. Amsterdam: Elsevier.

Taavitsainen, I. and Pahta, P. (2000) Conventions of professional writing: The medical case report in a historical perspective. *Journal of English Linguistics* 28: 60–76.

Tsai, M. H. (2010) Managing topics of birth and death in doctor–patient communication. *Journal of Pragmatics* 42: 1350–63.

Van Rijn-van Tongeren, G. (1997). *Metaphor in Medical Texts*. Amsterdam: Rodopi.

Wang, J., Liang, S. I., and Ge, G. C. (2008) Establishment of a medical academic word list. *English for Specific Purposes* 27: 442–58.

Webber, P. (2002) The paper is now open for discussion. In E. Ventola, C. Shalom, and S. Thompson (eds.), *The Language of Conferencing*. 227–54. Frankfurt: Peter Lang.

Webber, P. (2005). Interactive features in medical conference monologue. *English for Specific Purposes* 24: 157–81.

West, C. (1984) *Routine Complications: Troubles with talk between doctors and patients*. Bloomington, IN: Indiana University Press.

Wood, A. and Head, M. (2004) "Just what the doctor ordered": The application of problem-based learning to EAP. *English for Specific Purposes* 23: 3–17.

14 English for Nursing

SUSAN BOSHER

Introduction

English for nursing is a relatively recent specialty within the field of English for specific purposes. It focusses on the specific ways in which nurses, in contrast to doctors and other health-care professionals and paraprofessionals, use English both in the clinical setting as well as in nursing education. Although in recent years numerous textbooks have been published in English for nursing, most of them focus on the clinical setting and are intended for internationally educated nurses who are seeking to enter the workforce in "Inner Circle" countries (Kachru 1985), such as Australia, Canada, the United Kingdom, and the United States. More significant, but also less recognized, are the large numbers of English as a second language (ESL) immigrants and, to a lesser extent, international students in Inner Circle countries who identify nursing as their major in two- and four-year colleges and universities. Many of these students do not make it through the prerequisite courses, and those who do often encounter difficulty succeeding once they are in nursing programs.

Various needs analyses have been conducted to determine the objective, subjective, and learning needs of immigrant and international students in undergraduate-degree nursing programs (Bosher 2006; Bosher and Smalkoski 2002; Hansen 2010; Hussin 2008). These needs analyses have identified various issues that create challenges for ESL nursing students: personal, academic, discipline-specific, cultural, and language. The results of these studies have led to the development of courses and materials in English for nursing (Bosher 2006, 2008a, 2010).

The Handbook of English for Specific Purposes, First Edition.
Edited by Brian Paltridge and Sue Starfield.
© 2013 John Wiley & Sons, Inc. Published 2013 by John Wiley & Sons, Inc.

Other needs analyses have sought to identify the language and communicative skills and tasks of nursing as a profession (Cameron 1998; Epp and Lewis 2008; Hussin 2002; Marston and Hansen 1985). The results of these studies have contributed to a more complete understanding of the discourse of nursing and the development of a taxonomy of language use in nursing. This chapter will synthesize the findings of these two major areas of research and then discuss several related areas of research that are more specialized in nature, for example, writing in nursing, the development of nursing-specific language proficiency tests, and linguistic modification of multiple-choice nursing exams as a means of leveling the playing field in the assessment of ESL students. Despite the growing body of research in English for nursing, there has been surprisingly little collaboration between ESL professionals and nurse educators. Such collaboration could go a long way to addressing the many obstacles ESL students encounter in nursing programs, as well as creating a more culturally inclusive environment in nursing education.

Academic Strategies and Skills

In a needs analysis of ESL students in a baccalaureate-degree[1] nursing program, Bosher (2006) found that both academic skills and clinical skills are necessary for success in nursing programs. Academic skills in nursing are similar to academic skills in the social and natural sciences. Nursing students need to apply reading strategies and skills to complex reading material, usually in textbook format; apply listening strategies and skills to lectures; take notes to supplement lecture outlines; study effectively for tests; participate actively in discussions; ask questions; and write research papers on various topics in nursing. Students must also be able to read and write critically, for example, question the way in which a problem has been defined, the data that have been gathered to investigate the problem, and solutions that have been proposed (Cameron 1998). In their papers, students must be able to handle conflicting or contradictory ideas in problem statements, support their ideas with outside sources, and incorporate critical thinking and moral reasoning into their writing.

Some language tasks and skills are more challenging for ESL nursing students than others. In one needs analysis (Bosher 2006), faculty and students rated 74 academic, language, and culture-related skills and tasks for their degree of difficulty. Although there was considerable variation reported by faculty in their experiences with ESL students, there was also considerable overlap in the skills and tasks that both faculty and students identified as particularly challenging for ESL students: taking multiple-choice tests; incorporating into practice Western perspectives on culturally sensitive topics, such as sexuality and mental health; using effective reading strategies; asking questions in class; editing papers for grammatical errors; organizing and presenting ideas clearly and effectively in papers; preparing for clinicals or the practical training in a hospital setting; asking personal questions of clients; and managing time effectively.

Discipline-Specific Skills

Needs analyses have also identified certain discipline-specific skills and tasks in nursing which ESL students find particularly challenging. The most frequently cited discipline-specific task is nursing care plans (Bosher 2001, 2011). These assignments require students to research the medical diagnosis of every patient they are assigned to care for and to write out a detailed plan of care that reflects the nursing process of assessing the client, determining an appropriate nursing diagnosis, creating appropriate goals or desired outcomes for the client, implementing the interventions that have been identified in the plan, and evaluating the client's progress toward achieving the desired outcomes. These care plans require students to think critically about data collected through both a physical and psychosocial assessment of the patient and to use theoretical information from multiple source texts, usually nursing course textbooks, to support their assessment, diagnosis, and intervention plan.

Other discipline-specific skills and tasks in the clinical setting include charting and change-of-shift reports (Bosher 2010). Students need to document accurately and appropriately the nursing care they provide and to give complete and accurate information in change-of-shift reports and telephone orders. Nurses also need interviewing skills to gather information from clients, therapeutic communication skills to help clients cope with their situation, and assertiveness skills to speak up in difficult situations.

Cultural Skills and Content

Research has also addressed the cultural content of nursing, the cultural expectations of nursing instructors and supervisors, and the culture of nursing itself, all of which can present challenges for students who may not share the same cultural assumptions as the majority of nurse educators and supervisors. Becoming a nurse means becoming a member of a discourse community and beginning to think, feel, and believe as others in that community do and to use language in ways that identify oneself as a member of that group (Bosher 2011; Hussin 2008). More often than not, however, what others think, feel, and believe may not be stated explicitly and may or may not be consistent with ESL students' own cultural beliefs, values, and expectations in the health-care setting (Bosher 2008; Hussin 2002). For example, different cultures have different ways of understanding and responding to mental illness, sexuality concerns, and death and dying (Bosher 2008), and students often encounter difficulty addressing these issues or responding to them as expected in Western settings.

Cultural expectations are often embedded in communication style, such that differences in style can lead to cross-cultural misunderstandings. For example, instructors and supervisors from Western backgrounds often expect students to be self-directed and assertive, but, as Hussin (2008: 365–6) explains, students from

Asian cultures may view "assertive behavior, such as expressing one's own ideas, as transgressing the concept of harmony" and that "to justify one's own opinions would show a lack of respect for teachers and their experience [and authority]." If ESL students lack initiative and assertiveness in the ways expected by Western instructors and supervisors, they may be viewed as lacking in problem-solving skills or the ability to engage in clinical reasoning (Hussin 2008). According to Hussin (2002), preceptors, or clinical supervisors, often complain that ESL students lack initiative, do not speak up for themselves, and do not participate actively in team meetings. In fact, students may have important things to say in a team meeting, but need more time to come up with the correct words. However, "in Western culture, significant delays in conversation may be interpreted as a lack of interest or a lack of knowledge . . . lead[ing] to [negative] assumptions about a student's competency (Ladyshewsky as cited in Hussin 2008: 366).

Language Tasks and Skills in the Clinical Setting

Numerous studies have identified the language tasks and skills that are used in nursing in the clinical setting (Cameron 1998; Epp and Lewis 2008; Hussin 2002, 2008; Marston and Hansen 1985). The work of these researchers spans different levels of nursing in three different countries – Australia, Canada, and the United States – and with the exception of Marston and Hansen (1985) includes observations of nurses and recordings of interactions in various clinical settings. The findings of these studies provide rich data for the development of English for nursing materials.

The various lists that have been generated of the language tasks and skills that are used in the clinical setting are extensive (Hussin 2002). However, the work of Epp and Lewis (2008) also identified how nurses spend their time interacting with others on the job, in other words, what percentage of time they spend engaging in each of these language tasks and skills. Their situation analysis included over 80 hours of observation of nurses in various clinical settings as part of the first step in developing a nursing-specific language proficiency test. It revealed that nurses in Canada spend over half of their time with clients (56 percent), compared with other professionals (34 percent) and the clients' families (10 percent). Half of their time is spent on three language tasks: asking for information (22 percent), explaining (21 percent), and giving instructions (9 percent), followed by informing (7 percent), responding to questions (6 percent), suggesting (6 percent), and describing (6 percent). Other language tasks nurses spend some time on are engaging in small talk (5 percent), discussing (5 percent), comforting (4 percent), making or receiving telephone calls (3 percent), asking for help (2 percent), offering to help (2 percent), clarifying (1 percent), and apologizing (1 percent).

Cameron (1998), who conducted a needs analysis of international students in a graduate-degree nursing program in the United States, also found that giving information to patients and families is a primary communicative behavior in the clinical setting. Some of the information that nurses must convey, he found, includes communicating who one is and what one knows with confidence, good news and bad news, and options that are available to patients and their families. Nurses also give patients information about their diagnosis and procedures for self-care, as part of their role as educators. They present cases to preceptors and physicians, a task that requires nurses to present facts and nursing care plans, justify as well as challenge representations and interpretations of facts, negotiate differences of opinions, and respond effectively to interruptions. In their role as patient advocate, nurses contact and give information to other health-care professionals, social workers, family members, and friends. This kind of communication can set up a chain of reported speech, when several people have been contacted, that needs to be communicated clearly and accurately to others.

In her needs analysis of migrant nurses in Australia, Hussin (2002) identified numerous language tasks that nurses must successfully complete in the clinical setting: (1) taking a nursing history of the patient; (2) writing nursing care plans; (3) giving and receiving change-of-shift reports or handovers; (4) writing progress notes, discharge summaries, incident reports, and referral letters; (5) making and receiving phone calls; (6) using language while providing nursing care; (7) teaching patients and families about health-care topics and how to provide care after discharge; and (8) participating in team meetings about patients.

To complete these tasks with patients and family members, Hussin (2002) identified a variety of informational and interpersonal language skills that nurses need to use. The informational skills nurses need are interviewing techniques, giving instructions, asking for cooperation, checking readiness, explaining medical information in language that is easy to understand, explaining procedures, asking for permission, giving feedback, understanding colloquial language, and teaching techniques.

To complete these tasks with colleagues, nurses need some of the same informational skills, but additional ones as well: giving instructions and explanations of procedures, as well as understanding them; understanding and giving directions; asking for repetition and clarification; asking for assistance and explanation; checking for readiness; understanding and presenting verbal information; making and receiving telephone calls; accurately conveying telephone messages; using appropriate medical terminology; completing, reading, and interpreting routine forms, charts, and instructions; completing medical histories; reading and interpreting medical records and histories; writing, reading, and interpreting notes and summaries; writing, reading and interpreting nursing care plans; and writing, reading, and interpreting letters and reports (Hussin 2002).

Because so much of nursing involves establishing a relationship with patients, the nurse's interpersonal use of English is also very important. The language tasks and skills needed for interpersonal communication in nursing include expressing empathy; offering reassurance; interpreting nonverbal cues; using attending behaviors, nonverbal communication, reflective listening techniques, and clarification devices; paraphrasing; summarizing; using assertive responses; and expressing personal opinion (Hussin 2002).

In addition to individual speech acts, some tasks may require the nurse to produce a sequence of speech acts (Hussin 2002). For example, in transferring a patient, a nurse might begin with offering assistance, then request help from a colleague for the lift. The nurse might then explain the procedure to the patient and give instructions, especially when a mechanical lifting device is involved. Then, before beginning the actual lift itself, the nurse might check whether the colleague is ready, offer reassurance to the patient, and check the patient's degree of comfort. So in this one interaction, the nurse might produce a series of seven speech acts, five of which are addressed to the patient, two of which to a colleague.

Part of understanding a sequence of speech acts is being able to identify the shift from one speech act to another (Hussin 2002). Preceptors frequently comment that ESL students have difficulty keeping up with verbal instructions. For example, a nurse might make a request of an ESL student, but then follow it with a complaint, a joke, and then a set of instructions. Meanwhile, the student may not understand that a request was made and instructions provided.

A sequence of speech acts can become a convention or standard procedure when people are expected to follow the sequence (Hussin 2008). For example, when taking vital signs, nurses are expected to follow six steps, each consisting of a separate speech act: (1) give information to the patient, (2) explain the procedure, (3) ask for cooperation, (4) encourage the patient, (5) reassure the patient, and (6) give feedback to the patient about their vital signs. Such conventions provide excellent opportunities for developing materials as well as for assessing competencies in English for nursing.

Needs analysis of ESL students in the clinical setting have helped to identify language tasks and skills that are the most challenging for ESL students and that should be included in course and materials development (Bosher and Smalkoski 2002). The results of a needs analysis of ESL students in an associate-degree nursing program identified certain communicative tasks in the clinical setting as most challenging for ESL students: asserting oneself with patients, co-workers, and nursing instructors; communicating clearly and effectively with elderly patients; understanding clients who speak nonstandard English; using stress and intonation, and nonverbal communication appropriately; understanding and using small talk with patients; and asking for clarification. Other challenges that ESL students face in the clinical setting were also identified: feeling self-confident and comfortable enough to ask for assistance from other students and nursing supervisors; understanding how culture influences interactions with clients; understanding directions given by instructors and following through with step-by-step procedures in performance tests and clinicals; understanding client protocols and information that is stated about clients during protocols; and documenting appropriately and correctly in clients' records (Bosher and Smalkoski 2002).

In her work with migrant nurses in Australia, Hussin (2008) identified four areas of concern regarding the clinical performance of ESL students. The first area of concern was that students were not communicating with patients while they were providing care. In other words, they were not explaining what they were doing and they were not reassuring patients while they were performing a task. Secondly, students were not indicating when they did not understand instructions. Rather, they tended to "nod and smile," and, as a result, it was not always clear if they had understood. Third, students' production of English, in particular their pronunciation, was often unclear, such that medical terminology was difficult to understand. Finally, students were not taking an active role in their interactions and meetings with professional colleagues. In the same study (Hussin 2008), ESL students identified additional areas of difficulty they were experiencing: interacting in clinical situations; being assertive; making and receiving telephone calls; and giving change-of-shift or handover reports.

Linguistic Content of Language Tasks and Skills in the Clinical Context

Much of the research that has been done in English for nursing has focussed on determining the linguistic content of the various tasks and skills that have been identified as important for nurses in the clinical setting (Cameron 1998; Epp and Lewis 2008; Hussin 2002; Marston and Hansen 1985). This content can be divided into seven categories: pronunciation, vocabulary, grammar, and discourse, as well as pragmatic, strategic, and sociolinguistic competence, each of which will be discussed in the following sections.

Pronunciation

Cameron (1998) identified accuracy in speech production as one of the most important needs in English for nursing. Spoken accuracy takes place at four levels: pronunciation, vocabulary, grammar, and discourse, in other words, from the smallest unit of sound – the phoneme – to extended text. Pronouncing initial and final consonants, as well as common prefixes and suffixes, are some ways in which phonemes can create challenges for ESL students (Hussin 2002). In addition, phonemic contrasts can lead to miscommunication. For example, if a nurse is unable to distinguish between the phonemes /l/ and /n/, as in *low blood pressure* vs. *no blood pressure* (Cameron, 1998), or /b/ and /p/, as in *Betadine* and *Pethidine* (Hussin 2002), the results could be serious indeed. Other examples of phonemic contrasts that could result in miscommunication are *feeling* vs. *feeding*; *level* vs. *label*, and *pain* vs. *pan* (Cameron 1998).

In addition to phonemes, nurses must accurately pronounce words that are specific to nursing (Cameron 1998), including medical terminology, diagnoses, procedures, and names of drugs, particularly within the context of change-of-shift reports and telephone calls (Hussin 2002). Acronyms and abbreviations must also be pronounced correctly (Cameron 1998).

Nurses must also accurately pronounce general words that are commonly used in nursing and be able to distinguish between words that are easily confused, such as numbers, for example, *15* vs. *50* and *19* vs. *90*, and words of frequency, for example, *time* vs. *term* (Cameron 1998). Patients' names also need to be pronounced correctly (Hussin 2002).

Stress and intonation are other important aspects of pronunciation. Indeed, mispronunciation at the suprasegmental level can lead to greater problems in communication than mispronunciation at the segmental level. Too many unstressed syllables combined with regular reductions in rapid speech can reduce a sentence to something incomprehensible, for example, *"All prees fay die"* instead of *"All previous five died"* (Cameron 1998). In addition, misplaced word stress can result in confusion, for example, *respirátory* instead of *réspiratory*. Difficulties with stress and intonation can also lead to misunderstandings when reading forms and instructions aloud to patients.

Finally, ESL students may find it difficult to interpret tone, or stress, that is used to emphasize a particular word, especially when the meaning is one of sarcasm, as in the following example: "Don't you just love his bedside manner?" (Hussin 2002).

Vocabulary

Vocabulary also plays an important role in accuracy of speech production in many ways. First, there is word choice. There are many synonymous terms that have different connotations, for example, *stomach, belly, tummy, abdomen*, and *gut* (Cameron 1998). These words all refer to the same part of the body, but their usage may vary depending on the age, gender, or even social class of the patient, as well as the formality of the situation. Nurses need to know when to use which word and also need to understand the range of words that are used to refer to key body parts. In addition, many terms in health care are similar, yet distinctive, in meaning, such as *medical conditions* and *diseases* (Cameron 1998). Nurses need to make sure that the terms they use are the most appropriate. For example, the answers to the following questions: *"Do you have any medical conditions?"* and *"Do you have any diseases?"* are likely to be quite different.

In addition to word choice, paraphrasing of technical information is an important skill for nurses. Nurses often need to use nontechnical words instead of technical terms, so that patients can understand what they are saying (Cameron 1998). For example, in psychiatric nursing, the term *suicidal ideation* is likely to be used among health-care professionals. However, when talking with patients, the nontechnical term *suicidal thoughts* is more likely to be understood, as in the question *"Do you have suicidal thoughts?"* or more commonly *"Have you ever thought of hurting or killing yourself?"* On the other hand, Marston and Hansen (1985) discuss the importance of choosing the most technical or precise term in charting, for example, *flaccid* rather than *flabby*, and *emaciated* rather than *undernourished*.

Marston and Hansen (1985) also discuss the importance of sub-technical vocabulary, that is, the vocabulary that underlies specialized vocabulary, words that are not taught or necessarily explained in nursing classes, but are frequently used with medical or technical terms, such as *administer*, *position*, and *record*.

Many abbreviations are also used in health care, in written documentation and in change-of-shift reports, as well as in informal exchanges of information about patients, for example, *ADLs* (activities of daily living) and *NPO* (nothing by mouth). In addition, some words are routinely shortened, for example, *peri* for *perineum* and *pisi* for *episiotomy* (Hussin 2002).

Idioms and metaphors are often used to express abstract concepts that are frequent topics of conversations between nurses and patients, concepts that relate to the self, pain, emotion, loss, recovery, healing, and connection to others (Cameron 1998). Examples of such idioms and metaphors are *to fall out, to be at the end of one's rope, to feel adrift, to feel tied down*, and *to go nuts*. Another aspect of vocabulary that is important for nurses are words that are used to describe the physical appearance (Cameron 1998) and emotional state of patients.

In addition to idioms, there are many two and three-word verbs that are used to describe health-related issues, for example, *to bring up, to hold on, to come down with, to turn up with*, and *to break out in* (Cameron 1998). Although many of these two and three-word verbs have one-word equivalents, for example, *contract* for *to come down with* and *develop* for *to break out in*, native English-speaking patients are more likely to use and understand the more informal two and three-word verbs. In addition, colloquial language can be challenging to understand (Hussin 2008), particularly if a nurse does not share the same language or cultural background as the patient.

Finally, some words that are commonly used in health care have different forms or parts of speech (Cameron 1998). For example, *to live, life, liveliness, alive*, and *lively* are all different forms of "*to live*." Nurses could confuse one form of a word with another, as in the following example: *"The donor doesn't need to be life"* instead of *"The donor doesn't need to be alive."*

Grammar

In addition to pronunciation and vocabulary, various syntactic and morphological rules of grammar also contribute to accuracy in speech production. Asking questions is consistently identified as an important language task in English for nursing in the clinical setting (Cameron 1998; Epp and Lewis 2008; Hussin 2002; Marston and Hansen 1985). It is the primary means of getting information from patients, a key communicative behavior in the clinical setting (Cameron 1998). To conduct an interview, nurses must be able to ask the right kind of question at the right time, for example, open-ended questions to initiate an interview or a new topic of discussion, such as *"How are you feeling today?"* Information questions, such as *"Where does it hurt?" "When did the pain start?" "How long does it last?"* and *"What does it feel like?"* help nurses probe a topic for more information. Yes/no questions, such as *"Are you in pain?"* and *"Are you able to sit up?"* are helpful for getting answers to specific questions. Knowing when to ask what type of question is important, but students also need to be able to form different question types correctly.

Some types of questions are less straightforward and require inferencing to interpret them correctly (Cameron 1998). Elliptical questions are those questions for which some words have been left out, for example, in the following second question: *"How does your left leg feel today? Your right leg?"* Tag questions, which Hussin (2002) identified as particularly problematic for ESL students, are statements that are followed by a short question phrase, usually a question that the interlocutor already knows the answer to, for example, *"You're not hungry today, are you?"* Intonation questions are statements that end with rising intonation and in that way indicate they are a question, rather than a statement, for example, *"You're not hungry today?"* (Cameron 1998). Some questions are intended to confirm information that the nurse already suspects, and in that sense, are different from information questions, for example, *"Are the cramps quite regular now?"* (Cameron 1998). Other questions contain an embedded evaluation of the situation, for example, *"How many of these cramps do you get in a row?"* or contain options, for example, *"Did you feel better after taking the medicine or did you just start feeling better anyway?"* (Cameron 1998).

Another grammatical structure that is helpful for getting information from patients is the imperative or command. To conduct an assessment, nurses must be able to give simple commands, such as *"cross your legs," "bend your elbow," "touch your finger to your nose,"* and *"follow the light"* (Cameron 1998).

In addition to giving commands, nurses must also understand instructions given by doctors and nurse supervisors. Instructions that are given directly or explicitly, using an imperative, as in *"Give Mr Davis his medication now,"* are generally easy to understand. But instructions that are implied or suggested are more difficult for ESL students, for example, *"Mr Davis looks like he needs some help with ambulation"* (rather than *"Could you help Mr Davis with ambulation?"*) and *"We're going to have to do some more blood tests today"* (rather than *"Could you request some blood tests for Mr Lee?"*) (Hussin 2002, 2008). Indeed, Hussin (2002) claims that implicitness is a key problem area for ESL students, who need help understanding grammatical structures that are used to give implicit instructions, such as *"It's time to . . . ," "You could do this . . . ,"* and *"It might be good to. . . . "* Other structures that can be difficult to understand when they are not stated explicitly are questions, for example, *"Now that you've seen Mrs Mitchell's care plan, what do you think?"* (rather than *"What do you think about the interventions in Mrs Mitchell's care plan?"*) (Hussin 2002).

Tense and aspect are also important in health care communication (Cameron 1998) and have been identified as an area of difficulty for ESL students, particularly the use of the past versus the present perfect in case notes (Hussin 2002). Verb tenses indicate when something took place or how long it lasted. For example, in the following sentence *"I haven't seen him since he went to the clinic,"* the time period is clear. However, in the following sentence *"I don't see him since he goes to the clinic,"* the time period is not clear. If ESL students do not use past tense markings accurately, there may need to be some negotiation of meaning to clarify any resulting confusion. Another verb tense that can be confusing for ESL students is the present progressive (Hussin 2002). Students may not understand that the present progressive can be used to refer to the near future rather than the immediate present, as in the sentence *"She's having an appendectomy."*

Aspect is important for determining agency or the doer of an action when that information is important to have (Bosher 2003). Sometimes the agent is understood or is not necessary, as in the example, *"The patient was diagnosed with diabetes."* However, in other cases, it is important to know who the agent is, as in the example *"The nurse on the night shift gave the patient the wrong dosage of medication."*

Modal verbs are used in health-care communication to indicate hypothetical compared to factual situations (Cameron 1998) and are often confusing for ESL students. For example, *"This shot doesn't hurt as much as other ones"* is factual. However, *"This shot should not hurt as much as the other ones"* is hypothetical. Modal verbs on multiple-choice nursing exams can also be a source of difficulty for ESL students (Bosher 2003). Modals are also used in giving implicit instructions, as in *"You could do this . . . "* and *"It might be good to . . . "* (Hussin 2002).

Reported speech is another aspect of grammar that is prominent in health-care communication (Cameron 1998). Grammar textbooks typically limit the discussion of reported speech to such constructions as *"She said that her back hurts"* and *"The patient reported that her pain was 8 on a scale of 1 to 10."* In actual speech, however, nurses and patients tend to keep direct speech in dialogue form, but to introduce it using various expressions, such as the verb *"to be + like,"* *"says,"* and *"goes/go."* For example, a nurse might refer to what a patient said as follows: "And as I was taking his signs, *he says,* "I wanna go out and smoke a cigarette." "And *he goes,* "Well, I see everybody out there smoking cigarettes." Similarly, a patient might report what his or her doctor said as follows: "But *he's like,* 'If you ride your bike, well, do whatever you think you can do.' *I was like,* 'Can I ride my bike?' "

Other structures are sometimes used to emphasize a directive to patients, for example, what-cleft sentences, which begin with *"what,"* and it-cleft sentences, which begin with *"it."* The important information in a cleft sentence is positioned to follow the cleft structure, bringing emphasis and focussing attention on that information (Cameron 1998). For example, in the sentence *"[What I want you to try and do] [is]* **drink** *lots of water,"* the emphasis is on *"drink."* In the sentence *"[It] [is] [**water**, and lots of it], that I want you to drink,"* the emphasis is on *"water."* By contrast, the same statement without a cleft structure is less emphatic: *"I want you to try and drink lots of water."*

Pronoun usage is another aspect of grammar that is both common and problematic in English for nursing (Cameron 1998). Students whose native languages do not distinguish between *he* and *she* may confuse the two in English, as in the following example: *"We want to know how much time if we transfer Grace Wagner to another hospital because **she** is in critical condition. If we transfer **him**, we will waste much time. Maybe we, you know, maybe **she** died during the transfer time."*

Other grammar issues identified as potentially problematic for ESL nursing students include word order, adverbs of time and frequency, and prepositions (Hussin 2002). Hussin (2008) also identified structures students would need to practice to become more assertive, for example, "I" statements, as in, *"I feel anxious if I don't get early feedback [about my performance]"* (Hussin 2008).

Marston and Hansen (1985) also identified several grammatical forms that students would need in their needs analysis of licensed practical nurses in the United States. In addition to asking questions, they identified describing spatial relationships; using relative clauses to answer questions about a patient or to specify a patient; and describing procedures. Grammatical structures that are needed to describe spatial relationships include passive constructions and prepositions of location, such as *is located at, is divided by, is connected to, is found at,* and *is enclosed by.* Relative clauses are an important way in which to modify or specify a person or a place one is referring to, for example, *"At 8:00, the nurse took the blood pressure of the patient [who usually has high blood pressure]"* and *"The patient [who is scheduled for surgery] wants a bath."* Grammatical structures that are needed to describe procedures include third person subjects, imperatives, passives, and expressions of time.

On the other hand, different grammatical rules apply with charting. Contrary to traditional grammar, a telegraphic style of writing is used, characterized by the deletion of subjects of sentences, forms of the verb *to be,* possessive pronouns, and articles (Marston and Hansen 1985).

Discourse

At the discourse level there are tasks that nurses must be able to accomplish that require the ability to understand and produce contextualized stretches of language in spoken or written form. As previously discussed, nurses must be able to produce and understand a series of speech acts (Cameron 1998). In addition, nurses must be able to recount what they have been told, for example, retell in a change-of-shift report what a patient has said. They must also be able to narrate a sequence of events from either their own perspective or the perspective of someone else. And, they must be able to describe their assessment and observations of patients.

Making and receiving telephone calls is another example of using language at the discourse level, which also requires the use of another channel of communication (Cameron 1998). Phone calls are especially difficult for ESL nurses due to the lack of nonverbal clues and the frequent presence of background noise. Hussin (2002) writes of ESL nurses who would walk away from a nurse's station when the phone rang or pretend it was not ringing. Skills that are important in making and receiving phone calls, which ESL students tend to have difficulty with, include identifying numbers, letters, and names of people over the telephone and distinguishing between the intonation patterns for statements and questions.

Pragmatic competence

Pragmatic competence refers to knowing how to use language effectively and appropriately to accomplish certain language tasks (Hedge 2000). The many speech acts that nurses need to perform in the clinical setting reflect the ability to use language in specific ways to accomplish certain tasks.

One of the challenges of pragmatic competence is understanding communicative intent when it is not stated explicitly (Cameron 1998). In these situations, inferencing skills are needed, both language based and socially based. Other related challenges include inferring a patient's emotional state or mental status by what the patient has communicated unintentionally and inferring relevant social information based on the nurse's understanding of local culture (Cameron 1998).

Strategic competence

Another level of communicative competence in the clinical setting involves being able to use different strategies to ensure mutual comprehension, also referred to as strategic competence (Canale 1983; Canale and Swain 1980; Hedge 2000). These strategies include clarifying meaning, checking comprehension, and demonstrating understanding (Hussin 2008). Interactive repair is another strategy to ensure mutual comprehension (Cameron 1998). In addition, nurses need to recognize nonverbal and verbal cues of understanding and misunderstanding (Cameron 1998), so they can initiate the use of strategies to ensure mutual understanding.

To clarify meaning, ESL students can ask for repetition (Hussin 2008), as in *"Could you repeat that, please?"* Asking clarification questions is another strategy, for example, *"**What** did you say we need to order from the pharmacy?"* Clarification strategies are especially important when making telephone calls, as there are no visual clues (Hussin 2002). Comprehension checks include such devices as *"Was that 's' for Sam or 'f' for Fred?"* and *"Was that one nine or nine one?"* (Hussin 2008). To check understanding, Cameron (1998) discusses the role of paraphrasing and reflecting back to patients and colleagues what they have said or implied. Confirmation checks can also be used in combination with questions to make sure the information nurses are getting from patients is accurate and complete (Cameron 1998).

These strategies are particularly important when talking with patients who are physically or mentally impaired in some way.

There are various ways in which students can demonstrate their understanding (Hussin 2008). First, they can repeat key words. For example, in response to the instruction, *"Could you call the kitchen and order a low-fat, low-salt diet for Mrs Green?"* students could repeat the words *". . . a low-fat, low-salt diet"* in their response. Another strategy is to paraphrase the instruction in the response, for example, *"Okay, I'll call the kitchen and ask if Mrs Green can have meals that are low in salt and fat."* Expansion statements, or statements that add information, are another way to demonstrate understanding. For example, *"Yes, Mrs Green said that she needed to lose some weight before her next operation – I'll call the kitchen right now."* Another way to show one has understood is to use elaboration questions, or questions that ask for more information, for example, *"Okay, I'll call the kitchen. Should I ask them to change the menu right away or for her next meal?"*

Sociolinguistic competence

Sociolinguistic competence refers to the ability to use language in ways that are appropriate to the context, the relationship between the persons involved, and the purpose of the interaction (Hedge 2000). Because ESL students often have difficulty with sociolinguistic competence, it is important that the rules of socio-linguistic behavior in the clinical setting are made explicit, for example, how to take turns and interrupt politely in conversations (Hussin 2002). Another key problem area for ESL students is assertion; nurses need to be able to interrupt politely but assertively (Hussin 2002, 2008).

Sociolinguistic competence also includes knowing how to direct an interview appropriately and, if interrupted or side tracked, to renew the topic, especially in the face of patient resistance (Cameron 1998). With content that is culturally sensitive, nurses need to be able to address the topic and gather the necessary information regardless of their degree of discomfort or their patient's. Other skills that nurses must have include communicating empathy and concern to a patient in ways that are culturally appropriate, but at the same time that communicate confidence and authority (Cameron 1998).

Nurses must also be able to adjust their speech based on their audience and the purpose for communication, but without changing the content itself. For example, when translating medical language into language that is appropriate to use with nonspecialists, nurses need to take into consideration their audience (Cameron 1998), whether adult patients, children, or family members. When making requests, nurses need to adjust the form and wording of the request, depending on the person the nurse is addressing and the purpose of the request, for example, whether the nurse is asking a doctor to examine a patient, another nurse to help lift a patient, a patient to lie down, or a visitor to step outside for a few minutes (Marston and Hansen 1985).

Cameron (1998) also discusses the importance of understanding cultural and dialectal variation in English, variation that is often based on regional or social variables, such as gender, age, class, race, and ethnicity.

In addition to professional interaction, social interaction is also an expected and important type of communication in the clinical setting (Cameron 1998). Language tasks that are especially useful in social interaction include greetings and leave taking; making small talk and giving compliments; telling stories of personal experience; extending invitations; making requests; giving apologies; using terms of address appropriately, given the degree of politeness and deference warranted by the situation; recognizing and deflecting inappropriate behavior; and using culturally appropriate nonverbal behavior. Marston and Hansen (1985) also discuss the need for nurses to know how to make small talk. To establish rapport with patients, nurses need to engage in social conversation, and small talk is often the first step.

Hussin (2008) discusses the importance of using visual cues to initiate a con-versation, such as flowers on a bedside table, photos of family members, cards from visitors, and any books or activities the patient is engaged in. In other words, mastering certain conventions involves not only learning the language that is used and the accompanying nonverbal behavior, but also the ability to interpret and use visual signs and symbols appropriately.

In sum, while research has identified many ways in which English is used in nursing in the clinical setting, the specific tasks and skills that have been identified can be categorized by the type of communicative competence they most contribute to: accuracy in production at the level of pronunciation, vocabulary, grammar, or discourse, or pragmatic, strategic, or sociolinguistic competence. This framework provides a useful and comprehensive taxonomy or structure within which to develop materials that address all aspects of linguistic content in English language use in the clinical setting.

Writing in Nursing

Another area of research in the field of English for nursing has been in writing in nursing. Some studies have looked at how students acquire discipline-specific literacy, most notably how they learn how to write nursing care plans (Bosher 2001, 2011; Leki 2003, 2007). Other studies have investigated how nurses develop skill in writing nursing notes in a second language (Parks and Maguire 1999). More broadly, there have been attempts to understand more about the genres of writing required in nursing programs (Gimenez 2008), as well as ways in which learning centers can support nursing students in their writing (Smukler and Kramer 1996).

There have also been calls for a change in paradigm in the role of writing in nursing. One of the few nurse educators to have collaborated with ESL professionals, Alster (2004) critiques the generally poor quality of writing in nursing, which unduly influences the writing of nursing students. She argues for a more open approach to writing that would provide students with a greater variety of writing assignments and that would encourage students to write in ways that are both more personally engaging, as well as grounded in critical thinking, for example, reflective journals about clinical experiences to which faculty would respond at the level of content only. Alster (2004) advocates a writing-to-learn approach in nursing that would more actively involve students in creating knowledge in the profession and in critiquing the ideas of others, processes that would also help to initiate students into the nursing discourse community.

Assessing Language Proficiency in Nursing

Some research has also focussed on developing a more valid and reliable means of assessing language proficiency in nursing. Although there have been previous occupation-specific tests for health professionals, including nursing (Douglas

2000; McNamara 1996), the Canadian English Language Benchmark Assessment for Nurses (CELBAN) was recently developed for use with internationally educated nurses who are seeking to re-enter the nursing profession in Canada (Epp and Lewis 2008). As mentioned earlier, the test development process included extensive videotaping of nurses in the clinical setting, followed by target language analysis, specifically situational language use by nurses, the types of language tasks used, and the percentage of time spent on each type of task. Findings from this analysis indicate that over half of nurses' time is spent with clients (56 percent) and about a third of their time with professionals (34 percent), followed by clients' families (10 percent). Over half of their time is spent asking for information (22 percent), explaining (21 percent), and giving instruction (9 percent), combined.

Linguistic Bias on Multiple-Choice Nursing Course Exams

Research has also focussed on the wording of multiple-choice items on nursing course exams as a major barrier to success for ESL nursing students (Bosher 2003; Bosher 2008b; Bosher and Bowles 2008). One study (Bosher and Bowles 2008) investigated the effects of unnecessary linguistic complexity on students' comprehension of test items. Linguistic modification, or the attempt to reduce the linguistic complexity of test items without affecting their construct validity, offers one way to reduce the language load of test items (Abedi and Lord 2001). While this methodology has been used successfully in K-12 settings, it has not been adopted as one way to level the playing field in the assessment of ESL nursing students (Bosher 2008b). Further research is needed to investigate the effects of linguistic modification on the test scores of ESL nursing students.

Suggestions for Future Research

Nurse educators in the United States are well aware of the increase in ESL students in their programs and of the difficulties many of these students encounter, as illustrated by the number of articles that have been published in nursing journals since the early 1990s. Although nursing organizations have long called for greater diversity in the nursing profession (AACN 1997), the US National League for Nursing (NLN) reported "no significant increase in minority enrollment or graduation" (Nugent et al. 2002: 31) from nursing programs between 1995–2000. Furthermore, few changes have been made in nursing education to meet the needs of an increasingly diverse student population (Mulready-Shick 2009).

Surprisingly, there has been little input from ESL faculty in efforts to address the needs of ESL nursing students, even though language is often cited as the most significant barrier to their success (Amaro, Abriam-Yago, and Yoder 2006; Yoder 1996). No articles in nursing journals have specifically called for English for nursing courses, or for collaborating in meaningful ways with ESL faculty to promote student success or to provide faculty development, despite indications that existing academic support is insufficient to meet the needs of ESL nursing students (Amaro et al. 2006). Thus, it is up to ESL professionals, specifically those in the field of English for specific purposes, to research the situation of ESL students in nursing programs at their institutions and to advocate for English for nursing courses and other ESL support services that could help increase the success of ESL students in nursing programs and in the profession.

NOTE

1   In the United States students can pursue an associate degree in nursing (ADN) at a two-year community college or a baccalaureate or bachelor of science degree in nursing (BSN) at a four-year college or university. Graduates from both programs take the same national nursing licensure exam, the NCLEX.

REFERENCES

Abedi, J. and Lord, C. (2001) The language factor in mathematics tests. *Applied Measurement in Education* 14: 219–34.

Alster, K. B. (2004) Writing in nursing education and nursing practice. In V. Zamel and R. Spack (eds.), *Crossing the Curriculum – Multilingual Learners in College Classrooms*. 163–80. Mahwah, NJ: Lawrence Erlbaum.

Amaro, D. J., Abriam-Yago, K., and Yoder, M. (2006) Perceived barriers for ethnically diverse students in nursing programs. *Journal of Nursing Education* 45: 247–54.

American Association of Colleges of Nursing (AACN) (1997) Position Statement on Diversity and Equality of Opportunity. Oct. 27. Washington, DC: AACN.

Bosher, S. (2001) Discipline-specific literacy in a second language: How ESL students learn to write successfully in a B.S.-degree nursing program. *ERIC Document 454 707.*

Bosher, S. (2003) Barriers to creating a more culturally diverse nursing profession: Linguistic bias in multiple-choice nursing exams. *Nursing Education Perspectives* 24: 25–34.

Bosher, S. (2006) ESL meets nursing: Developing an English for nursing course. In M. A. Snow and L. Kamhi-Stein (eds.), *Developing a New Course for Adult Learners*. 63–98. Alexandria, VA: TESOL.

Bosher, S. (2008a) *English for Nursing, Academic Skills*. Ann Arbor, MI: The University of Michigan Press.

Bosher, S. (2008b) Removing language as a barrier to success on multiple-choice nursing exams. In S. Bosher and M. Dexheimer Pharris (eds.), *Transforming Nursing Education: The Culturally Inclusive Environment*. 259–84. New York: Springer.

Bosher, S. (2010) English for nursing: Developing discipline-specific materials. In N. Harwood (ed.), *Materials in ELT:*

Theory and Practice. 346–72. Cambridge: Cambridge University Press.

Bosher, S. (2011) Acquiring discipline-specific literacy in a second language: A case study of an ESL nursing student. *Taiwan International ESP Journal* 2: 17–48.

Bosher, S. and Bowles, M. (2008) The effects of linguistic modification on ESL students' comprehension of nursing course test items. *Nursing Education Perspectives* 29: 165–72.

Bosher, S. and Smalkoski, K. (2002) From needs analysis to curriculum development: Designing a course in health-care communication for immigrant students in the USA. *English for Specific Purposes* 2: 59–79.

Cameron, R. (1998) Language-focused needs analysis for ESL-speaking nursing students in class and clinic. *Foreign Language Annals* 31: 203–18.

Canale, M. (1983) From communicative competence to communicative language pedagogy. In J. C. Richards and R. W. Schmidt (eds.), *Language and Communication.* 2–27. London: Longman.

Canale, M. and Swain, M. (1980) Theoretical bases of communicative approaches to second language teaching and testing. *Applied Linguistics* 1: 1–47.

Douglas, D. (2000) *Assessing Languages for Specific Purposes.* Cambridge: Cambridge University Press.

Epp, L. and Lewis, C. (2008) Innovation in language proficiency assessment: The Canadian English Language Benchmark Assessment for Nurses (CELBAN). In S. Bosher and M. Dexheimer Pharris (eds.), *Transforming Nursing Education: The Culturally Inclusive Environment.* 285–310. New York: Springer.

Gimenez, J. (2008) Beyond the academic essay: Discipline-specific writing in nursing and midwifery. *Journal of English for Academic Purposes* 7: 151–64.

Hansen, M. (2010) Barriers that non-native speakers of English face in a nursing program. Unpublished master's thesis. Hamline University, St Paul, Minnesota.

Hedge, T. (2000) *Teaching and Learning in the Language Classroom.* Oxford: Oxford University Press.

Hussin, V. (2002) An ESP program for students of nursing. In T. Orr (ed.), *English for Specific Purposes.* 25–39. Alexandria, VA: TESOL.

Hussin, V. (2008) Facilitating success for ESL nursing students in the clinical setting: Models of learning support. In S. Bosher and M. Dexheimer Pharris (eds.), *Transforming Nursing Education: The Culturally Inclusive Environment.* 363–86. New York: Springer.

Kachru, B. B. (1985) Standards, codification and sociolinguistic realism: The English language in the outer circle. In R. Quirk and H. Widdowson (eds.), *English in the World: Teaching and Learning the Language and Literatures.* 11–36. Cambridge: Cambridge University Press.

Leki, I. (2003). Living through college literacy: Nursing in a second language. *Written Communication* 20: 81–98.

Leki, I. (2007) *Undergraduates in a Second Language – Challenges and Complexities of Academic Literacy Development.* 63–120. Mahwah, NJ: Lawrence Erlbaum.

Marston, J. and Hansen, A. (1985) Clinically speaking: ESP for refugee nursing students. *MinneTESOL Journal* 5: 29–52.

McNamara, T. (1996) *Measuring Second Language Performance.* London: Longman.

Mulready-Shick, J. (2009) "A long little story:" Exploring the experiences of nursing students as English language learners. In K. M. Bailey and M. G. Santos (eds.), *Research on ESL in US community Colleges: People, Programs, and Potential.* 37–48. Ann Arbor, MI: The University of Michigan Press.

Nugent, K. E., Childs, G., Jones , R., Cook, P., and Ravenell, K. (2002) Call to action: The need to increase diversity in the nursing workforce. *Nursing Forum* 37: 28–32.

Parks, S. and Maguire, M. H. (1999) Coping with on-the-job writing in ESL: A constructivist-semiotic perspective. *Language Learning* 49: 43–6.

Smukler, B. and Kramer, D. (1996) Beyond basic skills: A collaboration between a resource center and a department of nursing for high-risk nursing students. *Research and Teaching in Developmental English* 13: 75–83.

Yoder, M. K. (1996) Instructional responses to ethnically diverse nursing students. *Journal of Nursing Education* 35: 315–21.

15   Thesis and Dissertation Writing

PAUL THOMPSON

Introduction

The terms "dissertation" and "thesis" are used differently in different regions of the world – in North America, the lengthy text produced as the culmination of doctoral research is generally referred to as a dissertation, while in the United Kingdom it is referred to as a thesis. This chapter follows British conventions by describing the extended piece of written work at the masters level as a dissertation and that at the doctoral level as a thesis.

Although many British undergraduate programs as well as postgraduate programs do require students to write a dissertation, the focus in this chapter is on post-graduate writing, either the masters dissertation or the doctoral thesis, and on how research conducted in this area can inform the teaching and support of such students, within the framework of English for specific purposes (ESP). Some space will be given to discussion of research into the writing practices of second language (L2) writers on masters courses, but the majority of the work discussed here is concerned with the PhD thesis. The doctoral thesis is still a relatively neglected area of research (Starfield and Ravelli 2006), although interest has grown as increasing numbers of students choose to study for a doctorate. In the United Kingdom, the number of doctorates awarded in 2009/10 was 15,610, compared with a figure of 10,660 in 2002/3 (http://www.hesa.ac.uk/). The majority of ESP research on theses and dissertations to date has appeared in either the journal *English for Specific Purposes* or the *Journal of English for Academic Purposes*, as is evident in the list of references at the end of this chapter. Reference is not made to the many manuals that have been written for thesis writers; as Paltridge (2002) has noted, published advice on thesis writing is often at odds with actual practice, and the research that is discussed here is empirically driven.

The Handbook of English for Specific Purposes, First Edition.
Edited by Brian Paltridge and Sue Starfield.
© 2013 John Wiley & Sons, Inc. Published 2013 by John Wiley & Sons, Inc.

A thesis or a dissertation is for many students the longest and most challenging piece of assessed writing that they will have to do in their degree program. The sheer size of the text and the complex task of planning one's research, of synthesizing one's reading, and of sustaining a coherent and extended argument, is an immense challenge for any student writer; this challenge is magnified when writing in a language that is not one's mother tongue, and in a foreign academic culture. Furthermore, as Leki, Cumming, and Silva (2008) observe, second language post-graduate students face not only linguistic difficulties but also considerable threats to their sense of identity, as they try to adjust to unfamiliar environments in which their disciplinary expertise is neither easily expressed nor immediately recognized.

This chapter begins by asking what type of text a PhD thesis is, its purpose who it is written for and who it is written by, and how a thesis is typically structured. This is followed by a review of genre descriptions of PhD theses. Attention then turns to a process view of doctoral research, which focusses on the individual and on the context in which research students study and write. Finally, questions concerning support and language guidance for thesis and dissertation writers are discussed, and suggestions for future research are made.

Purposes and Descriptions

As Paltridge (2002: 126) states, dissertations and theses differ from research articles in their purposes, scale, audience, and the requirements they need to meet. A thesis or dissertation is a text that is produced for assessment purposes, and the immediate audience is the examiner, or examiners. The length of a masters dissertation can be around 10,000–20,000 words while a doctoral thesis in a humanities or social science subject may be about 80,000–100,000 words long. Each typically presents an original and extensive piece of research conducted by the writer. In the case of the PhD thesis, in particular, the writer has to demonstrate to the examiners that he or she has made an original contribution to knowledge, and is an authority on the subject of research.

Providing a comprehensive definition of the forms and functions of such texts is difficult because there is considerable variation across disciplines, and also across different national educational systems. In the *Reading Academic Text* corpus of doctoral theses (Thompson 1999), for example, the shortest thesis is 10,000 words long (biotechnology) and the longest (history) is over 110,000 words (the word count refers to running text within the main body of the thesis and it does not include the list of references, appendices and all front matter).

With respect to form, Paltridge (2002) has proposed four types of thesis organization: "traditional simple," and "traditional complex" (after Thompson 1999), "topic-based" and the "compilation of research articles" (after Dong 1998). In the first of these, the thesis follows the structure of a scientific research report, with separate chapters for the introduction, methods, results, and discussion; this is often referred to as the "IMRD" model. The traditional complex thesis typically begins with an introduction and a review of the literature and then is followed by a sequence of chapters, each of which follows the IMRD pattern, before concluding with a general summary chapter. The topic-based thesis begins with an introductory chapter and then a series of chapters that are each based on a topic; such theses are common in the humanities, for example. The fourth form that Paltridge proposes is the compilation of published research articles. The compilation of articles is an increasingly common type of thesis in which most, if not all, of the sections of the thesis are articles, which have been published in international journals, and there may be an introductory and a concluding chapter appended, in which the author tries to give unity to the complete text. In some European countries, for example, Belgium and Sweden, doctoral students are expected to publish their articles in journals with high impact factors in order for these papers to qualify for a doctoral thesis.

This is not, however, a form model *per se* – the article-compilation thesis may use the complex traditional form, for example, with introductory and concluding chapters added at either end of a series of IMRD chapters, each of which has been published as a separate research article in international journals. What changes with the article-compilation thesis, however, is the audience. Thompson (1999) reported that supervisors in Agricultural Economics saw the examiners as the immediate audience for a thesis, and fellow researchers in the discipline as the audience for a research article. Supervisors in Agricultural Botany added fellow lab workers as a potential audience for a thesis (where a group of researchers were engaged on the same project). With the article-compilation thesis, then, the audience broadens to the wider research community (Dong 1998), and the rhetorical situation is considerably changed. Much research has been done on the genre of the research article (see Charles, Paltridge, this volume), and so the article-compilation thesis is not discussed further in this chapter. Table 15.1 below presents a simplified model of the typical patterns of rhetorical organization in the three types of thesis discussed in this chapter.

Swales (1990), in discussing the difference between theses and research articles, proposed that what differentiates the former from the latter is that theses employ larger quantities of metadiscourse; a thesis is a much longer text than the research

Table 15.1 Three forms of rhetorical organization for PhD theses

Traditional simple	Traditional complex	Topic-based
Introduction	Introduction	Introduction
[Literature Review]	Literature Review	Chapter: Topic 1
Methods	Chapter: IMRD	Chapter: Topic 2
Results	....	....
Discussion	Chapter: IMRD	Concluding chapter
	Conclusion	

article, and there is consequently a greater need to include sections of text that provide the reader with explanations about what is to come, and with references to other parts of the text that relate to what the author is discussing at a given point. Bunton (1999) investigated what he refers to as "higher level metatext" (metatext/metadiscourse which works at the chapter or thesis level); in 13 Hong Kong doctoral theses, he found that 57 percent of the metatext in the theses was at this higher level. He observed also that L2 writers still needed to do more to orient their readers, which suggest that the 57 percent is not a high enough proportion. Hyland (2004) analyzed metadiscourse in a corpus of 240 theses and dissertations written by Hong Kong Chinese students, and found that the most frequently used devices were hedges and transitions, followed by evidentials (references to sources of information from other texts) and engagement markers. Hedges mitigate the writer's commitment to a proposition, while transitions indicate additive, contrastive, and consequential steps within the discourse. Between the two types of texts, Hyland found that the doctoral theses used 35 percent more metadiscourse than the dissertations, and also that they used more interactional metadiscourse (hedges, boosters, attitude markers, *inter alia*) than the masters dissertations.

It should be noted that the category of the "topic-based" form of thesis tends to be a catch-all for a wide range of frameworks that do not fit into the traditional IMRD patterns, and this is either evidence that there is less conventionalization of form in research paradigms outside that of traditional experimental studies, or that further research needs to be done to categorize other patterns.

While it is understandable that the IMRD structure has tended to dominate the attention of ESP researchers, given that it is a widely used form, in recent years several researchers have argued that more attention needs to be given to alternative forms of writing and specifically to research that takes a qualitative (rather than quantitative) approach. Belcher and Hirvela (2005), for example, studied six L2 doctoral students who were writing a qualitative research dissertation, with the aim of understanding what motivated these students to choose a qualitative topic and also to find out how they viewed the linguistic demands. Three of the students had intrinsic motivation, and three had extrinsic motivation, but all six succeeded. One of the keys to success for these writers, Belcher and Hirvela proposed, was writing support from a sympathetic and experienced reader. Casanave (2010) goes further to propose that students should be encouraged to take risks when writing qualitative research, as, she argues, unconventional writing can lead to creative thinking.

Starfield and Ravelli (2006) investigated visual and verbal representations of what they term the "writerly self" in History and Sociology PhD theses. They propose that in the postmodern age there is a new form of topic-based thesis emerging in which the writer is constructed as a reflexive self that is not able to write with the classic detachment of positivism, such as one might find in traditional "scientific" writing. Writers, they argue, are playing with forms and looking for new ways to make meaning. One of the key questions for the postmodern writer is how to represent and position himself or herself textually.

Genre Descriptions

The most productive research approach to thesis and dissertation writing to date has been in the area of genre analysis. In this section, I briefly review the genre descriptions that have been made of some components of theses and dissertations: introductions, literature reviews, discussion sections, and conclusions.

Introductions

The classic framework for the genre analysis of introductions in research articles is Swales' (1990) Create a research space (CARS) model, which consists of three moves: (1) "Establishing a territory," (2) "Establishing a niche," and (3) "Occupying the niche," each of which contains a number of steps. Bunton (2002: 74) has developed a modified CARS model for PhD theses, which uses the same moves, but he introduces different optional steps within these moves. These include "defining terms" (within Move 1) and "thesis structure" (cf, the observation made above that dissertations and theses are characterized by the frequent of higher level metadiscourse which informs readers of the "bigger picture," as it were), "research questions/hypotheses," "method," and "theoretical position" (within Move 3).

Samraj (2008) looked at variation in the uses of "I" and of references to literature in the introductions of masters dissertations in three different disciplines (biology, philosophy, and linguistics) and found that the Philosophy students in her sample tended to construct a stronger authorial identity but they also established weaker intertextual links (there was less citation). Samraj also observed that not all the dissertation introductions in her sample conformed to Swales' CARS model.

Literature reviews

Kwan (2006) applied Bunton's framework for thesis introductions to an analysis of literature review chapters in 20 Hong Kong dissertations. She found that the two dominant moves in the literature review section were Moves 1 and 2, with Move 3 occurring less than a quarter of the times that Move 1 did.

Thompson (2009) argued that the three moves in Kwan's move model for literature reviews function to establish a strong case for the writer's own work on which he or she is to be evaluated. Thompson then took a corpus-informed approach to the analysis of evaluation in literature reviews in theses in four disciplines. He selected the words "problem," "data," and "evidence" (selected because they are key nouns – "key" as determined by the "KeyWords" tool in WordSmith Tools (Scott 2010) – in the literature review chapters), and showed that they play an important role in maintaining the writer's voice through the literature review, in patterns such as the following:

```
DET + ADJ [optional] + PROBLEM + [optional postmodification] +
BE + that/to (Example: "The fundamental problem is that ... ")
```

```
there + BE + ADV/ADJ [optional] + evidence + that/to (Example:
"There is little evidence to ... ")
```

The gaps in findings, theories, explanations or descriptions of previous researchers are thus identified as constituting problems that are in need of resolution, or evaluated in terms of how much evidence they provide to support a line of argument.

Both Kwan and Thompson conducted their research on native speaker authored theses. Akindele (2008), by contrast, looked at literature reviews written by Botswanan doctoral students and also interviewed the writers. He identified the ability to write critically about the literature as a major challenge facing these L2 writers.

Although citations are not confined to the literature review sections of a thesis, it is worth commenting on research that has been conducted on citation practices in thesis and dissertation writing here. Thompson (2006) categorized all instances of citation in a corpus of agricultural botany theses written by native speakers and investigated how writers position themselves and what they place focus on. In the introduction, literature review, and discussion sections, the tendency was to use non-integral citation types with a focus on information rather than on people (non-integral citations are citations that are placed outside the sentence, usually inside brackets). However, some writers did integrate the names of researchers into the syntax of the sentence, particularly where comparisons of a number of studies were made.

Petrić (2007) adapted Thompson's coding framework for her analysis of citation practices in masters dissertations written by L2 writers of English at a Central European university. She found that citation at this level was used primarily for knowledge display, but that higher-grade students used citations for a wider range of functions, in order to support the writer's line of thought.

Charles (2006) examined what she terms "research reports" (that is, reporting clauses used by writers to make reference to others' work) in thesis citations in two disciplines, and found much higher levels of integral citation use in the theses than were reported by Hyland (2002) in his analysis of research articles. Charles speculated that this was because the integral citation form is part of a more extended discussion of a reference, which is possible in a thesis where there is more room to elaborate than in a journal article.

Discussion sections

Dudley-Evans (1994) presented a nine-move model for discussion sections of masters dissertations and research articles, and Bitchener (2010b: 4) provides the following revised three-move model that is directed at writers of empirically based doctoral theses:

1. *Provide background information*
   a. restatement of aims, research questions, hypotheses
   b. restatement of key published research
   c. restatement of research/methodological approach

2. *Present a statement of result (SOR)*
   a. restatement of a key result
   b. expanded statement about a key result
3. *Evaluate/comment on results or findings in a. restatement of aims, research questions, hypotheses*
   a. explanation of result – suggest reasons for result
   b. (un)expected result – comment on whether it was an expected or unexpected result
   c. reference to previous research – compare result with previously published research
   d. exemplification – provide examples of result
   e. deduction or claim – make a more general claim arising from the result, e.g. drawing a conclusion or stating a hypothesis
   f. support from previous research – quote previous research to support the claim being made
   g. recommendation – make suggestion for future research
   h. justification for further research – explain why further research is recommended

In this framework, the writer is likely to repeat a cycle of 2 followed by 3, so that the pattern may be: 1 – 2 – 3 – 2 – 3 . . . (where the three dots indicate that the sequence 2 – 3 can be repeated several times).

Bitchener and Basturkmen (2006) conducted four in-depth interviews with L2 dissertation writers and their supervisors, and asked them how they perceived the task of writing the discussion of results section (DRS) of the dissertation. Students tended to see their language problems at the sentence level while the supervisors saw it in terms of creating clear meaning at the paragraph level, and in terms of understanding the rhetorical and organizational requirements of the genre. Cooley and Lewkowicz (1995, 1997) also reported that supervisors at the University of Hong Kong claimed that difficulties with surface forms and structures are less problematic than difficulties affecting the development of coherent ideas and arguments, and they also observed that difficulties with appropriate lexical choice tended to obscure meaning.

Conclusions

Bunton (2005) proposes that the generic structure of a conclusions chapter is not the same as that of a discussion chapter. The following is his model for a conclusions chapter, with a small amendment to Move 4 drawn from Thompson (2005):

Move 1: restatement of aims and research questions
Move 2: consolidation of present research (findings, limitations)
Move 3: practical and theoretical implications
Move 4: recommendations for further research
Move 5: concluding restatement.

Writers and Supervisors

We have so far talked about the thesis or dissertation primarily as a product. It is important to recognize, however, that the models that genre analysis have proposed are simply attempts at describing what is common to the texts that the analysts have examined and that these models need to be tested against examples of theses written in the local context. Doctoral students need to look at theses written in their subject area and see how they are structured and what the typical moves are in each section, rather than uncritically adopt the models suggested by genre analysts. It cannot be said that there is one single way to write a thesis, as Paltridge (2012) observes, but it is important for students to find out what conventions exist within their own discipline and also to find out how binding those conventions are. Students can learn about this by examining previous theses and also by asking their supervisors, advisors, and other researchers at their institution.

The final text emerges from a complex of processes, over a long period of time. The student writer may work individually or as a member of a group (within a funded research project for example), and much of the time is guided by one or more supervisors. Starfield (2010) observes that social sciences and humanities students do not work in teams, unlike science students, and international students in these contexts have few opportunities for informal learning about the research culture of their field. In a science subject, Shaw (1991) reported that supervisors tend to have a strong influence on choice of research topic, on research design, and on the writing of the literature review. In an arts or social science discipline, by contrast, the student may be expected to exercise greater independence (Turner 2003).

Recent research has illustrated how doctoral study is a socially mediated activity: Kwan (2009), for example, describes the interactions between students, supervisors and other advisors in the development of literature reviews by thesis writers at a Hong Kong university. Casanave and Li (2008) is a collection of fascinating papers that explore how graduate students learn the unwritten rules of participation in their research communities, how they learn to negotiate their relationships with supervisors and peers, and how they cope with the challenges to their sense of identity. Casanave (2008) draws on Lave and Wenger's (1991) concept of *community of practice* to describe graduate academic literacy work as "participatory practice" and she goes on to argue that the major challenge for graduate students is not simply one of achieving proficiency in English, but one of "learning what it means to participate fully, not superficially, in an academic community of practice" (Casanave 2008: 27).

The thesis can be seen, therefore, as the culmination of a multitude of experiences through which students are socialized into the values and the ways of doing that are conventional to a given research community (although it should be admitted that the concept of a research community itself is problematic, particularly in multidisciplinary research contexts). Included within these values are notions of what the goals of research writing are and of reader expectations, and it has been found that less successful students differ from their more successful counterparts in their understandings of these values, and that their perceptions diverge markedly from those of their supervisors (Belcher 1994). Conversely, more successful supervisors display and make explicit the values and practices that are held by their community, and provide students with the language, skills, and opportunities that they need in order to become fuller participants (Duff 2010: 176).

San Miguel and Nelson (2007) conducted research into the expectations of a supervisor by looking, firstly, at two assignments written by L2 professional doctorate students, and, secondly, at the responses of the supervisor to those assignments. In the assignments, the students were required to use practice-based knowledge in order to solve real-world problems, and the task required them to frame the research. The finding was that the higher rated text of the two placed theoretical knowledge before action knowledge and was judged to be better framed.

Swales (2004: 122–38) presents a valuable overview of the range of case studies that have been conducted on individual doctoral students, and supervisors, in the years 1984–1997. He cites James (1984: 112) who writes, "students need help with what they find most difficult. What they find most difficult can only be discovered by observing them on the [writing] job." The difficulties can be linguistic (under- or over-complexity of sentences, vocabulary difficulties, poor referencing, underuse or overuse of metadiscourse, and so on) or rhetorical (writing for the wrong audience, assuming too much knowledge on the part of the reader, and so on), and subject supervisors are not always able to make explicit what the linguistic and rhetorical problems are, nor how students can overcome them.

Difficulties can also arise from epistemological and cultural differences. Cadman (1997) makes the point that L2 texts can be culturally inappropriate, as well as structurally inappropriate. She writes of the difficulty for L2 writers of constructing a suitable personal voice in the text, through evaluation and stance, and describes working with a Thai PhD student to cultivate a more authoritative voice in the writing, over a period of a year. During this period, the writer gradually moves from a concern with small details to an attention to the "bigger picture." Cadman also emphasizes the value, within this process, of reflexive writing in allowing students the opportunity to develop a more confident identity.

Phan Le Ha (2009) presents a fascinating account of the interaction between an Indonesian Master's student and her supervisor (the researcher herself, for whom Vietnamese is a first language) at an Australian university, in which both her own experiences of nurturing a writer's voice in English and those of her student are narrated. The account gives a powerful insight into the feelings of alienation L2 writers can experience and the inferiority complexes that are inculcated in them through rejection of their prior experiences and voices. Phan Le Ha and her student, Arianto, challenge the norms of the dominant discourse, and forge their own writing spaces in English. While not all L2 dissertation and thesis writers may choose the same routes as Phan Le Ha and Arianto, the struggles of these to achieve their own identities as academics in English are highly revelatory. This article is also representative of an approach to English for academic purposes known as "Critical EAP" (Benesch 2001; see also Starfield, this volume), which challenges the predominant norms and questions the concept of initiating students into disciplinary communities, with the concomitant assumption that the students must adapt to the values of the power holders (or gatekeepers).

Dong (1998) surveyed 169 post-graduate L2 writers and their thesis and dissertation supervisors in two US universities, and found that the L2 writers were at a disadvantage not only because of linguistic challenges but also because they lacked an adequate support network for their writing, compared to their NS counterparts. Although both groups of students had equal access to support resources, the L2 student writers did not make use of them in the same way. In spite of the fact that science students tend to work in teams, the L2 writers expressed strong feelings of isolation, which derived to varying degrees from the difficulties they found in communicating with those around them, the sociocultural divides and in some cases a sense that their perspectives were not valued.

A linguistic marker of identity expression in a thesis is the first person pronoun singular. John (2009) investigated writer identity in a corpus of applied linguistics MA dissertations, written by English as L2 writers, and showed how dissertation writers use the first person pronoun singular to establish different aspects of their identity and roles as thesis writers: as a person, as "Academic: Scholar," and as "Academic: Organizer." John examined the changes in use of first person pronouns across thesis drafts, and charted the move from a more personal starting point of their thesis to the projection of a more scholarly persona as academic in the final version of the dissertation.

Teaching

Specialist EAP writing support may be provided to dissertation/thesis writers before they begin the research process, during the process or when they are writing chapters of the thesis (in what many people term the "writing up" phase – though it should be noted that many thesis writers engage in writing throughout the research process). Where teaching is provided well in advance of the writing of thesis chapters, it is likely that the focus will fall on interim genres, such as "assigned writing for supervision sessions," the "extended research proposal" (the names used in different national and institutional contexts vary), and on writing articles for publication, and the course will prepare students for writing those genres. Paltridge (1997), for example, describes a short course delivered to doctoral students on writing research proposals, which consisted of three sessions. The emphasis here was on the texts that students needed to produce on their way towards writing the thesis.

Casanave and Hubbard (1992) conducted a survey of graduate faculty about what writing they required of first-year doctoral students, and found the following range of types of writing assigned: critical summaries, problem-solving, brief research papers, linguistic research papers, non-critical summaries, lab reports, literature reviews, and case studies. Given this plethora of writing types, Casanave and Hubbard make a case for discipline-specific writing instruction. They also make the point that writing increases in importance across the years of doctoral study, and that therefore writing support needs to be offered across the whole period of registration rather than being focussed on in the first year.

Allison et al. (1998) conducted interviews with supervisors and a survey of graduate students. They raise questions about how teachers should structure doctoral writing skills sessions. One question they pose is as to whether the content should be organized by dealing with the component parts of the thesis in sequential order. Such an approach would look at how to write an introduction, then the literature review, followed by sessions on the methods, results and discussion sections. Teaching guides such as Swales and Feak (2004), Weissberg and Buker (1990) and Bitchener (2010a) work sequentially through the stages of abstract, introduction, literature review, and so on, and focus on the linguistic features of each of these sections. Paltridge and Starfield (2007), in their guide for supervisors, acknowledge that abstracts are usually written last, by placing their chapter on abstracts after the "conclusions" chapter.

John Swales and Christine Feak have published three short textbooks looking at different sections of the IMRD thesis: the abstract (Swales and Feak 2009), the introduction (Feak and Swales 2011), and the literature review (Feak and Swales 2009). These are based on a genre approach to the sections and make use of samples of student writing for illustration. Both the books on the abstract and the introduction include chapters that focus on thesis writing, and in the chapter on abstract writing, the authors make it clear that abstracts are important in the North American context where examiners are asked to comment explicitly on the acceptability of the abstract. It is worth observing too that institutional and national requirements for the length of an abstract can vary considerably: Russian thesis abstracts (Swales and Feak 2009) are on average 5,600 words in length, while the University of Birmingham, UK, states that abstracts should be 200 words long.

The field of study, the methodology used and theoretical persuasion are "prime determinants of models of organization" (Johns and Swales 2002). Consequently, in a heterogeneous class of graduate students, it cannot be taken for granted that all students will write a thesis that follows the IMRD model. Even within a homogeneous group (students from the same discipline), there is a possibility of variation because of differences in methodological approaches used.

A further difficulty may be that, within a homogeneous group, students may be at different stages of their research, and teaching therefore needs to accommodate this range of development. Richards (1988) reports on an interactive needs analysis exercise, conducted as part of an intensive ESP thesis-writing program, in which students were asked to analyze exemplar texts (methods chapters, for example) and then work on a piece of writing that was relevant to them at that point in their research. Kwan (2008) made the point that writing a literature review, for example, is an iterative process, which takes place at various stages during doctoral studies, and it is possible therefore to approach the writing of a literature review at different levels of complexity, to suit the needs of students at varying levels of development.

Students are often not sure what the conventions are in their discipline, and a useful activity, where resources are available, is to ask the students to find examples of the types of dissertation that they are going to write. Furthermore, in many EAP contexts the writing support advisor has not written a thesis in the same subject, if he or she has written a thesis at all. In such contexts it is important that the adviser has access to examples for information about what is expected of theses in the disciplines that the students aspire to belong to, either by locating published texts on the internet or by asking supervisors to guide them to relevant examples.

Starfield (2003) describes the use of the Bunton/Swales and Feak thesis introduction three-move model with humanities and social sciences students in doctoral writing workshops. In these workshops, she asked the students to apply the model to a sample introduction taken from a history thesis. In applying the generic model to an authentic instance of a thesis introduction (the model did not fit neatly to the example, it should be noted), students became aware of a vocabulary and method for defining moves and also developed an understanding of the range of options available to them.

As indicated above, it is also important for students to find out about the expectations and values of their disciplinary community, and through classroom activities they can be encouraged to act as researchers into the practices of their communities (Johns 1997). The teaching of advanced academic literacy requires sensitivity towards the contexts in which writers develop their texts and this sensitivity can be nurtured through structured literacy research activities (Thompson 2005). Differences in the expectations that supervisors and students have about each other's roles and responsibilities can lead to problems in situations where the supervisors and students come from different cultural and educational backgrounds, but there can also be problems where the two parties share cultural backgrounds but still have different expectations (see Paltridge and Starfield 2007; Paltridge and Woodrow 2012). Doctoral writing workshops can address the nature of expectations through discussion between student participants of what they expect their supervisors to do and what they believe is the student's responsibility. Paltridge (2003: 87) provides a list of questions that can form the basis for discussion, including questions such as:

- Is it the student's or the supervisor's responsibility to select a promising research topic?
- Who assumes responsibility for the methodology and the content of the dissertation, the supervisor or the student?
- Should the supervisor assist in the actual writing of the dissertation if the student has difficulties or does the student have full responsibility for presentation of the dissertation, including grammar and spelling?

Paltridge reports that students generally have similar views to their supervisors on procedural issues such as arranging meetings, but diverge on the three questions shown above. After discussing the questions in a workshop, students can be asked to carry on the discussion with their supervisors, so that the expectations are made explicit.

Writing has tended to be perceived to be as an "autonomous" (Street 1984) set of skills that have to be learned, but Aitchison and Lee (2006) argue that supervisors and students need to recognize the role that writing plays in knowledge creation, and therefore its centrality in the research process. This point is also made forcefully by Murray (2011) who proposes that doctoral students need to write regularly throughout their period of study; she suggests a range of activities for developing greater ease in writing and a set of writing strategies. Aitchison and Lee (2006) stress the importance of viewing writing as a social activity and they discuss the value of setting up writing groups for doctoral students: group activities can lead to an enhanced sense of identity, readership and community.

Areas for Further Research

This chapter has looked at how theses and dissertations are organized and at what research has uncovered about the linguistic features of different parts of such texts. We have also considered the implications of this research for writing support and instruction in EAP contexts. It is clear that there is considerable variation between and within disciplines as regards what is conventional and what is appropriate, and that there is a need for much more research into such differences.

A major development in this field is the move towards electronic theses. In several countries, universities are requiring students to submit their thesis in both paper and electronic form, usually in PDF format. This makes access to authentic representative texts much easier than in the past. Researchers can now obtain electronic copies of theses for linguistic analysis from university libraries, and either work with the PDF version or convert the PDF files to a text format, for use with corpus analysis tools such as concordancers (e.g. WordSmith Tools or AntConc). It will still be necessary to consult subject specialist informants in order to gather information about the values of the discipline, and about the relationship of sub-disciplines to each other and to the parent discipline, but the widening of access to large quantities of empirical evidence will greatly assist research (and teaching, too, as Starfield 2003 demonstrates) in this area.

As shown above, there has been some investigation of the various types of writing that doctoral students are required to produce at different stages of their research. At the end of the first year, for example, students may need to produce an extended research proposal, or some draft chapters, for review by a university panel. Paltridge (1997) describes a course that he developed which focussed on the thesis proposal, and in which, *inter alia*, students looked at exemplar proposals written by previous students in order to determine the structure of such texts. Because such interim texts are not in the public domain, they are typically only available to researchers and instructors locally, but there is still a need for more research on such texts to be conducted within institutions and then reported at an international level.

There is also scope for much more interview and student tracking research into the experiences of L2 thesis writers. Bitchener and Basturkmen (2006: 14), reflecting on their interviews with students and supervisors, write:

> From the interview data, we also became aware of the need for future research to go beyond the mere identification of writing difficulties as they appear in the written text and identify the specific causes of these difficulties.

Engagement in discussions with the student writers and close observations of their interactions with their supervisors, their peers, and with other academics in their communities of practice promises therefore to illuminate our understanding not only of *what* student writers find difficulties with, but also of *why* these things are difficult.

REFERENCES

Aitchison, C. and Lee, A. (2006) Research writing: Problems and pedagogies. *Teaching in Higher Education* 11: 265–78.

Akindele, O. (2008) A critical analysis of the literature review section. *English for Specific Purposes World* 7(1) Accessed May 25, 2011 at http://www.esp-world.info/articles_20/doc/graduate_writing_site.pdf.

Allison, D., Cooley, L., Lewkowicz, J., and Nunan, D. (1998) Dissertation writing in action: The development of a dissertation writing support program for ESL graduate research students. *English for Specific Purposes* 17: 199–217.

Belcher, D. and Hirvela, A. (2005) Writing the qualitative dissertation: What motivates and sustains commitment to a fuzzy genre? *Journal of English for Academic Purposes* 4: 187–205.

Belcher, D. (1994) The apprenticeship approach to advanced academic literacy: Graduate students and their mentors. *English for Specific Purposes* 13: 23–34.

Benesch, S. (2001) *Critical English for Academic Purposes: Theory, Politics, and Practice*. Mahwah, NJ: Lawrence Erlbaum.

Bitchener, J. (2010a) *Writing an Applied Linguistics Thesis or Dissertation: A Guide to Presenting Empirical Research*. Basingstoke, UK: Palgrave Macmillan.

Bitchener, J. (2010b) *A Genre Approach to Understanding Empirically-Based Thesis Writing Expectations*. Wellington, New Zealand: Ako Aotearoa. Accessed May 26, 2011 at http://akoaotearoa.ac.nz/download/ng/file/group-3300/a-genre-approach-to-understanding-empirically-based-thesis-writing.pdf.

Bitchener, J., and Basturkmen, H. (2006) Perceptions of the difficulties of postgraduate L2 thesis students writing the discussion section. *Journal of English for Academic Purposes* 5: 4–18.

Bunton, D. (1999) The use of higher level metatext in PhD theses. *English for Specific Purposes* 18: S41–S56.

Bunton, D. (2002) Generic moves in PhD thesis introductions. In J. Flowerdew (ed.), *Academic Discourse*. 57–75. London: Longman.

Bunton, D. (2005) The structure of PhD conclusion chapters. *Journal of English for Academic Purposes* 4: 207–24.

Cadman, K. (1997) Thesis writing for international students: A question of identity? *English for Specific Purposes* 16: 3–14.

Casanave, C. P. (2010) Taking risks?: A case study of three doctoral students writing qualitative dissertations at an American university in Japan. *Journal of Second Language Writing* 19: 1–16.

Casanave, C. and Hubbard, P. (1992) The Writing Assignments and Writing Problems of Doctoral Students: Faculty Perceptions, Pedagogical Issues, and Needed Research. *English for Specific Purposes* 11: 33–49.

Casanave, C. P. and Li, X. (eds.) (2008) *Learning the Literacy Practices of Graduate School: Insiders' Reflections on Academic Enculturation*. Ann Arbor, MI: University of Michigan Press.

Charles, M. (2006) Phraseological patterns in reporting clauses used in citation: A corpus-based study of theses in two disciplines. *English for Specific Purposes* 25: 310–31.

Cooley, L. and Lewkowicz, J. (1995) The writing needs of graduate students at the University of Hong Kong. *Hong Kong Papers in Linguistics and Language Teaching* 18: 121–3.

Cooley, L. and Lewkowicz, J. (1997) Developing awareness of the rhetorical and linguistic conventions of writing a thesis in English: Addressing the needs of ESL/EFL postgraduate students. In A. Duszak (ed.), *Culture and Styles of Academic Discourse*. 113–40. Berlin: Mouton de Gruyter.

Dong, Y. R. (1998) Non-native graduate students' thesis/dissertation writing in science: Self-reports by students and their advisors from two US institutions. *English for Specific Purposes* 17: 369–90.

Dudley-Evans, T. (1994) Genre analysis: An approach to text analysis in ESP. In M. Coulthard (ed.), *Advances in Written Text Analysis*. 219–28. London: Routledge.

Duff, P. (2010) Language socialization into academic discourse communities. *Annual Review of Applied Linguistics* 30: 169–92.

Feak, C. B. and Swales, J. (2009) *Telling a Research Story. Writing a Literature Review*. Ann Arbor, MI: University of Michigan Press.

Feak, C. B. and Swales, J. (2011) *Creating Contexts: Writing Introductions Across Genres*. Ann Arbor, MI: University of Michigan Press.

Hyland, K. (2002) Activity and evaluation: Reporting practices in academic writing. In J. Flowerdew (ed.), *Academic Discourse*. 115–30. London: Longman.

Hyland, K. (2004) Disciplinary interactions: Metadiscourse in L2 postgraduate writing. *Journal of Second Language Writing* 13: 133–51.

James, K. (1984) The writing of theses by speakers of English as a foreign language. In R. Williams, J. Swales, and J. Kirkman (eds.), *Common Ground: Shared Interests in ESP and Communications Studies*. 99–113. Oxford: Pergamon.

John, S. (2009) The influence of revision on first person pronoun use in thesis writing. *Writing & Pedagogy* 1: 227–47.

Johns, A. (1997) *Text, Role and Context: Developing Academic Literacies*. Cambridge: Cambridge University Press.

Johns, A. and Swales, J. (2002) Literacy and disciplinary practices: Opening and closing perspectives. *Journal of English for Academic Purposes* 1: 13–28.

Kwan, B. (2006) The schematic structure of literature reviews in doctoral theses of applied linguistics. *English for Specific Purposes* 25: 30–55.

Kwan, B. (2008) The nexus of reading, writing and researching in the doctoral undertaking of humanities and social sciences: Implications for literature reviewing. *English for Specific Purposes* 27: 42–56.

Kwan, B. (2009) Reading in preparation for writing a PhD thesis: Case studies of experiences. *Journal of English for Academic Purposes* 8: 180–91.

Lave, J. and Wenger, E. (1991) *Situated Learning: Legitimate Peripheral Participation*. Cambridge: Cambridge University Press

Leki, I., Cumming, A., and Silva, T. (2008) *A Synthesis of Research on Second Language Writing in English*. New York: Routledge.

Murray, R. (2011) *How to Write a Thesis*. 3rd ed. Milton Keynes, UK: Open University Press.

Paltridge, B. (1997) Thesis and dissertation writing: Preparing ESL students for research. *English for Specific Purposes* 16: 61–70.

Paltridge, B. (2002) Thesis and dissertation writing: An examination of published advice and actual practice. *English for Specific Purposes* 21: 125–43.

Paltridge, B. (2003) Teaching thesis and dissertation writing. *Hong Kong Journal of Applied Linguistics* 8: 78–96.

Paltridge, B. (2012) Theses and dissertations in English for specific purposes. In C. Chapelle (ed.), *The Encyclopedia of Applied Linguistics*. Oxford: Wiley-Blackwell.

Paltridge, B. and Starfield, S. (2007) *Thesis and Dissertation Writing in a Second Language: A Handbook For Supervisors*. London: Routledge.

Paltridge, B. and Woodrow, L. (2012) Thesis and dissertation writing: Moving beyond the text. In R. Tang. (ed.), *Academic Writing in a Second or Foreign Language: Issues and Challenges Facing ESL/EFL Academic Writers in Higher Education Contexts*. 88–104. London: Continuum.

Petrić, B. (2007) Rhetorical functions of citations in high- and low-rated master's theses. *Journal of English for Academic Purposes* 6: 238–53.

Phan, L. H. (2009) Strategic, passionate, but academic: Am I allowed in my writing? *Journal of English for Academic Purposes* 8: 134–46.

Richards, R. (1988) Thesis/dissertation writing for EFL students: An ESP course design. *English for Specific Purposes* 7: 171–80.

Samraj, B. (2008) A discourse analysis of Master's theses across disciplines with a focus on introductions. *Journal of English for Academic Purposes* 7: 55–67.

San Miguel, C. and Nelson, C. (2007) Key writing challenges of practice-based doctorates. *Journal of English for Academic Purposes* 6: 71–86.

Scott, M. (2010) *WordSmith Tools, Version 5*. Liverpool, UK: Lexical Analysis Software.

Shaw, P. (1991) Science research students' composing processes. *English for Specific Purposes* 10: 189–206.

Starfield, S. (2003) The evolution of a thesis writing course for Arts and Social Science students: What can applied linguistics offer? *Hong Kong Journal of Applied Linguistics* 8: 137–54.

Starfield, S. (2010) Fortunate travellers: Learning from the multiliterate lives of doctoral students. In M. Walker and P. Thomson (eds.), *The Routledge Doctoral Supervisor's Companion*. 138–46. London: Routledge.

Starfield, S. and Ravelli, L. (2006) "The writing of this thesis was a process that I could not explore with the positivistic detachment of the classical sociologist": Self and structure in New Humanities research theses. *Journal of English for Academic Purposes* 5: 222–43.

Street, B. (1984) *Literacy in Theory and Practice*. Cambridge: Cambridge University Press.

Swales, J. M. (1990) *Genre Analysis: English in Academic and Research Settings*. Cambridge: Cambridge University Press.

Swales, J. (2004) *Research Genres: Explorations and Applications.* Cambridge: Cambridge University Press.

Swales, J. and Feak, C. B. (2004) *Academic Writing for Graduate Students.* 2nd ed. Ann Arbor, MI: University of Michigan Press.

Swales, J. and Feak, C. B. (2009) *Abstracts and the Writing of Abstracts.* Ann Arbor, MI: University of Michigan Press.

Thompson, P. (1999) Exploring the contexts of writing: Interview with PhD supervisors. In P. Thompson (ed.), *Issues in EAP Writing Research and Instruction.* 37–54. Reading, UK: Centre for Applied Language Studies, University of Reading.

Thompson, P. (2005) Points of focus and position: Intertextual reference in PhD theses. *Journal of English for Academic Purposes* 4: 307–23.

Thompson, P. (2009) Literature reviews in applied PhD theses: Evidence and problems. In K. Hyland and G. Diani (eds.), *Academic Evaluation and Review Genres.* 50–67. Basingstoke, UK: Palgrave Macmillan.

Turner, J. (2003) Writing a PhD in the contemporary humanities. *Hong Kong Journal of Applied Linguistics* 8: 34–53.

Weissberg, R. and Buker, S. (1990) *Writing up Research.* Englewood Cliffs, NJ: Prentice Hall.

16 English for Research Publication Purposes

JOHN FLOWERDEW

Introduction

Academic writing for research publication takes place around the globe, involving, according to a recent account, 5.5 million scholars, 2,000 publishers and 17,500 research/higher education institutions (Lillis and Curry 2010). A number of factors have come together to create this publishing phenomenon. First, with the rapid development of university education and research internationally, there are now more and more university faculty members and research students wishing to publish their findings. Second, as a result of the internationalization of research – facilitated by global communication networks supported by the internet and ease of international travel – universities are competing globally with each other to produce more and more research publications, a process which is encouraged by the establishment of international league tables comparing universities, with research output being an important metric. Third, as a result of the first two factors, international publication is becoming more and more often a requirement of doctoral or even master's degree graduation. Fourth and last, but by no means least, given that English is now widely accepted as the international language of research, there is a widely accepted lingua franca to facilitate this process.

As an indication of the preeminence of English in research, using statistics from Lillis and Curry (2010) again, out of the 66,166 academic periodicals included in *Ulrich's Periodicals Directory*, (2009) 67 percent use some or all English; and within the Institute for Scientific Information (ISI), which includes the "top" journals, more than 95 percent of natural science journals and 90 percent of social science journals are published in all or some English (Lillis and Curry 2010). Again,

The Handbook of English for Specific Purposes, First Edition.
Edited by Brian Paltridge and Sue Starfield.
© 2013 John Wiley & Sons, Inc. Published 2013 by John Wiley & Sons, Inc.

while a lot of this research is published by Anglophones, more and more is being published now by non-Anglophone scholars, or, rather, scholars who use English as their second, or professional, language, sometimes referred to as EAL (English as an additional language) writers.

To take just one example country where this is happening, Pérez-Llantada, Gibson, and Plo (2011) present the case of Spain. Pérez-Llantada et al. note that Spain, like many other countries, is increasingly impacted by the dominance of English. As one indicator of this, they note that there has been a decline in publication in Spanish language journals – from 5,309 articles in 1996 to 2,744 in 2006 – and a corresponding increase in English-language publications – from 19,820 papers in 1996 to 39,115 in 2006. Pérez-Llantada et al. adduce three reasons for this. First, and most important, is the Spanish academic reward system, which favors international publication. One of the criteria for promotion, for example, is publications in indexed journals and these are invariably published in English. Second, the increasing internationalization of teaching and research in Spain, has led to increased international academic exchange. Third, is the increasing amount of teaching that is conducted in English, as a result of student exchange programs, which require English as a lingua franca. The situation in Spain described by Pérez-Llantada et al. is not unlike that in many other countries.

There are tremendous benefits to this spread of English as the language of research. It means that scholars from all countries are able to access and publish in this international language. Ferguson (2007: 13) cites De Swaan's (2001) account of the impact of "external networks" in language spread:

> Languages . . . do not diminish in utility with use: on the contrary, the more speakers a language gains, the greater the potential number of interlocutors, the greater the production of texts, and the greater the utility of the language to all those already proficient in it.

So, extrapolating to research publication, the greater the number of scholars using English, the more research can be disseminated (to researchers who know English), and the more that research is disseminated in English, the more scholars will be encouraged to publish in English. The process is thus self-perpetuating. Ferguson takes the example of an academic journal *Angewandte Chemie*, which switched from publication in German to English. When the journal retitled itself as *Applied Chemistry*, there was a greater incentive for researchers to publish in English. Thus English is a self-perpetuating force; once it establishes a critical mass of users, more and more users are attracted to it.

Of course, there is a negative side to this: those scholars who do not have English will increasingly be excluded and those journals which cease to publish in particular languages will impoverish those languages in a process which Ferguson labels "domain loss" (see also Salager-Meyer 2008; Swales 1997; Tardy 2004). Furthermore, work not published in international English journals may be undervalued or ignored (a phenomenon referred to by Gibbs [1995] as "lost science") (see S. Cho 2004; Flowerdew 2001). And, finally, the Anglo-American discursive norms of journals may discriminate against the discursive norms of other languages (de Swaan 2001) and not accept what are perceived to be linguistic idiosyncrasies, or "non-standard" English (Ammon 2000: 112).

Inequalities in Academic Publishing

This brings us to consider the disparities within academic publishing. Within the international publishing "game" (Casanave 2002), there are various inequalities – Salager-Meyer (2008: 121) refers to "the stark disparities and inequities that exist in the world of scholarly publishing" – and various parameters have been applied to explain them. Importantly for this chapter, one disadvantage relates to language. Clearly, the Spanish scholars in Pérez-Llantada et al.'s example cited above are at a disadvantage vis-à-vis Anglophone scholars who will have acquired English as part of their upbringing, while Spanish scholars may have had only limited instruction in English. Within Kachru's (1992) model of the three concentric circles of English, Spain and other European countries, as well as China, Japan and the countries of Latin America, would be members of the outer circle, of those countries where English has only recently been introduced and does not have any historic tradition. Few people in these countries, historically, would be proficient in English. Countries in the expanding circle, those countries where English has a historic role – countries such as Hong Kong, India, Nigeria, Pakistan, Singapore – would likely find publication in English easier, English having perhaps already been established under the colonial regime. Those who would have least difficulty would be those for whom English is their native language, those from the inner circle countries, most notably Australia, Canada, Great Britain, and the United States.

Ferguson (2007: 20) uses a metaphor from economics, that of "location rent," to describe the disparity between Anglophone and EAL writers. Anglophone scholars, he argues, benefit from a resource, the production costs for which, they contribute very little to. EAL writers (and their governments and tax-payers who pay for their education), on the other hand, are required to spend more time and money acquiring this additional resource. Similarly, Van Parijs (2007) uses a different metaphor, describing Anglophone scholars as benefitting from a "free ride" when it comes to writing for publication. In addition to the cost of educating EAL writers, such writers require more time and money than their Anglophone counterparts in the actual act of writing. It is likely to take them longer to read and write, they may have to pay for editors and proofreaders and, other things being equal, the negotiating that they need to do with reviewers and editors is likely to be longer (Burrough-Boenisch 2003; Flowerdew 1999b; Lillis and Curry 2010). This is without mentioning the overlooked emotional burden that having to perform and be evaluated in an additional language carries with it (Flowerdew 2008).

Various surveys highlight this burden of having to write in a second language. Of the 585 Cantonese L1 academics in a survey I conducted (Flowerdew 1999a), over two-thirds felt that they were at a disadvantage compared with L1 writers in writing for publication. Similarly, Li's (2002) survey of mainland Chinese doctoral researchers discovered that almost 80 percent of these apprentice scholars felt themselves to be at a disadvantage. In a very recent study conducted by Ferguson, Pérez-Llantada, and Plo (2011), out of the 300 Spanish academics surveyed, 95 percent agreed that native speakers are at an advantage in international publishing.

In spite of the importance of this language disadvantage, some have argued that language is not the primary problem EAL scholars have in publication. In a study of reviewers' comments on submissions to *English for Specific Purposes*, Belcher (2007) has argued that language is not the major impediment to these writers. Instead, reviewers are more likely to mention a study's research design or literature review. Those submissions that are successful, Belcher argues, come from scholars who are willing to revise their articles and resubmit them, sometimes repeatedly, regardless of the language background of the writer. It needs to be borne in mind here, however, that submissions to *English for Specific Purposes* are likely to come from more proficient users of the English language than from scholars working in other, non-linguistic, fields.

One thing that seems to be true is that more and more EAL writers are publishing and becoming members of the editorial boards of international journals than was the case two or three decades ago. This is a point that has been made by Master (1999) with regard to papers published in *English for Specific Purposes* and by Swales (2004) with regard to *TESOL Quarterly*. Again, though, these are applied linguistics journals. Ferguson states that the bibliometric evidence is unclear on the success or otherwise of L2 writers, but that it does not support the argument that L2 scholars cannot succeed. He cites Wood (2001) who, based on data from *Nature* and *Science*, established that during one year (1997–8), 45.6 percent of writers were from L2 backgrounds. But then again, as Salager-Meyer, (2008) has noted, not all EAL writers are the same; some have had more privileges, such as living or studying in Anglophone countries, than others who have not benefitted in such a way. In the absence of statistical data on acceptance (and rejection) rates from international journals, the jury is still out on whether EAL writers suffer worse than L1 writers. Nevertheless, a warning from Hyland (2007: 87) needs to be heeded. Hyland writes that, "[in] a context where editors are overwhelmed with submissions and are often looking for reasons to reject manuscripts, non-standard language may serve as good a reason as any to justify this." In addition, this discussion of the success and failure rate of EAL writers fails to consider all of those scholars who never write for publication in English or who have given up doing so, because of language difficulties.

Another disadvantage that peripheral scholars have with regard to language – which, in fact, from a different perspective, might be considered an advantage and a privilege (Kramsch 1997) – is that they may be expected to write in two languages. As well as writing for publication in English, they may be expected to write for the local community in their first language. The pressures and dilemmas arising from such a situation are well brought out by Casanave (1998) in her study of Japanese scholars who return to Japan after doctoral study in the United States and by Shi (2002) in her study of the writing practices of Chinese scholars who have returned to China from the West.

Cutting across this language parameter of disadvantage is another parameter, that of the center and the periphery (Galtung 1971; Wallerstein 1974). Center and periphery is a model in political economy which claims that the countries in the "center" – the core industrial developed capitalist states focussed on capital-intensive industries – dominate and make dependent on them the "periphery" states – which act as mere purveyors of raw materials and producers of labour-intensive low quality goods. Although it is not impossible to move from a periphery situation to a center one, it is extremely difficult. In these terms, with regard to *English for research publication purposes* (ERPP), publication would take place unproblematically in the center countries, while it would be much more problematic in the periphery.

This dichotomy has been applied by Canagarajah (2002), himself a periphery scholar, in so far as he began his career in Jaffna, Sri Lanka (although he is now based in the United States). Based on his own experience and that of his colleagues in Jaffna, Canagarajah (1996, 2002) has described the many difficulties experienced by periphery scholars who want to publish in center journals. Periphery scholars may have difficulty not only with the English language. They may not have access to the latest books or journals; they may not have access to adequate, if any, research funding; they may have inadequate physical research facilities such as laboratories; and their university systems may not be structured in such a way as to encourage publication in international journals or even publication at all.

Another term used by some writers on academic publishing to refer to less privileged academics is that of "off-network" (Belcher 2007; Ferguson 2007; Swales 1987, 2004). This term draws attention to an important feature of successful international publication, the need for access to networks of people who can facilitate the process in order to act as a bridge between the center and the periphery (Lillis and Curry 2010). Issues concerning periphery, or off-network, scholars have been investigated in a range of geographical contexts including Hong Kong (see below), Korea (D. W. Cho 2009; S. Cho 2004), Poland (Duszak and Lewkowicz 2008), PRC (see below), Venezuela (Salager-Meyer 2008), Sudan (El Malik and Nesi 2008) and countries on the periphery of the European Union (Lillis and Curry 2010, see below).

All of the disadvantages for EAL writers, which have been outlined above, give rise to the need for measures to alleviate them. It is here that there is an important role for the English for specific purposes (ESP) researcher and practitioner. This can take the form of researching the specific nature of the favored target genre of the research community, the research article (RA); in investigating the social situation in which scholarly writers find themselves; and in applying the findings of this research to pedagogic intervention. These issues of research and pedagogy will take up the remainder of this chapter.

Approaches to Theory in ERPP

Discourse analysis

Much work has been done in ESP in describing the genre of the RA in rhetorical and linguistic terms. (Space precludes a discussion here of other members of the "genre set" that go with the RA, such as conference abstracts, conference presentations, submission letters, referee's reports, editorial letters, etc., see Räisänen 2002). This work, which can be broadly referred to as discourse analysis, has been conducted under the labels of genre analysis, corpus-based discourse analysis, and contrastive rhetoric (also referred to as intercultural rhetoric), among others. The relevance of this work to ERPP is that the more knowledge that there is available about the structure of the RA the more effective will be ESP practitioners in any pedagogical intervention that they might undertake in assisting writers – EAL writers, in particular, but also L1 writers – in writing effectively for publication. Other chapters in this volume review this work more thoroughly e.g. Paltridge this volume; Parkinson this volume), but studies specifically focussed on the RA can be briefly mentioned here.

Research on genre has shown how academic language is subject to systematic generic and disciplinary variation (e.g. Bhatia 1993; Hyland 2000; Swales 1990). Particularly worthy of note in the context of this chapter is the huge amount of work that, following Swales (1990), has been devoted to the research article. Swales' model for research article introductions, for example, has been further investigated by e.g. Anthony (1999), Nwogu (1990), Paltridge (1994), and Samraj (2002). Further work has focussed on other parts of the RA, e.g. discussion sections (e. g. Dudley-Evans 1994; Holmes 1997; Lewin and Fine 1996; Peacock 2002), results sections (e.g. Brett 1994; Bruce 2009; Kanoksilapathan 2007; Williams 1999; Yang and Allison 2003), and abstracts (e.g. Hyland and Tse 2005; Lorés Sanz 2004; Salager-Meyer 1992; Santos 1996). A main focus of this work is on schematic structure, the prototypical structural patterns that make up the genre and its parts, but work has also been done on lexico-grammar, how the parts (moves) are realized linguistically. Other features of the RA that have been investigated include metadiscourse (e.g. Hyland 1998), politeness (e.g. Myers 1989 and citation conventions (e.g. Dahl 2004; Hyland 1999, Thompson and Tribble 2001), among others.

Work on the RA has also been done within the contrastive rhetoric paradigm (e.g. Ahmad 1997; Burgess 2002; Dahl 2004; Lee 2000; Melander 1998; Melander, Swales, and Fredrickson 1997). The idea here is that writers from one language background may transfer features of the RA in their L1 to their writing in English. Knowledge of these likely areas of transfer can be focussed upon in any pedagogic intervention. Interestingly, contrastive rhetoric has been used to investigate some other more occluded professional academic genres (see e.g. Connor and Mauranen 1999; Yakhontova 2002) which space does not allow for any sort of detailed treatment of here.

Social constructivism and situated learning theory

In terms of how individuals actually go about writing for publication – the writing process, as opposed to the product, which is the focus of discourse analysis – the prevalent theoretical constructs for ERPP research are those of social constructivism (Bruffee 1986) and situated learning (Lave and Wenger 1991). These interrelated theories view writing as much broader than just "knowing various language structures and discourse strategies" (Grabe and Kaplan 1996). Writing is viewed by these theories as a situated social practice, involving various networks and communities. Individuals write in order to become members of communities of researchers and maintain relations with those communities. In order to become proficient ERPP practitioners, individuals need to learn not just the mechanics of writing, but how to gain access to and maintain relations with the relevant networks, to know what is acceptable rhetorically within those communities. As Hyland (2007: 88) emphasizes, "learning to write for a professional peer audience is the process by which novices are socialized into the academic community; it is the recognized route to insider status."

For this reason, the work of Lave and Wenger (1991) is much invoked in ERPP. Lave and Wenger (1991) developed the notion of "community of practice" as referring to a group of people who share an interest, craft, and/or profession. In sharing information and experiences, individuals within the group learn from each other. Professional communities of scholars involved in research and publication in particular fields of specialization are good examples of communities of practice (e.g. Casanave 2002). When someone joins a group, they initially spend time on the periphery in a sort of apprenticeship, perhaps performing some of the simpler tasks until they are ready to become full members. This process is described as "legitimate peripheral participation" (Lave and Wenger 1991). Learning to write for publication invariably takes the form of legitimate peripheral participation, because novices learn by a process of doing, by writing articles, submitting them for publication, and receiving feedback from the editors and reviewers. Communities of practice, by definition, vary in their make-up and their conventions. This means that what is expected in terms of writing in one discipline is likely to be different in another; this is referred to as its "situated" characteristic.

A social constructivist approach to research into writing for publication focusses on aspects of the publishing process such as peer review, negotiation with editors and reviewers and acceptance/rejection of papers. The work of Gosden in Japan was groundbreaking in investigating some of the social issues involved in publishing from an EAL perspective. In a first paper, Gosden (1992) surveyed editors of center science journals with regard to their attitudes towards non-native speaker (NNS) contributions. He found that the editors felt that their NNS contributors demonstrated a lack of clarity in their results sections, problematic research methodology, longer writing and submission time than L1 writers and problems stemming from what was perceived as their isolated situation, which included unfamiliarity with the target journal requirements, failure to review the literature adequately and failure to contextualize studies within the context of other work. In a second paper, Gosden (1995) focussed on the textual revisions involved in the writing of successful research articles by NNS novice Japanese researchers. In this case, "success" was judged from the processes of peer review, negotiation, revision, and eventual acceptance for publication of research articles in English-language scientific journals. In a third paper, Gosden (2003) analyzed referees' comments on scientific research articles. In this study, he noted the strong inter-personal dimension of reviewers' comments, with two thirds of the comments in his corpus of comments focussed on "interactional deficiencies" of the manuscripts under consideration. Gosden's conclusion was that novice researchers need to be made aware of "the need to interpret appropriately the motivation behind referees' comments" (Gosden 2003: 87).

Sociocultural factors of RA production such as those investigated by Gosden and others (see below) draw attention to the important role that power plays in this enterprize. As early as 1990, Swales (1990: 102) eloquently drew attention to this power factor, as follows:

> Despite an objective 'empiricist' repertoire, we are far away from a world in which power, allegiance and self-esteem play no part, however much they may seem absent from the frigid surface of RA discourse. And yet we find the research article, this key product of the knowledge-manufacture industry, to be a remarkable phenomenon, so cunningly engineered by rhetorical machining that it somehow still gives an impression of being but a simple description of relatively untransmuted raw material.

Another writer to emphasize the power factor in academic writing, including ERPP, is Casanave (2002: 30), who refers to all forms of academic literacy as "deeply social and political" and describes how EAL writers need to "wrestle with power-infused and entrenched academic cultures" (2002: 181). Casanave highlights the difficulties of EAL writers who write for publication in Chapter 7 of her book, "Writing Games" (Casanave 2000), pointing to the struggle EAL writers have in mastering what she refers to as "the rhetorical and linguistic resources needed for a successful publication," on the one hand, and "how to respond to, negotiate and compromise with reviewers, editors and co-authors," on the other.

Overlapping with Gosden's work in Japan was my own work in Hong Kong, with Cantonese L1 writers. Over an extended period, I investigated how Hong Kong Cantonese-L1 academics go about writing for publication in international journals. The first study published in this project (Flowerdew 1999a) was a quantitative survey focussing on perceptions, problems, and strategies employed in writing for international publication. Following the quantitative survey, I conducted a qualitative interview study with scholars across the disciplines, again focussing on perceptions, problems, and strategies. The next study (Flowerdew 2000) was a single case of an EAL scholar in mass communication from Hong Kong and his experience in publishing a scholarly article in an international refereed journal on his return from doctoral study in the United States. The investigation was presented as "a contribution to the important study of what it means to be a non-Anglophone researcher seeking international publication in English, but living and researching in a non-Anglophone country" (2000: 127, abstract). Following on from the case study was another interview study, this time with editors of journals in the fields of applied linguistics and language study (Flowerdew 2001), asking them about their perceptions of contributions from Hong Kong, in particular, and Asian and other periphery countries in general. In later work (Flowerdew 2007, 2008), I discussed the disadvantages experienced by EAL writers and invoked Goffman's notion of stigma to understand their position (Flowerdew 2008). Casanave (2008) critiqued this view, arguing against what she refers to as a "labeling" effect and I responded (Flowerdew 2009), arguing that my goal had been to articulate the position I see EAL writers potentially finding themselves in and suggesting some possible ways of resisting this positioning.

Broadly continuing my case study approach (Flowerdew 2000), Li published three separate cases of doctoral science students in Mainland China writing for publication. In the first of these, Li (2006a) focussed on a doctoral student in computer science and this student's work on alternative versions of a paper aimed at separate Chinese and international audiences. In the second of her studies to be reported here, Li (2006b), considered the publication efforts of a doctoral student of physics working towards international publication, demonstrating how the participant's writing processes and publication success were affected by the power relationships between the writer and his supervisors, on the one hand, and the writer and journal editors, on the other. This paper was contextualized within legitimate peripheral participation theory. In her third study, this time with a student of chemistry, Li (2007) again invoked community of practice theory. Using the student's process logs, his developing text, his bulletin board system message exchanges and post-hoc interviews, Li showed how the apprentice writer went about developing the first draft of a paper. This study demonstrated the complex interactions between the participant's engagement with the local research community, the laboratory data, his own experience and practice of writing research articles , and the global specialist research community.

In a later study, working together on data collected during Li's earlier studies, Flowerdew and Li (2007) showed how the doctoral science students focussed on in Li's earlier studies used copy and pasting strategies based on published work to develop their own writing for publication. As well as analyzing the students' strategies, the article considered the participants' justification for their practices and asked whether or not their practices constituted plagiarism (see also Starfield this volume).

In a final article based on Li's group of doctoral research students, Li and Flowerdew (2007) focussed on "shapers" (Burrough-Boenisch 2003), people who provided language correction for the doctoral science students involved in Li's studies. Three main sources of English-language correction assistance were identified: supervisors, peers, and language professionals.

In subsequent work, Flowerdew and Li (2009) and Li and Flowerdew (2007), addressed the issue of writing in English and Chinese on the part of established Hong Kong and Mainland scholars in the humanities and social sciences (HSS). The idea driving this research was to test the commonly held view that more work is published locally in these so-called "soft" disciplines (Lillis and Curry 2010) and to consider the tension at work between English and Chinese publication. In the first of these two studies, 20 academics across a range of HSS disciplines at an elite research-based university in China were interviewed. This study found that for the most part, in spite of official encouragement to publish in English, including financial inducements, for a range of reasons, these scholars preferred to publish in Chinese. The second of these studies involved interviews with 15 Hong Kong counterparts of the Mainland Chinese HSS scholars. The findings showed that these scholars were more motivated to publish in English both for institutionally driven reasons and through personal motivation. However, some of these Hong Kong scholars also publish in Chinese for the purpose of serving their target audiences at the local/regional level.

Overlapping with Flowerdew and Li, but using a similar case study approach, is the work of Lillis and Curry. Focussing on 50 education and psychology scholars writing for publication in 12 institutions over a period of eight years in Hungary, Portugal, Slovakia, and Spain, Lillis and Curry used an ethnographic "text-histories" approach to investigate ERPP practices in these non-Anglophone, "periphery" countries. Lillis and Curry's findings were published in a series of articles and later brought together in a book (Lillis and Curry 2010).

In common with Flowerdew and Li, Lillis and Curry (2010) view ERPP from a social practice perspective and contextualize such practice within globalization theory, with an emphasis on local practice and networked activity. Their book is contextualized within what Lillis and Curry refer to as "the politics of academic text production," positioned within the broader context of international knowledge production. Lillis and Curry emphasize how the role of English is sustained by institutional and national systems and their incentive and reward systems, which favor "international" publication (which, as they point out, is synonymous with publication in English). They demonstrate how the ERPP practices of the participants depend very much on "networked activity" and the role of local, national, and international networks in obtaining the resources necessary for successful publication in Anglophone "center" journals. Publication is viewed as very much a joint activity, rather than an individual one. Lillis and Curry (2010: 61) write that:

> Evidence of the significance of different kinds of network activity – in which scholars engage locally and transnationally – calls into question the predominant focus on individual competence in EAP (English for academic purposes) and academic writing research and pedagogy more widely.

In line with their view of ERRP as networked activity, Lillis and Curry examine in detail the role of "literacy brokers," people who assist in the task of successful publication. These may be friends, academic colleagues, editors, translators, or proofreaders. In the conclusion to their book, Lillis and Curry argue for a "de-centring" of the current model of academic publishing, with efforts needed to promote national journals, innovations in the practices of center journals in favor of non-Anglophone periphery scholars, and publishing practices which view research not as market-driven but as freely exchanged.

Methods used in ERPP research

In terms of methods, because it is problem-driven, as opposed to theory-driven, ERPP research employs a whole range of methods. In an earlier publication (Flowerdew 2005), I created a diagram to display the methods that I used in investigating ERPP in Hong Kong, as in Figure 16.1. The four circles of the figure represent the different foci of investigation. Starting in the top left quartile and going in a clockwise direction, these foci involve: (1) finding out what apprentice and/or experienced writers think about the process of writing for publication; (2) finding out what goes on in their minds when they are writing; (3) analyzing the

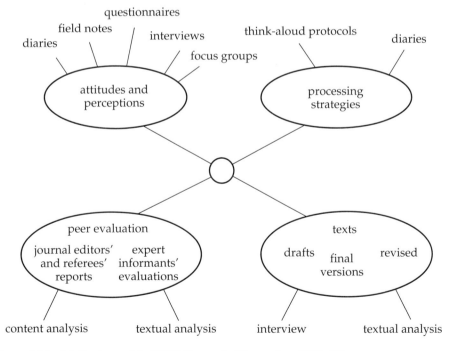

Figure 16.1   Methods used in ERPP Research (Flowerdew 2005: 68).

different versions of texts written by scholarly writers; and (4) obtaining and analyzing peer evaluation in the form of editors' and reviewers' reports and soliciting evaluations of manuscripts by specialist informants. Each of these foci is associated with particular research methods, as shown in the figure.

Within the extant research on ERPP, by far the most commonly used of those methods identified here is discourse/text analysis of one form or another (see above for references). With regard to the social dimension of ERPP, a very popular method has been the interview (e.g. S. Cho 2004; Giannoni 2008; Huang 2010; Pérez Llantada et al. 2011, also the work of Curry, Flowerdew, and of Li and of Lillis reviewed above). Another method has been to collect personal reflections on the writing experiences of bilingual writers (Aitchison, Kamler, and Lee 2010; Belcher and Connor 2001).

The ERPP Curriculum

Having reviewed the research base of ERPP, we now need to consider how the research may be applied to pedagogy. What should go into a course designed to prepare novice writers, especially EAL writers, in writing for publication? Kwan (2010) refers to these two aspects of what she calls "the discursive task" as, on the one hand, "communicating one's research through an RA" and, on the other hand, "communicating with gate-keepers about the RA" (see Figure 16.2 for Kwan's overall framework). While agreeing with this broad division, it should be noted that the two dimensions are interlinked: while creating the document, the writer will need to bear the needs of the gatekeepers in mind, and, in dealing with the gatekeepers, the writer will need to do this through the medium of language.

In communicating one's research through the RA, Kwan sets out particular competencies that need to be mastered. These include familiarity with the prototypical schematic structure of the genre and its parts (which are subject to disciplinary variation and variation across journals); command of discipline-specific citation language "to advance various rhetorical goals;" and metadiscourse "that signals one's degree of commitment to statements made" (2010: 57). These particular skills are in addition to generic writing skills such as "argumentation, coherence-building, and abstracting" (2010: 58).

A notable publication with regard to Kwan's first dimension, "communicating one's research through an RA," is a case study designed to use corpora in developing ERRP skills (Lee and Swales 2006). Lee and Swales (2006) had a heterogeneous group of graduate students at the University of Michigan create their personal corpora of research articles specific to their particular disciplines. These corpora were used as a resource for working on the writing required for the RA preparation on their higher degree programs. As noted elsewhere (Flowerdew and Li 2007), an issue that has to be confronted with this type of application is where to draw the borderline between reusing typical phraseological patterns, on the one hand, and copying longer sections of texts extracted from the corpus – a case of plagiarism – on the other (see Flowerdew and Li 2007, Pecorari 2003, 2006). Cargill

The discursive task

> communicating one's research through an RA
>
> > command of schematic structure
> >
> > command of discipline specific citation language and metadiscourse
> >
> > command of generic writing skills (e.g argumentation, coherence)
>
> communicating with gate-keepers about the RA
>
> > command of occluded genres
>
> strategic research conception
>
> > command of disciplinary academic rigour
> >
> > ability to find a "niche"
> >
> > ability to relate appropriately to the international community
>
> strategic management of research and publishing
>
> > manage time cycle
> >
> > ensure required amount of publications
> >
> > know appropriate journals

Figure 16.2   Kwan's model of the discursive task (based on Kwan 2010)

and O'Connor's (2009) handbook on research writing, uses a similar procedure to that reported by Lee and Swales.

With regard to "communication with gate-keepers," Kwan emphasizes that this involves what Swales (1996) refers to as "occluded" genres, which can be "difficult to handle" (Kwan 2010: 58). Reviewer comments tend to be indirect and can be misleading to the reader (Flowerdew and Dudley-Evans 2002; Gosden 2003). There is thus a need to develop the ability to interpret these documents, on the one hand, and to develop "discursive tactics to carry out revisions accordingly" (2010: 58), on the other.

In addition to the two dimensions discussed thus far, Kwan's competence framework for writing for publication has two further elements, both of which merit attention. The first of these is "strategic research conception." Here, the writer needs to ensure that, first, the research is conceived and conducted with appropriate disciplinary academic rigor, and that, second, it finds a niche in the literature in conformity with the "zeitgeist" (Berkenkotter and Huckin 1995) of the field (the spirit of the time), fitting into what elsewhere Bazerman (1980: 657–8) refers to as "the conversations of the discipline." Moreover, according to Kwan, researchers need to consider the relevance of their research to the international community. This can be particularly difficult for off-network scholars. Indeed, off-network scholars in humanities and social science fields, in particular, who may focus their research on local matters, need to consider how they can make their publications appeal to an international readership. It might also be added here that these researchers need to be able to decide what is appropriate for international publication and what is more appropriate for a local readership (Flowerdew and Li 2009; Li and Flowerdew 2007; Lillis and Curry 2010). Further-more, publishability will depend on the "fit" between a given article and the targeted journal.

The second additional competence identified by Kwan she refers to as "strate-gic management of research and publishing." Here, novice researchers need to consider how to manage their research and publication in such a way as to fit in with assessment schedules and the type and amount of publications expected by their institution at various academic ranks. To do this, these young researchers need to appreciate the length of time required to produce a manuscript and for it to go through the review process. They also need to know which journals to submit their work to and which journals to redirect their work to in the case of rejection. Indeed, it might be added that they need to know that rejection is the norm for most submissions and that initial rejection does not preclude resubmission.

A further dimension to Kwan's model she refers to as "competence in publish-ing the thesis-in-progress." This concerns publications produced during the doctorate, a requirement for which is becoming more and more common. One strategy here is to structure the thesis as a series of articles. Where this is not the case, then special skills are required in converting the thesis to articles and vice versa.

One publication possibility not envisioned by Kwan is that of joint-publication with a supervisor. In some science disciplines this is in fact the norm, where papers are published by teams of people. Here, competence is required in dividing up the work, in deciding who will do the writing, and so on.

Conclusion and Future Directions

This chapter has noted the preeminence of English as the international language of research and publication and the advantages and disadvantages of this situa-tion. The chapter has highlighted the disadvantages faced by EAL writers in particular, and periphery writers in general, of writing in English for publication. It has been argued that, in spite of its negative side, these disadvantages provide an important space for ESP researchers and practitioners. The chapter has reviewed the main approaches to research in ERPP, with discourse analysis and social constructivism/situated learning being the main theoretical approaches and a whole range of methods being used to pursue this research. In a final section, the chapter has considered the issue of pedagogy and suggested how an ERPP curriculum might look.

In the remaining space, some consideration will be given to the issue of disadvantage, and to how the situation might be improved, bearing in mind the role of ESP in this enterprise. One suggestion has been to discard the NS/NSS acronym and replace it with *L1 and L2 writers*, *EAL writers*, *international writers* (which to me is ambiguous) or to not make any distinction. This is a point made by many of the editors in Flowerdew's (2001) interview study. As Canagarajah (2006) has argued, in the wider scheme of things, the NS/NNS demarcation is already breaking down. English has become a contact language for both intra- and international relationships, not just in research and publication. In addition, for many writers, even if English is not their mother tongue, it is their L1 as far as their professional literacy practices are concerned. Taking away the labels will also reduce the stigma (Flowerdew 2008) attaching to EAL writers. An important step in this respect would be for journals to stop requiring writers to have their papers vetted by a "native-speaker" before submission. As Swales (2004) and Hyland (2006) have both argued, the degree of experience may be more important than the question of L1 and L2. Swales (2004), accordingly, suggests referring to "junior" and "senior" scholars.

Another suggestion is to open the door to different varieties of English in international publication. It is worth considering why it is that *English as a Lingua Franca* (ELF) (Nickerson this volume), a hybrid variety of English, is becoming more and more accepted in universities internationally, especially in spoken contexts, but has not become accepted as far as publication is concerned. The reason for this must be that writing is more conventional than speech, perhaps because it is easier for gatekeepers – publishers and editors in the case of ERPP – to control it. Ferguson (2007: 33) conceives of a move towards ELF occurring for ERPP in the longer term. He describes such a process as "the de-anglicization of English," glossing this process as:

> allowing bilingual EIL [English as an international language] authors to identify themselves, and be identified, as authoritative users of their own lingua franca variety (with its own peculiarities – see Ammon 2000) as opposed to imperfect writers of a standard British or American standard English.

As has been argued elsewhere (Flowerdew 2008; Flowerdew and Li 2009), there is a role for corpora here – collections of language written by international writers which are considered acceptable by the scientific community as a whole:

> In the long run . . . just as spoken corpora may help to characterize ELF in verbal communication (e.g. House 2003; Mauranen 2003; Seidlhofer 2004), large corpora for the various disciplines written by EAL writers might help to identify what is acceptable in terms of intelligibility in written academic English and what is not (Flowerdew 2008: 84).

Whether or not these perhaps utopian ideals come to pass, there will undoubtedly still be an important role for ESP in ERPP. The increase in international publication in English is unlikely to diminish and the difficulties experienced by EAL writers will remain. So we must ask the question, is the ESP profession prepared? The answer is that it is probably not. It can be argued that writing for publication should be an integral part of scholarly formation. However, not many universities offer such courses. Where such courses are offered, they may be run by individual academic departments or by language support centers. A well-prepared cadre of ESP practitioners would be in a position to claim this territory. However, where language support centers run such courses, those teaching on such courses usually do not have the sort of specialist training that this chapter has made clear is needed for such a task. As Hyland (2008) has written, this is a field where the research base is ahead of pedagogical practice. There is an urgent need, therefore, for ESP practitioners to up their game. This is a field where there is an important need and it is an area that offers unique challenges and opportunities for the ESP profession to demonstrate its value. It is time for ESP practitioners to respond.

REFERENCES

Ahmad, U. K. (1997) Research article introductions in Malay: Rhetoric in an emerging research community. In A. Duszak (ed.), *Culture and Styles of Academic Discourse*. 273–301. Berlin: Mouton de Gruyter.

Aitchison, C., Kamler, B., and Lee, A. (eds.) (2010) *Publishing Pedagogies for the Doctorate and Beyond*. London: Routledge.

Ammon, U. (2000) Towards more fairness in international English: Linguistic rights of non-native speakers? In R. Phillipson (ed.), *Rights to Language, Equity and Power in Education*. 111–16. Mahwah, NJ: Lawrence Erlbaum.

Anthony, L. (1999) Writing research article introductions in software engineering: How accurate is a standard model? *Transactions on Professional Communication* 42: 38–46.

Bazerman, C. (1980) A relationship between reading and writing: The conversational model. *College English* 41: 656–61.

Belcher, D. (2007) Seeking acceptance in an English only research world. *Journal of Second Language Writing* 16: 1–22.

Belcher, D. and Connor, U. (eds.) (2001) *Reflections on Multiliterate Lives*. Clevedon, UK: Multilingual Matters.

Berkenkotter, C. and Huckin, T. (1995) *Genre Knowledge in Disciplinary Communication: Cognition/Culture/Power*. Hillsdale, NJ: Lawrence Erlbaum.

Bhatia, V. K. (1993) *Analysing Genre: Language Use in Professional Settings*. London: Longman.

Brett, P. (1994) A genre analysis of the results section of sociology articles. *English for Specific Purposes* 13: 47–59.

Bruce, I. (2009) A genre analysis of the results sections in sociology and organic chemistry articles. *English for Specific Purposes* 28: 105–24.

Bruffee, K. A. (1986) Social construction, language, and the authority of knowledge: A bibliographic essay. *College English* 48: 773–90.

Burgess, S. (2002) Packed houses and intimate gatherings: Audience and rhetorical structure. In J. Flowerdew (ed.), *Academic Discourse*. 196–215. London: Pearson Education.

Burrough-Boenisch, J. (2003) Shapers of published non-native speaker research articles. *Journal of Second Language Writing* 12: 223–43.

Canagarajah, S. A. (1996) Nondiscursive requirements in academic publishing, material resources of periphery scholars, and the politics of knowledge production. *Written Communication* 13: 435–72.

Canagarajah, S. A.(2002) *A Geopolitics of Academic Writing*. Pittsburgh, PA: University of Pittsburgh Press.

Canagarajah, S. A. (2006) TESOL at 40: What are the issues? *TESOL Quarterly* 40: 9–34.

Cargill, M. and O'Connor, P. (2009) *Writing Scientific Research Articles: Strategy and Steps*. Oxford: Wiley-Blackwell.

Casanave, C. P. (1998) Transitions: The balancing act of bilingual academics. *Journal of Second Language Writing* 7: 175–204.

Casanave, C. P. (2002) *Writing Games: Multicultural Case Studies of Academic Literacy Practices in Higher Education*. Mahwah, NJ: Lawrence Erlbaum.

Casanave, C. P. (2008) The stigmatizing effect of Goffman's stigma label: A response to John Flowerdew. *Journal of English for Academic Purposes* 7: 264–67.

Cho, D. W. (2009) Science journal writing in an EFL context: The case of Korea. *English for Specific Purposes* 28: 230–39.

Cho, S. (2004) Challenges of entering discourse communities by publishing in English: Perspectives of non-native speaking doctoral students. *Journal of Language, Identity, and Education* 3: 47–72.

Connor, U. and Mauranen, A. (1999) Linguistic Analysis of Grant Proposals: European Union Research Grants. *English for Specific Purposes* 18: 47–62.

Dahl, T. (2004) Pragmatics of discourse. *Journal of Pragmatics* 36: 1807–1825.

De Swaan, A. (2001) English in the social sciences. In U. Ammon (ed.), *The Dominance of English as a Language of Science*. 71–83. Berlin: Mouton de Gruyter.

Dudley-Evans, T. (1994) Genre analysis: An approach to text analysis for ESP. In M. Coulthard (ed.), *Advances in Written Text Analysis*. 219–228. London: Routledge.

Duszak, A. and Lewkowicz, J. (2008) Publishing academic texts in English: A Polish perspective. *Journal of English for Academic Purposes* 7: 108–20.

El Malik, A. T. and Nesi, H. (2008). Publishing research in a second language: The case of Sudanese contributors to international medical journals. *Journal of English for Academic Purposes* 7: 87–96.

Ferguson, G. (2007) The global spread of English, scientific communication and ESP: Questions of equity, access and domain loss. *Ibérica* 13: 7–38.

Ferguson, G., Pérez-Llantada, C., and Plo, R. (2011) English as an international language of scientific publication: A study of attitudes. *World Englishes* 30: 41–59.

Flowerdew, J. (1999a) Writing for scholarly publication in English: The case of Hong Kong. *Journal of Second Language Writing* 8: 123–45.

Flowerdew, J. (1999b) Problems in writing for scholarly publication in English: The case of Hong Kong. *Journal of Second Language Writing* 8: 243–64.

Flowerdew, J. (2000) Discourse community, legitimate peripheral participation, and the non- native English-speaking scholar. *TESOL Quarterly* 34: 127–50.

Flowerdew, J. (2001) Attitudes of journal editors to non-native speaker contributions. *TESOL Quarterly* 35: 121–50.

Flowerdew, J. (2005) A multimethod approach to research into processes of scholarly writing for publication. In P. K. Matsuda and T. Silva (eds.), *Second Language Writing Research: Perspectives on the Process of Knowledge Construction*. 65–77. Mahwah, NJ: Lawrence Erlbaum.

Flowerdew, J. (2007) The non-Anglophone scholar on the periphery of scholarly communication. *AILA Review* 20: 14–27.

Flowerdew, J. (2008) Scholarly writers who use English as an additional language: What can Goffman's *"Stigma"* tell us? *Journal of English for Academic Purposes* 7: 77–86.

Flowerdew, J. (2009) Goffman's stigma and EAL writers: The author responds to Casanave. *Journal of English for Academic Purposes* 8: 69–72.

Flowerdew, J. and Dudley-Evans, T. (2002) Genre analysis of editorial letters to international journal contributors. *Applied Linguistics* 23: 463–89.

Flowerdew, J. and Li, Y. (2007) Language re-use among Chinese apprentice scientists writing for publication. *Applied Linguistics* 28: 440–65.

Flowerdew, J. and Li, Y. (2009) English or Chinese? The trade-off between local and international publication among Chinese academics in the humanities and social sciences. *Journal of Second Language Writing* 18: 17–29.

Galtung, J. (1971) A structural theory of imperialism. *Journal of Peace Research* 8: 81–117.

Giannoni, D. S. (2008) Medical writing at the periphery: The case of Italian journal editorials. *Journal of English for Academic Purposes* 7: 97–107.

Gibbs, W. W. (1995) Trends in scientific communication: Lost science in the third world. *Scientific American* 273: 76–83.

Gosden, H. (1992) Research writing and NNSs: From the editors. *Journal of Second Language Writing* 1: 123–39.

Gosden, H. (1995) Success in research article writing and revision: A social-constructionist perspective. *English for Specific Purposes* 13: 37–57.

Gosden, H. (2003) Why not give us the full story? Functions of referees' comments in peer reviews of scientific research papers. *Journal of English for Academic Purposes* 2: 87–101.

Grabe, W. and Kaplan, R. B. (1996) *Theory and Practice of Writing*. London: Longman.

Holmes, R. (1997) Genre analysis, and the social sciences: An investigation of the structure of research article discussion sections in three disciplines. *English for Specific Purposes* 16: 321–37.

House, J. (2003) English as a lingua franca: A threat to multilingualism. *Journal of Sociolinguistics* 7: 624–30.

Huang, J. C. (2010) Publishing and learning writing for publication in English: Perspectives of NNES PHD students in science. *Journal of English for Academic Purposes* 9: 33–44.

Hyland, K. (1998) Persuasion and context: The pragmatics of academic metadiscourse. *Journal of Pragmatics* 30: 437–55.

Hyland, K. (1999) Academic attribution: Citation and the construction of disciplinary knowledge. *Applied Linguistics* 20: 341–67.

Hyland, K. (2000) *Disciplinary Discourses: Social Interactions in Academic Writing*. London: Longman

Hyland, K. (2006) The "other" English: Thoughts on EAP and academic writing. *The European English Messenger* 15: 34–38.

Hyland, K. (2007) English for professional academic purposes: Writing for scholarly publication. In D. Belcher (ed.), *English for Specific Purposes in Theory and Practice*. 17–38. Ann Arbor, MI: University of Michigan Press.

Hyland, K. and Tse, P. (2005) *Evaluative that* constructions: Signaling stance in research abstracts. *Functions of Language* 12: 39–64.

Kachru, B. (1992) *The Other Tongue: English across Cultures*. Urbana, IL: University of Illinois Press.

Kanoksilapathan, B. (2007) Rhetorical moves in biochemistry research articles. In D. Biber, U. Connor, and T. A. Upton (eds.), *Discourse on the Move: Using Corpus Analysis to Describe Discourse Structure*. 73–119. Amsterdam: John Benjamins.

Kramsch, C. (1997) The Privilege of the non-native speaker. *PMLA* 112: 359–69.

Kwan, B. S. C. (2010) An investigation of instruction in research publishing in doctoral programs: The Hong Kong case. *Higher Education* 59: 55–68.

Lave, J. and Wenger, E. (1991) *Situated Learning: Legitimate Peripheral Participation*. Cambridge: Cambridge University Press.

Lee, D. and Swales, J. (2006) A corpus-based EAP course for NNS doctoral students: Moving from available specialized corpora to self-compiled corpora. *English for Specific Purposes* 25: 56–75.

Lee, S. (2000) Contrastive rhetorical study on Korean and English research paper introductions. *Pan-Pacific Association of Applied Linguistics* 4: 316–36.

Lewin, B. A. and Fine, J. (1996) The writing of research texts: Genre analysis and its applications. In G. Rijlaarsdam, H. van den Bergh, and M. Couzijn (eds.), *Theories, Models and Methodology in Writing Research*. 423–44. Amsterdam: Amsterdam University Press,

Li, Y. (2006a) Negotiating knowledge contribution to multiple discourse communities: A doctoral student of computer science writing for publication, *Journal of Second Language Writing* 15: 159–78.

Li, Y. (2006b) A doctoral student of physics writing for publication: A sociopolitically-oriented case study. *English for Specific Purposes* 25: 456–78.

Li, Y. (2007) Apprentice scholarly writing in a community of practice: An intraview of an NNES graduate student writing a research article. *TESOL Quarterly* 41: 55–79.

Li, Y. and Flowerdew, J. (2007) Shaping Chinese novice scientists' manuscripts for publication. *Journal of Second Language Writing* 16: 100–117.

Lillis, T. M. and Curry, M. J. (2010) *Academic Writing in a Global Context: The Politics and Practices of Publishing in English*. London: Routledge.

Lorés-Sanz, R. (2004) On RA abstracts: From rhetorical structure to thematic organisation. *English for Specific Purposes* 23: 280–302.

Master, P. (1999) Editorial. *English for Specific Purposes* 18: 102–4.

Mauranen, A. (2003). The corpus of English as lingua franca in academic settings. *TESOL Quarterly* 37: 513–27.

Melander, B. (1998) Culture or genre? Issues in the interpretation of cross-cultural differences in scientific papers. In I. Fortanet, S. Posteguillo, J. C. Palmer, and J. F. Coll, (eds.), *Genre Studies in English for Academic Purposes*. 211–26. Castello de la Plana, Spain: Publicacions de la Universitat Jaume I

Melander, B., Swales, J. M., and Fredrickson, K. M. (1997) Journal abstracts from three academic fields in the United States and Sweden: National or disciplinary proclivities? In A. Duszak, (ed.), *Culture and Styles of Academic Discourse*. 251–72. Berlin: Mouton de Gruyter.

Myers, G. (1989) The pragmatics of politeness in scientific articles. *Applied Linguistics* 10: 1–35.

Nwogu, K. N. (1990) *Discourse Variation in Medical Texts: Schema, Theme and Cohesion in Professional and Journalistic Accounts*. Monographs in Systematic Linguistics. Nottingham, UK: University of Nottingham.

Paltridge, B. (1994) Genre analysis and the identification of textual boundaries. *Applied Linguistics* 15: 288–99.

Peacock, M. (2002) Communicative moves in the discussion section of research articles. *System* 30: 479–97.

Pecorari, D. (2003) Good and original: Plagiarism and patchwriting in academic second-language writing. *Journal of Second Language Writing* 12: 317–45.

Pecorari, D. (2006) Visible and occluded citation features in postgraduate second-language writing. *English for Specific Purposes* 25: 4–29.

Pérez–Llantada, C., Gibson, F., and Plo, R. (2011) You don't say what you know, only what you can": The perceptions and practices of senior Spanish academics regarding research dissemination in English. *English for Specific Purposes* 30: 18–30.

Räisänen, C. (2002) The conference forum: A system of interrelated genres and discursive practices. In E. Ventola, C. Shalom and S. Thompson (eds.), *The Language of Conferencing*. 69–93. Frankfurt: Peter Lang.

Salager-Meyer, F. (1992) A text-type and move analysis study of verb tense and modality distribution in medical English abstracts. *English for Specific Purposes* 11: 93–113.

Salager-Meyer, F. (2008) Scientific publishing in developing countries: Challenges for the future. *Journal of English for Academic Purposes* 7: 121–32.

Samraj, B. (2002) Introductions in research articles: Variations across disciplines. *English for Specific Purposes* 21: 1–17.

Santos, M. B. D. (1996) The textual organization of research paper abstracts in applied linguistics. *Text* 16: 481–99.

Seidlhofer, B. (2004) Research perspectives on teaching English as a lingua franca. *Annual Review of Applied Linguistics* 24: 209–39.

Shi, L. (2002) How Western-trained Chinese TESOL professionals publish in their home environment. *TESOL Quarterly* 36: 625–34.

Swales, J. M. (1987) Utilizing the literatures in teaching the research paper. *TESOL Quarterly* 21: 41–68.

Swales, J. M. (1990) *Genre Analysis: English in Academic and Research Settings*. Cambridge: Cambridge University Press.

Swales, J. M. (1996) Occluded genres in the academy: The case of the submission letter. In E. Ventola and A. Mauranen (eds.), *Academic Writing: Intercultural and Textual Issues*. 45–58. Amsterdam: John Benjamins.

Swales, J. M. (1997) English as *Tyrannosaurus rex*. *World Englishes* 16: 373–82.

Swales, J. M. (2004) *Research Genres: Exploration and Applications*. Cambridge: Cambridge University Press.

Tardy, C. M. (2004) The role of English in scientific communication: Lingua franca or *Tyrannosaurus rex*? *Journal of English for Academic Purposes* 3: 247–69.

Thompson, P. and Tribble, C. (2001) Looking at citations: Using corpora in English for academic purposes. *Language Learning & Technology* 5: 91–105.

Ulrich's Periodicals Directory 2009. Accessed June 8, 2011 at http://www.ulrichsweb.com.

Van Parijs, P. (2007) Tackling the Anglophones' free ride: Fair linguistic cooperation with a global lingua franca. *AILA Review* 20: 72–87.

Wallerstein, I. (1974) *The Modern World-System: 1. Capitalist Agriculture and the Origins of the European World Economy in the 16th Century*. New York: Academic Press.

Williams, I. A. (1999) Results sections of medical research articles: Analysis of rhetorical categories for pedagogical purposes. *English for Specific Purposes* 18: 347–66.

Wood, A. (2001) International scientific English: The language of research

scientists around the world. In J.
Flowerdew and M. Peacock (eds.),
*Research Perspectives on English for
Academic Purposes*. 71–3. Cambridge:
Cambridge University Press

Yakhontova, T. (2002) "Selling or telling"?
The issue of cultural variation in
research genres. In J. Flowerdew (ed.),
Academic Discourse. 216–32. London and
New York: Longman.

Yang, R. and Allison, D. (2003) Research
articles in applied linguistics: Moving
from results to conclusions. *English for
Specific Purposes* 22: 365–85.

Part III ESP and Pedagogy

This section of the *Handbook* discusses issues that relate specifically to teaching and learning in English for specific purposes (ESP) settings. The main topics discussed are needs analysis and curriculum development, ESP and genre, ESP and assessment, and technology and ESP teaching and learning. Many of the books on ESP that are aimed at classroom teachers discuss methodology in relation to ESP teaching (e.g. Basturkmen 2006, 2010; Dudley-Evans and St John 1998; Master and Brinton 1998). There is also however a research literature on these topics that is discussed by each of the authors in this section of the book. Researchers in the area of ESP have moved from the view that ESP teaching is fundamentally the same no matter the context (Hutchinson and Waters 1987) to the view that each ESP situation needs to be examined in its own terms (Cheng 2011; Swales 1985). The social context of each ESP class is specific, as are the learning goals and objectives, the choice of materials and activities, the methodologies that are appropriate to the learners and their learning, as well as the ways in which the learning will be assessed (Cheng 2011). The use of language is also specific to the particular genres that the students need to be able to participate in (Hyland 2011), as are the "perceived needs and imagined futures" of our learners (Belcher 2006: 133).

In her chapter on needs analysis and curriculum development, Lynne Flowerdew outlines the history of needs analysis and what it means for curriculum development in ESP. She describes sources and methods of needs analysis, then discusses needs in relation to teaching English for academic purposes, English for occupational purposes, and English in the workplace. The chapter on genre and ESP by Brian Paltridge discusses language and discourse approaches to analyzing specific purpose genres as well as multimodality in specific purpose genres. The notion of genre as social action (Miller 1984) is given special attention, as are ways

The Handbook of English for Specific Purposes, First Edition.
Edited by Brian Paltridge and Sue Starfield.
© 2013 John Wiley & Sons, Inc. Published 2013 by John Wiley & Sons, Inc.

of narrowing the gap between text and context (Lillis 2008) in ESP genre research. The teaching and learning of specific purpose genres is then discussed and future directions for ESP genre studies are proposed.

In the chapter on ESP and assessment Dan Douglas discusses the theory and practice of assessment in ESP, then examines specific areas of learning, in particular, English for academic purposes, English for employment purposes, which include English for international aviation, Business English, English for court interpreters, and Health and Medical English, and, finally, English testing for immigration and asylum purposes. The chapter by Joel Bloch on technology and ESP discusses the use of technology in ESP classes, technology as a tool for language learning as well as ethical issues in relation to the use of technology in teaching and learning.

REFERENCES

Basturkmen, H. (2006) *Ideas and Options in English for Specific Purposes*. Mahwah, NJ: Lawrence Erlbaum.

Basturkmen, H. (2010) *Developing Courses in English for Specific Purposes*. Basingstoke, UK: Palgrave Macmillan.

Belcher, D. (2006) English for specific purposes: Teaching to perceived needs and imagined futures in worlds of work, study, and everyday life. *TESOL Quarterly* 40: 133–56.

Cheng, A. (2011) ESP classroom-based research: Basic considerations and future research questions. In D. Belcher, A. M. Johns, and B. Paltridge (eds.), *New Directions in English for Specific Purposes Research*. 44–72. Ann Arbor, MI: University of Michigan Press.

Dudley-Evans, T. and St John, M. J. (1998) *Developments in English for Specific Purposes: A Multi-Disciplinary Approach*. Cambridge: Cambridge University Press.

Hutchinson, T. and Waters, A. (1987) *English for Specific Purposes: A Learning-Centred Approach*. Cambridge: Cambridge University Press.

Hyland, K. (2011) Disciplinary specificity: Discourse, context and ESP. In D. Belcher, A. M. Johns, and B. Paltridge (eds.), *New Directions in English for Specific Purposes Research*. 6–24. Ann Arbor, MI: University of Michigan Press.

Lillis, T. (2008) Ethnography as method, methodology, and "deep theorizing." *Written Communication* 25: 353–88.

Master, P. and Brinton, D. (1998) (eds.), *New Ways in English for Specific Purposes*. Alexandria, VA: TESOL.

Miller, C. R. (1984) Genre as social action. *Quarterly Journal of Speech* 70: 151–67. Reprinted in Aviva Freedman and Peter Medway (eds.) (1994), *Genre and the New Rhetoric*. 23–42. London: Taylor & Francis.

Swales, J. M. (1985) The role of the textbook in EAP writing research. *English for Specific Purposes* 14: 3–18.

17 Needs Analysis and Curriculum Development in ESP

LYNNE FLOWERDEW

Introduction

Needs analysis, carried out to establish the "what" and the "how" of a course, is the first stage in ESP course development, followed by curriculum design, materials selection, methodology, assessment, and evaluation. However, these stages should not be seen as separate, proceeding in a linear fashion. Rather, as noted by Dudley-Evans and St John (1998), they are interdependent overlapping activities in a cyclical process. This conceptual distinction is neatly encapsulated by the diagrams in Figure 17.1 from Dudley-Evans and St John (1998: 121) showing how needs analysis is often ongoing, feeding back into various stages.

A broad, multi-faceted definition of *needs analysis* is provided by Hyland (2006: 73):

> *Needs analysis* refers to the techniques for collecting and assessing information relevant to course design: it is the means of establishing the *how* and *what* of a course. It is a continuous process, since we modify our teaching as we come to learn more about our students, and in this way it actually shades into *evaluation* – the means of establishing the effectiveness of a course. Needs is actually an umbrella term that embraces many aspects, incorporating learners' goals and backgrounds, their language proficiencies, their reasons for taking the course, their teaching and learning preferences, and the situations they will need to communicate in. Needs can involve what learners know, don't know or want to know, and can be collected and analyzed in a variety of ways.

The Handbook of English for Specific Purposes, First Edition.
Edited by Brian Paltridge and Sue Starfield.
© 2013 John Wiley & Sons, Inc. Published 2013 by John Wiley & Sons, Inc.

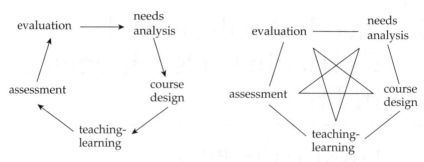

Figure 17.1   Linear vs. cyclical processes of needs analysis (Dudley-Evans and St John 1998: 121).

Having established the nature and the role of needs analysis in the overall course development process, I now review the different approaches needs analyses have embraced since the coming-of-age of English for specific purposes (ESP).

Needs analysis in ESP has a long history and is constantly evolving and redefining itself. Before the 1970s, needs analyses were based on teacher intuitions and sometimes informal analyses of students' needs, as noted by West (1994) in his landmark state-of-the-art article. It was in the 1970s that needs analysis first entered the literature on ESP as a formal concept and during this decade was largely defined in terms of the *target situation analysis*, (TSA), what learners are required to do with the foreign or second language in the target situation. Moreover, as West (1994) points out, needs analyses have a basis, either explicitly or implicitly, in theory (McDonough 1984), and also in principle, "The type of information sought during a needs analysis is usually closely related to the approach to teaching and learning and to syllabus design followed by the analysts" (Robinson 1991: 11–12). The concept of needs analysis, hand-in-hand with an underlying theory, was first established by the Council of Europe with their model for describing the language proficiency of adults whose jobs entailed working in different countries in, what was then, the European Economic Community. With a view to ensuring some degree of standardization across languages and countries, a semantically based model drawing on Wilkins' (1976) "notional-functional" syllabus design was proposed (Richterich and Chancerel 1977). This focus on functions culminated in Munby's (1978) communicative syllabus design, an ambitious undertaking to draw up a profile of communicative needs underpinned by Hymes' (1971) notion of communicative competence. This type of needs analysis is related to the skills-based approach; while an ESP syllabus might be defined at the macro-level in terms of the four traditional skills, for example, oral skills for business, the actual content of the course would be expressed by functions such as persuading, negotiating, and so on.

Richterich, and Chancerel (1997) put a particular emphasis on *present situation analysis* (PSA). A present situation analysis draws attention to the gap between what students are able to do with language at the beginning of the course and what they need to do at the end of the course. This is sometimes referred to as their "lacks." The *present situation analysis* also encompasses other aspects pertaining to the prevailing situation, including:

- personal information about the learners: factors which may affect the way they learn such as previous learning experiences, cultural information, reasons for attending the course and expectations of it and attitude to English;
- information about the language teaching environment (e.g. resources, administration matters).

Thus, broadly speaking, whereas the *target situation analysis* is concerned with "needs," the *present situation analysis* addresses learners' "lacks" and "wants," three aspects addressed at length in Hutchinson and Waters (1987) and also in Bruce's (2011) chapter on needs analysis. As Widdowson (1981) points out, while target needs are seen as goal-oriented, learner needs are more process-oriented when they refer to what the learner has to do to acquire the language. Another consideration concerns whether courses should be "wide-angled" or "narrow-angled," although as Basturkmen (2010) notes these two aspects should be seen on a continuum. For example, to take the case of Business English, a course focussing on broad academic skills encompassing many sub-fields such as marketing and accounting would fall at the "wide-angled" end of the continuum whereas a course on English for accountants would be relatively "narrow-angled." While both Hutchinson and Waters (1987) and Widdowson (1983) espoused a "wide-angle" approach to the curriculum, arguing that language and skills should be taught through a variety of topics, one reason being that students may find a "narrow-angle" approach demotivating, arguments in favor of a "narrow-angle" approach are put forward by Johns and Dudley-Evans (1991). A greater focus on the learner in needs analyses gave rise to the "negotiated" syllabus, which, as Brindley (1989) points out, can involve accommodation and compromise regarding not only what is to be learnt but also taking into account students' preferred ways of learning and cognitive style.

Hutchinson and Waters (1987) also formulate the *present situation analysis* in terms of the potential and constraints of the learning situation, that is, external factors that may include the resources and materials available and the prevailing attitude or culture. This more contextual, social, aspect of the language-teaching environment is referred to as a "means analysis" by Holliday (1994). What seems to be a key issue in discussion of the *target situation analysis* and *present situation analysis* concerns at what point they are considered in the whole needs analysis process vis-à-vis one another. Although Munby (1978) views the *present situation analysis* as a set of constraints (rather than in terms of its potential to be exploited) impinging on syllabus design including cultural, sociopolitical, logistical, administrative, psycho-pedagogic, and methodological factors, he considers them as something of an afterthought after the *target situation analysis* has been conducted. McDonough (1984), on the other hand, sees the *present situation analysis*, which involves "fundamental variables" specific to each individual teaching situation, as a prerequisite consideration to the *target situation analysis*, and in fact, Swales (1988) takes to task syllabus designers who procrastinate and postpone as late as possible dealing with the constraints associated with the *present situation analysis*. More recently, though, consideration of constraints has assumed more importance (see the four case studies in ESP course development in Basturkmen 2010). On a practical note, Robinson (1991: 9) observes, "one is likely to seek and find information relating to both the TSA and PSA simultaneously. Thus needs analysis may be seen as a combination of TSA and PSA."

This functional orientation to needs was a radical departure from the prevailing thinking at the time, which was to base student needs on a register analysis of ESP texts associated with a structural syllabus. Barber's (1985) "lexicostatistical" analysis of scientific prose is a prime example of this approach with its attention paid to grammatical structures such as the forms and use of the passive.

However, both the functional and register analysis approaches to needs have been criticized on various grounds. Long (2005), in his seminal publication on second language needs analysis, makes the point that syllabi grounded in notional-functional needs still relied, as before, on the intuitions of applied linguists and language teachers rather than domain specialists and tended to result in synthetic syllabi in which the target language items were presented as itemized lists. A failing of Munby's model was that its detailed specification of communicative events for a given participant contained no specification of the actual language forms realizing specific needs (Schutz and Derwing 1981). Neither did functional syllabi take account of empirical data. While the register analysis approach did provide somewhat sparse linguistic data on the target situation, little attempt was made to correlate grammatical findings with different sections of text and their respective rhetorical purposes or to seek advice from "specialist informants," as in later genre-analytic approaches (Swales 2004).

On account of the above failings, Long (2005) proposed task-based needs analyses as the unit of analysis for the following reasons. Job descriptions, which are formulated by domain experts on the background knowledge, performance standards, and tasks required, provide a more reliable source of data than those produced by language teachers and applied linguists. Task-based needs analyses reflect the dynamic qualities of the target discourse, thus revealing more than static, product-oriented text-based analyses. Whereas synthetic syllabi tend to be the outcome of needs analyses organized around functions, task-based needs analyses promote a more holistic analytical syllabus (see Johnson 2009 for detailed discussion on types of syllabi).

In the mid-1980s needs analyses based on samples of texts to inform writing syllabi progressed from a focus on register to a focus on rhetoric, in particular looking at the discourse of EST, English for science and technology, (see Trimble 1985). In the 1990s the focus shifted to a more genre-analytic perspective of the target discourses, embodying the concept of situated tasks (see Jordan 1997: 228–31 for an overview of register, discourse, and genre analysis). With needs articulated in terms of genres situated within the wider discourse communities in which they are produced and enacted, the ethnographic dimension of needs analysis received greater attention. As summarized in Hyland (2006: 66), an ethnographically oriented needs analysis seeks to achieve the following:

- Offer a comprehensive, detailed and "thick" description (Geertz 1973).
- Portray an insider's perspective, which gives precedence to the meaning of the event or situation to participants.
- Provide an account grounded in data collected from multiple sources that develops a conceptual framework.

The socio-rhetorical genre-analytic and more ethnographic approaches to needs analysis (see Jasso-Aguilar 2005) then began to embrace a more critical perspective, especially with regard to writing in the academy, influenced by the academic literacies (Lea and Street 1998) and critical EAP (Benesch 2001) movements. Both pose challenges to traditional needs analyses, as summarized by Starfield (2007: 883):

> The development of students' writing needs to be seen within its broader institutional setting, in terms of the dominant social and discursive practices that maintain and reproduce authority and power rather than as solely located within students themselves. Whereas traditional needs analysis tends to transform academic genres into "abstract, anonymous structures occurring anytime anywhere" (Prior 1995: 55), academic literacies approaches allow us to understand the complex situatedness and particularity of each classroom (Casanave 1995). Critical EAP (Benesch 2001) further challenges needs analysis approaches by arguing that within specific social contexts, students can exercise their right to challenge dominant discourses and unilateral socialization into preexisting sets of expectations.

Johns and Makalela (2011) give a brief history of needs assessment in ESP, tracing its development from a focus on "objective" needs to its more recent critical ethnographic stance serving to illuminate how the social contexts, expectations and intentions of all stakeholders have a bearing on the needs analysis process.

Sources and Methods

The next question to address is what sources and methods are used to collect data in needs analyses for ESP (see Long (ed.) 2005 for a thorough discussion and bibliography of needs analysis studies). While not aimed specifically at ESP, Long's account can be taken as representative of defining needs in ESP following his contention that "Instead of a one-size-fits-all approach, it is more defensible to view every course as involving specific purposes, the difference in each case being simply the precision with which it is possible to identify current or future uses of the L2" (2005: 10). Long cites the following as sources of information: published and unpublished literature, learners, teachers and applied linguists, domain experts, and triangulated sources (comparison of a range of data sources).

As for methods, Long (2005) notes that both inductive and deductive procedures (Berwick 1989) are used. The former includes expert intuitions, participant and non-participant observation, and unstructured interviews, while the latter involves surveys and questionnaires, structured interviews and, less commonly, criterion-referenced performance tests. Of interest is Long's comment that "Use of interviews is widely reported in needs analyses in ESP" (2005: 37). While not referring specifically to ESP, Long, citing Lincoln and Guba (1985), states that unstructured interviews are appropriate when the interviewer *"does not know what he or she doesn't know* and must therefore rely on the respondent to tell him or her." As the ESP teacher is more often than not the "non-knower," unstructured interviews with domain specialists would seem a good method to use initially for deriving categories for follow-up survey questionnaires or structured interviews.

Other methods for needs analyses in ESP could largely be seen as designed to collect ethnographically oriented information to gain an insider's view of the ESP situation. These would include detailed, longitudinal observations of the setting, focus group discussions, and analyses of participants' diaries and journals, in addition to the more quantitative data collection methods (see Brown 2009, for a discussion of qualitative vs. quantitative methods). The main criticism leveled against ethnographic methods, though, is that, while a rich understanding may be gleaned of what is specific to a particular context, the results may not be generalizable to other ESP settings. Ethnographic analyses can also usefully be supplemented by text-based analyses of the target genres. Corpus-based methodologies can help in this respect as they allow for analysis of large quantities of text (cf Biber 2006; Gavioli 2005), thereby providing a valid means of distinguishing between different EAP/ESP registers (see Bruce 2011 for a detailed discussion on these methods).

Moreover, as Hyland (2006: 68) notes, validity (an accurate reflection of the features being studied) and reliability (a consistent interpretation of the features) in needs analysis procedures can be achieved in three main ways:

Triangulation. Conclusions are developed using a range of data sources, research methods or investigators.
Prolonged engagement. The use of repeated observation and collection of sufficient data over a period of time.
Participant verification. The analysis is discussed with participants and its "reality" verified by them.

A helpful representation of aspects feeding into ESP curriculum development is given in Basturkmen (2010: 143), see Figure 17.2. While the "visible element" is the curriculum, this rests on a "below the surface" bedrock of needs analysis and investigations of specialist discourse, the latter often considered as being part of the needs analysis (see also Bruce 2011 who proposes a similar framework based on three interrelated stages).

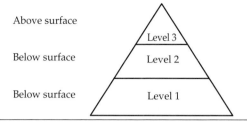

Above surface — Level 3

Below surface — Level 2

Below surface — Level 1

Level 1: Analyzing needs

Considerations

Situation analysis: What tasks are involved in the work or study area and what are the standards for their performance? Can the tasks be divided into sub-tasks?

What type of needs to investigate (for example, objective and/or subjective, immediate/long-term, skills and/or tasks)?

Which language-based skills or tasks do the students find difficult?

What is the nature of the students' difficulties in these language-based skills or tasks (for example, linguistic, conceptual, cultural)?

Level 2: Investigating specialist discourse

Considerations

Which linguistic forms and features to investigate (for example, those the students are weak in or unaware of, those members of the community of practice stress as important)?

What data to collect (for example, do relevant literature, descriptions, and corpora already exist or does primary data need to be collected)?

What approach to use in the investigation (for example, ethnography and/or text analysis)?

What primary data to collect (texts, marked scripts of students' writing, observations, self-reports, such as interviews)?

How to analyze the texts/discourse from the target community of practice or discipline (for example, whole or part of the texts, for specific features)?

How to devise pedagogical descriptions of discourse in the specialist area?

Level 3: Determining the curriculum

Considerations

How to focus on the course (for example, wide- or narrow-angled)

How to deliver the course (for example, web-based, classes, workshops, on-site or off-site)?

What units to include in the syllabus and how to sequence them (for example, genres, features of spoken discourse, conceptual content, easy to difficult, immediate to less immediate needs)?

How to evaluate learning (for example, with reference to the final or way-stage criteria or performance objectives used in the community of practice)?

What materials to develop and what types of tasks to include (for example, pedagogical descriptions of discourse and tasks that make use of activities of the work or study area)?

Figure 17.2 Needs analysis and curriculum development. Basturkmen, H. (2010: 143) *Developing Courses in English for Specific Purposes.* Basingstoke, UK: reproduced with permission of Palgrave Macmillan.

Needs Analysis in English for Academic Purposes (EAP)

Reports of various EAP-oriented needs analyses can be found in Jordan (1997) and, more recently, Hyland (2006). Needs analyses conducted in the academy usually take a skills-based approach at the macro-level and will be discussed from this perspective; for example, Paltridge et al. (2009) discuss needs specifically in relation to academic writing, which has been the focus of the majority of needs analyses conducted in the academy. Reading, listening to lectures, and participating in seminars and discussions figure far less in the literature. Below, needs analyses are discussed from the standpoint of major developments in the field with reference to specific programs and published textbooks.

Early EAP syllabi for writing were often derived from the material writer's own intuitive conception of needs supported by research studies on analyses of the target domain. Another observation is that the syllabus was not automatically determined by findings from the needs analysis (Hutchinson and Waters 1987). A similar point was made by Swales (1978) who stated that teaching syllabi need not necessarily reflect the priorities accorded to different skills in the academy. While Swales notes that the needs of science and engineering students at the University of Libya could be ranked in decreasing order of importance as *reading*, *listening*, *writing*, and *speaking*, given that students were exposed to receptive skills through their textbook material and lectures, he decided to focus on writing instead. In preparing the book, *Writing Scientific English*, Swales consulted the work of Herbert (1965) and Barber (1985) referred to earlier, for the grammatical structures to include in the syllabus based on register analysis. The treatment of some structures within a rhetorical perspective, such as definitions, presages the work of Trimble (1985) on rhetorical functions in EST. The general approach of Swales and Feak's (1994) *Academic Writing for Graduate Students* is also rhetorical, evolving, as stated by the writers, out of teaching experience and research.

Academic writing can also be based on needs derived from corpus linguistic studies, as evidenced by some of the tasks in Swales and Feak's (2000) later genre-based volume on research writing. For example, in their chapter on writing a literature review, explicit mention is made to the corpus research of Hyland (1999) and Marco (2000), which serves as needs analysis findings for addressing academic attribution and complex prepositional noun phrases respectively. Another ESP practitioner who draws on corpus data to formulate *product*-oriented needs is Bloch (2010) through research on a corpus of journal articles to determine the types and patterning of reporting verbs as rhetorical devices for inclusion in an EAP writing program.

A key ethnographic study is that by Prior (1995) who carried out a longitudinal, triangulated study on students' writing and professors' responses in graduate seminars. Prior's increasingly detailed research methodology explored how discourse and knowledge are dialogically constructed through an examination of the intellectual and social history of classroom interaction. Swales and Feak's volume

(2000) can also be considered as partly ethnographically motivated as they asked their students to act as ethnographers of their own situation by having them conduct mini-analyses of the language and discourse, very much in the spirit of Johns' (1997) socio-rhetorical approach to writing in the academy. Another ethnographic study is that by Chin (1994: 464) of a post-graduate journalism course. In addition to analyzing field notes, samples of student writing and transcribed audiotaped interviews with informants, Chin also examined the allocation of space and material resources in the department, deriving a "critical rereading of the department as a context for writing."

Chin's "critical rereading" of the situation heralds the work of Benesch (2001: 107–8) who problematizes the concept of needs, arguing as follows:

> The use of *needs analysis* to describe a tool for gathering data about institutional expectations is problematic for several reasons. . . . First, it conflates external requirements and students' desires as if they were congruent, not a possible area of study. Second, it hides the ideological battles that go on in academic life around curricular decision-making by highlighting only the final outcome of those charged decisions. . . . Third, it supports a notion of education as needs fulfillment, based on a theory of cultural deprivation . . .

For the above reasons, Benesch proposes, in addition to consideration of learners' *needs*, *wants*, and *lacks* as proposed in Hutchinson and Waters (1987: 108), a "rights analysis" for EAP writing: "Rights analysis is a theoretical tool for EAP teachers and students to consider possible responses to unfavorable social, institutional, and classroom conditions." However, Casanave (2004) questions whether employing a rights analysis would be appropriate in all EAP situations. While the students in Benesch's EAP classes were drawn from a US-based inner city and exposed to societal inequities, those of Swales are international students. For this reason, Swales takes a more accommodationist, pragmatic approach with the primary aim of acculturating students into the disciplinary discourses of their field, while at the same time, conceding that the field of EAP is no longer politically and culturally neutral (Swales 1997). "Rights" might also be conceived in terms of allowing students the right to choose their own tasks, as in the case of the negotiated syllabus. Frodesen (1995), for example, gives an account of a writing course in which major writing assignments were negotiated individually; however, one unexpected reaction by some students was their anxiety about having to define their own assignments.

Specific genres of writing in the academy have also been the focus of attention in needs analyses particularly thesis and dissertation writing, but with different emphases on the *needs*, *lacks*, and *wants* aspects. Paltridge's survey (2002) has revealed differences in perceived needs in terms of the advice on organization and structure given in guides and handbooks on thesis writing and what happens in practice. There was found to be a far wider range of thesis options in actual practice (traditional: simple; traditional: complex; topic-based; compilations of research articles), leading Paltridge to recommend that the rationale for the various choices and structural variation within theses need to be considered in syllabus design. A needs analysis focussing on students' *lacks* in thesis writing is that by Cooley and Lewkowicz (1997), who carried out a large, triangulated needs analysis through examination of student writing samples and questionnaires administered to students and supervisors. A somewhat different orientation to addressing students' lacks is proposed by Richards (1988) within an interactive needs analysis framework. After each individual assignment Richards referred students back to their advisors for feedback. This ongoing assessment was used to determine the course development in a summative manner, a point noted earlier by Hyland (2006). Evaluation of materials and methodologies provides another mechanism to feed into needs analyses. Starfield's (2004) students on a thesis-writing course reported a sense of empowerment through accessing corpus data to glean the phraseologies used by experts in authoritative writing; the evaluative comments from Starfield's students could be taken as evidence of student *wants* for corpus-based pedagogies. The accounts of syllabi for thesis writing by Richards (1988) and Starfield (2004) illustrate that needs analyses and other stages of the ESP curriculum development process are interdependent, feeding into the assessment and evaluation stages of syllabus design, as noted earlier in this chapter.

Moving to a specific disciplinary field of writing, that of legal discourse, EALP (English for academic legal purposes) presents several challenges to the ESP teacher, as revealed through various types of needs analysis. First, most of the published textbooks target first language (L1) learners; a survey by Candlin, Bhatia, and Jensen (2002) showed only 6 out of 56 legal writing books to be aimed at the second language (L2) learner. Moreover, the extent to which these textbooks can be used is problematic as different countries have different jurisdictions limiting the transfer of published materials across national, cultural, and legal boundaries. One contentious issue concerns to what extent a syllabus for teaching EALP can or should be content-based. Northcott's (2009: 170) needs analysis study in the UK presents this dilemma when she states that students "cannot learn how to write a legal essay without understanding how to read law reports. This in turn presupposes understanding the socio-legal context within which these texts are interpreted, hence the need for learners to become familiar with aspects of the UK legal system." Candlin et al. (2002: 314), however, are quite categorical that legal EALP should focus on the linguistic and socio-discursive aspects of legal writing, with authentic legal texts "used for teaching accurate, authentic legal writing, not legal content."

As far as needs analyses for academic reading are concerned, the same situation pertaining to academic writing prevailed in the 1970s–1980s. In other words, curricula were derived from the writer of the materials own intuitions, were based on rhetorical functions, (Trimble 1985) and tended to take a "wide-angle" approach drawing on material from a variety of scientific topics. A case in point is the *Reading and Thinking in English Series* (Widdowson 1980), comprising four graded books using a combined notional-functional approach. Implicitly, they can be said to acknowledge learner needs in terms of level as they progress from a focus on how basic grammar structures and vocabulary are used to express concepts such as processes in simplified text, moving to functional categories in authentic text in the final book in the series.

This implicit approach to needs analysis intuitively targeting learner *lacks* contrasts sharply with more recent reading materials development projects, which take a much more holistic and learner-centerd approach. One such study is that by Holme and Chalauisaeng (2006), who, like Richards (1988), espouse Tudor's (1996) iterative concept of needs into course design, that is, a method that does not frame needs as solely residing in an objective assessment of the target situation but one in which the learner is considered "in the evolving cultural dynamic that the class creates out of its negotiation with the target situation" (2006: 405). Their participatory appraisal (PA) model puts the learner at the heart of this dynamic needs analysis process by co-opting learners as co-researchers to determine their own needs and learning goals in an EAP reading program. In order to capture this iterative nature of needs analysis, Holme and Chalauisaeng employed two qualitative approaches, (1) participant observation and (2) semi-structured interviews, triangulated with quantitative instruments in the form of questionnaires collected over a period of several months. Of interest, is that occasionally the findings from qualitative observations were not borne out by the quantitative data. For example, while observations of the class's interactions and behavior indicated a strong shift in motivation, also expressed by student interest and involvement, this perception was not confirmed by the questionnaire data, which the authors explain by the fact that learners "were still coping with the residual feelings of language-learning failure that had dogged these students throughout their school years and beyond" (2006: 416). One lesson to be drawn from this study is the importance of triangulation, prolonged engagement, and participant verification for establishing validity and reliability of needs analysis procedures, as outlined in the first section of this chapter.

Evans, Hartshorn, and Anderson (2010), meanwhile, stress the importance of *responsiveness* in preparing content-based reading materials, noting that the curriculum should be responsive to the learners, above all, but also to stakeholders, program expectations, quality research (generated within a specific program as well as the language teaching profession in general), market demands and an ever-changing environment. Two aspects demand further comment here. The first is that over the past few years, higher education has shifted to a market-driven model, promoted in such a way as to ensure competition, maximum efficiency, and profits. How education is constructed discoursally as a commodity has been examined by Fairclough (1995). By responsiveness to environmental changes, Evans et al. (2010: 137) are referring to the role of the internet in shaping the curriculum. They state that students need to learn the differences between reading online and in-print materials, and exemplify strategies that will help students to be "efficient, effective readers of electronic materials." Evans et al.'s approach point to some very recent developments taken up in the final section of this chapter.

Needless to say, early EAP books on listening to lectures, such as *Study Listening: Understanding Lectures and Talks in English* (Lynch 1983), one in a series which also covers writing, reading, and speaking, paralleled those for writing and reading in that the materials were based on the writer's own intuitions on what aspects should be addressed. Of interest here is that Flowerdew and Miller's (1997) study of authentic lectures in Hong Kong found there to be a mismatch between listening skills in EAP textbooks and those required in mainstream classes. Moreover, other needs analyses of lectures have shown that this genre is not static but dynamic and evolving; for example, Stoller (2001) reports that Ferris and Tagg (1996) found that lectures in the US are becoming more interactive and less formal, making new demands on students.

One of the first studies to seriously consider the role of needs analysis in the lecture comprehension process is that by Schmidt (1981). One issue Schmidt discusses is to what extent findings from needs analyses carried out on one population are transferable to another situation. Citing materials by Candlin and Murphy (1976) prepared for engineering students in Saudi Arabia, based on a needs assessment carried out for foreign students in the United Kingdom, Schmidt points out that while this procedure constitutes a general way of assessing needs, it still "relies on the curriculum developer's intuition about the similarity of needs between two different populations" (1981: 200). Schmidt's main thesis in this article is to illustrate the advantages of a case study method over questionnaires and proficiency tests for assessing needs for lecture comprehension. A key advantage is that a case study allows for a more process- rather than product-oriented approach, as direct observation of a student with a follow-up interview can give insights into how a learner appears to acquire knowledge and the difficulties faced, for example, understanding a concept but being unable to record it in English. However, a drawback is that the findings may be unique to a particular student and not reflect general needs of the student population in the same context.

Schmidt's (1981) case study could be viewed as a precursor to later more ethnographic studies, briefly introduced in the first part of this chapter. One such study is that by Benson (1994) who situates his investigation of how lecturers and students view the L2 academic listening process within a broader framework of the "culture of learning." Working from a grounded, detailed "thick" description (Geertz 1973), Benson presents an illuminating rich tapestry of the meaning of this speech event through examination of minute patterns in motivation, interaction, roles (adopted or conferred), also considering the effect of hierarchical administrative planning on lecture content and related areas Through such densely textured ethnographic research, Benson hopes that wider conclusions about the "grander pattern may soon become apparent" (1994: 197). While "needs" are not explicitly referred to, nevertheless this ethnographic perspective has important implications for curriculum development (see Jackson 2002 for an account of an ethnographic investigation into the L2 case discussion in business). Of note is that Benson also underscores the creation of corpus data as a "worthy research goal" in order to gain further insights into the culture of learning in his ethnographic research. One such corpus of academic lectures is the needs-driven spoken corpus (NDSC) (Jones and Schmitt 2010) for informing discipline-specific vocabulary materials, on which subject lecturers and students were also consulted.

The above accounts all approach EAP needs from the four macro-skills perspective. But it should not be forgotten that both needs and curriculum development can never be completely neutral, being influenced by the analyst/developer's own ideology (cf the debate on wide- vs. narrow-angle courses and Benesch's concept of "rights" analysis). Johns' (Johns and Makalela 2011) reflections on the "frames" underpinning an EAP literacy curriculum, which adopts a critical ethnographic approach to the needs analysis, portray her beliefs that reading and writing should be integrated and grammar and the lexicon studied functionally.

Needs Analysis in English for Occupational Purposes (EOP)

The needs analyses for various types of academic purposes discussed in the previous section, with most concentrating on writing, are firmly rooted in the EAP environment. The needs analyses for English for occupational purposes (EOP) discussed in this section straddle both the academy and the professional workplace.

EOP in the academy

Needs analyses have been conducted targeting EOP needs for implementation in an EAP course. Belcher's (2006) overview article discusses several such needs analyses. Part 1 in *English for Specific Purposes* (Orr 2002) contains six case studies for learners in the university covering various EOP fields such as law, nursing, business, and tourism. Below I comment on a few carried out in the field of business and health care at the institutional and national level.

At the institutional level, Flowerdew (2010) describes how a module on proposal writing for the workplace for final-year science undergraduates was modified to take account of various constraints, such as some students' unwillingness to take a writing course which they could not see any immediate value in. Flowerdew's needs analysis pointed to a mismatch between the intended target *needs* and student *wants*; other needs analyses have highlighted mismatches between current EAP courses and EOP demands. At the national level, Bhatia and Candlin (2001) implemented a large-scale multimethod needs analysis project on business communication across five different tertiary institutions in Hong Kong (see Bargiela-Chiappini, Nickerson, and Planken 2007: 81–7 for more details of this project). They noted mismatches between current business programs in the academy and the skills demanded in the workplace. This aspect has also been commented on by Crosling and Ward (2002) who, based on the findings of their survey of oral communication needs carried out in Australia, found a mismatch between the formal deductively-oriented presentations common in English for business programs in the academy and the more informal inductive style in work-place situations. They suggest that universities focus on extending generic oral communication skills, building in assertiveness training when presenting view-points, and involving students in group work ideally taking place in cross-gender, cross-cultural and multidisciplinary setting, which can then be adapted in a job-focussed work environment. Meanwhile, Dovey (2006) discusses the issue of transferability from academic to professional contexts from the perspective of the "new vocationalism." Echoing the views of scholars in rhetorical genre studies (cf Devitt 2008) who emphasize the dynamic and fluid nature of genres which make them somewhat inaccessible to teaching, Dovey argues for a curriculum based on strategic needs which focus on "the ability to participate in/or manage the social and technical *processes* involved in leveraging knowledge" (2008: 395).

Similar concerns to those uncovered by needs analyses in business communica-tion outlined above have also been revealed by needs analyses targeting EOP health-care communication for designing curriculum in the academy (see Shi 2009 for a summary of studies on needs analyses in English for medical purposes). For example, Bosher and Smalkoski's (2002) findings from their ethnographic on-site observation of student nurses' difficulties included being assertive with clients and understanding how cultural values influence interactions with clients from backgrounds different from their own, not dissimilar to those needs identified by Crosling and Ward (2002). Meanwhile Leki's (2003) case study of a nursing student revealed the student's antipathy towards writing nonacademic disciplinary docu-ments, specifically the nursing care plan. Leki recounts how the student felt this task to be overly demanding on account of the fact that this genre in the academy required far more detailed writing than the notations used in clinical settings. This finding, in common with Flowerdew's (2010) analysis of student *wants*, illustrates the importance of taking into account motivational factors and how meaningful the tasks are perceived by students. Corpus analysis, mainly confined to EAP contexts in the past, is now being applied to health-care com-munication. Adolphs, Atkins, and Harvey's (2007) investigation of advice-seeking phone calls by the public to *NHS Direct* in the United Kingdom highlights the importance of interpersonal language, which, they state, has implications for training of health care professionals.

EOP in the workplace

The majority of needs analyses in workplace situations favor task-based needs analyses carried out through ethnographic on-site observations and often sup-plemented with more quantitative data, an approach advocated by Long (2005). For example, Jasso-Aguilar (2005) researched the daily tasks of Waikiki hotel maids through job shadowing. Garcia (2002) researched the communicative tasks of workers by visiting the factory floor. In fact, both of these studies adopt a *critical* ethnographic approach as they examine the power differentials existing in these social contexts (see also Starfield, this volume). While many needs analyses conducted in the occupational sector reveal clearly identifiable task-based language needs, this is not always the case as the needs may vary or the needs analysis targets future rather than immediate EOP needs (see Cowling 2007, who approaches needs analysis from a problematizing perspective).

There are two other aspects that are recurrent themes in accounts of needs analyses for EOP: internationalization and the use of English as a lingua franca (ELF), which go hand-in-hand. The international scope of English was recognized in the 1970s (Mackay and Mountford 1978, cited in Johns and Dudley-Evans 1991) for the transmission of science and technology and internal/international communication, in other words, tailored "to the outside world" (Johns and Price-Machado 2001: 43). As an example of the latter, Holliday's (1995) ethnographic approach to defining English language needs in an oil company in the Middle East underscores the importance of English as a lingua franca (Nickerson, this volume), not only for communication among local and expatriate staff within the company and within the international oil technology community, but also with the international commercial community.

Since Holliday's study, the use of English as a lingua franca in EOP contexts has proliferated with Nickerson (2005: 367) stating, "The dominance of English used as a *lingua franca* in international business contexts is now seemingly beyond dispute." Nickerson, like Dovey (2006), also argues for a focus on communication strategies, rather than product-based language skills in English for international business purposes syllabus design. What also needs to be taken into account in a strategy-based syllabus, as revealed by ethnographic observations (Gimenez 2001; Poncini 2004), is the role that culture plays in international communications. Of interest is that Gimenez' small-scale study on business negotiations revealed that some cultural differences seemed to be overridden by status-bound considerations. Corporate language policy is another consideration to take into account in regard to written communication (Evans 2010). More recently, the increasing globalization of legal practice has resulted in English also becoming the lingua franca of this field. This is especially true in the case of commercial lawyers who often represent international clients and who also need to equip themselves with business communication skills (Northcott 2009).

It is evident from this chapter that EAP rather than EOP has been the main focus of needs analysis enquiries. J. Flowerdew and Peacock (2001) attribute this to the fact that those EAP professionals situated in higher education are better positioned than EOP professionals to do research. Another reason could be that as EOP courses in the professional sector are often delivered by discipline-based practitioners rather than ESP specialists there is less focus on needs analyses to inform curriculum design; the teaching of Legal English to lawyers is a case in point (Northcott 2009). It is also evident that, apart from EAP, business communication, Legal English, and health care contexts dominate the literature on needs analysis. That these three fields have been singled out for attention is, as Belcher (2009: 2) acknowledges, because "the fastest growing branches of EOP are those associated with professions that are themselves constantly expanding and generating offshoots." The following section examines future avenues for expansion in needs analyses and curriculum development.

Further Directions

Two key forces are seen as driving future needs analyses and curriculum development in ESP: technologization and transnationalization, aspects of which are interrelated.

The increasing use of English as a lingua franca has been propelled by globalization. Globalization, in its turn, has been driven by advances in technological and communications innovations. To illustrate, several recent needs analyses have underscored the importance of email for efficient workplace written communication transnationally, both in Asian (Evans 2010) and European contexts (Louhiala-Salminen 2002; Rogerson-Revell 2007), and the importance of teleconferencing in oral communicative events for professional engineers in Malaysia (Kassim and Ali 2010). Not only has technology had a profound impact on modes of workplace communication, but it is also being increasingly used in analyses of English as a lingua francs workplace interactions. Whereas in the past monomodal corpora were used for analysis, multimodal corpora are now coming on-stream for capturing English as a lingua franca, transnational spoken interactions. Handford and Matous (2011) analyze face-to-face on-site spoken discourse in the construction industry and Bjørge (2010) the use of backchannelling in negotiations.

However, what about the use of technology for delivery of ESP courses? Belcher (2006: 149) signaled computer-mediated communication, CMC (e.g. blogs) as "an appealing and accessible but still largely unexamined means of motivating both oral and literate L2 proficiencies." Since then, these "new technologies" have been incorporated into design and delivery of courses, but this has mainly been in ESL/ EFL environments; ESP has yet to benefit fully from this era of "new technologies," but see Bloch (2008 and this volume) for application of technologies to EAP writing. Also, in this increasingly connected world, where communication is mediated by applications such as email, Skype and videoconferencing one would expect future ESP courses to adopt the communication tools of the field, similar to the line of thinking that ESP courses should mirror the activities and methodologies employed in real-life ESP situations (Robinson 1991).

Besides the changing nature of ESP being shaped by advances in technologization in this era of globalization, needs are also being redefined transnationally both in terms of learners' cultural identity (Belcher and Lukkarila 2011) and societal demands (cf Brecht and Rivers 2005).

Belcher and Lukkarila (2011) argue for broadening the scope of learner-centered needs analyses to focus on multilingual learners' self-perceived cultural identities, – how such learners see themselves – where they are from and who they want to become, in addition to what they want to do with language. Their research shows that both short- and long-term residents in the States "pointed to ethnolinguistic cultures of origin as the cultures with which they most identified themselves" (2011: 80). This research also has implications for needs analyses carried out at universities in the Asia-Pacific region with their increasing focus on internationalization.

With education now driven by market forces in a global competitive environment, content and language integrated learning (CLIL), where the integration of content and language is seen to allow for efficient pedagogy, is enjoying a resurgence of interest (see Wolff 2009 for an overview of this approach). One key initiative, coordinated by Beijing Foreign Studies University, is the restructuring of ESP programs in foreign language teaching universities in the Mainland to adopt a cross-disciplinary, language-plus-subject orientation (Zhu and Shen 2010). Another large-scale endeavor integrating language and content in ESP is that taking place in higher education within the new European framework of the Bologna reform designed to harmonize academic and quality assurance standards with a view to increasing mobility and international competitiveness (Fortanet-Gómez and Räisänen 2010). This language planning initiative in Europe seems to take us full circle back to the major aim of Richterich and Chancerel's needs analysis of the 1970s – to ensure some degree of standardization of language teaching across countries.

Concluding Remarks

Since West's landmark state-of-the-art survey of needs analysis in 1994, needs analyses carried out in ESP situations have assumed increasing importance; witness the number of articles on various types of needs analysis published in *English for Specific Purposes* over the last decade. Needs analyses have also taken on a more "problematizing" role with a plethora of different strands to consider. Needs, thus, are often complex, difficult to sort out, and may require a variety of responses in that there are often "competing needs and vested interests in defining and meeting [students'] needs" (Leki 2000: 104). These challenges are compounded by the changing nature of ESP in this increasingly technologized and globalized environment, but which nevertheless holds the promise of exciting possibilities for ESP practitioners.

REFERENCES

Adolphs, S., Atkins, S., and Harvey, K. (2007) Caught between professional requirements and interpersonal needs: Vague language in healthcare contexts. In J. Cutting (ed.), *Vague Language Explored*. 62–78. Basingstoke, UK: Palgrave Macmillan.

Barber, C. (1985). Some measurable characteristics of modern scientific prose. In J. M. Swales (ed.), *Episodes in ESP*. 3–14. New York: Prentice Hall.

Bargiela-Chiappini, F., Nickerson, C., and Planken, B. (2007) *Business Discourse*. Basingstoke, UK Palgrave Macmillan.

Basturkmen, H. (2010) *Developing Courses in English for Specific Purposes*. Basingstoke, UK: Palgrave Macmillan.

Belcher, D. (2006) English for specific purposes: Teaching to perceived needs and imagined futures in worlds of work, study, and everyday life. *TESOL Quarterly* 40: 133–56.

Belcher, D. (2009) What ESP is and can be: An introduction. In D. Belcher (ed.), *English for Specific Purposes in Theory and Practice*. 1–20. Ann Arbor, MI: University of Michigan Press.

Belcher, D. and Lukkarila, L. (2011) Identity in the ESP context: Putting the learner front and center in needs analysis. In D. Belcher, A. M. Johns, and B. Paltridge (eds.), *New Directions in English for Specific Purposes Research*. 73–93. Ann Arbor, MI: University of Michigan Press.

Benesch, S. (2001) *Critical English for Academic Purposes*. Mahwah, NJ: Lawrence Erlbaum.

Benson, M. (1994) Lecture listening in an ethnographic perspective. In J. Flowerdew (ed.), *Academic Listening: Research Perspectives*. 181–98. Cambridge: Cambridge University Press.

Berwick, R. (1989) Needs assessment in language programming: From theory to practice. In R. K. Johnson (ed.), *The Second Language Curriculum*. 48–62. Cambridge: Cambridge University Press.

Bhatia, V. and C. N. Candlin (eds.) (2001) *Teaching English to Meet the Needs of Business Education in Hong Kong*. Hong Kong: City University of Hong Kong Press.

Biber, D. (2006) *University Language. A Corpus-Based Study of Spoken and Written Registers*. Amsterdam: John Benjamins.

Bjørge, A. (2010) Conflict or cooperation: The use of backchannelling in ELF negotiations. *English for Specific Purposes* 29: 191–203.

Bloch, J. (2008) *Technologies in the Second Language Composition Classroom*. Ann Arbor, MI: University of Michigan Press.

Bloch, J. (2010) A concordance-based study of the use of reporting verbs as rhetorical devices in academic papers. *Journal of Writing Research* 2: 219–44.

Bosher, S. and Smalkoski. K. (2002) From needs analysis to curriculum development: Designing a course in health-care communication for immigrant students in the USA. *English for Specific Purposes* 21: 59–79.

Brecht, R. and Rivers, W. (2005) Language needs analysis at the societal level. In M. Long (ed.), *Second Language Needs Analysis*. 79–104. Cambridge: Cambridge University Press.

Brindley, G. (1989) The role of needs analysis in adult ESL programme design. In R. K. Johnson (ed.), *The Second Language Curriculum*. 63–78. Cambridge: Cambridge University Press.

Brown, J. D. (2009) Foreign and second language needs analysis. In M. Long and C. Doughty (eds.), *The Handbook of Language Teaching*. 269–93. Oxford: Wiley-Blackwell.

Bruce, I. (2011) *Theory and Concepts of English for Academic Purposes*. London: Palgrave Macmillan.

Candlin, C. N., Bhatia, V., and Jensen, C. (2002) Developing legal writing materials for English second language learners: Problems and perspectives. *English for Specific Purposes* 21: 299–320.

Candlin, C. N. and Murphy, D. (1976) *Engineering Discourse and Listening Comprehension*. Lancaster, UK: University of Lancaster.

Casanave, C. (1995) Local interactions: Constructing contexts for composing in a graduate sociology program. In D. Belcher and G. Braine (eds.), *Academic Writing in a Second Language. Essays on Research and Pedagogy*. 83–110. Norwood, NJ: Ablex Publishing Corporation.

Casanave, C. (2004) *Controversies in Second Language Writing*. Ann Arbor, MI: University of Michigan Press.

Chin, E. (1994) Redefining "context" in research on writing. *Written Communication* 11: 445–82.

Cooley, L. and Lewkowicz, J. (1997) Developing awareness of the rhetorical and linguistic conventions of writing a thesis in English: Addressing the needs of EFL/ESL postgraduate students. In A. Duszak (ed.), *Culture and Styles of Academic Discourse*. 113–29. Berlin: Mouton de Gruyter.

Cowling, J. (2007) Needs analysis: Planning a syllabus for a series of intensive workplace courses at a leading Japanese company. *English for Specific Purposes* 26: 426–42.

Crosling, G. and Ward, I. (2002) Oral communication: The workplace needs and uses of business graduate employees. *English for Specific Purposes* 21: 41–57.

Devitt, A. (2008) *Writing Genres*. Carbondale: Southern Illinois University Press.

Dovey, T. (2006) What purposes, specifically? Re-thinking purposes and specificity in the context of the "new vocationalism." *English for Specific Purposes* 25: 387–402.

Dudley-Evans, T. and St John, M. J. (1998) *Developments in English for Specific Purposes*. Cambridge: Cambridge University Press.

Evans, N., Hartshorn, J. and Anderson, N. (2010) A principled approach to content-based materials development for reading. In N. Harwood (ed.), *English Language Teaching Materials. Theory and Practice*. 131–56. Cambridge: Cambridge University Press.

Evans, S. (2010) Business as usual: The use of English in the professional world in Hong Kong. *English for Specific Purposes* 29: 153–67.

Fairclough, N. (1995) *Critical Discourse Analysis*. Harlow, UK: Longman.

Ferris, D. and Tagg, T. (1996) Academic oral communication needs of EAP learners: What subject-matter instructors actually require. *TESOL Quarterly* 30: 31–58.

Flowerdew, J. and Miller, L. (1997) The teaching of academic listening comprehension and the question of authenticity. *English for Specific Purposes* 17: 27–46.

Flowerdew, J. and Peacock, M. (2001) Issues in EAP: A preliminary perspective. In J. Flowerdew and M. Peacock (eds.), *Research Perspectives on English for Academic Purposes*. 8–24. Cambridge: Cambridge University Press.

Flowerdew, L. (2010) Devising and implementing a business proposal module: Constraints and compromises. *English for Specific Purposes* 29: 108–120.

Fortanet-Gómez, I. and Räisänen, C. (eds.) (2010) *ESP in European Higher Education: Integrating Language and Content*. Amsterdam: John Benjamins.

Frodesen, J. (1995) Negotiating the syllabus: A learning-centred, interactive approach to ESL graduate writing course design. In D. Belcher and G. Braine (eds.), *Academic Writing in a Second Language. Essays on Research and Pedagogy*. 331–50. Norwood, NJ: Ablex Publishing Corporation.

Garcia, P. (2002) An ESP program for union members in 25 factories. In T. Orr (ed.), *English for Specific Purposes*. 161–74. Alexandria, VA: TESOL.

Gavioli, L. (2005) *Exploring Corpora for ESP Learning*. Amsterdam: John Benjamins.

Geertz, C. (1973) Thick description: Towards an interpretive theory of culture. In *The Interpretation of Cultures: Selected Essays*. 3–30. New York: Basic Books.

Gimenez, J. (2001) Ethnographic observations in cross-cultural business negotiations between non-native speakers of English: An exploratory study. *English for Specific Purposes* 20: 169–93.

Handford, M. and Matous, P. (2011) Lexicogrammar in the international construction industry: A corpus-based case study of Japanese-Hong-Kongese on-site interactions in English. *English for Specific Purposes* 30: 87–100.

Herbert, A. J. (1965) *The Structure of Technical English*. London: Longman.

Holliday, A. (1994) *Appropriate Methodology and Social Context*. Cambridge: Cambridge University Press.

Holliday, A. (1995) Assessing English language needs within an institutional context: An ethnographic approach. *English for Specific Purposes* 14: 115–26.

Holme, R. and Chalauisaeng, B. (2006) The learner as needs analyst: The use of participatory appraisal in the EAP reading classroom. *English for Specific Purposes* 25: 403–19.

Hutchinson, T. and Waters, A. (1987) *English for Specific Purposes. A Learning-Centred Approach*. Cambridge: Cambridge University Press.

Hyland, K. (1999) Academic attribution: Citation and the construction of disciplinary knowledge. *Applied Linguistics* 20: 341–67.

Hyland, K. (2006) *English for Academic Purposes*. London: Routledge.

Hymes, D. (1971) *On Communicative Competence*. Philadelphia: University of Pennsylvania Press.

Jackson, J. (2002) The L2 case discussion in business: An ethnographic investigation. In J. Flowerdew (ed.), *Academic Discourse*. 268–86. London: Longman.

Jasso-Aguilar, R. (2005) Sources, methods and triangulation in needs analysis: A critical perspective in a case study of Waikiki hotel maids. In M. Long (ed.), *Second Language Needs Analysis*. 127–58. Cambridge: Cambridge University Press.

Johns, A. M. (1997) *Text, Role and Context*. Cambridge: Cambridge University Press.

Johns, A. M. and Dudley-Evans, T. (1991) English for specific purposes: International in scope, specific in purpose. *TESOL Quarterly* 25: 297–314.

Johns, A. M. and Makalela, L. (2011) Needs analysis, critical ethnography, and context: Perspectives from the client – and the consultant. In D. Belcher, A. M. Johns, and B. Paltridge (eds.), *New Directions in English for Specific Purposes Research*. 197–221. Ann Arbor, MI: University of Michigan Press.

Johns, A. M. and Price-Machado, D. (2001) English for specific purposes (ESP): Tailoring courses to students' needs – and to the outside world. In M. Celce-Murcia (ed.), *Teaching English as a Second or Foreign Language*. 43–54. Boston, MA: Heinle and Heinle.

Johnson, K. (2009) Foreign language syllabus design. In K. Knapp and B. Seiddlhofer (eds.), *Handbook of Foreign Language Communication and Learning*. 309–40. Berlin: Walter de Gruyter.

Jones, M. and Schmitt, N. (2010) Developing materials for discipline-specific vocabulary and phrases in academic seminars. In N. Harwood (ed.), *English Language Teaching Materials. Theory and Practice*. 225–50. Cambridge: Cambridge University Press.

Jordan, R. (1997) *English for Academic Purposes: A Guide and Resource Book for Teachers*. Cambridge: Cambridge University Press.

Kassim, H. and Ali, F. (2010) English communicative events and skills needed at the workplace: Feedback from the industry. *English for Specific Purposes* 29: 168–82.

Lea, M. and Street, B. (1998) Student writing in higher education: An academic literacies approach. *Studies in Higher Education* 23: 157–72.

Leki, I. (2000) Writing, literacy, and applied linguistics. *Annual Review of Applied Linguistics* 20: 99–115.

Leki, I. (2003) Living through college literacy. Nursing in a second language. *Written Communication* 20: 81–98.

Lincoln, Y. and Guba, E. (1985) *Naturalistic Enquiry*. Newbury Park, CA: Sage.

Long, M. (ed.) (2005) *Second Language Needs Analysis*. Cambridge: Cambridge University Press.

Long, M. (2005) Methodological issues in learner needs analysis. In M. Long (ed.), *Second Language Needs Analysis*. 19–76. Cambridge: Cambridge University Press.

Louhiala-Salminen, L. (2002) The fly's perspective: Discourse in the daily routine of a business manager. *English for Specific Purposes* 21: 211–31.

Lynch, T. (1983) *Study Listening: Understanding Lectures and Talks in English*. Cambridge: Cambridge University Press.

Mackay, R. and Mountford, A. (eds.) (1978) *English for Specific Purposes*. London: Longman.

Marco, M. J. (2000) Collocational frameworks in medical research papers. A genre-based study. *English for Specific Purposes* 19: 63–86.

McDonough, J. (1984) *ESP in Perspective*. London: Collins.

Munby, J. (1978) *Conmmunicative Syllabus Design*. Cambridge: Cambridge University Press.

Nickerson, C. (2005) Editorial. English as a *lingua franca* in international business contexts. *English for Specific Purposes* 24: 367–80.

Northcott, J. (2009) Teaching legal English: Contexts and cases. In D. Belcher (ed.), *English for Specific Purposes in Theory and Practice*. 165–85. Ann Arbor, MI: University of Michigan Press.

Orr, T. (ed.) (2002) *English for Specific Purposes*. Alexandria, VA: TESOL.

Paltridge, B. (2002). Thesis and dissertation writing: An examination of published advice and actual practice. *English for Specific Purposes*, 21: 125–43.

Paltridge, B., Harbon, L., Hirsch, D., Shen, H., Stevenson, M., Phakiti, A., and Woodrow, L. (2009) *Teaching Academic Writing: An Introduction for Teachers of Second Language Writers*. Ann Arbor, MI: University of Michigan Press.

Poncini, G. (2004) *Discursive Strategies in Multicultural Business Meetings*. Bern: Peter Lang.

Prior, P. (1995) Redefining the task: An ethnographic examination of writing and response in graduate seminars. In D. Belcher and G. Braine (eds.), *Academic Writing in a Second Language. Essays on Research and Pedagogy*. 47–82. Norwood, NJ: Ablex Publishing Corporation.

Richards, R. (1988) Thesis/dissertation writing for EFL students: An ESP course design. *English for Specific Purposes* 7: 171–80.

Richterich, R. and Chancerel, J. L. (1977) *Identifying the Needs of Adults Learning a Foreign Language*. Strasbourg: Council of Europe/Oxford: Pergamon.

Robinson, P. (1991) *ESP Today: A Practitioner's Guide*. Hemel Hampstead, UK: Prentice-Hall.

Rogerson-Revell, P. (2007) Using English for international business: A European case study. *English for Specific Purposes* 26: 103–20.

Schmidt, M. (1981) Needs assessment in English for specific purposes: The case study. In L. Selinker et al. (eds.), *English for Academic and Technical Purposes*. 199–210. Rowley, MA: Newbury House.

Schutz, N. and Derwing, B. (1981) The problem of needs assessment in English for specific purposes: Some theoretical and practical considerations. In R. Mackay and J. Palmer (eds.), *Languages for Specific Purposes*. 29–44. Rowley, MA: Newbury House.

Shi, L. (2009) English for medical purposes. In D. Belcher (ed.), *English for Specific Purposes in Theory and Practice*. 205–28. Ann Arbor, MI: University of Michigan Press.

Starfield, S. (2004) Why does this feel empowering? Thesis writing, concordancing and the "corporatising" university. In B. Norton and K. Toohey (eds.), *Critical Pedagogies and Language Learning*. 138–57. Cambridge: Cambridge University Press.

Starfield, S. (2007) New directions in student academic writing. In J. Cummins and C. Davison (eds.), *The*

International Handbook of English Language Teaching. 875–90. Norwell, MA: Springer.

Stoller, F. (2001) The curriculum renewal process in English for academic purposes. In J. Flowerdew and M. Peacock (eds.), *Research Perspectives on English for Academic Purposes*. 208–24. Cambridge: Cambridge University Press.

Swales, J. (1978) Writing "Writing Scientific English". In R. Mackay and A. Mountford (eds.), *English for Specific Purposes*. 43–55. London: Longman.

Swales, J. M. (ed.) (1988) *Episodes in ESP*. New York: Prentice Hall.

Swales, J. M. (1997) English as *Tyrannosaurus rex*. *World Englishes* 16: 373–82.

Swales, J. M. (2004) *Research Genres: Explorations and Applications*. Cambridge: Cambridge University Press.

Swales, J. M. and Feak, C. B. (1994) *Academic Writing for Graduate Students*. Ann Arbor, MI: University of Michigan Press.

Swales, J. M. and Feak, C. B. (2000) *English in Today's Research World*. Ann Arbor, MI: University of Michigan Press.

Trimble, L. (1985) *English for Science and Technology: A Discourse Approach*. Cambridge: Cambridge University Press.

Tudor, I. (1996) *Learner Centredness as Language Education*. Cambridge: Cambridge University Press.

West, R. (1994) Needs analysis in language teaching. *Language Teaching* 27: 1–19.

Widdowson, H. (ed.) (1980) *Reading and Thinking in English Series*. Oxford: Oxford University Press.

Widdowson, H. (1981) English for specific purposes: Criteria for course design. In L. Selinker, E. Tarone and V. Hanzeli. (eds.), *English for Academic and Technical Purposes*. 1–11. Rowley, MA: Newbury House.

Widdowson, H. (1983) *Learning Purpose and Language Use*. Oxford: Oxford University Press.

Wilkins, D. (1976) *Notional Syllabuses: A Taxonomy and its Relevance to Foreign Language Curriculum Development*. Oxford: Oxford University Press.

Wolff, D. (2009) Content and language integrated learning. In K. Knapp, and B. Seidlhofer (eds.), *Handbook of Foreign Language Communication and Learning*. 545–72. Berlin: Walter de Gruyter.

Zhu, M. and Shen, Y. (2010) On ESP development in foreign language teaching universities in China. In *Proceedings of 2010 ESP international conference, National Taipei University*. 253–63. Taiwan: Crane Publishing Company.

18 Genre and English for Specific Purposes

BRIAN PALTRIDGE

Introduction

The term "genre" was first introduced in the area of English for specific purposes (ESP) in 1981. Elaine Tarone and her colleagues (1981) use the term in their discussion of the use of the passive in research writing in the area of astrophysics while Swales (1981) uses the term in his seminal work on the discourse structure of research article introductions. Since then, genre has become an important notion in the area of English for specific purposes and has made a significant contribution to research in this area (see Bawarshi and Reiff 2010; Bax 2011; Bazerman, Bonini, and Figueiredo 2009; Bruce 2011; English 2011; Freedman and Medway 1994; Frow 2006; Gebhard and Harman 2011; Hyland 2002a, 2009a; Hyon 1996; Johns 2008; Johns et al. 2006; Martin and Rose 2008; Paltridge 1997, 2001a, 2012a; Rose and Martin 2012; Swales 1990, 2004, 2009; Tardy 2011a, 2011b for discussions of different perspectives on genre).

Genre, in ESP work, refers to communicative events such as seminar presentations, university lectures, academic essays, and business reports. ESP genre studies are based largely on Swales' (1981, 1990) work on the discourse structure and linguistic features of scientific reports. These studies have had a strong influence on the teaching of English for specific purposes and especially the teaching of academic writing to ESL graduate students. Swales (1990) proposes a definition of genre which has been extremely influential in ESP genre studies. He describes genre as a class of communicative events with some shared set of communicative purposes. The communicative purpose of a genre is recognized by the people who use it who, in turn, establish the constraints on what is generally acceptable in terms of how the text should be written or spoken, what issues it will address, and how it can do this. Instances of genres, however, vary in their prototypicality

The Handbook of English for Specific Purposes, First Edition.
Edited by Brian Paltridge and Sue Starfield.
© 2013 John Wiley & Sons, Inc. Published 2013 by John Wiley & Sons, Inc.

in that some instances may be highly typical examples of the particular genre, whereas others may be less so but still, nonetheless, be seen as instances of the particular genre. Swales points out that the name that a discourse community gives to a genre is important information for deciding on genre category membership, although, as Swales observes, this naming may require some further validation.

In his book, *Genre Analysis*, Swales (1990) argued that communicative purpose was the key factor that leads a person to decide whether a text is an instance of a particular genre or not. He has since, however, revised this view, saying that it is now clear that genres may have multiple purposes and these may be different for each of the participants involved (Askehave and Swales 2001). Also, instances of a genre that are very similar linguistically and rhetorically may have, in the words of Swales and Rogers (1995: 223) "startling differences in communicative purpose." The communicative purpose of a genre, further, may evolve over time, it may change, it may expand, or it may shrink (Swales 2004). Communicative purpose, further, can vary across cultures even when texts belong to the same genre category. Wang (2007, 2008), for example, examined newspaper commentates on the events of September 11th in Chinese and English and found that the aim of the Chinese texts was, primarily, to explain these events to their readership. The English texts, however, took on the role of making a case for, or debating, a particular point of view which, in turn, was reflected in how the texts were written. Tu (2010), in a study that looked at Chinese university self-introductions on the internet in Chinese and English, found that the main purpose of the Chinese texts was recruiting students to the institution whereas the English texts were mainly aimed at encouraging international collaborations and were organized in quite different ways and contained quite different content from the Chinese texts as a result of this. Communicative purpose, then, cannot always be used, by itself, to decide which genre category a text belongs to (or not) (Swales 2004).

ESP genre research has also considered the ways in which the use of one genre assumes, or depends on, the use of a number of other related genres, or the systems of genres (Bazerman 1994) of which the text is a part. Other writers use notions such as genre networks, genre chains, genre sets, and repertoires of genres to capture aspects of the relations between genres (Devitt 2004; Swales 2004; Tardy 2003). Tardy (2008) discusses how the notion of genre networks can be drawn on in academic writing programs, pointing out that while all of the complexities of these networks cannot be replicated in the classroom, teachers can, at least, take learners through part of the networks so they can understand how the texts they are writing are located in relation to other texts, and genres.

Genre, Discourse, and English for Specific Purposes

In ESP genre studies, the discourse structure of texts is typically described as being made up of a series of moves, each of which may contain one or more steps (see e.g. Swales, 1981, 1990, 2004). This is typically referred to as "move analysis." ESP genre studies have focussed on macro-level textual descriptions as well as sentence and clause-level choices within particular genres. More recently, ESP genre studies have considered contextual aspects of genres as well, taking up Swales' (1993) argument for the need to go beyond structural and linguistic examinations of texts in order to better understand social and contextual features of genres. Genre studies in ESP, then, have increasingly moved from linguistic descriptions, of their own, to studies which aim to understand why genres are shaped as they are, and how they achieve their particular goals. At the same time, analyses have moved, increasingly, from being "done by hand" to being computer-assisted (see e.g. Anthony and Lashkia 2003; Biber and Conrad 2009; Biber, Connor, and Upton 2009; Flowerdew 2005, Upton and Cohen 2009; Upton and Connor 2001), allowing for analyses to be based on a larger set of texts and, thereby, providing greater generalizability of the results.

Many of the ESP analyses of the discourse structure of texts have been based on Swales' (1981, 1990) work in this area. These studies have examined, for example, the discourse structures of research articles, masters theses and doctoral dissertations, job application and sales promotion letters, legislative documents, the graduate seminar, academic lectures, poster session discussions, and the texts that students read in university courses (see Bawarshi and Reiff 2010; Crookes 1986; Lin and Evans 2011; Paltridge 1997; Swales 1990, 2004 for reviews of this work). One model that has had a particular impact in ESP genre studies is what has come to be known as the CARS (create a research space) model. This model derives from the work of Swales (1981, 1990) and describes the typical discourse structure of the opening section of research articles; that is, the introduction. Swales shows how, in research article introductions, authors establish the territory of their research by showing how it is important and relevant in some way (Move 1: Establishing a research territory). The next move (Move 2: Establishing a niche) indicates the gap in previous research that the author's study aims to address while the third move (Move 3: Occupying the niche) states the purpose of the author's research and how it will fill the gap earlier sections of the introduction have identified. This model has since been applied to the introduction section of other genres such as theses and dissertations (see e.g. Bunton 2002; Paltridge and Starfield 2007). Cross-cultural examinations of the CARS model are summarized in Connor's (1996) *Contrastive Rhetoric* and in her (2011) *Intercultural Rhetoric in the Writing Classroom*. Taylor and Chen (1991) make an interesting observation between English and Chinese research article introductions showing how, in Chinese research articles at the time they were writing, there was much less of a focus on reviewing previous research, perhaps due to the difficulty in obtaining bibliographic resources at that time, but also, perhaps, because of issues of respect and face involved in reviewing and critiquing other scholars' work in Chinese settings.

Dudley-Evans (1999), Thompson (1999) and Paltridge (2002) have described discourse structures of thesis and dissertations written in English. Dudley-Evans describes the typical "IMRAD" (introduction–methods–results–discussion) pattern as being associated with what he terms a "traditional" dissertation. Thompson

(1999) further refines this category, dividing traditional dissertations into those that have "simple" and those that have "complex" patterns of organization. A further kind of dissertation is the "topic-based" dissertation. This type of dissertation typically commences with an introductory chapter, which is then followed by a series of chapters which have titles based on sub-topics of the topic under investigation. The dissertation then ends with a conclusion chapter. Dong (1998) describes doctoral dissertations that are based on a compilation of publishable research articles which are quite different from other sorts of doctoral dissertations. Particular sections (or part-genres) of theses and dissertations have also been examined such as dissertation acknowledgments, the literature review, discussion sections, and conclusions chapters (see Paltridge 2012a, 2012b; Paltridge and Starfield 2007; Paltridge et al. 2011, 2012; Swales 2004 for reviews and developments of this work). Theses and dissertations, of course, are more than just their discourse structures. They are very complex genres. They can have many readers and, as Pare, Starke-Meyerring, and McAlpine (2009) point out, many possible readings. Theses and dissertations, further, are part of a much larger genre set (Devitt 2004) that students need command of such as applications for admission, coursework assignments, comprehensive exams, dissertation proposals, and the dissertation itself, each of which is situated in a particular disciplinary context which influences how the text is produced, and, in turn read.

The analysis of discourse structures has not been confined to academic genres, however. Professional genres that have been examined in ESP research include corporate disclosure documents, letters of application, newspaper law reports, and popularized medical texts. Much of this work is informed by Bhatia's work such as his (1993) *Analyzing Genre: Language Use in Professional Settings* and his (Bhatia 2004) *Worlds of Written Discourse: A Genre-Based View*. Bhatia, and others (e.g. Askehave and Swales 2001; Flowerdew 2002; Swales 2004) suggest researchers might take a "text-first" or a "context-first" approach to the analysis of a particular genre. That is, they may start by looking at typical discourse patterns in the texts (a text-first approach), or they may commence with an examination of the context of the texts they want to investigate (a context-first approach) and then proceed to examine typical discourse patterns in the text (see Askehave and Swales 2001; Flowerdew 2011; Flowerdew and Wan 2010; Paltridge 2012; Swales 2004 for further discussion of this). There is no hard and fast rule on the sequence an analyst might take in carrying out their analysis. Rather, it depends on what the researcher is aiming to find out and the overall goal and purpose of the research.

Genre, Language and English for Specific Purposes

There has been an important shift in ESP genre studies from looking at language use, in general, to the use of language in specific settings and in specific genres. The work of Hyland (2002b, 2004a, 2008, 2009b, 2011), Biber (1988, 2006), Biber and Conrad (2009), Biber, Conrad, and Reppen (1994) Biber, Conrad, and Cortes

(2004) Biber et al. (2009), and Huckin (2003) has shown how the use of language varies across disciplines, and genres, and that this needs to be accounted for in studies that examine language use in specific purpose genres.

A number of corpora have been used in many ESP genre studies which give a greater level of reliability to the claims that can be made about genre-specific language. This includes the British academic spoken English (BASE Plus) corpus (http://www2.warwick.ac.uk/fac/soc/al/research/collect/base/), the British academic written English (BAWE Plus) corpus (http://www2.warwick.ac.uk/fac/soc/al/research/collect/bawe), the English as a lingua franca in academic settings corpus (ELFA) corpus (Mauranen 2010, 2011) (http://www.tay.fi/laitokset/kielet/engf/research/elfa/), the Michigan corpus of academic spoken English (MICASE) (http://www.lsa.umich.edu/eli/micase/index.htm) and the TOEFL spoken and written academic language corpus (Biber 2006). The BASE Plus corpus includes recordings of conference presentations, lectures and seminars, and interviews with academic staff. The MICASE contains data from a wide range of spoken academic genres. The ELFA corpus includes lectures, presentations, seminars, the dissertation defense, and conference discussions by speakers from a wide range of linguistic backgrounds. The TOEFL corpus contains examples of genres such as class sessions, office hour conversations, study group discussions, on-campus service encounters, text books, reading packs, university catalogues and brochures.

Corpus studies have also been carried out in areas other than English for academic purposes. These studies have examined, for example, Nobel Prize lectures, taxation websites, anti-discrimination bills, legal counsel opinions, persuasive and expository press genres, real estate discourse, emails in multinational corporations, sales letters, business faxes, company reports, and courtroom discourse (see e.g. Bargiela-Chiappini and Nickerson 1999; Bargiela-Chiappini, Nickerson, and Planken 2007; Bhatia and Gotti 2006; Flowerdew and Gotti 2006; Trosberg 2000 for examples of this work; also Gunnarsson 2009 for an extended discussion of the use of language in professional genres).

Corpora have also been extremely useful for ESP teachers in that they are able to show how language is used in the context of particular academic genres. Hyland's (2002c) study of the use of personal pronouns in Hong Kong student's academic writing is an example of this kind, as is Harwood's (2005) examination of the use of personal pronouns in academic research articles. Biber's (2006) *University Language* examines linguistic features of spoken and written academic genres as well as describes methodological tools for carrying out this kind of analysis. The appendix by Federica Barbieri in Biber and Conrad's (2009) *Register, Genre, and Style* provides an extensive summary of major corpus-based genre studies, approaches and methods of analysis used in the studies, and the findings of each of the studies, many of which are relevant to people working in the area of English for specific purposes (see L. Flowerdew 2011a, 2011b for further discussion of corpus studies in English for specific purposes research; Hyland 2012 for a corpus-based analysis of the relationship between authorial identity and disciplinarity in academic writing).

Genre, Multimodality, and ESP Research

In the very first volume of the journal *English for Specific Purposes*, DuBois (1980) wrote about the role of slides in conference presentations, many years before discussions of multimodality and ESP (and indeed multimodality and discourse analysis more generally). More recently, Miller (1998) has discussed the role of visual elements such as figures and tables in research papers, pointing out how these have increased in size and importance over the years. Indeed, as he and other researchers (e.g. Berkenkotter and Huckin (1995) have pointed out, some readers may "read" the visuals in research articles before they read the actual text. These visual components, however, have often been given less attention than the actual text in many ESP classes. As Miller (1998) points out, visuals in popular texts are different from visuals in academic texts. ESP teachers and students need to examine the relationship between visuals and the text in academic genres, how these visuals are glossed in the text, and the role they play in the author's overall presentation of their argument.

Johns (1998) reviews the role of visuals in specific purpose genres showing how, although these have been discussed in areas such as adult literacy and document design, they have only more recently been given focussed attention in ESP research. She then continues to consider how graphs, pictures and charts interact with texts in genres such as academic textbooks and how these are used to advance argumentation in the texts that students read and write in their academic classes. Swales and Feak (1995, 2004) suggest ways in which the relations between textual and visual representations of data can be considered in ESP classrooms, showing how writers do not simply transfer information from one format to another. Rather, the text that accompanies a visual representation is usually both a selective and interpretative commentary on the data. Writers need to decide how much information will be repeated in the text, and how much of the data will be interpreted for the reader.

Rowley-Jolivet (2002) also discusses visual elements in conference presentations. She examined 2048 visuals in 90 presentations given at conferences in the areas of geology, medicine, and physics. Rowley-Jolivet found there were four main kinds of visuals used in the presentations: scriptural (those that consist mainly of written text), numerical (such as mathematical formulae and numerical tables), figurative (such as photos and images such as X-rays or CAT scans), and graphical (such as maps, diagrams and charts). She compared this data to the published proceedings from the conference to see to what extent the visual data was typical of the genre of conference presentations. She found there were no scriptural representations in the written texts, fewer figurative and graphical representations than in the oral presentations, but considerably more graphical representations in the written texts, showing how the level of occurrence of these features is closely linked to the role and purpose of the particular genre. She also, importantly, points out the role of the visual elements in the conference presentations and how they aid comprehension of the presentations, especially for members of the audience who are non-native speakers of English. In her (2004) paper, Rowley-Jolivet examines these visual representations in terms of how they create textual relations and, in turn, coherence and information structure in the presentations and how these resources are exploited in the different scientific communities.

Tardy (2005, 2009) looked at the use of Microsoft PowerPoint presentation slides by multilingual writers in presentations that they prepared for an advanced writing class they were taking part in at a major US university. She shows how the students used these resources to express disciplinary identity through the use of organizational structures, vocabulary choice, use of images, and the color of their slides. They also expressed their cultural, educational and linguistic identities through their use of PowerPoint and their accompanying verbal commentary in ways that may not have been so easy for them to do in their written texts, alone. Molle and Prior (2008) take up the topic of multimodal genre systems in their discussion of a genre-based needs analysis for a number of graduate courses at a large US university. They found that the texts the students were producing were routinely hybrid and multimodal, highlighting the importance of going beyond purely linguistic descriptions of texts to ones that account for the complexities of the texts students are required to produce, and the processes through which they produce them.

ESP researchers have also begun to consider multimodality in digital genres and have made proposals for how genre analysis can be extended to account for the characteristics of non-linear, multimodal, web-mediated documents (see e.g. Askehave and Nielson 2005). Garzone (2002) considers whether traditional methods of analysis are appropriate for looking at online texts, suggesting these methods may need to be extended to take on a more semiotic, rather than solely linguistic approach. Miller and Shepherd (2004), in their discussion of digital genres (in their case blogs), show how digital genres draw not only on the potentialities of technology, but also rhetorical conventions from other, preceding, genres in ways that have merged into new conventional modes of expression. Researchers such as Bargiela-Chiappini (2005) have drawn on Lemke's (2002) notion of hypermodality, and the notions of presentational, orientational, and organizational meanings, to examine the interconnections between image, text and sound in online genres. Bargiela-Chiappini shows how these meanings, combined with features such as information accessibility and user-friendliness, have a strong impact on how these genres are constructed and, indeed, used (see Bateman 2008; Jewitt 2009; O'Halloran 2011; Prior 2009; this volume for further discussions of multimodal discourse analysis and ESP).

Genre as Social Action in ESP Research

ESP genre studies have been influenced by work in North American rhetorical genre studies (Artemeva 2008; Artemeva and Freedman 2008; Freedman 1999) to the point that, as some writers (e.g. Swales 2011a; Tardy 2011b) have pointed out, it may be harder to see clear divisions between some work in rhetorical genre studies and ESP work than it was when Hyon (1996) wrote her seminal article "Genre in three traditions." A key influence in rhetorical genre studies is Miller's (1984) notion of "genre as social action." In this view, a genre is defined, not in terms of "the substance or the form of discourse but on the action it is used to accomplish" (Miller 1984: 151). Genres in ESP research, then, are seen as socially situated actions (Berkenkotter and Huckin 1995; Tardy 2011c; Tardy and Swales 2008). In Tardy's (2011c: 57) words, genres "are often said to 'index' or reflect the socio-rhetorical contexts in which they exist." Pennycook (2010: 122) reinforces this point, saying that genres are not fixed textual categorizations but ways of "getting things done through language." We cannot, he argues, understand the use of language "without taking particular language practices in particular locations into account" (2010: 129). Different texts, roles, and contexts, further lead to different ways of doing things with language, different ways of joining in on disciplinary and professional conversations, and different "ways of belonging" (Johns 1997). Through our use of genres we say who we are and how we wish to be seen. Thus, in performing particular genres we present ourselves to the world and take on (or reproduce) particular identities.

Berkenkotter and Huckin's (1995) *Genre knowledge in disciplinary communication* is highly relevant to this discussion. Their work highlights the importance of considering the ways in which a genre is embedded in the communicative activities of the members of a particular disciplinary community, or profession. It also stresses the importance of understanding the functions of a genre from the point of view of the person who is using it. Berkenkotter and Huckin's work also aims to provide insights into the ways a person both acquires and uses genre knowledge as they participate in the knowledge-producing activities of their field or profession. It shows us how important the process of genre acquisition is in the learning of disciplinary genre knowledge. As Grabe and Kaplan (1996) observe, linguistic knowledge is necessary for effective communication, but not sufficient for users of specific purpose genres to achieve their goals. They need, as much, to understand the underlying views, assumptions, and aims of a field in which they are working, as much as they need control of the rhetorical and linguistic resources through which these views, assumptions, and aims are expressed.

It is crucial, then, for ESP researchers (and teachers) to have an understanding of the socially situated nature of genres and the role the genre is playing in the particular setting. Swales and Rogers (1995), in their examination of corporate mission statements, combine an analysis of mission statements with a contextual analysis and a set of case histories in order to gain insights into the role and function of this genre. They carried out interviews with writers of the mission statements, senior management and committee members as well as looked at policy documents in order to gain an understanding of the roles and history of these texts. They discuss how mission statements are extensions of the goals, values, and purposes of the corporations that publish them. What their study shows is the "added value" of carrying out a contextualized analysis of specific purpose genres in order to provide insights into the origins, development, and impact of genre "as a situated response to an emerging rhetorical need" (Swales and Rogers 1995: 237). As Swales and Rogers argue:

> Although there may be value in purely textual studies from cross-cultural or stylistic purposes, . . . a useful understanding of the role of genres in institutional and community affairs requires more sociocognitive input than the texts themselves provide (1995: 237).

Lillis (2008: 353), in her discussion of strategies for "closing the gap between text and context," suggests ways in which ESP researchers may contextualize their research as a way of "adding value" to their studies. These include what she terms "ethnography as method," "ethnography as methodology," and ethnography as "deep theorizing."

An example of ethnography as method is "talk around text." Talk around texts aims to get writers' perspectives on texts they have produced. Often this involves carrying out text-based interviews or using survey data to supplement the textual analysis. An example of this is Harwood's (2006) study of personal pronoun use in academic writing where he combined data analysis with text-based interviews. A further example is Nickerson's (2000) study of the genres and discourse strategies that Dutch writers working in multinational corporations employ when working in English where she used survey data to supplement the textual analysis of her study.

Ethnography as methodology involves using multiple data sources as well as a period of sustained involvement in the context in which the texts are produced to try to gain an understanding of the "dynamic and complex situated meanings and practices that are constituted in and by the writing" (Lillis 2008: 355). Curry and Lillis's (2010) book *Academic Writing in a Global Context*, where they employed text analysis, interviews, observations, document analysis, written correspondence, reviewers' and editors' comments to examine second language writers' experiences of getting published in English, is an example of this.

Ethnography as deep theorizing takes these two approaches a step further by considering how the language and orientation of the texts index (Bucholtz 2009; Bucholtz and Hall 2005; Ochs 1992) certain social structures, values, and relations in the same way that particular ways of speaking may point to, or index, a person's gender, social class or ethnic identity (Baker 2008; Litosseliti 2006). Starfield (2002, 2011) does this, for example, in her examination of first year students' writing in a former whites-only university in South Africa, as do Lillis and Curry (2010) in their study of second language scholars negotiating the peer-review and writing for publication process.

These studies parallel what Berkenkotter (2009: 18) terms a context-based, rhetorically-oriented, "wide-angle" approach to genre analysis that moves beyond solely text-based analysis to explore factors that influence the creation and reception of genres in particular social, cultural, and political settings (see Paltridge 2008; Paltridge and Starfield 2011; Paltridge and Wang 2011; Paltridge et al. 2011,

2012; Starfield 2010, 2011; Witte 1992 for further discussions of contextualized genre studies).

The Teaching and Learning of Specific Purpose Genres

Genre-based teaching emerged, in many ways, as a response to the process approach to teaching writing, with teachers and researchers arguing that process-based teaching does not address issues such as the requirements of particular writing tasks and variation in individual writing situations. It also, they argued, with its focus on personal meaning, gives students a false impression of what is required of them in academic settings (Horowitz 1986; Paltridge 2001b; Paltridge et al. 2009). The genre-based approach has not, however, been accepted without criticism. One key criticism has been that it is a product-based view of learning (only) and that it encourages learners to look for fixed patterns and formulae for their writing. Flowerdew (1993), in his proposal for a process approach to genre-based teaching, argues that models of genres should not be treated as fixed, rule governed patterns, but rather as prototypes which allow for individual variation. He also argues that genre-based teaching should incorporate "learning about" genres, rather than just the end product, or specific variety of genre. Badger and White (2000) take a similar view, arguing that process and genre-based approaches are complementary rather than in opposition to each other and that both have their place in the language learning classroom. As Johns (2008) argues, genre-based classrooms need to focus on both genre awareness and genre acquisition; that is, learners need to be given strategies for responding to new and different tasks and situations (genre awareness), at the same time as they need to acquire the genres that are important to them (genre acquisition).

Tardy (2006) examines the research in genre-based teaching and learning, in both first and second language contexts. As she points out, genre theory has gone beyond looking at genres as just "text types" (in the sense of rhetorical types such as such as argument, exposition, etc.) to considerations of genre as "a more social construct which shapes and is shaped by human activity" (2006: 79). Differences in the focus and learner groups in the studies she reviewed, however, made it difficult to draw conclusions as to the benefits of genre-based instruction. This, of course, is not a problem that lies just with genre-based studies. As Ortega (2010) points out in her work on research syntheses, in order to meaningfully compare the results of research on a particular topic, the studies that are examined must be sufficiently similar to each other in terms of their research questions, research design, research setting, and learner groups for meaningful comparisons to be made (see Norris and Ortega 2006, 2010 for further discussion of this). Small, single-site studies are, however, emerging in the literature which point to advances students can make in terms of their genre knowledge and ability to draw on this knowledge to successfully produce contextually appropriate texts in specific purpose settings.:

The work of Cheng (2006a, 2006b, 2007, 2008a, 2008b, 2011) is especially important in discussions of ESP genre-based teaching and learning. A common teaching strategy in genre-based classrooms is what is termed "metacommunicating" (Flowerdew 1993; Swales and Lindemann 2002); that is, the explicit analysis of examples of particular genres used in the classroom as a tool to heighten learners' awareness of genre-specific language features, rhetorical organization, and communicative purposes (Cheng 2011). In Cheng's (2008a: 68) research, he discusses how his student found genre "a supportive, explicit tool of learning" which he felt helped address other researchers' concerns about the product-oriented nature of ESP genre-based teaching. Dressen-Hammouda's (2008) study of a geology student's experiences in learning to write showed how he benefitted from a focus on genre, especially in relation to the acquisition of disciplinary identity. She argues, along with others, that the teaching of genres should include more than just linguistic and rhetorical features of genres. It should also focus on the disciplinary community's ways of perceiving, interpreting, and behaving; that is, the "ways of being, seeing, and acting" (2008: 238) that are particular to the student's disciplinary community.

Looking at a spoken academic genre, student presentations in the area of architecture, Morton (2009) also makes connections between disciplinary socialization and the mastery of a discipline's genres. She examined the rhetorical strategies that successful students employed to persuade their audience of the value of their design in a manner that was valued by experts in their discipline. The students she observed coordinated drawings, models, gesture, written text, and speech in a way that was immediately recognizable as components of a successful student presentation, despite having had little direct training in doing this. She saw, however, differences between how first year students and final year students did this, showing how disciplinary socialization proceeds in tandem with genre acquisition as students learn the "ways of doing and being" in their area of study.

Other authors such as Bawarshi and Reiff (2010), Flowerdew (1993, 2002, 2011), Henry and Roseberry (1998), Hyland (2004b, 2007, 2008), Hyon (1995, 1996, 2001, 2002), Johns (2002, 2008), Mustafa (1995), Paltridge (2001, 2007), Samraj (1995), and Tardy (2009) have discussed genre-based teaching. Johns (2008: 237) describes her experiences in genre-based teaching as an "on-going quest" for an approach "that is coherent and accessible to students while still promoting rhetorical flexibility and genre awareness." Tardy (2009: 287) observes, "despite its problematic normalizing effects, . . . writing and writers are tied to genre, even as they purposefully break generic conventions." As she concludes, the dynamic, contextual, and socio-rhetorical nature of genres can make them difficult to address in ESP classrooms, yet at the same time, genre is a concept that cannot be ignored.

Future Directions for ESP Genre Studies

In a review of genre and ELT published in 2007 (although written in 2001), I pointed to a number of areas in need of further research in the area of applied genre studies. Some of these areas have been addressed in the research literature that has been published since then. For example, we now have a better understanding of the benefits of genre-based instruction in ESP settings. We have, thanks especially to corpus studies, a better understanding of genre-specific language, and we have a better understanding of the relationship between text and context and how this impacts upon the language choices that language users make in their performance of particular genres. We have also learnt more about the historical, social, and ideological underpinnings of particular genres and how these influence what people say and do in their use of particular genres.

The area of research known as contrastive rhetoric has also been expanded to consider intercultural issues (see e.g. Connor 2004, 2011; Connor, Nagelhout, and Rozcyki 2008) and attention has been paid to the notion of a *"tertium comparationis"* (a comparable platform) (Connor and Moreno 2005; Moreno 2008) in these studies to ensure that texts that are being compared are indeed comparable (see Perales-Escudero and Swales 2011 for further discussion of this). Contrastive genre studies have also begun to take on a critical perspective that questions normative and essentialist assumptions about differences between languages and cultures (see Kubota 2010). We are also gaining a better understanding of the multiliteracies (Cope and Kalantzis 2000) requirements of our students' academic and professional lives. We have, then, come a long way in the area of genre-focussed ESP research, even if there is, still, a lot that needs to be done (see Belcher, Johns, and Paltridge 2011; Paltridge 2009; Swales 2011b for discussions of future directions in ESP research).

REFERENCES

Anthony, L. and Lashkia, G. V. (2003) Mover: A machine learning tool to assist in the reading and writing of technical papers. *IEEE Transactions on Professional Communication* 46: 185–93.

Artemeva, N. (2008) Toward a unified theory of genre learning. *Journal of Business and Technical Communication* 22: 160–85.

Artemeva, N. and Freedman, A. (eds.) (2008) *Rhetorical Genre Studies and Beyond*. Winnipeg: Inkshed Publications. Accessed August 2, 2011 at http://http-server.carleton.ca/~nartemev/Artemeva & Freedman Rhetorical Genre Studies and beyond.pdf.

Askehave, I. and Nielson, A. E. (2005) What are the characteristics of digital genres? Genre theory from a multimodal perspective. Proceedings of the 38th Hawaii International Conference on System Sciences. Accessed Sept. 18, 2010 at http://doi.ieeecomputersociety.org/10.1109/HICSS.2005.687.

Askehave, I. and Swales, J. M. (2001) Genre identification and communicative purpose: A problem and possible solution, *Applied Linguistics* 22: 195–212.

Badger, R. and White, G. (2000) A process genre approach to teaching writing. *ELT Journal* 54: 153–60.

Baker, P. (2008) *Sexed Texts: Language, Gender and Sexuality*. London: Equinox.

Bargiela-Chiappini, F. (2005) In memory of the business letter: Multimedia, genres and social action in a banking website.

In P. Gillearts and M. Gotti (eds.), *Genre Variation in Business Letters*. 99–122. Bern: Peter Lang.

Bargiela-Chiappini, F. and Nickerson, C. (eds.) (1999) *Writing Business: Genres, Media and Discourses*. London: Longman.

Bargiela-Chiappini, F., Nickerson, C., and Planken, B. (2007) *Business Discourse*. Basingstoke, UK: Palgrave Macmillan.

Bateman, J. A. (2008) *Multimodality and Genre: A Foundation for Systematic Analysis*. Basingstoke, UK: Palgrave Macmillan.

Bax, S. (2011) *Discourse and Genre: Analyzing Language in Context*. Basingstoke, UK: Palgrave Macmillan.

Bazerman, C. (1994) Systems of genres and the enactment of social intentions. In A. Freedman and P. Medway (eds.), *Genre and the New Rhetoric*. 79–101. London: Taylor & Francis.

Bazerman, C., Bonini, A., and Figueiredo, D. (eds.) (2009) *Genre in a Changing World*. West Lafayette, IN: Parlor Press.

Bawarshi, A. and Reiff, M. J. (2010) *Genre: An Introduction to History, Theory, Research, and Pedagogy*. West Lafayette, IN: Parlor Press.

Belcher, D., Johns, A. M., and Paltridge, B. (eds.) (2011) *New Directions in English for Specific Purposes Research*. Ann Arbor, MI: University of Michigan Press.

Berkenkotter, C. (2009) A case for historical "wide-angle" genre analysis: A personal retrospective. *Ibérica: Journal of the European Association of Language for Specific Purposes* 18: 9–21.

Berkenkotter, C. and Huckin, T. N. (1995) *Genre Knowledge in Disciplinary Communication: Cognition/Culture/Power*. Hillsdale, NJ: Lawrence Erlbaum.

Bhatia, V. K. (1993) *Analysing Genre: Language Use in Professional Settings*. London: Longman.

Bhatia, V. K. (2004) *Worlds of Written Discourse: A Genre-Based View*. London: Continuum.

Bhatia, V. K. and Gotti, M. (eds.) (2006) *Explorations in Specialized Genres*. Bern: Peter Lang.

Biber, D. (1988) *Variation Across Speech and Writing*. Cambridge: Cambridge University Press.

Biber, D. (2006) *University Language. A Corpus-Based Study of Spoken and Written Registers*. Amsterdam: John Benjamins.

Biber, D. and Conrad, S. (2009) *Register, Genre, and Style*. Cambridge: Cambridge University Press.

Biber, D., Conrad, S., and Cortes, V. (2004) *If you look at . . . :* Lexical bundles in university teaching and textbooks. *Applied Linguistics* 25: 371–405.

Biber, D., Conrad, S., and Reppen, R. (1994) Corpus-based approaches to issues in applied linguistics. *Applied Linguistics* 15: 169–89.

Biber, D., Connor, U., and Upton, T. A. (eds.) (2009) *Discourse on the Move: Using Corpus Analysis to Describe Discourse Structure*. Amsterdam: John Benjamins.

Bruce, I. (2011) *Theory and Concepts of English for Academic Purposes*. Basingstoke, UK: Palgrave Macmillan.

Bucholtz, M. (2009) From stance to style: Gender, interaction, and indexicality in Mexican youth slang. In A. Jaffe (ed.), *Stance: Sociolinguistic Perspectives*. 146–70. Oxford: Oxford University Press.

Bucholtz, M. and Hall, K. (2005) Identity and interaction: A sociocultural linguistic approach. *Discourse Studies* 7: 585–614.

Bunton, D. (2002) Generic moves in PhD thesis Introductions. In J. Flowerdew (ed.), *Academic Discourse*. 57–75. London: Longman.

Cheng, A. (2006a) Analyzing and enacting academic criticism: The case of an L2 graduate learner of academic writing. *Journal of Second Language Writing* 15: 279–306.

Cheng, A. (2006b) Understanding learners and learning in ESP genre-based writing instruction. *English for Specific Purposes* 25: 76–89.

Cheng, A. (2007) Transferring generic features and recontextualizing genre awareness: Understanding writing performance in the ESP genre-based literacy framework. *English for Specific Purposes* 26: 287–307.

Cheng, A. (2008a) Analyzing genre exemplars in preparation for writing: The case of an L2 graduate student in the ESP genre-based instructional framework of academic literacy. *Applied Linguistics* 29: 50–71.

Cheng, A. (2008b) Individualized engagement with genre in literacy tasks. *English for Specific Purposes* 27: 387–411.

Cheng, A. (2011) ESP classroom research: Basic considerations and future research questions. In D. Belcher, A. M. Johns, and B. Paltridge (eds.), *New Directions in English for Specific Purposes Research*. 44–72. Ann Arbor, MI: University of Michigan Press.

Connor, U. (1996) *Contrastive Rhetoric*. Cambridge: Cambridge University Press.

Connor, U. (2004) Intercultural rhetoric research: Beyond texts. *Journal of English for Academic Purposes* 3: 291–304.

Connor, U. (2011) *Intercultural Rhetoric in the Writing Classroom*. Ann Arbor, MI: University of Michigan Press.

Connor, U. and Moreno, A. (2005) Tertium comparationis: A vital component in contrastive rhetoric research. In P. Bruthiaux, D. Atkinson, W. G. Eggington, W. Grabe, and V. Ramanathan (eds.), *Directions in Applied Linguistics*. 153–64. Clevedon, UK: Multilingual Matters.

Connor, U., Nagelhout, E., and Rozycki, W. (eds.) (2008) *Contrastive Rhetoric: Reaching to Intercultural Rhetoric*. Amsterdam: John Benjamins.

Cope, B. and Kalantzis, M. (2000) (eds.) *Multiliteracies: Literacy Learning and the Design of Social Futures*. London: Routledge.

Crookes, G. (1986) Towards a validated analysis of scientific text structure. *Applied Linguistics* 7: 57–70.

Devitt, A. (2004) *Writing Genres*. Carbondale, IL: Southern Illinois University Press.

Dong, Y. R. (1998) Non-native speaker graduate students' thesis/dissertation writing in science: Self-reports by students and their advisors from two US institutions. *English for Specific Purposes* 17: 369–90.

Dressen-Hammouda, D. (2008) From novice to disciplinary expert: Disciplinary identity and genre mastery. *English for Specific Purposes* 27: 233–52.

DuBois, B. L. (1980) The use of slides in biomedical speeches. *The ESP Journal* 1: 45–50.

Dudley-Evans, T. (1999) The dissertation: A case of neglect? In P. Thompson (ed.), *Issues in EAP Writing Research and Instruction*. 28–36. Reading, UK: Centre for Applied Language Studies, University of Reading.

English, F. (2011) *Student Writing and Genre: Reconfiguring Academic Knowledge*. London: Continuum.

Flowerdew, J. (1993) An educational, or process, approach to the teaching of professional genres. *ELT Journal* 47: 305–16.

Flowerdew, J. (2002) Genre in the classroom: A linguistic approach. In A. Johns (ed.), *Genre in the Classroom: Multiple Perspectives*. 91–102. Mahwah, NJ: Lawrence Erlbaum.

Flowerdew, J. and Gotti, M. (eds.) (2006) *Studies in Specialized Discourse*. Bern: Peter Lang.

Flowerdew, J. (2011) Reconciling contrasting approaches to genre analysis: The whole can equal more than the sum of the parts. In D. Belcher, A. M. Johns, and B. Paltridge (eds.), *New Directions in English for Specific Purposes Research*. 119–44. Ann Arbor, MI: University of Michigan Press.

Flowerdew, J. and Wan, A. (2010) The linguistic and the contextual in applied genre analysis: The case of the company audit report. *English for Specific Purposes* 29: 78–93.

Flowerdew, L. (2011a) ESP and corpus studies. In D. Belcher, A. M. Johns, and B. Paltridge (eds.), *New Directions in English for Specific Purposes Research*. 222–51. Ann Arbor, MI: University of Michigan Press.

Flowerdew, L. (2011b) *Corpora and Language Education*. Basingstoke, UK: Palgrave Macmillan.

Freedman, A. (1999) Beyond the text: Towards understanding the teaching and learning of genres. *TESOL Quarterly* 33: 764–8.

Freedman, A. and Medway, P. (eds.) (1994) *Genre and the New Rhetoric*. London: Taylor & Francis.

Frow, J. (2006) *Genre*. London: Routledge.

Garzone, G. (2002) Describing e-commerce communication. Which models and categories for text analysis? In P. Evangelisti Allori and E. Ventola (eds.) *TEXTUS* 15: 279–96.

Gebhard, M. and Harman, R. (2011) Reconsidering genre theory in K–12 schools: A response to school reforms in the United States. *Journal of Second Language Writing* 20: 45–55.

Grabe, W. and Kaplan, R. B. (1996) *Theory and Practice of Writing. An Applied Linguistic Perspective*. London: Longman.

Gunnarsson, B. (2009) *Professional Discourse*. London: Continuum.

Harwood, N. (2005) "We do not seem to have a theory . . . the theory I present here attempts to full this gap": Inclusive and exclusive pronouns in academic writing. *Applied Linguistics* 26: 343–75.

Harwood, N. (2006) (In) appropriate personal pronoun use in political science: A qualitative study and a proposed heuristic for future research. *Written Communication* 23: 424–50.

Henry, A. and Roseberry, R. L. (1998) An evaluation of a genre-based approach to the teaching of EAP/ESP writing. *TESOL Quarterly* 32: 147–56.

Horowitz, D. (1986) Process not product: Less than meets the eye. *TESOL Quarterly* 8: 37–42.

Hyland, K. (2002a) Genre: Language, context and literacy. *Annual Review of Applied Linguistics* 22: 113–35.

Hyland, K. (2002b) Specificity revisited: How far should we go? *English for Specific Purposes* 21: 385–95.

Hyland, K. (2002c) Authority and invisibility: Authorial identity in academic writing. *Journal of Pragmatics* 34: 1091–112.

Hyland, K. (2004a) *Disciplinary Discourses: Social Interactions in Academic Writing*. 2nd edn. Ann Arbor, MI: The University of Michigan Press.

Hyland, K. (2004b) *Genre and Second Language Writing*. Ann Arbor, MI: The University of Michigan Press.

Hyland, K. (2007) Genre pedagogy: Language, literacy and L2 writing instruction. *Journal of Second Language Writing* 16: 148–64.

Hyland, K. (2008) Genre and academic writing in the disciplines. *Language Teaching*, 41: 543–62.

Hyland, K. (2009a) Genre analysis. In K. Malmkjær (ed.), *Routledge Encyclopedia of Linguistics*. 210–13. 3rd edn. London: Routledge.

Hyland, K. (2009b) *Academic Discourse*. London: Continuum.

Hyland, K. (2011) Disciplinary specificity: Discourse, context and ESP. In D. Belcher, A. M. Johns, and B. Paltridge (eds.), *New Directions in English for Specific Purposes Research*. 6–24. Ann Arbor, MI: University of Michigan Press.

Hyland, K. (2012) *Disciplinary Identities: Individuality and Community in Academic Discourse*. Cambridge: Cambridge University Press.

Hyon, S. (1995) A genre-based approach to ESL reading: Implications for North America and Australia. PhD dissertation. University of Michigan.

Hyon, S. (1996) Genre in three traditions: Implications for ESL. *TESOL Quarterly* 30: 693–722.

Hyon, S. (2001) Long-term effects of genre-based instruction: A follow-up study of an EAP reading course. *English for Specific Purposes* 20: 417–38.

Hyon, S. (2002) Genre and ESL reading: A classroom study. In A. M. Johns (ed.), *Genre in the Classroom: Multiple Perspectives*. 121–41. Mahwah, NJ: Lawrence Erlbaum.

Jewitt, C. (ed.) (2009) *The Routledge Handbook of Multimodal Analysis*. London: Routledge.

Johns, A. M. (1997) *Text, Role and Context: Developing Academic Literacies*. Cambridge: Cambridge University Press.

Johns, A. M. (1998) The visual and the verbal: A case study in Macroeconimics. *English for Specific Purposes* 17: 183–97.

Johns, A. M. (ed.) (2002) *Genre in the Classroom: Multiple Perspectives*. Mahwah, NJ: Lawrence Erlbaum.

Johns, A. M. (2008) Genre awareness for the novice student: An on-going quest. *Language Teaching* 41: 237–52.

Johns, A. M., Bawarshi, A., Coe, R. M., Hyland, K., Paltridge, B., Reiff, M. J., and Tardy, C. M. (2006) Crossing the boundaries of genre studies: Commentaries by experts. *Journal of Second Language Writing* 15: 234–49.

Kubota, R. (2010) Cross-cultural perspectives on writing: Contrastive rhetoric. In N. H. Hornberger and S. L. McKay (eds.), *Sociolinguistics and Language Education*. 265–89. Clevedon, UK: Multilingual Matters.

Lillis, T. (2008) Ethnography as method, methodology, and "deep theorizing." *Written Communication* 25: 353–88.

Lillis, T. and Curry, M. J. (2010) *Academic Writing in a Global Context: The Politics and Practices of Publishing in English*. London: Routledge.

Lin, L. and Evans, S. (2011) Structural patterns in empirical research articles: A cross-disciplinary study. *English for Specific Purposes*. 31: 150–60.

Litosseleti, L. (2006) *Gender and Language: Theory and Practice*. London: Hodder.

Martin, J. R. and Rose, D. (2008) *Genre Relations: Mapping Culture*. London: Equinox.

Mauranen, A. (2010) English as an academic lingua franca: The ELFA project. *English for Specific Purposes* 29: 183–90.

Mauranen, A. (2011) English as a lingua franca in ESP. In D. Belcher, A. M. Johns, and B. Paltridge (eds.), *New Directions in English for Specific Purposes Research*. 94–117. Ann Arbor, MI: University of Michigan Press.

Miller, C. R. (1984) Genre as social action. *Quarterly Journal of Speech* 70: 151–67. Reprinted in A. Freedman and P. Medway (eds.) (1994) *Genre and the New Rhetoric*. 23–42. London: Taylor & Francis.

Miller, C. R. and Shepherd, D. (2004) Blogging as social action: A genre analysis of the weblog. Accessed Sept. 16, 2010 at http://blog.lib.umn.edu/ blogosphere/blogging_as_social_ action_a_genre_analysis_of_the_ weblog.html

Miller, T. (1998) Visual persuasion: A comparison of visuals in academic texts and the popular press. *English for Specific Purposes* 17: 29–46.

Molle, D. and Prior, P. (2008). Multimodal genre systems in EAP writing pedagogy: reflecting on a needs analysis. *TESOL Quarterly* 42: 541–66.

Moreno, A. (2008) The importance of comparable corpora in cross-cultural studies. In U. Connor, E. Nagelhout, and W. Rozycki (eds.), *Contrastive Rhetoric: Reaching to Intercultural Rhetoric*. 25–41. Amsterdam: Benjamins.

Morton, J. (2009) Genre and disciplinary competence: A case study of contextualization in an academic speech genre. *English for Specific Purposes* 28: 217–29.

Mustafa, Z. (1995) The effect of genre awareness on linguistic transfer. *English for Specific Purposes* 14: 247–56.

Nickerson, C. (2000) *Playing the Corporate Game: An Investigation of the Genres and Discourse Strategies in English used by Dutch Writers Working in Multinational Corporations.* Amsterdam: Adophi.

Norris, J. and Ortega, L. (eds.) (2006) *Synthesizing Research on Language Learning and Teaching.* Amsterdam: John Benjamins.

Norris, J. and Ortega, L. (2010) Research synthesis. *Language Teaching* 43: 461–79.

Ochs, E. (1992) Indexing gender. In A. Duranti and C. Goodwin (eds.), *Rethinking Context: Language as an Interactive Phenomenon.* 335–58. Cambridge: Cambridge University Press.

O'Halloran, K. (2011) Multimodal discourse analysis. In K. Hyland and B. Paltridge (eds.), *Continuum Companion to Discourse Analysis.* 120–37. London: Continuum.

Ortega, L. (2010) Research synthesis. In B. Paltridge and A. Phakiti (eds.), *Continuum Companion to Research Methods in Applied Linguistics.* 111–26. London: Continuum.

Paltridge, B. (1997) *Genre, Frames and Writing in Research Settings.* Amsterdam and Philadelphia: John Benjamins.

Paltridge, B. (2001a) *Genre and the Language Learning Classroom.* Ann Arbor, MI: University of Michigan Press.

Paltridge, B. (2001b) Linguistic research and EAP pedagogy. In J. Flowerdew and M. Peacock (eds.), *Research Perspectives on English for Academic Purposes.* 55–70. Cambridge: Cambridge University Press.

Paltridge, B. (2002) Thesis and dissertation writing: An examination of published advice and actual practice. *English for Specific Purposes* 21: 125–43.

Paltridge, B. (2007) Approaches to genre in ELT. In J. Cummins and C. Davison (eds.), *The International Handbook of English Language Teaching*, Volume 2. 931–44. Norwell, MA: Springer.

Paltridge, B. (2008) Textographies and the researching and teaching of writing. *Iberica* 15: 9–24. Accessed Feb. 3, 2012 at www.aelfe.org/documents/02_15_Paltridge.pdf.

Paltridge, B. (2009) Where have we come from and where are we now? In D. Belcher (ed.), *English for Specific Purposes in Theory and Practice.* 289–96. Ann Arbor, MI: University of Michigan Press.

Paltridge, B. (2012a) *Discourse Analysis.* 2nd edn. London: Continuum.

Paltridge, B. (2012b) Theses and dissertations in English for specific purposes. In C. Chapelle (ed.) *The Encyclopedia of Applied Linguistics.* Oxford: Wiley-Blackwell.

Paltridge, B., Harbon, L., Hirsh, D., Phakiti, A., Shen, H., Stevenson, M., and Woodrow, L. (2009) *Teaching Academic Writing: An Introduction for Teachers of Second Language Writers.* Ann Arbor, MI: University of Michigan Press.

Paltridge, B. and Starfield, S. (2007) *Thesis and Dissertation Writing in a Second Language.* London: Routledge.

Paltridge, B. and Starfield, S. (2011) Research in English for specific purposes. In E. Hinkel (ed.), *Handbook of Research in Second Language Teaching and Learning.* Vol 2. 106–22 London: Routledge

Paltridge, B., Starfield, S., Ravelli, L., and Nicholson, S. (2011) Doctoral writing in the visual and performing arts: Issues and debates. *International Journal of Art and Design Education* 30: 88–101.

Paltridge, B., Starfield, S., Ravelli, L., Nicholson, S., and Tuckwell, K. (2012) Doctoral writing in the visual and performing arts: Two ends of a continuum. *Studies in Higher Education* 37: 989–1003.

Paltridge, B. and Wang, W. (2011) Contextualising ESP research: Media discourses in China and Australia. In D. Belcher, A. M. Johns, and B. Paltridge (eds.), *New Directions in English for*

Specific Purposes Research. 25–43. Ann Arbor, MI: University of Michigan Press.

Pare, A., Starke-Meyerring, D., and McAlpine, L. (2009) The dissertation as multi-genre: Many readers, many readings. In C. Bazerman, A. Bonini, and Figueiredo, D. (eds.), *Genre in a Changing World*. 179–93. West Lafayette, IN: Parlor Press.

Pennycook, A. (2010) *Language as a Local Practice*. London: Routledge.

Perales-Escudero, M. and Swales, J. M. (2011) Tracing convergence and divergence in pairs of Spanish and English research article abstracts: The case of *Ibérica. Ibercia* 21: 49-70.

Prior, P. (2009) From speech genres to mediated multimodal genre systems: Bakhtin, Voloshinov, and the question of writing. In C. Bazerman, A. Bonini, and D. Figueiredo (eds.), *Genre in a Changing World*. 17–34. West Lafayette, IN: Parlor Press.

Rose, D. and Martin, J. R. (2012) *Learning to Write/Reading to Learn: Genre, Knowledge and Pedagogy in the Sydney School*. London: Equinox.

Rowley-Jolivet, E. (2002) Visual discourse in scientific conference papers. *English for Specific Purposes* 21: 19–40.

Rowley-Jolivet, E. (2004) Different visions, different visuals: A social semiotic analysis of filed-specific visual composition in scientific conference presentations. *Visual Communication* 3: 145–75.

Samraj, B. (1995) The nature of academic writing in an interdisciplinary field. PhD dissertation. University of Michigan.

Starfield, S. (2002) "I'm a second-language English speaker": Negotiating writer identity and authority in Sociology One. *Language, Identity, and Education* 1: 121–40.

Starfield, S. (2010) Ethnographies. In B. Paltridge and A. Phakiti (eds.),

Continuum Companion to Research Methods in Applied Linguistics. 50–65. London: Continuum.

Starfield, S. (2011) Doing critical ethnographic research into academic writing: The theory of the methodology. In D. Belcher, A. M. Johns, and B. Paltridge (eds.), *New Directions in English for Specific Purposes Research*. 174–96. Ann Arbor, MI: University of Michigan Press.

Swales, J. M. (1981) Aspects of article Introductions. *Aston ESP Research Reports* No 1. Birmingham, UK: Language Studies Unit, The University of Aston. Republished University of Michigan Press 2011.

Swales, J. M. (1990) *Genre Analysis: English in Academic and Research Settings*. Cambridge: Cambridge University Press.

Swales, J. M. (1993) Genre and engagement. *Revue Belge de Philologie et d'Histoire* 71(3): 689–98.

Swales, J. M. (2004) *Research Genres: Explorations and Applications*. Cambridge: Cambridge University Press.

Swales, J. M. (2009) Worlds of genre – Metaphors of genre. In C. Bazerman, A. Bonini, and D. Figueiredo (eds.), *Genre in a Changing World*. 3–16. West Lafayette, IN: Parlor Press.

Swales, J. M. (2011a) Coda: Reflections on the future of genre and L2 writing. *Journal of Second Language Writing* 20: 83–5.

Swales, J. M. (2011b) Envoi. In D. Belcher, A. M. Johns, and B. Paltridge (eds.), *New Directions in English for Specific Purposes Research*. 271–74. Ann Arbor, MI: University of Michigan Press.

Swales, J. M. and Feak, C. B. (1995) From information transfer to data commentary. In T. Miller (ed.), *Functional Approaches to Written Text: Classroom Applications*. 64–76. Washington, DC: United States Information Agency.

Swales, J. M. and Feak, C. B. (2004) *Academic Writing for Graduate Students: Essential Tasks and Skills.* 2nd edn. Ann Arbor, MI: University of Michigan Press.

Swales, J. M. and Lindemann, S. (2002) Teaching the literature review to international graduate students. In A. M. Johns (ed.), *Genre in the Classroom: Multiple Perspectives.* 105–19. Mahwah, NJ: Lawrence Erlbaum.

Swales, John, M. and P. Rogers. 1995. Discourse and the projection of corporate culture: The mission statement. *Discourse and Society*, 6, 223-42.

Tardy, C. M. (2003) A genre system view of the funding of academic research. *Written Communication* 20: 7–36.

Tardy, C. M. (2005) Expressions of disciplinarity and individuality in a multimodal genre. *Computers and Composition* 22: 319–36.

Tardy, C. M. (2006) Researching first and second language genre learning: A comparative review and a look ahead. *Journal of Second Language Writing* 15: 79–101.

Tardy, C. M. (2008). Multimodality and the teaching of advanced academic writing: a genre systems perspective on speaking-writing connections. In A. Hirvela and D. Belcher (eds.), *The Oral/Literate Connection: Perspectives on L2 Speaking, Writing, and other Media Interactions.* 191–208. Ann Arbor, MI: University of Michigan Press.

Tardy, C. M. (2009) *Building Genre Knowledge.* West Lafayette, IN: Parlor Press.

Tardy, C. M. (2011a) ESP and multi-method approaches to genre analysis. In D. Belcher, A. M. Johns, and B. Paltridge (eds.), *New Directions in English for Specific Purposes Research.* 145–73. Ann Arbor, MI: University of Michigan Press.

Tardy, C. M. (2011b) The history and future of genre in second language writing.

Journal of Second Language Writing 20: 1–5.

Tardy, C. M. (2011c) Genre analysis. In K. Hyland and B. Paltridge (eds.), *Continuum Companion to Discourse Analysis.* 54–68. London: Continuum.

Tardy, C. M. and J. M. Swales (2007) Form, text organization, genre, coherence, and cohesion. In C. Bazerman (ed.), *Handbook of Writing Research.* 565–81. Mahwah, NJ: Lawrence Erlbaum.

Tarone, E., Dwyer, S., Gillette, S., and Ickes, V. (1981) On the use of the passive in two astrophysics journal papers. *The ESP Journal* 1: 123–40.

Taylor, G. and Chen, T. (1991) Linguistic, cultural, and subcultural issues in contrastive discourse analysis: Anglo-American and Chinese scientific texts. *Applied Linguistics* 1: 319–36.

Thompson, P. (1999) Exploring the contexts of writing: Interviews with PhD supervisors. In P. Thompson (ed.), *Issues in EAP Writing Research and Instruction.* 37–54. Reading, UK: Centre for Applied Language Studies, University of Reading.

Trosberg, A. (ed.) (2000) *Analysing Professional Discourses.* Amsterdam: John Benjamins.

Tu, W. (2010) How universities in China introduce themselves in Chinese and English on the internet: A contrastive genre study. MEd thesis. University of Sydney.

Upton, T. A. and Cohen, M. A. (2009) An approach to corpus-based discourse analysis: The move analysis as example. *Discourse Studies* 11: 585–605.

Upton, T. and Connor, U. (2001) Using computerized corpus analysis to investigate the textlinguistic discourse moves of a genre. *English for Specific Purposes* 20: 313–29.

Wang, W. (2007) *Genre across Languages and Cultures: Newspaper Commentaries in China and Australia.* Saarbruecken, Germany: VDM Verlag Dr. Müller.

Wang, W. (2008) Newspaper commentaries on terrorism in China and Australia: A contrastive genre study. In U. Connor, E. Nagelhout, and W. Rozycki (eds.), *Contrastive Rhetoric: Reaching to Intercultural Rhetoric*. 169–91. Amsterdam: John Benjamins.

Witte, S. (1992) Context, text and intertext: Towards a constructionist semiotic of writing. *Written Communication* 9: 237–308.

19 ESP and Assessment

DAN DOUGLAS

Introduction

Assessment in English for specific purposes (ESP) is in principle no different from other areas of language assessment. Language assessment practitioners must take account of test purpose, test taker characteristics, and the target language use situation. All language assessment specialists adhere to accepted principles of measurement, including providing evidence for test reliability, validity, and impact. Finally, professional language testers are bound by international standards of ethics which require, among other considerations, respect for the humanity and dignity of test takers, not knowingly allowing the misuse of test scores, and considering the effects of their tests on test takers, teachers, score users, and society in general (ILTA 2000). ESP assessment is held to these same principles. The traditional needs analysis in ESP covers the purpose of the assessment, the personal, educational, and knowledge characteristics of the test takers, and the context of specific purpose language use. Test developers must offer evidence that the tests they design provide consistent measurements of specific purpose language ability, that the inferences and decisions based on test performance are warranted, and that the consequences of the test are the intended ones and are beneficial for test takers. They are equally bound by professional ethical standards. If all this is true, in what ways can we reasonably distinguish assessment in ESP from other areas of language assessment?

The simple answer, of course, is that ESP assessment takes place in ESP programs. Assessment instruments are needed in specific purpose courses, as in all language programs, first, to give learners an opportunity to show what they have learned and what they can do with the language they have learned by being given the same instructions and the same input under the same conditions. Tests are

The Handbook of English for Specific Purposes, First Edition.
Edited by Brian Paltridge and Sue Starfield.
© 2013 John Wiley & Sons, Inc. Published 2013 by John Wiley & Sons, Inc.

needed secondly to get a "second opinion" about students' progress and help confirm teachers' own assessments and help them make decisions about students' needs. Thirdly, tests are needed to provide for some standardization by which teachers and other stakeholders judge performance and progress, allowing for comparisons of students with each other and against performance criteria generated either within the ESP program or externally. Finally tests help to ensure that student progress is judged in the same way from one time to the next, in other words, that the assessments are reliable. These are reasons for formal testing in any language-teaching program and ESP programs are no different in their need for assessment instruments that reflect the content and methodology of the courses, which we assume are themselves based on an analysis of the target language use situation. Traditionally, ESP courses and assessments have been contrasted with "general English" courses and assessments, though this distinction has been somewhat blurred in recent years (Douglas 2010), particularly since the publication of Bachman and Palmer's book, *Language Testing in Practice* (1996; revised 2010 as *Language Assessment in Practice*). All language tests require the developers to define the purpose of the test, conduct a needs analysis, collect language use data in context, analyze the target communicative tasks and language, and develop test tasks that reflect the target tasks. We can apply to language tests, I believe, what Long (2005: 1) has said about language courses: "Every language course should be considered a course for specific purposes, varying only (and considerably, to be sure) in the precision with which learner needs can be specified. . . . "

ESP assessment instruments are usually defined fairly narrowly to reflect a specific area of language use such as English for academic writing, English for nursing, Aviation English, or Business English, for example. Thus, ESP tests are based on our understanding of three qualities of specific purpose language: first, that language use varies with context, second, that specific purpose language is precise, and third that there is an interaction between specific purpose language and specific purpose background knowledge. With regard to contextual variation, it is well known that physicians use language differently from air traffic controllers, university students in economics use language differently from students in chemistry, and football/soccer players use language differently on the field than do ice hockey players on the rink. Furthermore, physicians use English differently when talking with other medical practitioners than when talking with patients, though both contexts would be categorized under the heading of Medical English. Cotos (2011) showed, by means of corpus analyses of published research article introductions in 50 different academic disciplines, that the discourse conventions of each discipline showed both similarities and differences across disciplines. Context has been defined variously over the years, but the classic features of context proposed by Hymes (1974) are still useful today: situation, participants, ends (purposes), act sequence (organization, content), key (tone), instrumentalities (language, medium), norms of interaction, and genre. The manipulation of these aspects of context in ESP tests challenge test takers to respond to differences in communicative context in ways perhaps more finely tuned than in more general language assessments. Secondly, regarding the notion that specific purpose language is precise, what outsiders refer to as unnecessary "gobbledygook" in academic, vocational, and technical fields, in fact reflects practitioners in those fields wishing to be more precise and accurate in their communication. Legal language, or "legalese," is the most-often cited example of such precision:

> I give my Agent the power to exercise or perform any act, power, duty, right, or obligation whatsoever that I have or may hereafter acquire, relating to any person, matter, transaction, or property, real or personal, tangible or intangible, now owned or hereafter acquired by me, including, without limitation, the following specifically enumerated powers. I grant to my Agent full power and authority to do everything necessary in exercising any of the powers herein granted as fully as I might or could do if personally present, with full power of substitution or revocation, hereby ratifying and confirming all that my Agent shall lawfully do or cause to be done by virtue of this Power of Attorney and the powers herein granted (Plain Language Association International 2009).

Although the language is this paragraph might seem unnecessarily obtuse to non-lawyers, I would suggest that the reason for its jargonish tone is the legal mind's desire for precision, covering all possible contingencies, and mitigating the possibility for misinterpretation or ambiguity. This is the second distinguishing feature of specific purpose language.

Finally, an important distinction between assessment in ESP and assessment in other areas of language teaching/learning is the relationship between language ability and background knowledge. In traditional, non-specific purpose assessment, content, or background knowledge has often been viewed as a confounding factor, masking "true" language ability and producing "construct irrelevant variance" (Douglas 2000; Fulcher 2000; Messick 1989). However, over the years, practitioners have gradually come to the realization that language knowledge and background knowledge are very difficult to distinguish in practice and that, although specific purpose testers are not in the business of assessing professional, vocational, or academic competence in specific purpose fields (Davies 2001), such competence is inextricably linked to language performance in those fields (Chapelle 1998; Douglas 2000, 2005; Fulcher 2000).

In this chapter I want to review recent literature on ESP testing, beginning with work on the theory and practice of specific purpose assessment, and then deal with various areas of ESP, including the testing of English for academic purposes for both learners and teachers; the testing of English for employment and vocational purposes in the fields of aviation, business, health, and medicine, and more broadly-defined workplace English; and testing for the purposes of immigration and asylum.

The Theory and Practice of Assessment in ESP

One would imagine that, after the number of years English for specific purposes teaching and assessment have been part of the profession of applied linguistics and language pedagogy (See Swales 1985 for a discussion of early examples of

ESP pedagogy, and Douglas 2000 for a discussion of early ESP assessment), the construct of specific purpose English ability – an understanding of what it is we assess in a test of ESP – would be fairly well established among assessment practitioners. To some degree this is the case but there are at least two theoretical issues that affect the practice of ESP testing: whether the construct of specific purpose language ability actually exists and the related issue of how the criteria for assessing specific purpose language performances should be derived. Davies (2001) argues that while the concept of *variation* in LSP has theoretical status, that of *varieties* does not, and that the principle of distinct specific purpose language abilities has more to do with content than with language: "LSP testing cannot be about testing for subject specific knowledge. It must be about testing for the ability/abilities to manipulate language functions appropriately in a wide variety of ways. This might mean no distinction between a general proficiency test and an LSP test" (2001: 143). Davies thus argues that the only justification for developing specific purpose language tests is to achieve face validity, and he equates degree of specificity with test difficulty.

Taking a different approach to the question of the specific purpose language test construct, Jacoby and McNamara (1999) grappled with the problem of determining performance assessment criteria in a test of Medical English and evaluations of conference presentation rehearsals. They found that, in the case of a Medical English assessment, the Occupational English Test (OET), the language-based criteria failed to capture critical features of the performance that supervising physicians deemed necessary for on-the-job communication. They got some clues as to the nature of these features from an analysis of physics conference presentation rehearsal critiques by practicing physicists. They found that the physicists hardly distinguished between native and non-native English speakers in making their evaluations of the rehearsal performance but rather focussed on criteria derived from their experience with actual conference presentations:

> In the OET, the rating scale for overall assessment is rooted in a comparison with a normative construction of native-speaker 'flexibility and range,' while in the rehearsal feedback, the assessment [of overall quality] is more holistically conceived, unrelated to comparisons with native speakers, and rooted in the complex task of presenting an effective conference talk (Jacoby and McNamara 1999: 233).

In my view, the weakness in Davies's argument is that he focusses entirely on the purely linguistic elements of specific purpose communication. As Jacoby and McNamara point out, however, there is more to it than that. A specific purpose language performance depends upon relevant non-linguistic knowledge that is, I think, inextricably interwoven with language knowledge in the performance. As Jacoby and McNamara put it,

> To assess special-purpose performance with general linguistic criteria, however, seems oddly out of synch with long-held fundamental positions in special-purpose language pedagogy and research, e.g. that special-purpose language is only a means to the acquisition of non-linguistic knowledge and skills; that using the traditional

four linguistic skills to delineate special-purpose performance is inadequate to capture real-world communicative cultures and activities; and that special-purpose performance is by definition task-related, context-related, specific, and local . . . (Jacoby and McNamara 1999: 234).

It should always be a part of the construct of specific purpose tests that learners' specific purpose language needs include not only linguistic knowledge but also background knowledge relevant to the communicative context in which learners need to operate. Thus, the theoretical underpinnings of specific purpose assessment must be expanded to include not only strictly linguistic features but also features of the context of interest to test takers and score users. As Fulcher (2000: 491) puts it, "some aspects of context may need to be defined as construct rather than error if they are found to be part of the meaning of test scores." With regard to context in ESP assessment, Davies (2008) grapples with the problem of authenticity. He points out, quite rightly, that tests can only *simulate* authenticity, but appears to take the view that authenticity is a unified whole and that tests are either authentic or they are not: "...tests simply cannot be authentic: what they can (all they can) do is to simulate authenticity" (2008: 69–70). Others (e.g. Bachman 1991; Douglas 2000) have taken the view that authenticity is a matter of degree related to the features of specific purpose context that are simulated in the test tasks, as argued in the previous section of this chapter. Indeed, Douglas (2005) has proposed a "continuum of specificity" ranging from less authentic and specific tests to those that are more so.

In conclusion, it seems to me that the construct of specific purpose language ability does indeed exist, that there is a case to be made for varying degrees of authenticity and specificity in ESP tests, and that the criteria for assessing specific purpose language performances should be derived from the specific purpose context itself. In the remainder of this chapter, then, this is the view that underlies the evaluation of research and development in ESP assessment.

English for Academic Purposes

English for academic purposes (EAP) assessment has evolved mainly with an emphasis on proficiency tests with reference to norms established for determining learners' levels of ability for mainstream classrooms and admission to tertiary education, and a secondary and more recent focus on criterion-referencing with respect to standards set for learners' attainments and public accountability in education (Cumming 2009). A third strand of academic ESP is in the area of English as a foreign language (EFL) teacher certification (Elder 2001).

There has been a fair amount of research into salient issues in the assessment of academic English in recent years. For example, Banerjee and Wall (2006) devised and validated an assessment checklist for pre-sessional academic English courses. Brooks (2009) looked at the co-construction of discourse in speaking tests and found that interaction with other learners resulted in more complex, linguistically demanding discourse than interaction with an examiner. Davidson and Cho (2001), in their case study of academic English assessment in one institution, argued that context in ESP refers both to the specific purpose language use situation and to the context in which the test is used. They suggest moving to more field-specific tests with an orientation toward academic units rather than toward ESL classes on the grounds that what academic learners need is information about their language use in their major fields, not that in more generic ESL classes. Elder, Bright, and Bennett (2007) investigated the relationship between diagnostic test performance and grades of learners in various academic disciplines as well as comparing writing produced in an assessment context with perceived requirements in academic disciplines. They found, perhaps unsurprisingly, that while a certain level of academic English was necessary for full engagement in academic disciplines, level of English ability was not always reflected in academic outcomes: "This is of course is as it should be. If language proficiency were all that mattered, then native speakers would be automatically assured of an easy passage through their academic courses . . ." (2007: 53). Gebril (2009) studied the generalizability of reading-to-write tasks compared with independent writing tasks and found that the reading-to-write tasks provided as reliable results as the independent writing tasks. Iwashita (2005) investigated the lexical range of test takers with respect to speaking task differences and found that while the number of words used in academic speaking tasks differed little by proficiency level, vocabulary use varied more by task type. Krekeler (2006) revisited the effect of background knowledge on ESP reading test performance and found a strong effect unrelated to threshold level. In other words, background knowledge did affect test performance but its effect was unpredictable with respect to the level of English proficiency. Qian (2007) grappled with the problems of assessing university students' English at the completion of their university studies, comparing the well-known international IELTS with a locally-produced test. He found that the local test compared favorably with IELTS and discussed the potential washback effect of both tests on teaching and learning. Finally, Read (2008) studied the use of a diagnostic test to identify academic language needs, based on an "assumption that academic language support will be more effective if students recognize for themselves the extent of their language needs and make a commitment to attend to them" (2008: 189). It is clear that academic English assessment accounts for a major portion of research in ESP testing.

With regard to mainstream proficiency testing for academic placement and admission, Davies (2008) provides an historical account of the development of British academic English proficiency testing through the lens of the International English Language Testing System (IELTS), arguing that the history of IELTS is as reflective of the development of the discipline of language testing as of the development of a particular test. Davies' work complements that by Spolsky (1995). Research on IELTS validity includes work by Moore and Morton (2005), O'Loughlin (2008), and Weir et al. (2009a, 2009b). With regard to the development of the Test of English as a Foreign Language (TOEFL; www.ets.org/toefl/) program, the introduction of the internet-based TOEFL iBT has been the subject of quite a lot of research and commentary in recent years, including a review by Alderson (2009) and validity arguments and evidence by Chapelle, Enright, and Jamieson (2008) and Sawaki, Stricker, and Oranje (2009). Biber et al. (2004) present the results of a corpus-based analysis of university language use as background for the TOEFL iBT. One the whole, these two large-scale academic English tests have been shown to be valid for the purposes for which they were developed, but there is much other research and development work in academic English outside the IELTS and TOEFL programs. A relatively new large-scale test of academic English, the Pearson Test of English Academic (PTE Academic; www.pearsonpte.com/pteacademic), was launched globally in 2009 and provides an online test of reading, writing, speaking, and listening, with the performances scored automatically by computer. Research has been carried out with regard to the validity and reliability of the test (Pearson 2010) and both the automated writing assessment tool (Landauer, Latham, and Foltz 2003) and the automated speech assessor (Pearson 2008). Other tests of academic English, with more regional clienteles that have been the subject of recent research and review include the British Test of English for Educational Purposes (Slaght and Howell 2007), the Canadian English Language Assessment (Turner 2005), and the College English Test, in China (Zheng and Cheng 2008).

Regarding the focus on developing tests for accountability and research to understand the language demands of learners in schools, this has been particularly prevalent in the United States where so called "no child left behind" legislation dating from 2002 has mandated tests to monitor progress and achievement in, among other subjects, English language and literacy (see Bailey 2007; Cumming 2009). The Center for Research on Evaluation, Standards, and Student Testing (CRESST), at the University of California at Los Angeles, has been particularly active in conducting research in this area (see, for example, Bailey 2007; Bailey and Butler 2004; Behrens et al. 2010; Kim and Herman, 2010). The Center is dedicated to providing sound data and evidence for the improvement of student evaluation for accountability and decision-making (CRESST 2010). There is, of course, interest in this area of academic English assessment outside the United States. For example, Cheng, Klinger, and Zeng (2007) explore the challenges of assessing the literacy of immigrant children in Canadian schools, while Cummins (2000) outlines the problems of assessing bilingual children in British schools.

A tangentially related EAP focus has been on the use of tests for certifying the English language skills of prospective and practicing English teachers. Elder (2001) outlines some of the problematic aspects of tests for teachers, including *specificity* – what is the domain of English for teaching? – *authenticity* – what task features are characteristic of the English teaching domain? – and *non-language factors* – what place do such factors as teaching skills or strategic competence have in the assessment of English for teaching? Consolo (2006) also grapples with the language domains non-native English speaking EFL teachers require for teaching as well as the level of English competence they expect to achieve to succeed in their teaching. The result of Consolo's study suggests that there is considerable uncertainty about these issues. In a major innovation in the assessment of English teachers' knowledge, Cambridge ESOL Examinations launched the Teaching Knowledge Test (www.cambridgeesol.org/exams/teaching-awards/tkt.html) in 2005 (Ashton and Khalifa 2005) as a first qualification for ESL teachers worldwide. The test was designed to measure subject knowledge (concepts and terminology in the discipline of ESL pedagogy), pedagogical knowledge (general principles of language teaching and learning), and pedagogical content knowledge (specialized knowledge of how to present language knowledge in a way that learners can understand). The new test was subjected to an evidence-based validation exercise prior to its launch and has been found to show high reliability and adequate quality assurance with respect to the purpose for which it was developed (Khalifa 2008). In a discussion conducted on the language testing online discussion list (LTEST-L) during the time of writing this chapter, it was found that certification of English teachers can exist at various administrative levels, including institutional, city, state/provincial, and national levels. Such certification is mandated in many parts of the world, including Europe, the Far East, the Middle East, and North America (Yin 2011), and this is clearly an important emerging area of research and development in ESP assessment.

Another area of teacher certification assessment is in the uniquely North American field of English tests for international teaching assistants (ITAs). Plough, Briggs, and Van Bonn (2010), for example, found that pronunciation and listening comprehension were the most important features in evaluating the speaking proficiency of prospective ITAs in an oral performance test. Saif (2006) found a positive relationship between a needs-based oral test and the content, teaching, classroom activities, and learning outcomes of an ITA training program. Finally, Wylie and Tannenbaum (2006) report on a standard-setting exercise for the TOEFL Academic Speaking Test (TAST; http://www.ets.org/research/policy_research_reports/rr-06-07_toeflibt-01), employing a panel of experts to determine what score level was deemed adequate for teaching.

English for Employment Purposes

The second major branch of ESP assessment is English for employment, vocational, and professional purposes, including an analysis of the PhonePass (Versant) test for employment purposes (Chun 2006), language testing in the military (Green and Wall 2005), English for the workplace (Lumley 2003; Lumley and Qian 2003; O'Loughlin 2008; Qian 2005), and the use of the IELTS general training module for vocational purposes (Smith and Haslett 2008). Specific areas of research and development also include English for international aviation, Business English, English for court interpreters, and Health and Medical English, as discussed below.

Aviation English

The International Civil Aviation Organization (ICAO) instituted a requirement that pilots and air traffic controllers involved in international aviation be certified as to their proficiency in English, the official language of international civil aviation, by a revised date of March, 2011. In order to meet this requirement, national civil aviation organizations began searching for tests of Aviation English. Well in advance of the deadline, test development companies began producing such tests. In a survey conducted by the Lancaster Language Testing Research Group (Alderson 2009) it was found that among several such tests available, little evidence was found regarding their quality, particularly in terms of the validity of interpretations of test performance. The survey team concluded that they "can have little confidence in the meaningfulness, reliability, and validity of several of the aviation language tests currently available for licensure" (2010: 51), and recommend that some international organization begin to monitor the quality of tests in this critical area of assessment; indeed, the International Language Testing Association has begun consultations with the ICAO for this very purpose. The Lancaster researchers also expressed concern for the validity of the ICAO scale for rating professional Aviation English, and some research has been undertaken to address such concerns. For example, Knoch (2009) reports on a standard-setting exercise in which users of the ICAO scale and pilots themselves were invited to give their views on the validity of the scale and descriptors as well as on the recorded performances of pilots with regard to the scale. Knoch concludes by asserting the importance of employing such stakeholder groups in the development and validation of ESP assessment scales. Read and Knoch (2009) provide an overview of the issues involved in the development and interpretation of tests of Aviation English.

Business English

The major contribution to the field of the assessment of Business English in the last few years is O'Sullivan (2006) *Issues in Business English: The Revision of the Cambridge Business English Certificates*. Its subtitle notwithstanding, a major portion of the book is devoted to a cogent discussion of the theory of specific purpose language assessment with examples drawn from major Business English tests. O'Sullivan argues that the construct of Business English is clearly definable but that work still needs to be done in the area of linking test tasks to language knowledge. The venerable Test of English as an International Language (TOEIC; http://www.ets.org/toeic), a business-oriented test of reading and listening since 1979, introduced speaking and writing components in 2006 in response to criticisms that learners who scored quite high on the reading and listening components, were "seriously deficient with regard to overall communicative ability" (Powers 2010: 2). The new test components have been subjected to validation studies and have been found to relate consistently to test takers' self-assessment of spoken and written abilities (Powers et al. 2009). In'nami and Koizumi (2012) carried out an analysis of the factor structure of the revised TOEIC and found support both for the separate reporting of reading and listening scores as well as for reporting a single composite score. Finally, in another area of Business English assessment, Qian (2005) conducted a study of the measurement of lexical richness in Business English writing.

Court interpreters

The field of certification of court interpreters has generated interest in the language-testing field, particularly in the United States, where the certification of interpreters in federal courts is mandated by law. Stansfield et al. (2003) describe the development of the Federal Court Interpreter Certification Examination (FCICE), which consists of a multiple-choice written component serving as a screening test for the second part, a criterion referenced oral examination. Stansfield and Hewitt (2005) report on a validation study of the FCICE that found that the written examination appropriately predicted performance on the oral examination. While not strictly related to the field of courtroom English, there is also useful background research on the task of providing linguistic evidence in court cases: Van Naerssen (2009) reports on relevant factors in making a connection between assessing language proficiency to providing evidence on the likelihood of a defendant or witness being capable of understanding laws and testimony in a trial.

Health/Medical English

The use of English language tests for determining the ability of internationally-trained health professionals to practice in English speaking environments has been a topic of concern in the ESP field for a number of years and continues to be of interest to researchers. Inoue (2009) discusses the development of a discourse-based rating scale for a health sciences communication test, arguing that this type of scale offers a more useful mans of diagnosing candidates' language skills as well as a more valid means of communicating test results than does a scale based on rater impressions. O'Neill et al. (2007) report on the use of the IELTS test for evaluating the English skills of nursing candidates, while Read and Wette (2009) consider the use of IELTS for the registration of health professionals in New Zealand. The O'Neill et al. study in particular touches on the controversy among language testing professionals regarding the advisability, indeed ethical issues, of using a test developed for one purpose, e.g. academic admissions, for another purpose, e.g. validating the language abilities of health professionals. In order to use a test of academic English for professional language certification, empirical evidence must be provided to show that interpreting test performance for a purpose other than that for which the test was designed is valid (Douglas 2000). For example, Eggly, Musial, and Smulowitz (1999) found that in spite of medical graduates scoring highly on the TOEIC and the Speaking Proficiency English Assessment Kit, neither of which had been validated for use in medical settings, ratings by both colleagues and patients in clinical communicative settings suggested that many of them displayed weaknesses in their professional communicative abilities. The Read and Wette (2009) study showed that test takers may prefer a test such as the IELTS over a more specific purpose test, such as the Occupational English Test (OET; www.occupationalenglishtest.org/), because of its lower fees and the availability of preparatory courses and practice materials.

From a test validation viewpoint, however, the use of a test designed for one purpose for another purpose without accompanying evidence supporting such a use, is questionable at best and at worst unethical.

English Testing for Immigration and Asylum

Language assessment instruments have been used for the purpose of determining the ethnicity and/or the suitability of applicants for immigration and political asylum for decades (millennia, if one accepts the evidence of the Biblical "shibboleth test" (Spolsky 1995), and research into the validity as well as the ethics of such uses has become of recent concern. An entire issue of the journal *Language Assessment Quarterly* was devoted in 2009 to these concerns. In this issue, McNamara (2009a) considers the role of language testers with regard to the use of a linguistically demanding citizenship test in Australia; Blackledge (2009a), Cooke (2009), and Saville (2009) look at issues involved in migrant language assessment in the United Kingdom; and Kunnan (2009) discusses the political, economic, and legal contexts of the language requirement of the US naturalization test. A book has also been published on the topic of assessment in the context of migration and citizenship (Extra, Spotti, and Avermaet 2009), dealing mainly with the testing of languages in Europe. Some chapters deal with English for immigration and asylum purposes, including that by Gales (2009) on the US situation, Blackledge (2009b) on that in the United Kingdom, and McNamara (2009b) on the Australian context. Finally, there is a chapter on the important topic of language and social identity in McNamara and Roever's book, *Language Testing: The Social Dimension* (2006) in which they discuss the use of language assessments of various kinds to identify acceptable and unacceptable members of ethnic and national groups. They confirm the view (Messick 1989) that all language tests imply values and that tests, both well-designed and improperly designed ones, can be used for unethical purposes to deny, for example, refugee status, political asylum, legal immigration, and citizenship. They conclude that in the language-testing field the tools needed to recognize and act upon such unethical political and social uses of language tests are still lacking today.

Conclusion

This review of recent theory and practice in ESP assessment suggests that the field has matured since its inception to the point where "mainstream" or "general" English language assessment has begun to be indistinguishable from specific purpose assessment. Indeed, it would be hard to find a test nowadays whose developers did not claim that it was based on an analysis of a target language use situation and reflected the communicative needs of specific groups of learners. Nevertheless, ESP assessment is clearly a definable sub-field of language assessment, with its focus on assessing ability to use language precisely to perform relevant tasks in authentic contexts while integrating appropriate aspects of field-specific background knowledge. There remains debate in the field about the nature of the construct of specific purpose language ability, and much research is being conducted to investigate this issue. Overall, there is a wide variety of research and development activity in ESP assessment around the world both among large test development companies and individual applied linguists and language testers.

A final word about the future of ESP assessment, touching on issues of the use of technology for test development, delivery, scoring, and score reporting, as well as the use of electronic corpora for the development of ESP tests. For test development, there is a range of course management and test development software, such as Blackboard (www.blackboard.com), or QuestionMark (www.questionmark.com/). In general terms, currently available software is useful for developing fairly basic multiple-choice and blank-filling tasks, and they allow for the inclusion of video, audio, and graphics as part of the input. They may not provide the flexibility ESP testers often require for highly authentic tasks, however, and it may be that purpose-built software will need to be developed for more sophisticated input and response features. With regard to test delivery, as Chapelle and Douglas (2006) point out, computers and the internet offer language testers a number of options for enhancing the authenticity of both test input and test response: full motion video, coordinated text and sound, and color graphics provide multimodal opportunities for context-rich tests. This is particularly true for ESP tests in which workplace, professional, and academic situations can more realistically be simulated than is possible with paper-based tests. At the same time, it should be emphasized that mere delivery of tests by computer will not automatically guarantee authenticity, for there are some situations in which paper-based input is the more authentic medium and the focus must be on replicating the target language use situation as authentically as possible, including the use of computers and the internet where these are a part of the target situation, and the use of other media when these are more realistic. The automated scoring of written and spoken test responses is a rapidly developing field, and is used now in major testing programs such as TOEFL and the Pearson Test of English. Natural language processing (NLP) by computers is becoming more and more sophisticated as researchers understand the nature of language and communication more deeply and are able to simulate human communication via computer (Chapelle and Douglas 2006), but few testing programs are ready to replace human raters entirely with automated systems (an exception is the Pearson Test of English). Research (e.g. Chodorow and Burstein 2004) has suggested that human raters may attend to the complexities of human language in ways that computers are so far unable to match, and Douglas (2010) notes that with regard to automated scoring of language tests, a certain amount of skepticism is warranted and such programs should probably be used only in low-stakes assessment situations. Moreover, they are expensive and likely to be beyond the means of all but the largest test development operations. Finally, a promising technological tool in the test development field is the use of electronic ESP corpora – large bodies of text drawn from specific purpose contexts – and powerful programs that allow for the analysis of the texts so that test developers can more fully understand ESP discourse (e.g. Biber et al. 2004; Taylor 2004). They are also used to validate language tests by showing the relationship between the language used in the test and that used in target situations. Technology, in other words, offers ESP assessment not only means for the delivery of tests but also tools for test development, scoring, and validation.

REFERENCES

Alderson, J. C. (2009) Test review: Test of English as a Foreign Language™: Internet-based Test (TOEFL iBT®). *Language Testing* 26: 621–31

Ashton, M. and Khalifa, H. (2005) A New Test for Teachers: Cambridge ESOL Teaching Knowledge Test. *Modern English Teacher* 14(1): 65–9.

Bachman, L. (1991) What Does Language Testing Have to Offer? *TESOL Quarterly* 25: 671–704.

Bachman, L. and Palmer, A. (1996) *Language Testing in Practice*. Oxford: Oxford University Press.

Bailey, A. (2007) *The Language Demands of School: Putting Academic English to the Test*. New Haven, CT: Yale University Press.

Bailey, A. and Butler, F. (2004) Ethical considerations in the assessment of the language and content knowledge of US school-age learners. *Language Assessment Quarterly* 1(2/3): 177–93.

Banerjee, J. and Wall, D. (2006) Assessing and Reporting Performances on Pre-Sessional EAP Courses: Developing a Final Assessment Checklist and Investigating its Validity. *Journal of English for Academic Purposes* 5: 50–69.

Behrens, J., Mislevy, R., DiCerbo, K., and Levy, R. (2010) *An Evidence Centered Design for Learning and Assessment in the Digital World*. CRESST Report778. Los Angeles: Center for Research on Evaluation, Standards and Student Testing (CRESST). Accessed March 8, 2011 at http://www.cse.ucla.edu/products/reports/R778.pdf.

Biber, D., Conrad, S., Reppen, R., Byrd, P., Helt,. M., Clark, V., Cortes, V., Csomay, E., and Urzua, A. (2004) *Representing Language Use in the University: Analysis of the TOEFL® 2000 Spoken and Written Academic Language Corpus (TOEFL Monograph No. TOEFL-MS-25)*. Princeton, NJ: Educational Testing Service.

Blackledge, A. (2009a) "As a country we do expect": The further extension of language testing regimes in the United Kingdom. *Language Assessment Quarterly* 6(1): 6–16.

Blackledge, A. (2009b) Inventing English as a convenient fiction: Language testing regimes in the United Kingdom. In G. Extra, M. Spotti, and P. Avermaet (eds.), *Language Testing, Migration, and Citizenship*. 66–86. London: Continuum.

Brooks, L. (2009) Interacting in pairs in a test of oral proficiency: Co-constructing a better performance, *Language Testing* 26: 341–66.

Chapelle, C. (1998) Construct Definition and Validity Inquiry in SLA Research. In L. Bachman and A. Cohen (eds.), *Interfaces Between Second Language Acquisition and Language Testing Research*. Cambridge: Cambridge University Press.

Chapelle, C., and Douglas, D. (2006) *Assessing Language Through Computer Technology*. Cambridge: Cambridge University Press.

Chapelle, C., Enright, M., and Jamieson, J. (2008) *Building a Validity Argument for the Test of English as a Foreign Language*. New York: Routledge.

Cheng, L., Klinger, D., and Zheng, Y. (2007) The challenges of the Ontario secondary school literacy test for second language students. *Language Testing* 24(2): 185–208.

Chodorow, M. and Burstein, J. (2004) *Beyond Essay Length: Evaluating E-Performance on TOEFL Essays*. TOEFL Research Report No. RR–73. Princeton, NJ: Educational Testing Service.

Chun, C. (2006) An analysis of a language test for employment: The authenticity of the Phonepass Test. *Language Assessment Quarterly* 3: 295–306.

Consolo, D. (2006) On a (re)definition of oral language proficiency for EFL teachers: Perspectives and contributions from current research. *Melbourne Papers in Language Testing* 11(1): 1–28.

Cooke, M. (2009) Barrier or entitlement? The language and citizenship agenda in the United Kingdom. *Language Assessment Quarterly* 6: 71–77.

Cotos, E. (2011) Potential of automated writing evaluation feedback. *CALICO Journal* 28(2): 420–59.

CRESST (2010) *Stepping Up: CRESST: Advancing Assessment, Evaluation, and Technology Worldwide*. Los Angeles: National Center for Research on Evaluation, Standards, and Student Testing. Accessed March 9, 2011at http://www.cse.ucla.edu/CRESST_Center_Overview.pdf.

Cumming, A. (2009) Language assessment in education: Tests, curricula, and teaching. *Annual Review of Applied Linguistics* 29: 90–100.

Cummins, J. (2000) *Language, Power, and Pedagogy: Bilingual Children in the Crossfire*. Clevedon, UK: Multilingual Matters.

Davidson, F. and Cho, Y. (2001) Issues in EAP test development: What one institution and its history tell us. In J. Flowerdew and M. Peacock (eds.), *Research Perspectives on English for Academic Purposes*. 286–97. Cambridge: Cambridge University Press.

Davies, A. (2001) The logic of testing languages for specific purposes. *Language Testing* 18: 133–48.

Davies, A. (2008) *Assessing Academic English: Testing English Proficiency 1950–1989 – the IELTS Solution*. Cambridge: Cambridge University Press.

Douglas, D. (2000) *Assessing Languages for Specific Purposes*. Cambridge: Cambridge University Press.

Douglas, D. (2005) Testing languages for specific purposes. In E. Hinkel (ed.), *Handbook of Research in Second Language Teaching and Learning*. 857–68. Mahwah, NJ: Lawrence Erlbaum.

Douglas, D. (2010) *Understanding Language Testing*. London: Hodder Education.

Eggly, S., Musial, J., and Smulowitz, J. (1999) The relationship between English language proficiency and success as a medical resident. *English for Specific Purposes* 18: 201–08.

Elder, C. (2001) Assessing the Language Proficiency of Teachers: Are There Any Border Controls? *Language Testing* 18: 149–70.

Elder, C, Bright, C. and Bennett, S. (2007) The Role of Language Proficiency in Academic Success: Perspectives from a New Zealand University. *Melbourne Papers in Language Testing* 12(1): 24–58.

Extra, G., Spotti, M., and Avermaet., P. V. (eds.) (2009) *Language Testing, Migration, and Citizenship*. London: Continuum.

Fulcher, G. (2000) The "communicative" legacy in language testing. *System* 28: 483–97.

Gales, T. (2009) The language barrier between immigration and citizenship in the United States. In G. Extra, M. Spotti and P. V. Avermaet (eds.) *Language Testing, Migration, and Citizenship*. 189–210. London: Continuum.

Gebril, A. (2009) Score generalisability of academic writing tasks: Does one test method fit it all? *Language Testing* 26: 507–31.

Green, R. and Wall, D. (2005) Language Testing in the Military: Problems,

Politics and Progress. *Language Testing* 22: 379–98.

Hymes, D. (1974) *Foundations in Sociolinguistics: An Ethnographic Approach*. Philadelphia, PA: University of Pennsylvania Press.

ILTA (2000) ILTA Code of Ethics. Accessed Jan. 18, 2011 at http://www.iltaonline. com/images/pdfs/ILTA_Code.pdf.

In'nami, Y. and Koizumi, R. (2012) Factor structure of the revised TOEIC® test: A multiple-sample analysis. *Language Testing* 29: 131–52.

Inoue, M. (2009) Health sciences communication skills test: The development of a rating scale. *Melbourne Papers in Language Testing* 14(1): 55–91.

Iwashita, N. (2005) An Investigation of lexical profiles in performance on EAP speaking tasks. *Spaan Fellow Working Papers in Second or Foreign Language Assessment* 3: 101–12.

Jacoby, S. and McNamara, T. (1999) Locating competence. *English for Specific Purposes* 1: 213–41.

Khalifa, H. (2008) Testing Teaching Knowledge: Developing a Quality Instrument to Support Professional Development. In L. Taylor and C. Weir (eds.), *Multilingualism and Assessment: Achieving Transparency, Assuring Quality, and Sustaining Diversity*. 191–202. Cambridge: UCLES/Cambridge University Press.

Kim, J. and Herman, J. (2010) When to exit ELL students: Monitoring success and failure in mainstream classrooms after ELLs' reclassification. CRESST Report 779. Los Angeles: Center for Research on Evaluation, Standards, and Student Testing (CRESST). Accessed March 8, 2011 at http://www.cse.ucla.edu/ products/reports/R779.pdf.

Knoch, U. (2009) Collaborating with ESP Stakeholders in Rating Scale Validation: The Case of the ICAO Rating Scale. *Spaan Fellow Working Papers in Second or Foreign Language Assessment* 7: 21–46.

Krekeler, C. (2006) Language for special academic purposes (LSAP) Testing: The effect of background knowledge revisited. *Language Testing* 23: 99–130.

Kunnan, A. (2009) Testing for citizenship: The U.S. Naturalization Test. *Language Assessment Quarterly* 6: 89–97.

Landauer, T., Latham, D., and Foltz, P. (2003) Automatic essay assessment. *Assessment in Education: Principles, Policy and Practice* 10: 295–308.

Long, M. (ed.) (2005) *Second Language Needs Analysis*. Cambridge: Cambridge University Press.

Lumley, T. (2003) Assessing English for employment. In C. Coombe and N. Hubley (eds.), *Assessment Practices*. Alexandria, VA: TESOL.

Lumley, T. and Qian, D. (2003) Assessing English for employment in Hong Kong. In C. Coombe and N. Hubley (eds.), *Assessment Practices*. Alexandria, VA: TESOL.

McNamara, T. (2009a) Australia: The dictation test redux? *Language Assessment Quarterly* 6: 106–11.

McNamara, T. (2009b) The spectre of the dictation test: Language testing for immigration and citizenship in Australia. In G. Extra, M. Spotti, and P. V. Avermaet (eds.), *Language Testing, Migration, and Citizenship*. 224–41. London: Continuum.

McNamara, T. and Roever, C. (2006) *Language Testing: The Social Dimension*. London: Blackwell.

Messick, S. (1989) Validity. In R. Linn (ed.), *Educational Measurement*. 13–23. New York: Macmillan.

Moore, T. and Morton, J. (2005) Dimensions of difference: A comparison of university writing and IELTS writing. *Journal of English for Academic Purposes* 4: 43–66.

O'Loughlin, K. (2008) The use of IELTS for university selection in Australia: A case study. *British Council/IELTS Australia Research Reports, Vol. 8*. Canberra: British Council /IELTS Australia.

O'Neill, T., Buckendahl, C., Plake, B., and Taylor, L. (2007) Recommending a nursing-specific passing standard for the IELTS examination. *Language Assessment Quarterly* 4: 295–317.

Pearson (2008) Versant English Test: Test Description and Validation Summary. Accessed March 8, 2011 at http://pearsonpte.com/SiteCollectionDocuments/Versant_English_Test_Test_Description_and_Validation_Summary.pdf.

Pearson (2010) Validity and reliability in PTE Academic. Accessed Feb. 2, 2012 at www.pearsonpte.com/SiteCollectionDocuments/ValidityReportUS.pdf

Plain Language Association International (2009) Accessed Jan. 19, 2011 at http://www.plainlanguagenetwork.org/Samples/index.html.

Plough, I., Briggs, S., and Van Bonn, S. (2010) A multi-method analysis of evaluation criteria used to assess the speaking proficiency of graduate student instructors. *Language Testing* 27: 235–60.

Powers, D. (2010) *The Case for a Comprehensive, Four-skills Assessment of English Language Proficiency*. TOEIC Policy and Research Reports Number 12. Princeton, NJ: Educational Testing Service.

Powers, D., Kim, H. J., Yu, F., Weng, V., and VanWinkle, W. (2009) *The TOEIC® Speaking and Writing Tests: Relations to Test-Taker Perceptions of Proficiency in English*. TOEIC Research Report Number 4. Princeton, NJ: Educational Testing Service.

Qian, D. (2005) Measuring lexical richness in business English writing: A study of Chinese learners. *The Hong Kong Linguist* 25: 36–42.

Qian, D. (2007) Assessing university students: Searching for an English language exit test. *RELC Journal* 38: 18–37.

Read, J. (2008) Identifying academic language needs through diagnostic assessment. *Journal of English for Academic Purposes* 7: 180–90.

Read, J. and Knoch, U. (2009) Clearing the air: Applied linguistic perspectives on aviation communication. *Australian Review of Applied Linguistics* 32(2): 1–21.

Read, J. and Wette, R. (2009) Achieving English proficiency for professional registration: The experience of overseas-qualified health professionals in the New Zealand context. In J. Osborne (ed.), *IELTS Research Reports* Volume 10. Canberra: IELTS Australia. Accessed Feb. 2, 2012 at www.ielts.org/pdf/Vol10_Full_report.pdf.

Saif, S. (2006) Aiming for positive washback: A case study of international teaching assistants. *Language Testing*, 23: 1–34.

Saville, N. (2009) Language assessment in the management of international migration: A framework for considering the issues. *Language Assessment Quarterly* 6: 17–29.

Sawaki, Y., Stricker, L., and Oranje, A. (2009) Factor structure of the TOEFL Internet-based test. *Language Testing* 26: 5–30.

Spolsky, B. (1995) *Measured Words*. Oxford: Oxford University Press.

Stansfield, C., Hewitt, W., Romberger, W., and Van Der Heide, M. (2003) The Federal Court Interpreter Certification Examination. *ATA Chronicle* 32(11): 29–34.

Stansfield, C. and Hewitt, W. (2005) Examining the predictive validity of a screening test for court interpreters. *Language Testing* 22: 438–62.

Swales, J. M. (ed.) (1985) *Episodes in ESP*. Oxford: Pergamon Press.

Taylor, L. (2004) Testing times: Research directions and issues for Cambridge ESOL examinations. *TESOL Quarterly* 38: 141–46.

Turner, C. (2005) Canadian academic English language (CAEL) assessment. In S. Stoynoff and C. Chapelle (eds.), *ESOL Tests and Testing: A Resource for Teachers and Administrators.* 49–53. Alexandria, VA: TESOL.

Van Naerssen, M. (2009) Going from language proficiency to linguistic evidence in court cases. In L. Taylor and C. Weir (eds.), *Language Testing Matters: Investigating the Wider Social and Educational Impact of Assessment*: 36–58. Proceedings of the ALTE Cambridge Conference, April 2008. *Studies in Language Testing* 31. Cambridge: UCLES/Cambridge University Press.

Weir, C., Hawkey, R., Green, A., and Devi, S. (2009b) The cognitive processes underlying the academic reading construct as measured by IELTS. *British Council/IDP Australia Research Reports* 9: 157–89.

Weir, C, Hawkey, R., Green, A., Devi, S., and Unaldi, A. (2009a) The relationship between the academic reading construct as measured by IELTS and the reading experiences of students in their first year of study at a British university. *British Council/IDP Australia Research Reports* 9: 97–156.

Wylie, E. C. and Tannenbaum, R. (2006) *TOEFL® Academic Speaking Test: Setting a Cut Score for International Teaching Assistants (ETS Research Memorandum No. RM-06-01)*. Princeton, NJ: Educational Testing Service.

Yin, M. (2011) Summary of online discussion of threshold policies/language requirements for teachers/teacher-trainees. Accessed Feb. 8, 2011 at http://www.ltest-l@lists.psu.edu.

Zheng, Y. and Cheng, L. (2008) College English Test (CET) in China. *Language Testing* 25: 408–17.

20 Technology and ESP

JOEL BLOCH

Introduction

The use of technology in ESP classes

Technology has long played a major role in the teaching of English for specific purposes (ESP) in two distinct ways. First, as a tool for helping with traditional types of language learning and, second, as a space for creating new forms of communicating. All areas of ESP pedagogy have been impacted by the ongoing development of new technologies. Spoken English teachers, for example, can use programs like Audacity not only to create their own recordings or podcasts but also to allow students to monitor a visual pattern of their spoken language. Audacity is a free program frequently used for podcasting but has been implemented by ESP teachers for specific pedagogical goals.

Technologies have also been used in a variety of ESP classes to create contexts for communicating with oral, literate, and visual modes of discourse. These include synchronous forms of discourse, such as chat, where the participants interact in the same time frame, or asynchronous forms, such as email, listservs, Twitter, or blogging, or newer forms of technologies, such as Facebook where the reader/writer can interact using any of these modes of discourse. The problem arises, then, in choosing which technologies are most appropriate for the types of learning found in the classroom, which raises a further question: how does the choice of a technology or technologies affect those goals for learning?

Decisions about the choice of technologies can be linked to the more traditional decisions made about the goals for a curriculum. ESP teachers have long relied on needs assessment for selecting the goals of their curricula. Hyland (2002) has argued that an ESP curriculum begins with a needs assessment of the learner.

The Handbook of English for Specific Purposes, First Edition.
Edited by Brian Paltridge and Sue Starfield.
© 2013 John Wiley & Sons, Inc. Published 2013 by John Wiley & Sons, Inc.

Dudley-Evans and St John (1998) describe different types of needs analysis as differentiating between objective needs (leaning how to use a technology, subjective needs (feeling comfortable using the technology), and analysis of the current situation (such as the lack of an ability to evaluate search materials). Louhiala-Salminen, Charles, and Kankaanranta (2005) argue that language learners need to acquire a sense of themselves as communicators who can interpret both the contextual and presuppositional clues within an exchange as well as an understanding of the discourse and cultural practices of the other participants. Each new technology may support a different sense of these communicative interactions, which may require a different set of goals to be incorporated into an ESP curriculum. In discussing business proposals, for example, Flowerdew (2010) finds that an important function of business communication is to establish rapport with the client. How this rapport is accomplished in a multimodal environment may differ from how it was established in a face-to-face context. For example, the use of email has been a central focus of research for establishing and perpetuating these kinds of relationships in an online context.

Language learners need to understand the often complex relationships between language and social context in order to become effective communicators. Jensen (2009), for example, examined the kinds of metadiscourse used in email to establish and maintain relationships between a buyer and a seller. Although email is still a popular and familiar tool, the ever-increasing use of other technologies, such as Facebook or Twitter, for these kinds of online interactions, often necessitate the direct teaching of the use of these technologies in the ESP classroom. A much different context for interacting can be created in an international business meeting held online using a technology like Elluminate (www.elluminate.com) or Adobe Connect, which may involve different kinds of interactions using different language strategies than used in a face-to-face meeting.

Such examples illustrate how traditional learner needs may manifest themselves differently in a technologically enhanced environment. With the newer technologies, direct teaching has become even more important. Newer technologies have tended to integrate different forms of environments. Many environments allow video, audio, and textual communication to occur at the same time. Some of the newer communication tools allow participants to conduct backchannel conversations while a speaker is giving a presentation, which has occasionally led to embarrassing situations. While many language learners may be familiar with these technologies, their use for the specific goals of the ESP classroom may not be as familiar. Therefore, directly teaching these technologies may again be necessary. Students and teachers may need to create blogs and Facebook pages, as well as to communicate with each other via Twitter and email, in order to learn the discoursal strategies most suitable for use with these technologies.

This need becomes more important when incorporating the variety of social contexts in which a technology can be used into the classroom. In a study of communication in the workplace, Crosling and Ward (2002) found a large variety of different forms of communication used for different communication types across a variety of social contexts. In the following years, many of the forms of communication they discussed have utilized various technologies, creating complex rela-tionships for oral and written interactions. Each technology supports the use of various forms of language, some may be appropriate and some may not, for a given context. For example, students may need to know when to switch between formal and informal forms when sending email.

However, using inappropriate language can cause not only breakdowns in communication but also can cause embarrassing and career threatening situations. Many of these forms of language have been affected by these new technologies (e.g. Crystal 2001). While it cannot be determined which technology will produce which form of discourse (e.g. Feenberg 1999), certain technologies seem to affect which discourses can appear in different contexts. Employees may update their status on Facebook or chat online with the person in the next cube so that they can continue to work on their computers at the same time. In other situations, team members may still gather in groups and talk face to face. Conferencing soft-ware may be used to support global interactions. In all such cases, there has been a great increase in the amount of communication and in locations where individu-als can communicate and a corresponding need to understand the role of the technologies used in these contexts.

Understanding the role of technology in these various and sometimes interlock-ing contexts has become extremely important, for example, for teachers, preparing students for careers where the choice of technology can be extremely critical. For example, when is it preferable to communicate with chat or email, by updating a Facebook page, or sending out a tweet? How do these choices affect the relation-ships between the sender and the receivers of information? How much privacy is required for an exchange of this information? Where are the participants physi-cally located and what kinds of information are they sharing, and, in a global context, what languages do the participants primarily speak?

The experiences with these technologies that students bring from both inside and outside the classroom may be invaluable in their future careers. Many years ago when the internet was first becoming popular, employers were worried that their employees would waste their time online; however, Sproull and Kiesler (1991) pointed out that these employees could also use their skills in workplace contexts. Today, the same skills students may bring for using social media sites may be applicable to their careers as corporations may use Facebook, virtual worlds, gaming, or blogs as part of their corporate marketing. Nickerson, Ger-ritsen, and van Meurs (2005) discuss the importance for students in ESP classes to reflect on the role of English around them, in particular how businesses may use English to promote their products.

In all these examples, the use of technology can be applicable across all types of ESP classrooms. Each technology has created its own norms and values for the use of language, some of which have also affected how language is used in face-to-face contexts (e.g. Crystal 2001; Myers 2010). Understanding the nature of these languages is especially important for ESP teachers who need to immerse their students in these types of technologies in response to their needs to use English, often as a lingua franca, in a variety of technology-based contexts.

The choice of which technologies to use involves an assessment between the types of relationships one is engaged in and the nature of the language most appropriate (Crystal 2001). As technology becomes more a factor in ESP education as a tool for language learning, as a site for varied and authentic materials, and as a place for publishing and sharing work, the impact of technology has become more complicated and often more controversial as well.

Technology as Tool for Language Learning

From the introduction of the stand-alone computer into the classroom, through the development of local networks (LAN), wide-area networks (WAN), the internet, and the World Wide Web to new mobile technologies, ESP teachers have been able to exploit the ability to share, produce, and use the vast amount of materials available outside the classroom. As Belcher (2004) points out, technology has often been used in ESP teaching as a tool for bringing language experiences from outside the classroom that are relevant for the teaching of English for a variety of purposes. Belcher gives the example of research by Shi, Corcos, and Storey (2001), who videotaped hospital discourse to bring to the language-learning classroom the authentic languages used outside the classroom.

Concordancing sites (see Nesi, this volume) are another technology that can facilitate the traditional concerns of ESP teachers for incorporating authentic forms of language. Hyland (2002), for example, argues for the importance of specificity of these forms of language. Concordancing has been particularly favored by ESP teachers since these sites can provide lexical and syntactic examples from authentic texts in specific areas of discourse. The use of concordancing is also an interesting example of how technological changes can affect the pedagogical value of a technology. Concordancing is an older technology that was primarily accessible to a few researchers in the field of linguistics. However, the development of stand-alone concordance programs, such as MonoConc 2.2 and Wordsmith, and the development of the World Wide Web have dramatically changed who could access these programs and how they could be used.

The stand-alone programs have allowed teachers to develop their own corpus, each potentially reflecting a genre or type of language that could be researched or used for developing materials. The internet allows corpora, whether they are small teacher-developed corpora or a large corpus like the Corpus of Contemporary American English (http://corpus.byu.edu/coca/) to be accessed by anyone, at any time, at any place, and for any purpose through the use of web-based interfaces that are designed to meet the specific needs of the users (Bloch 2009). Interfaces such as the one used by the View (corpus.byu.edu/bnc), for example, allow the user to search by lexical item and part of speech. Interfaces can allow the designer to access corpora according to whatever rules the designer feels are most relevant. The interface of the View, for example, offers pull-down menus so that the user can easily specify which part of speech is to be searched. MICASE (http://micase.elicorpora.info/), which was designed by the University of Michigan, allows the user to answer a series of questions, the answers to which will guide the search of the corpus.

The availability of corpora like the View, which contain both formal and informal forms of language, or MICASE, which contains different forms of language taken from different oral contexts, illustrates the various approaches available for incorporating this kind of specificity and how these approaches are incorporated in the design of the interface. MICASE, for example, allows the user to further specify language produced in different contexts or by different types of speakers with different backgrounds. A more narrowly defined approach to using the internet as a tool is the use of online dictionaries that are dedicated to specific areas of interest. InvestorWords.com, for example, offers fairly extensive definitions of lexical items related to business. Science Dictionary (http://www.sciencedictionary.org) offers definitions of scientific terms across a variety of fields.

ESP teachers are beginning to exploit these changes in design. Lee and Swales (2006: 72) discuss how they implemented the use of concordancing with language learners to achieve what they call "technology enhanced rhetorical consciousness-raising." This study, along with other studies of similar implementations (e.g. Yoon 2008; Yoon and Hirvela 2004), illustrate both the successes and frustrations of this process, some of which can be attributed to the design or architecture of the site itself. Both these concordancing sites and dictionary sites can be integrated into a learning network by directly inserting their URLs into a student's paper using the comment function in word processing programs like Microsoft Word. If a teacher or peer reviewer comments about a problem in the text that these sites could help with, the learner can directly click to that site.

One of the strengths of the internet for ESP teaching is the availability of different types of both oral and written texts. In their discussion of creating materials for an academic English program, Dudley-Evans and St John (1998) suggest that the ESP teacher find copies of syllabi and other course materials. Teachers and researchers in search of "authentic" materials need only turn on their computers to find these materials, including newspapers, magazines, scientific journals, news broadcasts, and lectures, all of which provide new ways for examining specific forms of language.

Another important resource for developing these kinds of materials has been the growth of open-access university courses where the lectures, class notes, and occasionally readings are freely accessible to everyone. Concepts, such as "open access," where materials are placed into a "commons" which anyone can use, have allowed for entire courses to be placed on the internet. Teachers interested in bringing in specific and authentic examples of classroom materials have an almost unlimited number of courses to choose from. Often complete materials for courses, for example, can be found on MIT's OpenCourseWare site (http://ocw.mit.edu/courses/electrical-engineering-and-computer-science) and Carnegie Mellon's Open Learning Initiative site (http://oli.web.cmu.edu/openlearning/index.php). Many universities, such as Yale (http://oyc.yale.edu) and The University of California, Berkeley (http://webcast.berkeley.edu) provide both audio and visual copies of lectures that can be used for language practice. From their computers, students can read course materials, listen to lectures, or study how professors lecture. Open access audio materials can be found on the websites of news organizations like the British Broadcasting Company (www.bbc.co.uk) or National Public Radio (www.npr.org), which make podcasts of their programs available.

Video-hosting sites like YouTube and Hulu (www.hulu.com) use closed captioning on many of their videos, which students can use to listen to and read at the same time. Oral forms of discourse, such as podcasts, have tended to be longer pieces. Radio stations frequently use podcasts to store past shows, providing teachers with a large up-to-the minute listening materials. Free programs like Audacity allow students to create their own podcasts. The ease of storage has allowed these podcasts to be stored for free online so they can be shared with an unlimited audience, as are blogs and other forms of multimodal texts. Sites for storing video texts, like YouTube (www.youtube.com) or Vimeo (www.vimeo.com), can greatly expand the audience for student work, helping them rethink their relationship between themselves and their audiences and how these relationships affect their use of language.

A major question that ESP teachers and students have to face with the availability of these materials is how to evaluate and successfully use them in the classroom. One of the greatest strengths of the internet, its role as a repository for raw information that has not been vetted by gatekeepers, has meant that students and teachers must take greater responsibility for evaluating the materials they download (Stapleton and Helms-Park 2006). In her study of the relationship between research and pedagogy in the evaluation of materials for Business English, Chan (2009) creates a framework that can be used for evaluating materials for business classes, which can also be applied to examining how various technologies can be used in a business context. Using email as a tool or a form of literacy, for example, is not simply a question of choosing an appropriate form of language but also involves understanding the often complex social relationships that can exist in a business setting. Choosing to whom a reply should be sent or who needs to be copied in can involve a complex understanding of the relationships within a particular social context. How one technology supplants another or may be used in conjunction with another technology illustrates what Chan calls the channeling of research into pedagogy. Researchers need to examine the same qualities of "authenticity, suitability, and credibility" (2009: 134) that Chan has identified as factors in evaluating any type of ESP material.

The new forms of digital literacies bring with them new challenges beyond simply integrating them into the classroom. When choosing an appropriate technology for use in the classroom, ESP teachers may need to consider what the nature of the literacy is and the type of authorship that is best supported by each technology. The choice of technology can therefore reflect the teacher's approach to the types of writing being used in the class. Synchronous forms of discourse tend to produce short forms of more informal language, as does Twitter, which is limited to 140 characters per tweet. The language of email can be either formal or informal, while listserv and discussion boards can produce more in-depth discussions using more formal forms of language. Blogs can be used to help students develop their ideas as well as various rhetorical strategies that can stand alone or be incorporated into formal print texts (Bloch 2007).

However, blogs can also be used as texts that students write simply to express their ideas, as millions of people do every day. They can be contextualized into specific contexts for different kinds of audiences, as businesses do as part of marketing campaigns. They can be integrated with other forms of discourse to create new forms of multimodal texts. The same argument can be made about podcasts. They, too, can be tools for helping students develop speaking and listening skills, but they can also be seen as aural texts that, like blogs, can be published autonomously or integrated into specific contexts for specific audiences.

Other forms of authorship can be supported by other types of technologies. Wikis, as illustrated by their best-known example, Wikipedia (www.wikipedia.com), have been shown to support the collaborative creation of texts. Kuteeva (2011), for example, examined whether the use of wikis affected how students wrote academic discourse. The growing importance of working collaboratively, often in different physical spaces, has also been supported by a large number of tools that have been referred to as cloud computing. The cloud refers to the storage of both the program, such as a word processing program or a spreadsheet, as well as the files, on the internet so that they can be accessed simultaneously from different locations without having to send the users' files by email so that only one person can work on it at a time. Cloud sites, such as Google Docs (www.google.com/google-d-s/presentations) and Zoho (www.zoho.com) often contain a suite of programs for facilitating such collaboration.

ESP teachers also need to take into account changes in how different technologies are valued in different contexts, both by their students and in the society in general. Email, which has been one of the most popular technologies for classroom use, has been replaced by text messaging by certain groups of users as the favorite means of communicating. While teachers can often create uses for these new technologies based on their own teaching experiences, it can be useful to notice how these technologies are valued outside the classroom, which may cause the teacher to rethink how they can be adapted for classroom use. For example, I attended a lecture where many in the audience were using Twitter to backchannel or comment on the lecture in real time. Many of my students were also using these technologies. Therefore, I adapted text messaging and Twitter as a form of instantaneous peer review for oral presentations. Each student gave an email address or phone number, and the other students sent them their evaluations and questions. Teachers are often placed in this situation of having to adapt technologies for the specific kinds of language pedagogies they want to employ.

Despite the constraints of the architecture of the technology, teachers can work around these constraints through their implementation of the technology. In an academic writing class, for example, we found that blogs were not a good tool for creating social interactions among the students. Therefore, we decided to use their blogs as texts that the students could use in developing their ideas. They could use their classmates' blogs, for example, to support their own ideas, express ideas they had difficulty in putting into words, or finding issues they could disagree with.

The burden of implementing technologies has frequently fallen on the teacher. Teachers have rarely been able to use technologies "right out of the box." Most of these technologies were not developed specifically for language learning, so teachers have had to develop methodologies for using these technologies. Part of the implementation problem has been choosing the most appropriate technology for the classroom problem the teacher wants to address. Each new technology, such as Facebook or Twitter, poses its own challenges and opportunities for ESP teachers that have to be addressed in the implementation process.

ESP teachers therefore require a level of flexibility in deciding the kinds of tools they would like to use. Nickerson (2005) found that there has been a growing interest in different strategies used in various forms of communications. However, these tools cannot be thought of as being independent from each other, just as forms of language use cannot be seen as being independent but involve thinking about what problems one needs to solve and then which tool is the best way of solving them. The additional amount of writing that the use of many of these technologies support, as well as the different ways this information is being used, is the challenge ESP teachers must face in integrating these tools into new forms of learning environments.

Technology as a Communicative Space

One of the greatest changes that the internet has brought has been in the ability to create new materials and to share materials across the Web. Tim Berners-Lee (1999), the principal designer of the World Wide Web, has written that his goal was to make the Web a place where anyone could be an author. This shift to the Web has particularly affected how we read and write and consequently how ESP can be taught. New forms of multimodal writing (see Prior, this volume) have incorporated various types of digitized texts – written, image, aural – into new forms of texts. New approaches to multimodal literacies allow students to combine texts, podcasts, and images or videos together to express personal experiences or ideas through different media. These changes have meant that some of the same technologies that are discussed as tools for language learning are also used as spaces where students will be creating and sharing their own texts.

Choosing digital media as a form of text raises many of the same questions ESP teachers have raised about the use of traditional forms of discourse: how do different types of texts create different forms of discourse, how will the students benefit from learning the creations of these forms of discourse, or what cultural differences, if any, exists in how such texts are written and read. For example, digital storytelling, where creators integrate print, visual, and oral texts together (e.g. Lambert 2010), has become a popular technology for general language teaching. Digital stories support the use of, for example, traditional narrative and expository genres, which can be augmented by images, videos, and music. In ESP contexts, digital storytelling can be a useful technology for professionals in medical fields or social working fields where telling stories can be an important component of the work (see examples at wuww.storycenter.org). By mixing texts, images, video, and music these types of multimodal texts have challenged our concept of genre, as Prior (2005: 28) has argued, with "more complex and less certain classifications."

At the same time, the use of digital storytelling raises important issues in how one textual mode affects the expression of other forms (e.g. Kress 2003), how changing audiences affect how texts are created, and how different forms of literacy may be valued differently, all of which are important when working with intertextual writing. Businesses have been trying to exploit literacy spaces such as Facebook and Twitter both for internal and external communications. In a business setting, a blog can be used to connect a company with its clients or customers, as can other forms of social networking. Many professions such as journalism have seen traditional print writing migrate to online digital forms.

ESP teachers have long used multimodal forms of literacy, whether supported by technology or not. Business, scientific, and technical forms of writing have always relied on visual representation to express ideas. The introduction of technology can be seen as building upon these older forms of expression in sometimes, newer, more complex ways. Besides introducing new forms of literacy, the development of new technologies has affected how older technologies are used. Although heavily criticized, a simple Microsoft PowerPoint presentation can integrate text, images, video, and aural forms. However, traditional approaches to using PowerPoint have changed in response to criticisms (e.g. Tufte 2003) that the architecture of PowerPoint seems to at least encourage users to present information in highly structured ways, either by using the preinstalled bullets or by cramming a large amount of text onto one slide. New approaches have limited the amount of text per slide to a few words and have placed a greater emphasis on visual representations.

Alternative approaches to presenting information online, such as Prezi (www.prezi.com), allow information to be created and presented in much different formats. Online meeting platforms, which are increasingly used for global interactions, allow for new ways of integrating these presentations in online contexts. New cloud technologies allow these presentations to be collaboratively created and shared. These new technologies have made the presentation of information a potentially important topic for a variety of ESP classes for how technology can affect the use of language in different contexts.

The collaborative nature of wikis, cloud computing, and even sometimes blogging illustrates how each new form of digital literacy can support a somewhat different form of authorship, which can be an important consideration in the classroom (e.g. Ivanič 1998). When hypertext first became a popular form of literacy, particularly in the design of web pages, Bolter (2001) argued that it decentralized the role of the author since the reader could click away to a new page at any time and therefore could no longer be controlled by the author. On the other hand, blogs have a flexibility that allow them to be used for groups as well as for individuals, so blogging can be used for more personal expression or for group contributions, depending on how the blog is set up. In business areas, both approaches can be used and therefore both may be appropriate for the ESP class.

The proliferation of digital texts has led to major controversies over whether reading these new forms of texts is different or "shallower" than reading traditional print texts (e.g. Carr 2010; Turkle 2011). Should texts be seen as varieties of literacy practices that are affected by the social, cultural, and economic contexts in which they are created or read or do different forms of texts involve more or less complex cognitive processes that affect how information is structured and ultimately how it is learnt, an issue that is central to a discussion of technology for academic purposes? The question of whether one form of digital text may be more complex than other forms has raised major questions for many years about how literacy should be viewed.

The use of many new technologies is not simply an aid to learning the language but reflects a need for students to learn to participate in their learning communities, often through the use of these different digital literacy practices. Email, chat, Twitter, blogs, and Facebook all may have more important roles outside the classroom than they do inside the classroom. Social networking has become an increasingly important literacy site where individuals have to feel comfortable exchanging data and making contacts with other people. However, sometimes learning the English of a specific context involves more than just learning to use the most prevalent forms of language found in that context. Today's new media can help students further immerse themselves in many more areas of the process of knowledge construction and the associated uses of language in their specific areas of interest.

Much has been discussed about the value of immersion in ESP pedagogy in both academic and workplace environments. In her review of ESP pedagogies, Belcher (2004) describes a number of field trips that teachers use as ways of immersing students in their disciplinary discourse. Technology has made the internet into a vast field trip that allows students both to gather information and sometimes interact with people all over the world. The various forms of online discourse can allow students to interact with others in their field both in real time and at each other's convenience. Open access sites and virtual worlds can make materials available across many disciplines and areas of interest.

The dilemma faced by both ESP students and teachers is that they may feel overwhelmed by the amount of this authentic information on the internet. We often refer to this as information overload. However, as Clay Shirky (2008) once put it, there is no such thing as information overload but only poor filtering. There are a variety of tools available for creating personal learning environments (PLE) where the students can customize their learning environment and keep it constantly updated. Aggregation is one way of filtering this information to lessen the overload. An aggregation site like Netvibes (www.netvibes.com), for example, can be used to organize the website feeds that alert the user to any updates to a site into a personal learning environment (PLE) that can be easily monitored and shared, a process that can contribute to the development of newer and more complex learning networks. In my PLE, for example, I have one tab for storing my students' blogs, another for journals I follow, another for blogs, and another for "fun" sites and news. Another way of organizing information that can be used by the individual or by others is through tagging. Tagging involves placing small bits of data to mark a site according to one's own interest. Whenever a member of the group finds a relevant piece of information, it can be tagged and automatically shared by all the participants.

The tremendous expansion of technology has meant that technology is being used today in various ways across every possible context. Such an expansion has raised an old question that ESP teachers have long asked: "what do you need/ want from the course?" (Dudley-Evans and St John 1998: 127). If the answer to this question includes technology literacy, then ESP teachers need to be prepared to work with helping the students learn to use, adapt, and implement these tools, just as they themselves have had to do.

The Ethical Controversies Over the use of Technology

The use of technology in ESP has raised a variety of legal and ethical issues for teachers. One of the most contentious ethical issues has been over the use and distribution of intellectual property and the related changes in attitudes towards plagiarism. These issues have been interrelated for a long time, but by facilitating the ease by which what is considered to be intellectual property, that is all materials placed in a fixed medium, is copied and distributed, the growth of the internet has foregrounded these issues as one of the central ethical concerns of education and the society as a whole throughout the world. New controversies surrounding plagiarism and the use of intellectual property have sometimes required ESP teachers to rethink the ethical considerations in using technologies. As Lawrence Lessing (2009), a well-known American intellectual property lawyer has put it, never before have so many of our uses of intellectual property been affected by legal constraints. The development of a simple corpus for use in class may entail legal and economic considerations that teachers can have difficulty understanding. The rights and constraints governing the use of intellectual property are usually a result of a mixture of local and international laws and rules. However, every teacher and student is to varying degrees affected by these concerns, particularly in the growing globalized society.

American law, as with the laws of many countries, differentiates between the commercial use and the educational use of intellectual property. Because intellectual property is treated differently than is physical property, users have rights that do not apply to other forms of property. Academic writing would be impossible if writers did not have the ability to borrow ideas and pieces of texts without permission. How much can be borrowed can depend on the amount and kind, as well as any economic consequences of such borrowing. Plagiarism, too, can be seen in such complex ways that are equally subject to much debate (e.g. Pecorari

2008; Sunderland-Smith 2008). Rightly or wrongly, the internet is frequently blamed for the so-called "plagiarism epidemic" that is frustrating teachers all over the world.

For the ESP teacher, what makes the internet such a rich source of authentic materials, as well as a space for students to interact and share work, is also what can cause great legal and ethical confusion. It is important for ESP teachers to understand both the rights and constraints that technology has imposed on the use of intellectual property since virtually every usage has been affected by the development of these new technologies. Can a teacher download an article from the internet and share it with her students? Can students use visual and audio materials from the internet? The answers to these questions are often unclear. The internet has frequently been "implicated" in the increase in the number of cases of plagiarism because of the ease of which intellectual property can be cut and pasted. Because of the variability of how plagiarism is defined across a variety of contexts, the ESP teacher needs to be aware of such variations and how to integrate learning to use intellectual property with the rules for how to use it.

The ethical concerns over the use of technology go beyond discussing whose concept of ownership will govern the distribution and attribution of materials over the internet. Issues relating to access to the internet, the speed and quality of access, the rights to uncensored materials, and the ability to participate equally in the production of internet materials have been seen as basic attributes of the development of the internet. Teachers have long been concerned with the digital divide, but today this divide does not refer only to owning a computer but also to accessing the internet. The science fiction writer, William Gibson (1999), who previously popularized the term "Cyberspace," has said "The future is here. It's just not evenly distributed yet (cited in O'Reilly 2002: para 1)."

Every discussion of the use of technology in a globalized field such as ESP has to acknowledge the limits to the distribution of these technologies due to both economic and political issues. The issues of distribution of technologies do not always fall along traditional economic divides; some so-called "developing" countries have made greater investments in their networks than developing countries. We have seen these developments in how technologies have been used in various protest movements. Nevertheless, there remain disparities in the ability to access materials. One response to this disparity has been the proliferation of open-access materials as discussed above. Open access journals, such as *Language, Learning, & Technology* (llt.msu.edu) and the *Journal of Writing Research* (http://jowr.org/current.html) provide teachers and researchers with free access to a variety of forms of research.

The nature of technological literacy has therefore raised both pedagogical and ethical concerns that can be incorporated into the ESP curriculum. In discussing the teaching of academic genres, Tardy (2009) discusses the immersion of students into the genres they are studying as a basic goal of a literacy classroom. Such immersion requires a thorough understanding not only of how to use these technologies but also of the ethical concerns for using these technologies across different genres. The popularity of a particular technology, both in the society and in the classroom, seems to raise an ever more complex set of issues. One question that has particularly perplexed many ESP teachers is how to use a site like Wikipedia (www.wikipedia) for searching for information or how to use social networking sites such as Facebook for connecting with students or as sites for literacy or sharing information.

Many teachers have recognized that these sites are widely used by their students for literacy acts and various other forms of communication and represent an important new way of communicating. Should these reasons themselves justify the use of a site like Facebook in the classroom? One of the central issues has been around privacy, especially since Facebook seems to redefine what is meant by privacy. There have also been concerns about how easy it is to delete information that individuals may no longer want or feel embarrassed by since many employers search for potential employees on Facebook sites before hiring them. On the other hand, using Facebook can be an important skill for students to have. This problem exemplifies the dilemma many ESP teachers face in trying to balance the needs of students with the ethical concerns surrounding the use of a technology.

Conclusion

Despite the growing importance of other languages on the internet, the use of English as a lingua franca remains a primary focus for this discussion of technology and ESP. However, research into the uses of these technologies has been shown to be inconsistent. In a survey of the use of technology in EAP classes in the United Kingdom, Jarvis (2004) found large gaps between the usefulness with which technology was perceived and its actual usage in the classroom. In their study of using a concordancing program with language learners, Lee and Swales (2006) described the research on the use of technology with language learners as "thin." Since this research was published, the roles of technology and its availability have evolved and some of the earlier conclusions may no longer be true. However, some of the problems with teacher training and accessibility, as Jarvis pointed out, still remain.

One major problem that needs to be researched more is how to implement the new technologies constantly being introduced. We have discussed the relationship of technology to achieving these kinds of goals; that is, determining the specific needs of the learner and then choosing a technology or technologies to support attaining that goal, or in some cases, a recognition that learning to use the technology itself can fulfill the needs of the learner. Macro-level economic changes have also greatly impacted the role technology can play in the ESP classroom. The evolution of the knowledge economy has placed a great deal of importance on the ability to use these new forms of technology.

As a result, teachers can be overwhelmed by both the number of resources and the need to draw upon resources from as many places as possible for help in implementing the most appropriate tools. Formerly popular technologies like email and blogging are slowly being usurped by Twitter and Facebook. We have begun to see dramatic shifts towards a greater reliance on mobile devices for what only computers were used for in the past. The Gartner Group, a leading technology consulting firm, coined the term "The Hype Cycle" (Fenn 1999) to describe the cycle many technologies go through. According to this assumption, a technology passes through an initial "Peak of Inflated Expectations" and then descends to a "Trough of Disillusionment" from which it rises to a "Slope of Enlightenment" and finally to the "Plateau of Productivity." Technologies such as email, blogging, or social networking have all gone through such phases. Initial expectations about the value of a technology are countered by strong criticisms and sometimes a shift from one technology to another. For teachers, this cycle can be greatly affected by how many teachers are able to use a technology and share their experiences with other teachers. Today, technologies like Twitter and Facebook are passing through these stages as teachers begin to research how best to use them in their classrooms.

The introduction of these new technologies, not unpredictably, has produced a backlash concerning the types of relationships they are promoting. Many of the criticisms, such as the problem with searching or with multitasking, has created a need for more direct teaching of how these technologies can be most effectively used. The use of the internet has created additional factors that need to be included in any checklist for evaluating materials. For example, how ubiquitous are these technologies and how can they be adapted to different contexts? Changes in how information is being distributed may have a similar impact. The mobility of smartphones and various tablets now being used have changed how information is being created and accessed. Apps that can be put on your cellphone have replaced applications on your computer. Even the applications that are on your hard drive are slowly being replaced by cloud applications that can be accessed from anywhere on the internet.

The explosion in new technologies raises additional questions concerning how sustainable these technologies are. New tools are being continually released, which provides more opportunities for classroom use but also more areas of confusion that teachers have to negotiate. There are many questions a teacher must consider before choosing a tool: What kinds of language are produced? What kinds of social relationships does the tool affect? How are the tools valued in the educational institution? In the larger society? There are other issues, however, that are particularly unique to the economic nature of technology today. A technology that a teacher may count on may suddenly disappear if it no longer appears to be economically feasible. A technology that was once free to use may begin to charge fees that are too expensive for many teachers to absorb. In such cases, teachers must be adaptable enough to find alternatives that they may have to quickly master.

The choice of a technology, either as a tool or a communicative space, is therefore, never a neutral decision: it can both affect the learning process and be affected by how it is adapted in the classroom. What makes each technology support different forms of language are differences in the code or architecture of each technology (Lessing 1999). A blog and a tweet use the same underlying HTML code, but the restrictions put on the number of characters in Twitter, has affected the type of language being created. The ability of blogs to be easily updated, as with the ability of wikis to be easily edited, have affected which kinds of social relationships can be best accomplished with each technology. How the technology can constrain the production of language can also affect the types of language. Synchronous forms of discourse need to be produced quickly and thus are often used in discussion type situations. Asynchronous forms of discourse can be created with more reflection and thus may produce longer and more detailed forms of language. Synchronous forms require an immediate response and therefore may incorporate more oral forms of language. Asynchronous forms do not require an immediate audience and therefore may produce forms of discourse that more resemble writing. While these architectural constraints may limit some uses of technology, they can also provide opportunities to modify their implementation to the needs of the students.

The use of technological tools can also be constrained by the economic factors of the internet. The reason that teachers and students have so much space on the internet to publish their own work or to find an almost unlimited supply of materials is that server space, the computers where all these materials are stored, is becoming less and less expensive. The push for more mobile forms of computing, as well as the economic factors that may favor cloud computing, will inevitably affect teaching with technology, particularly in countries where cellphone use is more widespread than internet access. These economic factors have already caused some popular tools to disappear or become prohibitively expensive. The announcement by Yahoo that Delicious, a popular site for sharing information, would be discontinued was greeted with consternation by some teachers, forcing them to scramble to find new sites to aggregate information. There was a similar occurrence when Ning, a formerly free social networking site for teachers, announced it would begin to charge a fee.

The success or failure of a technology in a classroom has often depended not only upon the design of the technology but also the degree of training the teacher has received. Traditionally, training has been limited to in-house sessions, but the development of the internet has created global networks of teachers with whom a teacher can connect for continual training. Teachers, however, cannot only rely on the experience of other language teachers. There is a vast amount of research, anecdotes, and discussion on the use of technology that can be of vast importance in helping the ESP teacher decide about the appropriate use of technology. As Belcher (2004: 166) argues, one of the great strengths of ESP has been its "eagerness to be responsive "to the needs of the students. As new contexts for the use of technology interact with what Belcher calls the social situatedness of the ESP teacher, the ability of ESP practitioners to respond to these continual changes in the development of technology will be one of its greatest challenges.

REFERENCES

Belcher, D. (2004) Trends in teaching English for specific purposes. *Annual Review of Applied Linguistics* 24: 165–86.

Berners-Lee, T. (1999) *Weaving the Web: The Original Design and Ultimate Destiny of the World Wide Web*. New York: Harper Collins.

Bloch, J. (2007) Abdullah's blogging: A Generation 1.5 student enters the blogosphere. *Language Learning & Technology* 11: 128–41.

Bloch, J. (2009) The design of an online concordancing program for teaching about reporting verbs. *Language Learning & Technology* 13: 59–78.

Bolter, J. D. (2001) *Writing Space: Computers, Hypertext, and the Remediation of Print*. 2nd edn. Mahwah, NJ: Lawrence Erlbaum.

Carr, N. (2010) *The Shallows: What the Internet is Doing to our Brains*. New York: W.W. Norton.

Chan, C. S. C. (2009) Forging a link between research and pedagogy: A holistic framework for evaluating business English materials. *English for Specific Purposes* 28: 125–36.

Crosling, G. and Ward, I. (2002) Oral communication: The workplace needs and uses of business graduate employees. *English for Specific Purposes* 21: 41–57.

Crystal, D. (2001) *Language and the Internet*. Cambridge: Cambridge University Press.

Dudley-Evans, T. and St John, M. J. (1998) *Developments in English for Specific Purposes: A Multidisciplinary Approach*. Cambridge: Cambridge University Press.

Feenberg, A. (1999) *Questioning Technology*. London: Routledge.

Fenn, J. (1999) When to leap on the hype cycle. The Gartner Group. Accessed Feb. 21, 2011, http://www.cata.ca/files/PDF/Resource_Centres/hightech/reports/indepstudies/Whentoleaponthehypecycle.pdf.

Flowerdew, L. (2010) Devising and implementing a business proposal module: Constraints and compromises. *English for Specific Purposes* 29: 108–20.

Hyland, K. (2002) Specificity revisited: How far should we go now? *English for Specific Purposes* 21: 385–95.

Ivanič, R. (1998) *Writing and Identity: The Discoursal Construction of Identity in Academic Writing*. Amsterdam: John Benjamins.

Jarvis, H. (2004) Investigating the classroom applications of computers on EFL courses at higher education institutions in UK. *Journal of English for Academic Purposes* 3: 111–37.

Kress, G. (2003) *Literacy in the New Media Age*. London: Routledge.

Lambert, J. (2010) *Digital Storytelling: Capturing Lives, Creating Community*. 3rd edn. Berkeley, CA: Center for the Study of Digital Storytelling.

Lee, D. and Swales, J. M. (2006) A corpus-based EAP course for NNS doctoral students: Moving from available specialized corpora to self-compiled corpora. *English for Specific Purposes* 25: 56–75.

Lessing, L. (1999) *Code and other Laws of Cyberspace*. New York: Basic Books.

Lessing, L. (2009) *Remix: Making Art and Commerce Thrive in the Hybrid Economy*. New York: Penguin.

Louhiala-Salminen, L., Charles, M., and Kankaanranta, A. (2005) English as a lingua franca in Nordic corporate mergers: Two case companies. *English for Specific Purposes* 24: 401–21.

Myers, G. (2010) *Discourse of Blogs and Wikis*. London: Continuum Press.

Nickerson, C. (2005) English as a *lingua franca* in international business contexts. *English for Specific Purposes* 24: 367–80.

Nickerson, C., Gerritsen, M., and van Meurs., F. (2005) Raising student awareness of the use of English for specific business purposes in the European context: A staff–student project. *English for Specific Purposes* 24: 333–45.

O'Reilly, T. (2002) *Inventing the Future.* Accessed Apr. 29, 2011, http://www.oreillynet.com/pub/a/network/2002/04/09/future.html.

Pecorari, D. (2008) *Academic Writing and Plagiarism: A Linguistic Analysis.* London: Continuum.

Prior, P. (2005) Moving multimodality beyond the binaries: A response to Gunther Kress' "Gains and Losses." *Computers and Composition* 25: 23–30.

Shi, L., Corcos, R., and Storey, A. (2001) Using student performance data to develop an English course for clinical training. *English for Specific Purposes* 20: 267–91.

Shirky, C. (2008) *Here Comes Everybody: The Power of Organizing Without Organizations.* New York: Penguin.

Sproull, L. and Kiesler, S. (1991) *Connections: New Ways of Working in Networked Organizations.* Cambridge: MIT Press.

Stapleton, P. and Helms-Park, R. (2006) Evaluating web sources in an EAP course: Introducing a multi-trait instrument for feedback and assessment. *English for Specific Purposes* 25: 438–55.

Sunderland-Smith, W. (2008) *Plagiarism, the Internet and Student Learning: Improving Academic Integrity.* New York: Routledge.

Tardy, C. M. (2009) *Building Genre Knowledge.* West Lafayette, IN: Parlor Press.

Tufte, E. (2003) PowerPoint is evil, *Wired,* 11.09. Accessed Feb. 27, 2011 at http://www.wired.com/wired/archive/11.09/ppt2.html.

Turkle, S. (2011) *Alone Together: Why we Expect More From Technology and Less From Each Other.* New York: Basic Books.

Yoon, H. (2008) More than a linguistic reference: The influence of corpus technology on L2 academic writing. *Language Learning & Technology* 12: 31–48.

Yoon, H. and Hirvela, A. (2004) ESL student attitudes toward corpus use in L2 writing. *Journal of Second Language Writing* 13: 257–83.

Part IV Research Perspectives and Methodologies in ESP Research

In this section of the *Handbook*, the chapters comprehensively survey approaches to research in English for specific purposes (ESP), the perspectives that inform these approaches, and the methodologies they employ. Some of the chapters cover emerging themes such as multimodality while others such as intercultural rhetoric may be more familiar to readers. All chapters do however provide both a historical account of how the particular area has developed and a discussion of the most recent orientations to ESP research. The section provides an ideal gateway for students, practitioners, and researchers to update themselves on contemporary research perspectives in ESP. The perspectives explored in this section are corpus studies, intercultural rhetoric, English as a lingua franca (ELF), critical perspectives on ESP, gender and race, ethnography, and multimodality. Some of the areas discussed in fact draw on a number of approaches, researchers of intercultural rhetoric, for example, might adopt an ethnographic approach or decide that corpus studies would more suit their aims or perhaps adopt a combination of these two approaches.

Hilary Nesi's chapter provides a detailed account of the rapidly expanding field of corpus studies in its interface with ESP. Corpora may be especially useful for ESP practitioners who are "not always conversant with the professions and disciplines of their students, and may not have much intuitive understanding of the way language is used in certain specified domains." The chapter describes types of ESP corpora, discusses the role of contextual information, and methods of analysis in corpus studies as well as the pedagogical uses of corpora.

The Handbook of English for Specific Purposes, First Edition.
Edited by Brian Paltridge and Sue Starfield.
© 2013 John Wiley & Sons, Inc. Published 2013 by John Wiley & Sons, Inc.

In Ulla Connor and William Rozycki's chapter, the focus is on ESP and intercultural rhetoric, that is, the study of written discourse between and among individuals with different cultural backgrounds. The authors take us through the evolution of this field, current theories that inform research, discuss recent research and the methodologies adopted, and draw out the principles of carrying out research in intercultural rhetoric.

Catherine Nickerson's chapter highlights the interconnections between ESP and English as a lingua franca showing how ESP research can work to extend our understandings of how ELF is used across a wide spectrum of settings and in different geographical locations. The chapter offers a thorough review of studies on ELF in business and educational contexts and many of the themes discussed intersect with topics examined in other chapters of this volume such as the status of native-speaker models of English, the use of corpora and intercultural rhetoric.

Sue Starfield's chapter considers critical perspectives on ESP. She traces the origins of "the critical turn" in ESP, outlining the work of many of the theorists and educators whose work created a climate which facilitated the emergence of perspectives which argued that issues of unequal power and social inequality were of concern to ESP teachers and researchers. The chapter continues with a discussion of critical English for academic purposes (EAP), considers critical approaches to needs analysis, critical perspectives on learning and teaching genre and on plagiarism, concluding with a section on power and politics in academic publishing in English.

The chapter on gender and race in ESP research by Ryuko Kubota and Liz Chiang is an illustration of how the "critical turn" in applied linguistics research (Davies 2007; Pennycook 2004; Starfield, this volume), more generally, is being taken up in ESP research. The chapter focusses, in particular, on teaching immigrants for resettlement and work purposes, and the teaching of English for academic purposes.

In her chapter on ethnographic perspectives on ESP, Dacia Dressen-Hammouda reminds us that, from its earliest days, inasmuch as it has sought to locate texts within contexts and to understand the values that communities give to their texts, ESP has had an ethnographic orientation. In more recent times, with an increase in qualitative approaches to applied linguistics research, we are seeing more ethnographically oriented studies in ESP. The chapter reviews a number of these studies while considering the contribution that ethnographic perspectives afford ESP researchers.

In his state of the art review of multimodality and ESP research, Paul Prior challenges ESP research and pedagogy to move to more complex understandings of multimodality that are emerging across a range of fields (e.g. Kress and Van Leeuwen 2001). He highlights the need for studies that look at embodied semiotic practice within specific domains that, for example, attend to nonverbal forms of communication and the ways in which genre systems are multimodal and language and communication are understood as situated sociocultural practice.

REFERENCES

Davies, A. (2007) *An Introduction to Applied Linguistics: From Practice to Theory.* Second edition. Edinburgh: Edinburgh University Press.

Kress, G. and Van Leeuwen, T. (2001) *Multimodal Discourse: The Modes and Media of Contemporary Communication.* London: Arnold.

Pennycook, A. (2004) Critical applied linguistics. In A. Davies and C. Elder (eds.), *The Handbook of Applied Linguistics.* 784–807. Malden, MA: Blackwell.

21 ESP and Corpus Studies

HILARY NESI

Introduction

All proficient language users have implicit knowledge about register, word meaning and grammatical and lexical patterns. If this were not the case we would not be able to speak and write with any fluency. We often find it hard to explicate all that we intuitively know about language, however, and in any case we cannot always rely upon what we think we know. "Human intuition about language is highly specific, and not at all a good guide to what actually happens when the same people actually use [the] language, as Sinclair (1991: 4) points out. This is a strong argument for the use of corpora to inform language teaching generally. An additional case can be made for the use of corpora in ESP, in that ESP practitioners are not always conversant with the professions and disciplines of their students, and may not have much intuitive understanding of the way language is used in certain specified domains.

A distinction is often made between "corpus-based" investigations, which are undertaken to check the researcher's intuition about language use, and "corpus-driven" investigations, where the researcher approaches the corpus data with an open mind, to see what patterns emerge (Tognini-Bonelli 2001). The corpus-based and corpus-driven distinction can be equated with approaches used in data-driven learning (see e.g. Mishan 2004), where learners may be required to test a previously developed hypothesis, or to develop and explore their own research questions. In the classroom teachers may find it less risky to use corpus data as evidence to confirm what they already know, but in this case corpus investigations can still be corpus driven from the learners' perspective if teachers allow learners to reach their own conclusions. Amongst researchers the corpus driven approach

The Handbook of English for Specific Purposes, First Edition.
Edited by Brian Paltridge and Sue Starfield.
© 2013 John Wiley & Sons, Inc. Published 2013 by John Wiley & Sons, Inc.

is favored, as Gilquin and Gries (2009) found in their survey of 81 recent corpus linguistics studies. Exploratory corpus research may lead the ESP practitioner to new discoveries about the language used in the students' target situations, and hence to changes in the content of syllabi and materials.

Types of ESP Corpora

Sinclair (2004) defines a corpus as "a collection of pieces of language text in electronic form, selected according to external criteria to represent, as far as possible, a language or language variety as a source of data for linguistic research." The term "corpus" is sometimes used more loosely, however: Thompson (2006) comments on collections of texts or text samples which are referred to as corpora but are not in electronic form, and Handford (2010: 262) mentions a number of studies of spoken professional discourse which are described as corpus-based, but which do not really qualify as corpus studies because the data has not been fully transcribed.

At exactly what stage a collection of texts in electronic form qualifies to be described as a corpus is open to debate. A corpus needs to be large enough to represent a given language variety or type of text, and many types of corpus analysis can only be conducted if the corpus is annotated in some way, for example with part of speech tags and contextual information. Large influential general purpose corpora such as the British National Corpus are fully annotated and documented, and their compilers have had the resources to resolve copyright issues. Corpora for specific research or pedagogical purposes, however, are usually created by time-poor academics and teachers, as Krishnamurthy and Kosem (2007) point out. They therefore tend to be smaller, although they can still be representative of a specific language variety because the narrower the corpus domain, the fewer texts will be needed to represent it. ESP corpora are often only minimally annotated, but simple concordancing software can still reveal plenty of useful information in a corpus of plain text files. Copyright law may prevent the distribution of texts in electronic format, but if ESP practitioners do not have the resources to deal with such issues they can often sidestep them by compiling corpora solely for their own private use.

Bowker and Pearson (2002: 454) provide guidance on how to design and build a Language for specific purposes (LSP corpus), suggesting "you can get more useful information from a corpus that is small but well designed than from one that is large but is not customised to meet your needs." Baker (2006: 25) argues that creating one's own corpus leads the way to effective analysis:

> The process of finding and selecting texts, obtaining permissions, transferring to electronic format, checking and annotating files will result in the researcher gaining a much better "feel" for the data and its idiosyncrasies. This process may also provide the researcher with initial hypotheses as certain patterns are noticed – and such hypotheses could form the basis for the first stages of corpus research.

ESP corpora with restricted access

Krishnamurthy and Kosem (2007: 368) lament the fact that so many specialized corpora are only available within the institutions where they were created: "unfortunately, this means that there is little sharing of best practice, little institutional cooperation, and considerable duplication of effort." It could be argued that not all personal ESP corpora are worth sharing, however, because some texts are unique to a specific situation and are of little use as ESP exemplars for learners in other contexts. On the other hand some small private ESP corpora become well-known despite their restricted access, because the findings from their analysis are relevant to a wide range of learners. Perhaps the most notable example of this is Coxhead's Academic Corpus, used to create the Academic Word List (AWL) (Coxhead 2000, 2011). The AWL is now a staple resource for English for academic purposes (EAP) materials developers (see for example, Schmitt and Schmitt 2005, 2011). Some corpora have restricted access for commercial reasons. Access to the TOEFL 2000 Spoken and Written Academic Language Corpus (T2K–SWAL), for example, is restricted because it was sponsored by the Educational Testing Service (ETS) to inform their test design. Findings from the T2K–SWAL have been widely reported, however, for example in Biber et al. (2002), Biber, Conrad, and Cortes (2004), and Csomay (2006). CANBEC, the Business English component of the Cambridge and Nottingham Corpus of Discourse in English (CANCODE), is inaccessible to all but the Cambridge University Press research team, but CANBEC data are discussed in McCarthy and Handford (2004) and Handford (2010).

ESP corpora in the public domain

Apart from compiling their own corpora or relying on findings from other researchers' corpus analyses, ESP practitioners can turn to ready-made corpora that are in the public domain. Several general corpora contain sub-components of relevance to ESP; isolating these components makes it possible to identify the idiosyncracies of a particular genre or register which may not be so visible when analysing the entire corpus. Lee and Swales (2006) report on using academic texts from the *British National Corpus* (BNC) in an EAP class for doctoral students, for example. The BNC is now somewhat dated as no new texts have been added since 1994, but it contains nearly 15.8 million words of written academic English, plus about 440,000 words of spoken academic discourse, and about 1.3 million words from other events of possible interest to ESP practitioners, such as sales demonstrations, trades union meetings, consultations and interviews (Aston and Burnard 1998). Leitner and Hesselman (1996) examined sports reporting in the British, Indian and Ghanaian components of the International Corpus of English (ICE). Ten, one million word, components of the ICE are now available to researchers, and each of these includes academic writing, business letters, and spoken business and legal texts, as well as media, and social discourse.

A growing number of specialized corpora are available on CD-ROM, as downloads or to search online. For investigations of the language of science and technology the largest open access corpus is probably the Professional English Research Consortium (PERC) corpus, a 17 million-word collection of samples from academic journal articles. For English for business purposes (EBP) the Wolverhampton Business English Corpus (WBE) could be a useful resource. It contains over 10 million words from web sources, although it is rather outdated now, as the texts were collected in 1999–2000. Someya's Business Letter Corpus, described in his masters thesis (2000), can be accessed online, but mostly contains model letters from textbooks (Lee 2010). Good quality student writing in a range of academic disciplines is represented in the Michigan Corpus of Upper-Level Student Papers (MICUSP) (roughly 2.6 million words) and the British Academic Written English Corpus (BAWE) (roughly 6.5 million words). ESP spoken corpora include the Michigan Corpus of Spoken Academic English (MICASE) (roughly 1.8 million words) and the British Academic Spoken English Corpus (BASE) (roughly 1.6 million words).

Some publicly available corpora record the use of English in contexts where English is used for communication but not as a first language. The Vienna-Oxford International Corpus of English (VOICE) and the English as a Lingua Franca in Academic Settings (ELFA) corpus each contain about one million words, and feature experienced speakers of English as a lingua franca (ELF) (see Nickerson this volume) from many different language backgrounds. Other corpora, such as MICUSP, BAWE, and the Engineering Lecture Corpus (ELC), contain both first language (L1) and second language (L2) components. The ELC is a growing collection of lectures on comparable engineering topics delivered in English at universities in England, Italy, Malaysia, and New Zealand, and intended to reveal cultural similarities and differences in university lecturing styles.

Academic learner corpora

Some learner corpora, such as the HKUST Corpus of Learner English (John Flowerdew 1996) and the Corpus of Academic Learner English (CALE) (Callies and Zaytseva 2011) consist of student writing produced for communicative academic purposes, and can be considered ESP corpora. Others, such as the International Corpus of Learner English (Granger 1994, 2003), contain texts produced by students for writing practice rather than for authentic communicative purposes, and are intended to provide information about the contributors' interlanguage. Although such corpora can be used to inform materials design, syllabus design, language testing, and classroom methodology, as Granger (2003) explains, they are of greater relevance for EFL than for English for specific academic purposes (ESAP) or ESP.

Small collections of academic learner writing can be used to improve or evaluate the learning experiences of specific groups of students. Lynne Flowerdew (1998a), for example, compared cause and effect markers in a subsection of the HKUST Corpus of Learner English and in an expert corpus, Global Warming:

The Greenpeace Report. Her findings were intended to inform the design of materials for science and engineering students in Hong Kong. Issitt (2011) assessed the writing progress made by international pre-sessional students at Birmingham University by comparing texts produced at the beginning and end of their course of study. The quality of the students' post-course work was found to have measurably improved.

A further use of learner corpora entails involving the students themselves in the process of corpus creation. Seidlhofer (2000), for example, asked students to build corpora of their own summaries of research articles, and then to compare them with the originals. Lee and Swales (2006) asked students to compile and compare two corpora relevant to their own field of study: one of their own writing, and one of expert published writing. This proved to be a useful way of dealing with the lack of existing corpora to represent the disciplines of the course participants (pharmacology, biomedical statistics, and educational technology).

Lee and Swales (2006: 68) warn against over-generalizing from research articles to student writing, however, because student assignments often aim for a different communicative effect:

> Not all the texts by the apprentice writer (e.g. lab reports and essays) will have been written for the same purpose or with the same audience in mind as the expert texts, which were targeted at a specialist, journal audience. In particular, writers who are new to the field can hardly be expected to make confident claims, expertly survey the literature, draw strong conclusions etc. in the same way as an established writer can.

The choice of reference corpus against which to compare learner corpus writing should therefore be made with care. The reference corpus should be generically comparable to the learner corpus, and in this respect some native-speaker student writing will be no more suitable than expert writing, especially in cases where the student texts were produced on demand as exemplars for the corpus, with no real communicative purpose in mind. Native speaker students do not necessarily write well, or in the style that learners aspire to.

Research article corpora

Many ESP corpora are made up of research articles, partly because there is a long ESP tradition of research article analysis, dating from Swales' original work on article introductions (1981), and partly because research articles are readily accessible in electronic format and can easily be selected according to learners' specific disciplines and fields. Copyright permission may be difficult to obtain, however. The PERC corpus project team sent requests to more than 1,500 journals, for example, but at the time of writing fewer than a quarter of these had granted copyright clearance, and then only for text samples. This is a drawback because the location of words and patterns within the text is often relevant in ESP research, and cannot be fully explored if texts are not presented in their entirety. Copyright issues help to explain why so many corpora of research articles are restricted access and are only known to ESP practitioners via publications reporting their analysis.

Luckily, findings relating to private research article corpora can be replicated, checked or challenged by others with reference to new collections of research articles from the same or similar sources. Research articles are not "occluded" genres (Swales 1996) because they are available for anyone to access and investigate. A great deal of information about a research article can be extrapolated from the title, standing, and mission statement of the journal in which it was published. Moreover research articles have to make sense outside the immediate context in which they were produced, by virtue of the fact that they are distributed and read internationally.

The Role of Context

Knowing about context aids the interpretation of corpus data, just as corpus data can deepen our understanding of context. It is therefore desirable that the contextual information that aids the developer should be made available to subsequent corpus users. Widdowson (1998: 711–12) famously objected that "reality . . . does not travel with the text," and similarly Mishan (2004: 220) complained that corpus files are "denuded of the distinguishing features of their origins, and become part of one indistinguishable whole." This has implications for the use of corpora and corpus data in the ESP classroom, where teachers may want to draw attention to sources and discourse community cultures.

Corpus documentation

Contextual information can be embedded within corpus files. Information known as "documentation" is stored in a document header, and includes the title and source of the text, and information concerning its publication or distribution. Other information can be included too; the MICASE file headers, for example, identify the type of speech event each file represents, the discipline and level of participants, and the gender, age, and first language of the speakers, amongst other things. BAWE corpus file headers list the genre family, discipline, level, title, and grade band of each assignment, alongside the age, gender, and first language of the writer, and the number of years of secondary education they received in the United Kingdom. This kind of information can be used by researchers to filter corpus files and create sub-corpora for more specific investigations. A user of the BAWE corpus, for example, could choose to work only with texts of a particular genre type, or only with those produced for a particular discipline.

Corpus annotation

Some ESP corpora are tagged for part of speech (POS) and/or semantic categories, to enable the investigation of grammatical features and stylistic patterns. The

BAWE corpus, for example, has been POS tagged using the UCREL CLAWS7 Tagset, and semantically tagged using the UCREL semantic analysis system (USAS). Both systems are available from the University Centre for Computer Corpus Research on Language (UCREL) at Lancaster University in the United Kingdom. Annotations can also encode information about the original features that were lost during file conversion or transcription, such as formatting in written text, noises or activities which occurred during a speech event, or relevant pictures or graphics. Even if the missing data is not described in detail, a note indicating its absence and where it occurred in the text can help to clarify meaning. The spoken component of the HKCSE business corpus (Cheng 2004; Warren 2004) is annotated using Brazil's (1997) system for labelling spoken discourse, showing the prominence, tone and pitch of each tone unit in the original recordings. This degree of annotation is unusual in ESP corpora, however, because of the effort it requires.

Integrating files in other formats

O'Keeffe, McCarty, and Carter (2007) have drawn attention to the need for more audiovisually aligned spoken corpora which can link transcript fragments directly to corresponding audio or video clips. Media files exist to accompany MICASE and BASE, but the transcripts and multimodal elements have not so far been integrated in this way. The English Language Interview Corpus as a Second Language Application (ELISA) (http://www.uni-tuebingen.de/elisa) and the SACODEYL European Youth Language Project (www.um.es/sacodeyl), however, both offer audiovisually aligned corpus searches alongside language learning materials. The ELISA corpus, still under development, features native speakers of English talking about their professional careers. SACODEYL features teenage speakers of various European languages (Widmann, Kohn, and Ziai 2011), but the software tools have potential for ESP corpora, as proposed by Brick and Endacott (2009). Thompson (2010) describes how to use WordSmith Tools to align transcripts and audio files. The process is quite laborious, but file integration will become easier as more and better corpus tools are developed to create, annotate, and concordance multimodal files.

Fortanet-Gómez and Querol-Julián (2010) describe a corpus of lecture transcripts integrated with video recordings, slides and handouts. Use of files in different formats in this way can supplement corpus annotation and provide the user with an even more complete picture of the original context.

Other kinds of annotation

ESP corpora are usually mined for information relating to a range of research questions, by the original compiler in the case of small private corpora, or by multiple researchers in the case of large corpora sponsored by publishers or research funding agencies. If the same corpus can be used for a number of studies this helps to justify the considerable time and effort required to compile it. However some ESP corpora have been annotated expressly to address particular queries, so that specific features can be identified and quantified more easily during analysis. Thompson (2000), for example, examined citation practices in a corpus of PhD theses by marking the integral and non-integral citations within each thesis section, and Chuang and Nesi (2006) used their own tagging system to categorize every error they found in a small corpus of student assignments.

Lynne Flowerdew (1998b) suggested that it would be pedagogically useful if corpora were annotated to indicate communicative intention. In response to this, Durrant and Mathews-Aydinli (2011) drew on Swales' notion of generic moves and steps (Swales 1990) to annotate functions in the introduction sections of research articles and a sub-corpus of BAWE. This functional annotation enabled them to examine the language of moves and steps more closely, as they show in their analysis of formulaic sequences in the "indicating structure" step. Maynard and Leicher (2007) tagged 50 MICASE transcripts for pragmatic features such as "advice" and "disagreement." Their system is now being adapted to describe pragmatic features in the Engineering Lecture Corpus (ELC) in order to compare lecturing styles across different cultural contexts. The ELC is being annotated for typical lecture functions, such as "housekeeping, "humor, "stories," and "summaries" (see for example, Alsop 2011).

Swales (2002) argues that corpus analysis is essentially a bottom-up procedure, starting with what is apparent in the concordance line, whereas genre analysis should be top-down, starting with the macro-structure of the text. The annotation of corpus files for their generic and pragmatic features may help to address Swales' concerns, because output can be linked to rhetorical moves that have already been identified, or to sections of text that have already been analysed to discern the speaker's or writer's intent. There is a danger, however, that other corpus users may reject the compilers' interpretations, or find that they interfere with their own analytical procedures. The Singapore Corpus of Research in Education (SCoRE) (Peréz-Paredes and Alcaraz-Calero 2009) resolves this problem by offering the user a choice of multiple levels of annotation when conducting corpus searches. It is audiovisually aligned, and annotated for word class, syntax, and semantic features (all fairly objective categories) and for pragmatic and pedagogical features (more subjectively).

The role of contributors, informants, and stakeholders

Some ESP corpus developers collect ethnographic data such as interview transcripts, either to help them choose the texts to include in the corpus, or to help them interpret the corpus once it has been compiled. Gledhill (1996, 2000), for example, consulted specialist informants to help choose representative texts for his corpus of cancer research articles, and Bhatia et al. asked the advice of law professors when compiling their corpus of law cases (2004: 212). Hyland interviewed experienced research writers, who were able to "respond to texts as readers with insider community understandings of rhetorical effectiveness, while also discussing their own discoursal preferences and practices" (2001: 211). Warren (2004) writes of the importance of involving hotel staff when interpreting texts collected in hotels for the business component of the HKCSE. He concludes that "without input from the stakeholders it would have been difficult for the researcher to reach a firm understanding of the status of the discourse within the business organization, let alone make recommendations in terms of staff language training needs" (2004: 127–8).

The BAWE corpus was part of a project to identify genres of student writing in higher education. Interviews with academic staff and students aided the selection of texts to include, the identification of genre families, and the analysis of genres in terms of departmental requirements and expectations (Nesi and Gardner 2012). The project also relied heavily on stakeholder support to gather assignments at specific levels of study and in specific disciplines, especially in cases where contributors were reluctant to come forward (Alsop and Nesi 2009).

Although copyright may not be a problem, the gathering of unpublished texts in ESP contexts can prove difficult because of the "perceived lack of reciprocal gain" for those who contribute (McCarthy and Handford 2004: 171). McCarthy and Handford describe issues surrounding the collection of spoken data for CANBEC; many companies were invited to contribute, but the ratio of acceptance was only 1 in 20.

Unfortunately interview data and other related texts such as field notes, pre-publication drafts, reviewers' comments and so on are rarely included in corpus documentation, perhaps for reasons of confidentiality. As a result corpus informed teaching materials tend to emphasize the final product, and neglect the processes that lead up to text creation (Feak and Swales 2010).

Methods of Analysis

The two basic functions of corpus software tools are to generate word frequency lists and to generate key word in context (KWIC) concordance lines. Corpus tools are commonly called "concordancers" because of the widespread use of concordancing in corpus analysis, but this is in fact a misnomer for the new generation of corpus tools, as Krishnamurthy and Kosem 2007) point out. Nowadays corpus software can compare different corpora for significant differences, identify multi-word units, and list collocations for any given word in the corpus, with statistics to indicate collocational strength. Corpus query software such as the Word Sketch function in Sketch Engine can provide very detailed descriptions of the contexts in which a word is found. The Word Sketch is designed primarily for lexicographical purposes, however, and many ESP corpora are too small to benefit from its capabilities.

Searching for patterns in concordance lines

The key word in context (KWIC) concordance line typically displays each occurrence in the corpus of the search term or "node" in the center of a line of about 70 characters. The lines can be arranged to place in alphabetical order words preceding or following the search term; this enables collocational patterns to become more apparent in the text. The search term can be a full word form, a partial word form plus wildcard symbols to stand for one or more missing characters, or a lemma, if the corpus has been POS tagged. The use of the lemma feature enables a simultaneous search of all inflected forms of the same word. Closed and open phrase patterns can be searched for by entering a sequence of word forms, combining word forms and wild cards, or employing corpus query language (CQL) to specify a syntactic or semantic pattern.

Many explorations of small, specialized corpora have made effective use of simple concordancing procedures. For example Skelton, Wearn, and Hobbs (2000) used a corpus of doctor–patient consultations to build up concordance lines containing strings likely to indicate metaphoric use, such as *"as if," "as though," "look like,"* and *"feel like."* The concordance lines were then filtered manually to identify a range of metaphors such as "the body is a machine," typically used by doctors, "the body is a container for the self," typically used by patients, and "illness is fire," used by both doctors and patients.

Marco (2000) searched for the collocational frameworks *"the . . . of," "a . . . of,"* and *"be* (lemma) *. . . to"* in a corpus of 100 medical research articles. This enabled her to identify nominal elements that were typical of the genre, for example quantifying words such as *amount, degree, dose, extent,* and *frequency* in the *"the . . . of"* framework. Marco also found associations between certain phrases and certain moves. The phrase *determine/estimate the number/degree of,* for example, was typically found in the "occupying the niche" move in article introductions.

If a corpus is POS tagged, it is also possible to generate concordance lines containing sequences of words belonging to specified word classes, using corpus query language (CQL). CQL queries are placed within square brackets, and specific search items (words, lemmas, or POS tags) are enclosed within quotation marks. For example the query [word = "affect|change"] is a way of searching simultaneously for the word forms *affect* and *change,* while [lemma = "affect|change"] will find all inflected forms of the two lemmas, and [lemma = "change" & tag = "V.."] will limit findings to the verb *change,* rather than both the verb and the noun. Long queries can be built up in this way, helping the researcher to discover the distribution of grammatical patterns in association with particular words. Nesi and Moreton (2012), for example, used CQL to investigate how student writers used certain types of nouns (the so-called "shell" nouns) to create cohesion in text. Shell nouns can establish a link to the preceding message, as in the "th- + *noun*" pattern "**This fact** confirms the assumption that . . ." (identified via the CQL string [tag = "DD."] [lemma = "fact" & tag = "N.."]) or they can establish a link to the message that follows, as in the "*noun* + *clause*" pattern "**The fact that** this assumption has been confirmed . . ." (identified via the CQL string [lemma = "fact" & tag = "N.."] [word = "that|wh.*|to"]). Many researchers have examined such patterns by painstakingly sifting through concordance lines, rather than by using CQL (see for example Charles 2003, 2007), but CQL can speed up the process, thus encouraging more extensive explorations.

Wordlists

One of the commonest applications of corpus studies to ESP has been the production of wordlists for materials and test design. Yang (1986) created the one-million word Jiaotong Daxue English of Science and Technology (JDEST) corpus in order to assess how well the ESP materials he was using represented the language of his students' target situation. He distinguished between different types of words on the basis of their frequency and range: "sub-technical" words were widely distributed across a range of fields, while "technical" words had a peak distribution in one particular field. This technique was also used by Liu and Nesi (1999) to identify sub-technical and technical vocabulary in a small corpus of engineering textbooks written in English. In consultation with engineering lecturers, Liu and Nesi converted their technical and sub-technical wordlists into vocabulary tests, discovering that the Chinese students were less likely to recognize technical terms, even at the end of their degree course.

Wordlist creation can also serve as a first stage in a more complex research procedure. Giannoni (2010), for example, investigated the values expressed in disciplinary discourse by identifying the most value-laden items in wordlists generated for different domains of his research article corpus, and then examining the use of these words in context.

In ESP, comparisons between corpora and sub-corpora are common, to distinguish between disciplines, or between language use in specialist and in general-purpose contexts, or to identify discrepancies between the language used in teaching materials and the language used in the authentic texts the textbooks try to model (see for example, Cheng 2004). When comparative corpora differ in size, word frequency can be standardized. Charteris-Black (2000), for example, compared frequencies per million words in a small corpus from *The Economist* magazine and in the general magazine section of the Bank of English. Increasingly, however, statistical "key word" techniques are used to discover frequency differences across different corpora.

Key word analysis

"Key word" is the term used for the search word in a concordance line (the key word in context) but it can also refer to items that occur with significantly higher or lower frequency in a given collection of texts, as compared with another "reference" corpus. WordSmith Tools and Sketch Engine both have functions to identify key words of this sort, but use slightly different statistical methods.

Scott and Tribble's study of a small corpus of professional correspondence (2006, Chapter 7) uses WordSmith Tools and takes as its starting point a single key word, *hope*, to compare the correspondence between socially close and socially distant correspondents, and between colleagues and between people working in different organizations. Key words are also a good indicator of corpus topics: the "aboutness" of text (Scott and Tribble 2006: 55), and have often been used to characterize the lexis of technical as compared to general English texts. The BNC is a common reference corpus, used by Nelson (2000) in his study of Business English, Mudraya (2006) in her study of engineering textbooks (2006), and Chujo, Utiyama, and Nakamura (2007) in their study of research articles in the Corpus of Professional English (a forerunner of the PERC corpus).

N-grams

N-grams (or "lexical bundles") are strings of words that frequently recur in a corpus. For example *"the end of the"* is the most frequent four-word n-gram (called a 4-gram) in the British National Corpus. N-grams are also sometimes known as "clusters," especially when their contents have been partially specified, for example in order to generate only those combinations containing the words *"the"* or *"of."* They are easy to generate using corpus software, and are often used together with more qualitative discourse-oriented procedures. They usually reveal more about the genre of the corpus than its topic; n-grams in spoken and written texts tend to be constituted differently, for example, and some genres are more formulaic than others. N-grams have been examined in the T2K SWAL (Biber et al. 2004), BASE (Nesi and Basturkman 2006) and BAWE (Chen and Baker 2010). For more information about n-grams in the BNC see William Fletcher's Phrases in English (PIE) website, http://phrasesinenglish.org/.

Most researchers have chosen to examine four-word combinations. Allen (2009), for example, looked at frequent four-word strings (4-grams) in a corpus of Japanese EAP science writing, to identify divergence from typical usage in the BAWE and PERC corpora. Wickens and Spiro (2010) examined 4-grams in a small corpus of reflective writing produced for a masters program in Education, noting how they shed light on reflective practice. Römer (2008), however, found that 5-grams were useful as a means of exploring her three million-word corpus of book reviews. Most of the 5-grams in her corpus were either evaluative, or described the structure of the book under review.

N-grams may not be of much direct use for ESP teaching and learning, however. Jones and Haywood (2004) asked pre-sessional EAP students to explore lexical clusters in concordance lines and corpus extracts, but their productive use did not improve, and they reported difficulty remembering the sequences.

Pedagogical Uses of ESP Corpora

Although most studies of specialist corpora end with a summary of the pedagogical implications of their findings, researchers still need to communicate more with teachers and materials developers (Römer 2010). On the whole, practitioners have been slow to avail themselves of corpus resources, and some researchers (for example Swales 2002) have queried whether corpus analysis has any direct impact on ESP teaching and learning. A questionnaire survey of 30 EAP support units at UK universities distributed in 2002 found that 16 made no use of corpora at all

(Thompson 2006), and Jarvis (2004) found that concordancing was being used in only about one in ten ESP/EAP courses in the United Kingdom.

The role of corpora in ESP materials design

A number of studies have unfavorably compared what textbooks teach with what corpora reveal. Harwood (2005), for example, provides a summary of findings concerning the differences between corpus evidence and the information in academic writing textbooks. Such findings have led to revisions in ESP syllabus content and greater use of corpus data, especially in textbooks oriented towards the general EAP market, such as Thurston and Candlin (1997) and Schmitt and Schmitt (2005, 2011). Corpus findings are also beginning to influence materials in other ESP areas; recent titles relating to business, ICT, law, marketing, medicine, and finance in the Cambridge University Press Professional English series claim to be "corpus-based," and ESP textbooks in other series may well be "corpus-informed" even if they do not overtly refer to corpus data. Textbooks usually present mediated corpus data in concordance lines or in text excerpts, to provide examples to illustrate accepted usage, or for gap-filling and matching exercises. Thurston and Candlin (1998) advocate using a variety of corpus-based activities, because students can lose interest if they are overexposed to concordance lines. The fact that textbook writers have to select and edit corpus evidence because of space constraints probably makes analysis easier for students, as they are not presented with large amounts of raw corpus data.

Data-driven learning

Some ESP practitioners favor a more investigative approach where students direct their own learning. The program devized by Lee and Swales (2006), for example, included use of Thurston and Candlin's materials, but also the hands-on creation and examination of concordances, n-grams and wordlists. These kinds of activities constitute a form of data-driven learning (DDL), a term coined by Johns (1989) to describe his one-to-one writing consultations with international students at Birmingham University, where student and advisor explored online corpus data together to solve language problems the student had encountered. Johns' consultations are reported in his "kibbitzer" series, available at http://lexically.net/timjohns; these discuss corpus investigations of specific lexico-grammatical features, and often include an exercise or two derived from the corpus data. There are now also kibbitzers on the MICASE site.

   In its strong, unmediated form, DDL involves learners in a four-stage procedure (Kennedy and Miceli 2001: 82):

1.   formulate the question;
2.   devize a search strategy;
3.   observe the examples and select relevant ones; and
4.   draw conclusions.

This places heavy demands on learners, however. In order to successfully complete an investigation of this sort they need to be trained (Gavioli 2005) and they also need to be highly motivated (Hyland 2006). Dudley-Evans and St John (1998) point out that whereas it can take 30 minutes to present collocations deductively through DDL procedures, the same information could be summarized by the teacher in five minutes. They conclude that:

> with learners who are curious about language and enjoy working with computer programs the extra time spent using data-driven learning techniques is justified. For learners who are less curious about language and computers the benefits are considerably fewer.

Conclusion

Approaches to corpus work in relation to ESP are changing in response to developments in technology. On the one hand researchers are using more and more powerful corpus tools, and are gaining access to larger corpora. This is enabling them to discover more about the use of language for specific purposes and to make stronger, statistically supported claims. As they are becoming more complex and powerful, however, corpus tools may also be becoming less accessible to students and teachers. Krishnamurthy and Kosem (2007: 369) complain of "complicated query language, search, and screen displays which are often user-unfriendly, overcrowded with information and unexplained terminology, and bewildering arrays of words and numbers." This may drive some ESP practitioners away from hands-on corpus use, whilst at the same time it seems likely that ESP syllabi and materials will be increasingly informed by findings from corpus research. For classroom corpus activities, simpler corpus interfaces are needed, especially those which enable teachers and learners without programming skills to upload their own corpora, tailored to their own specific needs. After examining findings from twelve writing classroom concordancing studies, Yoon (2011) concluded that the two essential ingredients for learners' success were mastery of the software, and access to corpora that reflected their own writing purposes.

Also, while in some quarters there is a growing interest in sophisticated corpus linguistics techniques (see for example Biber et al. 2002, and the collection edited by Gries et al. 2010) there is evidence of an opposite tendency, towards a greater use of qualitative discourse-oriented techniques. The collection edited by Charles, Pecorari, and Hunston (2009), for example, contains a number of studies which analyze texts both manually and with the aid of corpus tools. As an illustration of this, the chapter by Hewings, Coffin, and North (2009) examines e-conferences produced for a course in complementary and alternative medicine, using the WordSmith Tools keyword function together with techniques from genre analysis (Martin 1989), the analysis of casual conversation (Eggins and Slade 1997) and classroom discourse analysis (Sinclair and Coulthard 1975).

It is important that ESP corpus research does not separate into two opposing camps, but draws on both the quantitative and the qualitative aspects of corpus study. The use of English for specific purposes is closely associated with the use of genres within discourse communities, entailing an understanding of context and communicative purposes. ESP practitioners are concerned with the frequency and distribution of lexico-grammatical features within genres, not independently of them.

Publicly Available Corpora Referred to in the Text

British Academic Spoken English Corpus (BASE) www.coventry.ac.uk/base
British Academic Written English Corpus (BAWE) www.coventry.ac.uk/bawe
Business Letter Corpus KWIC Concordancer
   http://www.someya-net.com/concordancer/
Corpus of English essays written by Asian university students.
   http://language.sakura.ne.jp/s/ceeause.html
English as a Lingua Franca in Academic Settings (ELFA)
   www.helsinki.fi/englanti/elfa/elfacorpus
Michigan Corpus of Spoken Academic English (MICASE)
   http://micase.elicorpora.info/
Michigan Corpus of Upper-Level Student Papers (MICUSP)
   http://micusp.elicorpora.info/
Professional English Research Consortium (PERC) Corpus
   www.perc21.org/corpus_project
Uppsala Student English Corpus (USE)
   www.engelska.uu.se/Forskning/engelsk_sprakvetenskap/
   Forskningsomraden/Electronic_Resource_Projects/USE-Corpus/
Vienna-Oxford International Corpus of English (VOICE) www.univie.ac.at/voice
Wolverhampton Business English Corpus (WBE) available via the Evaluations and
   Language Resources Distribution Agency (ELDA)
   http://www.elda.org/rubrique1.html

REFERENCES

Alsop, S. (2011) The Story element in engineering lectures: An analysis of one category of pragmatic mark-up. Poster presented at *ICAME 32: Trends and traditions in English corpus linguistics.* The University of Oslo. Accessed May 28, 2012 at http://www.uio.no/icame2011.

Alsop, S. and Nesi, H. (2009) Issues in the development of the British Academic Written English (BAWE) corpus. *Corpora* 4: 71–83.

Aston, G. and Burnard, L. (1998) *The BNC Handbook: Exploring the British National Corpus with SARA.* Edinburgh: Edinburgh University Press.

Baker, P. (2006) *Using Corpora in Discourse Analysis*. London: Continuum.

Bhatia, V., Langton, N., and Lung, J. (2004) Legal discourse: Opportunities and threats or corpus linguistics. In U. Connor and T. Upton (eds.), *Discourse in the Professions*. 203–31. Amsterdam: John Benjamins.

Biber, D., Conrad, S., and Cortes, V. (2004) *If you look at . . .* : Lexical bundles in university teaching and textbooks. *Applied Linguistics* 25: 371–405.

Biber, D., Conrad, S., Reppen, R., Byrd, P., and Helt, M. (2002) Speaking and writing in the university: A multi-dimensional comparison. *TESOL Quarterly* 36: 9–48.

Bowker, L. and Pearson, J. (2002) *Working with Specialized Language: A Practical Guide to Using Corpora*. London: Routledge.

Brazil, D. (1997) *The Communicative Role of Intonation in English*. Cambridge: Cambridge University Press.

Brick, B. and Endacott, N. (2009) Designing online EAP materials using annotated samples of Spoken Academic Discourse. Paper presented at the 44th SEAMEO RELC International Seminar *The Impact of Technology on Language Learning and Teaching: What, How and Why*. 20–22 April. Singapore: SEAMEO.

Callies, M. and Zaytseva, E. (2011) Introducing the corpus of academic learner English (CALE). Paper presented at *ICAME 32: Trends and Traditions in English Corpus Linguistics*. The University of Oslo. Accessed May 28, 2012 at http://www.uio.no/icame2011.

Charles, M. (2003) "This mystery": A corpus-based study of the use of nouns to construct stance in theses from two contrasting disciplines. *Journal of English for Academic Purposes* 2: 313–26.

Charles, M. (2007) Argument or evidence? Disciplinary variation in the use of the noun *that* pattern in stance construction. *English for Specific Purposes* 26: 203–18.

Charles, M., Pecorari, D., and Hunston, S. (eds.) (2009) *Academic Writing: At the Interface of Corpus and Discourse*. London: Continuum.

Charteris-Black, J. (2000) Metaphor and vocabulary teaching in ESP economics. *English for Specific Purposes* 19: 149–65.

Chen, Y. H. and Baker, P. (2010) Lexical Bundles in L1 and L2 Academic Writing. *Language Learning and Technology* 14: 30-49.

Cheng, W. (2004) //→ did you TOOK // ↗ from the miniBAR// What is the practical relevance of a corpus-driven language study to practitioners in Hong Kong's hotel industry? In U. Connor and T. Upton (eds.) *Discourse in the Professions: Perspectives from Corpus Linguistics*. 141–66. Amsterdam: John Benjamins.

Chuang, F. Y. and Nesi, H. (2006) An analysis of formal errors in a corpus of L2 English produced by Chinese students. *Corpora* 1: 251–71.

Chujo, K., Utiyama, M., and Nakamura, T. (2007) Extracting level-specific science and technology vocabulary from the corpus of professional English (CPE). In M. Davies, P. Rayson, S. Hunston, and P. Danielsson (eds.), *Proceedings of the Corpus Linguistics Conference*. Birmingham, UK: University of Birmingham. Accessed 11 July 2012. www5d.biglobe.ne.jp/~chujo/data/CLProceedings-Final.pdf

Coxhead, A. (2000) A new academic word list. *TESOL Quarterly* 34: 213–38.

Coxhead, A. (2011) The Academic Word List 10 years on: Research and teaching implications. *TESOL Quarterly* 45: 355–62.

Csomay, E. (2006) Academic talk in American university classrooms: Crossing the boundaries of oral-literate discourse? *Journal of English for Academic Purposes* 5: 117–35.

Dudley-Evans, T. and St John, M. J. (1998) *Developments in English for Specific*

Purposes: A Multi-Disciplinary Approach. Cambridge: Cambridge University Press.

Durrant, P. and Mathews-Aydinli, J. 2011. A function-first approach to identifying formulaic language in academic writing. *English for Specific Purposes* 30: 58–72.

Eggins, S. and Slade, D. (1997) *Analysing Casual Conversation.* London: Cassell.

Feak, C. B. and Swales, J. M. (2010) Writing for publication: Corpus-informed materials. In N. Harwood (ed.) *English Language Teaching Materials.* 279–300. Cambridge: Cambridge University Press.

Flowerdew, J. (1996) Concordancing in language learning. In M. Pennington (ed.), *The Power of CALL* 97–113. Houston, TX: Athelstan.

Flowerdew, L. (1998a) Integrating expert and interlanguage computer corpora findings on causality: Discoveries for teachers and students. *English for Specific Purposes* 17: 329–45.

Flowerdew, L. (1998b) Corpus linguistic techniques applied to textlinguistics. *System*, 26: 541–52.

Fortanet-Gómez, I. and Querol-Julián, M. (2010) The video corpus as a multimodal tool for teaching. In M. Carmen Campoy, Bellés-Fortuno, B., and Gea-Valor, M. L. (eds.), *Corpus-Based Approaches to English Language Teaching.* 261–70. London: Continuum.

Gavioli, L. (2005) *Exploring Corpora for ESP Learning.* Amsterdam: John Benjamins.

Giannoni, D. S. (2010) *Mapping Academic Values in the Disciplines.* Bern: Peter Lang.

Gilquin, G. and Gries, S. T. (2009) Corpora and experimental methods: A state-of-the-art review. *Corpus Linguistics and Linguistic Theory* 5: 1–26.

Gledhill, C. (1996) Science as a collocation: Phraseology in cancer research articles. In S. Botley, Glass, J., McEnery, T., and Wilson, A. (eds.), *Proceedings of Teaching and Language Corpora 1996* Vol. 9. 108–26. Lancaster, UK: Lancaster University UCREL Technical Papers.

Gledhill, C. (2000) The discourse function of collocation in research article introductions. *English for Specific Purposes* 19: 115–35.

Granger, S. (1994) The learner corpus: A revolution in applied linguistics. *English Today* 39: 25–9.

Granger, S. (2003) The international corpus of learner English: A new resource for foreign language learning and teaching and second language acquisition research. *TESOL Quarterly* 37: 538–46.

Gries, S. Th., Wulff, S., and Davies, M. (eds.) (2010) *Corpus Linguistic Applications: Current Studies, New Directions.* Amsterdam: Rodopi.

Handford, M. (2010) What can a corpus tell us about specialist genres? In A. O'Keeffe and M. McCarthy (eds.), *The Routledge Handbook of Corpus Linguistics.* 255–69. London: Routledge.

Harwood, N. (2005) What do we want EAP teaching materials for? *Journal of English for Academic Purposes* 4: 149–61.

Hewings, A., Coffin, C., and North, S. (2009) E-conferencing: Corpus and discourse insights. In M. Charles, D. Pecorari, and S. Hunston (eds.), *Academic Writing: At the Interface of Corpus and Discourse.* 129–51. London: Continuum.

Hyland, K. (2001) Bringing in the reader: Addressee features in academic articles. *Written Communication* 18: 549–74.

Hyland, K. (2006) *English for Academic Purposes.* London: Routledge.

Issitt, S. (2011) How an L2 learner corpus can identify areas of quantifiable improvement in students' written discourse. Proceedings of the CL2011 conference, Birmingham 20-22 July 2011. Abstract available at http://www.birmingham.ac.uk/research/activity/corpus/publications/conference-archives/2011-birmingham.aspx.

Jarvis, H. (2004) Investigating the classroom applications of computers on

EFL courses at higher education institutions in UK. *Journal of English for Academic Purposes* 3: 111–37.

Johns, T. (1989) Whence and whither classroom concordancing? In T. Bongaerts, P. de Haan, S. Lobbe, and H. Wekker (eds.), *Computer Applications in Language Learning*. 9–33. Dordrecht, the Netherlands: Foris.

Jones, M. and Haywood, S. (2004) Facilitating the acquisition of formulaic sequences: An exploratory study in an EAP context. In N. Schmitt (ed.), *Formulaic Sequences*. 269–92. Amsterdam: John Benjamins.

Kennedy, C. and Miceli, T. (2001) An evaluation of intermediate students' approaches to corpus investigation. *Language Learning and Technology* 5(3): 77–90.

Krishnamurthy, R. and Kosem, I. (2007) Issues in creating a corpus for EAP pedagogy and research. *Journal of English for Academic Purposes* 6: 356–73.

Lee, D. Y. W. (2010) What corpora are available? In A. O'Keeffe and M. McCarthy (eds.), *The Routledge Handbook of Corpus Linguistics*, 107–21. London: Routledge.

Lee, D. Y. W. and Swales, J. M. (2006) A corpus-based EAP course for NNS doctoral students: Moving from available specialized corpora to self-compiled corpora. *English for Specific Purposes* 25: 56–75.

Leitner, G. and Hesselman, M. (1996) What do you do with a ball in soccer?: Medium, mode, and pluricentricity in soccer reporting. *World Englishes* 15: 83–102.

Liu, J. and Nesi, H. (1999) Are we teaching the right words? A study of students' receptive knowledge of two types of vocabulary: "Subtechnical and technical." In H. Bool and P. Luford (eds.), *Academic Standards and Expectations: The Role of EAP*. 141–47. Nottingham: Nottingham University Press.

Marco, M. J. L. (2000) Collocational frameworks in medical research papers: A genre-based study. *English for Specific Purposes* 19: 63–86.

Martin, J. R. (1989) *Factual Writing: Exploring and Challenging Social Reality*. Oxford: Oxford University Press.

Maynard, C. and Leicher, S. (2007) Pragmatic annotation of an academic spoken corpus fro pedagogical purposes. In E. Fitzpatrick (ed.), *Corpus Linguistics Beyond the Word: Corpus Research from Phrase to Discourse*. 107–15. Amsterdam: Rodopi.

McCarthy, M. and Handford, M. (2004) "Invisible to us": A preliminary corpus-based study of spoken business English. In U. Connor and T. Upton (eds.), *Discourse in the Professions: Perspectives from Corpus Linguistics*. 167–201. Amsterdam: John Benjamins.

Mishan, F. (2004) Authenticating corpora for language learning: A problem and its resolution. *ELT Journal* 58: 219–27.

Mudraya, O. (2006) Engineering English: A lexical frequency instructional model. *English for Specific Purposes* 25: 235–56.

Nelson, M. (2000) A corpus-based study of the lexis of business English and business English teaching materials. Unpublished PhD thesis. University of Manchester.

Nesi, H. and Basturkman, H. (2006) Lexical bundles and discourse signalling in academic lectures. *International Journal of Corpus Linguistics* 11: 147–68.

Nesi, H. and Gardner, S. (2012) *Genres Across the Disciplines: Student Writing in Higher Education*. Cambridge: Cambridge University Press.

Nesi, H. and Moreton, E. (2012) EFL/ESL writers and the use of shell nouns. In R. Tang (ed.), *Academic Writing in a Second or Foreign Language: Issues and Challenges Facing ESL/EFL Academic Writers in Higher Education Contexts*. 126–45. London: Continuum.

O'Keeffe, A., McCarthy, M., and Carter, R. (2007) *From Corpus to Classroom:*

Language Use and Language Teaching. Cambridge: Cambridge University Press.

Peréz-Paredes, P. and Alcaraz-Calero, J. M. (2009) Developing annotation solutions for online data driven learning. *ReCALL* 21: 55–75.

Römer, U. (2008) Identification impossible? A corpus approach to realisations of evaluative meaning in academic writing. *Functions of Language* 15: 115–30.

Römer, U. (2010) Using general and specialised corpora in English language teaching: Past, present and future. In M. C. Campoy, Bellés-Fortuno, B., and Gea-Valor, M. L. (eds.), *Corpus-Based Approaches to English Language Teaching*. 18–38. London: Continuum.

Schmitt, D. and Schmitt, N. (2005) *Focus on Vocabulary: Mastering the Academic Wordlist*. London: Longman.

Schmitt, D. and Schmitt, N. (2011) *Focus on Vocabulary 2: Mastering the Academic Wordlist*. 2nd ed. London: Longman.

Scott, M. and Tribble, C. (2006) *Textual Patterns: Key Words and Corpus Analysis in Language Education*. Amsterdam: John Benjamins.

Seidlhofer, B. (2000) Operationalising intertextuality: Using learner corpora for learning. In L. Burnard and T. McEnery (eds.), *Rethinking Language Pedagogy from a Corpus Perspective*. 207–24. Frankfurt am Main: Peter Lang.

Sinclair, J. (1991) *Corpus, Concordance, Collocation*. Oxford: Oxford University Press.

Sinclair, J. (2004) Corpus and Text – Basic Principles. In M. Wynne (ed.), *Developing Linguistic Corpora: A Guide to Good Practice*. Accessed Feb. 2, 2012 at http://ota.ahds.ac.uk/documents/creating/dlc/chapter1.htm.

Sinclair, J. and Coulthard, M. (1975) *Towards an Analysis of Discourse: The English Used by Teachers and Pupils*. Oxford: Oxford University Press.

Skelton, J., Wearn, A., and Hobbs, R. (2000) A concordance-based study of metaphoric expressions used by general

practitioners and patients in consultation. *British Journal of General Practice* 52: 114–18.

Someya, Y. (1999) A corpus based study of lexical and grammatical features of written business English. Unpublished MA thesis, University of Tokyo. Accessed Feb. 3, 2012 at http://www.someya-net.com/09-MA/.

Swales, J. M. (1981) *Aspects of Article Introductions. Aston ESP Research Reports* No 1. Birmingham: Language Studies Unit, University of Aston at Birmingham. Republished University of Michigan Press (2011).

Swales, J. M. (1990) *Genre Analysis: English in Academic and Research Settings*. Cambridge: Cambridge University Press.

Swales, J. M. (1996) Occluded genres in the academy: The case of the submission letter. In E. Ventola and A. Mauranen (eds.), *Academic Writing: Intercultural and Textual Issues*. 45–58. Amsterdam: John Benjamins.

Swales, J. M. (2002) Integrated and fragmented worlds: EAP materials and corpus linguistics. In J. Flowerdew (ed.), *Academic Discourse*. 150–64. Harlow: Longman.

Thompson, P. (2000) Citation practices in PhD theses. In L. Burnard and T. McEnery (eds.), *Rethinking Language Pedagogy from a Corpus Perspective*. 91–102. Frankfurt: Peter Lang.

Thompson, P. (2006) Assessing the contribution of corpora to EAP practice. In Z. Kantaridou, I. Papadopoulou, and I. Mahili (eds.), *Motivation in Learning Language for Specific and Academic Purposes*. Macedonia: University of Macedonia.

Thompson, P. (2010) Building a specialised audio-visual corpus. In A. O'Keeffe and M. McCarthy (eds.), *The Routledge Handbook of Corpus Linguistics*. 93–103. London: Routledge.

Thurstun, J. and Candlin, C. N. (1997) *Exploring Academic English: A Workbook for Student Essay Writing*. Sydney:

National Centre for English Language Teaching and Research, Macquarie University.

Thurstun, J. and Candlin, C. N. (1998) Concordancing and the teaching of the vocabulary of academic English. *English for Specific Purposes* 17, 267–80.

Tognini Bonelli, E. (2001) *Corpus Linguistics at Work*. Amsterdam: John Benjamins.

Warren, M. (2004) //↓so what have YOU been WORKing on Recently //: Compiling a specialised corpus of spoken business English. In U. Connor and T. Upton (eds.), *Discourse in the Professions: Perspectives from Corpus Linguistics*. 115–40. Amsterdam: John Benjamins.

Wickens, P. and Spiro, J. (2010) Reflecting on Reflection: Identity and discourse on a Reflective Professional Development module.

Paper presented at the *43rd Annual BAAL Conference*, 9–11 September. University of Aberdeen, UK.

Widdowson, H. (1998) Context, community and authentic language. *TESOL Quarterly* 32: 705–16.

Widmann, J., Kohn, K., and Ziai, R. (2011) The SACODEYL search tool – exploiting corpora for language learning purposes. In A. Frankenberg-Garcia, L. Flowerdew, and G. Aston (eds.), *New Trends in Corpora and Language Learning*. 167–78. London: Continuum.

Yang, H. Z. (1986) A new technique for identifying scientific/technical terms and describing science texts. *Literary and Linguistic Computing* 1: 93–103.

Yoon, C. (2011) Concordancing in L2 writing class: An overview of research and issues. *Journal of English for Academic Purposes* 10: 130–39.

22 ESP and Intercultural Rhetoric

ULLA CONNOR AND WILLIAM ROZYCKI

Introduction

Intercultural rhetoric is the study of written discourse between and among individuals with different cultural backgrounds. Culturally preferred patterns of texts and interactions have been documented to exist in ESP settings (see e.g. Canagarajah 2001, and Enkvist 2001, among the literacy autobiographies in Belcher and Connor 2001, for personal accounts of experienced differences). Intercultural rhetoric examines these influences – positive and negative – of first language, culture, and education on the production of texts, with the aim of informing teachers and learners. Intercultural rhetoric includes the study of interactions – both spoken and written – that are part of text production. The identification of preferred patterns in texts and interactions across cultures and languages is important because the knowledge can inform English for specific purposes (ESP) teachers and advanced learners. For example, graduate students, post-doctoral researchers, and other novice academic writers can use a corpus of articles to compare their own rhetorical and organizational habits and lexico-grammatical choices with those of successful practitioners in the discipline. Teachers of writing for specific disciplines can benefit from the comparison of corpora of texts in different languages but in the same discipline, in order to identify potential pitfalls for their students. Such corpora comparisons thus help teachers to understand reasons for potential mismatches in the formulation of specific text types by students. Research article introductions are a well-studied example, where reliance on the practices in one's native language can lead to a mismatch with the expectations in the target language. Intercultural rhetoric research can also shed light on successful strategies for business negotiations in situations where a variety of languages and

The Handbook of English for Specific Purposes, First Edition.
Edited by Brian Paltridge and Sue Starfield.
© 2013 John Wiley & Sons, Inc. Published 2013 by John Wiley & Sons, Inc.

cultures interact to conduct commerce. In such cases, ethnographic studies are helpful to identify the differences in style and approach that may impede or promote successful communication. In addition to corpus studies and ethnography, intercultural rhetoric research draws on methodology from the fields of text and genre analysis. It also has connections with other related areas of study, such as English as a lingua franca, critical perspectives on ESP, and multimodality.

This chapter will describe the history of intercultural rhetoric and its current theory and research methods, illustrated by examples of recent topics and published research. Then, methodologies of intercultural rhetoric research will be discussed, from general principles to a step-by-step guide to research. Sample studies within ESP will highlight the range of methodologies used within this perspective. Applications of the research to ESP instruction will be described using a sample ESP program for international medical residents. Finally, future research directions for intercultural rhetoric in ESP settings will be explored.

The study of cross-cultural writing began with Robert Kaplan's (1966) attention to cultural differences in the writing of English as a second language (ESL) students for academic purposes at US universities. Kaplan's observations about ESL students' paragraph writing pioneered attention to cultural differences in the writing of ESL students. This focus on writing was relatively new in the area of ESL instruction for international students in the United States. The emphasis had been on the teaching of oral language skills.

Kaplan analyzed essays written in English by students with a variety of first language backgrounds and showed that there was negative transfer from the first language writing to these second language essays. Working under the influence of the Sapir-Whorf hypothesis (i.e. language and cognition are interconnected) and of the contrastive analysis tradition (i.e. errors in a second language are caused by interference from the first (Lado 1957), Kaplan showed how differences from English in these second language writing patterns can be linked to how a school essay is organized in other languages such as Arabic, Chinese, Russian, and Thai.

The diagram depicting cross-cultural differences in paragraph organization in Kaplan's (1966) article caught the attention of ESL teachers and is often still reproduced in ESL texts and teacher reference books. Intuitively attractive as the diagram is, it is a simplification. For example, the diagram does not differentiate any further than the "English," "Oriental," "Semitic," "Romance," and "Russian" essay types in the sample, and indicates the rhetoric of English essays as proceeding in a straight line, the rhetoric of Semitic essays as proceeding in a zigzag pattern, the rhetoric of Oriental essays as circling inward, and so on. Neither does the article include much research into the first language rhetorics in the sample. Although Kaplan advanced his research and further developed his thinking about the topic in a number of subsequent publications (e.g. Connor and Kaplan 1987; Grabe and Kaplan 1989); unfortunately, the diagram still gets used, often as a "straw person" argument to attack Kaplan's work.

Since Kaplan's first study, a wealth of research has compared writing patterns and styles in many languages and cultures. Further refinement of the hypothesis has included, apart from tacit and gradual modifications of the Whorfian hypothesis and contrastive analysis, studies of diverse types of writing: newspaper writing, academic writing, and professional writing of all sorts, particularly business writing. The expansion in research focus reflects the realization of the role of English as the international language of science and commerce, and the consequent development of English for specific purposes research in both the United States and in English as a foreign language (EFL) situations in other countries. These studies, falling within a sub-field of applied linguistics that originally was termed contrastive rhetoric, inform us about cultural and social practices and preferences that shape writing and communication, and on how writing is best taught to non-native speakers of English. The insights gained from contrastive rhetoric research have been important for teachers in order to better understand their students and the writing they produce.

Connor's (1996) *Contrastive Rhetoric: Cross-Cultural Aspects of Second-Language Writing* sets out to define contrastive rhetoric and establish it as a legitimate area of research in second language acquisition studies. The book reflected the interdisciplinary nature of this research and the resulting pluralism of the research methods. In building a theory of contrastive rhetoric, the influences on this newly defined field were identified. These influences included the two cornerstones of contrastive rhetoric, namely the transfer of first language patterns to a second language, and the theory of linguistic relativity (patterns of language and writing are culture-specific). New influences introduced in the book, however, were theories of rhetoric (writing as communication and persuasion that is affected by audience), text linguistics (texts and writing have systematic, analyzable variation), genre analysis (writing is task- and situation-based and results in discourse types), literacy (the activity of writing is embedded in culture), and translation (texts are translatable across cultures, but may take different styles and forms). The book defined contrastive rhetoric as "an area of research in second language acquisition that identifies problems in composition encountered by second language writers, and by referring to the rhetoric strategies of the first language, attempts to explain them" (1996: 5). The goal of the book was to give practical advice for researchers and teachers of ESL.

Connor's (1996) book brought about a renewed interest in the study of writing cross-culturally and an attention to the interdisciplinary potential of contrastive rhetoric. Subsequent years have witnessed several book-length publications on cross-cultural writing such as Panetta's (2001) edited book *Contrastive Rhetoric Revisited and Redefined* (on the use of contrastive rhetoric in first language contexts), Kassabgy, Ibrahim, and Aydelott's (2004) edited book *Contrastive Rhetoric: Issues, Insights, and Pedagogy* (focussing on writing and translation, diglossia, second language acquisition, and pragmatics), and McCool's (2009) *Writing Around the World: A Guide to Writing Across Cultures* (offering practical advice for global writers). Several other published volumes include chapters on intercultural writing, e.g. Manchón (2009), Palmer-Silveira, Ruiz-Garrido and Fortanet-Gómez (2006), Ruiz-Garrido, Palmer-Silveira and Fortanet-Gómez (2010), and a special issue of the *Journal of Asian Pacific Communication* (2005), edited by Li and Casanave.

Of these, Palmer-Silveira, Ruiz-Garrido and Fortanet-Gómez (2006) is a significant collection of research on the use of English in intercultural and international business communication. The breadth of the volume is ambitious; chapters range from empirical studies of intercultural business encounters, to genre analyses of a variety of business communicative activities, to insightful reflections on teaching implications for ESP. Noteworthy is the multinational representation of the studies, although the major focus is on European contexts. The special journal issue (2005) edited by Li and Casanave offers multiple perspectives on first language (L1) and second language (L2) academic and school literacies in the Asian-Pacific sphere, with an impressively international set of contributors from that region. But alongside this flourishing and expanding research and publication has come, from other scholars, criticism of contrastive rhetoric.

Critics such as Ruth Spack (1997) and Vivian Zamel (1997) have pointed to contrastive rhetoric's view of cultures as static and diminishing of the individual. Both Spack and Zamel admit that students' linguistic and cultural backgrounds shape their writing in English, but Zamel criticizes contrastive rhetoric for simplistically portraying cultures as "discrete, discontinuous, and predictable" (1997: 343). Spack criticizes contrastive rhetoric for "falling into the trap of developing and perpetuating stereotypes – and ultimately of underestimating students' knowledge and their writing skills" (1997: 767). Some other writers, such as Ryuko Kubota (e.g. 1999, 2002), adopt a postmodernist critical view of the discourse of those in power, in particular seeing in contrastive rhetoric's approach to the writing of Asian students a continuance of the "Orientalism" that Edward Said (1978) so famously lambasted. Kubota maintains that contrastive rhetoric has essentialized Asian writers. She believes that contrastive rhetoric stereotypes speakers or writers of a given language by suggesting they all speak and write in the same way. In Kubota's view, contrastive rhetoric holds that the "otherness" of these writers is deficient because it is not part of the dominant discourse. Though some of this criticism outlined above has been unfair, some was indeed warranted, and was useful in promoting a critical re-examination by contrastive rhetoric theorists. Subsequently, and to some degree motivated by these criticisms as well as reflecting natural progression within the field, new connections with four related areas of study have resulted: English for specific purposes, new literacy studies, study of culture, and translation studies. In particular, study of culture has led to a new conceptualization of culture that goes beyond notions of ethnic or national culture to encompass more granular and individual descriptions of culture. For more on the connections with these areas, see below, and also Connor (2011), which offers a detailed history of the development of contrastive rhetoric into intercultural rhetoric.

One of the most important of the above-named new connections has been the study of culture. Dwight Atkinson (2004) wrote about the need for contrastive rhetoric to change its view of culture from a "received" view of culture to an alternative view. A received view considers cultures as ethnic, national, and static; alternative views take into account the changing nature of global communication and the changing definitions of culture as described below. The most useful concept in Atkinson's discussion of new cultural concepts for intercultural rhetoric is the "large cultures" versus "small cultures" distinction (Holliday 1999). In the theory proposed by Holliday and promoted by Atkinson, legal culture, business culture, classroom culture, for example, can be discussed and analyzed using the same parameters as one uses for the broader culture: norms, values, social practices, roles, hierarchies, and artifacts. We have learned from genre studies, for example, that various discourse communities have their own norms regarding genre characteristics and their own social practices about how to produce and consume these genres. Different norms for research papers often exist from discipline to discipline. People in businesses know what a typical sales letter looks like and likely have a schema about how sales negotiations are expected to proceed.

A complex notion of the interactions of different cultural forces emerges when one analyzes the small, medium, and large cultures present in a given situation. National culture overlaps with other, smaller cultures such as professional-academic culture, classroom culture, student culture, and youth culture. This is important for teachers of writing to take into consideration in ESP situations, where the students may share a discipline such as business, engineering, or nursing, but may have diverse ages, different genders, and distinct national/ethnic and socioeconomic backgrounds.

The new definitions of culture establish the basis for the shift from contrastive rhetoric to intercultural rhetoric. Intercultural rhetoric also encompasses two other major shifts in the approach to texts, drawing in part on research from the new literacy studies movement (Street 1984,2001). The two major shifts are namely (1) studying texts in context, and (2) studying texts as part of intercultural interactions. Thus, intercultural rhetoric assumes that the study of writing is not limited to texts, but needs to consider the surrounding social contexts and practices; national cultures interact with disciplinary and other cultures in complex ways; and intercultural encounters – both spoken and written – entail interaction among interlocutors and require negotiation and accommodation. Communication is seen as always embedded in a social context, and this informs intercultural rhetoric research, including cross-cultural studies (comparison of the same concept in culture one and two) and studies of interactions in which writers with a variety of linguistic and social backgrounds negotiate through speaking and writing.

Examples of Recent Published Works

As the domain of writing in EAP has expanded from the teaching of essay writing to other genres in academic and professional contexts, genre analysis has provided researchers with methods of analysis that supplement the discourse analysis methods used in previous contrastive rhetoric research. The development of genre analysis (Bhatia 1993; Swales 1990) has been beneficial for intercultural rhetoric research as it has forced researchers to compare the same specific genre across different cultures, whereas previous to genre analysis there was the danger that apples were being compared to oranges rather than apples to apples. In addition, this focus on the rhetorical analysis of specific genres by genre analysts has led intercultural rhetoric research to expand into many additional academic and professional genres.

The number of comparative empirical genre analyses has been staggering in the past two decades. Published studies have compared the rhetorical moves and linguistic features of the research article in a number of disciplines in various countries (e.g. Bielski and Bielski 2008; Duszak 1994; Golebiowski 1998; Moreno 1998; Mur Dueñas 2008; Pabón Berbesí, and Dominguez 2008; Ventola and Mauranen 1991; and Vladimirou 2008). Among the findings from the research above is that Finnish scientists writing in English use connectors with less frequency and less variability than native-English speaking scientists in their research articles (Ventola and Mauranen 1991), and that Spanish academics writing in Spanish use fewer linguistic markers indicating personal engagement, thus presenting a less confident authorial voice than Anglophone academic writers (Mur Dueñas 2008). Other genres that have been studied across cultures include the business letter request (Kong 1998; Yli-Jokipii 1996), sales letter (Wolfe 2008; Zhu 1997), grant proposal (Connor and Mauranen 1999; Feng 2008), application letter (Upton and Connor 2001), web pages (McBride 2008), letter of recommendation (Precht 1998, 2000), and newspaper commentaries (Wang 2007, 2008). The referenced empirical studies above illustrate the expansion of the genres studied in English for specific purposes interculturally. Many of the above use rhetorical moves analysis (e.g. Connor and Mauranen 1999 and Feng 2008), but other linguistic analyses are also used to identify and explain cultural differences in writing for a specific genre. Mur Dueñas (2008) uses metadiscourse analysis to examine Spanish–English contrasts in academic research articles, while Wang (2007, 2008) applies systemic-functional appraisal theory (Martin and White 2005) to evaluate newspaper commentaries in Chinese and English. Wang finds that Chinese newspaper editorials offer more facts as evidence for their positions than English-language editorials, and that Chinese editorials focus on non-human or generic participants, while English counterpart texts address both generic and specific participants. He further finds that English-language editorial writers employ more linguistic devices (such as projection, concession, and modality) than Chinese-language editorial writers when establishing a proposition. Wang suggests that these linguistic devices reflect the fact that the Chinese newspaper, an organ of the government, serves to promote government views rather than private views, and so presents a more authoritarian voice. McBride (2008) uses multimodal analysis of English-language website navigation and comprehension to study the development of information literacy in Chilean Spanish-speaking college students. She finds that Chilean students often miss the left-side menu bars or indices on English-language websites because their familiar Spanish-language websites offer a design that places such menus or indices in a central position. Precht (1998, 2000) finds that American writers of letters of recommendation support their recommendation with personal stories of the applicant, whereas German writers of such letters list facts that they know about the applicant. British writers of letters of recommendations tend to include one minor criticism of the applicant in the body of their letters, unlike either German or American writers of the same genre. Wolfe (2008) reports that American writers of sales letters attempt to reduce power distance by addressing the reader personally, while Russian writers of sales letters maintain power distance by avoiding personal greetings, and that Russian writers offer a collective image of self in contrast to the American writers' representation of the self as individual and personal.

Methodology in Intercultural Rhetoric Research

Intercultural rhetoric research, like any good research, involves a planned and systematic way of developing a better understanding of the researched phenomenon. It requires careful steps in the planning, conducting, and reporting stages. Typically, researchers draw their idea for the study from previous research as well as from practical experiences. In the planning stage, a researcher identifies a topic, conducts a literature search, develops tentative questions, designs the data collection, and often conducts a pilot study.

In the conduct of a study, intercultural rhetoric researchers need to carefully follow the design features of *tertium comparationis* (a common platform of comparison) between texts. Connor and Moreno (2005) recommend that when two sets of texts – two L1 sets or a set of L1 and L2 – are compared, they need to be carefully compared with the basis of similarity constraints specified. Similarly, in the data analysis phase it is important to identify comparable textual units in the languages, which then have to be operationalized into appropriate linguistic forms. Cohesion and coherence, for example, may not express themselves using the same linguistic features in every language. Consider the analysis of cohesion. After Halliday and Hasan's *Cohesion in English* (1976) described the cohesion system of English in great detail, it became quite clear that the system could not be directly applied in another language for purposes of cohesion analysis. In English, a substitution may serve as an effective cohesive tie, e.g. "I want an ice cream cone. Do you want one?" but that may not be the case in other languages.

Similarly, coherence relations are not created using the same linguistic features in every language. In English, coherence is often achieved by the appropriate sequencing of given and new information. Each sentence offers a topic or given information, and new information or a comment follows. Then, the new information or comment becomes the topic of the next sentence. Such sequences in prose are interspersed with an occasional repetition of the topic to keep the reader involved and to help understanding. However, these coherence relations in English do not necessarily translate directly into coherence relations in other languages. Rather, it is the *equivalent* features that should be compared.

These equivalencies must be identified at all three levels: at the text level, when identifying texts for inclusion in one's research; at the conceptual level when identifying "moves" or communicative acts to be studied; and at the linguistic level, when studying the linguistic realizations that are used to realize the concepts at the middle level. A methodologically rigorous approach to *tertium comparationis* is likely to require equivalency testing in a multitude of domains. Table 22.1, adapted from Connor and Moreno (2005), shows the equivalency analysis at multiple levels and domains undertaken in the preparation of a corpus of English-language and Iberian Spanish-language research articles on business and economics.

Table 22.1 serves as an example of some of the features a researcher should attend to in selecting texts for comparative purposes. It is by no means an exhaustive list (e.g. equivalencies in linguistic realizations are absent from the table); ultimately each researcher must decide the features appropriate for equivalency based on the researcher's own goals in comparative analysis.

An invaluable tool for the comparison of textual features in two or more languages is the creation of a corpus of texts in one language for comparison with equivalent texts in another language. In the early years this was done by hand, with the result that researchers could meaningfully collect and analyze only a handful of texts in each corpus. With the remarkable advances in information technology over the past few decades, corpora can now easily be digitally collected, manipulated, and statistically analyzed. This allows for cross-comparison of far more specimens of text, lending greater power to findings in intercultural rhetoric research, as well as in other areas of study. The approach, methodology, and application of these powerful corpus tools are a welcome addition to applied linguistics, and together comprise the sub-field of corpus linguistics.

Corpus linguistic methods have been an important part of intercultural rhetoric research, in both academic and professional contexts. The rigor exercised in corpus linguistics in relation to corpus design, data collection, and data analysis is valuable. It is important, however, that such a rigorous approach to genre identification and comparison of texts across languages does not lead into purely statistical interpretations. We must not essentialize discourse communities or ignore individual variation in texts, since texts are ultimately created by individuals and are in fact produced in a dynamic social context.

Fortunately, the conceptualization of writing as a socially constructed activity has led intercultural rhetoric researchers to look beyond texts for reasons behind production and comprehension. Increasingly, research includes qualitative methods such as observations and interviews to help explain findings of comparative textual studies. The study by Moreno and Suárez (2008) is a good example of such contextualized intercultural text analysis. Their original study was a textual study of book reviews published in academic journals in Spanish in Spain and in international journals in English. The focus was on the frequency and type of critical comments. They found that the Spanish reviewers had markedly fewer critical (i.e. negative) instances of evaluation compared with the reviewers for international journals. To help understand these differences, Moreno and Suárez hypothesized different "writing cultures" (2008: 16) based on distinct small culture interactions. To confirm the hypothesis, they sent structured email interview surveys to the reviewers. After analyzing the reviewers' responses, Moreno and Suárez found that the differences between the two approaches to evaluation (by Spaniards and by international reviewers) can be explained by a different under-

Table 22.1 Similarity constraints used in the design of Moreno's (1998) corpus of research articles on business and economics (adapted, with permission, from Connor and Moreno 2005).

Tertium comparationis: *The platform of comparison*	*Specific prototypical features considered constants for comparison*
Text form	Scientific exposition
Genre	Research article
Mode	Written
Participants	
(a) writers	(a) academics, professionals, researchers
(b) readers	(b) academics, advanced students, researchers, social and business leaders
Style variety	Formal
Dialectal variety	Standard
Format features	
(a) length	(a) 2,000 to 16,000 words
(b) intertexuality	(b) reference to other texts
(c) visuality	(c) graphs, tables, drawings, footnotes, appendices
Point of view	Objective
Communicative purpose	For writer: to persuade readers of viewpoint
	For reader: to improve knowledge of recent research in the field
Global rhetorical strategy	Demonstrating a theory *or*
	discussing advantages of business models or practices *or*
	analyzing reasons for a given situation *or*
	proving the accuracy of a prediction
Subject matter	Business and economics
Level of expertise	Expert writers
Unit of analysis	Complete texts
Global superstructure	Introduction–procedure–discussion *or*
	problem–analysis–solution *or*
	situation–explanation *or*
	situation–analysis–forecast *or*
	problem–solution–evaluation
Predominant text types	Argumentation *or*
	Exposition *or*
	Description

standing about the purpose of the genre, a crucial difference in the size of the academic communities – whereby in the smaller and somewhat closed world of Spanish reviewers, any author you review may someday become your colleague, your mentor, or your administrative superior – and different editorial practices. In particular, Spanish reviewers of books were often requested by the *book authors themselves* to write the review.

In intercultural rhetoric research, semi-ethnographic approaches are also being used in the field where actual intercultural interactions take place in offices, business meetings, and other workplaces. There are no true, intensive long-term ethnographies, but many intercultural rhetoric studies apply ethnographic methods of observations, interviews, and field notes. These are used to better understand the textual data. These methods add richness and accuracy to the interpretation, and the approach could be called "semi-ethnographic." Connor's (1999) study of authentic international business communication in a Finnish fish brokerage can be cited as a semi-ethnographic intercultural rhetoric study. The researcher did not sit in the broker's office but was able to obtain the written records and annotate the data with regard to the purpose and wording of each piece of communication, based on interviews. The study was one of the first empirical studies of intercultural business communication, which argued for the emergence of a truly international English.

In reporting the results, the intercultural rhetoric researcher also follows the usual steps from drafting to revising and editing. It is important to keep in mind what the readers want to know; why the research was carried out; how it was conducted; what methods were used; what was discovered; and what the findings may mean for research and practice.

A Sample ESP Program for International Medical Residents

In the past few decades there has been an increasing awareness of the complexity of cultural interaction in health care discourse. In Australia, Canada, the United Kingdom, and the United States populations are from diverse linguistic and cultural backgrounds and are increasingly served by medical professionals with equally diverse origins. Discourse analysts such as Erickson and Rittenberg (1987) and Roberts and Sarangi (2005) have identified obstacles to effective communication that are linguistically expressed but are based on the differing paradigms from which patient and physician operate in the health sphere. Intercultural rhetoric can both inform and mediate these communicative challenges that exist in health care discourse.

What follows is a description of an intercultural rhetoric approach, including both field research and its application, to the ESP training of medical residents at a Midwestern US medical center. Elements in the approach include (1) a focus that reaches beyond texts to talk, (2) a broad view of culture that includes both large and small cultures, and (3) an understanding that all interactions involve accommodation and negotiation. We present a case study from health care to draw attention to the increasing need for intercultural ESP research, and its application, in the area of medicine. Though there exists a growing body of intercultural rhetoric research on the discourse of research articles and academic writing, as well as on the discourse and the genres of professional domains such as business, law, and even, increasingly, forensic sciences, little has been done in the area of health care and medicine. This is gradually changing as more and more applied linguists and ESP experts are invited to bring their theories and methods for researching and teaching the language of health care into both academic and practical situations.

Indiana University Health is a provider of services to four hospitals and more than a dozen clinics in central Indiana. Medical residents, who are graduates from medical schools in the United States or overseas, learn individual specialties through a three-year apprenticeship in which they treat patients under the supervision of board-certified specialist physician-educators. The Indiana Center for Intercultural Communication (ICIC), an ESP training provider led by an intercultural rhetoric scholar, partners with individual medical departments (e.g. Family Practice, Internal Medicine) to improve the communication skills of residents during their terms of clinical residency. The programs are proactive and can be divided into two parts: orientation workshops and assessment/individual training modules.

Orientation workshops are offered to the incoming first-year residents (both American-born and foreign-born) during their orientation period. A typical workshop begins with a simulation to raise intercultural awareness among the residents, adapted from Jameson (1993). Participants are assigned to represent one of three distinct simulated cultures, each with different in-group shared attitudes toward time management, politeness, food consumption, and other behavioral and communicative traits. At the end of the negotiations, participants are debriefed and asked to connect the experience with actual intercultural encounters in their memory. They are reminded that the cultural differences experienced in the simulation likely presage what they will experience in their interaction with patients in the clinics. A discussion of the dangers of stereotyping then follows, with an emphasis on the conceptualization of small cultures and the explanatory powers of such a conceptualization in dealing with individual patients.

The workshop then turns to the specifics of medical encounters. A number of critical incidents are presented, in which medical professionals have interacted with patients but in which the outcome is unintended and medically ineffective. The incidents are drawn both from the literature (e.g. Erickson and Rittenberg 1987) and from documented incidents within Indiana University Health. The workshop participants are asked to analyze what went wrong in each encounter. After the problem is identified and alternative actions discussed, participants are invited to role-play the same situation to bring about a more satisfying and effective encounter.

In the third and final part of the workshop, participants share reflections on their own experiences with cultural differences and communicative challenges.

Most of the incoming residents have some clinical experience as senior medical students or as interns, so they draw on these experiences to share with the others in the workshop. This leads to open-ended discussion, with workshop leaders drawing connections to the concepts of large and small cultures and accommodation and negotiation as these lived events are described, discussed, and analyzed.

By the end of the workshop, participants are expected to have gained an understanding of their own cultural biases, be aware of individual and group differences in politeness, body language, personal modesty, pain management, and attitudes about the cause of sickness. They are also guided in linguistic strategies to improve communication. Regarding the use of language, participants leave the workshop with specific advice to speak simply and without specialist language to patients, to check for understanding using active feedback, and to allow adequate time for responses from patients.

Apart from the workshops for incoming residents, ICIC has implemented an assessment and training program designed specifically for residents in family practice. This specialization attracts many international medical graduates (graduates of medical schools outside of North America) to the residency program. In fact, in some years all the incoming residents are international, with no direct prior experience of American clinics and patients. To meet the needs of these residents, primarily non-native speakers of English, ICIC researchers worked with educators and behavioral scientists in Indiana University Family Practice to develop an incoming assessment battery. The purpose of the battery was to identify residents in need of supplementary cultural and linguistic training, with the aim to ensure success in family practice for every resident. Douglas (2000) places language ability, content knowledge, and communicative ability in a framework that leads to specific purpose ability, and this model informs the assessment and training for family practice.

Each incoming resident takes the following battery (a–g) of assessment tools:

(a)   Standard test of grammar, vocabulary, listening, and reading (95 minutes)
(b)   Oral proficiency test (audio-taped, modified SPEAK test – 5 minutes)
(c)   Writing sample (written on the theme of professional goals – 20 minutes)
(d)   Language mastery self-evaluation (test takers score their perceived proficiency in English language listening, speaking, reading, and writing – 5 minutes)
(e)   Personal interview (audio-taped with interviewer notes, on origin, education, family situation, goals and aspirations, perceived communication competency – approximately 15 minutes, with added testing of medical vocabulary and a medical context role-play – 10 minutes)
(f)   Interpersonal Communication Assessment (developed by ICIC, this is a Likert-scaled series of statements about the clinical situation and the residency program, to which residents express their level of agreement or disagreement – 25 minutes)

(g)   Examination of the resident's Objective Standardized Clinical Exam
      (a videotaped assessment of clinical rounds with simulated patients, an
      instrument given to all incoming residents by IU Family Practice – approxi-
      mately 50 minutes).

Testing instruments (a) to (d) are typical of any ESP program and address the
present situation analysis (Dudley-Evans and St John 1998). Assessment (e)
addresses the subjective needs of the learner, as well as identifying further the
present situation. However, it is assessments (f) and (g) that characterize an intercultural rhetoric approach to assessment and training.

Assessment (f) was developed over a two-year period through extensive literature review, interviews with family practice educators, and focus group analysis
of veteran family practice residents, in order to identify the norms of the discourse
community in clinical family practice. After this initial research had identified the
norms of the clinical practice, assessment (f) was drawn up to test knowledge of
the norms. The norms were then expressed either correctly or incorrectly in the
tool that became assessment (f), and incoming residents express agreement or
disagreement with the statements. An example statement from the assessment tool
is, "Nurses and assistants follow the doctor's orders without question." Some of
the international residents come from cultures in which the doctor acts autonomously, outside a medical support team. This presents challenges for adjusting to
team medicine delivery in the clinics. An "agree" or "strongly agree" answer
to this question signals that the resident will need explicit training in the team
approach to health care delivery in the United States. The purpose of assessment
(f) is to test knowledge of the norms of the residency, in order to provide training
for those new residents who show a deficit in prior knowledge of these (often
non-explicit) norms. This assessment tool follows the model of Stern (1992), who
identifies cultural knowledge as "systematic conceptual knowledge about the
culture and society" and states that cultural competence "implies the ability to
recognize culturally significant facts, and a knowledge of the parameters within
which conduct is acceptable or unacceptable" (1992: 82). For a fuller account of
assessment tool (f), see Rozycki et al. (2011).

Assessment (g) is the tool that measures all the elements of job performance
ability – language use, cultural knowledge, and specialist medical knowledge –
together. While family practice specialists rate the resident's overall and specialized knowledge performance, ICIC trainers separately can assess the competence
of the resident in the nexus of language use (comprehension, pronunciation, register), cultural knowledge (body language, level of formality, bedside manner),
and medical knowledge application.

The component scores from this series of tests (a) to (g) are then analyzed by
ICIC personnel, and a decision made concerning training recommendations for
each resident. For some residents no training is recommended, for others a tailored
training regime, ranging in length from 3 to 30 hours, is recommended to the resi-
dence director of family practice.

Actual training, commenced as early as possible in the residency and designed to fit with the clinical schedules of the new residents, includes a broad range of mediation, from pronunciation practice and grammar review to the role-played making of requests and the giving of oral commands to medical team members. The end result of the ICIC resident training programs is to ensure that native-speaking residents have an awareness of cultural differences and the tools to promote better physician–patient communication, and additionally that international residents gain the linguistic skills and cultural knowledge to ensure their equal success in the residency programs. The assessment tools and training applications for medical residents largely arise through research in intercultural rhetoric in its broadest sense, including large and small culture study, discourse analysis of both written and spoken genres, and English as a lingua franca in science and medicine.

Future Directions

Future research in intercultural rhetoric in ESP settings is expected to continue with two related foci: the first on cross-cultural studies of specific genres, and the second on interactions in the production and comprehension of these genres. In academic settings, genres produced by students, such as theses and dissertations, and genres produced by academics, such as research articles, call for increased attention. Not only do we need to learn more about specific linguistic and textual features of these genres, but we also need to learn more about the contexts and processes of producing them. This means that, in addition to the published texts themselves, we need, for example, to study and understand draft revisions, correspondence with editors and reviewers, negotiations among co-authors This type of granular ethnographic research is the best way to identify the cultural differences that impede the success of academic writers in an L2 setting. Studying the research, writing, and publishing processes across languages and cultures (both large and small) will be invaluable for ESP instruction aimed at equipping students with the best tools for academic or career success. In addition to the academic genres where a considerable body of research already exists, we will see intercultural research turn also to fairly new genres of research such as conference proposals and grant proposals. Additionally, attention will be turned to hybrid text/oral genres such as research conference presentation. In professionals settings also, we will see a growth in the study of interactions – both spoken and written. In international business communication, studies that track down the specific language and discourse features in texts, as well as the strategies favored by participants with different backgrounds, will enlighten our understanding about what is needed for the most effective communication amongst intercultural negotiators of business deals.

Finally, the difficulty in formulating or defining standards of use for English as a lingua franca (see Nickerson, this volume) in international commerce points to a need also for application of intercultural rhetoric research. As English increasingly becomes the lingua franca of business and academic communication, variation from standards and norms will need to be addressed by ESP practition-ers. Intercultural rhetoric research is well situated to address this growing area of inquiry. It is often difficult for learners to know how much variation is tolerated within a discourse community, and research can at the same time both quantify this and also identify changes in the practices of disciplinary or professional fields as they become increasingly global in identity and membership. Intercultural rhetoric research can thus reveal the means and standards of features in a given genre, as well as the scope of variation that exists within that genre. Intercultural rhetoric can thereby serve the needs of ESP learners and instructors by identifying the norms of a given discourse community and also the leeway members have for negotiation and the degree of accommodation that can be expected in transactions across cultures within that given discourse.

REFERENCES

Atkinson, D. (2004) Contrasting rhetorics/ contrasting cultures: Why contrastive rhetoric needs a better conceptualization of culture. *Journal of English for Academic Purposes* 3: 277–89.

Belcher, D. and Connor, U. (eds.) (2001) *Reflections on Multiliterate Lives.* Clevedon, UK: Multilingual Matters.

Bhatia, V. K. (1993) *Analyzing Genre: Language Use in Professional Settings.* London: Longman.

Bielski, M. and Bielski, J. (2008) Analyzing medical language: A study of Polish/ English abstract translations. In S. Burgess and P. Martín-Martín (eds.), *English as an Additional Language in Research Publication and Communication.* 159–171. Bern: Peter Lang.

Canagarajah, S. (2001) The fortunate traveler: Shuttling between communities and literacies by economy class. In D. Belcher and U. Connor (eds.), *Reflections on Multiliterate Lives.* 23–37. Clevedon, UK: Multilingual Matters.

Connor, U. (1996) *Contrastive Rhetoric: Cross-Cultural Aspects of Second Language Writing.* Cambridge: Cambridge University Press.

Connor, U. (1999) How like you our fish? Accommodation in international business communication. In M. Hewings and C. Nickerson (eds.), *Business English:*

Research into Practice. 115–28. Harlow, UK: Longman.

Connor, U. (2011) *Intercultural Rhetoric in Second Language Writing.* Ann Arbor, MI: University of Michigan.

Connor, U. and Kaplan, R. B. (eds.) (1987) *Writing across Cultures. Analysis of L2 Text.* Reading, MA: Addison-Wesley.

Connor, U. and Mauranen, A. (1999) Linguistic analysis of grant proposals: European Union research grants. *English for Specific Purposes* 18: 47–62.

Connor, U. and Moreno, A. I. (2005) Tertium comparationis. A vital component in contrastive rhetoric research. In P. Bruthiaux, D. Atkinson, W. G. Eggington, W. Grabe and V. Ramanathan (eds.), *Directions in Applied Linguistics.* 153–64. Clevedon, UK: Multilingual Matters.

Douglas, D. (2000) *Assessing Languages for Specific Purposes.* Cambridge: Cambridge University Press.

Dudley-Evans, T. and St John, M. J. (1998) *Developments in English for Specific Purposes.* Cambridge: Cambridge University Press.

Duszak, A. (1994) Academic discourse and intellectual styles. *Journal of Pragmatics* 21: 291–313.

Enkvist, N. E. (2001) Reminiscences of a multilingual life: A personal case history.

In D. Belcher and U. Connor (eds.), *Reflections on Multiliterate Lives.* 51–9. Clevedon, UK: Multilingual Matters.

Erickson, F. and Rittenberg, W. (1987) Topic control and person control: A thorny problem for foreign physicians in interaction with American patients. *Discourse Processes* 10: 401–15.

Feng, H. (2008) A genre-based study of research grant proposals in China. In U. Connor, E. Nagelhout, and W. Rozycki (eds.), *Contrastive Rhetoric: Reaching to Intercultural Rhetoric.* 63–86. Amsterdam: John Benjamins.

Golebiowski, Z. (1998) Rhetorical approaches to scientific writing: An English-Polish contrastive study. *Text* 18: 67–102.

Grabe, W. and Kaplan, R. B. (1989) Writing in a second language: Contrastive rhetoric. In D. M. Johnson and D. H. Roen (eds.), *Richness in Writing: Empowering ESL Students.* 263–83. New York: Longman.

Halliday, M. A. K. and Hasan, R. (1976) *Cohesion in English.* Essex: Longman.

Holliday, A. (1999) Small cultures. *Applied Linguistics* 20: 237–64.

Jameson, D. A. (1993) Using a simulation to teach intercultural communication in business communication courses. *Bulletin of the Association for Business Communication*: 3–11.

Kaplan, R. B. (1966) Cultural thought patterns in intercultural education. *Language Learning* 16: 1–20.

Kassabgy, N., Ibrahim, Z., and Aydelott, S. (eds.) (2004), *Contrastive Rhetoric: Issues, Insights, and Pedagogy.* Cairo: University of Cairo Press.

Kong, K. C. C. (1998) Are simple business request letters really simple? A comparison of Chinese and English business request letters. *Text* 18: 103–41.

Kubota, R. (1999) Japanese culture constructed by discourses: Implications for applied linguistics research and ELT. *TESOL Quarterly* 33: 9–35.

Kubota, R. (2002) The author responds: (Un)Raveling racism in a nice field like TESOL. *TESOL Quarterly* 36: 86–92.

Lado, R. (1957) *Linguistics Across Cultures.* Ann Arbor, MI: University of Michigan Press.

Martin, J. R. and White, P. R. R. (2005) *The Language of Evaluation: Appraisal in English.* London: Palgrave Macmillan.

Manchón, R. (2009) *Writing in Foreign Language Contexts: Learning, Teaching, and Research.* Clevedon, UK and Buffalo, NY: Multilingual Matters.

McBride, K. (2008) English web page use in an EFL setting: A contrastive rhetoric view of the development of information literacy. In U. Connor, E. Nagelhout, and W. Rozycki (eds.), *Contrastive Rhetoric: Reaching to Intercultural Rhetoric.* 219–40. Amsterdam: John Benjamins.

McCool, M. (2009) *Writing Around the World: A Guide to Writing Across Cultures.* London: Continuum.

Moreno, A. I. (1998) The explicit signaling of premise-conclusion sequences in research articles: A contrastive framework. *Text* 18: 545–85.

Moreno, A. I. and Suárez, L. (2008) A study of critical attitude across English and Spanish academic book reviews. *Journal of English for Academic Purposes* 7: 15–26.

Mur Dueñas, P. (2008) Analysing engagement markers cross-culturally: The case of English and Spanish business management research articles. In S. Burgess and P. Martín-Martín (eds.), *English as an Additional Language in Research Publication and Communication.* 197–213. Bern: Peter Lang.

Pabón Berbesí, M. and C. L. Domínguez, C. L. (2008) Structure and function of the nominal group in English and Spanish in academic texts. In S. Burgess and P. Martín-Martín (eds.), *English as an Additional Language in Research Publication and Communication.* 215–33. Bern: Peter Lang.

Palmer–Silveira, J., Ruiz–Garrido, M., and Fortanet–Gómez, I. (2006) *Intercultural and International Business Communication: Theory, Research, and Teaching*. Berlin: Peter Lang.

Panetta, C. G. (2001) *Contrastive Rhetoric Revisited and Redefined*. Mahwah, NJ: Lawrence Erlbaum.

Precht, K. (1998) A cross-cultural comparison of letters of recommendation. *ESP Journal* 17: 241–65.

Precht, K. (2000) *Patterns of Stance in English*. Unpublished doctoral dissertation. Northern Arizona University.

Roberts, C. and Sarangi, S. (2005) Theme-oriented discourse analysis of medical encounters. *Medical Education* 39: 632–40.

Rozycki, W., Connor, U., Pylitt, L., and Logio, L. (2011) Assessing cultural knowledge among international medical graduates. In B. Hoekje and S. Tipton (eds.), *English Language and the Medical Profession: Instructing and Assessing the Communication Skills of International Physicians*. 111–32. Bingley, UK: Emerald Press.

Ruiz-Garrido, M., Palmer-Silveira, J., and Fortanet-Gómez, I. (2010) *English for Professional and Academic Purposes*. Amsterdam: Rodopi.

Said, E. (1978) *Orientalism*. New York: Pantheon.

Spack, R. (1997) The rhetorical construction of multilingual students. *TESOL Quarterly* 31: 765–74.

Stern, H. H. (1992) *Issues and Options in Language Teaching*. Oxford: Oxford University Press.

Street, B. V. (1984) *Literacy in Theory and Practice*. Cambridge: Cambridge University Press.

Street, B. V. (2001) Introduction. In B. V. Street (ed.), *Literacy and Development: Ethnographic Perspectives*. 1–17. London: Routledge.

Swales, J. M. (1990) *Genre Analysis: English in Academic and Research Settings*. Cambridge: Cambridge University Press.

Upton, T. and Connor, U. (2001) Using computerized corpus analysis to investigate the textlinguistic discourse moves of a genre. *English for Specific Purposes* 20: 313–29.

Ventola, E. and Mauranen, A. (1991) Non-native writing and native revising of scientific articles. In E. Ventola (ed.), *Functional and Systemic Linguistics: Approaches and Uses*. 457–92. Berlin: Mouton de Gruyter.

Vladimirou, D. (2008) Pronominal reference in linguists' writings: Explaining the English-speaking and the Greek-speaking academic communities. In S. Burgess and P. Martín-Martín (eds.), *English as an Additional Language in Research Publication and Communication*. 173–95. Bern: Peter Lang.

Wang, W. (2007) *Newspaper Commentaries in China and Australia: A Contrastive Genre Study*. Saarbruecken: VDM Verlag Dr Müller.

Wang, W. (2008) Newspaper commentaries on terrorism in China and Australia: A contrastive genre study. In U. Connor, E. Nagelhout, and W. Rozycki (eds.), *Contrastive Rhetoric: Reaching to Intercultural Rhetoric*. 169–91. Amsterdam: John Benjamins.

Wolfe, M. L. (2008) Different cultures, different discourses? In U. Connor, E. Nagelhout, and W. Rozycki (eds.), *Contrastive Rhetoric: Reaching to Intercultural Rhetoric*. 87–121. Amsterdam: John Benjamins.

Yli-Jokipii, H (1996) An approach to contrasting languages and cultures in the corporate context: Finnish, British, and American business letters and telefax messages. *Multilingua*, 15: 305–327.

Zamel, V. (1997) Toward a model of transculturation. *TESOL Quarterly* 31: 341–52.

Zhu, Y. (1997) An analysis of structural moves in Chinese sales letters. *Text* 17: 543–66.

23 English for Specific Purposes and English as a Lingua Franca

CATHERINE NICKERSON

Introduction

The field of English for Specific Purposes (ESP) owes its existence to the widespread and enduring use of English as a lingua franca (ELF) in domain specific interactions – at least to a certain extent. As numerous scholars have pointed out, English is both the most used language as an international lingua franca, as well as being the most investigated one (e.g. Bargiela-Chiappini, Nickerson, and Planken, 2013; Gerritsen and Nickerson 2009; Jenkins 2006; Knapp and Meierkord 2002; Louhiala-Salminen and Charles 2006; Mair 2003; Seidlhofer 2004). In business, in professional encounters, and in education, ELF interactions are commonplace occurrences regardless of geographical location, and in much web-based communication and most of the information technology enabled services (ITES) around the globe, ELF once again dominates. Scholars interested in the use of ESP, and the implications for teaching that their research reveals, have therefore frequently looked at ELF discourse in their investigations. There are also some indications that this has increased in recent years. In this chapter, I will show that ELF and ESP share much common ground. I will demonstrate that a number of the researchers that have contributed to our understanding of ELF, have done so by using an ESP approach. In fact, ESP, and the research methodologies that support it, can be seen to have made an important contribution to our understanding of what ELF is and how it is used.

The chapter will first give an overview of the key approaches, publications, and scholars that have characterized the ELF field, with particular reference to ESP. It will include the contribution made by ESP to ELF both in the past and in current research, and it will also explore how other approaches used in the investigation

The Handbook of English for Specific Purposes, First Edition.
Edited by Brian Paltridge and Sue Starfield.
© 2013 John Wiley & Sons, Inc. Published 2013 by John Wiley & Sons, Inc.

of ELF may be of some interest to ESP research in the future. In doing so, I will discuss how ELF has been viewed by ESP scholars and others, and the impact that this has had beyond the confines of ESP research. The chapter will look at ELF in different geographical locations, notably in Europe and in Asia, and it will briefly review ESP work that has been done on specific types of ELF interactions in business and the professions. My intention will be to show ESP research can do much to further our understanding of how ELF is used across many different domains within a society.

A number of landmark publications related to ELF are also of direct relevance to ESP. Several of these are comprised of ESP explorations, intended to facilitate the teaching of the particular interaction under investigation, others are publications that originated in other fields, or as a result of motivations other than teaching, but which nevertheless present findings or ideas that have consequences for how we view ESP. These include the influential sociolinguistic work by Graddol on the future of English alongside other languages on a global scale, the 2005 special issue of *English for Specific Purposes* on English as a lingua franca in business contexts, the 2010 special issue of *English for Specific Purposes* on ESP Research in Europe, the series of publications by Seidlhofer and colleagues from the wider field of applied linguistics that have sought to understand more about the nature of what ELF discourse is, and how this should be taught, and most recently the 2011 special issue of the *Journal of Pragmatics* that focusses on the use of ELF in the context of higher education. I will first discuss each of these, together with other similar research that has helped to shape our understanding of ELF in general, and ELF in specific contexts, and I will then go on to review the work in ELF that has appeared in English for specific purposes since the beginning of 2005 in academic, professional, and business contexts, with particular reference to the methodologies used.

From English as a Lingua Franca to Global English

The recent publications by David Graddol (e.g. Phillipson 2004, 2006) on the use of English across the globe, and its position compared to other widely used languages such as Hindi, Arabic, and Chinese (*Putonghua*) provide a useful introduction to the way in which English is used as a lingua franca in contemporary society, and how this may continue to develop in the future. In his 2006 report for the British Council, for instance, which looks at the use of global English and the English as a foreign language (EFL) industry, he reviews developments in the global demography and economy, changes in the use of technology and the structure of society, and finally how English can be compared now and in the future with other important world languages. He then goes on to look at the changes and future of English language education within the wider field of education, and then finally the implications of all these developments for the EFL industry. The report contains a great deal of invaluable background information for scholars interested in ELF, including the numbers of speakers currently estimated to be learning English around the world, and the impact that this is likely to have on native speakers of English who are rapidly losing their traditional linguistic advantage. He also makes two important points that are of direct relevance for ESP: (1) that the rise in the importance of global English will lead to a corresponding fall in the relevance of native speaker models both for the teaching of English and for how speakers (of global English) are evaluated, and (2) that English is now considered by many as a basic component of a person's general education, alongside other skills such as general literacy and computer literacy, and that this attitude towards English will continue to gain ground in the future. As I will discuss later in this section, several scholars have also identified these two trends in the course of their empirical investigations in ESP and they have gone on to speculate on what these will mean for the discipline in the future.

A part of Graddol's report deals with two other important developments in the discussion surrounding the use of English as a global lingua franca. The first of these is the critical discussion of the hegemonic role played by English, that has been prevalent in the work of scholars such as Canagarajah (1999), Pennycook (1998) and Phillipson (1992, 2003). As Graddol (2006) points out, the rise of global English and the corresponding decrease in the privileged position held by native speaker models, may provide a sustainable answer to the problems that have been viewed in the past as linguistic imperialism (Phillipson 1992). At the same time, global English requires a re-evaluation of learners' needs including the most appropriate teachers to teach it, the most appropriate textbooks to use, and the most appropriate accents to use as models. This is apparent in the work of scholars such as Nair-Venugopal (2009) for Malaysia, and Nickerson (2008) for India, for instance, who have underlined the need to meet the needs of local learners of English beyond the models provided by standardized Western teaching materials. Despite the large body of work in the past two decades that has revealed much about how English is used by foreign and second language users across the globe in business and professional communication, much of it used as a lingua franca, very few of these findings have as yet been incorporated into teaching materials (see Bargiela-Chiappini et al. 2013; Nelson 2006; and Nickerson 2005 for further discussion on this point). The second development that Graddol discusses is the increasing interest in ELF communication, and in particular the interest in the way in which non-native English speakers communicate together. As I will go on to discuss in more detail below, Graddol observes that "ELF suggests a radical reappraisal of the way English is taught, and even if few adopt ELF in its entirety, some of its ideas are likely to influence mainstream teaching and assessment practices in the future" (2006: 87). Drawing on Kachru's more recent work (Kachru 2004), Graddol (2006) observes that the rise of global English has led to a blurring of boundaries between what we understand by the terms "native speaker," "second-language speaker," and "foreign language user." Kachru suggests instead that it makes more sense to make a division between highly proficient speakers, i.e. speakers "who have a 'functional nativeness' regardless of how they learned or use the language" (Graddol 2006: 110) and those with lower proficiency who are not (yet) able to function in the same way (Kachru 2004). It seems plausible that this will also influence ESP as a field, since the blurring of these boundaries coupled with a focus on functional nativeness and a reassessment of the way in which English is taught, will also impact what we decide to investigate in our research.

Graddol (2006) refers to the Vienna-Oxford International Corpus of English (VOICE) project, directed by Barbara Seidlhofer, as being at the forefront of work on ELF communication specifically related to interactions between non-native speakers of English. The VOICE corpus is comprised of more than one million words of ELF transactions, mostly involving European ELF speakers. Among the speech events that are included in the corpus are meetings, interviews, service encounters and seminar discussions, suggesting that it should certainly be of interest to researchers looking at discourse from an ESP perspective (http://www.univie.ac.at/voice/page/corpus_description). The publications that have resulted from the project thus far, (e.g. Facchinetti, Crystal, and Seidlhofer 2010; Seidlhofer 2010) provide a rich source of information on the nature of ELF discourse in general and how this operates in at least some forms of specific discourse. Since ESP has traditionally had more focus on written forms of communication, rather than spoken forms of communication, the VOICE project and the publications emanating from it, may suggest some useful ways forward for ESP scholars interested in looking at either specific forms of spoken discourse, or at genres such as email that combine the features of spoken and written communication (e.g. Jensen 2009).

Seidlhofer and her colleagues (e.g. Jenkins 2000; Seidlhofer 2010; Seidlhofer and Jenkins 2003) suggest that the best approach in considering ELF interactions is to identify and then focus on those aspects of the interaction that are most likely to lead to problems, rather than using valuable time and resources on those that do not. Graddol (2006) observes that this approach has started to build a "lingua franca core" (LFC), i.e. a bank of problematic linguistic and discourse items that can be referred to for the design of both teaching and assessment materials. Several ESP researchers have pursued a similar approach, most notably including Rogerson-Revell (2007, 2008, 2010) who has investigated ELF discourse through the close text analysis of meetings at the European Commission, Charles and Marschan-Piekkari (2002) who used surveys and interviews to identify problems in the communication between managers at a large multinational corporation that used English as its official language, and Briguglio (2005) who investigated the ways in which English was used alongside other local languages in ELF interactions in Malaysia (see also Bargiela-Chiappini and Zhang this volume). This shift in emphasis towards the development of ELF models, as opposed to a reliance on native-speaker models, provides a challenging way forward for ESP.

Business English as a Lingua Franca

The 2005 special issue of the journal, *English for Specific Purposes* (*ESPJ*), on Business English as a lingua franca includes three articles that exemplify the work that has been done in ELF-related ESP research in business contexts. These three studies use different approaches to investigate different aspects of ELF communication and at the same time, each one also identifies an important aspect of ELF discourse that is of wider relevance for the field of ESP. The first of these is the study of the discourse of negotiation by Planken (2005), the second the investigation of English lingua franca communication at a bank and a paper manufacturer in joint ventures in Finland and Sweden by Louhiala-Salminen, Charles, and Kankaanranta (2005), and the third, the study of ELF interactions in the banking sector in Hong Kong by Chew (2005). In Planken's study, the focus is on the difference between the discourse produced in negotiation simulations by experienced ELF negotiators, and that produced by (advanced) ELF-speaking students with no prior experience in business negotiations. Planken (2005) demonstrates that the experienced negotiators used a varied set of discourse strategies that were all directly related to the business transaction in the negotiation, whereas the student negotiators used a much more limited set of strategies and they were also much more likely to talk off topic during the course of the negotiation. The study therefore suggests that despite high levels of language proficiency in English, the students also need to develop an appropriate set of *business* discourse strategies in order to become effective business negotiators. I will return to this point later in the discussion.

Chew's (2005) study of the use of English in the banking sector in Hong Kong reveals another aspect of ELF communication of relevance for ESP. Alongside a needs analysis survey of the English required in the Hong Kong banking sector, the study also includes a set of interviews with Cantonese-speaking bank personnel specifically designed to identify any difficulties that they faced when called upon to use English at work. Despite a long experience of using English as a lingua franca, Chew's respondents talked about their feelings of inadequacy or disempowerment when they needed to use English, mostly because they felt that they were not able to respond as quickly as those around them or because they either lacked the discourse strategies that they needed or they used a different set of strategies as a result of their national cultural background (Chew 2005). Other researchers have observed similar emotions in contexts other than Hong Kong, including Tanaka (2006) in Japan, and Gimenez (2002) in Argentina. Studies such as these would once again suggest that successfully communicating as an ELF speaker in a specific context entails more than the development of overall language proficiency; it requires speakers to develop a set of discourse strategies that are appropriate for the particular genre within which the person is operating, and likewise, it requires all speakers (including native speakers in particular) to develop an awareness of the discourse strategies used in ELF communication by specific national cultures. Many of these ideas are encapsulated in the third contribution to the special issue, the study of ELF communication by Louhiala-Salminen et al. (2005) at two joint ventures in Scandinavia.

A very important contribution to our understanding of ELF as it is used for English for specific business purposes is the concept of Business English as a lingua franca (BELF) as discussed by Louhiala-Salminen et al. (2005) and later elaborated on by Charles (2007). Louhiala-Salminen et al. observe that "BELF refers to English used as a 'neutral' and shared communication code" (2005: 403), which means that it is shared by the global business community without being a first language for anyone, while at the same time all of those involved can (and should) be viewed as legitimate users and not as "non-native speakers." Charles (2007: 264) comments further:

> BELF differs from ELF in that its domain is solely business, and its frame of reference is provided by the globalized business community. The *B* of BELF is thus the socio-pragmatic backdrop against which language – and any lexical or syntactic anomalies in it – is to be interpreted. Looked at from this angle, we can refer to the global business community as the "culture" that has created BELF, and within which BELF evolves.

Most recently, Kankaanranta and Louhiala-Salminen (2010) have shown in a study of BELF users' perceptions, that English is regarded as "simply work," or in other words, they see it as a skill that is simply necessary to get their work done. What this means is that ELF in business contexts is reliant on the business context for its interpretation, and the users themselves are also evaluated on their business acumen first, followed by their language proficiency. For speakers of languages other than English who want to be successful in business, and therefore for ESBP scholars with an interest in teaching applications, this is an important point, as it underlines the use of English as a business tool. In other words, the ability to communicate effectively in English provides support for business activities in the same way that being able to use Microsoft PowerPoint effectively also does or the ability to understand financial transactions. This is in line with Graddol's suggestion that English can now best be viewed as an important basic skill, which allows an individual to negotiate their way through the world of work. Viewed in this way, although undoubtedly a very important one, English becomes a skill that can be learned and applied in business or professional communication, disassociated from its original cultural roots (see also Bargiela-Chiappini and Zhang, this volume).

An important observation made by researchers interested in BELF is that it involves speakers in communication with each other, none of whom are speakers of English as a first language, and English is therefore a neutral tool. However, as Louhiala-Salminen et al. (2005) demonstrate in their discussion of the different discourse strategies used by Finns and Swedes in ELF, different national cultures may use very different strategies and these may be perceived very differently by speakers who originate from a different place. There is therefore an interaction between national culture and language skills. Gerritsen and Nickerson (2009) suggest that it is also useful to consider International Business English (IBE) as an additional categorization, alongside BELF – at least in theory – where IBE includes the presence of native-speakers of English. This is expanded further by Nickerson (2010) who uses an adaptation of Kachru's "circles of English" (Kachru 1985), to try to capture the increasing complexity inherent in business interactions, moving from interactions at the least complex level between two native speakers of English from the same national culture, through BELF where the speakers originate in different national cultures and then on to IBE at the most complex level, where native speakers are also involved. Several researchers have pointed out that native speakers of English tend to cause difficulties in interactions where ELF is being used, and although a detailed discussion of why this is the case is beyond the scope of this chapter, it is worth investigating further within ESP (see e.g. Bilbow 2002; Charles and Marschan-Piekkari 2002; Rogerson-Revell 2007, 2008). The work on BELF and on IBE by scholars interested in the use of English for business points again to the need to reassess the privileged position that has traditionally been held by native speaker models, and the perhaps more pressing need to understand much more about the nature of ELF communication and what leads both to success and to failure in a ELF interaction. This resonates with the work that I have discussed earlier in this chapter on the blurring of boundaries between native speakers, second language speakers and foreign language users, and the need to understand more about what constitutes *functional nativeness*.

ELF in Europe and ELF in Education

The 2010 special issue of *ESPJ* on ESP research in Europe also contains contributions that involve investigations into ELF – either in situations where English is produced by non-native speakers and used as a lingua franca, or in situations where English is included in texts as a lingua franca targeted at non-native speakers. These studies also exemplify the blurring of the boundaries between our conventional understanding of native, second and foreign language speakers. The study by Planken, van Meurs and Radlinska (2010) for instance looks at the use of English in advertising in Polish glossy magazines and investigates whether the target audience for those ads is able to comprehend them, and what their attitude is to the inclusion of English in the ads. Rather than looking at the nature of ELF produced, it therefore seeks to establish how ELF discourse is perceived. In terms of its methodology, the study draws on the field of document design and uses an experimental approach to the advertising texts it focusses on. The respondents in the survey are presented with texts and text fragments adapted from authentic advertising texts, and these are then used to test for both their attitudes to the use of English together with their ability to comprehend the meaning of those texts. Work like this is an established part of the research tradition of document design originating mostly in Belgium and the Netherlands (e.g. Hoeken et al. 2003; Jansen and Balijon 2002, etc.), and in recent years document design has also included a number of studies that have focussed on ELF communication and the impact that this communication has on its target audience (e.g. Gerritsen et al. 2007). Whereas ESP–ELF investigations have primarily been concerned with the production of ELF, document design ELF investigations are centered on the reception of ELF and its comprehensibility. Experimental studies in ELF are still relatively rare, but it seems plausible that they will make more contribution to ESP in the future and provide information of use in the design of appropriate teaching materials for ELF. As Graddol (2006) has suggested it is most useful to know what causes more problems for users of global English in ELF interactions.

A second study in the 2010 special issue by Wozniak (2010) looks at the English language needs of French mountain guides, using interviews, observation, and a questionnaire. In conventional terms, the guides are foreign language users who use ELF with other non-native speakers and IBE with native speakers of English, but in Kachru's terms, Wozniak's study is intended to assess the guides' needs in order to improve their *functional nativeness*, regardless of who they are interacting with. Finally, in the third relevant study in the special issue, Crawford Camiciottoli (2010) discusses the development of training for Italian students attending English medium education elsewhere in Europe as part of the Erasmus program on the basis of a corpus study. Once again, the European context in tertiary education suggests that researchers do not need to differentiate between native and non-native speakers in either the production or reception of English, as students are just as likely, or perhaps even more likely, to be listening to ELF as they are to a native speaker. Crawford Camiciottoli's study again underlines the decline in importance of native speaker models and the corresponding need to understand more about ELF models.

Outside of the work that has appeared in *ESPJ*, a 2011 special issue of the *Journal of Pragmatics* looks at ELF in university education. In the last decade in Europe in particular, the use of ELF at tertiary level and the attitudes towards its use have fundamentally changed, and it is this shift that the special issue investigates. The articles by Jenkins (2011) and by Haberland (2011) for instance focus on the increasing role played by global English in ELF interactions, and the sometimes uneasy relationship between native speakers and non-native speakers in such interactions, and the investigations by Björkman (2011) and Knapp (2011) look in more detail at the strategies or communicative functions that characterize academic ELF contexts (in Europe) and that may also lead to difficulties in the communication that takes place. Björkman's work in particular (e.g. Björkman 2009, 2010), and the close text analysis it involves, provides a great deal of information on how ELF is used. As she points out (Björkman 2010), however, although the use of ELF in tertiary contexts is widespread, the majority of studies have still focussed on native speaker models and relatively few have discussed non-native speakers. Exceptions to this are the work of Crawford Camiciottoli (2005, 2010), as I have discussed above, who has considered the discourse of non-native lectures, as well as how lectures can be adjusted to meet the needs of an international audience, and the work of Burrough-Boenisch (2005, 2006) who has looked in detail at the changes made by academic (mostly native speaker) editors in editing academic ELF discourse, such as that written by non-native speakers. Crawford Camiciottoli and Burrough-Boenisch both work with corpora and close text (discourse) analysis to deconstruct the nature of the discourse, and the changes or adjustments made in each case that they are interested in.

In the preceding three sections, I have looked at several landmark publications that have focussed on lingua franca interactions in English. These have suggested a number of approaches and recent developments in ELF research that also have relevance for those interested in ESP. Of major importance is the shift away from native speaker models, coupled with a blurring of the conventional boundaries between native speakers, ESL speakers and EFL speakers towards a categorization of speakers in terms of their *functional nativeness*. In the next section I focus on the methodologies that have been used in ELF research, particularly those methodologies that have also been incorporated into ESP. In doing so, I will look in detail at the approaches and methodologies used in recent work with a focus on ELF that has appeared in the *ESPJ* from the beginning of 2005 onwards, alongside other studies that have appeared elsewhere.

Approaches and Methodologies: Work in *ESPJ*

In the 2009 discussion of BELF provided by Gerritsen and Nickerson (2009: 181) the authors identify three methodologies that have characterized BELF research. As they suggest,

> BELF research is not in itself a methodology, nor indeed has it been associated with any one methodology in particular. [...] it is, rather, a rich area of research that has made use of a variety of different methodological approaches, each intended to reveal a different aspect of lingua franca communication.

Gerritsen and Nickerson identify survey research, the analysis of a corpus of data, and experimental research as the methodologies most prevalent in (B)ELF research, and they also observe that BELF researchers have usually incorporated a period of observation into their research in order to design the questionnaire or interview, in survey research, or to select the items for analysis or test items, in corpus and experimental research. Of these four, it is clear that ESP investigations focussing on ELF have also been characterized by survey research (e.g. Barbara et al.1996; Kaankanranta and Louhiala-Salminen 2010), and by corpus analysis (e.g. Li, Mead, and Mead 2000; Planken 2005), often preceded by a period of observation, it is only experimental research that has more rarely been used in ESP (but see Nickerson, Gerritson, and van Meurs 2005; Planken et al. 2010).

Some ESP–ELF studies have combined several different methodologies, for example the study of ELF writing at the Hong Kong Jockey Club (Baxter, Boswood, and Peirson-Smith 2002) which combined a corpus analysis, questionnaire, and interviews at the needs analysis stage in the project, followed by a genre focus and an analysis of the processes involved in producing that genre, which allowed the researchers to develop an appropriate training course in the second part of the project (see Bargiela-Chiappini et al. 2013 for further discussion). The type of genre analysis referred to by Baxter et al. (2002) in their work at the Hong Kong Jockey Club, has its origins in ESP (see Paltridge this volume for further discussion), and many researchers who have looked at the use of English as a lingua franca in business contexts, have also used an (ESP) genre approach, often together with a discourse analysis approach to identify the linguistic items that are associated with certain strategies. These researchers include scholars such as Akar (2002); Charles (1996); de Groot (2008); Louhiala-Salminen (2002); and Nickerson (2000). Indeed, in Vijay Bhatia's original work on genre and its applications in professional settings (Bhatia 1993) an analysis of ELF application letters is used to illustrate how differently different (national) cultures may operationalize the same genre. Several of the researchers mentioned above have continued to investigate this premise and to unpack the differences in discourse strategies (and their linguistic realizations) that are a consequence of national cultural differences. As I have discussed above, a very accessible example of this is Louhiala-Salminen et al.'s (2005) study of the differences between Finns and Swedes in their use of ELF and also in the ways in which those differences were perceived by both sides; whereas the Swedes were viewed by the Finns as too wordy, the Finns were viewed by the Swedes as too direct. It seems likely that this type of research will continue to be of interest, particularly with the shift in focus towards global English.

In recent work on ELF in business and industry published in *ESPJ*, a number of different methodologies have been used. The contrastive study of ELF and native-speaker email responses produced by Dutch and US corporations respectively by van Mulken and van der Meer (2005), for instance, is a genre study of written business discourse, and the study of intercultural business negotiations by Vuorela (2005) is a discourse-based study of spoken interactions. In later work, Gimenez (2006) and Forey and Lockwood (2007) each use a (systemic functional) genre approach to investigate the genre of the international business email and the genre of the calls made within the ITES industry respectively. Forey and Lockwood's work is of particular relevance for ELF as it underlines the economic importance of *functional nativeness* for emerging economies like India and the Philippines, which involves a combination of both proficiency and adaptability, so, on the one hand a high level of language proficiency such that the call center representative is able to communicate effectively across a wide spectrum of customers, and on the other hand an ability to adapt to their communication styles and communication preferences. As Nickerson's (2009) study of software engineers in Bangalore suggests, call center representatives may certainly become specialized in dealing with one area of the world which may be for instance Australia (native speakers of English) as opposed to China (non-native speakers of English), but they think of this in terms of whether or not they need to be more or less direct, or in terms of the medium of communication that works best with that group of customers, and not in terms of whether the person is a native or non-native speaker of English.

Four recent additional studies that have appeared in *ESPJ* are also worthy of mention, and together with the 2010 European ESP special issue, they are perhaps a cautious indication that the field has moved beyond a concern with the native-speaker of English and the traditional methodological approach of comparing native and non-native speaker discourse. Jensen's (2009) study of an email negotiation between a Danish company and a Taiwanese business contact is not only a useful example of (B)ELF and the importance of global English in business transactions, it also shows how different methodologies can be combined to say something meaningful about a relatively new genre. Jensen combines Hyland's (2005) concept of metadiscourse, an approach that has been most often associated with written discourse, together with Charles' (1996) categories of "old and new relationship negotiations" (Jensen 2009: 4), an approach that has most often been associated with spoken discourse in negotiations. In the first of the other three studies, Evans (2010) uses an extensive survey to show that English remains an important component in business in Hong Kong and has, in fact, increased in use over the past decade, despite predictions that it would decline as a result of the transition from being a British colony. In the second, Flowerdew and Wan (2010) combine genre analysis and ethnographic approaches to deconstruct the way in which company audit reports are produced in Hong Kong, for example, the written document is produced in English, but the writing process may involve English, Cantonese, and Putonghua. Finally, in the third, Bjørge (2010) works with a corpus of negotiations and transcriptions to investigate backchannelling in video recordings of simulated negotiations involving 51 students from 16 different nationalities.

In ELF–ESP investigations in professional and academic contexts, the same methodologies have also been used as those in business contexts, and similarly, the influence of (ESP) genre analysis has also been felt. Jackson (2005) for instance uses a survey methodology to identify the English language needs of pre-experience business students at a university in Hong Kong, and, outside of work published in *ESPJ*, the 2009 study by Gunnarsson (2009) is worth mentioning here in its application of genre analysis to trace the gradual shift from Swedish to English in a historical study of the increasing influence of ELF in Swedish academic discourse. Most recently, Mauranen, Hynninen, and Ranta (2010), give an account of the usefulness of corpus-based analysis in their description of the corpus of interactions included in the English as an academic lingua franca (ELFA) project at the University of Helsinki, and in other studies in *ESPJ*, Burrough-Boenisch (2005) uses an experimental respondent survey and a close text analysis to trace the changes made by native speakers and non-native speakers of English in ELF academic discourse. Tietze (2008) uses questionnaires, interviews, email correspondence, and telephone conversations to investigate the relationship between ELF and knowledge management in management education, and Kassim and Ali (2010) and Kaewpet (2009) use a survey questionnaire and set of interviews respectively, to investigate the ELF needs of engineering students in Malaysia (Kassim and Ali) and in Thailand (Kaewpet). Most recently, Pérez-Llantada, Plo, and Ferguson (2011) also use interviews to investigate the challenges that need to be met by Spanish academics in negotiating the dominance of English in academic discourse and the need to be proficient in ELF for academic purposes and finally, the 2010 study by Hincks of the difference in speaking rate and information content in ELF presentations compared to native (Swedish) presentations, uses a software analysis coupled with a close text (language) analysis to reveal a

23 percent decrease in speaking rate in ELF compared to Swedish and a corresponding reduction in information content (Hincks 2010). This fascinating study clearly demonstrates the difficulties posed for some speakers by the dominance of English.

In terms of methodologies and approach, the traditional approaches used in ESP investigations, often in combination with each other to provide triangulation, i.e. survey, corpus, discourse analysis, and genre analysis, have also been applied in studies on ELF. Studies in recent years also suggest less focus on a comparison between the language produced by native speakers and non-native speakers, and more interest in the production of ELF in specific contexts, and likewise, its production. As a result, the experimental work more associated with document design than it has been thus far with ESP would seem to provide a fruitful area of enquiry in the future, particularly in revealing more about the effects of ELF and global English, and the perceptions and attitudes of those that use it.

The Future of ELF Research in ESP

In this chapter I have reviewed relevant work in ELF and ESP from 2005 onwards. This has revealed a number of trends that are likely to impact the field of ESP in general in the future, and in particular the research that ESP scholars carry out. It seems clear that ELF communication will become of increasing importance within ESP, with a particular emphasis on the use of global English and a need for us to understand the nature of *functional nativeness*. As a result there will be a corresponding decrease in our reliance on, and perhaps interest in, native speaker models. The comparative studies that characterized the field into the beginning of this century will be of less interest, and there will be a corresponding increase in studies of ELF discourse between speakers originating from different places. Alongside this, there will be more interest in spoken forms of communication used for specific purposes, and ESP scholars will continue to investigate hybrid genres which combine the characteristics of both spoken and written discourse where ELF is prevalent, such as email negotiations, call center communications, academic lectures and so on. This will be the case across all social domains.

There will be an increased emphasis in ESP on ELF as it is used in Europe, and large-scale projects like VOICE and ELFA will generate findings of interest to ESP scholars looking at both professional and educational contexts. Similarly, scholars will also continue to build on this type of work in Asia, especially where the focus is on ELF communication around the region. This research, which provides invaluable information on an area of the world where ELF in the *avatar* of global English has perhaps been most widely felt in the course of the last decade, and confirms the importance of ELF within the ESP discipline. It also reaffirms the corresponding decrease within the discipline in interest in native speaker models. In the next decade then, it seems plausible that ESP will be increasingly challenged by the need to account for ELF models as well as for functional nativeness, and in doing so it will make a major contribution to our understanding of the ways in which the majority of the world's English speakers communicate.

REFERENCES

Akar, D. (2002) The macro contextual factors shaping business discourse: The Turkish case. *International Review of Applied Linguistics in Language Teaching* 40: 305–22.

Barbara, L., Celani, A., Collins, H., and Scott, M. (1996) A survey of communication patterns in the Brazilian business context. *English for Specific Purposes* 15: 57–71.

Bargiela-Chiappini, F., Nickerson, C., and Planken, B. (2013) *Business Discourse.* Second edition. Basingstoke, UK: Palgrave Macmillan.

Baxter, R., Boswood, T., and Peirson-Smith, A. (2002) An ESP program for management in the horse-racing business. In T. Orr (ed.), *English for Specific Purposes.* 117–146. Alexandria, VA: TESOL.

Bhatia, V. K. (1993) *Analysing Genre: Language in Professional Settings.* London: Longman.

Bjorge, A. K. (2010) Conflict or cooperation: The use of backchannelling in ELF negotiations. *English for Specific Purposes* 29: 191–203.

Björkman, B. (2009) From code to discourse in spoken ELF. In A. Mauranen and E. Ranta (eds.), *English as a Lingua Franca: Studies and findings.* 225–54. Newcastle, UK: Cambridge Scholars Press.

Björkman, B. (2010) So you think you can ELF: English as a lingua franca as the medium of instruction. *Hermes* 45: 77–99.

Björkman, B. (2011) Pragmatic strategies in English as an academic lingua franca: Ways of achieving communicative effectiveness? *Journal of Pragmatics* 43: 950–64.

Bilbow, G. (2002) Commissive speech act use in intercultural business meetings. *International Review of Applied Linguistics in Language Teaching* 40: 287–303.

Briguglio, C. (2005) Developing an understanding of English as a global language for a business setting. In F. Bargiela-Chiappini and M. Gotti (eds.), *Asian Business Discourse.* 313–44. Bern: Peter Lang.

Burrough-Boenisch, J. (2005) NS and NNS scientists' amendments of Dutch scientific English and their impact on hedging. *English for Specific Purposes* 24: 25–39.

Canagarajah, S. (1999) *Resisting Linguistic Imperialism in English Teaching.* Oxford: Oxford University Press.

Charles, M. (1996) Business negotiations: Interdependence between discourse and the business relationship. *English for Specific Purposes* 15: 19–36.

Charles, M. (2007) Language matters in global communication. *Journal of Business Communication* 44: 260–82.

Charles, M. and Marschan-Piekkari, R. (2002) Language training for enhanced horizontal communication: A challenge for MNCs. *Business Communication Quarterly* 65: 9–29.

Chew, S. K. (2005) An investigation of the English language skills used by new entrants in banks in Hong Kong. *English for Specific Purposes* 24: 423–35.

Crawford Camiciottoli, B. (2005) Adjusting a business lecture for an international audience: A case study. *English for Specific Purposes* 24: 183–99.

Crawford Camiciottoli, B. (2010) Meeting the challenges of European student mobility: Preparing Italian Erasmus students for business lectures in English. *English for Specific Purposes* 29: 268–80.

Evans, S. (2010) Business as usual: The use of English in the professional world in Hong Kong. *English for Specific Purposes* 29: 153–67.

Facchinetti, R., Crystal, D., and Seidlhofer, B. (eds.) (2010) *From International to Local English – and Back Again*. Frankfurt: Peter Lang.

Flowerdew, J. and Wan, A. (2010) The linguistic and the contextual in applied genre analysis: The case of the company audit report. *English for Specific Purposes* 29: 78–93.

Forey, G. and Lockwood, J. (2006) "I'd love to put someone in jail for this": An initial investigation of English in the business processing outsourcing (BPO) industry. *English for Specific Purposes* 26: 308–26.

Gerritsen, M. and Nickerson, C. (2009) BEFL: Business English as a lingua franca. In F. Bargiela-Chiappini (ed.), *The Handbook of Business Discourse*. 180–92. Edinburgh: Edinburgh University Press.

Gerritsen, M., Nickerson, C., van Hooft, A., van Meurs, F., Nederstigt, U., Starren, M., and Crijns, R. (2007) Selling their wares: English in product advertisements in Belgium, France, Germany, the Netherlands and Spain. *World Englishes* 26: 291–315.

Gimenez, J. (2002) New media and conflicting realities in multinational corporate communication: A case study. *International Review of Applied Linguistics in Language Teaching* 40: 323–44.

Gimenez, J. (2006) Embedded business emails: Meeting new demands in international business communication. *English for Specific Purposes* 25: 154–72.

Graddol, D. (2004) The future of language. *Science* 303(5662): 1329–331.

Graddol, D. (2006) *English Next*. London: British Council. Accessed Feb. 27, 2011 at http://www.britishcouncil.org/learning-research-englishnext.htm accessed.

Groot, E. de (2008) *English Annual Reports in Europe: A Study on the Identification and Reception of Genre Characteristics in Multimodal Annual Reports Originating in the Netherlands and in the United Kingdom*. The Netherlands: Centre for Language Studies, Radboud University Nijmegen.

Gunnarsson, B. L. (2009) *Professional Discourse*. London: Continuum.

Haberland, H. (2011) Ownership and maintenance of a language in transnational use: Should we leave our lingua franca alone? *Journal of Pragmatics* 43: 937–49.

Hincks, R. (2010) Speaking rate and information content in English lingua franca oral presentations. *English for Specific Purposes* 29: 4–18.

Hoeken, H., van der Brandt, C., Crijns, R., Dominguez, N., Hendriks, B., Planken, B., and Starren, M. (2003) International advertising in Western Europe: Should differences in uncertainty avoidance be considered when advertising in Belgium, France, the Netherlands and Spain? *The Journal of Business Communication* 40: 195–218.

Hyland, K. (2005) *Metadiscourse*. Continuum: London.

Jackson, J. (2005). An inter-university, cross-disciplinary analysis of business education: Perceptions of business faculty in Hong Kong. *English for Specific Purposes* 24: 293–306.

Jansen, C. and Balijon, S. (2002) How do people use instruction guides? Confirming and disconfirming patterns of use. *Document Design* 3: 195–204.

Jenkins, J. (2000) *The Phonology of English as an International Language: New Models, New Norms, New Goals*. Oxford: Oxford University Press.

Jenkins, J. (2006) Points of view and blind spots: ELF and SLA. *International Journal of Applied Linguistics* 16: 138–62.

Jenkins, J. (2011) Accommodating (to) ELF in the international university. *Journal of Pragmatics* 43: 926–36.

Jensen, A. (2009) Discourse strategies in professional e-mail negotiation: A case study. *English for Specific Purposes* 28: 4–18.

Kachru, B. (1985) Standards, codification and sociolinguistic realism. In R. Quirk and H. Widdowson (eds.), *English in the World: Teaching and Learning the Language and Literatures*. 11–30. Cambridge: Cambridge University Press for the British Council.

Kachru, B. (2004) *Asian Englishes: Beyond the Canon*. Hong Kong: Hong Kong University Press.

Kankaanranta, A. and Louhiala-Salminen, L. (2010) "English? – Oh, it's just work!": A study of BELF users' perceptions. *English for Specific Purposes* 29: 204–09.

Kassim, H. and Ali, F. (2010) English communicative events and skills needed at the workplace: Feedback from the industry. *English for Specific Purposes* 29: 168–82.

Knapp, A. (2011) Using English as a lingua franca for (mis-)managing conflict in an international university context: An example from a course in engineering. *Journal of Pragmatics* 43: 978–90.

Knapp, K. and Meierkord, C. (eds.) (2002) *Lingua Franca Communication*. Frankfurt: Peter Lang.

Kaewpet, C. (2009) Communication needs of Thai civil engineering students. *English for Specific Purposes* 28: 266–78.

Li, S., Mead, F., and Mead, K. (2000) An analysis of English in the workplace: The communication needs of textile and clothing merchandisers. *English for Specific Purposes* 19: 351–68.

Louhiala-Salminen, L. (2002) The fly's perspective: Discourse in the daily routine of a business manager. *English for Specific Purposes* 21: 211–31.

Louhiala-Salminen, L. and Charles, M. (2006) English as the lingua franca of international business communication: Whose English? What English? In J. Carlos Palmer-Silveira, M. F. Ruiz-Garrido, and I. Fortanet-Gómez (eds.), *Intercultural and international Business Communication*. 27–54. Bern: Peter Lang.

Louhiala-Salminen, L., Charles, M., and Kankaanranta, A. (2005) English as a lingua franca in Nordic corporate mergers: Two case companies. *English for Specific Purposes* 24: 401–21.

Mair, C. (ed.) (2003) *The Politics of English as a World Language*. Amsterdam and Atlanta, GA: Rodopi.

Mauranen, A., Hynninen, N., and Ranta, E. (2010) English as an academic lingua franca: The ELFA project. *English for Specific Purposes* 29: 183–190.

Nair-Venugopal, S. (2009) Localised perspectives: Malaysia. In F. Bargiela-Chiappini (ed.), *Handbook of Business Discourse*. 387–99. Edinburgh: Edinburgh University Press.

Nelson, M. (2006) Semantic associations in Business English: A corpus-based analysis. *English for Specific Purposes Journal* 25: 217–34.

Nickerson, C. (2000) *Playing the Corporate Language Game. An Investigation of the Genres and Discourse Strategies in English Used by Dutch Writers Working in Multinational Corporations*. Amsterdam and Atlanta, GA: Rodopi.

Nickerson, C. (2005) English as a lingua franca in international business contexts. *English for Specific Purposes* 24: 367–80.

Nickerson, C. (2008) Towards the creation of appropriate teaching materials for high proficiency ESL learners: The case of Indian management students. *TESL-EJ 12*.

Nickerson, C. (2009) The challenge of the multilingual workplace. In L. Louhiala-Salminen and A. Kankaanranta (eds.), *The Ascent of International Business Communication*. 193–204. Helsinki: Helsinki School of Economics.

Nickerson, C. (2010) The Englishes of business. In A. Kirkpatrick (ed.), *The Handbook of World Englishes*. 506–19. Oxford and New York: Routledge.

Nickerson, C., Gerritsen, M., and van Meurs, F. (2005) Raising student

awareness of the use of English for
specific business purposes in the
European context: A staff-student
project. *English for Specific Purposes* 24:
333–46.

Pennycook, A. (1998) *English and the
Discourses of Colonialism*. London:
Routledge.

Pérez-Llantada, C., Plo, R., and Ferguson,
G. R. (2011) "You don't say what you
know, only what you can": The
perceptions and practices of senior
Spanish academics regarding research
dissemination in English. *English for
Specific Purposes* 30: 18–30.

Phillipson, R. (1992) *Linguistic Imperialism*.
Oxford: Oxford University Press.

Phillipson, R. (2003) *English-Only Europe?
Challenging Language Policy*. London:
Routledge.

Planken, B. (2005) Managing rapport in
lingua franca sales negotiations: A
comparison of professional and aspiring
negotiators. *English for Specific Purposes*
24: 381–400.

Planken, B., van Meurs, F., and Radlinska,
A. (2010) The effects of the use of
English in Polish product
advertisements: Implications for English
for business purposes. *English for Specific
Purposes* 29: 225–42.

Rogerson-Revell, P. (2007) Using English in
international business: A European case
study. *English for Specific Purposes* 26:
103–20.

Rogerson-Revell, P. (2008) Participation
and performance in international
business meetings. *English for Specific
Purposes* 27: 338–60.

Rogerson-Revell, P. (2010) Can you spell
that for us non-native speakers?:
Accommodation Strategies in

International Business Meetings. *Journal
of Business Communication* 47: 432–54.

Seidlhofer, B. (2004) Research perspectives
on teaching English as a lingua franca.
Annual Review of Applied Linguistics 24:
209–39.

Seidlhofer, B. (2010) Lingua franca English
– the European context. In A.
Kirkpatrick (ed.), *The Routledge Handbook
of World Englishes*. 355–71. Oxford:
Routledge.

Seidlhofer, B. and Jenkins, J. (2003) English
as a lingua franca and the politics of
property. In C. Mair (ed.), *The Politics of
English as a World Language*. 139–54.
Amsterdam/Atlanta, GA: Rodopi.

Tanaka, H. (2006) Emerging English-
speaking business discourses in Japan.
Journal of Asian Pacific Communication 16:
25–50.

Tietze, S. (2008) The work of management
academics: An English language
perspective. *English for Specific Purposes*
27: 371–86.

van Mulken, M. and van der Meer, W.
(2005) Are you being served? A genre
analysis of American and Dutch
company replies to customer enquiries.
English for Specific Purposes 24: 93–109.

Vienna-Oxford International Corpus of
English (VOICE). Accessed Feb. 26, 2011
at http://www.univie.ac.at/voice/
page/what_is_voice.

Vuorela, T. (2005) How does a sales team
reach goals in intercultural business
negotiations? A case study. *English for
Specific Purposes* 24: 65–92.

Wozniak, S. (2010) Language needs
analysis from a perspective of
international professional mobility: The
case of French mountain guides. *English
for Specific Purposes* 29: 243–52.

24   Critical Perspectives on ESP

SUE STARFIELD

Introduction

> with the advent of the critical turn in ESP . . . has come greater licence to explore the socio-political, and equity dimensions of ESP in a world where English sits at the apex of the world language hierarchy (Ferguson 2007: 9).

Over a decade ago, Master (1998) demonstrated his awareness of this hierarchy when he expressed his concern about the global dominance of English, its predominant role in academic publication, and its capacity to pose a threat to the use of other languages in the domains not only of science, technology, and culture but in some cases to their very existence as languages. Addressing the role of English for specific purposes (ESP) specifically, he identified what he called "a subtle aspect of linguistic dominance" (1998: 720) in ESP if it was seen primarily as an instrument of very narrow technical training that neglected wider "sociocultural domains whose specific purpose is not only access to and success in education or employment but also individual self-betterment . . . for example, survival, literacy, and AIDS education" (1998: 721). He concluded that the "inclusion of the individual sociocultural perspective may help ESP adopt a critical stance that will work to hinder and control its own tendencies towards linguicism and linguistic imperialism" (1998: 271). These latter two terms refer to the "ideologies and structures where language is the means of effecting or maintaining an unequal allocation of power and resources" (Phillipson 1992: 55). At the same time, Master acknowledges that with the dominance of English comes additional responsibility for ESP practitioners and researchers who can be the gateway to access to the language and the power it vehicles for their students. This responsibility is in

The Handbook of English for Specific Purposes, First Edition.
Edited by Brian Paltridge and Sue Starfield.
© 2013 John Wiley & Sons, Inc. Published 2013 by John Wiley & Sons, Inc.

effect one of the key themes that critical research into ESP has sought to address and will be discussed at greater length below.

In the early years of ESP in the period after World War II, it was viewed by many in the West as a modern, more scientific and efficient approach to language learning and teaching than previous approaches and as helping to contribute to progress and development in developing countries (see Starfield 2012). Benesch (2001) in her book, *Critical English for Academic Purposes*, however points to the large scale ESP projects of the early periods as being driven less by goals of global progress and communication but more narrowly by British neocolonialism and American capitalism and imperialism. It is doubtful whether the early proponents of ESP could have anticipated either the global expansion of English or the critique that this expansion has occasioned. More recently, Belcher (2006: 134), while noting that ESP was initially often described as "needs-based, pragmatic, efficient, cost-effective and functional", acknowledged the developing critique of traditional ESP practices, commenting that these practices have variously also been described as "accommodationist," "assimiliationist," "market driven," and "colonizing."

While not wishing to set up overly simplistic binary oppositions, the contestation around these terms draws our attention to the development of critical perspectives in ESP that can be viewed as part of what Kubota and Chiang (this volume), and others, term the "critical turn" in applied linguistics and TESOL research. Their chapter also provides a useful framework for conceptualizing the different meanings of "critical" as does Pennycook (2011). The term "critical" can be seen to draw on several traditions including the work of the European critical theorists of the Frankfurt School such as Habermas, Adorno, and Marcuse; the work of Freire (1970, 1994) and others in critical pedagogy; the work of Michel Foucault (e.g. 1980); Pierre Bourdieu (e.g. 1991); Edward Said (1978); and more recently, work by Benesch (2001); Canagarajah (2002a, 2002b); Luke (2004), Pennycook (1994, 1997, 2001); and Phillipson (1992), among others, more specifically looking at the role of English in producing and reproducing unequal access to the resources, both material and symbolic that English affords. Poststructuralism, postmodernism and postcolonial theories further contribute to the difficulty of "pinning down" shared understandings of the "critical." While these influences will be discussed in greater detail below, all can be said to share a concern with how unequal power relations shape interaction and opportunity both in and outside of the classroom; with how identities of learners and teachers are shaped by discourse, by unequal access to resources for meaning making, and by broader social inequity, along with a commitment to promoting social justice and change. Moreover, they can be said to share an interest in interrogating the taken for granted, the naturalized and the normalized in daily life and asking us to consider how hegemony works to make unequal power relations of all kinds appear "just the way things are" (see also Luke 2004). Pennycook (1994: 168) argues that these sorts of processes promote the view that "both the spread of English and the teaching of English are natural, neutral and beneficial." It should be pointed out at this point however that "critical" is not used here to refer to discussions of higher order reading comprehension and reasoning processes (Luke 2004;

Pennycook 2001). Of course, not all of those referred to in this paragraph have commented on English language learning and teaching but it is their contribution to shaping the "critical turn" that is important to understand. It is fair to say that the early years of ESP were not characterized by much interest in these larger social concerns, in particular a concern with the role of English, as attested to be a number of the chapters in this volume. As Kubota and Chiang (this volume) point out, ESP has often been characterized as having a pragmatic orientation rather than a critical one and this has been a topic of debate in the 1990s and 2000s (see also Hyland this volume) and is discussed in more detail below.

According to Luke and Dooley (2011: 856), Freire's work has foregrounded language teaching and learning as "an act of political and cultural power with substantive material and social consequences and possibilities for learners and their communities." Freire's work (1970, 1994), at a time of decolonization, rather than the current era of globalization, asked learners and teachers to consciously name, question, and problematize oppressive relations of power, both within education and within society more broadly, that effectively excluded them from access to freedom. He also put forward a vision of pedagogy as providing hope, which Benesch (2001, 2009) discusses further as crucial to criticality in EAP.

The Frankfurt school was a group of European philosophers who before and after World War II developed what they called "critical theory" as a critique of traditional Marxism. Their work has been very influential in that it looked beyond economic oppression to try to understand how domination is enacted in advanced capitalist societies through mass culture and ideologies that could work to absorb and neutralize movements that sought social change (see also Pennycook 2001).

A key question for Michel Foucault (e.g. 1980) was the relationship between power and knowledge in Western societies as expressed in discourse. At any given period, discourse constructs what is true and sets limits to what is known and knowable, what can and cannot be said. The work of critical discourse analysts such as Norman Fairclough (1995) is heavily influenced by Foucault's thinking as is much poststructuralist thinking about pedagogy and the ways social power relations shape communicative practices and may restrict access to powerful discourses (Morgan 2007). Poststructuralism has also led to conceptualizations of identity as fluid and unstable as it is constructed in and through discourse, leading to a realization in language learning and teaching that identities are negotiable and that while learners are positioned in discourse they can exert agency (Morgan 2007).

Pierre Bourdieu's (1991) concepts of cultural capital, symbolic power, and habitus (how our bodily dispositions and habits are shaped by social class) as well as his theories of reproduction and schooling have all contributed to shaping the critical perspectives that frame the ESP work described below. His theory of symbolic power understands pedagogical contexts as hierarchically structured, socially differentiated fields of practice. Access to the dominant forms of language and academic literacies is unequal and only certain speakers (or writers) will be recognized as in possession of the legitimate language and have not only the "right to speak" but also the "power to impose reception" (to be listened to) (see also Norton 2000).

Edward Said's (1978) theory of Orientalism in which he puts forward a critique of how the West developed a discourse (in Foucault's terms) about the East (Orientalism) which portrays those societies and their inhabitants as "Other" in ways which facilitated colonialism and limited the identities available to them has influenced critical perspectives in ESP. Ellwood and Nakane (2009: 204), for example, argue that an "overarching stereotype which contrasts a silent East with an articulate West" held by both Australian teachers and the Japanese students in their EAP and mainstream university classes worked to reproduce and reinforce the silence of Japanese students in their classes. Critical approaches to both ESP and TESOL have argued that their work in developing and non-Western countries can be seen as extending Orientalist perceptions and deficit views of learners and of non-native scholars trying to publish in English by stereotyping and essentializing them (see for example, Kubota 2004; Pennycook 1994).

By its very nature, critical work in ESP has been and still is an area of contestation. Those who work in the field probably would not want it any other way. Pennycook's (2001: 8) characterization of critical applied linguistics as a "restive problematization of the given" invites a continuing reappraisal and critical reflection. While running the risk of gross oversimplification, the debates can be seen to center around two main questions: To what extent should ESP's "project" be an essentially pragmatic one? To what extent is it incumbent on teachers to "empower" students to challenge societies' inequities? In this chapter, I consider critical perspectives on research into English for academic purposes, perhaps the most well known sub-field of ESP in which critical work is being done. I then go on to consider critical approaches to needs analysis, critical perspectives on learning and teaching genre, and on plagiarism. The chapter concludes with a section on power and politics in academic publishing in English and a consideration of future directions for research.

Critical Perspectives on English for Academic Purposes

In her introduction to the special issues of the *Journal of English for Academic Purposes* devoted to critical English for academic purposes, Benesch (2009: 81) describes critical EAP (CEAP) as "widen[ing] the lens of academic purposes to take the sociopolitical context of teaching and learning into account." She reiterates that this should not be taken to mean that "CEAP overlooks on-the-ground requirements of academic genres and classroom interactions but, rather, that they are explored in relation to EAP students' and teachers' complex and overlapping social identities: class, race, gender, ethnicity, age and so on." Critical EAP, she continues, "considers hierarchical arrangements in the societies and institutions in which EAP takes place, examining power relations and their reciprocal relationship to the various players and materials involved."

The comments above remind us of the debates over the "real" goals of EAP instruction and the role of EAP instructors that began in the 1990s. To what extent does the pragmatic view of EAP – to help novice students acculturate to the expectations of the academy without challenging the *status quo* (Allison 1994) – still dominate the field? The pragmatic approach labeled critical EAP "political," as if, as Benesch (2001) and Pennycook (1997) pointed out, other approaches were ideologically neutral. Pennycook (1997: 258) termed the acculturation approach "vulgar pragmatism," arguing that it failed to show awareness of the role of English in "the spread of particular forms of culture and knowledge" and called for a "critical pragmatism." Benesch (2001: 51) did acknowledge that, "provoking a desire to interrogate the status quo . . . is not achieved by critical teachers imposing their vision or political agenda on students." Instead, drawing on Freire's work, she argued for a local and situated approach, which engages students into dialogue about the limits of what is possible and promotes hope. Her work at the City University of New York goes a considerable way in showing how teachers of EAP can have agency and work to change the structural conditions that limit their capacity for change. In her book, *Critical English for Academic Purposes* (Benesch 2001), she shows how in her negotiations with more powerful content professors she challenged existing, hitherto unquestioned classroom practices, encouraged students to consider actions that would enable them to do so too and also introduced subject matter in her linked classes that challenged students to reconsider many of their own assumptions. Morgan and Ramanathan (2005: 156) reframed the debate somewhat, acknowledging that while "one of the central rules of [EAP] instruction is to help students manage unfamiliar disciplinary content and text types, critical EAP develops as an embedded, co-occurring literacy strategy – to raise students' awareness of how academic content 'manages' them, . . . shaping their desires, world views, and life chances beyond the school." Thus "critical EAP literacies invigorate, rather than replace, conventional academic skill sets" (Morgan and Ramanathan 2005: 156). Taking up this debate on the nature of EAP as norm reinforcing or norm challenging, Harwood and Hadley (2004) proposed a "critical pragmatic approach" to teaching academic writing through introducing students to corpus-based research for investigating disciplinary literacy practices in their own fields of study. They did however acknowledge that Lea and Street's (1998) research into academic literacies, which revealed the extent to which individual tutors and lecturers' views of good writing varied even within a disciplinary field, could mitigate the effectiveness of such an approach.

Critical researchers have shown an awareness of the tensions inherent in trying to adopt critical perspectives within institutions that remain fundamentally unchanged. For example, Morgan (2009: 89) asks whether EAP teacher educators who do this may "inadvertently promote pedagogies of despair and pessimism." Reflecting critically on his own practices, he wonders whether the focus in his classes on the negative impacts of the spread of English globally could have led to a student's decision to abandon her teaching studies as she no longer wished to be part of the EAP profession. In his capacity as a teacher educator, Morgan (2009) wonders whether critical approaches have perhaps exaggerated the capacity for teachers to act as change agents, noting that many EAP teachers remain in marginalized contract positions.

The debate on the agency and ethical responsibility of teachers of CEAP is relocated by Appleby (2009: 109) to the context of an international development program in which a "complex set of power, gender and knowledge relations" both reproduce and contest the patriarchal and colonial discourses within and without the classroom as a group of white Australian women teachers critically reflect on the learner-centered Western discourses they bring with them. Many of the issues these teachers encounter in an apparently distant "third world" setting would not be that unfamiliar to teachers in the globalized EAP classrooms of many contemporary Western universities and colleges, what Singh and Doherty (2004: 09) have called "the contact zone of the global university." Contact zones refer to spaces and locations in which people with disparate historical trajectories and cultural identities "meet, clash, and grapple with each other, often in highly asymmetrical relations of domination and subordination" (Pratt 1991: 4). Viewing EAP as situated in the these global contact zones, where most EAP practitioners are working, enables us to understand that they arise out of the interplay of various, often contradictory forces: Western colonial and neocolonial practices; the marketization of Western higher education; the global spread of English language conflated with Western knowledge, and the demands of former colonized people for access to dominant language and knowledge resources on their own terms (Singh and Doherty 2004). Singh and Doherty's interviews with EAP teachers in Australian settings reveal the extent to which teachers may not only be positioning their students in discourses which can limit the students available identity options but how the commodification of EAP positions teachers and limits their access to discourses that might allow them to challenge these identity options.

Chun's (2009) analysis of the discourses of neoliberalism that shape preparatory EAP courses for international students wishing to enrol in North American universities explores the spaces available to EAP practitioners in these "corporatizing" (Starfield 2004a) environments. Not only are both the structure and location of these courses symptomatic of the commodification of higher education in that students pay high fees to enrol, EAP is itself packaged and marketed as a costly commodity. The textbooks used also can be seen to promote ideologies that support a neoliberal vision of a benign free-market economy. Finding that the international students in his classes seemed to withdraw from these lessons, Chun encouraged them to question what the images and texts meant to them and offer their alternative readings of these texts which he hoped would open up for them other identity options than those of the consumer.

Dudley-Evans (2001) claimed that the economic power of the full-fee paying international students at his university had been beneficial, leading to changes on the part of the academic departments in course content, teaching methods, and an acceptance of the role of the EAP teacher in a team-teaching capacity. It is debatable whether the current intense corporatization of the universities and the cutting back on EAP-type programs and resourcing more widely would facilitate the same degree of acceptance today. More recent studies of the subtle and not so subtle institutional pressures academic faculty experience to pass the work of international students enrolled at Western universities (see e.g. Baik 2010) high-light the complexity of the forces at play; large numbers of students who meet baseline, internationally recognized, English language proficiency test scores are recruited to fund these universities, often at huge cost, not solely financial, to themselves and their families (Banerjee and Wall 2006; Paltridge and Starfield 2007).

Much of the research within the critical tradition has been within the sub-field of English for academic purposes examining the struggles of undergraduate and post-graduate students, primarily non-native speakers of English, to acquire the academic literacies needed for successful study in Western higher education institutions. The notion that language needed to be understood within the contexts in which it was to be used has been central to ESP and EAP since their inception (Belcher 2006). While earlier ESP work introduced the notion of discourse community (Swales 1990) to bridge between texts and their contexts, critical work has argued that community in this view is often portrayed as having a homogenous and nonconflictual agreement over norms and values. Critical work argues that any context needs to be understood as sociohistorically and politically constituted and will be shaped by the power relations and inequality in the wider society (see for example Canagarajah 2002a; Ivanič 1998; Lillis 2001; Prior 1998; Starfield 2001, 2011). Prior's ethnographic research, for example, indicates the contingency of disciplinary norms, how these are constantly negotiated and renegotiated in terms of power and other social relations and cannot be seen to pre-exist the "task" in apriori ways. At the same time, much current research into academic discourse, while acknowledging that the construct of disciplinarity is "not an altogether happy one" (Hyland 2011: 11) continues to promote the view of discipline and community as in normative agreement, the norms being those of knowledgeable "insiders," thus avoiding discussions of how power relations shape these communities and how one becomes an "insider."

Gao's (2010) "micropolitical" ethnographic case studies of the language-learning strategies of students from mainland China at an English medium university in Hong Kong further point to the limits of understanding the university as a homogenous community of practice. The mainland Chinese speakers of Phutongua (Mandarin) in fact "entered a setting with complex and overlapping communities" (2010: 277) in which they struggled to engage with the local Cantonese speakers and also to create opportunities for speaking English.

Studies have looked at how students are positioned as second-language speakers by the dominant institutional discourses which fail to recognize the discourses the students bring with them from their homes or previous literacy practices (see for example Angélil-Carter 1997; Archer 2008; Starfield 2002; 2004b, 2011; Thesen 1997). As Northedge (2003) points out, academic discourses do not only exclude second language speakers but also those from lower socioeconomic backgrounds or minority groupings. These institutions are seen as reproducing existing societal inequalities and power relations and the EAP/ESP teachers' ability to challenge the status quo is called into question as they can also be positioned by the

institution in such a way (marginalized) that their capacity to change the dominant power relations is limited (Ivanič 1998; Lillis 2001; Starfield 2004a)

Critical Perspectives on Needs Analysis

Belcher (2006) reminds us that needs analysis has been one of the cornerstones of
the ESP approach and has always been research-based, with a move since the
1980s to include information about learners' subjective needs, their wants, investments and desires, and their memberships of multiple communities. While many
published studies of needs analyses in a range of contexts do not yet seem to have
fully taken on the challenge of critical approaches to EAP curriculum development, Benesch (2001) problematized and further expanded ESP's notion of needs
analysis from its focus on the target situation through her focus on "rights analysis," calling attention to the need to take into consideration learners' opportunities
for negotiation and resistance both within and beyond the language classroom.
The critically self-reflexive teacher, she argues, provides opportunities for students
to exercise agency and challenge "unreasonable and inequitable arrangements"
without neglecting to attend to meeting the learning needs that more traditionally
focussed needs analysis would suggest (2001: 108). As Morgan (2007: 1044) notes
"Benesch's pedagogy emphasizes dialogue and the importance of balancing pragmatic issues with transformative ones in the university context."

This tension is a concern for Johns and Makalela (2011) as they jointly and critically reflect on the stated and unstated assumptions and intentions that underlay
a needs analysis project funded by an external donor in a university setting in
rural South Africa in which they were both involved, Johns as external consultant
and Makalela as the academic "client." Rather than describing a successful needs
analysis carried out with traditional survey, interview, partial observation, and
discourse analytic methodology, their discussion highlights the limits of what is
possible for an external consultant who is not familiar with the political realities
and power relations of the local context to achieve within a brief time frame. It
suggests, perhaps, that local solutions may better serve the students in this very
disadvantaged setting.

Belcher and Lukkarila (2011) argue that needs analysis should take into account
contemporary understandings of identity through acknowledging students'
multiple and fluid identities and multiple community memberships. Identity is
experienced by their multilingual students as a complex, ongoing process of both
positioning and being positioned in multiple contexts. They urge EAP practitioners to try to understand the multiple, contradictory, and dynamically evolving
nature of learner needs as linked to their identities evolving over space and time.
They ask: "How much more enlightening would any target needs analysis be if
we considered not just what learners want to be able to **do** in a language but also
who they want to *become* through language?" (2011: 89; authors' emphases).

The vast majority of needs analyses of workplace contexts have not attempted
to adopt critical perspectives. Jasso-Aguilar's (2005) participant observation study

of the English language needed by hotel maids in Waikiki is one of the few to do so. Her multimethod needs analysis uncovered a gap between the hotel's perceptions of the English language skills needed by the maids and the maids' own perceptions of their needs in which the unequal power relations between management and the workers were implicated. She recommends that when conducting a needs analysis

> it is necessary to examine the social context in which the actors live their lives critically, as well as the power differentials involved. As researchers and curriculum designers we must strive for a critical perspective based upon dialogue with, rather than observation and manipulation of, people (2005: 150).

Similarly, Goldstein's (1997) critical ethnography of immigrant workers at a Canadian factory interrogated their multiple language needs and is able to shed light on why many of the workers were resistant to the English language courses on offer despite it seeming obvious that learning English would improve their life chances. Critical ethnography (see Anderson 1989; Carspecken 1996; Starfield 2011) adopts ethnographic research methods but consciously and reflexively considers the data gathered through broader social, political, and historical frames that have shaped the contexts in which the researcher is carrying out her observation.

Perspectives on Plagiarism

In the wake of Pennycook's (1996) seminal article on the construction of plagiarism in late twentieth-century Western academia which drew our attention to the intersection and interconnections of questions of the ownership of English, historically limited, peculiarly Western, essentially modernist constructs of authorship and originality, and the increased scrutiny of "apparent plagiarism," particularly of non-native speakers of English, a considerable amount of research has looked at plagiarism less as students' deliberate intention to deceive and more as a response to unfamiliar and frequently contradictory academic literacy practices, encompassing a set of strategies that students resort to out of a relative sense of powerlessness in the university. Whereas the pragmatic response to the increased "detection" of plagiarism might be to teach citation practices, paraphrasing and summarizing skills, studies working within critical frames have argued that the extensive textual borrowing of plagiarism is in fact a kind of "patchwriting," a developmental strategy adopted by new students as they attempt to acquire the privileged literacies of the academy while having little authority to do so (e.g. Abasi and Akbari 2008; Currie 1998; Howard 1999; Hull and Rose 1989; Pecorari 2008). Flowerdew and Li (2007) report on a "language re-use" writing strategy adopted by Chinese doctoral students in research science who are required to publish in Science Citation Index (SCI)-listed English language journals in order to graduate. To compensate for their limited English language resources, the students recycle formulaic language from already published articles and are adamant that this does not constitute plagiarism as the content is their own. The authors argue that the rhetorical and linguistic formulaicity of scientific discourse itself may in part encourage the students' language re-use. They also alert us to the tension that may lie in EAP teachers' recommendation of imitation as a learning strategy and use of genre pedagogy as a teaching tool as perhaps inadvertently fostering such textual borrowing (Flowerdew and Li 2007).

There is therefore a degree of agreement in the literature that plagiarism may not arise only out of a students' deliberate intention to deceive but may be being produced by the symbolic power of academic discourse itself as students with differing amounts of what counts as cultural capital enter the university and are unfamiliar with the dominant practices. The increased corporatization of the university referred to earlier and the concomitant increase in numbers of fee paying international students with fairly low levels of academic language proficiency combined with low levels of support for these students may have also increased the likelihood of student plagiarism as the stakes for them are particularly high (see e.g. Abasi and Akbari 2008).

While elsewhere in the academy the term "intertextuality" is positively connoted and regularly written about in academic analyses, it is viewed as "transgressive" or as plagiarism particularly in the texts of non-native speakers when they are seen to transgress institutional conventions (Chandrosoma et al. 2004). Studies have also pointed to native and non-native speaker student texts being assessed differently, with native speakers being "allowed" more transgressive intertextuality than non-native speakers, that is to say it is accepted by the marker that the ideas expressed could legitimately be the student's "own" ideas (Angélil-Carter 2000; Starfield 2002). The surveillance of the writing of non-native speaker students and academics appears to increase regularly, with more and more sophisticated technology being developed to "detect" plagiarism.

Ironically perhaps, while critical research findings consistently indicate the extent to which plagiarism, particularly of non-native speakers, is to a large extent inadvertent and the result of a lack of familiarity with dominant practices and the students' developing identity as an "author" (Gilmore et al. 2010; Ivanič 1998), universities regularly increase their surveillance and detection of plagiarism rather than the literacy scaffolding that could assist students (Abasi and Akbari 2008; Chandrasoma, Thompson, and Pennycook 2004). If we look critically then at the possibilities of our research effecting change at an institutional level we are obliged to admit that the scales are unevenly tipped.

Genre, Access, Power

The critical turn in EAP has led to an interrogation of the intentions and outcomes of explicit genre teaching, initially promoted as a pedagogy of access (see Benesch 2001; Cope and Kalantzis, 1993; Delpit 1988; Kubota and Lehner 2004). Both Benesch (2001) and Luke (1996), from slightly differing perspectives, claimed that by ignoring the ideological power of academic genres, EAP teachers might (unwittingly) be reproducing those same academic contexts that work to "limit the participation of non-native-speaking students in academic culture" (Benesch 1993: 713) leading to an unintentional transmission of these same genres of power (Luke 1996).

As Morgan and Ramanathan (2005: 155) argue a "politics of access" which sees as its main goal "the modeling of powerful genres and texts . . . may presume a degree of disciplinary stability and textual uniformity at variance with the co-constructed dynamics observed in discourse communities." They remind us that power is not solely located in texts but in how "text users" are located institutionally and socially.

One of the issues that explicit pedagogies have failed to deal with relates to the tacit nature of much genre knowledge and the extent to which it can be articulated and taught. In her attempt to identify the criteria research supervisors were using to describe the generic features of a successful research proposal (the gatekeeping genre students need to complete before being fully admitted to doctoral studies in Australia), Cadman (2002: 95) encountered the difficulties inherent in asking disciplinary insiders to articulate their generic criteria, with one of the supervisors stating "I like the student to surprise me by going beyond expectations." Cadman wonders how the multilingual students in her EAP program could meet this criterion or how she as a writing teacher would assist them. Similarly Starfield (2004b) found that a successful student's essay had met a number of unarticulated criteria that only emerged in her text-based interview with the marker. These included "the fact that he's done reading" and "what he shows is a real engagement with the theorist" which were not listed on the memorandum provided to the essay markers. Ben, the student, was only able to negotiate a successful identity for himself by drawing on textual resources he was familiar with from outside the academic context and extra-textual resources from other areas of his life.

Proponents of *rhetorical genre studies* (for example Artemeva 2008; Schryer 2011) have thus argued, from slightly different premises, that explicit genre teaching as suggested by ESP, fails to fully understand the implications of socially situated understandings of genre; that concepts such as discourse community are limited in their explanatory power (see also section on CEAP for more discussion) and have tended to favor a more immersion-based approach to genre pedagogy than an explicit teaching of text types and linguistic features (Bawarshi and Reiff 2010). However, the extent to which immersion type approaches or legitimate peripheral participation understandings of how learning occurs (Lave and Wenger 1991) either reproduce or alter existing relations of power remains a largely unaddressed question.

The pragmatist and the criticalist views on genre teaching were in all likelihood not as polarized as they may have initially appeared in the early debates. Certainly, the debate has been healthy in as much as it has led to a greater understanding of the various positions (Bawarshi and Reiff 2010). Paltridge (2001:121) sums this up when he explains how critical views "might explore the connections between discourse, language learning, language use, and the social and political contexts." Tardy (2009: 282) has recently acknowledged that her "biggest challenge" as a writing instructor is to "balance the need to help my students write in ways that are deemed appropriate and successful within various social groups with the need to help my students manipulate, break, and change genres and the power relationships embedded in them."

The Power and Politics of Publishing in English

The title of this section comes from the Introduction to the special issue of *TESOL Quarterly* on "Critical approaches to TESOL," edited by Alastair Pennycook in 1999 in which he directly identified academic publication as a political issue, posing a number of questions about who gets published in an international context. The questions raised earlier in this chapter over the debate around norms, whether English is a neutral medium for academic communication, and the impact of globalization, are all implicated when we consider the growing body of research in this area. The chapter by John Flowerdew (this volume) looks at writing for publication in greater detail; however, a chapter on critical perspectives in ESP would be incomplete if it failed to point to the fairly substantial and growing body of research in ESP/EAP in the decade since Swales (1997) asked whether English had become the *Tyrannosaurus rex* of the academic world – destroying other languages in its path – supporting claims such as Ferguson's (2007: 20) that "undeserved and substantial advantages accru[e] to native speakers from the global dominance of English, not least in the field of academic publication" (see e.g. Flowerdew 2007 and Uzuner 2008). Having said this, non-native scholars should not be construed as constituting a homogenous grouping, their access to resources both discursive and non-discursive (Canagarajah 1996) will be shaped by where they studied, where they are currently located, their access to support networks and so on (Salager-Meyer 2008).

Moving beyond the immediate context of individual researchers seeking to publish in prestigious journals, current research situates the production and reception of texts for publication within wider broader geopolitical and geolinguistic frames that highlight forces that sustain the dominance of English and its consequences (see e.g. Canagarajah 2002a). According to Lillis and Curry (2010: 9), 67 percent of the 66,166 academic periodicals listed in *Ulrich's Periodicals Directory* are published "using some or all English," with a similar situation prevailing in more than 95 percent of natural science journals indexed by the *Institute for Scientific Information* (ISI). Flowerdew (2007: 14) identifies the worldwide pressures on non-native scholars to publish in English as being "symptoms of globalization and the marketization of the academy," pointing out that these scholars will, in all likelihood, also need to develop the skills to publish in their native language as well. Market forces operating to restructure higher education have contributed to the rise of bibliometrics such as the use of impact factors, with individual academic departments, and academics themselves, rated and ranked on performance in these indexes (see Lillis and Curry 2010 for a more detailed analysis). Lillis and Curry's (2010) eight-year long ethnographic study of a number of European scholars writing for publication reveals a systematic disadvantaging of languages other than English in the global publication process and of those academics who are non-native speakers of English but who experience the daily pressure to publish in English for institutional recognition and reward. They also alert us to the possibility that an "over-emphasis on celebrating English as . . . [an] academic lingua franca," as providing opportunities for multilingual scholars, and its "implied neutral or positive perspective" ignores the very real differences that pertain to the evaluation of non-native speaker writing, particularly in international journals where English and international are typically synonymous (Lillis and Curry 2010: 22).

Canagarajah (1996) directly addressed the geopolitics of knowledge production via the issue of unequal access to the material or what he termed "non-discursive requirements" of access to publication by periphery scholars. These range from things such as paper for printing drafts on, access to recent journal articles (the cost of subscriptions) to funding to attend conferences, to paying editors and translators, to writing and researching in politically unstable or oppressive nations (see also Englander 2009; Lillis and Curry 2010; Salager-Meyer 2008). Canagarajah (2002b) also argues that dominant Western discursive norms such as those presented in the well-known CARS framework (Swales 1990) which focus on the "newness" of the research and the need to "market" ideas as "original" may not suit the needs of scholars in less competitive communities. Studies comparing the structure of research article introductions in similar disciplines across different languages that note the absence of a rhetorical move (Move 2) indicating a gap in previous research provide support for this view (see for example Hirano 2009). Again we are faced with some of the issues raised earlier in this chapter: to what extent should multilingual scholars be "enculturated" or inducted into the dominant genres and rhetorical forms: will Anglo-American rhetorical norms be reinforced (Salager-Meyer 2008); what is lost when this happens, what options do these writers have? Of course though, as Salager-Meyer (2008) points out, while language and discourse-related issues are factors in periphery researchers struggling to publish their work in "international" journals, it is the fundamental lack of resources to fund scientific research that limit researchers' ability to publish in many instances.

In her case study of a Chinese PhD student's attempts to publish in an "international" (English language) journal to meet a graduation requirement, Li (2006: 473) terms the final version of the published article a "sociopolitical artifact" in as much as it was shaped by accommodation, conflict, resistance, and the ambient unequal power relations between the student and more powerful others. These tensions encourage Li to critically reflect on whether a pragmatically-oriented or more sociopolitical approach might have best helped the student writer in her study and lead her to conclude that a critical pragmatism that incorporates knowledge of the "various power relations they are positioned in" through the publication process may be helpful to novice scholars in standard English for research purposes courses and facilitate their legitimate peripheral participation (2006: 476).

Ferguson (2007: 34) suggests working to cultivate a "greater sense of responsibility on the part of relatively privileged Anglophone researchers for assisting their non-Anglophone disciplinary peers with their English," although as he readily acknowledges this is unlikely to "have much impact on the larger problem of non-language based inequalities in academic publication which, because they are related to wider disorders of development and wealth distribution, are even more intractable." Nevertheless, as Uzuner (2008: 251) points out, academic communities have cause to be concerned about multilingual scholars' perceptions of prejudice as their limited participation "will impoverish knowledge production."

The good news is that there nevertheless is a growth in the acceptance rates of manuscripts by non-native speakers as documented by Ferguson (2007) and Benfield and Feak (2006). Lillis and Curry's (2010) work suggest that this is not necessarily at the expense of publication in local journals, both in English and in the local languages. A number of case studies of non-native scholars underline their persistence and development of strategies that facilitate eventual publications (e.g. Englander 2009; Li 2006). EAP researchers can thus, through such studies, contribute to promoting the "joy and pleasure involved in academic endeavours" (Lillis and Curry 2010: 176) and not only the pain and potential stigmatization (Flowerdew 2008).

Future Directions

The rapidly changing landscape of global higher education, the increase in what is being called English medium instruction across a range of countries, the consolidation of English as the dominant language of international publication, the emergence of lingua franca English in workplaces across the globe, the extent to which these developments contribute to greater access to rights, opportunities, and choices for the citizens of what remains, despite the claims for the benefits of globalization, a highly unequal world, are all topics that require more research by ESP practitioners and researchers working within critical frames. It is important for ESP practitioners to be mindful that their work, while contributing to improving equitable access to the "goods" that English affords, may also be contributing (unintentionally) to diminishing the status and power of other languages.

Studies such as Gao's "micropolitical" ethnographic case studies of the language learning strategies of students from mainland China studying at an "English medium" university in Hong Kong and Li's sociopolitical case study of a Chinese graduate student struggling to publish his research that investigate the lived realities and strategic choices individuals make about their learning within specific sociopolitical settings can only enrich our understandings of the complex worlds that our students, wherever they may be located, negotiate daily. Longitudinal studies such as Lillis and Curry's (2010) ethnographic case studies are urgently needed across a number of the areas mentioned in this chapter as we need to understand better how enculturation, to the extent that it occurs, changes and develops over time and in different contexts.

Speaking to the scientific community more broadly on the issue of what he calls "linguistic inequality" and the dominance of English in scientific publication, Tonkin (2011: 112) makes the interesting suggestion that it "change the rhetoric, by making it persistently clear to native English-speakers that they do indeed possess an advantage over speakers of other languages that they should set about voluntarily equalizing." This suggests potential shifts in research focus such as suggested by Uzuner (2008) to look at the extent to which monolingual English speaking novice scholars and multilingual novice scholars face similar challenges in getting published in dominant center journals.

Yongyan Li (2007: 74) pertinently asks how teachers of EAP can facilitate non-native English speaking apprentice scholars' successful writing for publication while helping them to develop their agency to challenge dominant norms "sanctioned in the Anglo-American publication world." She tells us that there is a lack of qualified EAP professionals to assist young scholars such as those who have participated in her case studies, to meet the onerous requirements for publication, and urges TESOL programs to develop such training as part of their programs. Once again we see, as Benesch (2009) has reminded us, that in critically oriented work, research and praxis (praxis being the reciprocal relationship between theory and practice) are always linked, as is the desire to respond to a perceived injustice.

REFERENCES

Abasi, A. R. and Akbari, N. (2008) Are we encouraging patchwriting? Reconsidering the role of the pedagogical context in ESL student writers' transgressive intertextuality. *English for Specific Purposes* 27: 267–84.

Allison, D. (1994) Comments on Sarah Benesch's "ESL, Ideology, and the Politics of Pragmatism": A Reader Reacts . . . . *TESOL Quarterly* 28: 618–23.

Anderson, G. L. (1989) Critical ethnography in education: Origins, current status, and new directions. *Review of Educational Research* 59: 249–70.

Angélil-Carter, S. (1997) Second language acquisition of spoken and written English: Acquiring the Skeptron. *TESOL Quarterly* 31: 263–87.

Angélil-Carter, S. (2000) *Stolen Language*. London: Longman.

Artemeva, N. (2008) Toward a unified theory of genre learning. *Journal of Business and Technical Communication* 22: 160–85.

Appleby, R. (2009) The spatial politics of gender in EAP classroom practice. *Journal of English for Academic Purposes* 8: 100–10.

Archer, A. (2008) "The place is suffering": Enabling dialogue between students' discourses and academic literacy conventions in engineering. *English for Specific Purposes* 27: 255–66.

Baik, C. (2010) Assessing linguistically diverse students in higher education: A study of academics' beliefs and practices.

Unpublished Doctor of Education thesis. The University of Melbourne, Australia.

Banerjee, J. and Wall, D. (2006) Assessing and reporting performances on pre-sessional EAP courses: Developing a final assessment checklist and investigating its validity. *Journal of English for Academic Purposes* 5: 50–69.

Bawarshi, A. S. and Reiff, M. J. (2010) *Genre: An Introduction to History, Theory, Research, and Pedagogy.* West Lafayette, IN: Parlor Press.

Belcher, D. (2006) English for specific purposes: Teaching to perceived needs and imagined futures in worlds of work, study and everyday life. *TESOL Quarterly* 40: 133–56.

Belcher, D. and Lukkarila, L. (2011) Identity in the ESP context: Putting the learner front and center in needs analysis. In D. Belcher, A. M. Johns, and B. Paltridge (eds.), *New Directions in English for Specific Purposes Research.* 73–93. Ann Arbor, MI: Michigan University Press.

Benesch, S. (1993) ESL, ideology, and the politics of pragmatism. *TESOL Quarterly* 27: 705–17.

Benesch, S. (2001) *Critical English for Academic Purposes.* Mahwah, NJ: Lawrence Erlbaum.

Benesch, S. (2009) Theorizing and practicing critical English for academic purposes. *Journal of English for Academic Purposes* 8: 81–5.

Benfield, J. R. and Feak C. B. (2006) How Authors Can Cope With the Burden of English as an International Language. *Chest* 129: 1728–730.

Bourdieu, P. (1991) *Language and Symbolic Power.* Cambridge, UK: Polity Press.

Cadman, K. (2002) English for academic possibilities: The research proposal as a contested site in postgraduate genre pedagogy. *Journal of English for Academic Purposes* 1: 85–104.

Canagarajah, A. S. (1996) "Non-discursive" requirements in academic publishing, material resources of periphery scholars, and the politics of knowledge production. *Written Communication* 13: 435–72.

Canagarajah, A. S. (2002a) *A Geopolitics of Academic Writing.* Pittsburgh, PA: University of Pittsburgh Press.

Canagarajah, A. S. (2002b) *Critical Academic Writing and Multilingual Students.* Ann Arbor, MI: Michigan University Press.

Carspecken, P. F. (1996) *Critical Ethnography in Educational Research.* New York: Routledge.

Chandrasoma, R., Thompson, C., and Pennycook, A. (2004) Beyond plagiarism: Transgressive and nontransgressive intertextuality. *Journal of Language, Identity & Education* 3: 171–93.

Chun, C. W. (2009) Contesting neoliberal discourses in EAP: Critical praxis in an IEP classroom. *Journal of English for Academic Purposes* 8: 111–20.

Cope, B. and Kalantzis, M. (eds.) (1993) *The Powers of Literacy: A Genre Approach to Teaching Writing.* London: Falmer Press.

Currie, P. (1998) Staying out of trouble: Apparent plagiarism and academic survival. *Journal of Second Language Writing* 7: 1–18.

Delpit L. (1988) The silenced dialogue: Power and pedagogy in educating other people's children. *Harvard Educational Review* 58: 280–98.

Dudley-Evans, T. (2001) Team-teaching in EAP: Changes and adaptations in the Birmingham approach. In J. Flowerdew and M. Peacock (eds.), *Research Perspectives on English for Academic Purposes.* 225–38. Cambridge: Cambridge University Press.

Ellwood, C. and Nakane, I. (2009) Privileging of speech in EAP and mainstream university classrooms: A critical evaluation of participation. *TESOL Quarterly* 43: 203–30.

Englander, K. (2009) Transformation of the identities of nonnative English-speaking scientists as a consequence of the social construction of revision. *Journal of Language, Identity and Education* 8: 35–53.

Fairclough, N. (1995) *Critical Discourse Analysis*. London: Longman.

Ferguson, G. (2007) The global spread of English, scientific communication and ESP: Questions of equity, access and domain loss. *Ibérica* 13: 7–38.

Flowerdew, J. (2007) The non-Anglophone scholar on the periphery of scientific communication. *AILA Review* 20: 14–27.

Flowerdew, J. (2008) Scholarly writers who use English as an additional language: What can Goffman's "Stigma" tell us? *Journal of English for Academic Purposes* 7: 7–86.

Flowerdew, J. and Li, Y. (2007) Language re-use among Chinese apprentice scientists writing for publication. *Applied Linguistics* 28: 440–65.

Foucault, M. (1980) *Power/Knowledge: Selected Interviews and Other Writings, 1972–1977*. New York: Pantheon.

Freire, P. (1970) *Pedagogy of the Oppressed*. New York: Continuum.

Freire, P. (1994) *Pedagogy of Hope: Reliving Pedagogy of the Oppressed*. New York: Continuum.

Gao, X. (2010) To be or not to be "part of them": Microplitical challenges in mainland Chinese students' learning of English in a multilingual university. *TESOL Quarterly* 44: 274–94.

Gilmore, J., Strickland, D., Timmerman, B., Maher, M., and Feldon, D. (2010) Weeds in the flower garden: An exploration of plagiarism in graduate students' research proposals and its connection to enculturation, ESL, and contextual factors. *International Journal for Educational Integrity* 6: 13–28.

Goldstein, T. (1997) *Two Languages at Work: Bilingual Life On The Production Floor*. Berlin: Mouton de Gruyter.

Harwood, N. and Hadley, G. (2004) Demystifying institutional practices: Critical pragmatism and the teaching of academic writing. *English for Specific Purposes* 23: 355–77.

Hirano, E. (2009) Research article introductions in English for specific purposes: A comparison between Brazilian Portuguese and English. *English for Specific Purposes* 28: 240–50.

Howard, R. M. (1999) *Standing in the Shadow of Giants: Plagiarists, Authors, Collaborators*. Westport, CT: Ablex.

Hull, G. and Rose, M. (1989) Rethinking remediation: Toward a social-cognitive understanding of problematic reading and writing. *Written Communication* 6: 139–54.

Hyland, K. (2011) Disciplinary specificity: Discourse, context and ESP. In D. Belcher A. M. Johns, and B. Paltridge (eds.), *New Directions in English for Specific Purposes Research*. 6–24. Ann Arbor, MI: Michigan University Press.

Ivanič, R. (1998) *Writing and Identity: The Discoursal Construction of Identity in Academic Writing*. Amsterdam: John Benjamins.

Jasso-Aguilar, R. (2005) Sources, methods, and triangulation in needs analysis: A critical perspective in a case study of Waikiki hotel maids. In M. H. Long (ed.), *Second Language Needs Analysis*. 127–68. Cambridge: Cambridge University Press.

Kubota, R. (2004) Critical multiculturalism and second language education. In B. Norton and K. Toohey (eds.), *Critical Pedagogies and Language Learning*. 30–52. Cambridge: Cambridge University Press.

Kubota, R. and Lehner, A. (2004) Toward critical constructive rhetoric. *Journal of Second Language Writing* 13: 7–27.

Lave, J. and E. Wenger (1991) *Situated Learning: Legitimate Peripheral Participation*. Cambridge: Cambridge University Press.

Lea, M. and Street, B. (1998) Student writing in Higher Education: An academic literacies approach. *Studies in Higher Education* 23: 157–72.

Li, Y. (2006) A doctoral student of physics writing for publication: A sociopolitically oriented case study. *English for Specific Purposes* 25: 456–78.

Li, Y. (2007) Apprentice scholarly writing in a community of practice: An intraview of an NNES graduate student writing a research article. *TESOL Quarterly* 41: 55–79.

Lillis, T. (2001) *Student Writing: Access, Regulation, Desire*. London: Routledge.

Lillis, T. and Curry, M. J. (2010) *Academic Writing in a Global Context: The Politics and Practice of Publishing in English*. Oxford: Routledge.

Luke, A. (1996) Genres of power? Literacy education and the production of capital. In R. Hasan and G. Williams (eds.), *Literacy in Society*. 308–38. London: Longman.

Luke, A. (2004) Two takes on the critical. In B. Norton and K. Toohey (eds.), *Critical Pedagogies and Language Learning*. 21–29. Cambridge: Cambridge University Press.

Luke, A. and Dooley, K. (2011) Critical literacy and second language learning. In E. Hinkel (ed.), *Handbook of Research in Second Language Teaching and Learning*. 856–67. New York: Routledge.

Master, P. (1998) Positive and negative aspects of the dominance of English. *TESOL Quarterly* 32: 716–27.

Morgan, B. (2007) Poststructuralism and applied linguistics. In J. Cummins and C. Davison (eds.), *International Handbook of English Language Teaching*. Part II. 1033–52. New York: Springer.

Morgan, B. (2009) Fostering transformative practitioners for critical EAP: Possibilities and challenges. *Journal of English for Academic Purposes* 8: 86–99.

Morgan, B. and Ramanathan, V. (2005) Critical literacies and language education: Global and local perspectives. *Annual Review of Applied Linguistics* 25: 151–69.

Northedge, A. (2003) Enabling participation in academic discourse. *Teaching in Higher Education* 8: 169–80.

Norton, B. (2000) *Identity and Language Learning. Gender, Ethnicity, and Educational Change*. Harlow, England: Pearson Education.

Paltridge, B. (2001) *Genre and the Language Learning Classroom*. Ann Arbor, MI: University of Michigan Press.

Paltridge, B. and Starfield, S. (2007) *Thesis and Dissertation Writing in a Second Language: A Handbook for Supervisors*. London: Routledge.

Pecorari, D. (2008) *Academic Writing and Plagiarism: A Linguistic Analysis*. London: Continuum.

Pennycook, A. (1994) *The Cultural Politics of English as an International Language*: New York: Longman.

Pennycook, A. (1996) Borrowing others' words: Text, ownership, memory and plagiarism. *TESOL Quarterly* 30: 201–30.

Pennycook, A. (1997) Vulgar pragmatism, critical pragmatism, and EAP. *English for Specific Purposes* 16: 253–69.

Pennycook, A. (1999) Introduction: Critical approaches to TESOL. *TESOL Quarterly*, 33: 329–48.

Pennycook, A. (2001) *Critical Applied Linguistics*. Mahwah, NJ: Lawrence Erlbaum.

Pennycook, A. (2011) Critical and alternative directions in applied linguistics. *Australian Review of Applied Linguistics* 33(16): 1–16. Accessed Feb. 3, 2012, http://www.nla.gov.au/openpublish/index.php/aral/article/view/2049/2463.

Phillipson, R. (1992) *Linguistic Imperialism*. Oxford: Oxford University Press.

Pratt, M. L. (1991) Arts of the contact zone. *Profession* 9: 33–40.

Prior, P. (1998) *Writing/Disciplinarity: A Sociohistoric Account of Literate Activity in the Academy*. Mahwah, NJ: Lawrence Erlbaum.

Said, E. (1978) *Orientalism*. London: Routledge and Kegan Paul.

Salager-Meyer, F. (2008) Scientific publishing in developing countries:

Challenges for the future. *Journal of English for Academic Purposes* 7: 121–32.

Schryer, C. (2011) Investigating texts in their social contexts: The promise and peril of rhetorical genre studies. In D. Starke-Meyerring, A. Paré, N. Artemeva, M. Horne, and L. Yousoubova (eds.), *Writing in Knowledge Societies. Perspectives on Writing*. Fort Collins, CO: The WAC Clearinghouse and Parlor Press. 31–52. Accessed May 29, 2012 at http://wac.colostate.edu/books/winks/.

Singh, P. and Doherty, C. (2004) Global cultural flows and pedagogic dilemmas: Teaching in the global university contact zone. *TESOL Quarterly* 38: 9–42.

Starfield, S. (2001) "I'll go with the group": Rethinking discourse community in EAP. In J. Flowerdew and M. Peacock (eds.), *Research Perspectives on English for Academic Purposes*. 132–47. Cambridge: Cambridge University Press.

Starfield, S. (2002) "I'm a second-language English speaker": Negotiating writer identity and authority in Sociology One. *Journal of Language, Identity, and Education* 1: 121–40.

Starfield, S. (2004a) "Why does this feel empowering"? Thesis writing, concordancing, and the "corporatising" university. In B. Norton and K. Toohey (eds.), *Critical Pedagogies and Language Learning*. 138–157. Cambridge: Cambridge University Press.

Starfield, S. (2004b) Wordpower: Negotiating success in a first-year sociology essay. In L. J. Ravelli and R. A. Ellis (eds.), *Analysing Academic Writing*. 66–83. London: Continuum.

Starfield, S. (2011) Doing critical ethnographic research into academic writing: The theory of the methodology. In D. Belcher, A. M. Johns, and B. Paltridge (eds.) *New Directions in English for Specific Purposes Research*. 174–96. Ann Arbor, MI: Michigan University Press.

Starfield, S. (2012) The historical development of languages for specific purposes. In C. A. Chapelle (ed.), *The Encyclopedia of Applied Linguistics*. Oxford: Wiley-Blackwell.

Swales, J. M. (1990) *Genre Analysis: English in Academic and Research Settings*. Cambridge: Cambridge University Press.

Swales, J. M. (1997) English as *Tyrannosaurus rex*. World Englishes 16: 373–82.

Tardy, C. M. (2009) *Building Genre Knowledge*. West Lafayette, IN: Parlor Press.

Thesen, L. (1997) Voices, discourses and transition: In search of new categories in EAP. *TESOL Quarterly* 31: 487–511.

Tonkin, H. (2011) Language and the ingenuity gap in science. *Critical Inquiry in Language Studies* 8: 105–11.

Uzuner, S. (2008) Multilingual scholars' participation in core/global academic communities: A literature review. *Journal of English for Academic Purposes* 7: 250–63.

25 Gender and Race in ESP Research

RYUKO KUBOTA AND LIZ T. CHIANG

Introduction

Issues of gender, race, and other social categories are underexplored in English for specific purposes (ESP) research. Even in the broader field of second language education, only recently did these topics, especially race, begin to attract explicit attention. The increased focus on these issues reflects the critical turn observed since the 1990s in teaching English to speakers of other languages – the field that encompasses ESP (Kumaravadivelu 2006). The critical turn is characterized by growing skepticism about modernist assumptions in which learners, teachers, language, and culture are conceptualized in a neutral, objective, and universal way regardless of differences.

The term "critical" in the "critical turn" has multiple meanings (Luke 2004; Pennycook 2004), although the recent trend can be characterized by a postmodern poststructuralist approach. This approach no longer views social product and practice, including language, language use, and language learning, as governed by a universal rule or representing a fixed unified truth but rather as socially and discursively constructed. This view rejects the understanding of learners as autonomous or homogeneous; instead, it takes into account heterogeneous backgrounds of individuals in terms of gender, race, ethnicity, age, sexual identity, and other social categories. These categories intersect with one another to form complex social relations as well as multiple and fluid identities. These identities are further viewed as *performed* or *doing* rather than the permanent *being*, allowing a possibility for resisting and appropriating power through engaging in linguistic practice. This approach problematizes normative linguistic and cultural practices and fixed characteristics attached to social categories. At the same time, such practice of

The Handbook of English for Specific Purposes, First Edition.
Edited by Brian Paltridge and Sue Starfield.
© 2013 John Wiley & Sons, Inc. Published 2013 by John Wiley & Sons, Inc.

problematizing assumptions constantly requires critical reflections. As such, meanings and understandings of language, gender, race, teaching, learning, and so on are never fixed and there is no truth outside discourses.

Pennycook (2004) calls this approach *problematizing practice* in discussing different critical approaches in recent second language research. He contrasts it with another critical approach represented by linguistic imperialism, language policy and planning, and critical discourse analysis, which critiques politics and ideologies embedded in the power struggle of domination/subordination. Pennycook names this approach *emancipatory modernism* and argues that this neo-Marxist approach is distinguished from the *problematizing practice* approach because its critique of ideology as false consciousness assumes the existence of an alternative truth (which *problematizing practice* rejects) and that the power is conceptualized as a one-way imposition rather than omnipresent and circulating.

These different approaches raise the following questions for ESP: In what ways can the role of gender, race, and other social categories be conceptualized in teaching and learning ESP? Which approach(es) to critical inquiry does research on these social categories support? Should *emancipatory modernism* or the *problematizing practice* approach be the main focus? What is the tension between these approaches? And how does ESP's tendency to pragmatism influence inquiries into gender, race, and other categories?

This chapter focuses on gender, race, and other social categories discussed in the field of second language education and sociolinguistics and provides conceptual foundations. This discussion is followed by an overview of how these issues are discussed in two areas within ESP: teaching language to adult immigrants for resettlement and work purposes and teaching English for academic purposes (EAP). Finally, some future directions are offered. The limited attention to gender, race, and other categories in ESP is linked to its emphasis on pragmatism. Thus, we first examine the relationship between pragmatism and social categories by reviewing the criticisms of pragmatism and needs analysis in ESP.

Pragmatism Contested: Critical Approaches and their Relevance to Gender and Race

ESP addresses pragmatic concerns in academic settings in secondary or higher education and various occupational contexts including teaching English to immigrants and refugees for facilitating resettlement purposes (Belcher 2009). It is distinguished from teaching general purpose English in that it aims to fulfil specific goals and needs in a certain profession or discipline (Dudley-Evans and St John 1998). As such, pragmatism arising from academic or professional needs often characterizes ESP.

However, pragmatism in ESP has been problematized. Critics such as Pennycook (1997) and Benesch (2001) argue that ESP's instrumental focus overlooks the political nature of content knowledge, language, and culture, while legitimating the taken-for-granted forms and understandings of these categories. Citing Cherryholmes (1988), Pennycook (1997) argues that vulgar pragmatism, which ESP often promotes, is concerned with functional efficiency built upon the existing standards and conventions reproducing the social and institutional order. The dominant discourses and social practices are unquestioned, while normative assumptions are supported by universalism and neutrality. Such principles underlying ESP's vulgar pragmatism overlook the role of gender, race, or other differences in teaching and learning. In contrast, critical pragmatism promotes critical reflection and action not based on universal standards but in accordance with situational ethics and moral choices.

Another contentious topic is needs analysis, a central component of ESP. Although any teaching is and should be built upon certain needs, teaching ESP foregrounds the awareness of the specific needs that exist in a particular institution, profession, or individual. Hutchinson and Waters (1987: 54) identify two kinds of needs: "*target needs* (i.e. what the learner needs to do in the target situation) and *learner needs* (i.e. what the learner needs to do in order to learn)." Benesch (2001) argues that, despite its good intention to conceptualize needs as multidimensional, this dual meaning of needs still takes the target needs for granted as neutral and pre-existing, thereby relegating instruction and learning merely to the fulfilment of external demands. Alternatively, Benesch proposes *rights analysis,* which enables learners to know the rights that they are entitled to in their context. Critical understandings of needs further problematize the linguistic and content standards that these needs are identified against. Pennycook (1997) questions the neutrality of language – ranging from the norms of English for specific purposes (academic, business, etc.) to the notion of English as an international language – as well as the content knowledge of the discipline or profession (i.e. academic canon, the mainstream way of knowing).

What should be added to this critique of needs analysis is the neutral view of the learner, which is closely linked to learners' backgrounds. In the discourse of needs analysis, learners are viewed as individuals with varied levels of discrepancy between their linguistic or professional knowledge/skill and the target needs. However, in performing certain skills, what learners actually experience in a specific discipline or profession might differ depending on their individual attributes such as gender, race, class, nationality, accent, age, religion, and sexual identity. These attributes, along with the contexts where social relations are established, shape the learner identities which are multiple, fluid, and contested (Norton 2000, 2010). Furthermore, these social categories in the larger society are constitutive of hierarchies of power, positioning individuals in unequal statuses.

This indicates that using, teaching, and learning language in a specific academic or professional context is not about fitting predetermined target goals into a one-sized learner characteristic; rather it is about navigating the complex relations of power structured through interactions among people from diverse gender, racial, linguistic, socioeconomic, and other backgrounds. Consistent with the critical turn mentioned earlier, integrating these issues in ESP research would shed light on how social categories and their intersectionality influence the actual experiences of learners in a particular academic/professional context and how such experiences challenge the existing assumptions and practices in the context.

To give an example, learning to become effective physicians and nurses in English as a second language would involve not only acquiring specialized vocabulary and literacy skills to process technical reports but also critical awareness of how social categories might influence *communication*, a crucial component of medical practice. In North American medical contexts, physicians are predominantly males whereas nurses are females. There are generally more White physicians and nurses than those of color. The ways male and female physicians communicate with patients are likely to differ – female physicians tend to use mitigated devices in conveying directives and they are less likely to interrupt patients (West 1984, 1990). Common images of physicians and nurses also differ – while physicians are typically represented as technically knowledgeable and competent, nurses are seen as caring, warm, patient, and sympathetic, even though their training overlaps in many respects (see Lupton 1995). Such differences are certainly compounded by the interlocutors' gender, race, culture, accent, age, and so on in a particular interactional context. How do such gender and race dynamics impact communication among participants and ultimately the treatment of the patient? What racial and gender stereotypes are constructed about service providers/recipients and how do they affect communication? What identities do ESP learners have and how do these identities influence their learning and professional experiences? How should ESP learners and instructors be prepared for such sociolinguistic and institutional complexity?

Discussing these questions would be facilitated by understanding how gender, race, and other social categories are conceptualized and how they are investigated in scholarly fields. In what follows, we provide conceptual overviews on gender, race, and other categories.

Shifting Conceptualizations of Gender and Inquiry into Identity

In the past two decades, gender has attracted greater attention in sociolinguistics and applied linguistics research. Consistent with feminist studies, the contemporary approach to research on language use and gender is characterized by postmodern, poststructuralist, and constructivist approaches to gender difference (Cameron 2005; Higgins 2010; Kubota 2003; Pavlenko 2001; Sunderland 2000). In short, the current understanding of gender reflects a shift from earlier approaches that focussed either on male dominance or gender difference to a diversity/constructivist approach.

As represented in works by Lakoff (1975) and Tannen (1990), the earlier approach assumed a male/female binary as given and explored how men and women used language differently. The seminal work of Lakoff (1975) described women's language use as powerless, dependent, and inferior to men's and thus representative of the gender domination/subordination relationship. While this perspective fore-grounded female inferiority vis-à-vis male dominance, Tannen (1990) explained gender difference as arising from different patterns of socialization, thereby viewing gender difference as analogous to cultural difference. Regardless of these conceptual differences, these approaches view gender difference in language use as a fixed gender-specific universal phenomenon, reflecting a modernist binary model that juxtaposes men and women. The understanding of gender difference as fixed underestimates possibilities for women's resistance and complies with the existing patriarchal structures, implying that women ought to change their language use if they want to be successful in the male-dominated world. It is also important to point out that this approach to gender does not take other social categories (e.g. race, class, sexual identities) into consideration (Mills 2008). In feminism, this monolithic lens of womanhood from a White middle-class woman's perspective has been problematized in postcolonial or black feminism, which illuminates the positionalities and experiences of women of color constructed in racial, gender, and socioeconomic relations of power (Collins 1998; Minh-ha 1989; Mohanty 2003).

In contrast, the diversity/constructivist stance conceptualizes gender as fluid, agentive, and yet socially and historically constructed. It is informed by postmodern skepticism of essentialism, universalism, and objectivism as well as the poststructuralist notion of discursive construction of knowledge. It also parallels the *problematizing practice* approach to critical applied linguistics mentioned earlier. In a poststructuralist view, gendered meanings are constructed by discourses or "systems of power/knowledge (Foucault 1980) that regulate and assign value to all forms of semiotic activity" (Morgan 2007: 1036). More specifically, through our everyday experiences of reading, viewing, hearing, and talking about what women, men, girls, and boys do, say, and think, our specific understanding of gender and gender differences are shaped, circulated, and confirmed. This view does not assume any pre-existing gender difference; rather, gender difference is considered to be a product of discursive construction. One related notion is per-formativity (Butler 1999), which views gender as a set of repeated performed acts rather than a predetermined category. Although such performed acts are discursively constrained by social expectations, they do not preclude subversive acts or appropriation and creation of alternative expectations. In these perspectives, gender is conceptualized as *becoming* and *doing,* rather than *being.*

This leads to a question of how to conceptualize identity. In the field of applied linguistics, identity is currently understood as social, historical, and discursive construction rather than fixed personal traits in psychological terms (Block 2007, 2009; Miller and Kubota forthcoming; Norton 2000, 2010). Identity is formed through complex social interactions in immediate contexts where an individual plays multiple roles as a family member, worker, student, or research participant as well as in broader imagined communities in which discourses define groups of people in specific ways (Angélil-Carter 1997). Identity also involves not only gender but also other social categories including race, ethnicity, class, sexuality, religion, language, and so on, As such, identity is plural, fluid, and often contra-dictory, indexing both individual and collective processes of negotiation (Thesen 1997).

Although the diversity/constructivist understanding of gender has provided renewed perspectives, it poses an important question: How can systematic gender inequality in social institutions like workplaces, schools, and courts be challenged and transformed? This question points to the importance of theorizing gender not merely from an individual point of view but also as a collective experience within the system of inequalities (McElhinny 2003). Applied to ESP, this leads to a ques-tion of how researchers and practitioners can address gender inequalities in the real world where learners of ESP are likely to encounter them. The diversity/constructivist stance is certainly useful for understanding the plural and fluid nature of gender identities and the discursive construction of people's beliefs about gender difference. However, it may not provide concrete tools for achieving gender equality in academic and vocational settings. In this sense, the *emancipatory modernism* approach mentioned earlier might be useful. As seen in the following section, one conceptual approach to race foregrounds racism as a central concern, which is contrasted with the postmodern poststructuralist approach to gender in which sexism does not constitute the main issue.

Conceptualization of Race and Critical Race Theory

Race has received greater attention in recent applied linguistics scholarship but it has not been discussed as widely as issues of gender. Race is a socially constructed notion. Scientists agree that there is no scientific evidence that race exists biologi-cally as almost all human genes are shared. Nonetheless, ideas of race are real – they produce a discourse that shapes people's sense of which racialized group Self and Other belong to (Kubota and Lin 2009). As a system of sorting people based on phenotypes (i.e. observable physical features), race exists as a social and discursive category. A concept related to race is ethnicity. While race has a phenotypical undertone, ethnicity has to do with cultural traits such as language, religion, customs, and so on. In contemporary discourse, race and ethnicity are often used interchangeably perhaps because the current liberal discourse tends to obfuscate the distinction between race and culture.

In fact, the contemporary discourse often conflates the idea of race with *culture*, a more benign term than race (Bonilla-Silva 2003; May 2009). Thus, cultural dif-ference discussed casually, academically, or professionally often overlaps the idea of racial difference. Paralleling the approach to gender that views gender differ-ence as cultural difference (Tannen 1990), racial difference perceived in cultural terms often functions to fix and essentialize the difference as an intrinsic attribute of certain groups of people. This resonates with liberal multiculturalism which celebrates and romanticizes cultural difference, while contradictorily emphasizing colorblind equality of people as belonging to one human race (Kubota 2004). While this belief in human sameness is consistent with the scientific evidence of race, it overlooks the socially constructed racial difference which legitimates racial inequalities in social structures and people's lived experiences, which critical race theory (CRT) (Crenshaw et al. 1995) confronts as discussed below.

Some conceptual understandings of race parallel discussions of gender. Similar to the diversity/constructivist approach to gender, the current conceptualization of race views race as socially, discursively, and historically constructed. Specific meanings about racialized groups of people are produced through this process. As such, the meanings attached to race are unstable, shifting, and diverse rather than fixed, unchanging, and universal. This means that physical appearance does not necessarily correspond to how people define who they or others are racially. Just like some popular films, in which racial crossing occurs in casting (e.g. *My Geisha, Memoirs of a Geisha*, etc.), people in real life may take on a racial identity that is outside of what is perceived by Self or Others, though this is not always perceived uncontroversially. Moreover, identities of individuals from mixed race backgrounds illuminate a hybrid, conflicted, and evolving nature, producing varied positionalities across time and space (Kamada 2009).

While the constructivist and anti-essentialist conceptualization of race overlaps that of gender, CRT focusses explicitly on problems of racism and the superiority of whiteness with an aim to establish racial equality in social spheres. CRT was developed in the field of legal studies in the United States in the 1980s to critically examine how the supposedly fair and objective legal system actually disadvantages racially and socioeconomically marginalized populations, perpetuating racial inequalities (Crenshaw et al. 1995). CRT has been introduced to the field of education (Ladson-Billings and Tate 1995) and recently to second language education (Curtis and Romney 2006; Kubota and Lin 2009). Central to CRT is the recognition that racism is deeply ingrained in our society and thus colorblind attitudes and policies would not solve existing problems. Sharing with the diversity/constructivist approach to gender, CRT conceptualizes race as a social and historical invention and recognizes the multiplicity of experiences and subjectivities of people of color that are shaped by complex interplay between race and other social categories. However, the primary goal of CRT is to eliminate racial injustice by drawing attention to the collective and consistent experience of oppression with a larger goal of ending all forms of oppression.

This goal is to be accomplished through counter-storytelling of people of color. In exposing their silenced voices about their everyday race-based experiences of pain and injuries, counter-storytelling challenges the majoritarian stories that are told by and continue to benefit the racially privileged (Solórzano and Yosso 2002). From a positivist point of view, counter-storytelling is criticized as lacking objectivity and generalizability. Yet such notions are in and of themselves the product of Eurocentric traditions that have excluded people of color in knowledge production in mainstream academe. Counter-storytelling thus illuminates marginalized knowledge in a new discursive space.

Collective experience of racism indicates that racism is not just personal prejudice or bigotry. It exists institutionally, disadvantaging certain groups of people seeking access to social services or professional participation while privileging others. Furthermore, racism exists epistemologically, assigning superiority to certain knowledge (e.g. historical perspective) that reflects the view of the dominant group. This understanding of racism provides us with a greater conceptual leverage in putting critical work into practice.

As evident from the above discussion, CRT shares some conceptual underpinnings with the diversity/constructivist approach to gender. Yet, CRT provides a greater emphasis on problematizing and transforming unequal relations of power. It thus corresponds more to the *emancipatory modernism* approach. This, however, does not necessarily imply that sexism is more difficult to address, though sexist language and sexism in general may not completely parallel racist language (e.g. hate speech) and racism (Mills 2008). For instance, a feminist approach can constitute a branch of CRT, critiquing oppression of women within White patriarchy and colonialism (see Wing 2003). Some feminist sociolinguists also argue that while the attention of inquiry within the diversity/constructivist approach to gender has shifted from structural oppression in the patriarchal system to the local construction of gendered meanings in immediate contexts, both dimensions – larger societal factors and local processes – can be investigated (Mills 2008). Many ESP learners and teachers are women and people of color. Racial and gender inequalities are likely to pervade professional contexts, influencing the experiences of these individuals. These issues need to be addressed in both local and broader contexts in order to achieve individual professional advancement and structural justice in society.

Other Social Categories and Intersectionality

Other social categories (e.g. age, class, language, religion, sexual identity) impact social practices and identities in academic and professional settings. It is important to take these categories into consideration because gender and race do not shape our experiences in isolation; rather, they intersect with other categories in complex ways in social contexts. Of these social categories, recent research has paid increased attention to the plural nature of language and linguistic attributes of language users. Conversely, other categories have received relatively marginal attention in research (e.g. social class and privileged students – Vandrick 2009; social class and language use – Rampton 2010; sexual identity in instructional settings – Curran 2006; Liddicoat 2009; Nelson 2009, 2010; religion – Karmani and Makoni 2005; Wong and Canagarajah 2009). In this section, we focus our discussion on linguistic difference.

One linguistic attribute increasingly discussed in the last decade is non-native speakerness as opposed to the concept of the native speaker which has been problematized in such domains as second language acquisition research (Firth and Wagner 2007), language teaching (Cook 2007; Holliday 2008), linguistic imperialism (Phillipson 1992), world Englishes (Kachru 1982), and English as a lingua franca (Jenkins 2000). In these scholarly discussions, the concept of the native speaker is problematized as producing and legitimating a norm that alienates both non-native varieties of language and non-native speakers as illegitimate. In language teaching contexts, the superiority of the native speaker is reflected in the selection of teaching materials and teaching staff.

One issue addressed often is non-native accents. An accent indexes one's habitus (a system of embodied dispositions imbued by individual attributes – Bourdieu 1984), which is reassembled to produce cultural capital (i.e. education, skills, and knowledge) (Luke 2009). Speaking in a non-native or non-standard accent thus disadvantages the speaker in converting his or her cultural capital into economic and/or symbolic capital. Furthermore, perceived accent is not just a linguistic matter; it is intertwined with the speaker's race as perceived by others. As Rubin (1992) shows, listeners are likely to identify a heavier accent in English when the speech they hear is associated with a speaker with non-White racial background. Other qualitative inquiries illuminate biases against native speakers of English who are non-White (Curtis and Romney 2006). Furthermore, research in Canada indicates that résumés for job applications with foreign-sounding names (e.g. Chinese, Indian) are disadvantaged compared to those with Anglophone surnames in being chosen for interviews (Oreopoulos 2009). This indicates that (non)native speakerness often becomes a proxy of race. It is important to note that linguistic biases are far more tolerated than racial prejudice. Thus, linguistic categorization (e.g. assigning the ESL label to immigrant children of color who are native English speakers – Motha 2006) masks a race-based sorting system of people. These issues are significant for ESP because non-native accents and non-White racialized backgrounds characterize many of the learners in professional contexts. It is essential to raise ESP teachers' and learners' awareness of these challenges and explore strategies to overcome them.

Problematizing the linguistic norm, however, poses the following contentious question for ESP, especially in second language contexts where the dominant population is native English speakers: How does this view accommodate the pragmatic concerns of ESP? Some professional fields have certain expectations for acceptable language use and it is tied to the fulfilment of the demands of service recipients. When the perceived effectiveness of service is linked to profit-making, meeting customers' expectations becomes crucial. Thus, the more the field is linked to commercial operations, the more difficult it becomes to promote a diversity/hybridity perspective. EAP might be more accommodating but language and discourse constitute gate-keeping criteria. A clash between pragmatic demands and progressive ideas certainly applies to gender and race as well, but social sanction against sexism and racism would allow more tolerance toward diverse norms in hiring, promotion, and so on. Yet, it is important to reiterate that linguistic intolerance might mask racial intolerance. It is this blurring boundary between language and race that we must pay attention to.

In the following sections, we present how issues discussed thus far are addressed in two areas of ESP: teaching English to adult immigrants for resettlement and work purposes, and teaching EAP.

Teaching Language to Adult Immigrants for Resettlement and Work Purposes

The experiences of adult immigrants and refugees learning English for resettlement and work purposes have been studied by qualitative studies outside of ESP proper with a specific focus on the role of gender in language learning. However, issues of race and other social categories are underexplored in these studies despite the fact that many of them focus on immigrants and refugees of color.

Some of these studies questioned the prevalent assumption that English language skills enable socioeconomic mobility and a better life for working-class immigrants and refugees. Goldstein (1997) and Harper, Pierce, and Burnaby (1996) examined English classes offered at factories in Canada for unskilled immigrant women workers. These classes aimed to integrate the women into the English-speaking workforce and to facilitate communication with the managers. For these women, however, speaking English to co-workers from the same linguistic background was perceived as an insult and would jeopardize their friendship. Conversely, speaking their native language at work maintained their solidarity and the stability of employment. For many of them, learning English during lunchtime was a social activity rather than a means to increase active participation in the factory or obtain better positions with higher salaries. From the employer's perspective, keeping the employees' English skills at a low level would prevent them from demanding better work conditions (Harper et al. 1996). In the US context, Gordon (2004) observed that employers structured tasks to obviate the need for English skills. This indicates that regardless of the availability of English language training, these immigrant women workers are confined at the bottom of the economic system with their implicit consent and contentment.

This does not necessarily mean that all women are locked into low-paying unskilled jobs or that this applies to men in the same way, although research findings are not always consistent. A few Portuguese female factory workers in Goldstein's (1997) study did get promoted to managerial positions. However, these women tended to have had prior English-learning experiences. This situation of Portuguese men at the same factory was similar, except that these men had more exposure to English speakers due to the nature of their work (Goldstein 1997; see also Rockhill 1987). Conversely, a study on Lao refugee men and women in the United States (Gordon 2004) did not find that men were advantaged over women in terms of socioeconomic advancement. They were equally constrained in low-paid unskilled employment that required little proficiency in English.

Another study conducted in the United States on refugee women (Warriner 2007) parallels the Canadian studies in terms of the irrelevancy of English proficiency in employment, although the nature of the ESL program was slightly different. This government-supported program focussed on life/employment skills and academic skills required for high school completion. The instruction lasted only for three to six months and a standardized test was required to gauge readiness for job interviews and to obtain high school credentials. Regardless of the level of English proficiency, however, the women only obtained low-wage employment. They were caught between foregoing their current jobs to obtain additional language training and giving up further training in order to keep employed despite low wages.

With regard to gendered identity as a worker or as a new citizen, immigrant and refugee women often experience dilemmas and ironies. While many women have aspirations to work and learn English in order to contribute to the family income, many are unable to fulfil their desires due to resistance from their husband or other obstacles such as lack of childcare (Gordon 2004; Kouritzin 2000; Menard-Warwick 2004; Rockhill 1987; Warriner 2004). Some women's investment in learning English is confined to the family domain – i.e. to help their children become linguistically integrated into the school (Menard-Warwick 2004; Skilton-Sylvester 2002).

Male immigrant learners of English may also face the need to negotiate their identity, although only a few studies have examined men's experiences. Goldstein (1997) shows how a Portuguese male supervisor at the factory displayed his male authority in assisting younger Portuguese women with English skills necessary for supervisory tasks. In the case of a Mexican immigrant man in the United States (Menard-Warwick 2006), a serious work injury shifted his identity characterized by physical masculinity to a technical one. It also reformulated his linguistic identity from an inadequate speaker of English to a literate user of English with computer skills.

Overall, studies that have investigated immigrant and refugee women's engagement in learning English generally have revealed that developing English skills has not necessarily led to socioeconomic mobility; rather it has been more linked to establishing solidarity and friendship among co-workers or performing the role as an educated mother in a new environment. In contrast, a few studies that have examined the experiences of immigrant men have revealed a mixed picture; learning English is sometimes linked to socioeconomic mobility but sometimes not.

Many of the recent studies discussed above draw on Norton's (2000) conceptualization of identity as multiple and shifting, which is influenced by feminist poststructuralist theory, and the view of language learning as investment (Gordon 2004; Kouritzin 2000; Menard-Warwick 2004, 2006; Skilton-Sylvester 2002; Warriner 2004). These studies reveal how gendered identities are intertwined with the presence or absence of language learning opportunities, which were closely linked to their family circumstances. They fall under the diversity/constructivist paradigm of understanding gender. However, as discussed earlier, this paradigm tends not to directly confront sexism and gender inequalities embedded in the social and economic system. The Canadian studies that found little connection between English learning and socioeconomic mobility challenge future ESP research in that even if these women (and perhaps men) learned English and sought better career opportunities, they might not actually succeed. This is due to various social injustices, such as sexism, racism, accent discrimination, homophobia, and Islamophobia, that exist within the current neoliberal socioeconomic system. Future ESP research might investigate how teaching ESP maintains or challenges a hierarchy of power and how it could improve the lives of immigrants and refugees.

Teaching EAP

In the area of teaching EAP, researchers have addressed several topics relevant to this chapter: e.g. gendered practice in academic writing activities and publications, cultured practice of academic writing, and inquiry into gender and other social categories in EAP classrooms. While gender has been discussed in some publications, issues of race have not been explicitly discussed; instead, race or ethnicity is implied in the discussions of cultural difference in the published works reviewed below. With regard to theoretical orientations, unlike the research on teaching English to immigrants or refugees reviewed above, poststructuralist analysis of gender does not dominate the research.

Though not directly addressing EAP, research by Johnson (1992) provides some interesting insight into gender in academic writing. Focussing on peer response, Johnson (1992) examined international female graduate students' written responses to papers composed by their peers in order to investigate how the gender of the addressees influenced their use of compliments. The results showed that unlike the native English-speaking (NES) women peer reviewers who used more compliments to female addressees than to male addressees (Johnson and Roen 1992), the non-native English-speaking (NNES) women students did not vary complimenting strategies according to the gender of the addressee to the same extent. While this finding appears to indicate the need for NNES women writers to acquire gendered discourse strategies in the target discourse community, such strategies may negatively impact the effectiveness of writing in the male-dominant academic discourse. In fact, Johnson and Roen (1992) found that female-linked complimenting strategies – e.g. the use of positive evaluations, intensifiers, personal references – were perceived as less effective by both male and female NES writers. This indicates a challenge for NNES female academic writers to negotiate the tension between acquiring gendered discourse strategies and negotiating male dominance in academic discourse.

Gendered discourse features found in published works also demonstrate both similarities and differences between men and women. Examining a corpus of book reviews written by male and female reviewers in philosophy and biology and conducting interviews with selected reviewers, Tse and Hyland (2008) conclude that the discourse strategies used by male and female reviewers were overall more similar than different but more different between the disciplines than within the disciplines. They also found gender difference prominent particularly in biology with regard to the gender of the author of the book (i.e. male reviewers were more critical of male authors), reflecting competitiveness within the discipline, which reflects structural gender inequalities.

These results echo the findings of Belcher (2009). Following up on an earlier call for affirming non-adversarial argumentation in academic writing which is likely to be preferred by women and non-Anglophone scholars (Belcher 1997), Belcher (2009) examined three major US-based academic journals of language studies published between 1996 and 2006 to investigate whether the articles written by women and English as an international language (EIL) scholars increased in number and whether their articles manifested implicit and less confrontational gap statements as expected by their gender and cultural backgrounds. Belcher indeed observed a larger number of female and EIL contributors but NES female scholars used more explicit gap statements in 2006 than in 1996 and EIL scholars overwhelmingly used explicit gap statements. Belcher speculates that this alignment with male-based academic discourse may have to do with the authors' concerns of rhetorical effectiveness, publishability, and perceived impact of their work.

The findings that EIL writers are prone to use mainstream male-based academic English discourse strategies that are less implicit, nuanced, or intimate are intriguing. These writers have tended to be viewed as novices in Western academic communities and positioned as maintaining their cultural rhetorical traditions that are incompatible with English conventions, as indicated by traditional research in contrastive rhetoric. As discussed earlier, the contemporary discourse often substitutes the idea of race with the more acceptable concept of culture. In this sense, the subtext of cultural differences discussed in the context of written discourse features implies racial or ethnic differences of L2 writers (Kubota 2003, 2010). The traditional contrastive rhetoric research has highlighted cultural differences in rhetorical features between English and other languages, just like research on gender in language use previously focussed on fixed gender differences. However, just as first language (L1) and second language (L2) female and male writers' actual use of discourse strategies in English academic writing is not constrained by fixed gender difference but rather reflects complex negotiation of discourse strategies in multiple relations of power, written discourse features used by L2 writers from diverse cultures are multiple and fluid. This reflects a complex negotiation of writer identities in relation to the audience and the context as well as the dynamic and diverse nature of language and discourse (see Archer 2008). Thus, while some L2 writers find little trouble acculturating into the academic English discourse community (Cheng 2006) or even favor the rhetoric of academic English over that of their native language (Shi 2003), others may prefer a more humbling writing style (Belcher 1997; Canagarajah 2001). This indicates a multiplicity of writer identities that cannot be reduced to a fixed category of homogeneous L2 writers.

With regard to pedagogy, advocates of critical EAP have addressed issues of gender. For instance, in an EAP class linked to a psychology course, Benesch (1998) had her students read a story about a girl with anorexia. Using a feminist approach that foregrounds expression of multiple voices based on personal experiences, Benesch engaged students in understandings about anorexia not only from a psychological perspective but also in relation to sociocultural construction of femininity. In a study of four White female EAP teachers in East Timor, Appleby (2009) discussed a clash between Western values of gender egalitarianism that these teachers wanted to introduce and the local male-dominant social practices that the students were accustomed to. These teachers also faced ironic contradictions of wanting to be egalitarian while being authoritarian to impose gender equality. Grey (2009) taught an EAP course on business communication in Australia. Through a poststructuralist lens, she explored how a hybrid computer-generated composite image of a person presented by a group of students disrupted the conventional notions of gender, race, and sexuality, and challenged students' possible biases.

Besides these useful studies, issues of gender and race in EAP are underexplored. This is related to the pragmatism of EAP that emphasizes preparing students for other disciplines rather than engaging them intellectually in academic contents. The orientations of ESP inquiry are mixed; some research focuses on gender or cultural difference with or without the awareness of issues of power, while others draw on either *emancipatory modernism* or the *problematizing practice* paradigm.

Conclusion and Future Directions

In this chapter, we have provided a theoretical overview of gender, race, and other social categories as well as their intersectionality. We have also reviewed how these categories are addressed in selected studies in ESP. These studies have illuminated issues of gender; however, other categories remain largely underexplored. Within the two sub-fields of ESP reviewed, recent studies on teaching English to immigrants and refugees tend to use a diversity/constructivist approach to explore the multiple and fluid identities of women (and some men). Research related to EAP raises issues of gendered or culturally influenced discourse strategies in writing that involve contradictions and complexities. It also proposes and problematizes pedagogy that disrupts normative expectations of gender.

To conclude, we would like to propose some issues for future exploration. First, social injustices such as sexism, racism, and homophobia should be explicitly addressed in research and pedagogy. These problems, manifested as discursive practices, pose real-life challenges especially for many of our ESP learners in professional fields. Research can expose the mechanisms of exclusion and suggest possible strategies to cope with and overcome challenges for both teachers and students. Second, gendered, and racialized positionalities of ESP teachers need to be investigated in more detail. This would involve examinations of how power relations between teacher and student are mediated by gender, race, accent, and other categories and how such relations impact understandings of Self and Other as well as approaches to teaching and learning. Gendered and racialized teacher identities need to be investigated in relation to privilege or marginalization. Third, the historical development of CRT raises the question of how CRT can be integrated into teaching English for legal purposes. The students learning English for this purpose in White-dominant societies are likely to be racial and linguistic minorities who can play an important role in challenging racial discrimination in the legal system. Drawing students' attention to this theory would constitute an important component of critical ESP. Fourth, it is necessary to explore contextual understanding of *needs* by taking into consideration how the learner's gender, race, class, and other backgrounds shape social practices in a specific professional context. In other words, we need to know how needs vary according to the backgrounds of the participants in a particular context. Lastly, our sociopolitical engagement in ESP research and teaching with explicit attention to gender, race, and other categories would be supported by a good balance between *emancipatory modernism*, which critiques ideologies and structural inequalities, and *problematizing practices*, which mobilize notions of heterogeneity, hybrid identities, and multiplicity of meaning.

REFERENCES

Appleby, R. (2009) The spatial politics of gender in EAP classroom practice. *Journal of English for Academic Purposes* 8: 100–10.

Angélil-Carter, S. (1997) Second language acquisition of spoken and written English: Acquiring the skeptron. *TESOL Quarterly* 31: 263–87.

Archer, A. (2008) "The place is suffering": Enabling dialogue between students' discourses and academic literacy conventions in engineering. *English for Academic Purposes* 27: 255–66.

Belcher, D. (1997) An argument for nonadversarial argumentation: On the relevance of the feminist critique of academic discourse to L2 writing pedagogy. *Journal of Second Language Writing* 6: 1–21.

Belcher, D. (ed.) (2009) *English for Specific Purposes in Theory and Practice*. Ann Arbor, MI: University of Michigan Press.

Benesch, S. (1998) Anorexia: A feminist EAP curriculum. In T. Smoke (ed.), *Adult ESL: Politics, Pedagogy, and Participation in Classrooms and Community Programs*. 101–14. Mahwah, NJ: Lawrence Erlbaum.

Benesch, S. (2001) *Critical English for Academic Purposes: Theory, Politics, and*

Practice. Mahwah, NJ: Lawrence Erlbaum.

Block, D. (2007) *Second Language Identities*. London: Continuum.

Block, D. (2009) Identity in applied linguistics: The need for conceptual exploration. In V. Cook (ed.) *Contemporary Applied Linguistics: Volume 1 Language Teaching and Learning*. 215–32. London: Continuum.

Bonilla-Silva, E. (2003) *Racism without Racists: Color-Blind Racism and the Persistence of Racial Inequality in the United States*. Lanham, MD: Lowman and Littlefield.

Bourdieu, P. (1984) *Distinction: A Social Critique of the Judgment of Taste*. Cambridge, MA: Harvard University Press.

Butler, J. (1999) *Gender Trouble: Feminism and the Subversion of Identity (Tenth Anniversary Edition)*. London: Routledge.

Cameron, D. (2005) Language, gender, and sexuality: Current issues and new directions. *Applied Linguistics* 26: 482–502.

Canagarajah, S. (2001) The fortunate traveler: Shuttling between communities and literacies by economy class. In D. Belcher and U. Connor (eds.), *Reflections* on *Multiliterate Lives*. 23–37. Clevedon, UK: Multilingual Matters.

Cheng, A. (2006) Analyzing and enacting academic criticism: The case of an L2 graduate learner of academic writing. *Journal of Second Language Writing* 15: 279–306.

Cherryholmes, C. (1988) *Power and Criticism: Poststructural Investigations in Education*. New York: Teachers College Press.

Collins, P. H. (1998) *Fighting Words: Black Women and the Search for Justice*. Minnesota, MN: University of Minnesota Press.

Cook, V. (2007) The goals of ELT: Reproducing native-speakers or promoting multicompetence among second language users? In J. Cummins and C. Davison (eds.), *International Handbook of English Language Education* vol. 1. 237–48. Norwell, MA: Springer.

Crenshaw, K., Gotanda, N., Peller, G., and Thomas, K. (1995) Introduction. In K. Crenshaw, N. Gotanda, G. Peller and K. Thomas (eds.), *Critical Race Theory: The Key Writings That Formed the Movement*. xiii–xxxii. New York: The New Press.

Curran, G. (2006) Responding to students' normative questions about gays: Putting queer theory into practice in an Australian ESL class. *Journal of Language, Identity, & Education* 5: 85–96.

Curtis, A. and Romney, M. (eds.) (2006) *Color, Race, and English Language Teaching: Shades of Meaning*. Mahwah, NJ: Lawrence Erlbaum.

Dudley-Evans, T. and St John, M. J. (1998) *Developments in ESP: A Multi-Disciplinary Approach*. Cambridge: Cambridge University Press.

Firth, A. and Wagner, J. (2007) Second/foreign language learning as a social accomplishment: Elaborations on a receonceptualized SLA. *The Modern Language Journal* 91: 800–19.

Foucault, M. (1980) *Power/Knowledge: Selected Interviews and Other Writings,* 1972–1977. C. Gordon (ed.) New York: Pantheon Books.

Goldstein, T. (1997) *Two Languages at Work: Bilingual Life on the Production Floor*. Berlin: Mouton de Gruyter.

Gordon, D. (2004) "I'm tired. You clean and cook." Shifting gender identities and second language socialization. *TESOL Quarterly* 38: 437–57.

Grey, M. (2009) Ethnographers of difference in a critical EAP community – becoming. *Journal of English for Academic Purposes* 8: 121–33.

Harper, H., Peirce, B., and Burnaby, B. (1996) English-in-the-workplace for garment workers: A feminist project? *Gender and Education* 8: 5–19.

Higgins, C. (2010) Gendered identities in language education. In N. H. Hornberger and S. L. McKay (eds.), *Sociolinguistics and Education*. 370–97. Clevedon, UK: Multilingual Matters.

Holliday, A. (2008) Standards of English and politics of inclusion. *Language Teaching* 41: 119–30.

Hutchinson, T. and Waters, A. (1987) *English for Specific Purposes: A Learning-Centred Approach*. Cambridge: Cambridge University Press.

Jenkins, J. (2000) *Phonology of English as an International Language*. Oxford: Oxford University Press.

Johnson, D. M. (1992) Interpersonal involvement in discourse: Gender variation in L2 writers' complimenting strategies. *Journal of Second Language Writing* 1: 195–215.

Johnson, D. M. and Roen, D. H. (1992) Complimenting and involvement in peer review: Gender variation. *Language in Society* 21: 27–57.

Kachru, B. B. (ed.) (1982) *The Other Tongue: English Across Cultures*. Urbana, IL: University of Illinois Press.

Kamada, L. (2009) *Hybrid Identities and Adolescent Girls: Being "Half" in Japan*. Clevedon, UK: Multilingual Matters.

Karmani, S. and Makoni, S. (eds.) (2005) Special Issue: Islam and English in the post-9/11 era. *Journal of Language, Identity, and Education*: 4(2).

Kouritzin, S. (2000) Immigrant mothers redefine access to ESL classes: Contradiction and ambivalence. *Journal of Multilingual and Multicultural Development* 21: 14–32.

Kubota, R. (2003) New approaches to race, class, and gender in second language writing. *Journal of Second Language Writing* 12: 31–47.

Kubota, R. (2004) Critical multiculturalism and second language education. In B. Norton and K. Toohey (eds.) *Critical Pedagogies and Language Learning*. 30–52. Cambridge: Cambridge University Press.

Kubota, R. (2010) Cross-cultural perspectives on writing: Contrastive rhetoric. In N. H. Hornberger and S. L. McKay (eds.), *Sociolinguistics and Education*. 265–89. Clevedon, UK: Multilingual Matters.

Kubota, R. and Lin, A. (2009) Race, culture, and identities in second language education: Introduction to research and practice. In R. Kubota and A. Lin (eds.), *Race, Culture, and Identity in Second Language Education: Exploring Critically Engaged Practice*. 1–22. New York: Routledge.

Kumaravadivelu, B. (2006) TESOL methods: Changing tracks, challenging trends. *TESOL Quarterly* 40: 59–81.

Ladson-Billings, G. and Tate, W. (1995) Toward a critical race theory of education. *Teachers College Record* 97: 47–68.

Lakoff, R. (1975) *Language and Woman's Place*. New York: Harper & Row.

Liddicoat, A. J. (2009) Sexual identity as linguistic failure: Trajectories of interaction in the heteronormative language classroom. *Journal of Language, Identity, and Education* 8: 191–202.

Luke, A. (2004) Two takes on the critical. In B. Norton and K. Toohey (eds.), *Critical Pedagogies and Language Learning*. 21–29. Cambridge: Cambridge University Press.

Luke, A. (2009) Race and language as capital in school: A sociological template for language-education reform. In R. Kubota and A. Lin (eds.), *Race, Culture, and Identities in Second Language Education: Exploring Critically Engaged Practice*. 286–308. New York: Routledge.

Lupton, D. (1995) Perspectives on power, communication and the medical encounter: Implications for nursing theory and practice. *Nursing Inquiry* 2: 157–65.

May, S. (2009) Critical multiculturalism and education. In J. A. Banks (ed.), *The Routledge International Companion to Multicultural Education*. 33–48. New York: Routledge.

McElhinny, B. (2003) Theorizing gender in sociolinguistics and linguistic anthropology. In J. Holmes and M. Meyerhoff (eds.), *The Handbook of Language and Gender*. 21–42. Malden, MA: Blackwell.

Menard-Warwick, J. (2004) "I always had the desire to progress a little": Gendered narratives of immigrant language learners. *Journal of Language, Identity, and Education* 3: 295–311.

Menard-Warwick, J. (2006) "The think about work": Gendered narratives of a transnational, trilingual Mexicano. *International Journal of Bilingual Education and Bilingualism* 9: 359–73.

Miller, E. and R. Kubota (forthcoming). Second language learning and identity construction. In J. Herschensohn and M. Young-Sholten (eds.), *The Cambridge Handbook of Second Language Acquisition*. Cambridge: Cambridge University Press.

Mills, S. (2008) *Language and Sexism*. Cambridge: Cambridge University Press.

Minh-ha, T. T. (1989) *Woman, Native, Other*. Bloomington and Indianapolis, IN: Indiana University Press.

Mohanty, C. T. (2003) *Feminism Without Borders: Decolonizing Theory, Practicing Solidarity*. Durham, NC: Duke University Press.

Morgan, B. (2007) Poststructuralism and applied linguistics: Complementary approaches to identity and culture in ELT. In J. Cummins and C. Davison (eds.), *International Handbook of English Language Teaching*. 1033–52. Norwell, MA: Springer.

Motha, S. (2006) Racializing ESOL teacher identities in U.S. K-12 public schools. *TESOL Quarterly* 40: 495–518.

Nelson, C. D. (2009) *Sexual Identities in English Language Education*. New York: Routledge.

Nelson, C. D. (2010) A gay immigrant student's perspective: Unspeakable acts in the language class. *TESOL Quarterly* 44: 441–64.

Norton, B. (2000) *Identity and Language Learning: Gender, Ethnicity and Educational Change*. London: Longman.

Norton, B. (2010) Language and Identity. In N. H. Hornberger and S. L. McKay (eds.), *Sociolinguistics and Education*. 349–69. Clevedon, UK: Multilingual Matters.

Oreopoulos, P. (2009) Why do skilled immigrants struggle in the labor market? A field experiment with six thousand résumés. Working Paper Series no. 09–03. Metropolis, BC: Centre of Excellence for Research on Immigration and Diversity. Accessed Feb. 16, 2011 at http://mbc.metropolis.net/assets/uploads/files/wp/2009/WP09-03.pdf.

Pavlenko, A. (2001) Bilingualism, gender, and ideology. *The International Journal of Bilingualism* 5: 117–51.

Pennycook, A. (1997) Vulgar pragmatism, critical pragmatism, and EAP. *English for Specific Purposes* 16: 253–69.

Pennycook, A. (2004) Critical applied linguistics. In A. Davies and C. Elder (eds.), *The Handbook of Applied Linguistics*. 784–807. Malden, MA: Blackwell.

Phillipson, R. (1992) *Linguistic Imperialism*. Oxford: Oxford University Press.

Rampton, B. (2010) Social class and sociolinguistics. *Applied Linguistics Review* 1: 1–21.

Rockhill, K. (1987) Gender, language and the politics of literacy. *British Journal of Sociology of Education* 8: 153–67.

Rubin, D. L. (1992) Nonlanguage factors affecting undergraduates' judgments of non-native English-speaking teaching assistants. *Research in Higher Education* 33: 511–31.

Shi, L. (2003) Writing in two cultures: Chinese professors return from the West. *The Canadian Modern Language Review* 59: 369–91.

Skilton-Sylvester, E. (2002) Should I stay or should I go? Investigating Cambodian women's participation and investment in adult ESL programs. *Adult Education Quarterly* 53: 9–26.

Solórzano, D. G. and Yosso, T. J. (2002) Critical race methodology: Counter-story telling as an analytical framework for education research. *Qualitative Inquiry* 8: 23–44.

Sunderland, J. (2000) Issues of language and gender in second and foreign language education. *Language Teaching* 33: 203–23.

Tannen, D. (1990) *You Just Don't Understand*. New York: William Morrow Paperbacks.

Thesen, L. (1997) Voices, discourses and transition: In search of new categories in EAP. *TESOL Quarterly* 31: 487–511.

Tse, P. and Hyland, K. (2008) "Robot kung fu": Gender and professional identity in biology and philosophy reviews. *Journal of Pragmatics* 40: 1232–248.

Vandrick, S. (2009) *Interrogating Privilege: Reflections of a Second Language Educator*. Ann Arbor, MI: University of Michigan Press.

Warriner, D. (2004) "The days now is very hard for my family": The negotiation and construction of gendered work identities among newly arrived women refugees. *Journal of Language, Identity, and Education* 3: 279–94.

Warriner, D. S. (2007) "It's just the nature of the beast": Re-imagining the literacies of schooling in adult ESL education. *Linguistics and Education* 18: 305–24.

West, C. (1984) When the doctor is a "lady": Power, status and gender in physician-patient encounters. *Symbolic Interaction* 7: 87–106.

West, C. (1990) Not just "doctors' orders": Directive-response speech sequences in patients' visits to women and men physicians. *Discourse Society* 1: 85–1 12.

Wing, A. K. (ed.) (2003) *Critical Race Feminism: A Reader*. 2nd ed. New York: New York University Press.

Wong, M. S. and Canagarajah, S. (eds.) (2009) *Christian and Critical English Language Educators in Dialogue: Pedagogical And Ethical Dilemmas*. New York: Routledge.

26 Ethnographic Approaches to ESP Research

DACIA DRESSEN-HAMMOUDA

Introduction

There is wide agreement that English for specific purposes (ESP) is largely a teaching-materials driven and learner-centered approach (Dudley-Evans and St John 1998). This focus has developed concurrently with the "social turn" (Gee 1990) in language and literacy studies, which considers that language use cannot be properly described and understood outside its context of social use. As a result, much of the research carried out in ESP over the past decades has been done so with the express intent of improving teaching methods by improving our understandings of language use. This concern has led to a situation where ESP teaching practice and research have become closely entwined. As noted by Hewings (2002a: v) in his introductory editorial for *English for Specific Purposes*, one of the "great strength[s]" of ESP has been its

> ability to maintain a balance between, on the one hand, the report of sound and interesting research and, on the other, discussion of its implications for pedagogical practice relevant to a wide range of teaching contexts.

In many respects, the motivation to provide authentic descriptions of specialized language-in-context for teaching purposes early on pushed ESP practitioners to try to combine aspects of both quantitative and qualitative approaches into their research methods. Ramani et al. (1988: 83), for example, identify the "first explicit call for an ethnographic approach" in ESP as having originated with Swales' (1985: 219) argument that:

The Handbook of English for Specific Purposes, First Edition.
Edited by Brian Paltridge and Sue Starfield.
© 2013 John Wiley & Sons, Inc. Published 2013 by John Wiley & Sons, Inc.

it is not only texts that we need to understand, but the roles texts have in their environments; the values congruent and conflictive, placed on them by occupational, professional and disciplinary memberships; and the expectation these memberships have on the patternings of the genres they participate in.

Without necessarily carrying out actual ethnographies, ESP studies since the 1980s have demonstrated a desire to develop a more ethnographic, or social-use-centered, orientation. This orientation can be seen, for example, in articles from the earlier volumes of the journal, *English for Specific Purposes*, where qualitative techniques and contextual analyses of sociopolitical or socioeducational factors were used to meet a shared research goal of providing more authentic descriptions of specific purpose language use to improve teaching materials. Qualitative and ethnographic-oriented approaches have since become increasingly accepted as part of ESP research practice, as can be seen in the growing number of studies using such methods which have been published in the field's major journals. A survey carried out for the purposes of this chapter, which looked at publications in *English for Specific Purposes*, the *Journal of English for Academic Purposes*, and the *Journal of Second Language Writing* (see qualitative and ethnographic approaches in ESP research below) shows that for each ten-year period since the early 1980s, that number has tripled.

What is an Ethnographic Approach to Research?

The move to a more sociocultural orientation in ESP research has caused scholars to devise increasingly complex ways to provide contextual understandings of texts. One way in which scholars have done this has been to integrate various ethnographic and qualitative approaches and techniques into their research practice. Harklau's (2005, 2011) discussion of ethnography lays down some of the key features of an ethnographic approach:

> The term ethnography refers to a range of diverse and ever-changing research approaches . . . originating in anthropological and sociological research and characterized by first-hand, naturalistic, sustained observation and participation in a particular social setting. The purpose of ethnography is to come to a deeper understanding of how individuals view and participate in their own social and cultural worlds (Harklau 2005: 179).

However, while all ethnographic research is necessarily qualitative, not all qualitative research is necessarily ethnographic. In-depth interviews and focus groups, for example, are valuable methods of qualitative inquiry, but do not constitute ethnography if carried out independently of other methods and without sustained involvement in the research setting. Ethnography, thus, specifically implies a "triangulation" of research methods (Davis 1995; Lazaraton 1995; Lillis 2008; Starfield 2010; Watson-Gegeo 1988). Triangulation is one important distinctive feature of ethnographic research in that it "requires the researcher to approach an issue, topic or event in a variety of ways in order to validate the findings" (Johns and Makalela 2011: 202). Other distinctive features of ethnographic research include sustained engagement over time, participant observation and critical reflection about the role of the researcher (Harklau 2011; Lillis 2008; Starfield 2010, 2012).

Harklau (2011) identifies two overarching trends in qualitative research in applied linguistics. On the one hand, there are sociocultural approaches oriented toward describing the ecological context of language learning, such as ethnographies and case studies. On the other, there are approaches such as conversation analysis and genre analysis, which examine the construction of social realities through discourse using audio, video, or textual data. Within these two broad groups, there is however considerable overlap among categories: discourse-based researchers often highlight the usefulness of including interpretive and empirical orientations in their analysis of discourse, and socioculturally-focused researchers combine their research methods with a focus on language in new and opportune ways. While "felicitous and generative," such combinations cause philosophical and methodological incompatibilities, however, that may be left unrecognized or unaddressed by researchers (Harklau 2011: 182).

A further issue is that scholars may be vague about the ontological and epistemological basis for their research practices and intellectual histories (Harklau 2011; Lillis 2008; Street 1997). As Harklau (2011: 183) observes, such implicit, underlying forces result in the homogenization of "largely implicit understandings of qualitative research in [the] field" such that scholars often assume a stance which implies that carrying out qualitative or ethnographic-like methods (case study, grounded theory, thick description, practitioner inquiry) is necessary, but without explaining why they do it, nor what it adds, apart from noting that it creates more nuanced explanations of the phenomena being studied. Such variability in approaches has led to the situation described by Lillis (2008) who has observed that in some studies, researchers might treat ethnography as a simple "method" for gaining information about context, or conversely as a "methodology" intended to build more holistic understandings of language and literacy phenomena.

As a result, the incorporation of ethnographic approaches into research practices may be carried out with researchers picking and choosing from among the available approaches in ways which suit their immediate research needs, but without reflection as to the full implications of what ethnographic methods actually bring to the understanding of language-learning or literacy acquisition, nor what the use of ethnographic approaches implies for the research itself.

Scollon and Scollon (2001) have identified several key characteristics they find common to all ethnographic studies. Ethnographic studies are seen to share four procedures; that is, *fieldwork, participant observation, strange making* (the process by which researchers resolve the particular stance they take when they are both participants and observers in a social setting) and *contrastive observation*. They also include *members' generalizations* about the significance of the data. Members' generalizations are then contrasted with the observations made by the researcher. These types of data are enhanced by accounts of *individual members' experiences*. Finally, the interpretation the analyst has given to the event is validated by inviting *participant feedback* on the analyst's data and interpretations.

The necessity of designing ethnographic approaches to gain "emic" (i.e. insiders') perspectives to create trustworthiness points to one final consequence from not making one's epistemological and ontological orientations explicit, and this is the failure to explore the effects that we, as researchers, necessarily have on the outcome of our research. A critical stance is one of the key legacies of the social turn in language and literacy studies (Street 1997). In this regard, the comfortable givens and complacency that result from being satisfied with "etic" (or outsiders') descriptions of sociocultural context in fact contradict the original justifications for the social turn in language and literacy research, by glossing over the fundamental observation that all language interactions are inherently dynamic, and shaped by complex interactions of social, institutional, and historical forces (see Bakhtin 1981),

Lillis (2008) describes a set of strategies which, in an incremental fashion, allow ESP researchers to move between emic and etic perspectives depending on research motives, and beyond the disconnect between text and context when researching academic writing. She identifies three levels of ethnography currently used in studies that have a qualitative research orientation: "ethnography as method," "ethnography as methodology," and "ethnography as deep theorizing."

Lillis gives *talk around text* as an example of "ethnography as method." She pinpoints a number of limitations with this kind of technique, however. As she notes, text in this approach is treated as a complex phenomenon, but the talk around it "tends to be treated as straightforwardly transparent, a simple reflection of the writer's perspective" (2008: 361). Although it is important to take talk into account, she cautions that it must be read on at least three different levels: (1) as a "realist" tale; (2) as indexing relevant aspects of the community of practice, of self, and of writing; and (3) as a performative indicator of the power relations between researcher and writers being researched and how this influences the outcome of the talk (Lillis 2008). As a consequence, she argues strongly for using other methods of research, other than just talk-around-text.

The second level of ethnographic research Lillis (2008) identifies is "ethnography as methodology." Ethnography as methodology differs from ethnography as method through its long-term site and actor engagement, drawing from the idea that "long conversations" (Maybin 2006) are a useful means for gathering information. As examples of possible methods she cites literacy history interviews, where the researcher "elicits autobiographical accounts of language and academic literacy learning to frame current practices and perspectives" (Lillis 2008: 362). The literacy history interview incites continued research through "cyclical dialogue around texts over a period of time" (2008: 362). As she argues, the longer dialogue allows the analyst to explore the writer-participant's evolving relationship with discourses, writing practices, and identity while opening up possibilities for the writer-participant to offer up relevant observations to the researcher.

A further way in which ethnography as methodology differs from ethnography as method is the practice of collecting and analyzing multiple sources of data to build more "holistic" understandings of the text-context interaction. To create such holistic understandings, the various data collected need to reflect both *thick descriptive practices* (Geertz 1973), by observing and collecting "everything that may prove (potentially) to be significant, building up a detailed pictures of places, people, and resources" (Lillis 2008: 368) using journals, field notes, or photos, as well as *thick participative practices* (Sarangi 2006,2007), which involves "a form of [researcher] socialization in order to achieve a threshold for interpretive understanding" (Lillis 2008: 367). Such data, she argues, help "remind the researcher of the importance of staying located in writers' specific sociohistorical trajectories and to avoid reading the data (in this case, people's lives and perspectives) through any straightforward theoretical (etic) lens" (2008: 372). One limitation of ethnography as methodology Lillis identifies, however, is that while it allows the researcher to more effectively bridge the gap between text and context, "there is often no parallel move . . . circulating back from context to text" (2008: 374). In other words, while such approaches effectively bring the researcher to more fully reflect on the complexities of context, they do not push the researcher to come back full circle by seeing how context is actually textualized. For this reason, she moves on to a third level of ethnography, as a way of developing ever more nuanced ways of relating text and context.

The third level of ethnography is what Lillis, following Blommaert (2007), calls "ethnography as deep theorizing." Using this perspective on ethnography can, she claims, narrow the gap between text and context by using two context-sensitive categories drawn from linguistic ethnography: *indexicality* and *orientation*. This involves consideration of how the language and orientation of the texts "index" (Bucholtz and Hall 2005; Ochs 1992) certain social structures, values, and relations in the same way that particular ways of speaking may point to, or index, a person's gender, social class, or ethnic identity (Litosseliti 2006). Indexicality, here, acts as a mediational category that helps bridge the gap between text and context, thereby "radically challeng[ing] the dichotomy between language and culture" (Lillis 2008: 381).

Moving beyond comfortable predictability in research practices and narrow assumptions about the nature of social action, then, requires taking a critical stance on the research and the research process. As Street (1997), Starfield (2011), and others argue, one of the most basic actions one can undertake to develop a critical stance is to make one's epistemological and theoretical background explicit, because this background "(implicitly or explicitly) informs the questions that researchers ask; the assumptions which we make; and the procedures, methods and approaches we use to carry out research" (Norton 1995: 569). In addition, only a critical approach to research can produce the sort of deep theorizing (Lillis 2008) necessary to producing trustworthy accounts of literate practice, by reducing the gap between text and context. In other words, "critical ethnographic work, and the understandings of context it affords, can illuminate not only how texts are produced and received but also how contexts for writing are constituted and what constitutes context" (Starfield 2011: 176). Given its focus on researcher reflexivity and location and attention to unequal power relations and legitimacy, the critical approach to ethnography described by Starfield (2011) betters allows researchers to bridge the gap between text and context by showing greater sensitivity to issues of agency and to the power of indexicality, or "how texts point to (index) specific discourses on identity, writing, academia and power" (Starfield 2011: 177).

One ESP-oriented approach which captures many of these characteristics is Swales' (1998) "textography." Textography is an approach to the analysis of written texts which combines text analysis with ethnographic techniques such as surveys, interviews, and other data sources in order to examine what texts are like, and why. It looks critically "at the texts themselves, as well as the context of production and interpretation of the texts" (Paltridge 2004: 84) in order to provide a more situated and contextualized basis for understanding writing than might be obtained by just looking at texts alone. Devitt (2004: 65) underscores how important textographical examinations are of particular writers writing particular texts in order to "expose different realities." Textography's ability to explain individual behavior within the context of its social and cultural context, thus, goes beyond the researcher's perspective by grounding explanations of behavior in observations of actual practice. In addition, a textography collects *members' generalizations* about the significance of discoursal artifacts, through text-based interviews and other data sources. Paltridge (2008) and Paltridge et al. (2011) demonstrate a number of ways in which a textography can be carried out, illustrating how combining textual and ethnographic approaches can help uncover the "outside forces" (Hyland 2003) which shape individual writing and literacy practices, including both what is possible to say or do and the assumptions made by more expert members about those writers who have less experience with the community's norms and expectations.

Qualitative and Ethnographic Research in ESP

To investigate the extent to which such qualitative and ethnographic approaches have made their way into ESP research practices, three international peer-reviewed journals in ESP, the *English for Specific Purposes* journal (preceded by *The ESP Journal*, 1980–1985), the *Journal of Second Language Writing*, and *Journal of English for Academic Purposes*, were surveyed to identify research reports that have used qualitative and/or ethnographic methods. These journals were chosen as representative of the field of ESP because the articles published relate specifically to ESP concerns; Hewings (2002b), for example, has identified *English for Specific Purposes* as the field's "flagship journal." In addition, the three journals are taken to be interrelated because authors publishing in one of the journals also typically tend to publish in one or both of the other journals, as well. Specifically, the survey sought to identify what qualitative methods were used most often and whether

Table 26.1 Number of studies using qualitative methods per journal

Journal name	Time period	Number of qualitative studies	Total number of publications	%
English for Specific Purposes	1980–2010	51	548	9
Journal of Second Language Writing	1992–2010	21	278	7.5
Journal of English for Academic Purposes	2002–2010	13	176	7.4
Total number of articles		85	1002	8.4

the use of ethnographic approaches has increased over time in the research that has been published in these journals.

In this survey, studies were identified as using qualitative methods if authors used at least one, if not a combination of, qualitative methods including: surveys, questionnaires, interviews, case studies, textography, "ethnography," "qualitative analysis," participant and non-participant observation, evaluations, onsite visits, focus group interviews, writer reflections, peer reviews, think-aloud protocol, researchers' own intuitions as non-native speakers, narrative, literacy histories, network histories, and a situation or contextual analysis of wider sociocultural, sociohistorical, sociopolitical or socioeducational factors.

The survey period spanned 30 years (1980–2010). During this period, 85 articles (8.4 percent) were identified as using some combination of qualitative methods (see Table 26.1). As similarly observed in the field of applied linguistics more generally (Gao, Li, and Lü 2001), the number of ESP-based studies using a qualitative research orientation has grown over time (see Figure 26.1). While in the early 1980s and throughout much of the 1990s, only a couple of articles using qualitative approaches were published each year, between 1999–2007 this number doubled, and doubled again between 2008–2010. However, compared to Gao et al.'s (2001) study, which surveyed the growth of qualitative methods and relative decline of quantitative methods in four major applied linguistics journals over roughly the same period, the current survey found significantly fewer studies using qualitative methods in the three ESP journals examined (Table 26.1). This difference is likely to be due to an important methodological distinction made here between qualitative studies and quantitative, text-based analysis. Gao et al. (2001), in contrast, included all textual analyses in their count of qualitative methods.

The findings of the current survey are more in line with Harklau (2011), who identified only 17 applied linguistics studies out of 230 (7.4 percent) that used some form of the term "ethnography." In the three ESP journals surveyed, "ethnography" as a practice also appeared quite limited. Only 7 studies out of 85

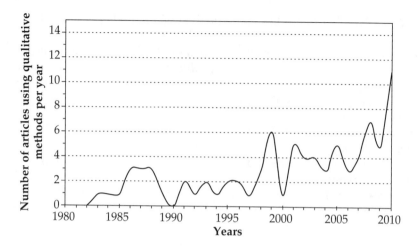

Figure 26.1 Expansion of qualitative approaches into ESP research practices (1980–2010).

(8.2 percent) used some form of the word "ethnography" in their methods description, such as "learner ethnography," "ethnographic approach," "ethnography of lecturers," "ethnographic account of course design," "a more ethnographic analysis of the production context," "a text-ethnographic study" or "an ethnographically oriented study of disciplinary practices"; just six articles used some form of the term in the title.

As similarly observed by Harklau (2011), the interview study was by far the most frequently used qualitative approach in the journals I examined, followed by surveys or questionnaires, and contextual analysis. However, the number and types of qualitative approaches used have grown significantly in recent years. Since the mid-1990s, case studies, non-participant observations, qualitative analyses, social network analyses, different types of ethnography (e.g. learner ethnography, ethnography of lecturers), and authors' own intuitions as native speakers have become more frequent. In more recent years (2004–2010), still other qualitative methods have appeared, including reader response, critical contrastive rhetoric, critical reading/rewriting, narrative, simulated blind manuscript review, the analysis of video recordings and focus groups.

Based on the results of this small survey, we can conclude that ESP scholars have adopted a wide range of qualitative and ethnography-inspired methods in their research, even if for the most part, they do not carry out full-blown ethnographies in the sense that they did not use multiple data sources and did not engage in sustained involvement in the field. The reasons for this qualitative shift, as noted earlier, find their origins in the increasing attention paid to the broader, more contextual aspects of ESP practice. As noted by Bhatia and Gotti (2006: 9–10) for example, ESP scholars' increased interest in developing their understanding of text/context interactions has resulted in a "powerful multidimensional and multi-perspectived framework [which] handle[s] not only the text but also the context" such that "emphases on text and context have almost been reversed."

Some Current Ethnographic Orientations in ESP Research

Table 26.2 summarizes some of the main points that have been raised in this chapter concerning ethnographic approaches as a research perspective and methodology. It will be used as a basis to discuss a number of recent studies from ESP that used an ethnographic approach. Here, I limit my review of ethnographic studies in ESP to those concerned explicitly with describing how non-native speakers of English learn to navigate and manage the communicative imperatives of interacting in situated settings (professional, academic, etc.). In addition, given the field's specific concerns of designing effective descriptions for teaching purposes using text/context interactions, I have also focussed on those studies that combine an analysis of textual and ethnographic data to explore the processes of text production in its situated contexts.

One illustration of an ESP-oriented ethnographic approach that is centrally relevant to ESP concerns is Johns and Makalela's (2011) critical approach to devising needs analysis. As they indicate at the outset of their book chapter, needs assessment is often treated as though it were an "objective" endeavor, although it is most certainly influenced by the background assumptions and expectations of each party – the "client" as well as the "consultant" – which, when in conflict or unstated, can adversely affect the outcome of the proposed assessment. Based on the authors' own experience, they describe the importance of following the guidelines of critical ethnography described by Madison (2003) in devising a needs analysis, in order to be able to "predict our own potential to do harm" and to "make a contribution to equity, freedom and justice" (Johns and Makalela 2011: 217). At the same time, they underscore a claim made by critical ethnographers by applying it to ESP researchers' and teachers' work which "cannot be 'objective,' and free from [their] own frames, intentions and purposes."

Another key example of ethnographic research in ESP is Starfield's (2010, 2011) critical ethnographic study of the ways in which student writers negotiated their textual identities through writing over the course of a year, in the context of the final years of official apartheid in South Africa. To address the concerns raised intially, namely why Black students for whom English was an additional language were encountering higher failure rates in their discipline-based courses than were the White students, Starfield engaged in both "thick descriptive practices" (Geertz 1973) and "thick participatory practices" (Sarangi 2006). She conducted both non-participant and participant observations in multiple teaching/learning contexts, conducted in-depth semi-structured interviews, collected documents including students' essays, tests and exams, the student handbook used in class, and also

Table 26.2   Summary of surveyed ethnographic approaches and analytical focus

	Ethnographic approach or principles	*Methodological focus*
Scollon and Scollon (2001)	Fieldwork	Members' generalizations
	Participant observation	Discourse, practices
	Strange-making	Individual experiences
Watson-Gegeo (1988)	Contrastive observation	Participant feedback/validation
	Triangulation of methods and focus on:	People's behavior in a particular setting
	– individual behavior	The behavior's social organization
	– whole system ("holistic") analysis	– social rules
	– differences between contexts	– interactional expectations
	– "emic" perspective	– cultural values
Lillis (2008)	Ethnography as method	Talk-around-text
	Ethnography as methodology	– text-focussed talk
	– long-term site engagement	– writer-focussed talk
	– multiple data sources	Thick descriptive practices (Geertz 1973)
	– researchers' influence on outcome	– places, people, resources
	Ethnography as deep theorizing	Thick participative practices (Sarangi 2006)
		– researcher socialization
		Mediational categories of text-context
		– indexicality
		– orientation
Starfield (2011)	Critical ethnography	Reflexively designed research practice
		Theoretical assumptions made explicit
		Assumes that social processes are historically and structurally located in unequal power reations
		Assumes unequal access to linguistic resources and legitimacy
		Sensitivity to the relative autonomy of human agent within social systems
		Exploration of how relations of domination are sustained
		Recognizes the power of indexicality
		Homogeneity of culture/community refuted

student-published newspapers and political pamphlets. She collected data in multiple sites and took extensive fieldnotes about what went on in lecture halls, tutorials, graders' meetings, weekly tutor briefings, in the office of one of the tutors, and in hall conversations. She engaged in "thick participation," noting that "in some respects [she] was like a student" (Starfield 2010: 60) by attending all weekly lectures with several hundred students, plus a weekly tutorial with a group of 30 students, and by reading all of the students' course materials. In this way, she was able to develop a critical perspective, looking at the ways in which some Black students' academic writing success was related to ways in which they successfully constructed identities in political and union organizations outside the university, or how the student handbook used in class vehicled a point of view in which the identities of students from disadvantaged backgrounds were at odds with "mainstream" identities. Finally, she triangulated her results by having her evolving interpretations evaluated by participants via a series of semi-structured interviews with both students and staff, thereby creating trustworthiness.

Some of the implications of Starfield's study for the field of ESP are, like for Johns and Makalela (2011), the necessity of assuming a critical stance in all research and teaching work. However, this explicitly calls for reflexivity on the part of the researcher, who makes explicit not only her or his own epistemological assumptions but also the role played during the research through interactions with the study participants (Starfield 2012). It also calls for unambiguously making clear the implications of unequal power and legitimacy involved in all social interactions, and in exploring the repercussions of this imbalance with the social actors involved.

Lillis and Curry's longitudinal study of how scholars from four national contexts (Hungary, Slovakia, Spain, and Portugal) manage their participation in expanding research networks is yet another illustration of ethnographic research in ESP. By studying how scholars gained access to essential resources for publication in English-medium journals (Curry and Lillis 2010; Lillis and Curry 2006, 2010), they have devised what they call a "text-oriented ethnographic" approach which involved collecting and analyzing both textual and ethnographic data in a sustained manner (at the time of the 2010 publications, the study had already been running for nine years). Ethnographic data included (1) observations of participants' activity in context; (2) repeated semi-structured interviews with each of the participants; and (3) concomitant and ongoing communication with participants via email, mail and the telephone. The textual data included drafts of the participants' texts and correspondence with editors, reviewers, and colleagues (manuscripts, comments, revised texts). Overall, they "made 60 field visits, conducted approximately 260 interviews, collected around 1200 texts by participants and 500 items of correspondence between participants and editors . . . [constructed] 240 text histories [and obtained] scholars' perspectives on their experiences" (Curry and Lillis 2010: 283).

The aim of Lillis and Curry's study was to document the participants' "text histories," by exploring how the manuscripts changed as they crossed boundaries in both local and national contexts as well as international contexts, as negotiated from the point of view of the authors participating in the study. To get at this perspective, a number of methodological tools were used: *text histories*, which were based on the manuscripts, comments and revised versions of their texts as well as interviews with authors; *talk around text*, which was collected via interviews with authors and all correspondence related to the evolving manuscripts; *academic research networks*, by which the researchers examined authors' social and research networks; *heuristics for tracking changes across drafts*; and *indexicality* and *orientation*, or the underlying meaning gleamed about stance from textual features in the manuscripts and comments from reviewers.

Of course, as Lillis (2008: 356) cautions, "isolating data extracts in the way [one does in the research article] runs counter to the holistic 'pull' of ethnography whereby . . . a key aim is the weaving together of data in order to understand a particular phenomenon." The publication of their study in book form (i.e. Lillis and Curry 2010) gives a greater sense of the complexity involved in the study than was possible to capture with shorter, article-length research reports. Doubtless, this is a major reason why such studies tend to be rare in ESP, as it is difficult to convey the full scope of an ethnographic approach when having to choose what to focus on from the wealth and range of ethnographic data, within the constraints of a single research article.

In this regard, the longitudinal study partially reported on in Dressen-Hammouda (2008 forthcoming) falls into this situation. Whereas Lillis and Curry have examined the publication difficulties encountered by non-native speakers of English, the work I have been developing since Dressen (2002a) deals with the topic of disciplinary acculturation, and on describing what changes in genre knowledge, practices, identity, perspectives, attitudes, and ideology need to occur within an individual as she or he moves into a new disciplinary community and is granted "membership" as a researcher. To explore this theme, my study combines both etic and emic qualitative approaches to create two overlapping stories which examine the acculturation process from the inside and out. On the one hand, an individual's progress is tracked over an eight-year period, as he moves from being a third-year undergraduate in geology to a research/teaching faculty member two years into his tenure. On the other, the story is also told against the sociohistorical and cultural backdrop of disciplinary history and the description of its members' practices, in order to shed more light onto understanding what necessarily happens to individuals during the process of disciplinary acculturation.

My study brings together a wide range of qualitative methodological approaches to bear on the examination of disciplinary acculturation, including sociohistorical analysis, literacy narratives, text-based interviews, long conversations about disciplinary and writing practices taking place over several years, shorter conversations about geological history and practice using focus groups, accounts of members' generalizations, case studies, my own stance as a researcher involved in observation-participation and quasi "strange-maker," analyses of a wide range of textual artifacts (field notebooks, drawings, field reports, conference abstracts, research articles, dissertation chapters, and course lecture notes) and tracking the changes in the individual student's and other participants' textual artifacts over time using "recontextualization" (Berkenkotter 2001; Bernstein 1990; Dressen 2002; Linell 1998) and standard deviation analysis of linguistic features of the texts (Dressen-Hammouda 2012). Some of the study's implications for the field of ESP include how successful disciplinary acculturation and genre mastery requires becoming proficient in a disciplinary culture's implicit and indexical system, and how much useful understanding there is to be gleaned about general learning processes from a close study of individual behavior and agency.

Concluding Remarks

A number of voices caution that ESP research still has not gone far enough in answering fundamental questions relative to bridging the gap between texts and contexts in both spoken and written genres. In a series of publications, Cheng (2006a, 2006b, 2007, 2008a, 2008b, 2011), for example, raises the issue of how little we still know about how people learn genres, despite the large number of studies carried out on the topic (see Bawarshi and Reiff 2010; Tardy 2006 for a discussions of these studies). Cheng (2007) identifies the reason for this gap as stemming from researchers' overwhelming attention to text. He observes "some researchers have previously argued that the judgment on whether a genre has been mastered rests with the discoursal and linguistic realization in [a learner's] text of a target genre" (Pang 2002: 154). Cheng challenges today's ESP research as still being too closely focused on *what* people learn – the "acquisition of increasing complex genres" (Cheng 2006b: 79), or the text – rather than on *how* they learn it, or the context.

In the past decade ESP research has, however, gone the way of complexifying language and teaching descriptions, even to the point of no longer having any choice but to continue going down that road. Thanks to an impressive collection of ethnographic studies on literacy development, we have now learned much about the nature of discoursal expertise and literacy (Barton and Hamilton 1998; Beaufort 1999, 2007; Berkenkotter and Huckin 1995; Geisler 1994; Haas 1994; Herrington 1981; Ivanič 1998; Lillis and Curry 2010; Myers 1990; Prior 1998). From such studies, we have learned that the world of others' words shapes the complex of abilities and knowledge that enable people to function in and contribute to specific situations. Thus, a writer in the disciplines, the sciences, and the professions today needs to know not only how to write a specific genre exemplar but also when to write it and under what circumstances.

Hyland (2002, 2009) makes a strong argument for using ethnographic approaches to research in order to preserve the usefulness of ESP research for teaching purposes. He points to our research community's increasing knowledge about the specificity of disciplinary writing tasks and to the wide variation seen in genre exemplars across disciplines and professions. Such distinctions have been brought to light not only by a sizeable collection of survey studies, but additionally by ethnographic methods. As he notes, ethnographic studies paint a more accurate, albeit complicated, picture of generic norms and of literacy that can only be of benefit to our learners.

REFERENCES

Bakhtin, M. (1981) *The Dialogic Imagination*. M. Holquist (ed.), C. Emerson, and M. Holquist (trans.). Austin, TX: University of Texas Press.

Barton, D. and Hamilton, M. (1998) *Local Literacies: Reading and Writing in One Community*. London: Routledge.

Bawarshi, A. and Reiff, M. J. (2010) *Genre: An Introduction to History, Theory, Research, and Pedagogy*. West Lafayette, IN: Parlor Press.

Beaufort, A. (1999) *Writing in the Real World: Making the Transition From School to Work*. New York: Teachers College Press.

Beaufort, A. (2007) *College Writing and Beyond: A New Framework for University Writing Instruction*. Logan, UT: Utah State University Press.

Berkenkotter, C. (2001) Genre systems at work: DSM-IV and rhetorical recontextualization in psychotherapy paperwork. *Written Communication* 18: 326–49.

Berkenkotter, C. and Huckin, T. (1995) *Genre Knowledge in Disciplinary Communication: Cognition, Culture, Power*. Hillsdale, NJ: Lawrence Erlbaum.

Bernstein, B. (1990) *Class, Codes, and Control. Vol.4: The Structuring of Pedagogic Discourse*. London: Routledge.

Bhatia, V. K. and Gotti, M. (eds.) (2006) *Explorations in Specialized Genres*. Bern: Peter Lang.

Blommaert, J. (2007) On scope and depth in linguistic ethnography. *Journal of Sociolinguistics* 11: 682–88.

Bucholtz, M. and Hall, K. (2005) Identity and interaction: A sociocultural linguistic approach. *Discourse Studies* 7: 585–614.

Cheng, A. (2006a) Analyzing and enacting academic criticism: The case of an L2 graduate learner of academic writing. *Journal of Second Language Writing* 15: 279–306.

Cheng, A. (2006b) Understanding learners and learning in ESP genre-based writing instruction. *English for Specific Purposes* 25: 76–89.

Cheng, A. (2007) Transferring generic features and recontextualizing genre awareness: Understanding writing performance in the ESP genre-based literacy framework. *English for Specific Purposes* 26: 287–307.

Cheng, A. (2008a) Analyzing genre exemplars in preparation for writing: The case of an L2 graduate student in the ESP genre-based instructional framework of academic literacy. *Applied Linguistics* 29: 50–71.

Cheng, A. (2008b) Individualized engagement with genre in literacy tasks. *English for Specific Purposes* 27: 387–411.

Cheng, A. (2011) ESP classroom research: Basic considerations and future research questions. In D. Belcher, A. M. Johns, and B. Paltridge (eds.), *New Directions in English for Specific Purposes Research*. 44–72. Ann Arbor, MI: University of Michigan Press.

Curry, M. J. and Lillis, T. (2010) Academic research networks: Accessing resources for English-medium publishing. *English for Specific Purposes* 29: 281–95.

Davis, K. (1995) Qualitative theory and methods in applied linguistics research. *TESOL Quarterly* 29: 427–53.

Devitt, A. (2004) *Writing Genres.* Carbondale, IL: Southern Illinois University Press.

Dressen, D. (2002) *Accounting for Fieldwork in Three Areas of Modern Geology: A Situated Analysis of Textual Silences and Saliences.* Unpublished PhD dissertation, The University of Michigan.

Dressen-Hammouda, D. (2008) From novice to disciplinary expert: Disciplinary becoming and genre mastery. *English for Specific Purposes* 27: 233–52.

Dressen-Hammouda, D. (2012) Measuring the construction of discoursal expertise through corpus-based genre analysis. In A. Boulton, S. Carter-Thomas and E. Rowley-Jolivet (eds.), *Corpus-Informed Research and Learning in ESP: Issues and Applications.* 193–214. Amsterdam: John Benjamins.

Dudley-Evans, T. and St John, M. J. (1998) *Developments in English for Specific Purposes: A Multi-Disciplinary Approach.* Cambridge: Cambridge University Press.

Gao, Y., Li, L., and Lü, J. (2001) Trends in research methods in applied linguistics: China and the West. *English for Specific Purposes* 20: 1–14.

Gee, J. (1990) *Social Linguistics and Literacies: Ideology in Discourses.* London: Falmer Press.

Geertz, C. (1973) *Local Knowledge: Further Essays in Interpretive Anthropology.* New York: Basic Books.

Geisler, C. (1994) *Academic Literacy and the Nature of Expertise: Reading, Writing, and Knowing in Academic Philosophy.* Hillsdale, NJ: Lawrence Erlbaum.

Haas, C. (1994) Learning to read biology: One student's rhetorical development in college. *Written Communication* 11: 43–84.

Harklau, L. (2005) Ethnography and ethnographic research on second language teaching and learning. In E. Hinkel (ed.), *Handbook of Research in Second Language Teaching and Learning.* 179–94. Mahwah, NJ: Lawrence Erlbaum.

Harklau, L. (2011) Approaches and methods in recent qualitative research. In E. Hinkel (ed.), *Handbook of Research in Second Language Teaching and Learning, Vol. 2.* 175–89. London: Routledge.

Herrington, A. (1981) Writing to learn: Writing across the disciplines. *College English* 43: 379–87.

Hewings, M. (2002a) Editorial. *English for Specific Purposes* 21: v–vi.

Hewings, M. (2002b) A history of ESP through English for Specific Purposes. *English for Specific Purposes World.* Accessed Feb. 22, 2011 at http://www.esp-world.info/Articles_3/Hewings_paper.htm.

Hyland, K. (2002) Specificity revisited: How far should we go now? *English for Specific Purposes* 21: 385–95.

Hyland, K. (2003) Genre-based pedagogies: A social response to process. *Journal of Second Language Writing* 12: 17–29.

Hyland, K. (2009) *Teaching and Researching Writing.* 2nd ed. London: Longman.

Ivanič, R. (1998) *Writing and Identity: The Discoursal Construction of Identity in Academic Writing.* Amsterdam: John Benjamins.

Johns, A. and Makalela, L. (2011) Needs analysis, critical ethnography, and context: Perspectives from the client and the consultant. In D. Belcher, A. M. Johns, and B. Paltridge (eds.), *New Directions in English for Specific Purposes Research.* 197–221. Ann Arbor, MI: The University of Michigan Press.

Lazaraton, A. (1995) Qualitative research in applied linguistics: A progress report. *TESOL Quarterly* 29: 455–72.

Lillis, T. (2008) Ethnography as method, methodology, and "deep theorizing": Closing the gap between text and context in academic writing research. *Written Communication* 25: 353–88.

Lillis, T. and Curry, M. J. (2006) Professional academic writing by multilingual scholars: Interactions with literacy brokers in the production of English-medium texts. *Written Communication* 23: 3–35.

Lillis, T. and Curry, M. J. (2010). *Academic Writing in a Global Context: The Politics and Practices of Publishing in English.* London: Routledge.

Linell, P. (1998) Discourse across boundaries: On recontextualizations and the blending of voices in professional discourse. *Text* 18: 143–57.

Maybin, J. (2006) *Children's Voices. Talk, Knowledge and Identity.* Basingstoke, UK: Palgrave Macmillan.

Madison, D. S. (2005) *Critical Ethnography: Method, Ethics, and Performance.* Thousand Oaks, CA: Sage.

Myers, G. (1990) *Writing Biology: Texts in the Construction of Scientific Knowledge.* Madison, WI: University of Wisconsin Press.

Norton B. (1995) The theory of methodology in qualitative research. *TESOL Quarterly* 29: 569–76.

Ochs, E. (1992) Indexing gender. In A. Duranti and C. Goodwin (eds.), *Rethinking Context: Language as an Interactive Phenomenon.* 335–58. Cambridge: Cambridge University Press.

Paltridge, B. (2004) The exegesis as a genre: An ethnographic examination. In L. Ravelli and R. Ellis (eds.), *Analyzing Academic Writing: Contextualised Frameworks.* 84–103. London: Continuum.

Paltridge, B. (2008) Textographies and the researching and teaching of writing. *Iberica* 15: 9–23. Accessed Feb. 3, 2012 at www.aelfe.org/documents/02_15_Paltridge.pdf.

Paltridge, B., Starfield, S., Ravelli, L., Nicholsen, S., and Tuckwell, K. (2011) Doctoral writing in the visual and performing arts: Two ends of a continuum. *Studies in Higher Education.* DOI: 10.1080/03075079.2011.562285.

Pang, T. (2002) Textual analysis and contextual awareness building: A comparison of two approaches to teaching genre. 145–61. In A. M. Johns (ed.), *Genre in the Classroom: Multiple Perspectives.* Mahwah, NJ: Lawrence Erlbaum.

Prior, P. (1998) *Writing/Disciplinarity: A Sociohistoric Account of Literate Activity in the Academy.* Mahwah, NJ: Lawrence Erlbaum.

Ramani, E., Chacko, T., Singh, S. J., and Glendinning, E. (1988) An ethnographic approach to syllabus design: A case study of the Indian Institute of Science, Bangalore. *English for Specific Purposes* 7: 81–90.

Sarangi, S. (2006) The conditions and consequences of professional discourse studies. In R. Kiely, P. Rea-Dickins, H. Woodfield, and G. Clibbon (eds.), *Language, Culture and Identity in Applied Linguistics.* 199–220. London: Equinox.

Sarangi, S. (2007) The anatomy of interpretation: Coming to terms with the analyst's paradox in professional discourse studies [Editorial]. *Text* 27: 567–84.

Scollon, R. and Scollon, S. W. (2001) *Intercultural Communication: A Discourse Approach.* Oxford: Blackwell.

Starfield, S. (2010) Ethnographies. In B. Paltridge and A. Phakiti (eds.), *Continuum Companion to Research Methods in Applied Linguistics.* 50-65. London: Continuum.

Starfield, S. (2011) Doing critical ethnographic research into academic writing: The theory of methodology. In D. Belcher, A. M. Johns, and B. Paltridge (eds.), *New Directions in English for Specific Purposes Research.* 174–96. Ann Arbor, MI: The University of Michigan Press.

Starfield, S. (2012) Researcher reflexivity. In C. Chapelle (ed.), *The Encyclopedia of Applied Linguistics.* Oxford: Wiley-Blackwell.

Street, B. (1997) The implications of the "New Literacy Studies" for literacy education. *English in Education* 31(3): 45–59.

Swales, J. M. (1985) *ESP:* The heart of the matter or the end of the affair? In R. Quirk and H. G. Widdowson (eds.), *English in the World.* 212–23. Cambridge: Cambridge University Press.

Swales, J. M. (1998) *Other Floors, Other Voices: A Textography of a Small University Building.* Mahwah, NJ: Lawrence Erlbaum.

Tardy, C. (2006) Researching first and second language genre learning: A comparative review and a look ahead. *Journal of Second Language Writing* 15: 79–101.

Watson-Gegeo, K. (1988) Ethnography in ESL: Defining the essentials. *TESOL Quarterly* 22: 575–92.

27 Multimodality and ESP Research

PAUL PRIOR

Introduction

English for Specific Purposes (ESP) research and pedagogy developed initially against conceptualizations of a general English language competence, a single language system target that could be described by some grammar (not yet determined) linked to a lexicon and articulated through a phonological and orthographic system, a competence that generally appeared to be mode-free. Along with contemporary moves in ethnomethodology (e.g. Cicourel 1973; Garfinkel 1967) and the ethnography of communication/sociolinguistics (e.g. Gumperz 1982; Hymes 1974), ESP emerged as a counter to the dominant vision of general language competence, articulating a notion of language as more heterogeneous, dialogic, and situated, as a mosaic of registers and genres organized around specific domains of social practice – disciplines, professions, workplaces, recreation, home, and community/public life. The shift from idealized speakers of unified national languages to more situated, practice-oriented notions of discourse might have made mode and multimodality a central concern of ESP. Looking at situated practices and socialization into such practices (see Duff 2010, for a review of research on academic discourse socialization) could draw attention not only to the different patterns of use in specific modes (e.g. differences between oral and written language use), but also to the way multiple modes are simultaneously involved in situated acts (and chains of acts) of representation and communication. Written texts are always visual as well as linguistic, even without images; consider, for example, the effect of writing the beginning of this sentence in bold, capital, italic letters: ***WRITTEN TEXTS ARE ALWAYS VISUAL AS WELL AS LINGUISTIC.***

The Handbook of English for Specific Purposes, First Edition.
Edited by Brian Paltridge and Sue Starfield.
© 2013 John Wiley & Sons, Inc. Published 2013 by John Wiley & Sons, Inc.

Face-to-face communication blends talk, gesture, proxemics, and situated use of artifacts and tools, including use of literate and visual materials (e.g. situated production and reception of words and graphs on a chalk or white board in classes and workplaces; joint reading of directions for games, medical tests, or use of tools). Communicative practice in all domains involves chains of acts, representations and people across spaces and over time. The accelerating shift in recent years from studies of single, monomodal genres to studies of multimodal genre systems or chains has been a response to this recognition (see Bazerman 2004; Molle and Prior 2008; Swales 2004). In short, the lived experience of situated activity – and all activity must be situated – is (and always has been) multisemiotic.

Nevertheless, multimodality seems to have remained a somewhat peripheral area of ESP research as traditional language theories have continued to shape questions and methods. As Belcher (2006: 149) noted in her overview of ESP (published in a special 40th anniversary issue of *TESOL Quarterly*), "Although there have been numerous studies of academic and professional genres, the ESP gaze has been focussed more often on written than spoken genres and on products rather than processes." And as I have argued (Prior 1998), notions of speech and discourse communities that have been at the center of ESP theory have typically sought the same kind of system of rules governing language performance that traditional linguists envisioned for national languages, although for smaller circles (a discipline, a profession, a classroom or workplace) and perhaps with a sometimes wider range of phenomena (rules of use as well as of form). In my read of core journals in the field, *English for Academic Purposes* and *English for Specific Purposes*, the dominant research questions continue to be questions of language forms in monomodal frames (e.g. use of metadiscourse in a particular written genre; pronouns in conference presentations). Mode in such studies is simply a transparent and trivial container of language. Occasionally, there is a limited cross-modal comparison of language features (e.g. comparison of metadiscourse in medical talk and text). Methodologically, such studies involve analysis of texts, textual transcripts of talk, or corpora as opposed to a fuller, situated study of sociocultural activity.

This chapter does not aim to offer a comprehensive review of all relevant work in ESP, but instead to consider some of the ways that questions of multimodality have been broached and framed as well as ways multimodality might be understood as a central, critical dimension of ESP research. Of course, the question of how *mode* and *multimodality* fits into ESP research depends on what we mean by this term, and its meanings have been neither stable nor fixed. I will first consider three ways that multimodality has been explored in ESP and related fields and consider some studies that illustrate these approaches. In order to sketch what a full engagement with multimodal and semiotic practices might mean for ESP research, I will then turn to two particular cases, considering the place of embodied activity in specialized domains and illustrative work on one academic field (biology). I will close with a call for research frameworks that take up the semiotic, multimodal, character of situated sociocultural practices more widely and seriously than is typical in ESP research.

Speaking and Listening, Reading and Writing: The Four-Mode Scheme

One fairly conventional notion of mode that has been present in ESP for decades is the simple scheme of four linguistic modes (sometimes referred to as skills): reading, writing, speaking, and listening. This scheme structures the first section of this *Handbook* (ESP and Language Skills), with chapters devoted to each of the four modes plus one for vocabulary. Mode in this scheme is defined as a way of using language, with the basic modal binary of orality and literacy further subdivided into productive and receptive uses. In these terms, multimodality might then refer to the way these four modes of language work together and are used in a specific domain. ESP needs analyses have pretty routinely asked how language needs and uses in specific domains are distributed across the four-mode scheme.

The four-mode scheme and elaborations on it (e.g. attention to particular kinds of reading or writing, speaking or listening) have been a staple of ESP needs analysis since its formation, particularly in studies that use questionnaires to identify situation- and role-specific communicative needs in particular domains. Johns (1981), for example, developed a questionnaire for academic English needs, in which faculty were asked to rate the importance of the four language skills (reading, writing, speaking and listening) as well as of specific forms of each (e.g. reading textbooks, examination questions or journals in the field; writing reports, essay answers, or critiques; talking in class or for oral reports). Studying the language needs of textile and clothing merchandisers in a Hong Kong firm that traded internationally, So-Mui and Mead (2000) offered another kind of elaboration of the scheme as they probed the typical and preferred *channels* of oral and written communication (telephone, face-to-face, fax, email, letters, telex, standard forms). Kassim and Ali (2010) report on an English needs analysis for engineers in Malaysia. Using questionnaires, they asked about uses of oral language with different categories of people (e.g. clients, local colleagues, international colleagues, subcontractors or suppliers) and probed various dimensions of oral language use including purpose (e.g. conflict resolution, instructions, social conversation), theme (e.g. work vs. social), format (e.g. presentation vs. conversation), and again certain technologically-mediated channels (i.e. with questions on teleconferencing and telephone, but face-to-face otherwise implied). In a study that blended questionnaires, interviews, and observation to present a language analysis for French mountain guides, Wozniak (2010) discusses mode in terms of language skills (reading specialized documents, engaging in general conversations, engaging in professional conversations, writing) and of dimensions of the participant structure (whether conversations are with native or nonnative speakers).

At a basic level, this four-mode scheme is grounded in a non-trivial interest in mode as it envisions communicative competence and practice in specific sociocultural domains as distributed across a finely differentiated modal profile. However, this four-mode scheme is largely taken for granted theoretically and typically not associated with the idea of multimodality. Thus, current interest in multimodality has not grown out of attention to these four modes of language use, but rather from a new school, which I will call *multimodality studies*, that emerged in the 1990s and has rapidly gained attention in multiple disciplinary and educational settings.

Multimodality Studies and ESP in a Digital Age

Multimodality studies is particularly associated with the work of Gunther Kress and Theo Van Leeuwen (e.g. 1996, 2001) and their colleagues, and tends to be grounded in systemic-functional linguistics (Halliday 1978). Broadly, Kress (2003) has argued that new digital technologies of information and communication (of production, storage, distribution) have radically altered the semiotic landscape, moving the world from a long, stable period of print literacy – itself spurred by another technological innovation, the printing press, that overturned a longer history of chirographic (handwriting) literacy. In Kress's account, the emerging digital age is defined by a shift from the practices and values of written prose to those of the highly visual representations found in digitally-driven new media technologies (digital film, computer animation, digital photography, computer-aided graphs, diagrams, and illustrations, much now on the Web or at least designed with web distribution in mind). Kress (2003, 2005) has argued that print linguistic text and visual image have distinctly, even radically, different patterns of semiotic affordances for conveying meaning. I have argued (Prior 2005) that Kress's focus on artifacts rather than practices, representation of modal affordances as mutually exclusive binaries, and sharply defined periodization of semiotic history is quite problematic. However, there is no doubt that multimodality studies has had a wide influence and has done much to focus attention on semiotics.

Kress and Van Leeuwen (2001) argue persuasively for the value of identifying general semiotic operations, like chunking of information, that are realized in varied ways across modes (and often through the simultaneous deployment of multiple modes) rather than relying on single-mode accounts (e.g. of paragraphing in writing, of turns at talk, of visual framing for images). They define modes as "semiotic resources" that "can be realized in more than one production medium" (Kress and Van Leeuwen 2001: 21–22). Key to their definition is socioculturally organized attention to, and conventionalization of, some semiotic resource and the resulting practical abstraction from its material medium. Language, they say, is a mode because it can be realized in speech or writing. Speech is a mode because it can be in the air or on paper. It is important to recognize that their definition of mode is quite different from the everyday notion expressed in the four modes (speaking, listening, writing, reading). For example, among the modes they identify are voice, gesture, narrative, color, furniture, and plastic. Thinking about digital screens and increasingly visual print, Kress and Van Leeuwen (2001) emphasized that texts routinely (necessarily) achieve meaning through the orchestration of multiple simultaneous modes. A screen might combine voiceover, music, video, and linguistic text; the linguistic text may even be animated with motion and sound. A print magazine article might use words, images, color, and furniture as modes to convey its social meanings. A face-to-face conversation involves talk, gesture, proxemics, and other channels (olfactory, touch) to achieve its sense.

Taking up multimodality studies in ESP, Royce (2002: 192) argued:

> If making sense of (and constructing) texts requires the ability to understand the combined potential of various modes for making meaning, TESOL professionals need to be able to talk and think seriously about multimodal communication because they need to help learners develop *multimodal communicative competence.*

Taking science textbooks as an example, Royce analyzes the mix of verbal (written) and visual modes, emphasizing the different kinds of intersemiotic relations that contribute complementarily to the meaning potential of the material. Although only one chapter in her book explicitly highlights connections to English for specific purposes (ESP)/English for academic purposes (EAP), O'Halloran's (2004a) collection offers chapters that take up a multimodality studies approach to specific sites of cultural practice, including exemplary analyses of the architectural design of the Sydney Opera House (O'Toole 2004), of a museum exhibition in Singapore (Pang 2004), of feature films (O'Halloran 2004b), and of print (Yeun 2004) and TV (Baldry 2004) advertisements. Guo (2004) makes connections to ESP/EAP explicit in a chapter analyzing the designed, functional character of the visual-linguistic relations in two figures of a biology textbook. Summing up the implications of this kind of analysis, Guo (2004: 215) suggests:

> we ESP/EAP teachers and researchers need to take seriously the multimodal nature of meaning-making in academic apprenticeship and professional life and refocus our research and teaching agenda to better prepare our students for their current and future academic and professional life.

A striking feature of O'Halloran's collection, and of multimodality studies in general, is the almost exclusive focus on texts and other semiotic objects. Multimodality studies rarely involve close attention to how people make, distribute, or use multimodal texts and objects.

Given the strong focus on the revolutionary character of technological changes, it is not surprising that for some researchers the term multimodality simply seems to signify digital media and texts, to name the ways new affordances of digital technologies and screens lead to noisy new deployments of multiple modes (linguistic text, visuals, and sound) that replace the staid simplicity of a monomodal print past. For example, Nickerson and Planken (2009), relying heavily on Kress's work, frame their discussion of multimodality in English for specific business purposes almost entirely around digital media – blogs, home pages, press releases, and websites, posted on the Web. In keeping with work in multimodality studies, these digital sites are represented entirely as an issue of the structuring of texts (screens mostly, but perhaps paper), not as a question of composing and using such texts in activity. Shipka (2011) has critiqued the ways that many literacy researchers seem to conflate multimodality with digitality, either explicitly or implicitly (e.g. all examples of multimodality turning out to be electronic), and she offers alternative theoretical and pedagogical grounds for understanding rhetorically agile activity in all kinds of semiotic objects, focussing especially on practices of multimodal re-mediation and re-purposing.

In short, multimodality studies has focussed sharp attention on new media and the digital revolution, has especially emphasized the role of the visual in the current communicative economy, and has recognized that multiple modes operate together in any particular semiotic object. For multimodality studies, in the age of digital media, the *design* of semiotic objects has become the key issue. However, another hallmark of multimodality studies to date has been its narrow focus on semiotic objects (a fact that seems more a matter of methodological habit than a theoretical imperative). Although multimodality studies has argued for attention to practice, analyses have focussed attention almost exclusively on texts, screens, and semiotic objects. Where practices are mentioned, they are almost always inferred from, or imagined off, the pages, screens, and three-dimensional objects under analysis as opposed to being described through observational and ethnographic attention to the dynamics of situated semiotic activity.

Multimodality as Semiotic Practice: Situated and Ethnographic Research

As studies of language in specific domains emerged across fields (i.e. not only in ESP), attention turned to situations of use as well as domains of language and often to embodied semiotic practices as well as semiotic artifacts. This kind of practice orientation appears, for example, in mediated discourse analysis (e.g. Scollon 2001, 2008; Norris 2004; Norris and Jones 2005), in ethnomethodological studies of workplaces (e.g. Heath and Luff 2000), and broadly in situated and ethnographic approaches to communicative practices (e.g. Agha 2007; Duranti and Goodwin 1992; Silverstein and Urban 1996). Increasingly, studies that look at face-to-face interaction look beyond oral language, attending also to gesture and other nonverbals, situated use of tools, and the indexical coupling of discourse with environments (see e.g. Goodwin 2007; Streeck 2009). Since the 1990s, studies of academic enculturation (see e.g. Belcher 1994; Casanave 1995, 2002; Prior 1998) have taken up a more longitudinal perspective that highlights multiple sites of activity and multiple genres (foregrounded and backgrounded, in talk and text). Reflecting on these developments, Swales (2000) pushed LSP to engage in both deeper and more extensive ways with the complexity of practices in specialized cultural domains. Swales' (2000) review of work in Language for specific purposes (LSP) focussed attention on the shift in attention from single genres to genre systems (Bazerman 1994), sets, or repertoires (with examples of chains that moved from talk to text, text to talk, or that prominently combined both text and talk, as in scripted oral presentations with use of visuals); to consider more carefully issues of mode (channel) of communication – glossed in business contexts as "letter, phone, fax, email, etc." (Bazerman 1994: 66) – and to recognize the growing prevalence of settings that are multimedia and multilingual.

In fact, an ethnographic orientation to specialized discourse practices and their multimodal character has been a part of ESP research from its formation. Dubois (1980: 49), in the first issue of *The ESP Journal*, reported on the integration of slides in biomedical conference papers. Her analysis not only focussed on the integration of visual and verbal information in the slides, but also paid attention to the situated practices of speakers, with observations such as the following:

> Speakers present their introductions and summaries/conclusions standing at the lectern, facing toward the audience; almost all use written aids prepared in advance. Some refer to notes, while others actually read prepared text. At the margins of the speech, certain speakers call attention to the general content of the slide:
> > ... and if we could have the first slide, this is the key illustration from that paper. Now, on the vertical axis, you have cardiac index, and in the horizontal axis, you have the saturation in the pulmonary artery. (3781)
> without necessarily repeating everything it contains.

Situated attention to conference presentations has been a particularly productive arena for considering the multimodal character of semiotic practices. Shalom (1993) analyzed the way written text, visuals, and varied kinds of presentational and interactive talk were displayed in different kinds of conference events (plenary lecture, roundtable, poster) at an ecology conference. Räisänen (1998) analyzed interlinked systems of genres around conference presentations in automotive safety engineering and described such conference presentations as multisemiotic genre performances, noting the mix of slides (often containing images of graphs and mathematics) with talk that often displayed multiple registers and, frequently, edited video (e.g. replayed in slow motion). Based on filmed data of conference sessions in geology, medicine, and physics, Rowley-Jolivet (2002) analyzed the use of visuals, attending to how written language, graphical, numerical, and figurative visuals were projected, including whether in color or black-and-white, the frequency and periodicity of visual projections per paper, and the various ways that spatial organization was used to convey semantic relations (e.g. given–new, cause–effect, general–particular).

Academic courses and disciplinary research sites are like conference presentations in that they routinely blend talk, text, visuals, and other semiotics. Ochs, Jacoby, and Gonzales (1994) examined how physicists linguistically and gesturally animated graphic whiteboard representations of experimental results in the meetings of a physics research group. In undertaking an ethnographic needs analysis for academic writing in several disciplines (architecture, civil engineering, and music), Molle and Prior (2008: 544) found that texts and genre systems were multimodal, "that multiple modes or media co-existed not only at every level of the texts (from sections to phrases) but also throughout the writing process." Roth

(2009) closely traces the thinking-in-action of a physics professor presenting a lecture in a university course on thermodynamics; he analyzes the unfolding communicative and epistemic work of gesture, graphic drawing, proxemics, gaze, written and oral language, and mathematical representations (oral and written).

Ethnographically informed studies have also considered how multimodal practices are related to discourse enculturation. Johns (1998) described an undergraduate student's work in an economics class. In considering interactions between visual and verbal representations, Johns went beyond the products in the class (student or instructional) and considered how the student's visual note taking (focussed on graphs and diagrams) shaped her test-taking and paper-writing processes, and her learning of economics. Examining field reports, conference papers, and eventually published articles and drawing on interview data, Dressen-Hammouda (Dressen 2002; Dressen-Hammouda 2008) suggests that a doctoral student in geology was learning to manage complex semiotic frameworks grounded in field experience through certain textual practices (silence as well as explicit and disguised representations of research activity in the field) as he developed increasing mastery of specialized lexical and thematic markers of the discipline. Medway (2002) explored the multiple semiotics (drawing, mathematics, words) of architectural students' sketchbooks (which were common but not required), considering the diverse material found in these books as a fuzzy genre important to professional enculturation. Tardy (2009) examined how several graduate students in different disciplines engaged in multimodal genre networks as they learned the staged and blended semiotic practices of presenting slides for presentations in classrooms, research groups, conferences, and other settings. She also highlighted the use of multiple semiotics (numerical, graphic, and linguistic) in students' course papers. Paltridge (2004) analyzed the way art and design master's projects blend a visual-material art project (paintings, digital and material objects, installations, events) with a textual exegesis that contextualized the art. Such multisemiotic blends of discourse and material can be found in many social practices. Roozen (2009) articulates the way visual and generic materials may be linked in chains of practice across sites and over time. His analysis documents how a student repurposed her extensive fan art and fiction engagements across multiple school and non-school activities over years. He focusses in particular on how, as she studied for a graduate MA examination in English, she produced in her notebook a *Spy vs. Spy* comic (a visual-textual blend she used in her fan fiction/art) to aid her understanding of Kenneth Burke's (1969) pentad, particularly his notions of agents, acts, agency, and scenes. Like the common distinction in writing across the curriculum between learning to write and writing to learn, these studies point to students learning to make visual representations but also (e.g. in Roozen's, Medway's, and Johns' studies) of students drawing to learn.

Situated and ethnographic research on professional settings also points to multimodal chains of activity. For example, in a study of land surveyors in Hong Kong, which drew on observational protocols and participant logs of communication, Cheng and Mok (2008) mapped out complex multilingual as well as multimodal chains of genres and communicative events in this workplace. To consider further how ethnographic studies of discourse practices, whether conducted in direct service of ESP/EAP or not, have informed and may continue to inform ESP, I will turn next to considering how close attention to embodied activity in the world reshapes understanding of situated cultural practices and then take up one particular cultural domain, that of biological sciences, to consider how multiple situated studies of a cultural domain of practice begin to sketch our a different notion of needs.

Embodied Activity-in-the-World: Reimagining Situated Needs and Socialization

Working from an artifact-centered approach, Dressen-Hammouda's (Dressen 2002; Dressen-Hammouda 2008) analyses (discussed in the last section of this chapter) did not offer insight into specifically *how* the geology student developed semiotic practices in the course of multiple years of disciplinary enculturation. In contrast, Goodwin (1994, 2007) examines another site of field enculturation and activity as he traces the *professional vision* of archeologists in the field. Goodwin (2007: 205) argues for the critical role of *environmentally coupled gestures* in realizing the joint work of seeing "relevant structure in the complex visual field provided by the emerging soil of an excavation" and highlights the way that enculturation and the work itself involves "the mutual interplay of multiple semiotic fields, including the moving hand, the dirt which the hand is articulating, the accompanying talk, the participation framework constituted through the positions of the participants' bodies, local sequential organization, the larger activity that these actions are embedded within" (Goodwin 2007: 210). In short, archeological practice, as Goodwin describes it, is done and learned through moment-to-moment embodied activity tightly coupled to objects, environments, and other people in the world.

Following the work of an interdisciplinary and multinational team researching soil processes at the edge of the Amazonian rain forest, Latour (1999) also notes the way the environment was marked and labeled, selectively sampled and ordered, tested and described through varied semiotic means. His analysis begins to connect the dots among such environmentally-coupled semiotic processes as laying stakes in the rainforest, spitting on dirt and rolling it in the hands to determine its composition, comparing dirt samples to the Munsell color chart to identify their color, making a cross-sectional map of the soil strata, and writing up – based on the data collected in the field and brought back to a laboratory in France – a research report for journal publication.

Drawing on the dialogic notion of *semiotic remediation* (the way situated activity routinely involves semiotic performances that are re-represented and re-used across chains of activity (see Prior and Hengst 2010; Prior et al. 2006), Prior (2010) analyzes the situated practices of a university Art and Design group (mainly two professors and two non-native English speakers (NNES) graduate research assistants) as they worked to re-make an online, interactive art object called *IO*. The analysis traces how, across multiple meetings over 11 months, they chained together acts of writing, drawing, talking, computer programming, electronic databasing (of image and text), and gesturing (in the air, over paper, whiteboards, and screens). Haviland (2007) analyzed the semiotic *transpositions* in a master's class for a string quartet as instructors moved from miming the playing of instruments (sometimes in the air, sometimes bowing on fingers) to playing their own instruments or bowing on the student's instrument as the student fingered the notes; in this setting, the music instructors evoked the score through gestures, vocal song, humming, and other sounds as they characterized the score verbally and metaphorically. Using elicited visual representations of writing along with in-depth interviews, Prior and Shipka (2003) consider the embodied and materially-, spatially-, and temporally-organized character of literate composing, highlighting the way undergraduate students, graduate students, and professors displayed varied ESSPs (environment-selecting and -structuring practices) aimed at supporting the participants intellectual engagements and composing processes. Johnson-Eiola (2005) likewise examined how the organization of spaces, tools, and repeated remediations of sound were used by an advanced graduate student in music as he engaged in digital composing.

Workplace studies display similarly embodied and environmentally coupled practices. Fraiberg's (2010) analyses of meetings and work at an Israeli high-tech company highlight complex multilingual as well as multimodal and technologically mediated practices as participants planned product development and business strategies. Whether in information (and control) centers (Heath and Luff 2000), auto repair shops (Streeck 2009), or hospital operating rooms (Zemel et al. 2008), close studies of situated and embodied activity repeatedly point to the relevance of embodied activity to specialized domains of activity and their associated communicative practices. Studies of environmentally coupled and discursively animated embodied action point to the specialized ways that bodies act and interact in what have been widely conceptualized in ESP simply as special-purpose domains of language.

The Case of Biology: Academic Needs as Embodied, Multimodal Genre Systems

Among academic fields that EAP is interested in, biology happens to be one that has been studied in particularly intense ways that illustrate the range of semiotic resources that might be taken up in ESP research. Studies of representational practice have highlighted the way biology texts are routinely multimedia genres (Lemke 1998). Dubois's (1980) study of slides at biology conferences (mentioned earlier) made that point, as did Rowley-Jolivet's (2002) analyses of medical presentations two decades later. In a longitudinal case study of the writing of several established biologists across popular and technical genres, Myers (1990) compared the very different kinds and functions of graphs and visual images (annotated and captioned) in popular science articles from those in the original technical articles. By grounding analysis of textual differences between narratives of nature (in popular texts) and narratives of science (in technical papers) in extended, ethnographic case studies, Myers was also able to make visible some of the distributed authorship of the popular texts. He found, for example, that magazine editors extensively rewrote and re-imaged the scientists' texts. In their ethnographic account of a laboratory studying neurologically active chemicals at the Salk Institute, Latour and Woolgar (1986) described the cascades of inscriptions that were also tied to material transformations. The cascades typically involved transformations of graphic and numerical data from raw formats to summarized versions in articles. At the same time, the laboratory also was engaged in transforming the brains of animals into isolated chemical substances that could be experimentally tested, another kind of semiotic and material transformation.

Where multimodality studies have so far been focussed on interpretive accounts of how images on page, screen or other surface might structure the meanings that idealized readers take from them, research on visual practices in biological laboratories has focussed on environmentally coupled gestures and talk, as scientists engage in the work of interpreting visual data and visualizing conceptual understanding. In a molecular genetics lab, Amman and Knorr-Cetina (1990) documented the practices of inspecting autoradiograph films (x-ray films of radioactively marked DNA and RNA strands). They noted the way scientists jointly held the films up to the light, constructing their professional seeing of the films through talk. Amman and Knorr-Cetina were particularly struck that, unlike in conversational analyses of everyday talk that routinely find a strong preference for agreement, the scientists' talk displayed a strong preference for disagreement. Alač and Hutchins (2004) and Alač (2005) offer very close analysis of the embodied and coordinated talk, gesture, drawing, and writing of neuroscientists as they read, and learn to read, fMRI images of brain regions from computer screens. Becvar, Hollan, and Hutchins (2005) trace the way a biology professor and research assistants in a biochemistry laboratory aligned visual and verbal representations with a stabilized representational gesture as they worked to represent the theoretical spatiotemporal dynamics of a protein moving to bind with another protein. In combination, these studies of laboratory research and practice in biology, of popular and technical genres, and of apprentice-like enculturation processes make it clear that multimodality is about more than multiple modes inscribed in conference slides, textbooks, and journal articles, that it is also about deeply embodied multiple modalities of engagement in the world.

Conclusion

In one fashion or another, ESP research has long evidenced an interest in the multimodal character of specialized communication. However, interest in modality, along with other dimensions of practice, has been attenuated by the very strong focus in ESP research on language features of texts (even if the texts are transcripts of talk). A growing body of ESP research on the multimodal character of situated practices – along with clear theoretical and methodological developments in related fields studying cognition, action, communication, and learning in varied sociocultural settings – suggest that ESP will need to embrace theory and research that traces embodied semiotic activity as well as that analyzes multimodal semiotic objects. However, attention to semiotic practice should not be seen as simply another technical element in the ESP toolkit. In calling for a critical ethnographic practice in ESP (see also Benesch 2001), Starfield (2011) noted the power of historically situated visual and material artifacts and actions in making the social worlds of writing and academic work. Following first-year sociology students at a South African University after the end of apartheid, she found that race was read by instructors from handwriting styles of anonymous papers (made so as to elide racial prejudices) as well as by skin color in embodied interactions of schooling. The materiality of writing technologies and the materiality of violent clashes with police alike signified the social order of the campus. A clearer focus on semiotic practices then should not be limited to close analysis of focally situated activity, but rather should aim to weave a textured portrait of social and communicative orders that is both deep and broad, that is as sensitive to the microphysics of power as to the indexical character of disciplinary, workplace or community knowledge. Within that framework, ESP accounts of communicative needs will truly be able to go beyond questions of different language forms in talk and writing or the use of visual diagrams and numerical data in certain canonical genres in order to trace the multiple, material semiotics of embodied, situated, and chained social practices.

REFERENCES

Agha, A. (2007) *Language and Social Relations*. Cambridge: Cambridge University Press.

Alač, M. (2005) From trash to treasure: Learning about brain images through multimodality. *Semiotica* 156: 177–202.

Alač, M. and Hutchins, E. (2004) I see what you are saying: Action as cognition in fMRI brain mapping practice. *Journal of Cognition and Culture* 4: 629–61.

Amman, K. and Knorr-Cetina, K. (1990) The fixation of (visual) evidence. In M. Lynch and S. Woolgar (eds.), *Representation in Scientific Practice.* 85–122. Cambridge, MA: MIT Press.

Baldry, A. (2004) Phase and transition, type and instance: Patterns in media texts as seen through a multimodal concordancer. In K. O'Halloran (ed.), *Multimodal Discourse Analysis: Systemic Functional Perspectives.* 83–108. London and New York: Continuum.

Bazerman, C. (1994) Systems of genres and the enactment of social intentions. In A. Freedman and P. Medway (eds.), *Genre and the New Rhetoric.* 83–96. London: Taylor & Francis.

Bazerman, C. (2004) Speech acts, genres, and activity systems: How texts organize activity and people. In C. Bazerman and P. Prior (eds.), *What Writing Does and How It Does It: An Introduction to Analyzing Texts and Textual Practices.*

79–101. Mahwah, NJ: Lawrence
Erlbaum.

Becvar, L., Hollan, A. J., and Hutchins, E.
(2005) Hands as molecules:
Representational gestures used for
developing theory in a scientific
laboratory. *Semiotica* 156: 89–112.

Belcher, D. (1994) The apprenticeship
approach to advanced academic literacy:
Graduate students and their mentors.
English for SpecificPurposes 13: 23–34.

Belcher, D. (2006) English for specific
purposes: Teaching to perceived and
imagined futures in worlds of work,
study, and everyday life. *TESOL
Quarterly* 40: 133–56.

Benesch, S. (2001) *Critical English for
Academic Purposes: Theory, Politics, and
Practice*. Mahwah, NJ: Lawrence
Erlbaum.

Burke, K. (1969) *A Grammar of Motives*.
Berkeley, CA: University of California
Press.

Casanave, C. (1995) Local interactions:
Constructing contexts for composing in
a graduate sociology program. In D.
Belcher and G. Braine (eds.), *Academic
Writing in a Second Language: Essays on
Research and Pedagogy*. 83–110. Norwood,
NJ: Ablex.

Casanave, C. (2002) *Writing Games:
Multicultural case Studies of Academic
Literacy Practices in Higher Education*.
Mahwah, NJ: Lawrence Erlbaum.

Cheng, W. and Mok, E. (2008) Discourse
processes and products: Land surveyors
in Hong Kong. *English for Specific
Purposes* 27: 57–73.

Cicourel, A. (1973) *Cognitive Sociology:
Language and Meaning in Social
Interaction*. Harmondsworth, UK:
Penguin.

Dressen, D. (2002) Identifying textual
silence in scientific research articles:
Recontextualizations of the field account
in Geology. *Hermes, Journal of Linguistics*
28: 81–108.

Dressen-Hammouda, D. (2008) From
novice to disciplinary expert:

Disciplinary identity and genre mastery.
English for Specific Purposes 27: 233–52.

Dubois, B. L. (1980) The use of slides in
biomedical speeches. *The ESP Journal* 1:
45–50.

Duff, P. (2010) Language socialization into
academic discourse communities.
Annual Review of Applied Linguistics 30:
169–92.

Duranti, A. and Goodwin, C. (eds.) (1992)
*Rethinking Context: Language as an
Interactive Phenomenon*. Cambridge:
Cambridge University Press.

Fraiberg, S. (2010) Composition 2.0:
Toward a multilingual and multimodal
framework. *College Composition and
Communication* 62: 100–26.

Garfinkel, H. (1967) *Studies in
Ethnomethodology*. Englewood Cliffs, NJ:
Prentice Hall.

Goodwin, C. (1994) Professional vision.
American Anthropologist 96: 606–33.

Goodwin, C. (2007) Environmentally
coupled gestures. In S. Duncan, J.
Cassell, and E. Levy (eds.), *Gesture and
the Dynamic Dimension of Language:
Essays in Honor of David McNeill*.
195–212. Amsterdam: John Benjamins.

Gumperz, J. (1982) *Discourse Strategies*.
Cambridge: Cambridge University Press.

Guo, L. (2004) Multimodality in a biology
textbook. In K. O'Halloran (ed.),
*Multimodal Discourse Analysis: Systemic
Functional Perspectives*. 196–219. London
and New York: Continuum.

Halliday, M. A. K. (1978) *Language as Social
Semiotic: The Social Interpretation of
Language and Meaning*. London: Edward
Arnold.

Haviland, J. (2007) Master speakers, master
gesturers: A string quartet master class.
In S. Duncan, J. Cassell, and E. Levy
(eds.), *Gesture and The Dynamic
Dimension of Language: Essays in Honor of
David McNeill*. 147–72. Amsterdam: John
Benjamins.

Heath, C. and Luff, P. (2000) *Technology in
Action*. Cambridge: Cambridge
University Press.

Hymes, D. (1974) *Foundations in Sociolinguistics: An Ethnographic Approach*. Philadelphia, PA: The University of Pennsylvania Press.

Johns, A. M. (1981) Necessary English: A faculty survey. *TESOL Quarterly* 15: 51–7.

Johns, A. M. (1998) The visual and the verbal: A case study in macroeconomics. *English for Specific Purposes* 17: 183–97.

Johnson-Eiola, J. (2005) *Datacloud: Toward a New Theory of Online Work*. Cresskill, NJ: Hampton Press.

Kassim, H, and Ali, F. (2010) English communicative events and skills needed at the workplace: Feedback from the industry. *English for Specific Purposes* 29: 168–82.

Kress, G. (2003) *Literacy in the New Media Age*. New York: Routledge.

Kress, G. (2005) Gains and losses: New forms of texts, knowledge, and learning. *Computers and Composition* 22: 5–22.

Kress, G. and Van Leeuwen, T. (1996) *Reading Images: The Grammar of Visual Design*. London: Routledge.

Kress, G. and Van Leeuwen, T. (2001) *Multimodal Discourse: The Modes and Media of Contemporary Communication*. London: Arnold.

Latour, B. (1999) *Pandora's Hope: Essays on the Reality of Science Studies*. Cambridge, MA: Harvard University Press.

Latour, B. and Woolgar, S. (1986) *Laboratory Life: The Social Construction of Scientific Facts*. Princeton, NJ: Princeton University Press.

Lemke, J. (1998) Multiplying meaning: Visual and verbal semiotics in scientific text. In J. Martin and R. Veel (eds.), *Reading Science: Critical and Functional Perspectives on Discourses of Science*. 87–113. London: Routledge.

Medway, P. (2002) Fuzzy genres and community identities: The case of architecture students' sketchbooks. In R. Coe, L. Lingard, and T. Teslenko (eds.), *The Rhetoric and Ideology of Genre*. 123–53. Cresskill, NJ: Hampton.

Molle, D. and Prior, P. (2008) Multimodal genre systems in EAP writing pedagogy: Reflecting on a needs analysis. *TESOL Quarterly* 42: 541–66.

Myers, G. (1990) *Writing Biology: Texts in the Social Construction of Scientific Knowledge*. Madison, WI: University of Wisconsin Press.

Nickerson, C. and Planken, B. (2009) English for specific business purposes: Written business English and the increasing influence of multimodality. In D. Belcher (ed.), *English for Specific Purposes in Theory and Practice*. 127–42. Ann Arbor, MI: University of Michigan Press.

Norris, S. (2004) *Analyzing Multimodal Interaction: A Methodological Framework*. New York: Routledge.

Norris, S. and Jones, R. (eds.) (2005) *Discourse in Action: Introducing Mediated Discourse Analysis*. New York: Routledge.

Ochs, E, Jacoby, S. and Gonzales, P. (1994) Interpretive journeys: How scientists talk and travel through graphic spaces. *Configurations* 2: 151–71.

O'Halloran, K. (ed.) (2004a) *Multimodal Discourse Analysis: Systemic Functional Perspectives*. London and New York: Continuum.

O'Halloran, K. (2004b) Visual semiosis in film. In K. O'Halloran (ed.), *Multimodal Discourse Analysis: Systemic Functional Perspectives*. 109–30. London and New York: Continuum.

O'Toole, M. (2004) *Opera Ludentes*: The Sydney Opera House at work and play. In K. O'Halloran (ed.), *Multimodal Discourse Analysis: Systemic Functional Perspectives*. 11–27. London and New York: Continuum.

Paltridge, B. (2004) The exegesis as a genre: An ethnographic examination. In L. Ravelli and R. Ellis (eds.), *Analysing Academic Writing: Contextualized Frameworks*. 84–103. London and New York: Continuum.

Pang, A. (2004) Making history in *From Colony to Nation*: A multimodal analysis of a museum exhibition in Singapore. In K. O'Halloran (ed.), *Multimodal Discourse Analysis: Systemic Functional Perspectives*. 28–54. London and New York: Continuum.

Prior, P. (1998) *Writing/Disciplinarity: A Sociohistoric Account of Literate Activity in the Academy*. Mahwah, NJ: Lawrence Erlbaum.

Prior, P. (2005) Moving multimodality beyond the binaries: A response to Gunther Kress's "Gains and losses." *Computers and Composition* 22: 23–30.

Prior, P. (2010) Remaking IO: Semiotic remediation in the design process. In P. Prior and J. Hengst (eds.), *Exploring Semiotic Remediation as Discourse Practice*. 206–234. Basingtoke, UK: Palgrave MacMillan.

Prior, P. and Hengst, J. (eds.) (2010) *Exploring Semiotic Remediation as Discourse Practice*. Basingtoke, UK: Palgrave MacMillan.

Prior, P., Julie Hengst, J., Kevin Roozen, K., and Shipka, J. (2006) "I'll be the Sun": From reported speech to semiotic remediation practices. *Text and Talk* 26: 733–66.

Prior, P. and Shipka, J. (2003) Chronotopic lamination: Tracing the contours of literate activity. In C. Bazerman and D. Russell (eds.), *Writing Selves, Writing Societies: Research from Activity Perspectives*. 180–238. Fort Collins, CO: WAC Clearinghouse and Mind, Culture, and Activity. Accessed May 20, 2011 at http://wac.colostate.edu/books/selves_societies/.

Räisänen, C. (1998) *The Conference Forum as a System of Genres: A Sociocultural Study of Academic Conference Practices in Automotive Crash-Safety Engineering*. Gothenburg Studies in English 76. Göteborg, Sweden: Acta Universitatis Gothoburgensis.

Roth, W. M. (2009) Realizing Vygotsky's program concerning language and thought: Tracking knowing (ideas, conceptions, beliefs) in real time. *Language and Education* 23: 295–311.

Roozen, K. (2009) "Fan fic-ing" English Studies: A case study exploring the interplay of vernacular literacies and disciplinary engagement. *Research in the Teaching of English* 44: 136–69.

Rowley-Jolivet, E. (2002) Visual discourse in scientific conference papers: A genre-based study. *English for Specific Purposes* 21: 19–40.

Royce, T. (2002) Multimodality in the TESOL classroom: Exploring visual-verbal synergy. *TESOL Quarterly* 36: 191–205.

Scollon, R. (2001) *Mediated Discourse: The Nexus of Practice*. New York: Routledge.

Scollon, R. (2008) Discourse itineraries: Nine processes of resemiotiziation. In V. Bhatia, J. Flowerdew, and R. Jones (eds.) *Advances in Discourse Studies*. 233–44. London: Routledge.

Shalom, C. (1993) Established and evolving spoken research process genres: Plenary lecture and poster session discussions at academic conferences. *English for Specific Purposes* 12: 37–50.

Shipka, J. (2011) *Toward a Composition Made Whole*. Pittsburgh, PA: University of Pittsburgh Press.

Silverstein, M. and Urban, G. (1996) (eds.), *Natural Histories of Discourse*. Chicago, IL: University of Chicago Press.

So-mui, F. L. and Mead, K. (2000) An analysis of English in the workplace: The communication needs of textile and clothing merchandisers. *English for Specific Purposes* 19: 351–68.

Starfield, S. (2011) Doing critical ethnographic research into academic writing: The theory of methodology. In D. Belcher, A. M. Johns and B. Paltridge (eds.), *New Directions in English for Specific Purposes Research*. 174–96. Ann Arbor, MI: University of Michigan Press.

Streeck, J. (2009) *Gesturecraft: The Manu-Facture of Meaning*. Amsterdam and Philadelphia: John Benjamins.

Swales, J. M. (2000). Language for specific purposes. *Annual Review of Applied Linguistics* 20: 59–76.

Swales, J. M. (2004) *Research Genres: Explorations and Applications.* Cambridge: Cambridge University Press.

Tardy, C. (2009) *Building Genre Knowledge.* West Lafayette, IN: Parlor Press.

Wozniak, S. (2010) Language needs analysis from a perspective of international professional mobility: The case of French mountain guides. *English for Specific Purposes* 29: 243–52.

Yuen, C. Y. (2004) The construal of ideational meaning in print advertisements. In K. O'Halloran (ed.), *Multimodal Discourse Analysis: Systemic Functional Perspectives.* 163–95. London and New York: Continuum.

Zemel, A., Koschman, A. T., LeBaron, C., and Feltovich, P. (2008) "What are we missing?" Usability's indexical ground. *Computer Supported Cooperative Work* 17: 63–85.

28 The Future of ESP Research: Resources for Access and Choice

DIANE BELCHER

Introduction

> If we are to encourage research that is pragmatic in the sense of looking at the everyday contexts of teaching, I would argue that this should be a critical . . . pragmatism, a position that . . . insists that while we do have to get on with our teaching, we also have to think very seriously about the broader implications of everything we do (Pennycook 1997: 267).

Those of us drawn to a specific purposes approach to English language teaching and to research in support of that endeavor are very likely to value English for specific purpose's (ESP) construal of learner-centeredness, its commitment to meeting the specific needs of specific learners in the contexts, or target situations, they wish to function in (Belcher 2009). Looked at from a critical theoretical vantage point, as Pennycook (1997) and others over the past decade and more have, ESP's goals may appear in a less-than-flattering light as a "pedagogy of cultural accommodation" (Bawarshi and Reiff 2010: 53) rather than of "cultural alternatives" (Pennycook 1997: 264). ESP's laudable goal of finding out what culture, or community, language learners hope to join and then helping them meet the discoursal requirements of that community can be seen, from a more critical perspective, as encouraging learners to conform to others' expectations. From this perspective, ESP appears to privilege a transmission, not transformative, pedagogy, to be convention-bound and prescriptive in its apparently socially reproductive teaching objectives. Benesch has argued (2001; see also Bawarshi and Reiff 2010) that eagerness to help learners become fully-functioning members of various communities can ultimately limit their participation, insofar as normative

The Handbook of English for Specific Purposes, First Edition.
Edited by Brian Paltridge and Sue Starfield.
© 2013 John Wiley & Sons, Inc. Published 2013 by John Wiley & Sons, Inc.

cultural practices, which often disadvantage those who are culturally different, are reinforced through such pedagogy. Yet, as Casanave (1995, 2002) has remarked in her critique of the discourse community construct, communities not only change those who enter them but are changed by those who become part of them. Helping learners negotiate expected communicative practices, Hyland (2004) has pointed out, also equips them with the tools needed to critique those practices. Thus we are not really faced, as Pennycook (1997) has also pointedly observed, with an either/or choice – to promote either acculturation or critique – for learners can be provided with what they need to join a community and also supported in thinking critically about that community's requirements.

   To do this, to enable access to communities and awareness of cultural alternatives within and beyond them, however, and do it effectively, can make an already daunting teaching task even more challenging (Belcher 2004, 2006). As professionals accustomed to doing research in their own local contexts, mainly in the form of current and target needs analysis, but mindful of learner rights too (Benesch 2001), ESP practitioners should be able to look to, and, ideally, contribute to, published research as a resource that will facilitate their praxis. For research to better play this supportive, pragmatic (and critically pragmatic) role, it will need to extend its recent trajectory of both broadening and deepening our understanding of (1) the communicative practices, or discourses, learners need to feel comfortable enough with to use and critique, (2) the communities of practice (CoP) learners wish to be part of, and (3) the community of ESP practitioners' efforts to mediate specific-purpose-driven learning.

Practices: Learning from Discourses Written, Spoken, and Digital

In his concluding remarks in a recent edited volume on ESP research, Swales (2011) laments that only one of its contributors focusses on spoken discourse. ESP researchers have, in fact, devoted the lion's share of their attention to written discourse, no doubt largely because examples of written discourse are more readily obtained and analyzed than speech samples. Despite several decades of text-linguistic research, however, much about written discourse remains to be examined.

Written discourse

While early text-oriented ESP research focussed on register analysis, or "lexico-statistics" (Swales, 1988: 189), Swales (1990), interested in the rhetorical motivation of texts in the context of discourse communities, ushered in a more top-down approach to written discourse analysis that ESP is now almost synonymous with, namely, genre analysis, or discourse-level analysis of socially-agreed upon ways of meeting communicative purposes. Unlike many other types of linguistic analysis, genre analysis considers whole texts, such as, job application letters, in their context of use. Swales-style genre analysis, known as move (rhetorical strategies) analysis, remains a highly productive analytical tool not only for the much-analyzed genre of the research article, which is now receiving more cross-linguistic attention (as in Hirano 2009) but for many other written genres as well, including such "occluded" genres (Swales 2004: 18) as statements of purpose in graduate program applications (Samraj and Monk 2008). More recently ESP genre analysts have begun to pay serious attention to intertextuality and interdiscursivity (Bhatia 2009) and the related concepts of genre chains, sets, and networks (Bhatia 2004; Swales 2004; Tardy 2011; Tardy and Swales 2008). Genre analysis has thus been moving beyond a focus on genres as isolated phenomena and toward more contextualized genre research, inspired, in part, by Swales' (1998) "textography" approach, a combination of document analysis and thick ethnographic description (see J. Flowerdew 2011; Paltridge and Wang 2011; Tardy 2009, 2011).

Yet bottom-up approaches have by no means disappeared, and, in fact, have had new life breathed into them with the advent of corpus tools, utilizing software to facilitate analysis of millions of words of text focussing on multiple textual features, using, for example, Biber's (1992) multidimensional analysis. Corpus tools now enable comparison of lexico-grammatical patterns in learner and expert corpora, as in Hyland's (2008) work with student and published texts (see also Frankenberg-Garcia, Flowerdew, and Aston 2011). Sizable corpora of unpublished student texts, notably MICUSP, the Michigan Corpus of Upper Level Student Papers (http://micusp.elicorpora.info/; Römer and Wulff 2010), and BAWE, the British Academic Written English corpus. (http://www2.warwick.ac.uk/fac/ soc/al/research/collect/bawe/; Nesi 2011), have recently been compiled and made publicly available. Though relatively small (compared to, for instance, the Bank of English), these student text corpora are indicative of what can be done in the building of specialized electronic databases and what their future uses might be, that is, what might be learned about writing at various stages of tertiary study across the disciplines (Swales 2011: 274) has noted, however, that a crucial question for those interested in corpus-based research is "what a corpus is most good for and what it is less good for." Bruce (2010: 162) has pointed out that what corpus data is obviously not very good at is telling us much about "discoursal settings." We may have access to more text than ever before, but without the context of the texts' production and consumption. Hyland (2000), however, who has enlisted specialist informants to enrich his own analysis of discipline-specific corpus data, has shown us that corpus-based research need not be viewed or treated as context-free.

The past decade has also seen a significant bridging of bottom-up and top-down perspectives (L. Flowerdew 2005) has offered a persuasive rationale for linking corpus with genre analytic approaches and a guide to studies that are leading the way forward in this direction (see also Biber, Connor, and Upton 2007; and L. Flowerdew 2011). How corpus-informed genre studies could also include a critical dimension has been suggested by Kandil and Belcher (2011), who combine critical discourse analysis with use of corpus tools to open a window on genre uptake, or, in the case of their study, to see how power may be exercised over genre consumers' world views.

Spoken discourse

Combined macro and micro-analytic approaches can, of course, be equally useful for investigating spoken discourse, which as noted earlier, has so far received far less attention in ESP than written discourse has. Technology is definitely making a difference, as we now can collect recordings of spoken interactions that, like written discourse, can be compiled in corpora and analyzed with the help of software (MICASE, the Michigan Corpus of Academic Spoken English (http://micase.elicorpora.info/), for example, provides access to both sound files and orthographic transcriptions of 15 categories of academic speech events, such as, lectures and advising consultations (Simpson-Vlach and Leicher 2006). An analogous corpus, the BASE, or British Academic Spoken English corpus (http://www2.warwick.ac.uk/fac/soc/al/research/collect/base/), includes video as well as audio recordings and text transcripts (Thompson and Nesi 2001). The Wulff, Swales, and Keller (2009) study of spoken discourse at a small academic conference shows how relatively easy it is, with audio equipment, transcription, and corpus tools, to construct a small spoken corpus that can be readily mined for analysis. Only very recently, however, has there been an attempt to build a corpus with transcription that is more than orthographic (Pickering and Byrd 2008) have argued that much is lost in corpus studies of spoken discourse that treat spoken data as written text. With the development of the Hong Kong Corpus of Spoken English (Warren 2006), comprised of academic and business interactions, we now have a corpus with prosodic transcriptions. Constructing such a corpus is obviously a laborious undertaking, but this and other corpora like it built in the future promise to enable greater access to the "acoustical realizations" (Pickering and Byrd: 115) of authentic spoken discourse.

Research on spoken discourse is also pioneering in an area in which written discourse research has lagged behind, namely, studies of English as a lingua franca (ELF) (Nickerson, this volume; Swales and Tardy 2008). Given that most speakers of English use it as an additional language, often with other EAL speakers (Graddol 2006), there clearly is a need for research on ELF, which may indeed pervade the discourse of both the current and target situations for the majority of students of English around the world. Mauranen (2011) argues that it is in spoken interaction that we best see how ELF is negotiated by its users and is developing, and that it is research on ELF interaction that promises to move us beyond the native speaker ideal, toward a conceptualization of communicative effectiveness as "constructed jointly by all actors involved" (2011: 94). The English as a Lingua Franca in Academic Settings (ELFA) corpus, a database comprised of spoken ELF in academic settings in Finland, and the research that the corpus has made possible (Mauranen, Hynninen, and Ranta 2010), are models for ELF research in other ESP contexts, which could, Mauranen (2011: 112) contends, revolutionize our notion of "communicative success."

Digital discourse

Digital discourse, viewed by many as a hybrid, with features of both written and spoken discourse (Bloch 2008, this volume), has only recently begun to receive the research attention it deserves. What remains to be seen is whether or not digital discourse will level the playing field for English language learners by enabling greater access to information, exposure to authentic language use, and the ability to instantaneously communicate with other English users no matter where in the world they are (see Lam 2000). Or, will digital discourse pose greater-than-ever hurdles to communication: a steeper learning curve and heavier financial burdens, with its hardware, software, and Internet access requirements? What we can be certain of is that there are new genres and communication environments that English language learners are confronted with and often eager to participate in. Some ESP researchers have already turned their attention to email as a genre (Gimenez 2006). Others have considered how writing in an e-environment can affect composing processes (Stapleton 2010). Social media, or Web 2.0, however, have so far received limited attention (but see Bloch 2008 on blogs; Kuteeva 2011 on wikis; Yi 2009 on instant messaging). It is now probably a truism to say that Facebook, Twitter, and mobile devices in general are transforming the communication means and styles, not to mention the social and political lives, of many. We know too little about how such modes of communication pose both problems and opportunities for English language learning,

Communities of Practice: Mapping Academic, Occupational, and Other Domains

Bawarshi and Reiff (2010) have characterized ESP as preferring to see communicative practices from a discourse community perspective, with a community's needs for and use of discourse uppermost in mind. Interestingly, Bawarshi and Reiff also assert that despite obvious interest in context, ESP tends to treat it as a black box, primarily as a starting point from which to view text. It is indeed arguably the case that text, whether written, spoken, or digital, has received much more attention than context in ESP, especially when compared to the ethnographic work in fields such as rhetorical studies (see for example, Beaufort 2000), and that much can be learned from such situated naturalistic inquiry. However, it can also be argued that no sub-field interested in language education has attempted more than ESP has to consider discourse in a diverse array of academic, occupational, and private and public life contexts, or communities of practice (Wenger 1998), a term now often preferred over discourse community (perhaps because of the unidirectional view of socialization associated with the latter; see Casanave 1995, 2002; but also, for a CoP critique, Haneda 2006).

English for academic purposes

Although ESP researchers are interested in contexts other than the academic, English for academic purposes (EAP) has received by far the most attention (Hewings 2002). If one looks at the two most prestigious and influential journals in ESP, one finds far more than half the articles in *English for Specific Purposes* focussing on EAP, and the other journal entirely devoted to it, the *Journal of English for Academic Purposes*. Why EAP so often is the center of attention is not difficult to fathom (Belcher 2006). Not only are most researchers located in academia itself, but academy-based researchers have access to research sites on their own campuses and to research funds, in addition to being professionally rewarded for doing research. This abundance of researcher attention, however, does not at all mean we now know all we need to know about EAP. As Hyland has suggested in his argument for renewed commitment to specificity (2011) and elsewhere (2006), the more we learn about EAP, the more we realize how varied EAP contexts are, and the more aware we are of how much remains to be discovered in support of "equipping students with the communicative skills to participate in particular academic cultures" (2011: 22).

The bulk of EAP research, again not surprisingly given the number of researchers in higher education, has concentrated on post-secondary student needs, and in this context, graduate-level learners have frequently been focussed on. Yet some disciplinary contexts have been addressed more than others, with less attention given to the arts and humanities than to the natural and social sciences (on the former, see Starfield and Ravelli 2006). There have also been relatively few attempts at longitudinal ethnographic-style studies of graduate students (among the few, Casanave 2002; Tardy 2009), or indeed of students at any other level of study (but see Leki 2007; Spack 1997). Few have also followed Prior's (1998) lead in examining the interplay of oral and written communication (see also Rubin and Kang 2008) in the complex activity systems that graduate students participate in.

Less looked at than the needs of graduate students are those of undergraduates. The challenges of focussing on this group, who in the first years of study may have only a vague notion of what direction their studies will take, are obvious. Despite the limited amount of research in this area, the contributions of researchers concentrating on undergraduate EAP have been significant and influential. With the diverse "socioliteracies" needs (Johns 1997: 20) of undergraduates, and hence their overarching need for "rhetorical flexibility" (Johns 2008: 238), in mind, Johns has advocated a student-as-ethnographers approach to data collection across the curriculum, encouraging students to compile literacy portfolios of sample writing assignments and readings. Now, with corpora like MICASE and MICUSP available, as well as online access to course materials, student-ethnographers and EAP specialists need not be limited in their investigations to classrooms and faculty they can physically access (see for example, Lee's, 2009, analysis of MICASE academic lectures). Johns (2009) has also pointed out the need to consider academic venues beyond the classroom (as has Benesch 2001), such as, faculty offices, where students can engage in clarification and negotiation of assignments. Of course, venues in and out of the classroom are often sites of unequal power relations, and as Starfield (2011: 190) has compellingly demonstrated through her own work with South African undergraduates, "the broader theoretical perspectives" of critical ethnographic methodology offer a potent means of examining "conditions and discourses" (2011: 174), whether at the undergraduate or any other level.

Relatively recent is the attention to the needs of professional academics, what Hyland (2009) refers to as English for professional academic purposes (EPAP). As any novice faculty member is well aware, academic language and literacy challenges do not end with attainment of one's highest degree. Especially for academics based in what Canagarajah (2002: 43) has referred to as the "periphery," non-English-dominant settings, the demands of contributing to English-medium international research conversations loom large. Research such as the impressive longitudinal ethnographic study of Curry and Lillis (2010), with participants in four countries, is giving us a much fuller picture of EAL academics' needs. Curry and Lillis observe that it is not only textual support but social networks, local and transnational, often forged through face-to-face communication at conferences, that are needed for participation in the English-dominated world of scholarly publication. EAL academics may not just be expected to contribute to scholarship in English, however. Now gaining more notice is the challenge EAL academics face juggling the demands of being research-active in two very typologically different languages and academic cultures (Casanave 2002; J. Flowerdew and Li 2009). Much more needs to be learned about the role EAP can play in support of EAL scholars and more equitable global knowledge dissemination and access.

Least examined of all academic levels is that of pre-tertiary language learners. While ESP (including EAP) has not traditionally been engaged in research on the contexts of younger learners, in fact, as Cruickshank (2009) has pointed out, the support offered to pre-tertiary EAL students should be considered EAP. Given the pace of global migrations, Cruickshank notes, there is some urgency in the need for extending our research purview to these learners, who may have had limited formal language study, or in the case of refugees, almost no formal study of anything at all. What might be learned, Cruickhank argues, about the "language-content nexus" (2009: 35) in secondary schools, may well be of value for post-secondary academia too, where language and other content-area faculty dialogue tends to be infrequent (see Benesch 2001). At both the primary and secondary levels, much of the language-support research that has been carried out has been done by systemic functional linguists (SFL) in Australia (Christie and Derewianka, 2008) and more recently in the United States (Gebhard, Harman, and Seger 2007). A fusion of SFL and ESP perspectives (Gebhard and Harman 2011; Hyland 2004) may be particularly efficacious for younger learners' academic contexts. Outside of ESL (English as a second language) environments, in EFL settings where English-language instruction is often now required of very young learners (for example, Japan and Korea), we know even less about the specific needs of such learners and their instructors, and how EAP specialists, with their needs analysis expertise, might help.

English for occupational purposes

Probably two of the most examined contexts in English for occupational purposes (EOP) are the rapidly expanding professional areas of business (EBP) (Bargiela-Chiappini and Zhang, this volume) and medicine (EMP) (Ferguson this volume; Belcher 2009) Yet, as we have seen is the case with many EAP areas, much remains under-investigated in these and many other occupational communities.

With the global reach of many companies and their need for a common corporate language for multicultural personnel, it is easy to understand why EBP researchers are among those in EOP most active in research on English as an international language (Planken and Nickerson 2009). Much BELF (Business English as a lingua franca) research has originated in the European Union, but Asia is a more and more frequent BELF research venue. EBP researchers are also in the forefront in research on multimodal, new media communication (Nickerson and Planken 2009), but so far much of this research has focussed on email and corporate websites, with little attention to such web-mediated communication as podcasts and videoconferencing.

Medical English specialists have in recent years moved beyond focussing primarily on the medical research article (Shi 2009) towards more occluded genres, such as nursing care plans (Hussin 2004), a particularly challenging literacy task for immigrant nurses-in-training in English-dominant settings, where there is a shortage of domestic health care workers. In countries attempting to build a more international patient base, such as Thailand, there is a felt need for more research on how to prepare clinic and hospital staff for interaction with English-language patients. EMP, in fact, stands out among EOP research areas in its interest in professional–non-professional communication, as in doctor–nurse–patient interactions (Shi 2009). Perhaps because of this interest, EMP researchers have taken a more critical approach than have many other EOP researchers, not infrequently focussing on the needs of the least powerful in Medical English interactions, patients (Candlin 2002). Other EOP researchers might consider extending their research focus to those who must interact with business, law or other professionals in a language the clients may feel distinctly disadvantaged in.

Many other occupational areas have also benefitted from attention in ESP, from tax accountants (J. Flowerdew 2011) to mountain guides (Wozniak 2010). The fact that such specialized EOP inquiry exists has little to little to do with research funding agencies or institutions and much to do with the need ESP practitioners feel to perform their own just-in-time research. The challenges of working in previously un-researched settings may be partly responsible for the novel approaches taken in them, approaches that could be beneficial in many other ESP research sites as well.

Unfortunately, but understandably, few have followed in the footsteps of Jasso-Aguilar (1999), who was truly a participant/observer in her data collection on the needs of Hawaiian hotel maids. Undergoing on-the-job hotel housekeeping training herself, Jasso-Aguilar was able to see the needs of the maids from their own perspective, decidedly different from that of hotel management. Equally innovative was the needs assessment reported on by Garcia (2002), focussed on factory workers in Chicago. Not only were the workers' factory-floor communication needs considered, but their personal and professional life goals too, as well as their needs as individuals and group participants, as labor union members. Lillis and Walkó's (2009: 489) observation about EAP is equally relevant to EOP and to ESP overall: that there has been much more focus on learners as individuals than on "networks of activity." Nor has there been much consideration of the ancillary role that English itself may play in activity networks where it is just one of the languages needed (for an exception, see Cheng and Mok 2008, on land surveyors in Hong Kong).

English for community membership purposes

ESP has traditionally not been well-attuned to the needs of language learners outside their school or employment contexts, though a few researchers, especially those informed by systemic functional linguistics and critical pedagogy, have pointed us in the direction of everyday communication needs, especially of adult immigrant learners.

As is the case with younger learners, the everyday needs of adult language and literacy learners have been the focus of attention most notably of systemic functional linguists in Australia. SFL educators have developed sequenced genre- and register-based curricula, with relevant themes such as public transportation, to address the immediate and less-easily-defined future community membership needs of adults at many different proficiency levels (De Silva Joyce and Hood 2009). What content and sequencing are optimal, De Silva Joyce and Hood have noted, are topics that could benefit from further research, as indeed could the question of how well any such approach succeeds in meeting the expansive range of evolving needs of a diverse adult learner population.

In another immigrant-welcoming nation, Canada, there has also been a concerted effort to meet the challenge of preparing newcomer adults for community membership, including citizenship, in their new homeland. Morgan and Fleming (2009: 265), in their critical evaluation of such language teaching efforts, have observed that the instruction may be informed by a normative notion of national community and citizenry more than by the actual needs and desires of "diasporic" adult learners. Morgan and Fleming's critique suggests the potential of a combined critical theoretical and ESP-oriented approach to investigating how to prepare adult learners for everyday contexts with awareness of options, among which would be the possibility of not fully accommodating to expectations of the immigrant-receiving community.

Not all English-language learners are committed to life in a single nation-state, however. Researchers such as Yi (2009) have considered an increasingly prevalent phenomenon, language learners whose goal is to feel at home in more than one national setting and language. More studies like Yi's, focussing on transnational identity, could help us better understand the needs of a new generation of language users who look forward to a lifetime of border-crossing mobility.

The ESP Practitioner Community: Building Knowledge of the Nature and Nurture of ESP Expertise

Some in ESP might well argue that the community that ESP professionals know the least about is their own. How do those interested in language education become ESP specialists? How do those actively engaged in ESP praxis exercise and hone their expertise? How do ESP practitioners know that what they do results in the learning outcomes that they and their students desire? These are questions that too few have attempted to address.

Reflecting on the education of novice ESP educators

What we do know about the education of those interested in specific-purpose-driven teaching is that there is little preparatory coursework available. Very few programs in Teaching English to speakers of other languages (TESOL), applied linguistics, or language education offer ESP as an area of specialization, though relatively more provide elective classes in the ESP approach. Given the limited formal ESP pre-service options, it is no surprise that ESP professional education has not been a popular research topic, though calls for development of more instruction in specific-purpose areas, such as Medical English, are not uncommon (Shi 2009). Perhaps there would be more ESP teacher education opportunities if those who have developed them focussed their own analytical lenses on how they have designed and implemented these courses. One such example is Morgan's (2009: 88–9) analysis of a course he created to prepare novice teachers to take a critical approach to EAP instruction, and hence be able to "look at the 'bigger picture,'" aware of "the larger socio-political and economic conditions . . . that shape educational agendas." More self-reflective accounts of course design might inspire not only more pre-service EAP/ESP curriculum development but also more similarly reflective teacher educator practice.

Understanding the practices of ESP practitioners

Much of the published sharing of ESP practitioner reflections on what's been done and seems to work, or action research, has focussed, as might be expected, on needs analysis, with less attention to materials development and coping with specialist knowledge needs.

While it is not difficult to find reports on needs analyses that have led to rich data on needs in almost any context about which there is published ESP research, there are approaches to needs assessment that have only more recently been explored. Consideration of learner identity, for example, has been suggested. (Belcher and Lukkarila 2011) as one way to discover learners' outside-of-school everyday and long-term language use aims as well as first language maintenance concerns. Learner and expert corpora, referred to earlier, offer another means of enhancing assessment of current and target needs, while also providing learners with tools for analysis of their own needs. Lee and Swales (2006) have reported on their efforts to promote learner autonomy by teaching students to build and analyze their own corpora, with their own texts and online published articles from their fields of study. With custom-made corpora, learners can be taught how to determine their needs without reliance on an instructor or native speaker inform-ant. The limitations of ESP professionals themselves as needs assessors have recently been contemplated by Johns and Makalela (2011). In their critical ethnog-raphy of an ESP consultant's attempts to assess and address EAP needs at a South African university, Johns and Makalela report on what happens when the self-reflexive critical ethnographic microscope is turned on such a project, with full acknowledgment of the difficulty of ever being "free of our own frames, inten-tions, and purposes" (2011: 217). Their findings suggest the advantages, both for ESP practitioners and those they seek to help, of collaborative inquiry with stake-holders, combining "etic" and "emic" perspectives on efforts to bring about change, and avoid doing harm, in a local context.

Many studies reporting on needs analysis include at least brief descriptions of the resulting materials. Few ESP specialists, however, have offered for close inspection their own materials development processes and products. Swales (2009) is among those few who have (for others, see Harwood 2010). That pub-lished analyses of materials development are rare no doubt has much to do with how under-valued instructional materials themselves are by many researchers and research institutions (Swales 1995). Swales' own work provides a model for future materials development chronicles.

One of the most vexing issues for ESP praxis is the need for at least some spe-cialist knowledge. While many have addressed this issue, reporting on develop-ment of less specialized courses or collaboration with subject specialists (Belcher 2009), Walker (2011) has recently suggested, with reference to his own instruc-tional practice, that corpus tools offer a particularly effective way of meeting this ESP practitioner need. Case studies, with autoethnographic data, of how other ESP instructors have similarly met their content knowledge needs would be revealing.

Learning about ESP learning

With limited awareness of how learners learn in ESP classrooms, promoting advancements in ESP professional expertise would seem to be a fairly utopian goal. Possibly because ESP has so much faith in the value of materials and tasks developed in response to well executed needs analysis, few ESP studies have focussed on teacher efficacy and closely examined the relationship between teaching and learning.

Cheng (2011a), an eloquent advocate of ESP classroom-based research, has extensively examined, perhaps more than anyone else so far, how students learn in specific-purpose-oriented classes. Cheng's (2008, 2011b) research methods, including fine-grained analysis of such case study data as student comments on the generic moves in discipline-specific text samples, are clearly labor-intensive but revelatory. His findings have provided abundant evidence that his use of a genre analysis approach addressed his own and his students' goals by equipping them with "a self-directed learning tool to develop . . . genre knowledge and their autonomy as learners" (2011a: 59; see also Negretti and Kuteeva 2011). Classroom-based studies analogous to Cheng's, focussed on other teaching and assessment strategies, hold the potential for greatly expanding our now limited knowledge of what may actually be accomplished in ESP instructional contexts.

Conclusion

In an editorial for an issue of the journal *English for Specific Purposes*, Paltridge (2009: 1), noting the wide range of countries represented by the contributors, remarked that for ESP research, "there is no Inner Circle," a reference to Kachru's (1992) famous configuration of the English-speaking world as concentric circles, with the inner circle consisting of countries where native English speakers are dominant. Paltridge observed that for those engaged in ESP, English is "the property of its users, native and non-native speakers alike". Probably no research sub-field in English-language teaching (ELT) is more truly international in its foci and its researchers than is ESP. Its commitment to local current and target situation analysis, carried out by anyone engaged in the ESP approach, means that research and theory, as well as pedagogical materials and tasks, developed by professionals far removed from the situations of interest are not automatically assumed to be either authoritative or relevant.

Because of its vantage point privileging the local, or "glocal" (globalized local; Robertson 1995) context, ESP researchers are in a position to substantially contribute to moving ELT beyond a native speaker model. Especially promising are recent ESP research developments that help establish a foundation for empowering students to engage in ongoing discovery and determination of their needs as language learners (Cheng 2011a; Lee and Swales 2006), able to decide who they want to see as models in their particular context, such as, other more proficient English-as-a-lingua-franca users (Mauranen 2011), and to what extent they want to meet the expectations of English-language speakers in positions of power in their schools and professions, cyber and "real life" communities. With its current research trajectory, ESP appears well on its way toward constructing a knowledge base facilitative of pedagogical praxis that, rather than simply focussing on pragmatically helping students of English meet others' expectations, supports growth in their ability to feel ownership of a language that, along with their other lingua-cultural affiliations and competences, increases access to a world of options.

REFERENCES

Bawarshi, A. and Reiff, M. J. (2010) *Genre: An Introduction to History, Theory, Research, and Pedagogy*. West Lafayette, IN: Parlor Press.

Beaufort, A. (2000) Learning the trade: A social apprenticeship model for gaining writing expertise. *Written Communication* 17: 185–223.

Belcher, D. (2004) Trends in teaching English for specific purposes. *Annual Review of Applied Linguistics* 24: 165–86.

Belcher, D. (2006) English for specific purposes: Teaching to perceived needs and imagined futures in worlds of work, study, and everyday life. *TESOL Quarterly* 40: 133–56.

Belcher, D. (2009) What ESP is and can be: An introduction. In D. Belcher (ed.), *English for Specific Purposes in Theory and Practice* 1–20. Ann Arbor, MI: University of Michigan Press.

Belcher, D. and Lukkarila, L. (2011) Identity in the ESP context: Putting the learner front and center in needs analysis. In D. Belcher, A. M. Johns, and B. Paltridge (eds.), *New directions in English for Specific Purposes Research*. 73–93. Ann Arbor, MI: University of Michigan Press.

Benesch, S. (2001) *Critical English for Academic Purposes: Theory, Politics, and Practice*. Mahwah, NJ: Lawrence Erlbaum.

Bhatia, V. (2004) *Worlds of Written Discourse*. London: Continuum.

Bhatia, V. (2009) Intertextual patterns in English legal discourse. In D Belcher (ed.), *English for Specific Purposes in Theory and Practice*. 186–204. Ann Arbor, MI: University of Michigan Press.

Biber, D. (1992) On the complexity of discourse complexity: A multidimensional analysis *Discourse Processes* 15: 133–63.

Biber, D., Connor, U., and Upton, T. (2007) *Discourse on the Move: Using Corpus Analysis to Describe Discourse Structure*. Amsterdam: John Benjamins.

Bloch, J. (2008) Blogging as a bridge between multiple forms of literacy: The use of blogs in an academic writing class. In D. Belcher and A. Hirvela (eds.), *English for Specific Purposes in Theory and Practice*. 288–309. Ann Arbor, MI: University of Michigan Press.

Bruce, I. (2010) Textual and discoursal resources used in the essay genre in sociology and English. *Journal of English for Academic Purposes* 9: 153–66.

Canagarajah, A. S. (2002) *A Geopolitics of Academic Writing*. Pittsburgh, PA: University of Pittsburgh Press.

Candlin, S. (2002) A triple jeopardy: What can discourse analysts offer health professionals? In C. N. Candlin (ed.), *Research and Practice in Professional Discourse*. 293–308. Hong Kong: City University of Hong Kong Press.

Casanave, C. P. (1995) Local interactions: Constructing contexts for composing in a graduate sociology program. In D. Belcher and G. Braine (eds.), *Academic Writing in a Second Language*. 83–112. Norwood, NJ: Ablex.

Casanave, C. P. (2002) *Writing Games: Multicultural Case Studies of Academic Literacy Practices in Higher Education*. Mahwah, NJ: Lawrence Erlbaum.

Cheng, A. (2008) Individualized engagement with genre in literacy tasks. *English for Specific Purposes* 27: 387–411.

Cheng, A. (2011a) ESP classroom research: Basic considerations and future research questions. In D. Belcher, A. M. Johns and B. Paltridge (eds.), *New Directions in English for Specific Purposes Research*. 44–72. Ann Arbor, MI: University of Michigan Press.

Cheng, A. (2011b) Language features as the pathways to genre: Students' attention to non-prototypical features and its implications. *Journal of Second Language Writing* 20: 69–82.

Cheng, W. and Mok, E. (2008) Discourse processes and products: Land surveyors in Hong Kong. *English for Specific Purposes* 27: 57–73.

Christie, F and Derewianka, B. (2008) *School Discourse: Learning to Write Across the Years of Schooling*. London: Continuum.

Cruickshank, K. (2009) EAP in secondary schools. In D. Belcher (ed.), *English for Specific Purposes in Theory and Practice*. 22–40. Ann Arbor, MI: University of Michigan Press.

Curry, M. J. and Lillis, T. (2010) Academic research networks: Accessing resources for English-medium publishing. *English for Specific Purposes* 29: 281–95.

De Silva Joyce, H. and Hood, S. (2009) English for community membership: Planning for actual and potential needs. In D. Belcher (ed.), *English for Specific Purposes in Theory and Practice*. 244–63. Ann Arbor MI: University of Michigan Press.

Flowerdew, J. (2011) Reconciling contrasting approaches to genre analysis: The whole can equal more than the sum of the parts. In D. Belcher, A. M. Johns, and B. Paltridge (eds.), *New Directions in English for Specific Purposes Research*. 119–44. Ann Arbor, MI: University of Michigan Press.

Flowerdew, J. and Li, Y. (2009) English or Chinese? The trade-off between local and international publication among Chinese academics in the humanities and social sciences. *Journal of Second Language Writing* 18: 1–16.

Flowerdew, L. (2005) An integration of corpus-based and genre-based approaches to text analysis in EAP/ESP: Countering criticisms against corpus-based methodologies. *English for Specific Purposes* 24: 321–32.

Flowerdew, L. (2011) ESP and corpus studies. In D. Belcher, A. M. Johns, and B. Paltridge (eds.), *New Directions in English for Specific Purposes Research*. 222–51. Ann Arbor, MI: University of Michigan Press.

Frankenberg-Garcia, A., Flowerdew, L., and Aston, G. (eds.), (2011) *New Trends In Corpora And Language Learning*. London: Continuum.

Garcia, P. (2002) An ESP program for entry-level manufacturing workers. In T. Orr (ed.), *English for specific purposes*. 161–74. Alexandria, VA: TESOL.

Gebhard, M. and Harman, R. (2011) Reconsidering genre theory in K-12 schools: A response to school reforms in the United States. *Journal of Second Language Writing* 20: 45–55.

Gebhard, M, Harman, R., and Seger, W. (2007) Reclaiming recess in urban schools: Learning the language of persuasion. *Language Arts* 84: 419–30.

Gimenez, J. (2006) Embedded business emails: Meeting new demands in international business communication. *English for Specific Purposes* 25: 154–72.

Graddol, D. (2006) *English Next*. London: The British Council.

Haneda, M. (2006) Classrooms as communities of practice: A reevaluation. *TESOL Quarterly* 40: 807–17.

Harwood, N. (ed.), (2010) *English Language Teaching Materials: Theory And Practice*. Cambridge: Cambridge University Press.

Hewings, M. (2002) A history of ESP through *English for Specific Purposes*. *English for Specific Purposes World* 1. Available at http://www.esp-world.info/Articles_3/Hewings_paper.htm.

Hirano, E. (2009) Research article introductions in English for specific purposes: A comparison between Brazilian Portuguese and English. *English for Specific Purposes* 28: 240–50.

Hussin, V. (2002) An ESP program for students of nursing. In T. Orr (ed.), *English for Specific Purposes*. 25–40. Alexandria, VA: TESOL.

Hyland, K. (2000) *Disciplinary Discourses: Social Interactions in Academic Writing*. London: Longman.

Hyland, K. (2004) *Genre and Second Language Writing*. Ann Arbor, MI: University of Michigan Press.

Hyland, K. (2006) *English for Academic Purposes: An Advanced Resource Book*. London: Routledge.

Hyland, K. (2008) As can be seen: Lexical bundles and disciplinary variation. *English for Specific Purposes* 27: 4–21.

Hyland, K. (2009) English for professional academic purposes. In Diane Belcher (ed.), *English for Specific Purposes in Theory and Practice*. 83–105. Ann Arbor, MI: University of Michigan Press.

Hyland, Ken. (2011) Disciplinary specificity: Discourse, context, and ESP. In D. Belcher, A. Johns, and B. Paltridge (eds.), *New Directions in English for Specific Purposes Research*. 6–24. Ann Arbor, MI: University of Michigan Press.

Jasso-Aguilar, R. (1999) Sources, methods and triangulation in needs analysis: A critical perspective in a case study of Waikiki hotel maids. *English for Specific Purposes* 18: 27–46.

Johns, A. M. (1997) *Text, Role, and Context: Developing Academic Literacies*. Cambridge: Cambridge University Press.

Johns, A. M (2008) Genre awareness for the novice academic student: An ongoing quest. *Language Teaching* 41: 237–52.

Johns, A. M. (2009) Tertiary undergraduate EAP: Problems and possibilities. In D. Belcher (ed.), *English for Specific Purposes in Theory and Practice*. 41–59. Ann Arbor, MI: University of Michigan Press.

Johns, A. M. and Makalela, L. (2011) Needs analysis, critical ethnography, and context: Perspectives from the client – and the consultant. In D. Belcher, A. M. Johns, and B. Paltridge. (eds.), *New Directions in English for Specific Purposes Research*. 197–221. Ann Arbor, MI: University of Michigan Press.

Kachru, B. (1992) *The Other Tongue: English Across Cultures*. Urbana, IL: University of Illinois Press.

Kandil, M. and Belcher, D. (2011) ESP and corpus-informed critical discourse analysis: Understanding the power of genres of power. In D. Belcher, A. M. Johns, and B. Paltridge (eds.), *New Directions in English for Specific Purposes Research*. 252–70. Ann Arbor. MI: University of Michigan Press.

Kuteeva, M. (2011) Wikis and academic writing: Changing the writer–reader relationship. *English for Specific Purposes* 31: 44–57.

Lam, E. (2000) L2 literacy and the design of the self: A case study of a teenager writing on the Internet. *TESOL Quarterly* 34: 457–83.

Lee, J. (2009) Size matters: An exploratory comparison of small- and large-class university lecture introductions. *English for Specific Purposes* 28: 42–57.

Lee, D. and Swales, J. M. (2006) A corpus-based EAP course for NNS doctoral students: Moving from available specialized corpora to self-compiled corpora. *English for Specific Purposes* 25: 56–75.

Leki, I. (2007) *Undergraduates in a Second Language: Challenges and Complexities of Academic Literacy Development*. New York: Lawrence Erlbaum.

Lillis, T. and Walkó, Z. (2008) Review of *English for Academic Purposes*, by K. Hyland. *English for Specific Purposes* 27: 487–90.

Mauranen, A. (2011) English as the lingua franca of the academic world. In D. Belcher, A. M. Johns, and B. Paltridge (eds.), *New Directions in English for*

Specific Purposes Research. 94–117. Ann Arbor, MI: University of Michigan Press.

Mauranen, A., Hynninen, N., and Ranta, E. (2010) English as an academic lingua franca: The ELFA project. *English for Specific Purposes* 29: 183–90.

Morgan, B. (2009) Fostering transformative practitioners for critical EAP: Possibilities and challenges. *Journal of English for Academic Purposes* 8: 86–99.

Morgan, B. and Fleming, D. (2009) Critical citizenship practices in ESP and ESL Programs: Canadian and global perspectives. In D. Belcher (ed.), *English for Specific Purposes in Theory and Practice.* 264–88. Ann Arbor, MI: University of Michigan Press.

Negretti, R. and Kuteeva, M. (2011) Fostering metacognitive genre awareness in L2 academic reading and writing: A case study of pre-service English teachers. *Journal of Second Language Writing* 20: 95–110.

Nesi, H. (2011) BAWE: An introduction to a new resource. In A. Frankenberg-Garcia, L. Flowerdew, and G. Aston. (eds.), *New Trends in Corpora and Language Learning.* 212–28. London: Continuum.

Nickerson, C. and Planken, B. (2009) English for specific business purposes: Written business English and the increasing influence of multimodality. In D. Belcher (ed.), *English for Specific Purposes in Theory and Practice.* 127–42. Ann Arbor, MI: University of Michigan Press.

Paltridge, B. (2009) Editorial. *English for Specific Purposes* 28: 1–3.

Paltridge, B. and Wang, W. (2011) Contextualizing ESP research: Media discourses in China and Australia. In D. Belcher, A. M. Johns and B. Paltridge (eds.), *New Directions in English for Specific Purposes Research.* 25–43. Ann Arbor, MI: University of Michigan Press.

Pennycook, A. (1997) Vulgar pragmatism, critical pragmatism, and EAP. *English for Specific Purposes* 16: 253–69.

Pickering, L. and Byrd, P. (2008) An investigation of relationships between spoken and written academic English: Lexical bundles in the AWL and in MICASE. In D. Belcher and A. Hirvela (eds.), *The Oral-Literate Connection: Perspectives on L2 Speaking, Writing, and other Media Interactions.* 110–32. Ann Arbor, MI: University of Michigan Press.

Planken, B. and Nickerson, C. (2009) English for specific business purposes: Intercultural issues and the use of business English. In D. Belcher (ed.), *English for Specific Purposes in Theory and Practice.* 107–26. Ann Arbor, MI: University of Michigan Press.

Prior, P. (1998) *Writing/Disciplinarity: A Sociohistoric Account of Literate Activity in the Academy.* Mahwah, NJ: Lawrence Erlbaum.

Robertson, R. (1995) Glocalization: Time-space and homogeneity-heterogeneity. In M. Featherstone, S. Lash and R. Robertson. (eds.), *Global Modernities.* 25–44. London: Sage.

Römer, U. and Wulff, S. (2010) Applying corpus methods to written academic texts: Explorations of MICUSP. *Journal of Writing Research* 2: 99–127.

Rubin, D. and Kang, O. (2008) Writing to speak: What goes on across the two-way street. In D. Belcher and A. Hirvela (eds.), *The Oral-Literate Connection: Perspectives on L2 Speaking, Writing, and Other Media Interactions.* 210–25. Ann Arbor, MI: University of Michigan Press.

Samraj, B. and Monk, L. (2008) The statement of purpose in graduate program applications: Genre structure and disciplinary variation. *English for Specific Purposes* 27: 193–211.

Shi, L. (2009) English for medical purposes. In D. Belcher (ed.), *English for Specific Purposes in Theory and Practice.* 205–28. Ann Arbor, MI: University of Michigan Press.

Simpson-Vlach, R. and Leicher, S. (2006) *The MICASE Handbook: A Resource for Users of the Michigan Corpus of Academic*

Spoken English. Ann Arbor, MI: University of Michigan Press.

Spack, R. (1997) The acquisition of academic literacy in a second language: A longitudinal case study. *Written Communication* 14: 3–62.

Stapleton, P. (2010) Writing in an electronic age: A case study of L2 composing processes. *Journal of English for Academic Purposes* 9: 295–307.

Starfield, S. (2011) Doing critical ethnographic research into academic writing: The theory of the methodology. In D. Belcher, A. M. Johns, and B. Paltridge (eds.), *New Directions in English for Specific Purposes Research*. 174–96. Ann Arbor, MI: University of Michigan Press.

Starfield, S. and Ravelli, L. (2006) "The writing of this thesis was a process that I could not explore with the positivistic detachment of the classical sociologist": Self and structure in *New Humanities* research theses. *Journal of English for Academic Purposes* 5: 222–43.

Swales, J. M. (1988) *Episodes in ESP: A Source and Reference Book on the Development of English for Science and Technology*. New York: Prentice Hall.

Swales, J. M. (1990) *Genre Analysis: English in Academic and Research Settings*. Cambridge: Cambridge University Press.

Swales, J. M. (1995) The role of the textbook in EAP writing research. *English for Specific Purposes* 14: 3–18.

Swales, J. M. (1998) *Other Floors, Other Voices: A Textography of a Small University Building*. Mahwah: Lawrence Erlbaum.

Swales, J. M. (2004) *Research Genres: Explorations and Applications*. Cambridge: Cambridge University Press.

Swales, J. M. (2009) When there is no perfect text: Approaches to the EAP practitioner's dilemma. *Journal of English for Academic Purposes* 8: 5–15.

Swales, J. M. (2011) Envoi. In D. Belcher, A. M. Johns, and B. Paltridge. (eds.), *New Directions in English for Specific Purposes*

Research. 271–74. Ann Arbor, MI: University of Michigan Press.

Tardy, C. (2009) *Building Genre Knowledge*. West Lafayette, IN: Parlor Press.

Tardy, C. (2011) ESP and multi-method approaches to genre analysis. In D. Belcher, A. M. Johns, and B. Paltridge. (eds.), *New Directions in English for Specific Purposes Research*. 145–73. Ann Arbor, MI: University of Michigan Press.

Tardy, C. and J. M. Swales (2008) Form, text organization, genre, coherence, and cohesion. In C. Bazerman (ed.), *Handbook of Research on Writing*. 565–81. New York: Taylor and Francis.

Thompson, P. and Nesi, H. (2001) The British Academic Spoken English. BASE) corpus project. *Language Teaching Research* 5: 263–64.

Walker, C. (2011) How a corpus-based study of the factors which influence collocation can help in the teaching of business English. *English for Specific Purposes* 30: 101–12.

Warren, M. (2006) Because of the role of er front office um in hotel: Lexical cohesion and discourse intonation. *International Journal of Corpus Linguistics* 11: 305–23.

Wenger, E. (1998) *Communities of Practice: Learning, Meaning and Identity*. Cambridge: Cambridge University Press.

Wozniak, S. (2010) Language needs analysis from a perspective of international professional mobility: The case of French mountain guides. *English for Specific Purposes* 29: 243–52.

Wulff, S., Swales, J. M., and Keller, K. (2009) "We have about seven minutes for questions": The discussion sessions from a specialized conference. *English for Specific Purposes* 28: 79–92.

Yi, Y. (2009) Adolescent literacy and identity construction among 1.5 generation students: From a transnational perspective. *Journal of Asian Pacific Communication* 19: 100–29.

Index

abbreviations 269, 271
Abo Mosallem, E. 220
Academic Formulas List 126–7
Academic Keywords List 140
academic learning corpora 138–41,
    410–11
academic literacies 97, 144, 145
academic publishing, inequalities in 303–6
academic purposes, English for *see* English
    for academic purposes (EAP)
Academic Word List (AWL) 120–1, 123,
    139, 254, 409
    see also Coxhead, A.
Academic Writing for Graduate Students
    (Swales and Feak) 107
Academic Writing in a Global Context (Curry
    and Lillis) 355
accents 489
acculturation 465
acronyms 269
active listening 57
Adamson, H. D. 11
Adams-Smith, D. 10
Adobe Connect 386
Adolphs, S. 338
Adorno, T. 462
aggregation 394
Aguilar, M. 143
Ainsworth-Vaughn, N. 244
air traffic control, language of 227

air traffic controllers (ATCs) 42, 43–4, 56,
    229
Aitchison, C. 295
Akhtar, K. 10
Akindele, O. 288
Ala , M. 529
Alderson, C. 43, 44, 239
Alderson, J. C. 373
Ali, F. 455, 521
Allan, K. 245
Allen, J. P. B. 78
Allison, D. 65, 293
Allwright, J. 254, 256
Allwright, R. 254, 256
Alster, K. B. 277
American Association for Business
    Communication (ABC) 200
Amman, K. 529
*Analyzing Genre: Language Use in
    Professional Settings* (Bhatia) 16, 350
Anderson, N. 335
Angewandte Chemie (Applied Chemistry) 302
Anglia Ruskin University, UK 194
Anglophone countries 247
Anglophone literature 195
Anglophone scholars 303, 474
Angouri, J. 159, 178
annotation 413–14
    corpus 412–13
annual reports 103, 104